GENERAL ROBERT E. LEE.

FROM THE PORTRAIT BY ELDER, PRESENTED TO THE UNIVERSITY OF VIRGINIA
BY THE STUDENTS OF THE SESSION OF 1870-71.
AND ALUMNI.

MEMOIRS

OF

ROBERT E. LEE

HIS MILITARY AND PERSONAL HISTORY

EMBRACING

A LARGE AMOUNT OF INFORMATION HITHERTO UNPUBLISHED

BY

A. L. LONG

FORMERLY MILITARY SECRETARY TO GEN. LEE, AFTERWARD BRIG.-GEN. AND CHIEF OF
ARTILLERY SECOND CORPS, ARMY OF NORTHERN VIRGINIA

TOGETHER WITH

INCIDENTS RELATING TO HIS PRIVATE LIFE SUBSEQUENT
TO THE WAR

COLLECTED AND EDITED WITH THE ASSISTANCE

OF

MARCUS J. WRIGHT

FORMERLY BRIG.-GEN. ARMY OF TENNESSEE, AND AGENT OF THE UNITED STATES FOR
THE COLLECTION OF CONFEDERATE RECORDS

ILLUSTRATED.

THE BLUE AND GREY PRESS

Published by
THE BLUE AND GREY PRESS
A division of Book Sales, Inc.
114 Northfield Avenue
Edison, NJ 08837

ISBN 0-89009-694-5

Manufactured in the United States of America.

(FAC-SIMILE OF THE DEDICATION WRITTEN BY GENERAL LONG ON A SLATE USED BY THE BLIND.)

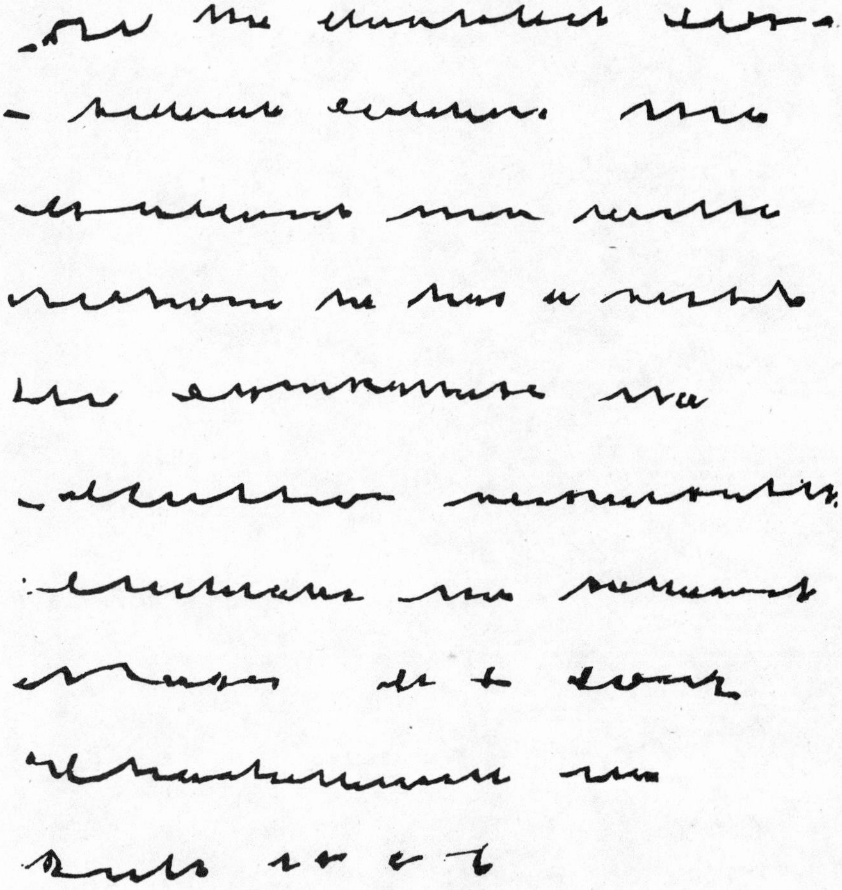

To the Disabled Confederate Soldiers,

THE GALLANT MEN WITH WHOM HE HAS A RIGHT TO SYMPATHIZE,

THE AUTHOR RESPECTFULLY DEDICATES THE FOLLOWING PAGES.

A. L. LONG, CHARLOTTESVILLE, VA.

JULY 28, 1886.

PREFACE.

To overcome the inactivity to which loss of sight has for some years subjected me, I have sought occupation in recording the recollection of familiar events. Having obtained a slate prepared for the use of the blind, I soon learned to write with a moderate degree of legibility. In order to excite a pleasing interest in my work, I undertook something that might prove of future benefit. Having served on General Lee's personal staff during the most important period of his military career, I began an eye-witness narrative of his campaigns in the war between the States. In the execution of my work I received valuable assistance from my wife and daughter, my two sons, and Miss Lucy Shackelford (now Mrs. Charles Walker), all of whom lovingly and faithfully served me as copyists and readers. I am also indebted to Colonel C. S. Venable of General Lee's staff, Major Green Peyton of Rodes's staff, and Major S. V. Southall of my own staff, for indispensable aid in reviewing my manuscript, informing me of facts that had not come to my knowledge or reminding me of such as had escaped my recollection. My work is now completed, and I offer it to the public, hoping it may prove of value as a record of events which passed under my own observation, and many of which have been described directly from my notes made at the time of their occurrence. It is not intended to be a history of the war in detail, but a statement of my personal knowledge of General Lee's life, actions, and character, and of the part played by him in the great events of which he was the ruling spirit.

1

After receiving my manuscript the publishers desired a change of plan which would embrace some of the interesting social and domestic features of General Lee's life. This part of the work has been edited and conducted through an arrangement with the publishers by General Marcus J. Wright, formerly of the Confederate Army of Tennessee, but now, and for some years past, agent of the United States War Department for the collection of Confederate records. My wife has rendered important aid in this part of the work by contributing personal incidents and other valuable material obtained through her friendly relations with the family of General Lee. It is also proper to acknowledge the use of the publications of Rev. J. W. Jones, Colonel Walter H. Taylor, Miss Emily Mason, the Southern Historical Society papers, Swinton, and the Report of the Congressional Committee on the Conduct of the War (Federal). I have had occasion to refer to the *Memoirs* of General Grant and *The Campaigns of General J. E. B. Stuart*, by Major H. B. McClellan. I have been greatly encouraged in the publication of this work by the cordial concurrence of General G. W. Custis Lee, General W. H. F. Lee, Major R. E. Lee, Miss Mildred Lee, Governor Fitz Lee, and other members of the family.

I further desire to acknowledge my indebtedness to Colonel R. N. Scott, U. S. A., for opportunity afforded me at the War Records Office of studying official reports, maps, and the confidential letter-books of General Lee, relating to the events described in the present volume, many of which have never hitherto been published, and which will prove of great value and interest both in rightly understanding military operations and in estimating the character and genius of that great soldier.

A. L. LONG.

PUBLISHERS' NOTE.

GENERAL LEE, less fortunate than General Grant, was over-taken by death before he could complete his design of writing and publishing to the world his personal narrative of the important events in which he figured. In offering this work to the public the Publishers consider it a consummation of that intention, and they further believe that in the selection of General Long as the writer these Memoirs become as nearly an autobiography as any it would be possible to obtain from another hand than that of General Lee himself.

It was only during the last years of his life. that General Lee seriously contemplated writing a history of his campaigns. He had been repeatedly urged to do so by friends, was offered large inducements by publishers, and even from foreign countries came urgent requests for his story. To most of these solicitations he returned a negative answer. Under date of October 25, 1865, he says: "I cannot now undertake the work you propose, nor can I enter into an engagement which I may never be able to accomplish. It will be some time before the truth can be known, and I do not think that time has yet arrived." To a request from a German officer for the right of translation he writes on March 13, 1866: "It has been my desire to write a history of the campaigns in Virginia, but I have not yet been able to commence it." It would appear that he began to collect materials for this purpose shortly after this date, and wrote to the various corps and division commanders asking reports of operations for the last campaigns of the war. He writes to Colonel Taylor, his late adjutant-general: "I am desirous that the bravery and devotion of the Army of Northern Virginia shall be correctly transmitted to posterity. This

3

is the only tribute that can now be paid to the worth of its
noble officers and soldiers.''

That the desire expressed in these letters became a settled
intention, and that General Lee had made some progress in
the collection of material, is shown in a letter to Mr. C. F.
Lee, Jr., which is kindly placed at our service:

" LEXINGTON, VA., 6th June, 1870.

"My Dear Cassius: I am very much obliged to you for
your letter of the 1st and the interest you evince in the character of the people of the South and their defence of the
rights which they believed were guaranteed by the Constitution.   The reputation of individuals is of minor importance
to the opinion which posterity may form of the motives which
governed the South in their late struggle for the maintenance
of the principles of the Constitution.   I hope, therefore, a true
history will be written and justice be done them.   A history of
the military events of the period would also be desirable.   I
have had it in view to write one of the campaigns in Virginia,
in which I was more particularly engaged.   I have already collected some materials for the work, but lack so much that I
wish to obtain that I have not commenced the narrative.   I
am very much obliged to you for the offer of the materials
which you have collected.   I think it probable that I have
all the official reports, and I would not like to resort to any
other source for a statement of facts. . . . .

"I am, very truly, your cousin,
"R. E. LEE.

" C. F. LEE, JR., Alexandria, Va."

General Lee's death occurred four months after the date of
this letter, and there was found to be but little done in the ful-
filment of his expressed purpose.

The narrative of General Long includes many valuable contributions made by the members of General Lee's family, and
is, in the main, based upon his own notes made at the time of
the occurrences spoken of.   The writer, moreover, had the
advantage of an intimate personal association with General Lee
under conditions which ensured the most perfect mutual con-

fidence and trust. The following letter to General Long expresses how high an opinion of the author was entertained by General Lee, and how desirous he was to associate him with himself in the coming campaigns:

"RICHMOND, 19th Apr., 1862.

"MY DEAR MAJOR: I have taken the liberty to apply for your appointment as my military secretary, which you may have observed, under a late law of Congress, has the rank and pay of colonel of cavalry. I had endeavored to obtain your promotion in another way which probably would have been more agreeable to you, but, failing in that, I have taken this course. If confirmed by the Senate, I will inform you, and you must let me know whether the situation is agreeable to you. If it is not and you prefer remaining where you are, or if any other situation is more agreeable to you, let me know, and I will do what I can to obtain it for you. At all events, understand not to consider yourself obliged to accept the one offered. . . . .

"Yours truly,
"R. E. LEE.

"MAJOR A. L. LONG."

The delicacy with which this offer of personal service was made marks a distinguishing characteristic of the writer.

The acceptance by General Long began an acquaintance and service which closed only with the close of the war. Shortly afterward General Long received from General Lee the following testimonial:

"General A. L. Long entered the Confederate service in 1861, and has served continuously till the surrender of the Army of Northern Virginia, 9th April, 1865. His conduct during that time has been marked by zeal and gallantry. A graduate of the Military Academy at West Point, in addition to a military education, he has long experience in the military service.

"He was with me as chief of artillery in the winter of 1861–62 in the Southern department, and became a member of my staff when appointed to the command of the Army of Northern Virginia. He was promoted brigadier-general in 1863, and made

chief of artillery of the Second Army Corps, Army of Northern Virginia, which position he held till the surrender of the army, 9th April, 1865.   R. E. LEE,
                                                    "*General.*"

In the preparation of these memoirs the author has been influenced by the intention of General Lee as indicated in the foregoing letters. He has sought to include only such accounts of the military operations as were legitimate subjects of record and were confirmed by General Lee's reports. Contributions of a personal nature from relatives, friends, and associates have been included in the text, as serving to illustrate the traits of character which made Lee so famous in his generation.

The addition to General Long's work of the official reports of General Lee, as well as of a great number of confidential letters and despatches which form the only official record of the movements and operations of the Army of Northern Virginia for the period which they cover, will give to this work unique interest and exceptional value. Letters and confidential extracts from the private letter-books of General Lee, heretofore unpublished, as well as the returns of organization of the army and tables of reports of its strength, have been placed at the service of General Long through the courtesy of Colonel R. N. Scott, at the head of the Bureau of War Records in Washington.

The assistance given by General Marcus J. Wright in the compilation of records and returns, and especially in the preparation of the chapters relating to the last years of General Lee's life, has been of great importance and service, and materially contributes to the completeness and the value of the work.

TABLE OF CONTENTS.

CHAPTER I.

GENEALOGY.

CHAPTER II.

EARLY LIFE.

CHAPTER III.

THE MEXICAN WAR.

CHAPTER IV.

THE INDIAN CAMPAIGN.

CHAPTER V.

A DIVIDED COUNTRY.

CHAPTER VI.

OPENING OF THE CIVIL WAR.

CHAPTER VII.

THE WEST VIRGINIA CAMPAIGN.

CHAPTER VIII.

THE SOUTH COAST DEFENCES.

CHAPTER IX.

THE PENINSULAR CAMPAIGN.

CHAPTER X.

THE SEVEN DAYS' FIGHT.

CHAPTER XI.

POPE OUTGENERALLED.

CHAPTER XII.

THE ADVANCE INTO MARYLAND.

CHAPTER XIII.

FREDERICKSBURG.

CHAPTER XIV.

CHANCELLORSVILLE.

CHAPTER XV.

GETTYSBURG.

CHAPTER XIX.

THE SIEGE OF PETERSBURG.

CHAPTER XX.

THE SIEGE CONTINUED.

CHAPTER XXI.

FROM PETERSBURG TO APPOMATTOX.

CHAPTER XXII.

GENERAL LEE AS A SOLDIER.

CHAPTER XXIII.

PRESIDENT OF WASHINGTON COLLEGE.

CHAPTER XXIV.

HOME AND SOCIETY LIFE.

CHAPTER XXV.

DEATH AND MEMORIAL CEREMONIES.

CHAPTER XXVI.

THE WORLD'S ESTIMATE.

APPENDIX.

LIST OF PLATES AND MAPS.

PLATES.

FAC-SIMILES OF GENERAL LEE'S FIELD-MAPS.

MEMOIRS

OF

ROBERT E. LEE.

CHAPTER I.

GENEALOGY.

The Lee Family.—Richard Lee Emigrates to Virginia.—"President Lee."—His Celebrated Sons.—Henry Lee and his Descendants.—The Military and Civil Record of
"Light-horse Harry."—An Affecting Incident.—Prominence of the Lee Family.

IT is the boast of American society and civilization that men
have risen to eminence in nearly all departments of life
unaided by the advantages incidental to hereditary preferment.
Nevertheless, the people of this country do not fail to place a
proper value on respectable and illustrious lineage, and when a
man in any way or through any circumstances has attained distinction in the world, there is a natural curiosity in the minds
of his countrymen to know both his origin and the history of
those from whom he has descended.

General Robert E. Lee comes of a family illustrious in both
England and America—one, as history attests, worthy of him
as he was worthy of it. But his renown is due mainly to the
part he himself has played both in peace and war, which has
at once reflected honor on the memory of his ancestors and
added to his own name a noble distinction of which his descendants may justly be proud.

To those who have the curiosity or desire to know "from
whence came this Virginian," it is proper to state that his
ancestry may be clearly traced to the Norman Conquest. The
founder of the family, Launcelot Lee, came originally from

17

Loudun, France. He entered England with William the Conqueror, distinguished himself at the battle of Hastings, and acquired an estate in Essex.

A later member of the family, Lionel Lee, took part in the third Crusade, following Richard Cœur de Lion in 1192 to Palestine, at the head of a company of "gentlemen cavaliers." He displayed great gallantry at the siege of Acre, and in return for his services was made earl of Litchfield, while another estate, afterward called "Ditchly," was bestowed upon the family. The armor worn by Lionel Lee in the crusade may still be seen in the Horse Armory of the Tower of London.

The line of descent of General Lee can be traced directly from Richard Lee, a younger son of the earl of Litchfield, who was the fifth from Sir Henry Lee, knight of the Garter in the reign of Queen Elizabeth. This Richard Lee in 1641, during the reign of Charles I. of England, came to America as colonial secretary under the governorship of Sir William Berkeley. He was possessed of a handsome person, fine talents, and popular manners, and by these qualities was enabled to secure influence over the colonists. He aided Sir William in keeping Virginia firm in her allegiance to the Crown during the civil war between the Cavaliers and Roundheads. After the triumph of the latter he was of great assistance to the governor in making the most advantageous terms with the Protector, Cromwell, through an acknowledgment of the authority of the Commonwealth, which in return conferred free sovereignty on Virginia.

It will thus be seen that the Lees were at once and at this early period of history fully identified with the country of their adoption.

The county of Westmoreland, with its diversity of hill and dale, its mild climate, fertile soil, and attractive scenery, at an early period won the attention of the Washingtons, Fairfaxes, Lees, and other distinguished families, and they naturally established their homes in this attractive situation. Here they evinced many of the traits, characteristics, and customs of English society. Frequently they made the country ring with the merry sound of the horn and the hound as they swept through field and wood in pursuit of the wily fox or the bounding stag. In the life and habits of these people and others of like descent and customs was formed the germ of that martial spirit which characterizes what is called the "chivalry of Virginia." In later days General Lee has been heard to relate with enthusiasm how as a boy he had followed the hunt (not infrequently on foot) for hours over hill and valley, without fatigue. These exhilarating exercises tended to greatly strengthen the limbs, expand the chest, and give vigor to a constitution which in after-life rendered him able to endure the greatest hardships of war.

Richard Lee, second son of the Richard above named, was born in Virginia in 1646. He was educated in England, graduated in law, and returned to Virginia, where he took an active part in the colonial legislation. His fourth son, Thomas Lee, was one of the first of the family to establish himself in the county of Westmoreland. He attained high distinction both in America and England, and grew to be one of the most prominent men in the early history of Virginia, in which province he became successively president of the council and governor of the colony, being the first native-born American who held the latter office under the British Crown. He is known in colonial history as "President Lee." The fine mansion of Stratford in Westmoreland county, the birthplace of several famous members of the family, was built for Thomas Lee by the East India Company, aided by an ample donation from the privy purse of Queen Caroline, his previous residence having been burned. This edifice still stands, and is very substantially built, the walls of the first story being two and a half feet thick, and those of the second story two feet. It contained originally about seventeen rooms, though one writer credits it with one hundred rooms, and another declares that the stables contained one hundred stalls for horses.

Thomas Lee died in 1756. He left eight children, six sons and two daughters. Several of his sons occupied prominent places in the colonial history of America. Three of them, Richard Henry, Francis Lightfoot, and Arthur Lee, deserve particular mention from their connection with our Revolutionary history.

Richard Henry Lee early entered the House of Burgesses of

Virginia, and afterward became a distinguished member of
the Continental Congress. To him is due that stirring resolution of the 10th of June, 1776, which proclaimed to the
world that America was full-grown and ready to take its allotted place in the family of nations—the resolution "that these
United Colonies are, and of right ought to be, free and independent States; that they are absolved from all allegiance to
the British Crown; and that all political connection between
them and Great Britain is, and ought to be, totally absolved."

Francis Lightfoot Lee was also a member of the Continental
Congress, and was one of the signers of the Declaration of
Independence; while Arthur Lee was sent on an important
foreign mission on behalf of the new republic.

Returning to Richard Lee, of the second generation of the
family in America, and the father of Thomas Lee just described, we must now consider the descent of his fifth son,
Henry, the direct ancestor of the subject of these memoirs.
Henry Lee filled no prominent place in colonial history. His
life was that of a student, though, like his brothers, he occupied a seat in the early councils of the colony. He married a
Miss Bland, and had three children, of whom we are concerned
only with the second son, Henry.

This Henry Lee became a member of the House of Burgesses,
and took an active part in all the exciting political events of
the time. He was married in 1753 to Lucy Grymes, reported
to be a descendant of General Thomas Grymes of Cromwell's
army. He left a large family, six sons and five daughters, the
oldest of whom, born in 1756, near Dumfries on the Potomac,
bore the name of his father, and in addition to the distinguished part he performed in the Revolutionary War attained
the higher distinction of being the father of Robert E. Lee,
the noblest figure of a long and illustrious line.

At an early age this third Henry Lee in direct descent was
sent to Princeton College, where he distinguished himself as
a student. He was preparing for the practice of the law, and
was just about embarking for England to pursue his studies,
when hostilities with the mother-country changed his plans.
He was then nineteen years of age. Abandoning his inten-

tion of going to England, he raised a company of cavalry, and soon after the battle of Lexington joined Washington. His energy and ability quickly gained for him a high reputation. Speedily promoted to the rank of lieutenant-colonel, he was assigned to the command of an independent corps composed of infantry and cavalry, known as "Lee's Legion." His services were conspicuous during the war, and at the close of the Revolution no one had acquired a more permanent and deserved reputation than "Light-horse Harry." About the year 1781 he married his cousin, the daughter of Col. Philip Ludwell Lee of Stratford. Soon after the close of the war he was elected to Congress, and afterward became governor of Virginia, to which office he was three times elected. He was one of those who earnestly favored General Washington as the first President.

About the year 1790 he lost his wife, who had borne him four children, all of whom died in childhood except his son Henry. From the office of governor he returned to private life, and was subsequently married to Mrs. Anne Hill Carter, daughter of Mr. Charles Carter of Shirley. On account of the political agitation of the country he was again induced to enter public life, and in the winter of 1798–99 he became a member of the General Assembly. He was also re-elected to Congress, notwithstanding the tide of opposition then running against the Federals.

On the death of General Washington he prepared the eulogy, by direction of Congress, in which occur the memorable words which have become indissolubly attached to the name of the hero of the Revolution: "First in war, first in peace, and first in the hearts of his countrymen."

The children of his second marriage were Charles Carter Lee of Powhattan; Sidney Smith Lee, a commander in the United States navy in 1860, and afterward of the Confederate States navy; General Robert Edward Lee; and two daughters, Anne and Mildred.

Of these children, Robert Edward was born in the Stratford mansion, and in the same room in which were born two of the signers of the Declaration of Independence, Richard Henry and

Francis Lightfoot Lee.   In 1811, Henry Lee removed with his family to Alexandria for the purpose of educating his children, and whilst here was offered and accepted a major-general's commission in the United States army during the second war with England.   In 1814 he was in Baltimore, the guest of Mr. Alexander C. Hansen, at the time when the house of that gentleman was attacked by a mob.   His visitor took part in the defence of the house, in which duty he received serious injuries, from whose effects he never recovered.

About the close of the year 1817 declining health induced him to visit the West Indies, but finding that the tropical climate did not afford him the relief he expected, he determined to return to his native shores.   While on his return voyage, failing strength caused him to direct his course to the coast of Georgia, and to claim the hospitality of the daughter of his old friend and comrade, General Greene, who occupied her father's residence on Cumberland Island.   After lingering a short time at this hospitable mansion, his noble spirit took its flight to join those who had preceded him.   Nearly half a century later that event was brought in the most striking manner to the knowledge of the writer of this work, who was then accompanying General Lee, during the Civil War, on a tour of inspection along the coasts of Georgia and Florida.   While passing through the channel that separates Cumberland Island from the main land, the steamer stopped at a plantation wharf, and the general then asked me to accompany him on a sacred mission.   After following for some distance a road shaded with live-oak and magnolia, we passed through a gate opening into extensive grounds dotted with groups of olive, orange, and lemon trees, intermingled with brilliant subtropical shrubbery.   In the midst of these grounds arose an extensive pile of buildings whose unfinished state bore evidence that the design of the projector exceeded his means of execution.   This was the residence of General Greene.   We entered a spacious hall, and after admiring for a moment the richly-carved frames of the ample windows that lighted it and the stairway that wound its spiral course along the unfinished walls of shell and mortar, we descended a flight of steps into a garden, which, though neglected, exhibited signs of taste and cultivation. Passing on, we came to a dilapidated wall enclosing a neglected cemetery. The general then, in a voice of emotion, informed me that he was visiting the grave of his father. He went alone to the tomb, and after a few moments of silence plucked a flower and slowly retraced his steps, leaving the lonely grave to the guardianship of the crumbling stones and the spirit of the restless waves that perpetually beat against the neighboring shore. We returned in silence to the steamer, and no allusion was ever made to this act of filial devotion.

The brief genealogical record here given might have been greatly extended had it seemed desirable to present in full detail the posts of honor obtained and the distinguished services performed by the ancestors of Robert E. Lee. The few facts we have stated will suffice to show the prominent position held by the Lees in England, and their essential influence and importance in the colonial history of Virginia and in the struggle through which the independence of America was achieved. Always on the patriotic side, and doing noble duty alike in the legislative hall and on the battlefield, they stand high among the leaders in that series of great events through which the fetters of tyranny were broken and another star added to the galaxy of civilized nations. Alike in England and America this family has always occupied an honorable position and been held in high esteem, and the pages of its history are nowhere sullied by a deed of which any of its members need to be ashamed. From the date of its origin members of the family have gained distinction as warriors, until, through Launcelot Lee, Lionel Lee, and "Light-horse Harry," the culminating point is reached in Robert E. Lee, the greatest commander of modern times, and a military genius who may fairly be placed in comparison with the noted captains of the world as in some respects the noblest and ablest of them all.

CHAPTER II.

EARLY LIFE.

Birth and Boyhood of Robert E. Lee.—Sent to West Point.—Descriptive Letter.—He is appointed Lieutenant of Engineers.—His Marriage.—Testimony of Friends as to his Character.—His Engineering Service at St. Louis.—Stationed in New York Harbor.

ROBERT EDWARD LEE, the fourth child of General Henry Lee, was born at Stratford, the ancient manor-house of the Lee family in Virginia, on the 19th of January, 1807. His name was taken from those of his maternal uncles, Robert and Edward Carter of Shirley.

In order to avail himself of better opportunities for the education of his children, General Lee left Stratford when his son Robert was four years old and removed to Alexandria. In this city the family lived successively on Cameron street, on Orinoco street, and in the house known as The Parsonage. Persons are yet living who remember Robert Lee in those his days of childhood, and who have an abiding recollection of his thoughtfulness of character and of his earnestness in the performance of every duty.

He was, indeed, in a somewhat trying position for one of his tender years. His father had been compelled, through declining health, to repair to the West Indies in search of relief, while his mother was a confirmed invalid. Of his brothers, one was a student at Harvard, another was in the navy; one of his sisters was in delicate health, and for a considerable period absent from home, while the other was too young to be of much use in household duties; so that many domestic cares fell upon Robert. Though but eleven years of age at the period of his father's death, the boy was old beyond his years, and of a thoughtfulness, a sense of filial obligation, and a warm affection for his parents that aided him to accept respon-

24

sibilities and perform duties of which few boys of his age would have been capable.

Little is known of the events of his early life, but that little redounds to his credit. His character at this period is admirably summarized in a passage of a letter written by his father from the West Indies: "Robert, who was always good, will be confirmed in his happy turn of mind by his ever-watchful and affectionate mother."

It is undoubted, indeed, that the lessons of this judicious and loving mother bore an important part in the formation of the estimable character which her noble son in after years displayed. She taught him in his years of childhood to "practise self-denial and self-control, as well as the strictest economy in all financial concerns"—lessons which were destined to bear ample fruit in his subsequent life.

As we have said, many of the cares of the household devolved upon the child, who did the marketing, attended to housekeeping duties, managed outdoor affairs, looked after his mother's horses, and acted the "little man" to an extent and with a discretion unusual in a boy of his age.

His warm affection for his mother undoubtedly had its share in this devotion to duties usually distasteful to growing lads, and it was particularly shown in the pathetically earnest care which he took of this patient invalid. Discarding schoolboy frolics, he would hurry home from his studies to see that his mother had her daily drive, and might be seen carrying her to her carriage, affectionately arranging her cushions, and earnestly endeavoring to entertain her, gravely assuring her that unless she was cheerful she would derive no benefit from her airing.

In confirmation of the statements here made we are fortunately enabled to give the testimony of near relatives of Robert E. Lee as to his youthful character and habits. From one of his cousins we have the following interesting remarks:

"I remember him well as a boy at school to Mr. Leary at the Alexandria Academy, and afterward at school to Mr. Hallowell when his school was in the house now occupied by Mr. Turner, and his mother lived next door. I recollect his uniformly correct deportment at school and elsewhere, and his attention to

his studies.   What impressed me most in my youthful days
was his devotion to his mother, who, as you know, was for
many years an invalid; she used to say he was son and daughter to her.   He was her housekeeper, relieved her of all domestic cares, looked after the horses, rode out in the carriage with
her, and did the marketing for the family.''

Another cousin offers the following testimony in a letter addressed to Mrs. Lee after the death of her noble husband:

"Aunt Lee's health was bad: your husband was everything
to her.   He kept house under his mother's directions.   She was
one of the most methodical and beautiful of managers, always
cheerful and dignified.   I think Robert's disposition was very
like his mother's.

"You remember Nat, who was Aunt Lee's dining-room servant: after her death his health became very bad; your husband
took him to the South, had the best medical advice, comfortable room, and everything that could be done to restore him,
and attended to him himself.   When your husband was going
to Mr. Hallowell's school he would come out at twelve o'clock,
have their carriage gotten, and go out with aunt to ride, doing
and saying everything to amuse her.   In her last illness he
mixed every dose of medicine she took, and he nursed her
night and day.   If Robert left the room she kept her eyes on
the door till he returned.   He never left her but for a short
time.''

An incident related by one of his friends strikingly shows the
high moral sense to which he had early attained, and the influence which it exerted upon all with whom he came into contact.   At that period life in Virginia retained much of the
rollicking character of its eighteenth-century conditions, and
the boy chanced, during a vacation, to find himself an invited
guest in a house where these undesirable customs were kept up.
The host was a fascinating gentleman, possessed of all graces
of mind and manner, yet, while not dissipated, his mode of
life was such as to shock the sterner sense of morality of his
youthful visitor.   Robert made no comment on what he saw,
but his unspoken rebuke proved more efficacious than any
words of reproach could have done.   The night before his

departure his host came to his bedside, and in affecting language sought to excuse himself for the wild life into which he had fallen. He offered his sorrow for the loss of those dearest to him as a reason for habits which he could not seek to defend, and he impressively warned his young guest to beware of similar habits, advised him to persist in his commendable course of life, and earnestly promised that he would himself endeavor to reform if but to render himself worthy of the respect and affection of one of so estimable a character.

In his school-duties Robert was as diligent, attentive, and methodical as at home. Mr. William B. Leary, an Irish gentleman, was his first teacher. Shortly after the war a meeting took place between the teacher and his now-famous pupil at Lexington, and again when General Lee was returning from Georgia his old teacher came from a long distance to meet him, and they had a very pleasant interview.

When the growing youth reached an age in which it became necessary to seriously consider his future life and vocation, he himself seems to have selected the military profession, and decided to make an application for admission to West Point. His object in this was partly the desire to relieve his mother of the burden of his support, but there is reason to believe that the army was his deliberate choice as a profession, and that his mind had a natural tendency toward military science, to which it proved in after years to be so peculiarly adapted. When it was fully decided that he should prepare himself for admission to West Point he was sent with this object to the school of Mr. Benjamin Hallowell, an able teacher of mathematics and well suited to give the youthful aspirant the necessary preliminary education. His record in this school can best be shown by the following letter from Mr. Hallowell:

"Robert E. Lee entered my school in Alexandria, Va., in the winter of 1824–25, to study mathematics preparatory to his going to West Point. He was a most exemplary student in every respect. He was never behind-time at his studies; never failed in a single recitation; was perfectly observant of the rules and regulations of the institution; was gentlemanly, unobtrusive, and respectful in all his deportment to teachers and his

fellow-students. His specialty was finishing up. He imparted
a finish and a neatness, as he proceeded, to everything he undertook. One of the branches of mathematics he studied with
me was conic sections, in which some of the diagrams were
very complicated. He drew the diagrams on a slate; and
although he well knew that the one he was drawing would
have to be removed to make room for another, he drew each
one with as much accuracy and finish, lettering and all, as if it
were to be engraved and printed. The same traits he exhibited at my school he carried with him to West Point, where,
I have been told, he never received a mark of demerit, and
graduated at the head of his class.''

We may add here one further passage from the letter of his
cousin to Mrs. Lee, which gives some interesting information
on this point in Robert E. Lee's life:

''I know your dead husband was most anxious to go to West
Point, both to relieve his mother and to have a military education. Your aunt Lewis interested herself very much in obtaining his commission, and took him to Washington and introduced him to General Jackson. He was so much pleased with
our beloved Robert that he got him his appointment.''

In 1825, when he was eighteen years of age, he entered West
Point as a cadet. Concerning his life while in this institution
we have little information. It was undoubtedly that of an
earnest and diligent student, too absorbed in his studies to have
many social relaxations or to indulge in any of those truant
escapades which are apt to form the telling events in schoolboy
life. In respect to his standing at this institution interesting
information is volunteered by Colonel Macomb, U. S. A., who
entered the Military Academy in 1828, the year before Lee's
graduation. He found that Cadet Robert E. Lee was then the
prominent figure in the corps of cadets, being adjutant of battalion. Yet the formality which has always existed between
''plebs'' and older classes permitted only admiration at a distance, and this admiration only ripened into intimate acquaint-
anceship five years afterward when the two young men met in
Washington.

In the year 1829, at the completion of his four years' course, he graduated, bearing off the second highest honors of the institution. During his whole course he had never received a demerit mark for any breach of rules or neglect of duty. He was highly esteemed by his comrades, and was noted for studious habits and commendable conduct. He avoided tobacco and intoxicating liquors, used no profane or immoral language, and throughout his whole student-life performed no act which his pious mother could not have fully approved.

Throughout his whole life, indeed, he never used tobacco, and, though in rare cases he would drink a glass of wine, he strictly avoided whiskey or brandy and did his utmost to favor temperance in others. The intemperate habits of many of the persons under his command were always a source of pain to him, and several anecdotes are told of his quiet manner of administering reproof to young men who had over-indulged in strong liquor. Indeed, on more than one occasion he refused to promote officers addicted to intoxication, saying, "I cannot consent to place in the control of others one who cannot control himself."

Immediately after his graduation he received the appointment of second lieutenant of Engineers in the army of the United States, and was employed for several years thereafter on the seacoast defences in engineering duty.

It may be well to append at this point some interesting extracts from a letter which the writer has received from a near relative of General Lee, which are of special value as the testimony of one who was closely associated with him in his youth, and as serving to fill out the somewhat meagre information heretofore extant concerning the events of his early life :

"My first recollection of Robert Lee was during his mother's residence in Alexandria. His father was absent at the time, I think, in the West Indies, from which trip he never returned. I have no recollection of ever seeing him. From my earliest remembrance of my aunt she was a very delicate woman, and was thus left at the death of General Lee with the entire charge of five children, Carter, Anne, Smith, Robert, and Mildred. Robert, when I first remember him, was, I should say, a youth of some fifteen or sixteen years. I was frequently with the

Arlington family at my aunt's, but, being very young, passing events made very little impression on my mind. Robert was six years my senior, and when there my intercourse was principally with Bella Carter, our cousin, who lived with them for a time, while Robert and Mildred would be engrossed with Mary Custis. I remember hearing Robert spoken of frequently as a youth of great promise, his devotion to his mother and the help he afforded her in all her business and household matters commented on with admiration—particularly his devotion to his sister Anne, afterward Mrs. Judge Marshall of Baltimore. The first time I remember being struck with his manly beauty and attractiveness of manner was when he returned home after his first two years at West Point. He came with his mother and family on a visit to my father's. He was dressed in his cadet uniform of West Point, gray with white bullet buttons, and every one was filled with admiration of his fine appearance and lovely manners. I think he was about nineteen. Again, I remember being for some time with him at my grandfather Randolph's in Fauquier. I think it was the fall after he graduated. The house was filled with the young people of the family of both sexes. He was very much matured since I had last seen him, splendid-looking—as full of life, fun, and particularly of teasing, as any of us.

"But I have often said since he entered on his brilliant career that, although we all admired him for his remarkable beauty and attractive manners, I did not see anything in him that prepared me for his so far outstripping all his compeers. The first time this idea presented itself to me was during one of my visits to Arlington after my marriage. We were all seated around the table at night, Robert reading. I looked up and my eye fell upon his face in perfect repose, and the thought at once passed through my mind: 'You certainly look more like a great man than any one I have ever seen.' The same idea presented itself to me as I looked at him in Christ Church, Alexandria, during the same visit. Again, he spent some time at my father's in the fall of 1831, shortly after his own marriage and just before mine. He was then, as of old, bright, animated, and charming. I did not see him again until, I think, the fall of 1836. He was returning from the Springs with his wife, who was in distressing ill-health, and I never saw a man so changed and saddened. It has always been painful to me to think of him as he was then. The last time I saw Robert Lee, except for a short time at Richmond on his way to the South the spring before his death, was at my own house the summer after the Mexican War. He was then looking very well, and was more than usually agreeable and interesting from his fund of anecdote connected with the war, which was of course at that time fresh in his memory. In closing I will make one more statement, which is, that I knew Robert Lee from the time I can first recollect, and I never remember hearing him censured for anything in my life.''

Another letter from the same writer furnishes the following interesting quotation :

''There is one more trait in General Lee's character which I must mention here, which was his beautiful neatness and love of order. Young men are very apt to think it beneath them, and *little*, to give much attention to these small matters, and I have often brought up to those of my own family the beautiful neatness of Robert Lee. His wife told me, after his return from the Mexican War, that he had brought back every article of clothing he had taken with him, and a bottle of brandy which he had taken in case of sickness, *unopened*.''

The Mary Custis referred to in the foregoing letter was the daughter and heiress of Washington Parke Custis of Arlington and granddaughter of the wife of General Washington. For years Robert Lee had been an occasional visitor at Arlington, and while he was yet a boy had been strongly attracted to the lovely young heiress—an intimacy which ripened into love as the youthful pair approached years of maturity. Mary Custis had received a fine classical education, and with the accompanying advantages of wealth and position was deemed by her father worthy of a match superior to that offered by a young man devoted to a military career. Yet the handsome cadet captured the heart of the Virginia heiress, and he returned to West Point from a visit home the plighted lover of Mary Custis. It was the first love for them both, and was destined to be a lasting one. Their marriage took place two years after his graduation, and was attended with an amusing circumstance which is worth relating.

The wedding took place at Arlington on the evening of Thursday, June 30, 1831. The ceremony, which was witnessed by a large circle of guests, was performed in the right-hand drawing-room of that fine old mansion by the Rev. William Meade, afterward bishop of Virginia. The attendants on the bride and groom, as given by one of the bridesmaids, were the following: First bridesmaid and groomsman, Miss Catharine Mason and Lieutenant Sidney Smith Lee ; second, Miss Mary Goldsborough and Lieutenant Thomas Kennedy ; third, Miss Marietta Turner and Lieutenant Chambers; fourth, Miss Angela Lewis and Mr. Tillman; fifth, Miss Julia Calvert and Lieutenant Prentiss; sixth, Miss Britannia Peter and Lieutenant Thomas Turner.

The amusing circumstance above referred to, as related by a person present at the wedding, is the following: In the early evening preceding the hour fixed for the wedding a heavy thunderstorm came up, rather unfortunately for the Rev. Mr. Meade, who was yet on the road, and who reached the house thoroughly drenched. It was impossible for him to conduct a marriage ceremony without some change of raiment, and they were obliged to supply him with a suit of clothes belonging to Mr. Custis, the father of the bride. Unluckily for the fit of these garments, Mr. Custis was short and stout, the clergyman tall and thin, and he presented a highly ridiculous appearance to those who saw him in his borrowed plumage. However, the ample folds of the surplice covered all defects of raiment, and the guests generally were unaware of the awkward predicament of the dignified divine.

This was before the days of marriage-journeys, and the festivities were concluded in the mansion, the ceremony being followed by a handsome supper, while the large bridal-party were entertained at Arlington until the evening of the following Monday, when an entertainment was given at the house of General John Mason. The newly-married couple at once settled down to housekeeping in the good old style.

This match was considered a brilliant one for Lieutenant Lee, his wife being looked upon as a great heiress, possessed of a large landed estate and a multitude of slaves. Yet she has often been heard to declare that the advantage of the wedding was largely on her side, since her husband's management of her estate was so skilful and judicious as to make it more valuable and remunerative than she could possibly have done. His profession, however, obliged him to be nearly always absent from home, which was probably a main reason for her father's objection to the marriage.

The property of Miss Custis embraced two mansions, with the accompanying lands: Arlington, on the Virginia heights opposite the city of Washington, and the White House, on the Pamunky River. Arlington is beautifully situated, and commands a view of Washington, Georgetown, and a long stretch of the Potomac, with a wooded background of distant hills and valleys. It was surrounded by groves of stately trees, except in front, where the hill slopes gracefully downward to the low lands bordering the river. This fine old mansion was seized by the Federal Government at the commencement of the Civil War, and occupied by the Federal troops as a camping-ground. It contained valuable relics, many of which were taken away, and never recovered by the family. The White House, on the Pamunky, was the scene of the marriage of General Washington with the widow Custis. This place was also occupied by the Federal troops, and burned— accidentally, no doubt, as some of the Federal officers took every precaution to preserve it on account of its historical associations.

Years afterward, Mrs. Lee, desiring to see once more this beloved home of her dearest memories, came alone to Arlington. Too much of an invalid even to get out of her carriage, she looked sadly around and asked for a cup of water from the spring, and then ordered the driver to take her away. The desecration which had come upon the beloved home of her youth and of so many years of happy married life was too great for the sorrowing invalid to endure.

The fate of the two mansions of the Custis family strongly

illustrates the ravages of war. The White House, as we have said, was burned to the ground, and "not a blade of grass left to mark the culture of more than a hundred years." Arlington was desolated by the war, its groves cut down, its furniture carried off, its precious relics of Washington scattered over the North, and only the shell was left of the beautiful home of the past. The estate finally became the property of the United States Government, and the grounds were converted into a soldiers' cemetery.

We may very briefly finish our account of General Lee's married life by stating that there were born to him seven children. These were, in order of birth, G. W. Custis, Mary, W. H. Fitzhugh, Annie, Agnes, Robert, and Mildred. Of these children, two are dead—Agnes, who died after her father, and Annie, who died October 20, 1862. That General Lee was always exceedingly fond of his family is evidenced in his letters to his wife and children, examples of which will be given in a later portion of this work. They are full of expressions of affection and of wise fatherly advice, and prove that in the very tempest of war the heart of the great soldier was with his loved ones at home, and that he could turn from ordering some momentous movement in the field to write home words of tender sentiment and admonition, and hope of domestic bliss, as if his only cares were those of peaceful life. It is remarkable how little of war and how much of Christian feeling and family affection these letters contain.

General Lee tells an interesting anecdote in connection with one of his sons (Custis), which may fitly be quoted here: When a very little child his father took him to walk one winter's day in the snow, holding him by the hand. Soon the boy dropped behind. Looking over his shoulder, he saw Custis imitating his every movement, with head and shoulders erect, putting his little feet exactly in his father's footprints. "When I saw this," said the general, "I said to myself, 'It behooves me to walk very straight, when this fellow is already following in my tracks.'"

Shortly after his graduation Lieutenant Lee was sent on

engineering duty to Old Point, Virginia. Here he remained for several years. In 1835 he was assigned to a new field of duty, being appointed assistant astronomer on the commission for marking out the boundary-line between Ohio and Michigan. In 1836 he was promoted to the rank of first lieutenant, and in 1838 was made captain in the Engineer corps.

In regard to his life during this period interesting information has been volunteered by some of his friends who were intimately associated with him at that time both professionally and socially. Mr. James Eveleth relates that he was a clerk in the Engineer department at Fortress Monroe when Lieutenant Robert E. Lee reported there for his first service after graduating at the Academy, and from that time (1829) until 1834, Lee served at Fortress Monroe as assistant to Captain Andrew Talcott, who was in charge of the construction of the fortifications for the defence of Hampton Roads. In 1834, Lee was transferred to Washington as assistant to the chief engineer. Mr. Eveleth was also transferred, on July 1, 1835, as clerk in the Engineer department at Washington, thus keeping up his acquaintance with Robert E. Lee. During all this time Lee enjoyed the affectionate consideration and high appreciation of his brother-officers, as well as of all who came in contact with him. There never was a man more universally beloved and respected. He was conspicuous in the mind of Mr. Eveleth for never having uttered a word among his most intimate associates that might not have been spoken in the presence of the most refined woman. It can always be said of him that he was never heard to speak disparagingly of any one, and when any one was heard so to speak in his presence he would always recall some trait of excellence in the absent one. Mr. Eveleth calls to mind with peculiar interest the affectionate relations existing between Lieutenant Lee and Lieutenant J. E. Johnston, the latter being known to his intimates as Colonel Johnston. It is interesting to think of these two men passing on in unbroken friendship throughout their long and very distinguished careers. He has seen them meet after separation with the affectionate demonstrations of two school-friends.

Every incident relative to the life, associates, and habits of the young lieutenant at this period is of interest as a guide-post on the road to the great distinction which he afterward attained. We are fortunate in being able to give some further information, obtained from his intimate friends. General Meigs describes his daily habits in the following words:

"In 1836–37, Lieutenant Lee was stationed at Washington as assistant to Chief Engineer Colonel Gratiot, and, having married the daughter of G. W. Custis of Arlington, he resided at that place, riding his horse into town every morning in time for the opening of the office at nine o'clock. As all public offices in those days closed at three precisely, his figure, mounted upon a compact Virginia bay horse, was to be seen every afternoon on Pennsylvania Avenue on his return to Arlington. This habit of constant exercise in all kinds of weather, not on wheels, but in the saddle, no doubt contributed to the vigor of his health and the endurance which enabled him to stand the cares, toils, and exposures of many campaigns."

Mrs. Kennan adds that often on his return from the city to Arlington he would stop and make a call on her family at their house in Tudor Place, Georgetown, and that he was always genial and ready to enter into the interests and pleasures of others.

Colonel Macomb, whose remembrance of the cadet-life of General Lee we have already given, adds the following reminiscences of his life in Washington at the period which we have now reached. At that time the colonel had the good fortune to be one of the "mess" at Mrs. Ulrich's, where the Riggs House now stands. The "mess" was composed of Joseph E. Johnston, James H. Prentiss, Thomas J. Lee, Augustus Canfield (who afterward married Miss Cass), James F. Izzard, and John Macomb. Lee was an occasional member of the "mess." Although married and residing at Arlington, yet, being on duty in the Engineer department, he found himself frequently under the necessity of remaining in Washington on account of the roads, which were at times impassable. Besides these young officers there were some distinguished men in the mess: Mahlon Dickerson, Secretary of the Navy; William C. Rives,

who had been minister to France, and who was at this time
Senator from Virginia; Hugh Swinton Legaré of South Carolina, an eminent lawyer, then member of Congress from South
Carolina, but at an earlier period minister to The Hague; and
Joel R. Poinsett, Secretary of War. The presence of the latter
frequently brought General Eustis, his brother-in-law, into the
membership of the "mess." Mrs. Ulrich felt great partiality
for the young officers of the "mess," and would refuse all
applications from persons whom she thought would not be
acceptable and congenial to them. Under these circumstances
it may be understood that the inmates of her house were excep-
tionally agreeable to each other. Messrs. Legaré and Dickerson often discussed the Greek poets, etc., to the edification of
the young soldiers, whose training had been in a different line.
An incident which illustrates the gayety of these young officers
is here recalled: As Lieutenant Lee was about to start for Arlington on one occasion on his spirited Virginia horse, seeing
Macomb approach, he hailed him, saying, "Come, get up with
me." To the surprise of Lee, Macomb approached, put his
foot in the stirrup, and mounted behind him. Thereupon they
rode down Pennsylvania Avenue, and just as they were in front
of the President's House they met the Hon. Levi Woodbury,
Secretary of the Treasury, to whom they both bowed with great
dignity. A more astonished gentleman has not been seen
before or since.

In the spring of 1857, Captain Macomb was ordered to Mexico. He went by the Southern route, and spent at San Antonio
a delightful week with Colonel Lee, who was then stationed
there as lieutenant-colonel of the Second Cavalry. They
renewed their old acquaintance, with the custom of visiting the
ladies, and had a lively time. This was Colonel Macomb's
last interview with his old friend, whom he remembers of all
the men of his acquaintance as the most beloved and admired
by both men and women. No one was ever jealous of him;
all delighted to do him honor. Colonel Macomb recalls that,
while stationed at Santa Fé, New Mexico, news came of the
alarming illness of General Scott, which led, among the officers,
to the discussion of his probable successor. It was universally

agreed that Lee would be the man. This shows the estimation of his compeers.*

As everything illustrative of the early life and the developing character of the great hero of the Civil War must possess an interest for his very numerous friends and admirers, we feel sure that we will be excused for adding to the reminiscences above given the following testimony from Mr. F. Schneider. It is of a different bearing from the foregoing, and clearly indicates important traits of character, showing a precision of idea, a clear conception of what he wanted, a close attention to minute details, and a faithful discharge of even the smallest obligation, which had much to do with the subsequent success of the man.

Mr. Schneider had a blacksmith-shop on the corner of Twentieth and G streets. Upon the first occasion of his acquaintance (1835) Lieutenant Lee was riding into the city from Arlington to his office, and happening to see Mr. Schneider shoeing a horse, he dismounted and inquired into his manner of shoeing horses. Being satisfied, he gave particular directions and left his horse to be shod. When he returned from the office he lifted each foot of the horse carefully, then nodded his head, and said to Mr. Schneider, "You are the first man I have ever come across that could shoe a horse by my directions." From that time all the Arlington horses were

* Colonel Macomb was present at the marriage of Lieutenant Sidney Smith Lee of the navy, brother of Robert E. Lee, who married Miss Mason, in the old Christ Church at Alexandria. The party were first entertained at General John Mason's house at Claremont. They then went to Arlington, where the festivities were continued. Lieutenant Robert Lee and his friends took part in this old Virginia frolic. Seven young men were bivouacked in one of the larger rooms at Arlington. Captain Canfield, one of the number, made much fun for the party. In the morning the negro servant made so much noise on the bare floor, bringing wood and making fires, that Canfield called out, " Moses, why not come up on the pony ?" At this point Mr. Custis threw the door wide open and called out, " 'Sleep no more ; Macbeth hath murdered sleep.' "

Every night before the party retired punch was bounteously dispensed from a punch-bowl which had belonged to General Washington. In the bottom of the bowl was a painting of a ship, the hull resting in the bottom, the mast projecting to the brim. The rule was to drink down to the hull—a rule strictly observed.

As this bowl has a history, it may be stated that it was presented to General Washington by Colonel Fitzhugh, a former aide-de-camp, who afterward left Virginia and settled in the Genesee Valley in Western New York.

sent to Mr. Schneider to be shod. When ordered to Mexico his high regard for Mr. Schneider led him to go from the War Department to his shop to bid him good-bye. The year before the Civil War repairing and fencing was done at Arlington, and Colonel Lee came to Mr. Schneider to have made a peculiar gate-latch that could be opened without dismounting. He wanted a dozen, and Mr. Schneider said, "Well, colonel, I will make one. If that pleases you, I will make eleven more." He came a few days after the one was ready for him. He took it with him and had it put on the gate, then came back and said, "Make the eleven. It is the very thing I want, and could not be improved." Since Mr. Schneider has retired from business one of the general's daughters was visiting at the surgeon-general's. She wanted a fan mended, and asked General Barnes to send it to her father's friend, Mr. Schneider. This was done, and Mr. Schneider was most happy to repair the fan. Mr. Schneider says his heart always warmed at the sight of Lee: it was pleasant to serve him. He would listen to suggestions which Mr. Schneider felt free to make, and was always reasonable and just. Among the books of Mr. Schneider's extensive library is the *Life of General Lee*, by John Esten Cooke, and in his catalogue, printed by himself, he appends in a footnote the following incident:

"In the fall of 1860 the general rode over from Arlington to the iron-foundry of Mr. Schneider, corner of Eighteenth and Pennsylvania Avenue, and drew from his pocket the draft of a peculiar kind of coulter which he requested to be cast for him to use in breaking up a lot of heavy meadow-sod. The price of the coulter was fixed at two dollars, and the colonel's old market-man called for it a day or two after. A few months passed and the peaceful pursuits of agriculture were exchanged for the strife and turmoil of war. General Lee pitched his tent in the South, and the quiet scenes of Arlington knew him no more. Late in 1861, amid the stirring scenes that were enacting around him, whilst all the cares and responsibilities of his position were resting upon General Lee, Mr. Schneider received by the hands of a little boy two one-dollar gold-pieces with a brief note of apology."

We now approach a somewhat important period in General Lee's life—that in which he was first to clearly show the material of which he was made and his fine ability as an engineer. In the year 1837 he received orders to proceed to St. Louis, which city at that time was threatened with a serious disaster from the deflection of the main current of the Mississippi River to the Illinois side, and the danger of its cutting a new channel through the bottom-lands. Here he was to make surveys and consider the best means of averting this threatened peril, which would make of St. Louis an inland city, and to report to the Department at Washington. In addition, he was entrusted with other duties connected with the navigation of the Mississippi, the details of which we can best give in the words of General Meigs, quartermaster-general U. S. A., who, then a lieutenant, accompanied the young engineer as his assistant, and who furnishes for this work the following valuable account of their operations:

In the summer of 1837, Lieutenant Robert E. Lee, corps of Engineers, was ordered by the Engineer department to proceed to the Mississippi River, and, with an appropriation made by Congress for the purpose, to make examination, plans, and estimates for the improvement of the navigation of the Mississippi at the harbor of St. Louis, where sandbars threatened to interfere with the use of the water-front of the city, known as the levee, upon which they were encroaching, and where the main channel of the river showed a tendency to change from the Missouri to the Illinois shore. He was also instructed to make surveys and plans for improving the navigation of this river near the point where the Des Moines enters it from the west, and above and about the mouth of Rock River, which enters from the east. At both these points the river flows over ledges of rocks, with a narrow and tortuous channel. During the season of low water all steamboats at these points were obliged to discharge at least a part of their cargo, which was placed upon what were then known as "keel-boats" and towed by horses along the shores to the head of the rapids. The country about these rapids was only then being

surveyed and opened for settlement. No railroad had at that
time crossed the Alleghanies.

Lieutenant Lee left Washington about June, accompanied
by Lieutenant Meigs as his assistant. They went by the way
of the Pennsylvania Canal to Pittsburg, where they took a
steamer and descended to Louisville, stopping at Cincinnati
(both of these were then small cities, compared with what they
are to-day). At Louisville they found a small steamboat which
had just been completed under the supervision of Captain
Shreeves, famous as the inventor and operator of the "snag-
boat." His son-in-law, Captain Morehead, was the captain of
the surveying boat; and here, with the aid of the boatmen,
Lieutenant Lee organized and outfitted a strong surveying-
party of river-men. The steamer proceeded to the Des Moines
rapids, touching at St. Louis on the way. (St. Louis's principal distinction then was that it was the headquarters of the
North-western fur trade. Ashley, Chouteau, and Sandford had
there their principal offices, and thence despatched expeditions
which penetrated the Rocky Mountains and fought battles in
Oregon and Washington Territories with the Canadian voya-
geurs and Scotch servants of the Hudson Bay Company.)
Arrived at the lower or Des Moines rapids of the Mississippi,
the party attempted to pass the rapids in their steamer, and
quickly experienced the difficulties of the navigation by finding themselves fast on the rocks of one of the lower channels.
All efforts to float the steamer failed, and the party proceeded
to make their survey of these rapids while using the steamer as
a base of operations, the surveying-parties leaving the steamer
in small boats in the morning and returning at night.

Having completed the survey of the Des Moines rapids,
they took passage in a steamer which they found at the head
of the rapids, and ascended to Rock Island. There they discovered another steamer wrecked upon a rock in the Rock
Island rapids; her hull was stove in and her lower deck was
partly under water, but her upper cabin, with its staterooms,
was dry and habitable. Holes made for removing the engines
yawned in the cabin-floor. Lieutenant Lee made this wreck
his base of operations during the survey of the upper rapids.

From the stern, after the day's work was over, the young men
of the party replenished the larder by fishing for blue catfish,
pike, and pickerel. About the end of October the work on
this part of the river was finished, and they returned to the
Des Moines rapids on a passing steamer. At these rapids they
found the banks lined with birch-bark canoes and Indian tepees,
a tribe of Chippewas having assembled there to receive the fall
distribution of presents from the agents. Owing to a rise in
the river, they now found themselves able to float their own
steamer, in which they returned to St. Louis.

Here the second story of a warehouse on the levee was
rented as an office, where the maps giving the results of their
surveys of the upper river were prepared. While the reduction
of their notes to the form of maps was going on parties were
placed in the field on each bank of the river. Signals were
established, and the river was thoroughly triangulated and
sounded from the mouth of the Missouri to some distance
below St. Louis. These surveys were completed and mapped,
and the party broke up. The men were discharged, and Lieutenant Lee and Lieutenant Meigs returned to Washington,
laying up their steamer for the winter on the Ohio, and passing through Wheeling by way of the Cumberland road. At
Frederick, Md., they took cars on the Baltimore and Ohio
Railroad, crossing some divides by horse-power. No locomo-
tive had at that time reached Frederick.

Lieutenant Lee made up his report, in which he recommended the improvement of the two rapids by the straighten-
ing and widening of the channels and by blasting and moving
the rocks which obstructed navigation. He recommended, in
regard to the St. Louis problem, the proper course of the dikes
to deflect the currents and to close at low water the eastern or
Illinois channel by connecting Bloody Island with the eastern
shore.

These reports and maps were published by Congress, which
for many years continued to make appropriations for the execution of the work designed and recommended by Lieutenant
Lee.

Probably the only survivor of that expedition is General

Meigs, who takes pleasure in contributing this reminiscence to the memoirs of General Lee. It was the beginning of the permanent improvement of the upper Mississippi River. At that time only a few log houses, traders' stores, and military posts existed on the shores of the rapids and for hundreds of miles above. The land had never been surveyed or brought into the market.

The preliminary survey above described was not the whole of Lieutenant Lee's connection with the improvement of the Mississippi. For some years thereafter he superintended the progress of the work at the points designated. During the prosecution of this work at St. Louis there was much free criticism and adverse prediction indulged in by the people of the threatened city. Heedless of this public clamor, the young Engineer officer pursued the even tenor of his way, and finally convinced his critics by the best of logic, that of success, that there might be some intelligence and ability outside of political assemblies and newspaper offices.

General Lee has described to the writer of this work the general method in which he achieved success in this difficult undertaking. His method was to force the current back into its original channel by driving piles and constructing cribs and wing-dams. The eddies thus created caused a deposit of sediment to be made between the dams, which gradually filled up the place where the wash-out had occurred with solid matter, and diverted the unsteady stream back into its original course.

Operations at the rapids also were prosecuted in accordance with the plans and under the directions of Lieutenant Lee, and an available channel gradually formed. Many years later, the commerce of the river requiring larger boats than could safely venture through the Des Moines channel, a ship-canal was constructed on the western shore of the river at this place, notwithstanding the fact that railroads then lined both shores of the stream. The commerce thus made available has supplied the wants of the millions who have since made of the upper Mississippi and of the plains of the Red River of the North the granary of North America. Cities have sprung up which, like

Minneapolis and St. Paul, count their inhabitants by the hun, dred thousands; St. Louis, then a small town with a few thousand inhabitants, has grown into a noble city peopled by more than three hundred and fifty thousand souls; and the worthless prairie-land of that day has now been largely converted into city lots of immense value. It is not claimed here that the engineering skill of Lieutenant Lee was in any sense the cause of this prosperity, but simply that he performed services that helped to render it possible.

Although we have said so much in regard to the appearance and character of Robert E. Lee, yet General Meigs's testimony to that effect is so valuable, when we consider his opportunities of thoroughly knowing him, that we cannot omit it. He expresses himself as remembering with pleasure and affection "his intimate associations with Lieutenant Lee, a man then in the vigor of youthful strength, with a noble and commanding presence, and an admirable, graceful, and athletic figure. He was one with whom nobody ever wished or ventured to take a liberty, though kind and generous to his subordinates, admired by all women, and respected by all men. He was the model of a soldier and the beau ideal of a Christian man."

Some letters of General Lee, written at this period, are sufficiently characteristic to be of interest to the reader, and we may be excused for quoting them. One, written to his wife and dated "Louisville, June 5, 1839," contains the following passage :

"You do not know how much I have missed you and the children, my dear Mary. To be alone in a crowd is very solitary. In the woods I feel sympathy with the trees and birds, in whose company I take delight, but experience no interest in a strange crowd. I hope you are all well and will continue so, and therefore must again urge upon you to be very prudent and careful of those dear children. If I could only get a squeeze at that little fellow turning up his sweet mouth to 'keese Baba'! You must not let him run wild in my absence, and will have to exercise firm authority over all of them. This will not require severity, or even strictness, but constant attention and an unwavering course. Mildness and forbearance, tempered by firmness and judgment, will strengthen their affection for you, while it will maintain your control over them.''

We are fortunately enabled to add to this a letter of much value as detailing incidents in the life of the young lieutenant of Engineers while on duty in the West. The Dick referred to may remain incognito, as his personality is of no importance to the narrative. The letter is addressed externally to ''Lieut. J. E. Johnston, Topographical Engineers, Washington, D. C.,'' but internally '' My Dear Colonel,'' the title by which General Johnston was then familiarly known to his intimate friends:

"St. Louis, 26th July, 1839.

'' My Dear Colonel : Upon my return here some few days since from the Rapids I found your letter of the 1st. It did me good to hear of the boys, especially as it was all good. Kan's fishing-project I fear is more natural than feasible, and its merits in so benighted a place as Washington will never be appreciated. I now contemplate you, therefore, as one of the stars in General Scott's staff. While up the river I fell in with Dick, and escorted him from Galena to Burlington, his headquarters. General Brooke happened at Galena while we were there, and, besides the pleasure of meeting him again, we had much sport in fighting the battles of Old Point over again. But it was done temperately and in a temperance manner, for the general has forsworn strong potations, and our refreshment consisted of only soda-water and ice-cream, delicacies that had been untasted by the general for the last *nine* years, and four times a day did we pay our respects to the fountain and freezer. Dick had been up to Dubuque to let out one of his roads, and, finding some spare days on his hands, 'accoutred as he was,' he plunged into a pleasure-party for the Falls of St. Anthony that came along in fine spirits with music playing and colors flying. Would you like to hear of his apparel? A little short-sleeved, short-waisted, short-skirted, brown linen coat, well acquainted with the washboard, and intended for a smaller man than our friend; a faded blue calico shirt; domestic cloth pants; a pair of commodious brogans; and a hat torn, broken, and discolored. Now, hear him laugh as he presents himself for a dance, arms akimbo, and you have him before you. I believe, though, it was a concerted thing with him, for whom should he meet but his Indian friend 'Hole-in-the-Day' and his faithful *Red She*, who showed him his old blanket that she religiously wrapt herself in, but upon examining *his* fingers her good copper rings were not there! He complains bitterly of his present waste of life, looks thin and dispirited, and is acquainted with the cry of every child in Iowa. He is well practised in pork-eating and promiscuous sleeping, and is a friend to Quakers, or rather their pretty daughters. . . . .

"News recently arrived that the Sioux had fallen upon a party of Chippeways and taken one hundred and thirty scalps. The *Hole-in-the-Day*, Dick's friend, had gone in advance with the larger party, and they did not come up with him. It is expected that this chief, who is represented as an uncommon man, will take ample revenge, and this may give rise to fresh trouble. You will see the full accounts in the papers. . . . .

"Bliss is well at the Rapids, with the whole fleet, and I hope jerking out the stones fast.

"R. E. Lee."

We must pass with more rapidity over the few subsequent years of his career. As already said, he was made captain of Engineers in 1838. In 1840 he resumed his legitimate duties of military engineer, and in 1842 was sent to Fort Hamilton in New York harbor, where he was occupied for several years in improving the defences. In 1844 he was appointed on the board of visitors to the Military Academy at West Point. These services occupied him until the year 1846, when the breaking out of hostilities between the United States and Mexico opened a wider field for the exercise of his abilities as a military engineer, and offered his first opportunity for that practical education in the art of war which was afterward to bear such abundant fruit.

CHAPTER III.

THE MEXICAN WAR.

Causes of the War.—A Daring Scout.—Siege of Vera Cruz.—Cerro Gordo.—Passage of the Pedregal.—Contreras, Churubusco, Chapultepec.—Letter from Mexico.—Testimony of Generals Wilcox and Hunt.—Encomium from General Johnston.

IN 1846 war was declared between the United States and the neighboring republic of Mexico—a war in which Robert E. Lee bore a prominent part, and in which he gained great distinction both as an able engineer and as a gallant and daring soldier. His connection with this war forms so important a chapter in his history that some brief account of its causes and the general course of its events becomes here necessary.

Texas while yet a sub-province of the republic of Mexico had attracted a considerable population of immigrants from the United States, who confided in the promise of the Mexican Cortes, promulgated in 1824, that as soon as it had gained sufficient importance it should be erected into an independent state of the republic, and be made "free, sovereign, and independent in whatever exclusively related to its internal government and administration."

The foreign immigration which took place on the faith of this proclamation called forth in 1830 a counter-decree from Bustamente, then President or tyrant of the republic, in which he prohibited the ingress of foreigners. To execute his edicts he introduced a considerable force of Mexican soldiers into Texas, which was thus virtually placed under military rule.

This act called forth strong opposition among the inhabitants, and the soldiers were forced to leave the country. Bustamente's rule ended in 1832, he being succeeded by Santa Anna as President. Shortly afterward Texas petitioned to be erected into a separate state, as promised in the act of 1824. Austin, the agent sent by the Texans to the capital city, being

47

unable to obtain any reply to his petition from the Mexican
Government, wrote to the Texan authorities and advised them
to organize a state government without waiting for the action
of the Mexican Congress.

This action was considered treasonable, and Austin was
arrested and imprisoned for over a year. Santa Anna had
meanwhile overthrown the Mexican constitution and made
himself military dictator of the "republic of Mexico," so
called. The people of Texas resented this usurpation, organized a state government, and raised troops to resist the invasion
which they had every reason to expect. They were not mistaken. Troops invaded the province, and an engagement took
place at Gonzales on the 2d of October, 1835.

This was the first step in a war which resulted in the independence of Texas. In the battle of San Jacinto, April 21,
1836, the Mexicans suffered a complete defeat, and Santa Anna
was taken prisoner. One of the terms of his release was the
recognition of the independence of Texas, which had been
erected into a republic on the 17th of March, with David G.
Burnett for its first President.

On the 3d of March, 1837, the independence of this new
power was recognized by the United States, two years afterward by France and England, and very soon by most of the
European states.

As early as August 4, 1837, Texas proposed to unite herself
with the United States. This proposition was declined by the
administration of President Van Buren, and was not entertained till the term of President Tyler, when a resolution of
Congress was passed setting forth the terms of a union of the
republic of Texas with the United States. This proposition
was formally adopted by the people of Texas assembled in
convention on July 4, 1845, and a new constitution was formed
preparatory to the admission of the young republic as a State
of the Federal Union.

The independence of Texas had never been acknowledged
by Mexico, and this action of the United States Government
gave serious offence, which was evidenced by a remonstrance
from General Almonte, the Mexican minister resident at Wash-

ington, who immediately afterward demanded his passports and left the country. All friendly intercourse between the United States and Mexico now ceased. Mr. Polk, who was then Pres-ident, apprehending an invasion of Texan soil, sent General Zachary Taylor, with about five thousand men, to guard the new State of the American Union. Early in August, 1845, he took position at Corpus Christi, near the mouth of the Neuces River. On the 13th of January, 1846, he was ordered to ad-vance to the Rio Grande, and reached the east bank of that river on March 28th, where he erected a fortress, called Fort Brown, directly opposite the Mexican city of Matamoras.

On the 26th of April, General Ampudia, the Mexican com-mander, gave notice that he considered hostilities commenced, and on the same day a force of 63 American soldiers were attacked on the Texan side of the river, and all killed or captured. This was the first blood shed in the war.

Two other battles took place on Texan soil—one near Palo Alto, where a Mexican army of about 6000 men was defeated; and the other at Resaca de la Palma, where the same army was utterly routed and the soil of Texas freed of its invaders.

A few days afterward General Taylor crossed the river, took possession of Matamoras, and carried the war definitely into Mexican territory. Fifty thousand volunteers were called for, and the army of General Taylor was rapidly reinforced by recruits from Texas and the adjoining States.

The plan of military operations now adopted at Washington was to invade Mexico on three different lines: one was from Matamoras to the interior, under the lead of General Taylor; another toward New Mexico and California, under the lead of General Kearney; while a third column, under General Wool, was to seize the northern departments of Mexico. With the last column Captain Lee first entered the field of war.

The young officer of Engineers remained with General Wool's command until ordered to join the expedition of General Scott, and while with it he performed very important service, as in-stanced in the story, related by himself, of a scouting-expedi-tion. This incident is of such interest as illustrative of the romance of war and of the daring of its hero that we here

briefly repeat it, as told by a friend who had heard him personally relate it:

Shortly before the battle of Buena Vista, General Wool,
being ignorant of the position and movements of the enemy,
but having been positively assured that Santa Anna had crossed
the mountains and was encamped with his whole army at a
point only twenty miles distant, determined to send out a
scouting-party to ascertain the truth of this report. Captain
Lee, who was present, at once volunteered to perform this
duty. His offer was accepted, and he was directed to procure
a guide and order a company of cavalry to meet him at the
outer picket-line as escort. By some means, however, he
missed the picket-post and his escort, and ere long found himself several miles beyond the lines with no company but his
guide. This was a young Mexican who knew the country,
and whom Captain Lee had promised the contents of a pocket-
pistol if he should play false.

Dangerous as it was to proceed alone, to return was to
abandon the enterprise for that night, and the daring scout
galloped on. At a point about five miles from the reported
place of encampment of the Mexican army the moonlight
displayed numerous tracks of mules and wagons in the road.
No artillery-tracks were visible, but these might have been
obliterated by the others, and there was abundant reason to
conclude that a strong foraging- or reconnoitering-party had
passed here. The information thus obtained would have satisfied many officers, yet it was not sufficiently positive for
Captain Lee, who determined to go on till he reached the
picket-posts of the enemy.

To his surprise, he found no pickets. He concluded that he
had missed them as he had those of his own army, and had
ridden within the Mexican lines. In confirmation of this
opinion, he soon found himself in view of what appeared to
be large camp-fires on a hillside at no great distance. His
guide, who was by this time in a pitiable state of fright,
begged him earnestly to return, saying that there was a stream
of water just beyond, and that he knew that Santa Anna's
whole army was encamped on the other side.

But the daring scout was not yet quite satisfied, and, directing the guide to await his return, he galloped boldly forward. Soon he perceived what appeared to be the white tents of a large encampment. Reaching the banks of the stream, he heard beyond it loud talking and the usual noises of a camp.

By this time, however, he was near enough to be able to make better use of the moonlight, and discovered that his white tents were simply a large *flock of sheep*, and that his army was a train of wagons and the drovers of a large herd of cattle, mules, etc. Riding into their camp, he quickly learned from them that Santa Anna had not yet crossed the mountains, and that there were no Mexican forces in that locality.

He galloped back with this important news to the army, where he found his friends in a state of serious apprehension as to his safety, the intended escort having reported his disappearance. "But," said General Lee, "the most delighted man to see me was the old Mexican, the father of my guide, with whom I had been last seen by any of our people, and whom General Wool had arrested and proposed to hang if I was not forthcoming."

Though he had ridden forty miles that night, he was in the saddle again after a three hours' rest. He guided a body of cavalry to and far beyond the point to which he had gone the night before, and succeeded in ascertaining definitely the position, force, etc. of the enemy.

The signal victory of General Taylor at Buena Vista, February, 1847, in which a force of 20,000 Mexicans under Santa Anna was put to rout by 5000 Americans, virtually ended the war in the northern Mexican states. Meanwhile, during January and February, 1847, General Scott was collecting a large force in the neighborhood of Tampico to operate against Vera Cruz and the city of Mexico. Captain R. E. Lee joined this force by the particular request of General Scott.

About the last of February, General Scott embarked his troops and sailed for Vera Cruz, and on the 9th of March landed his army of 12,000 men a short distance south of that city, which he immediately proceeded to invest. The city was surrounded by a wall and defended by a powerful fortress, the castle of San Juan de Ulloa, the number of guns being about 400. It was garrisoned by 5000 Mexican troops under General Morales.

The establishment of batteries and the other details of the siege were directed by Captain Lee, who prosecuted his labors with such vigor that by the 22d the batteries were ready to commence the bombardment which resulted on the 29th in the surrender of Vera Cruz and the adjacent fortifications. For his services on this occasion Captain Lee was favorably mentioned by General Scott in his report of the siege of Vera Cruz. Having gained a secure base of operations, General Scott advanced toward the city of Mexico; but on reaching Cerro Gordo, the point where the National Road emerges from the Tierra Caliente, he found himself confronted by General Santa Anna with a numerous army, which this general had, in spite of his defeat at Buena Vista, thoroughly reorganized and put in position to oppose Scott's advance.

Cerro Gordo was of such formidable strength that a direct attack was deemed injudicious, and therefore it became necessary to adopt other means for its reduction. In the words of General Scott, "Reconnoissances were pushed in search of some practicable route other than the winding, zigzag road among the spurs of mountains, with heavy batteries at every turn. The reconnoissances were conducted with vigor under Captain Lee at the head of a body of pioneers, and at the end of the third day a passable way for light batteries was accomplished without alarming the enemy, giving the possibility of turning the extreme left of his line of defence and capturing his whole army, except the reserve, that lay a mile or two higher up the road. Santa Anna said that he had not believed a goat could have approached him in that direction. Hence the surprise and the results were the greater."

A large force was sent along the route thus made passable, and, though it was discovered by the enemy before it had quite reached the point desired, it had gained a position which enabled it to storm and carry the heights of Cerro Gordo and rout the Mexican army, Santa Anna being defeated and forced to retire with great loss. General Scott, in his report of this battle, says:

"I am compelled to make special mention of Captain R. E. Lee, Engineer. This officer was again indefatigable during these operations in reconnoissances as daring as laborious, and of the utmost value. Nor was he less conspicuous in planting batteries and in conducting columns to their stations under the heavy fire of the enemy."

An interesting incident which occurred during one of the reconnoissances mentioned by General Scott was related to the writer by John Fitzwalter, who acted as a guide to Captain Lee during this campaign, and who himself was so daring as to gain from the Mexicans the title of Juan Diablo, or, to put it in plain English, John the Devil.

During the reconnoissance in question Captain Lee had ventured too far from his supporting column, and unexpectedly found himself in the midst of the enemy and in a position of great danger. He was forced to take refuge beneath a fallen tree, near which was a spring to which the Mexicans frequently came for water. While he lay hidden in this perilous covert hostile soldiers frequently passed over the tree, and even sat down on it and entered into conversation, without discovering the somewhat nervous individual beneath it. He was obliged to remain there until the coming of night enabled him to retire from the dangerous locality.

It may not be amiss to mention at this point that Captain Lee was not the only one of his family who took part in these operations. His elder brother, Lieutenant Sidney Smith Lee of the navy, served in the bombardment of Vera Cruz in command of a detachment of seamen who worked the guns in the trenches. These guns were under the general direction of Captain Lee, who has often been heard to relate with what anxiety after each discharge he would look to see if his brother was safe, and how reassured he felt when he saw his white teeth gleaming through the smoke.

Early in these operations Captain Lee had been appointed on the personal staff of General Scott, who had the greatest confidence in his judgment and ability, and was always strongly influenced by his opinion in council.

In the subsequent campaign in the Valley of Mexico to Captain Lee is mainly due the capture of Contreras and the reduction of Churubusco—successes which opened the way for General Scott to the walls of Mexico.

A distinguished officer (General Henry J. Hunt) who participated in the Mexican campaign thus describes the operations at Contreras:

"On the 19th of August, 1847, General Scott's headquarters were at San Augustin, a small village four or five miles south of Churubusco. The main road running south from the city of Mexico forks at Churubusco, one branch going to San Augustin, while the other runs in a south-westerly direction, and passes to the east of Contreras and of a somewhat elevated plateau beyond or south of Contreras. The distances from Churubusco to the plateau and from the plateau to San Augustin are each about equal to the distance from San Augustin to Churubusco. This triangular space, included between the two roads and a ridge of hills south of San Augustin as the third side, is called the Pedregal. This Pedregal is a vast surface of volcanic rocks and scoria broken into every possible form, presenting sharp ridges and deep fissures, exceedingly difficult even in the daytime for the passage of infantry, and utterly impassable for artillery, cavalry, or single horsemen. There are occasional intervals, especially near San Augustin, where small fields have been made and tilled; but these little oases grow smaller and more infrequent toward the west, and a mile or two from the plateau cease altogether, so that the country from above Contreras to the range of hills on the south is an almost unbroken field of desolation, such as lava would present if in a state of ebullition. Indeed, it appears like a sea of such lava suddenly congealed, with here and there a clump of hardy bushes and dwarf trees which have managed to force an existence from the apparently sterile rocks. By taking advantage of the·small open spaces a difficult, crooked, and hardly passable road—not much better than a mule-track— had been opened from San Augustin to the plateau, in front of which it joins the road from the city of Mexico. On this plateau General Valencia had intrenched his fine division, about six thousand strong, with twenty-four guns, which com-

Gen. Scott's troops crossing the Pedregal, Mexico, Aug. 19th, 1847.   Pages 54-5.

pletely commanded the approach from San Augustin. A mile or more north of Contreras and the neighboring hamlet of Anselda, and on the main city road, lay General Santa Anna with a portion of the reserves of the Mexican army.

"On the morning of the 19th, General Scott ordered Pillow's and Twiggs's divisions to move from San Augustin toward the plateau, the ground having been previously carefully reconnoitered by Captain R. E. Lee, assisted by Lieutenants Beauregard and Tower of the Engineers. Pillow was directed to improve the road with his force, and, if possible, make it practicable for artillery, while Twiggs was thrown in advance to protect the working-parties.

"General Scott in his official report, written that same day, says: 'By three o'clock this afternoon the advanced divisions came to a point where the new road could not be continued except under the direct fire of twenty-two pieces of the enemy's artillery (most of them of large calibre), placed in a camp strongly intrenched to oppose our operations, surrounded by every advantage of ground, and, besides, being reinforced hourly by immense bodies of cavalry and infantry, which, coming from the city over an excellent road beyond the volcanic fields, were consequently entirely beyond the reach of our cavalry and artillery.

"'Arriving on the ground an hour later, I found that Pillow's and Twiggs's divisions had advanced to dislodge the enemy, picking their way (all officers on foot) along his front, and extending themselves toward the road from the city and the enemy's left. . . . . The battle, though mainly stationary, continued to rage with great violence until nightfall.'

"In the mean time, portions of Riley's, Persifer Smith's, Shields's, and Cadwallader's brigades had made their way across the Pedregal to Contreras, whence they watched the approach of the Mexican troops from the city. Captain Lee accompanied these troops, and the nature of the ground can perhaps best be understood by the description given of it by one who passed over it at the time.

"He says: 'Late in the morning of the 19th the brigade of which my regiment was a part (Riley's) was sent out from San

Augustin in the direction of Contreras.   We soon struck a
region over which it was said no horses could go, and men
only with difficulty.

" ' No road was available; my regiment was in advance, my
company leading, and its point of direction was a church-spire
near or at Contreras.   Taking the lead, we soon struck the
Pedregal (a field of volcanic rock like boiling scoria suddenly
solidified), pathless, precipitous, and generally compelling rapid
gait in order to spring from point to point of rock, on which
two feet could not rest, and which cut through our shoes.   A
fall upon this sharp material would have seriously cut and injured one, whilst the effort to climb some of it cut the hands.

" ' Such was the general character of the portion crossed by
my regiment, and I believe by the brigades, though many, not
pushing as I did, may have picked out a circuitous and better
route.

" ' Just before reaching the main road from Contreras to the
city of Mexico we reached a watery ravine, the sides of which
were nearly perpendicular, up which I had to be pushed and
then to pull others.

" ' On looking back over this bed of lava or scoria, I saw the
troops, much scattered, picking their way very slowly, while
of my own company, some eighty or ninety strong, only five
men crossed with me or during some twenty minutes after.

" ' With these five I examined the country beyond, and struck
upon the small guard of a paymaster's park, which, from the
character of the country over which we had passed, was deemed
perfectly safe from capture.

" ' My men gained a paymaster's chest well filled with bags
of silver dollars, and the firing and fuss we made both frightened the guard with the belief that the infernals were upon
them and made our men hasten to our support.

" ' Before sundown all of Riley's—and, I believe, of Cadwallader's, Smith's, and Pierce's brigades—were over, and by nine
o'clock a council of war, presided over by Persifer Smith and
counselled by Captain R. E. Lee, was held at the church.

" ' I have always understood that what was devised and finally
determined upon was suggested by Captain Lee; at all events,

the council was closed by his saying that he desired to return to General Scott with the decision of General Smith, and that, as it was late, the decision must be given as soon as possible, since General Scott wished him to return in time to give directions for co-operation.

"'During the council and for hours after the rain fell in torrents, whilst the darkness was so intense that one could move only by groping.

"'To illustrate: my company again led the way to gain the Mexican rear, and when, after two hours of motion, light broke sufficiently to enable us to see a companion a few feet off, we had not moved four hundred yards, and the only persons present were half a dozen officers and one guide.

"'Captain Lee left the council to join General Scott. History gives him the credit of having succeeded, but it has always seemed incredible to me when I recollect the distance amid darkness and storm, and the dangers of the Pedregal which he must have traversed, and that, too, I believe, entirely unaccompanied. Scarcely a step could have been taken without danger of death; but that to him, a true soldier, was the willing risk of duty in a good cause. I would not believe it could have been made, that passage of the Pedregal, if he had not said he made it.'

"General Scott in the report from which we have already quoted, says of this same night: 'It was already dark, and the cold rain had begun to fall in torrents on our unsheltered troops. Wet, hungry, and without the possibility of sleep, all our gallant corps, I learn, are full of confidence, and only wait for the last hour of darkness to gain the position whence to storm and carry the position of the enemy. Of the seven officers despatched since about sundown from my position, opposite the enemy's centre, and on this side of the field of rocks and lava, to communicate instructions to the hamlet (Contreras), not one has succeeded in getting through those difficulties, increased by darkness. They have all returned.

"'But the gallant and indefatigable Captain Lee of the Engineers, who has been constantly with the operating forces, is just in from Shields, Smith, Cadwallader, etc. to report as above, and to request that a powerful diversion be made against the centre of the intrenched camp to-morrow morning.

" 'Brigadier-general Twiggs, cut off from the portion of his division beyond the impracticable ground, and Captain Lee, are gone to collect the forces remaining on this side, with which to make that diversion about five o'clock in the morning.'*

"The troops were collected, the diversion made, and the result of the combined movement, made possible only by Captain Lee's services, was the brilliant victory of Contreras early on the following morning.

"Subsequently, General Scott, whilst giving testimony before a court of inquiry, had occasion to refer to these operations, and he thus speaks of the service rendered on this occasion by Captain Lee:

" 'Captain Lee, Engineers, came to me from the hamlet with a message from Brigadier-general Smith, I think, about the same time (midnight). He, having passed over the difficult ground by daylight, found it just possible to return to San Augustin in the dark—*the greatest feat of physical and moral courage performed by any individual, in my knowledge, pending the campaign.*'

"When we remember that Captain Lee left the council-room at Contreras to pass over miles of such ground as we have described, in a pitch-dark night, without light or company, with the additional danger of wandering either to the right or left and thus falling into the hands of Valencia or Santa Anna, the risk of being met by some of those straggling bands of Mexicans which we had seen in the Pedregal, with no guide but the wind as it drove the cold rain in torrents against his face, or an occasional flash of lightning to give him a momentary glimpse of the country around him,—it will be acknowledged that General Scott, considering the object for which this was done, the manner of doing it, and the results, has characterized this deed of devotion by the only terms, exalted as they are, that could appropriately describe it."†

* See *Ex. Doc. No. 65, Senate, 1st Session 30th Cong.*, p. 73.

† General Hunt has given the following interesting incident which occurred at the meeting of the Massachusetts Branch Cincinnati Society, held at Boston, July 4, 1871:

In the battle that followed the events so fully described by General Hunt, Captain Lee bore an important part. The movement against the enemy commenced at three o'clock in the morning, a tedious march through darkness, rain, and mud, under the guidance of Captain Lee, bringing the assailing columns by sunrise to an elevation in the rear of the enemy's forces. An assault was at once made, the intrenchments of the enemy stormed, and in seventeen minutes after the charge was ordered the surprised Mexicans were in full flight and the American flag floating proudly over their works.

The subsequent movements may be briefly described. The victory of Contreras being complete, General Scott next advanced to Coyoacan, a strongly-fortified place, which Captain Lee was sent to reconnoitre with Captain Kearney's troop, First Dragoons, supported by Major Loring's rifle regiment. Another reconnoissance was sent under Lieutenant Stevens of the Engineers toward the strongly-fortified convent of San Pablo in the hamlet of Churubusco, one mile distant. Captain Lee, having completed his first reconnoissance, was next ordered to conduct Pierce's brigade, by a third road, to a point from which an attack could be made on the enemy's right and rear, thus favoring the movement on the convent and tending to cut off the line of retreat to the capital. Shields

* Upon that occasion General Silas Casey was admitted to the society. As usual, a speech of welcome was made. With admirable taste he ignored in his acknowledgment the Civil War, but gave them interesting points on the Mexican War (he commanded the stormers of Twiggs's division at Chapultepec), and in his speech he referred to me. So, as usual on such occasions, they had me up. I was 'dead broke' on matter for a speech, but it occurred to me that, as the Pedregal was fresh in my mind, I would give them a little more Mexican history, and I recited, glibly enough, the story. Of course I did not mention the name of the hero. I saw that they all thought it was General Casey. I kept dark until the close, amidst repeated demands of ' Name him! Name him!' When I got through and the name was again vociferously demanded, I replied, ' It is a name of which the old army was and is justly proud—that of Robert E. Lee, then a captain of Engineers, and since world-wide in fame as the distinguished leader of the Confederate armies.'

" For a moment there was unbroken silence, then such a storm of applause as is seldom heard. I remarked that I had been desirous to test the society, which represented all shades of political opinions, and was glad to see they could recognize heroism and greatness even in a former enemy."

was ordered to follow Pierce closely and to take command of the left wing.

The battle, thus ordered, soon raged violently along the whole line. Shields, in particular, was hard pressed and in danger of being overwhelmed by the hosts of the foe. Tidings of this threatened disaster were brought to General Scott by Captain Lee, who was at once ordered to conduct two troops of the Second Dragoons and the Rifles to the support of the left wing. The contest ended in the repulse of the enemy and a brilliant victory for General Scott's army.

This victory was followed by another, on the 8th of September, at the Molino del Rey. The troops were now rapidly approaching the capital city of Mexico, and the Engineer officers, Captain Lee, Lieutenant Beauregard, and others, were kept engaged in reconnoissances, which they performed with great daring and success. Then succeeded one of the most daring exploits of the war, that brilliant charge by which were stormed the heights of Chapultepec, a steep hill bristling with walls, mines, and batteries, yet up which our infantry columns rushed with a fiery valor and impetuosity which the Mexicans were quite unable to withstand. The heights were carried and the enemy put to flight.

In this brilliant affair Captain Lee was wounded, and, though eager to advance, was compelled to retire from loss of blood. In his official report General Scott again spoke of him in words of the highest compliment, remarking that he was "as distinguished for felicitous execution as for science and daring," and further stated that "Captain Lee, so constantly distinguished, also bore important orders from me (September 13th) until he fainted from a wound and the loss of two nights' sleep at the batteries."

It is evident, in fact, that General Scott had formed an exalted opinion of the valor and military genius of his young captain of Engineers. He makes, indeed, throughout the reports of his Mexican campaign frequent mention of three officers of the Engineer corps who were afterward to achieve high distinction in another field—Captain R. E. Lee, First Lieutenant P. G. T. Beauregard, and Second Lieutenant G.

B. McClellan.   Yet there is every evidence that Captain Lee was his special favorite, and there is hardly a despatch in which his name is not honorably mentioned.   We may add to the above the statement made by the Hon. Reverdy Johnson, that he "had heard General Scott more than once say that his success in Mexico was largely due to the skill, valor, and undaunted energy of Robert E. Lee."   Years afterward General Scott was heard to declare, "Lee is the greatest military genius in America."

These brilliant services were not left without that recognition which is most dear to the heart of a soldier.   Lee was steadily promoted.   His gallant conduct at Cerro Gordo brought him the brevet rank of major; his services at Contreras and Churubusco brought him the additional brevet of lieutenant-colonel; and after Chapultepec he was nominated for the brevet rank of colonel—distinctions fully earned by his skill and valor.

The victory last mentioned was immediately followed by the capture of the forts which guarded the roads leading into the city and the occupation of the Mexican capital.   This virtually ended the war.   There was some guerilla warfare, but no battles of importance, after this achievement, the Mexicans giving up the contest as hopeless.

The terms on which peace was granted, as is well known, were highly advantageous to the United States, and perhaps in no just sense disadvantageous to Mexico, for the provinces which were ceded to the United States, though they have been raised to such a high value by Anglo-Saxon enterprise and energy, were almost worthless in the hands of the supine Mexicans.   The indemnity which the Mexican Government received for these provinces was probably of more value to it, at that time, than the provinces themselves, and possibly the vast wealth in gold and silver which they contained might have yet been undiscovered had the Mexican rule continued, as it had remained undiscovered for previous centuries of Spanish dominion.

The remarks here made are preparatory to a quotation which we design to make from a hitherto unpublished letter by General Lee, in which he shows a shrewd political judgment and a correct idea of the proper method of dealing with vacillating diplomatists, though it savors rather of the soldier than of the politician. The letter also contains a passage indicative of General Lee's quiet love of a joke which is too good to omit. It is dated "City of Mexico, 12 April, 1848," and is written to one of his young lady-cousins. We quote only those parts of public interest, beginning with the witticism alluded to:

"It seems that all in Alexandria are progressing as usual, and that nothing will stop their marrying and being given in marriage. Tell Miss —— she had better dismiss that young divine and marry a soldier. There is some chance of the latter being shot, but it requires a particular dispensation of Providence to rid her of the former. Since the reception of your letter we have had the official notification of the ratification of the treaty by our Senate, brought on by Major Graham, and have learned of the arrival at Vera Cruz of the commissioner, Mr. Sevier, who has been preceded by the attorney-general, Mr. Clifford. I fear this hot despatch of envoys will cause the Mexicans to believe that we are over-anxious to accept their terms, and that they will be as coy, in proportion as we appear eager, to ratify on their part. They are very shrewd, and it will be difficult to get them to act before trying the strength of the new commissioner and making an effort for a mitigation of terms. The opportunity afforded them for pow-wowing they will be sure not to lose, but the time thus consumed, so precious to us, we cannot regain. In my humble opinion it would have been better to have sent out the naked instrument to General Butler, with instructions to submit it to the Mexican Government, and if within the prescribed time they thought proper to ratify it to pay them down the three millions and march the army home; but if not, to tear up the paper and make his arrangements to take the country up to the line from Tehuantepec to Osaqualco or whatever other southern boundary they should think proper for the United States. I think we might reasonably expect that they would lose no time in ratifying the present treaty. I might make a rough diplomatist, but a tolerably quick one."

The same letter gives us some insight into the methods by which Colonel Lee managed to kill dull time during his long detention in the city of Mexico. We may be pardoned for making a further quotation:

"I rode out a few days since for the first time to the church of Our Lady of Remedios. It is situated upon a hill at the termination of the mountains west of the city, and is said to be the spot to which Cortez retreated after being driven from the city on the memorable *Noche Triste.* I saw the cedar tree at Popotla, some miles nearer the city, in which it is said he passed a portion of that night. The 'trees of the Noche Triste,' so called from their blooming about the period of that event, are now in full bloom. The flower is a round ellipsoid, and of the most magnificent scarlet color I ever saw. I have two of them in my cup before me now. I wish I could send them to you. The holy image was standing on a large silver maguey-plant, with a rich crown on her head and an immense silver petticoat on. There were no votaries at her shrine, which was truly magnificent, but near the entrance of the church on either side were the offerings of those whom she had relieved. They consist of representations in wax of the parts of the human body that she had cured of the diseases with which they had been affected. And I may say there were all parts. I saw many heads severed from the trunks. Whether they represented those that she had restored I could not learn. It would be a difficult feat."

We should be glad to give further details of his life while thus detained in the city of Mexico waiting on the slow movements of diplomacy. But there is no such information extant. Undoubtedly he was not idle during those slow-moving months, but occupied himself in exploring the surrounding country and in studies incidental to his profession. He was too full of health, vitality, earnestness, and ambition to be willing to rest content while there were new progress to make and new information to be attained; and as he was free from those small vices and cared not for those petty pastimes in which so many of his companions passed their hours of leisure, there can be no doubt that his energy took the direction of study and observation, and that he was steadily though unknowingly fitting himself for the great part which he was destined in the future to play.

In fact, as regards this we are not confined to conjecture, but may relate an anecdote in point as told by General Magruder:

"After the fall of Mexico, when the American army was enjoying the ease and relaxation which it had bought by toil and blood, a brilliant assembly of officers sat over their wine discussing the operations of the capture and indulging hopes of a speedy return to the United States.

"One among them rose to propose the health of the captain of Engineers who had found a way for the army within the city, and then it was remarked that Captain Lee was absent. Magruder was despatched to bring him to the hall, and, departing on his mission, at last found the object of his search in a remote room of the palace busy on a map.

"Magruder accosted his friend and reproached him for his absence. The earnest worker looked up from his labors with a calm, mild gaze which we all remember, and, pointing to his instruments, shook his head.

"'But,' said Magruder in his impetuous way, 'this is mere drudgery. Make somebody else do it and come with me.'

"'No,' was the reply—'no, I am but doing my duty.'"

It is but just to add that we are indebted for much of our information concerning Captain Lee's life and exploits in Mexico to General Wilcox, who has kindly prepared for this work a long and valuable series of reminiscences of the Mexican War, and of Lee's connection therewith. In addition to the laudatory quotations from Scott's reports, General Wilcox presents some similarly favorable remarks from other prominent commanders in that war. General Persifer Smith, in his report of Contreras and Churubusco, says: "In adverting to the conduct of the staff I wish to record particularly my admiration of the conduct of Captain Lee of the Engineers. His reconnoissances, though pushed far beyond the bounds of prudence, were conducted with so much skill that their fruits were of the utmost value, the soundness of his judgment and his personal daring being equally conspicuous." General Shields,

CAPTAIN R. E. LEE

FROM A PORTRAIT TAKEN IN 1852

who with General Pierce attacked in the rear of Churubusco, in his report says: "As my command arrived I established the right upon a point recommended by Captain Lee of the Engineers, in whose skill and judgment I had the utmost confidence."

A testimonial to the same effect is given by General Twiggs in his report of the battle of Cerro Gordo, in which his division carried the heights and stormed the fortifications of the enemy. He remarks: "Although whatever I may say may add little to the good reputation of Captain Lee of the Engineer corps, yet I must indulge in the pleasure of speaking of the invaluable services which he rendered me from the time I left the main road until he conducted Riley's brigade to its position in rear of the enemy's strong work on the Jalapa road. I consulted him with confidence and adopted his suggestions with assurance. His gallantry and good conduct on both days, 17th and 18th of April, deserve the highest praise."

Colonel Riley, in his report of the same engagement, says: "Although not appropriately within the range of this report, yet, coming under my immediate observation, I cannot refrain from bearing testimony to the intrepid coolness and gallantry exhibited by Captain Lee of the Engineers when conducting the advance of my brigade under the heavy flank fire of the enemy."

General Twiggs, in his report of the battle of Contreras, further says: "To Captain Lee of the Engineers I have again the pleasure of tendering my thanks for the exceedingly valuable services rendered throughout the whole of these operations."

General Wilcox first made the acquaintance of Robert E. Lee at the siege of Vera Cruz, and says of him at that time: "I was much impressed with his fine appearance, either on horse or foot. Then he was in full manly vigor, *and the handsomest man in the army.*"

General Wilcox concludes: "I have given a brief outline of the operations in Mexico, in order that the references made to Captain Lee in the official reports of his superiors might be properly appreciated. It will be seen that the compliments

won by him were deserved—that he was active, untiring, skilful, courageous, and of good judgment.   He is referred to as
making roads over difficult routes, locating and constructing
batteries, bringing over the Pedregal in the night important
information that enabled the commanding general to give
orders exactly applicable to the field of Contreras, and which
were so brilliantly executed at an early hour the next morning,
and in which the diversion under Colonel Ransom, directed by
Captain Lee, had such good results, having been converted into
a real attack.   The quotations then show on what important
missions he was sent during the conflict at Churubusco; that
then he was sent to look at the base and hospital at Mixcoac,
to see that it was made as secure as possible, for at it were the
sick and wounded, reserve ordnance, etc.; and, finally, that he
was wounded at Chapultepec slightly, and pretty well worn out
from excessive work by night and day.   It could hardly have
been otherwise than that a captain with such encomiums from
his superiors would be greatly distinguished should occasion
ever be presented.   All who knew him were prepared to accept
him at once as a general when he was assigned to the command
of the Army of Northern Virginia, and his success, great as it
was, was only what had been anticipated.

"C. M. WILCOX."

To General Hunt, who has already contributed so freely to
this chapter, we are indebted for other reminiscences of Captain Lee of a very interesting character.   The first of the two
anecdotes given below relates to an earlier period of Lee's life,
but, as it is referred to in the second, an incident of the Mexican War, they are both given here.   They yield important
glimpses into the personal feelings and character of the subject of this memoir:

"In 1843–44, I was stationed at Fort Hamilton, New York
harbor.   Captain Lee was the Engineer officer in charge of the
works there, and I saw much of him.   He was then about
thirty-five years of age, as fine-looking a man as one would
wish to see, of perfect figure and strikingly handsome.   Quiet
and dignified in manner, of cheerful disposition, always pleas-

ant and considerate, he seemed to me the perfect type of *a gentleman.* His family, then with him, consisted of Mrs. Lee, their little daughter Mary, and the two boys, Rooney (W. H. F.) and Custis, and formed a charming portion of our little society. He was a vestryman of the little parish church of Fort Hamilton, of which the post-chaplain was the rector, and as thorough in the discharge of his church as of other duties.

"But the Tractarian movement had reached America; Tract No. XC. had been published. Puseyism was a bone of contention. The excitement invaded our little parish, and it created feeling, for the 'Low-Church' members vehemently suspected the rector of 'High-Church' views because of certain suspicious prayers that he used to which they had not been accustomed. From all this Captain Lee kept aloof, and, as he was altogether too important a member to make his views a matter of indifference, various were the efforts made to draw him out—each party hoping for his powerful support—but without success, for he always contrived in some pleasant way to avoid any expression of opinion that would commit him to either faction.

"One evening he came into the quarters of one of us youngsters, where a number of officers and one or two of the neighbors were assembled. Soon the inevitable subject came up and was discussed with considerable warmth, and, on the parts of two or three, with some feeling. Captain Lee was quiet, but, to those who understood him, evidently amused at the efforts to draw him out. On some direct attempt to do so he turned to me and in his impressive, grave manner said, 'I am glad to see that you keep aloof from the dispute that is disturbing our little parish. That is right, and we must not get mixed up in it; we must support each other in that. But I must give you some advice about it, in order that we may understand each other: *Beware of Pussyism! Pussyism* is always bad, and may lead to unchristian feeling; therefore beware of *Pussyism!*'

"The ludicrous turn given by his pronunciation, and its aptness to the feeling that one or two had displayed, ended the matter in a general burst of laughter, for the manner more than the words conveyed his meaning. It became rather a joke at my expense, however, for sometimes when several of us met he would look at me in a grave way, shake his head, and say, 'Keep clear of this *Pussyism!*' And that was as near as they ever got to committing Captain Lee to a Church quarrel.

"There were several young officers at Fort Hamilton at the time, some of whom afterward became prominent—notably Duncan, who so greatly distinguished himself in the Mexican War, and Sedgwick, between whom and Captain Lee a warm friendship existed, and who was killed at Spottsylvania fighting his old comrade.

"After leaving Fort Hamilton I met Captain Lee but once or twice until he came to Vera Cruz with General Scott, in the spring of 1847, when our old relations, which had been as intimate as the difference in our ages would permit, were renewed. After the surrender of Vera Cruz there was a report that the churches in town would not be opened for service, for fear that they might be 'desecrated by the heretics.' The object and effect of this upon the people could be easily divined, and General Scott sent to the proper authorities to *borrow* a couple of churches for the ensuing Sunday, as he had excellent chaplains. The hint was taken, and the churches all opened. There was one outside the walls near which one of our batteries had been constructed, and the edifice was somewhat injured in the cannonade, but it too was opened.

"As I had not been to church for a long time, I availed myself of this opportunity, but already on my arrival found the place crowded. As with all Catholic churches in that country, there were no pews. The congregation—mostly women—were on their knees in the body of the church, whilst the galleries and all other available space were filled by our volunteers, full of curiosity, for but few of them had ever seen the Catholic service. It was but a few years since the 'Native American' excitement, accompanied by violent demonstrations against Catholics, and the sacking of their churches in some of our large towns, had raged, and the feeling was not yet entirely over.

"I found not only that the church was full, but the door was blocked by a crowd of our soldiers. Patiently making my way, I finally got inside the door where I could see the altar. All present were on their knees or standing except on the left, where midway of the church a single bench had been brought and set against the wall. On this bench, in full uniform, epaulettes, and sword, sat General Scott and his staff, the general himself at the end nearest the altar, then his aid, Lieutenant Williams, then Captain Lee, Lieutenants Beauregard, Say, etc. The bench seemed full, but a few minutes afterward, looking in that direction, I caught Captain Lee's eye. He was evidently looking for this opportunity, for he motioned me toward him and made a movement indicating that there was room for me beside him. I had been longer in Mexico than these new-comers, and in my dilapidated old campaign dress felt that I would be a little out of place in the brilliant party. However, standing was tiresome, and I gradually picked my way to the bench, and found that he had a place ready for me by his side.

"It was evident that the service was a special one. Soon the acolytes were going round the church making the worshippers close up until a clear space was formed all round the congregation. Then one of the acolytes went to the altar, lighted a large thick wax candle, and brought it to General Scott. At first the general did not seem to comprehend it, but, taking in the situation, he took the candle and immediately handed it to Mr. Williams. The volunteers stared with open mouths. It was understood that General Scott, if successful in his campaign, must be a Presidential candidate at the next election. Hostility to the Catholic Church was *the* element with the 'American' party. The matter was getting interesting. In a moment or two the acolyte returned with another, but not so large or honorable a candle as the first. Finding the first one in the aid's hands and General Scott unprovided, he looked rather dazed, but acted promptly—blew out his light, went back to the altar, got another large one, and brought it to the general, who had to take it. I, being next to Williams, carefully looked away, and saw *nothing* until the acolyte returned with the smaller candle lighted for *me*, which I took, and others were given to Captain Lee and the rest of the staff.

"Then we were requested to rise, were wheeled 'by twos' to the left, which brought General Scott in front of me and Captain Lee on my right. Soon a side-door opened just in front of General Scott, and an array of priests in gorgeous vestments filed out and formed in our front. Everything was clear enough now—a Church procession, in which General Scott and his staff—including poor me in my shabby old undress—had the place of honor. I looked at Captain Lee. He had that dignified, quiet appearance habitual to him, and looked as if the carrying of candles in religious processions was an ordinary thing with him. The music—and very good music it was—commenced, and the procession moved round the church. We had passed the altar, when an idea occurred to me upon which I could not refrain from acting, and I touched Captain Lee's elbow. He very properly gave me a rebuking look, but upon my repeating the touch he bent his head toward me and whispered, 'What is it?'—'Captain Lee?'—'Well?'—'I really hope there is no *Pussyism* in all this?' I glanced at him; his face retained its quiet appearance, but the corners of his eyes and mouth were twitching in the struggle to preserve his gravity.

"After we got into the City of Mexico, I frequently met him, but he was always busy. In the ensuing spring he examined the western part of the valley, and on his daily return to the city generally passed through Tacubaya, two miles west of it, where my battery was stationed, occupying a large hacienda in the suburbs, with gardens and orange-groves in blossom, in which there were great numbers of beautiful humming-birds. It was a pleasant spot, and Captain Lee almost always stopped for half an hour with me to enjoy its beauties. I remember nothing special in these visits except his desire to heal the differences between General Scott and some of his subordinate officers and the efforts he was making in that direction, about which he conversed with me. He was a peacemaker by nature."

We are fortunate in being able to add to the foregoing record the following highly valuable testimony, contributed expressly to this work by General Joseph E. Johnston, one of the ablest and most distinguished commanders in the Confederate army. Like all who knew Robert E. Lee, General Johnston testifies to his noble character and agreeable manner, and concludes with an interesting instance of his warm sympathy:

"No one among men but his own brothers had better opportunity to know General Lee than I. We entered the Military Academy together as classmates, and formed then a friendship never impaired. It was formed very soon after we met, from the fact that my father served under his in the celebrated Lee's Legion. We had the same intimate associates, who thought, as I did, that no other youth or man so united the qualities that win warm friendship and command high respect. For he was full of sympathy and kindness, genial and fond of gay conversation, and even of fun, that made him the most agreeable of companions, while his correctness of demeanor and language and attention to all duties, personal and official, and a dignity as much a part of himself as the elegance of his person, gave him a superiority that every one acknowledged in his heart. He was the only one of all the men I have known who could laugh at the faults and follies of his friends in such a manner as to make them ashamed without touching their affection for him, and to confirm their respect and sense of his superiority.

"I saw strong evidence of the sympathy of his nature the morning after the first engagement of our troops in the Valley of Mexico. I had lost a cherished young relative in that action, known to General Lee only as my relative. Meeting me, he suddenly saw in my face the effect of that loss, burst into tears, and expressed his deep sympathy as tenderly in words as his lovely wife would have done.   J. E. JOHNSTON."

CHAPTER IV.

THE INDIAN CAMPAIGN.

On Engineering Duty at Baltimore.—Made Superintendent of West Point.—Promoted Lieutenant-colonel of Second Cavalry.—Regiment Ordered to Texas.—Character of Indian Warfare.—Campaigning against the Comanches.—The Cortinas Raid.—Return to Arlington.

AFTER the conclusion of the treaty negotiations with Mexico, Colonel Lee returned home with the army, and was again assigned to duty in the corps of military Engineers, and stationed at Soller's Point, near Baltimore, where he was placed in charge of the defensive works there constructing. His successive assignment to duty in connection with the erection of fortifications at such important points as Hampton Roads, New York harbor, and Baltimore gives evidence that he was highly esteemed as a military engineer, and the character of the works upon which he was thus engaged still attests his ability in this direction. In fact, to his thorough training in engineering science was added a quick and correct perception which enabled him to quickly grasp the military requisites of a situation and to make the best possible provision for its defence.

An incident occurred during this period of his life which it will be of interest to transcribe, both as showing the high estimation in which he was then held as a soldier and his exalted sense of the duty he owed to his country. It was related by Jefferson Davis in his address at the Lee Memorial meeting in Richmond, November 3, 1870:

"He came from Mexico crowned with honors, covered by brevets, and recognized, young as he was, as one of the ablest of his country's soldiers. And to prove that he was estimated then as such, not only by his associates, but by foreigners also, I may mention that when he was a captain of Engineers, sta-

tioned in Baltimore, the Cuban Junta in New York selected
him to be their leader in the revolutionary effort in that island.
They were anxious to secure his services, and offered him every
temptation that ambition could desire, and pecuniary emoluments far beyond any which he could hope otherwise to acquire.
He thought the matter over, and, I remember, came to Washington to consult me as to what he should do. After a brief
discussion of the complex character of the military problem
which was presented, he turned from the consideration of that
view of the question by stating that the point on which he
wished particularly to consult me was as to the propriety of
entertaining the proposition which had been made to him. He
had been educated in the service of the United States, and felt
it wrong to accept service in the army of a foreign power while
he held his commission. Such was his extreme delicacy, such
the nice sense of honor of the gallant gentleman we deplore.
But when Virginia, the State to which he owed his first and
last allegiance, withdrew from the Union, and thus terminated
his relations to it, the same nice sense of honor and duty which
had guided him on a former occasion had a different application
and led him to share her fortune for good or for evil.''

For three years, from 1849 to 1852, Colonel Lee was engaged
in the construction of the fortifications at Baltimore. His service there ended on September 1, 1852, on which date he was
appointed superintendent of the Military Academy of West
Point, to succeed Captain Brewerton. In this position he
remained till April 1, 1855, when he was promoted to a command in the cavalry arm of the service. This, under the law,
incapacitated him for further duty as superintendent of West
Point, and he was succeeded in that office by Major J. G.
Barnard.

His administration had been a highly efficient and successful
one. He improved the discipline of the Academy and brought
it up as a military institution to a higher proficiency than it
had ever previously attained. During his administration the
course of study was extended, under order of the Secretary of
War, dated August 28, 1854, to five years, and several improve-
ments were made to the Academy and its surroundings. These

consisted of a new wharf and road, a spacious and excellent riding-hall, etc.

We may at this point fitly quote from a private letter written by Colonel Lee on August 6, 1853, to a young friend of his who was about to engage in business, as serving to show the personal interest which he then and always took in whatever concerned the welfare of his friends and acquaintances. He appears to have been—and was, in fact—the confidant and adviser of a great number of the young men belonging to the best class of Virginia families. To him they were constantly writing for information, assistance, encouragement, and advice, and upon his opinion they based their own actions:

"I am glad to find that you have also a prospect of employment with Mr. Manning. Choose between them that which best affords a prospect of advancement and improvement. You are perhaps aware that a young man entering on railroad service, and bringing no experience, is expected to take a subordinate position, no matter what his qualifications, at the bottom of the ladder, and to prove by his work his capabilities for advancement. Bear this constantly in mind, my dear Conny, and work your own promotion. Recollect what depends on your exertions, and how much you owe your mother's love, sister's affection, the expectations of family and friends. You must excuse my anxiety on your behalf, my interest in your welfare, and my ardent desire to see you do justice to yourself and credit to your name."

The great acquisition of territory that followed the Mexican War and the frequent Indian outbreaks in the frontier States and Territories rendered an increase of the army necessary for the protection of the greatly-extended border-line and of the new population that was crowding into the fertile region of the West. Therefore, Congress in 1855 passed an act authorizing the raising of two new regiments of infantry and two of cavalry. The principal grades in these regiments were filled by selections from those officers who had most highly distinguished themselves in the war with Mexico.

Of the two new cavalry regiments, the First was placed under the command of Colonel E. V. Sumner, with Brevet

Colonel J. E. Johnston as lieutenant-colonel, while the same grade in the Second Cavalry, which was commanded by Colonel A. S. Johnston, was assigned to Brevet Colonel R. E. Lee. As soon as these regiments were organized and equipped, the First Cavalry was assigned to Kansas, while the Second was sent to Western Texas for the defence of the settlers and domesticated Indians against the incursions of the nomadic tribes which infested those regions, and which embraced as their most formidable members the Comanches, the Apaches, and their kindred tribes.

During the fall and winter of 1855–56 the Second Cavalry was recruited and organized at Jefferson Barracks. Colonel Lee in this work brought to bear with great effect his fine power of organization and discipline. The winter at Jefferson Barracks was so severe that little could be done in the way of drilling and setting up the regiment, but when spring opened that branch of regimental work was pushed forward with great activity, and the regiment rapidly acquired proficiency in drill and the rules of discipline. Colonel Lee contributed much to this desirable end by his influence and example. When the spring had sufficiently advanced to ensure firm roads over the alluvial soil of Missouri and Arkansas the Second Cavalry began its long march to Western Texas. Colonel A. S. Johnston and Colonel Hardee were the only field officers present, Colonel Lee and Major Thomas having obtained leave of absence to transact personal business. The route taken led the regiment past Forts Smith and Wachita. The latter fort was at that time garrisoned by two batteries of artillery; Major H. J. Hunt commanded the post. When the regiment approached the fort it was received with a salute of thirteen guns, which Colonel Johnston at the head of his regiment most gracefully acknowledged. Johnston was in the prime of life, tall and graceful, with a superb military bearing. The regiment encamped in the vicinity of the fort. After completing their arrangements all officers partook of a collation that had been provided for them by the officers of Fort Wachita—an entertainment which was greatly enjoyed by both guests and hosts.

Johnston gave his regiment a day's rest ere he proceeded on his march.   The officers of the regiment frequently spoke of Colonel Lee in the highest terms of praise, and seemed to look forward with pleasure to the time when he should join them.   The writer, who was at that time stationed, at Fort Wachita, was in a position to understand the character of the service that awaited the new cavalry regiment, and this it may be of interest to describe.

The theatre on which this gallant regiment was to operate was the region embraced by the Rio Grande on the south and the Arkansas River on the north, and extending from the western boundary of the Indian Territory to the eastern confines of New Mexico.   This extensive territory was occupied exclusively by wild animals and Comanche Indians.

The Comanches were the hereditary lords of this immense domain, and for generations it had been their custom to levy contributions on their neighbors with an unsparing hand. They were also in the habit of making frequent raids into the northern Mexican states, and sometimes extended their excursions to the confines of Louisiana and Arkansas, murdering and pillaging the defenceless inhabitants, and then returning to their strongholds with immense booty.   They were often pursued, but, being well mounted on strong, active ponies, almost invariably eluded their pursuers.   Since the admission of Texas into the Union and the acquisition of New Mexico and other Mexican territory, the United States had made constant efforts to suppress Indian depredations on our Western frontiers and in the newly-acquired territories.

The system of defence adopted was the establishment of a chain of military posts on the Western frontier and in the Indian country.   The military establishment of the United States being on a very meagre scale, these posts were insufficiently garrisoned to afford entire protection.   At the time the Second Cavalry was ordered to Texas the Comanches had been unusually active in their predatory excursions.   It was therefore expected that the regiment would have to perform much arduous service.   A finer body of troops than the Second Cavalry was never seen.

The colonel was a perfect soldier, and his subalterns were

unsurpassed for ability and conduct. As a proof of the superiority of these officers it may be said that this regiment turned out during the war more distinguished men than any other regiment in the army. Besides Johnston, Lee, Hardee, and Thomas, it furnished Van Dorn, Palmer, Hood, Fitz Lee, Stoneman, Kirby Smith, Fields, and others not remembered, all of whom became general officers in either the Confederate or the Federal service.

As soon as the regiment reached its destination it was split up into detachments which were sent on expeditions in different directions. In order to illustrate the character of the service which it was required to perform, the writer may give an example that came within his personal knowledge. In the spring of 1854 a party of emigrants was pursuing its way through the western part of Texas. It was accompanied by a newly-married couple, a Mr. and Mrs. Wilson. They were both young, and had determined to cast their lot in Western Texas. The party was discovered just before it reached its destination by a band of Comanches, who attacked and murdered all with the exception of Mrs. Wilson, whose youth and beauty excited the admiration of the Comanche chief. The news of this massacre was reported at a military post by a mail-party the day after it happened. A mounted company was at once sent in pursuit of the marauders, accompanied by an experienced guide. On reaching the place of the massacre it appeared from signs that the Comanche band was large and had proceeded with its booty in a north-western direction toward the confines of New Mexico. A rapid pursuit was immediately instituted, and after many long and wearisome marches succeeded in overtaking the hostiles among the Pecos Hills, not far from Santa Fé. They were immediately attacked and defeated. Mrs. Wilson was found with them, and rescued and sent to Santa Fé, where she was kindly received and finally returned to her friends.

The Second Cavalry was employed in the arduous and dangerous duty thus assigned to it until the outbreak of the Civil War, and performed much useful service in repressing the activity of its savage foes and in punishing them for their outrages.

The "memorandum-book" kept by Colonel Lee during this period furnishes interesting information concerning his own movements and those of the regiment, and from these notes and his letters we can gain a fair idea of his life during the Indian campaign.

From these memoranda we learn that he left Alexandria on February 12, 1856, to join his regiment, and reached it at Fort Mason, Texas, on March 25th. He was then directed by Colonel Johnston to proceed to Camp Cooper—situated in the Comanche Reserve on the Clear Fork of the Brazos, thirty-five miles from its mouth—and take command of the first and fifth squadrons of the regiment, there stationed. He reached this post on April 9th, and writes under date of the 12th to the following effect:

"We are on the Comanche Reserve, with the Indian camps below us on the river belonging to Catumseh's band, whom the Government is endeavoring to humanize. It will be uphill work, I fear. Catumseh has been to see me, and we have had a talk, very tedious on his part and very sententious on mine. I hailed him as a friend as long as his conduct and that of his tribe deserved it, but would meet him as an enemy the first moment he failed to keep his word. The rest of the tribe (about a thousand, it is said) live north of us, and are hostile. Yesterday I returned his visit, and remained a short time at his lodge. He informed me that he had six wives. They are riding in and out of camp all day, their paint and 'ornaments' rendering them more hideous than nature made them, and the whole race is extremely uninteresting."

Shortly afterward Colonel Lee with five companies made an expedition to the head-waters of the Brazos and Wachita rivers, which occupied him several months. The principal result of this expedition was the acquisition of geographical information, for at that time the Comanches were on their annual pilgrimage to the north of the Arkansas River in search of game for their winter supply of provisions.

Of his subsequent life in Texas interesting glimpses are obtained from his letters. The Comanches seem to have made plentiful work for the soldiers. Thus on August 25, 1856, he speaks of a party of these restless savages who had been on a maurauding expedition into Mexico, "which is a cloak to cover all their thefts and murders." They were then seeking to steal north around the cavalry camp, divided into small parties to escape detection. He was about to send out a company of troopers in pursuit, with directions to follow them for twenty days if necessary. He says: "These people give a world of trouble to man and horse, and, poor creatures! they are not worth it."

Again, in January, 1857, he reports several encounters between the troops and maurauding Indians, who were severely punished. "It is a distressing state of things that requires the application of such treatment, but it is the only corrective they understand, the only way in which they can be brought to keep within their own limits."

During this period, however, he himself was absent from his command, having been summoned to Fort Brown, on the Rio Grande, to serve on a court-martial. Here his chief enjoyment seems to have been in the natural surroundings. He writes: "My daily walks are alone, up and down the banks of the river, and my pleasure is derived from my own thoughts and from the sight of the flowers and animals I there meet with. The birds of the Rio Grande form a constant source of interest, and are as numerous as they are beautiful in plumage. I wish I could get for you the roots of some of the luxuriant vines that cover everything, or the seeds of the innumerable flowers."

He returned to Camp Cooper on April 18, 1857. On July 23d orders came for Colonel Johnston to report in person at Washington and to turn over to his lieutenant-colonel the command of the regiment. On October 21st Lee received notice by telegraph of the death of G. W. P. Custis, his wife's father, and returned to Arlington, reaching there on November 11th.

An officer who served under him during this period writes of him as follows, bearing the same testimony as all of his friends: "He examined everything thoroughly and conscientiously until master of every detail, ever too conscientious to act under imperfect knowledge of any subject submitted to him. And with all his stern sense of duty he attracted the love, admiration, and confidence of all. The little children always hailed his approach with glee, his sincerity, kindliness of nature, and cordial manners attracting their unreserved confidence."

Returning to Texas after his visit home, he resumed command of the regiment. As to the character of his life there we have already said enough. There were no serious encounters with the Indians, but a multitude of petty affrays, sufficient to break the monotony of camp-life, yet not of such importance as to claim special attention. He was in Washington again in the autumn of 1859, and on this occasion played a part in the famous "John Brown raid," which we shall describe in the next chapter.

After this affair he returned to duty with his regiment, under orders from headquarters of February 9, 1860, which assigned him to the command of the department of Texas. Reaching there on February 20th, he found work prepared for him in the pursuit of one Cortinas, a notorious brigand who had been crossing the Rio Grande and committing depredations on Texan soil. Efforts were made to overtake and arrest this land-pirate, but without success. The vicinity of Mexican territory and the supineness of the Mexican authorities gave him every opportunity to cross and recross the river at will, now making a raid into Texas, now seeking a covert in Mexico, after the established and time-honored custom of the brigands of the Rio Grande.

Colonel Lee's journal contains the following notes in reference to this troublesome individual:

"March 16th. Continued my route, report having reached me that Cortinas was ascending the Rio Grande.

"March 20th. Could get no account of Cortinas's whereabouts, or learn that he had ever ascended the Rio Grande higher than La Mesa.

"April 10th. Resumed journey; nearly all the ranches on the road have been burned—those spared by Cortinas burned by the Rangers.

"April 11th. Resumed journey; reached the scene of Cortinas's defeat by Major Heintzelman.

"May 7th. Have been engaged corresponding with the Mexican authorities; succeeded in getting them to issue orders for the arrest of Cortinas. . . . . He has left the frontier and withdrawn to the Ceritos with his property, horses, etc."

These few extracts will give some slight idea of the difficulties experienced by these frontier garrisons, which had to guard with a few troopers a long and thinly-inhabited frontier, and were prevented, for fear of international complications, from following brigands and savages across the river into Mexican territory, while the Mexicans themselves made little or no effort to suppress these outrages—perhaps winked at them.

Had Colonel Lee received the privilege of pursuing his foes upon Mexican soil, as some of his successors in the frontier department have done, the story of these marauders would probably have been a very different one. As he remarked in the letter quoted in our last chapter, he might have made "a rough diplomatist, but a tolerably quick one."

Events, however, were arising which were destined to abruptly end this active but unsatisfactory life on the frontier, and to bring him into a field of operations more worthy of his talents, and one destined to give him a worldwide fame. The detail of the causes and character of these events must be left to a subsequent chapter.

CHAPTER V.

A DIVIDED COUNTRY.

Colonel's Lee's Views on Slavery.—The John Brown Raid.—Letters on Secession.—
Mr. Lincoln Inaugurated.—Fort Sumter Bombarded.—Virginia Secedes.—Lee,
Blair, and Scott.—Lee Resigns his Commission.—Appointed Commander-in-chief
of the Virginia Forces.

WE have in the preceding chapters covered the earlier
events in the life of Robert E. Lee, and brought our
work up to the date of the opening of one of the most stupendous events of modern times, the terrible Civil War between
the Northern and Southern sections of the United States. It is
now necessary to go back and briefly consider the preliminary
events leading to this contest, and their effect upon Lee's beliefs
and feelings, as expressed in letters from Texas dating back for
several years before the era of secession.

The most exciting political question of that era was the irri-
tating one of slavery, which had aroused the feelings of con-
testants on both sides of the much-debated problem to a degree
of passion seldom before known in our Congressional chambers,
and was dangerously heating the minds of the whole people,
both South and North. This question, which a few years before was confined to a few political fanatics, had rapidly spread
over the Northern and North-western States, and now nearly
divided the political parties of those sections.

This rapid spread of abolitionism and of the spirit of dissen-
sion caused the conservatives of both the North and the South
to feel serious alarm for the safety of the Union. Colonel Lee
was of the latter class, being by education a firm supporter of
constitutional liberty. In a letter from Texas dated December
27, 1856, he thus expresses himself:

" . . . . I have just received the *Alexandria Gazette* from
the 20th of November to the 18th of December, inclusive.

Besides the usual good reading matter, I am interested in the relation of local affairs, and infer from the quiet and ordinary course of events that all is going on well, especially (I hope) at Arlington.

"The steamer also brought the President's Message, the reports of the various heads of departments, etc., so that we are assured that the Government is in operation and the Union in existence. . . . . I was much pleased with the President's Message. His views of the systematic and progressive efforts of certain people at the North to interfere with and change the domestic institutions of the South are truthfully and faithfully expressed. The consequences of their plans and purposes are also clearly set forth. These people must be aware that their object is both unlawful and foreign to them and to their duty, and that this institution, for which they are irresponsible and non-accountable, can only be changed by *them* through the agency of a civil and servile war.

"There are few, I believe, in this enlightened age who will not acknowledge that slavery as an institution is a moral and political evil. It is idle to expatiate on its disadvantages. I think it is a greater evil to the white than to the colored race. While my feelings are strongly enlisted in behalf of the latter, my sympathies are more deeply engaged for the former. The blacks are immeasurably better off here than in Africa, morally, physically, and socially. The painful discipline they are undergoing is necessary for their further instruction as a race, and will prepare them, I hope, for better things. How long their servitude may be necessary is known and ordered by a merciful Providence. Their emancipation will sooner result from the mild and melting influences of Christianity than from the storm and tempest of fiery controversy. This influence, though slow, is sure. The doctrines and miracles of our Saviour have required nearly two thousand years to convert but a small portion of the human race, and even among Christian nations what gross errors still exist! While we see the course of the final abolition of human slavery is still onward, and give it the aid of our prayers, let us leave the progress as well as the results in the hand of Him who sees the end, who chooses to work by slow influences, and with whom a thousand years are but as a single day. Although the Abolitionist must know this—must know that he has neither the right nor the power of operating, except by moral means; that to benefit the slave he must not excite angry feelings in the master; that, although he may not approve the mode by which Providence accomplishes its purpose, the results will be the same; and that the reasons he gives for interference in matters he has no concern with holds good for every kind of interference with our neighbor,— still, I fear he will persevere in his evil course.

". . . . Is it not strange that the descendants of those Pilgrim Fathers who crossed the Atlantic to preserve their own freedom have always proved the most intolerant of the spiritual liberty of others?"

The political excitement in 1857 continued to be increased by the contest between the Pro-slavery and Free-soil parties for political supremacy in Kansas, until it was at such a height that argument was superseded by the pistol and the rifle. Several bloody encounters ensued. The district was so overrun by riot and bloodshed that it became necessary to sustain the civil authority by a large military force. The troops soon ended the disturbances, dispersed the political factions, and forced their leaders, through fear of punishment, to flee from the Territory.

This event, however, served to greatly intensify the prevailing political excitement. The Abolition party had already, in 1856, proved strong enough not only to nominate a candidate, John C. Fremont, for the Presidency, but to gain for him 114 electoral votes, being but 60 votes less than those cast for James Buchanan, the successful candidate. In the interval between this election and that of 1860 the strength of the Antislavery party rapidly augmented, and there was much reason to believe that it would be successful in its next effort. By the autumn of 1858 the country had become greatly aroused through the agitation incidental to the approaching Presidential campaign and the heated debates in Congress. During the succeeding year this political excitement was raised to a dangerous pitch by an event which then occurred, and which, as Lee was directly connected with it, needs to be described more in detail.

The event referred to is what is known in the history of that period as the "John Brown raid." John Brown, a fanatical leader of the Free-soil party, who with his sons had played a prominent part in the Kansas difficulties, had since the suppression of that outbreak been secretly engaged in organizing a plan for the production of a servile insurrection in the South. In October, 1859, with the aid of a party of sixteen whites and five blacks, into whom he had infused his own enthusiasm and reckless disdain of consequences, he actually invaded Virginia, and seized the Government arsenal and other buildings at Harper's Ferry, with a desperate boldness that created the greatest consternation in the town and the surrounding country.

The moment that news of this invasion reached Washington the Government authorities took active measures to oppose it and capture the insurgents. General Scott was absent from Washington at the time, but Colonel Lee happened to be present, having shortly before arrived from Texas on a visit to his family at Arlington. He was immediately sent for by the Secretary of War, and asked to take command of a battalion of marines and proceed to Harper's Ferry, at which point a force of militia, hastily gathered from the adjoining counties, had previously assembled.

Colonel Lee, on arriving at Harper's Ferry, found that the insurgents had already failed in their main object, that of stirring up the slaves of the vicinity to join them as a nucleus for spreading the fire of insurrection throughout the negro population of the South. The occupation of the Government buildings under cover of night was the extent of their success, and they were here closely confined by the beleaguering militia. With a considerable degree of shrewdness, however, Brown had ordered the seizure of some of the principal citizens, whom he held as hostages in the engine-house in the armory yard, to which he had retired with his adherents.

Colonel Lee on arriving at once stationed his marines around this building, and sent Lieutenant J. E. B. Stuart, who accompanied him with a flag of truce to demand the surrender of the insurgents, promising to protect them and secure them a legal trial. This demand Brown refused to comply with, and required on his part permission to march out with his men, arms, and prisoners as far as the second toll-gate. At this point he proposed to release his prisoners, and would then be ready to fight the troops if he could not escape.

It was out of the question to accept such a proposal. The envoy remonstrated with the insurgents, and tried to convince them of their folly. He only received for answer that if attacked they would kill their hostages. Among the latter was Colonel Lewis Washington, who resided in that neighborhood, and who at this moment boldly exclaimed, "Never mind *us*— fire!" Colonel Lee is reported to have remarked, on hearing these words, "The old Revolutionary blood does tell."

Before sending Lieutenant Stuart to hold this parley Colonel Lee had devised a scheme of action which was to be put into effect if the insurgents should refuse to surrender. In this event the lieutenant was directed to raise his arm as a signal, when the marines would rush upon the door of the engine-house, and so occupy the insurgents by the suddenness of their attack as to save the lives of the prisoners. The scheme was successfully executed. The marines rushed upon the door, forced it in, captured the building, and released the hostages uninjured. The result here described is briefly but clearly given in Lee's memorandum-book:

"Waited until daylight, as a number of citizens were held as hostages whose lives were threatened. Tuesday about sunrise, with twelve marines under Lieutenant Green, broke in the door of the engine-house, secured the insurgents, and released the prisoners unhurt. All the insurgents killed or mortally wounded but four—John Brown, Stevens, Coppie, and Shields."

The insurgents in their turn had fired upon their invaders with some effect. They would probably have been lynched by the excited citizens but for the presence of Colonel Lee and his marines. He handed them over to the civil authorities, as directed from Washington, and returned to Arlington.

We have, in the preceding chapter, briefly described the life of Colonel Lee during the last year of his residence in Texas.

Then in command of the department, he was, as we have seen, kept busily engaged in the pursuit of the brigand Cortinas and in other duties. In the midst of his arduous labors he from time to time cast anxious glances at the threatening aspect of the political horizon, and with a foreboding heart watched the cloud grow darker and more angry until the storm burst in the North and rolled South, whence it thundered back until the popular tempest rent the country in twain. The triumph of the party that had caused so much alarm throughout the South by the election of Mr. Lincoln to the Presidency in 1860 spread consternation among the conservatives of both sections, and especially among those of the South, since the radical hostility was directed principally at them. Nevertheless, there were many who hoped that the fears of the despondent were groundless, and that the country would be saved. But when Congress assembled in December it was soon discovered that the spirit of conciliation had departed from the deliberative body of the nation, and that there was no prospect of an amicable settlement of the political questions that had divided the country; and therefore the Southern representatives advised their constituents to prepare for a withdrawal from the Union—peaceably if possible, forcibly if necessary.

South Carolina, being the first to act, passed her ordinance of secession about the last of December, and the other Cotton States speedily followed her example.

From Texas in January, 1861, Colonel Lee expresses himself on the condition of the country as follows:

"I received Everett's *Life of General Washington*, which you sent me, and enjoyed its perusal. How his spirit would be grieved could he see the wreck of his mighty labors! I will not, however, permit myself to believe, until all the ground for hope has gone, that the fruit of his noble deeds will be destroyed and that his precious advice and virtuous example will so soon be forgotten by his countrymen. As far as I can judge from the papers, we are between a state of anarchy and civil war. May God avert both of these evils from us! I fear that mankind for years will not be sufficiently Christianized to bear the absence of restraint and force. I see that four States have declared themselves out of the Union: four more will apparently follow their example. Then, if the Border States are brought into the gulf of revolution, one half of the country will be arrayed against the other. I must try and be patient and await the end, for I can do nothing to hasten or retard it."

From the above it may be observed with what pain and regret Colonel Lee witnessed the progressive steps leading toward the dissolution of the Union. In further illustration of this feeling, and of the political knowledge and wisdom of the writer, we may quote from another letter of the same date. It is addressed to his son from "Fort Mason, Texas, January 23, 1861," and contains the following highly interesting passage:

"The South, in my opinion, has been aggrieved by the acts of the North, as you say. I feel the aggression, and am willing to take every proper step for redress. It is the principle I contend for, not individual or private benefit. As an American citizen I take great pride in my country, her prosperity, and her institutions, and would defend any State if her rights were invaded. But I can anticipate no greater calamity for the country than a dissolution of the Union. It would be an accumulation of all the evils we complain of, and I am willing to sacrifice everything but honor for its preservation. I hope, therefore, that all constitutional means will be exhausted before there is a resort to force. Secession is nothing but revolution. The framers of our Constitution never exhausted so much labor, wisdom, and forbearance in its formation, and surrounded it with so many guards and securities, if it was intended to be broken by every member of the Confederacy at will. It is intended for 'perpetual union,' so expressed in the preamble, and for the establishment of a government, not a compact, which can only be dissolved by revolution or the the consent of all the people in convention assembled. It is idle to talk of secession. Anarchy would have been established, and not a government, by Washington, Hamilton, Jefferson, Madison, and all the other patriots of the Revolution. . . . . Still, a Union that can only be maintained by swords and bayonets, and in which strife and civil war are to take the place of brotherly love and kindness, has no charm for me. I shall mourn for my country and for the welfare and progress of mankind. If the Union is dissolved and the Government disrupted, I shall return to my native State and share the miseries of my people, and save in defence will draw my sword on none.''

In February, 1861, the seven Cotton States united themselves into an independent republic under the designation of the Confederate States of America, and selected for its capital Montgomery, Alabama. The Border slaveholding States still adhered to the Union, hoping that after party passion should subside the final separation of the States would be prevented, and that the government under which they had attained a remarkable degree of wealth and prosperity would be preserved. At that time there was much speculation as to the policy Mr. Lincoln would adopt, and his inaugural address was awaited with impatience. At his inauguration on the 4th of March the address in which he declared his future policy was regarded as enigmatical, and various opinions were formed as to the probable course of the new President on the exciting questions which agitated the country. It was generally believed that his course would be conservative; at least it was thought that "honest old Abe," as Mr. Lincoln was familiarly called, would be governed by a desire for conciliation. It is probable that the intention of Mr. Lincoln was at first to adopt a national policy, as in his inaugural address, which seemed calm and dispassionate, he assured the country that he had no purpose to interfere with the institution of slavery *where it already existed*, and that, in his opinion, he had no right to do so. Yet he denounced the doctrine of the right of secession from the Union as unconstitutional, and declared his firm purpose to hold, occupy, and possess the places and property in the South belonging to the Federal Government. This announcement was received in the South as equivalent to a declaration of war.

Wishing to effect an amicable adjustment of the questions at issue, especially that of the surrender of Fort Sumter, the new Confederacy sent commissioners to Washington for that purpose. They were, however, not officially received by Mr. Lin-

coln, but were led to believe that his intentions toward the Confederacy were amicable, and that he would in due time order a
peaceable surrender of Fort Sumter. With that belief the commissioners returned to Montgomery. Soon after the departure
of the Confederate commissioners from Washington, Mr. Lincoln sent a formidable expedition to Charleston harbor for the
relief of the fort. As soon as the attitude of Mr. Lincoln was
discovered at Montgomery the Confederate authorities ordered
the immediate reduction of Fort Sumter. Before attacking the
place General Beauregard demanded its peaceable surrender,
which being refused by its commander, Major Anderson, the
fort was assailed by all the Confederate batteries which could
be brought to bear upon it. After a bombardment of thirty-
two hours Major Anderson was forced to capitulate on the 13th
of April, 1861.

On the 15th of April, the second day after the fall of Fort
Sumter, Mr. Lincoln issued a proclamation calling for 75,000
volunteers, and a few days later he issued proclamations ordering
the blockade of the Southern ports and suspending the writ of
habeas corpus. These acts were immediately resented by Virginia, North Carolina, Tennessee, and Missouri by the withdrawal of these States from the Union and their entrance into
the Southern Confederacy, while Kentucky refused to comply
with the call for troops and declared a neutrality. Maryland
also refused to furnish troops, but from her geographical position was forced to submit. On the other hand, the non-slave-
holding States obeyed the President's proclamation and promptly
furnished troops.

Seeing the gigantic preparations which were being made by
the United States to coerce them, the Southern States with
similar activity prepared for their defence. The rupture which
had thus divided the country reduced the officers of the army
and navy to the alternative of either appearing in arms against
their native States or of resigning their commissions in the
service of the United States. All those of Southern birth,
with few exceptions, adopted this latter course, and joined their
fellow-countrymen "for weal or woe." Colonel Lee, who had
been summoned from Texas to report in person to the com-

mander-in-chief at Washington, reached that city on March
1st, and was there at the time of the events above described.

On the 17th of April, 1861, the ordinance of secession was
passed in the convention of Virginia. This cast the die for
Colonel Lee. The sentiments expressed in his letters and his
strong sense of the debt of allegiance he owed to his native
State effectually prevented him from remaining any longer an
officer of the United States army, and obliged him by every
sentiment of duty and affection to cast his lot with the State
of his nativity and with the numerous friends and relatives who
made this State their natal home. Yet his final decision was
not reached without severe mental trouble, nor without efforts
on the side of the Government to preserve his highly-valued
services to the Federal army. In fact, an offer of a most allur-
ing character, and which must have won over any one with less
than his supreme sense of duty, was made to him—no less an
offer, in short, than the supreme command of the Federal
army.

That this fact has been denied we are aware, yet there exists
indubitable evidence of it. We have been fortunate enough to
obtain a highly valuable letter from a near relative of General
Lee describing a conversation with Mrs. Lee on this subject.
This letter, it is true, does not settle the point in question, but
it gives information no longer attainable concerning General
Lee's feelings and actions at that time which is of the utmost
importance. We extract the most significant portions of this
letter:

"The first time I saw her (Mrs. Lee), shortly after the breaking
out of the war, she related to me all that Robert Lee had suffered
at the time of his resignation—that from the first commencement of our troubles he had decided that in the event of Virginia's secession duty (which had ever been his watchword)
would compel him to follow. She told me what a sore trial it
was to him to leave the old army, to give up the flag of the
Union, to separate from so many of his old associates (*particularly* General Scott, for whom he always felt the greatest
regard), and to be censured by many whose good opinion he
valued. She told me of the interviews between General Scott

and himself, in which he used every argument he could bring
to bear to induce him to remain with the Union. She mentioned an interview he had with Blair, in which he taunted
him with its being his dislike to parting with the negro which
made him remain with the South. This accusation Robert
Lee indignantly denied, saying that if he owned all the negroes
in the South he would gladly yield them up for the preservation
of the Union. She mentioned that General Scott, in one of
their interviews, said that in the event of his resignation, which
from his advanced age must soon become a necessity, if Robert
had remained with the North he (General Scott) believed he
would be given the command of the Union army. *She did not
say* that any offer had been made by the Government, but that
in the event of his resignation he (General Scott) felt sure that
Robert Lee would be offered his position. This may have been
only General Scott's own opinion, formed from his admiration
and appreciation of his high qualities as a soldier. I remember hearing at the time that General Scott had pronounced him
the officer who had most distinguished himself in the Mexican
War, and also that he had advised his Government to leave no
stone unturned, if possible, to secure him to their side, saying
at the same time that Robert Lee would be worth fifty thousand
men to them.''

In regard to this offer of the command of the army by Mr.
Blair to Colonel Lee, as referred to in the foregoing letter, we
have positive corroborative evidence, submitted by a person to
whom Mr. Blair himself stated it as a fact. This evidence
occurs in a letter written by a well-known resident of Washington, and from which we take the following extract:

"I have never seen the account (of the offer to General Lee
of the command of the Federal army) worded just as I had it
from Mr. Blair. The following is an accurate—I think a very
nearly verbatim—report of it:

"MR. BLAIR: I come to you on the part of President Lincoln to ask whether any inducement that he can offer will prevail on you to take command of the Union army?

"COLONEL LEE: If I owned the four millions of slaves, I
would cheerfully sacrifice them to the preservation of the

Union, but to lift my hand against my own State and people is impossible."

The most valuable testimony concerning this question, however, is that of General Lee himself, as given in a letter addressed to the Hon. Reverdy Johnson of date February 25, 1868. In this letter he uses the following language:

"I never intimated to any one that I desired the command of the United States army, nor did I ever have a conversation but with one gentleman, Mr. Francis Preston Blair, on the subject, which was at his invitation, and, as I understood, at the instance of President Lincoln.

"After listening to his remarks I declined the offer he made me to take command of the army that was to be brought into the field, stating, as candidly and courteously as I could, that, though opposed to secession and deprecating war, I could take no part in an invasion of the Southern States.

"I went directly from the interview with Mr. Blair to the office of General Scott—told him of the proposition that had been made to me and my decision. Upon reflection after returning home, I concluded that I ought no longer to retain any commission I held in the United States army, and on the second morning thereafter I forwarded my resignation to General Scott.

"At the time I hoped that peace would have been preserved —that some way would be found to save the country from the calamities of war; and I then had no other intention than to pass the remainder of my life as a private citizen.

"Two days afterward, on the invitation of the governor of Virginia, I repaired to Richmond, found that the convention then in session had passed the ordinance withdrawing the State from the Union, and accepted the commission of commander of its forces which was tendered me. These are the simple facts of the case."

The Mr. Blair who made this offer to Colonel Lee has heretofore been stated to have been Montgomery Blair, Postmaster-General of President Lincoln's Cabinet. The letter here quoted, however, settles the fact that it was Francis Preston Blair, Sr., father of Montgomery Blair, who was then a member of Mr. Lincoln's Cabinet.　Mr. F. P. Blair held no official position.

In the interviews between General Scott and Colonel Lee it is stated that the veteran commander earnestly sought to persuade the younger officer not to throw up his commission, telling him that it would be the greatest mistake of his life. But to all his pleadings Colonel Lee returned but one answer— that his sense of duty was stronger with him than any prospects of advancement, replying to the appeal not to send in his resignation in the following words: "I am compelled to: I cannot consult my own feelings in this matter."

The final result of the endeavors here indicated was Colonel Lee's resignation of his commission in the United States army, as indicated in the following letter addressed to General Scott:

"ARLINGTON, VA., April 20, 1861.

"GENERAL: Since my interview with you on the 18th inst. I have felt that I ought not longer to retain my commission in the army.　I therefore tender my resignation, which I request you will recommend for acceptance.　It would have been presented at once, but for the struggle it has cost me to separate myself from a service to which I have devoted the best years of my life and all the ability I possessed.　During the whole of that time—more than a quarter of a century—I have experienced nothing but kindness from my superiors and a most cordial friendship from my comrades.　To no one, general, have I been as much indebted as to yourself for uniform kindness and consideration, and it has always been my ardent desire to merit your approbation.　I shall carry to the grave the most grateful recollections of your kind consideration, and your name and fame will always be dear to me.

"Save in the defence of my native State, I never desire again to draw my sword.　Be pleased to accept my most earnest wishes for the continuance of your happiness and prosperity, and believe me most truly yours,

"R. E. LEE."

From the foregoing letter it will be seen what anguish

Colonel Lee must have felt in parting from his old commander and the service in which for thirty years he had occupied an honorable and distinguished position, and which still allured him with the most brilliant prospects. All must acknowledge that no selfish or unpatriotic motive influenced him in refusing to draw his sword against his native State, to which from early boyhood he had been taught by the wisest and the purest in the land he owed his first allegiance. Here it is also just to remark that all of those who resigned their commissions in the service of the United States to cast their lot with their native States were influenced by the same pure and unselfish motives.

On the same day in which this graceful and dignified letter was penned Colonel Lee wrote to his sister, Mrs. Marshall, then residing in Baltimore, expressing the same sentiments with the same earnestness and feeling:

"My Dear Sister : I am grieved at my inability to see you. I have been waiting for a more convenient season, which has brought to many before me deep and lasting regret. Now we are in a state of war which will yield to nothing. The whole South is in a state of revolution, into which Virginia, after a long struggle, has been drawn; and, though I recognize no necessity for this state of things, and would have forborne and pleaded to the end for redress of grievances, real or supposed, yet in my own person I had to meet the question whether I should take part against my native State. With all my devotion to the Union, and the feeling of loyalty and duty of an American citizen, I have not been able to make up my mind to raise my hand against my relatives, my children, my home. I have therefore resigned my commission in the army, and, save in defence of my native State, with the sincere hope that my poor services may never be needed, I hope I may never be called on to draw my sword.

"I know you will blame me, but you must think as kindly of me as you can, and believe that I have endeavored to do what I thought right. To show you the feeling and struggle it has cost me I send a copy of my letter to General Scott which accompanied my letter of resignation. I have no time for more.

. . . . May God guard and protect you and yours, and shower upon you every blessing, is the prayer of your devoted brother,

"R. E. LEE."

That General Lee sacrificed much in this action need scarcely be said. In addition to the high position offered him in the United States army, he yielded his private fortune, with his beautiful home, Arlington, a home endeared by historic associations and by many years of happy married life, a home of unsurpassed beauty of situation, and adorned with all that men most value, now destined to be the sport of rude soldiers, its priceless relics scattered, its beautiful surroundings desecrated, its choicest attractions destroyed. That this would be its fate he could not well have doubted. That he might become a houseless wanderer upon the face of the earth was within the limits of probability. He was daring all, risking all, for a principle, yet duty was a far stronger force in his soul than earthly advancement, and there is nothing to show that these considerations ruled with him for a moment. Not, "What will be to me most profitable?" but, "What does duty command?" was the question which forced itself upon his attention, and the instant he had decided upon this vital point all lesser considerations dropped from his mind, and he gave himself heart and soul to the service of his native State.

As soon as it was known that Colonel Lee had retired from the United States army the governor of Virginia tendered him the appointment of major-general and commander-in-chief of the forces of Virginia, and on the 23d of April, in the presence of the Convention and of a large assemblage of citizens, Mr. Janney, president of the Convention, presented to him his commission in the following address:

"In the name of the people of our native State, here represented, I bid you a cordial and heartfelt welcome to this hall, in which we may almost hear the echoes of the voices of the statesmen, the soldiers, and the sages of bygone days who have borne your name and whose blood now flows in your veins. We met in the month of February last charged with the solemn duty of protecting the rights, the honor, and the interests of the people of this commonwealth. We differed for a time as to the best means of accomplishing that object, but there never was at any moment a shade of difference among us as to the great object itself; and now, Virginia having taken her position, as far as the power of this Convention extends, we stand animated by one impulse, governed by one desire and one determination, and that is, that she shall be defended, and that no spot on her soil shall be polluted by the foot of an invader.

"When the necessity of having a leader for our forces became apparent, all hearts and all eyes, by the impulse of an instinct which is a surer guide than reason itself, turned to the old county of Westmoreland. We knew how prolific she had been in other days of heroes and statesmen ; we knew she had given birth to the Father of his country, to Richard Henry Lee, to Monroe, and last, though not least, to your own gallant father; and we knew well by your deeds that her productive power was not exhausted. Sir, we watched with the most profound and intense interest the triumphal march of the army led by General Scott, to which you were attached, from Vera Cruz to the capital of Mexico. We read of the sanguinary conflicts and the blood-stained fields, in all of which victory perched upon our banners. We knew of the unfading lustre which was shed upon the American arms by that campaign, and we knew also what your modesty has always disclaimed, that no small share of the glory of those achievements was due to your valor and your military genius.

"Sir, one of the proudest recollections of my life will be that I yesterday had the honor of submitting to this body the confirmation of the nomination, made by the governor of this State, of you as commander-in-chief of the naval and military forces of this commonwealth. I rose to put the question, and when I asked if this body would advise and consent to that appointment, there rushed from the hearts to the tongues of all the members an affirmative response, which told with an emphasis that could leave no doubt of the feeling whence it emanated. I put the negative of the question for form's sake, but there was an unbroken silence.

"Sir, we have by this unanimous vote expressed our convictions that you are at this day, among the living citizens of Virginia, first in war, and we pray God most fervently that you may so conduct the operations committed to your charge that it may soon be said of you that you are first in peace, and when that time comes you will have gained the still prouder distinction of being first in the hearts of your countrymen.

"Yesterday your mother, Virginia, placed her sword in your hands upon the implied condition—which we know you will keep to the letter and in the spirit—that you will draw it only in defence, and that you will fall with it in your hand rather than the object for which it was placed there shall fail."

To this he replied :

"MR. PRESIDENT AND GENTLEMEN OF THE CONVENTION: Profoundly impressed with the solemnity of the occasion, for which I must say I was not prepared, I accept the position assigned me by your partiality. I would have much preferred had your choice fallen upon an abler man. Trusting in Almighty God, an approving conscience, and the aid of my fellow-citizens, I devote myself to the service of my native State, in whose behalf alone will I ever again draw my sword."

The impressiveness of the scene was much enhanced by the striking person and graceful manner of General Lee, who then appeared in the full vigor of manhood. Referring to the above scene, Hon. A. H. Stephens says:

"All the force which personal appearance could add to the power and impressiveness of the words, as well as the sentiments uttered by him, was imparted by his manly form and the great dignity as well as grace in his every action and movement. All these, combined, sent home to the breast of every one the conviction that he was thoroughly impressed himself with the full consciousness of the immense responsibility he had assumed. A more deeply interesting or solemn scene of the character I never witnessed."

At this time General Lee was in the prime of a healthful and vigorous life. He was fifty-four years of age, a man of finely-shaped and well-knit body, and of fully-developed faculties of mind. He was of graceful manner and grave and dignified bearing, though he could be kind and even playful on occasion. All his previous life, all the training of mind and body he had undergone, had been devoted to the building up of a nature capable of a great enterprise, of physical powers and intellectual development fitted to the mighty work now before him, and he entered the arena of civil war fully prepared to undertake and to perform one of the most stupendous labors ever engaged in by mortal man.

CHAPTER VI.

OPENING OF THE CIVIL WAR.

Military Contrast of North and South.—General Lee organizes an Army.—Topography of Seat of War.—Lines of Operation.—Federal Advance.—Battle of Manassas.—Result of the Victory.—The Author's First Interview with General Lee.

AT the commencement of hostilities there was great inequality between the North and the South in all essentials necessary for the vigorous prosecution of war.

With the Northern States remained a thoroughly-organized government, with all of its machinery intact and capable of a rapid expansion to meet sudden emergencies. The army and navy, though small, had a complete organization, which formed a nucleus about which forces of any magnitude might be rapidly gathered. There was also a treasury into which flowed the revenue of a wealthy and prosperous nation, ever ready to furnish the sinews of war.

On the other hand, the Southern States were destitute of everything requisite even for defence, except the stout hearts and ready hands of their sons and the scanty supplies found in the arsenals and the navy-yards within their borders.

On the secession of Virginia, Governor Letcher called into service the entire military force of the State, which consisted of an unorganized militia, a few companies of volunteers which had been previously armed and equipped, and the cadets of the State military institution, two or three hundred in number.

The other Southern States were no better provided for than Virginia. The cadets and volunteers were the only available force that could be obtained for the seizure of the Gosport navy-yard and the arsenal at Harper's Ferry.

When General Lee accepted the command of the forces of Virginia, he was not ignorant of her unprovided condition, and

100

he was fully aware of the immense responsibility he assumed in undertaking her defence with the inadequate means at hand. But his native State was threatened with what he regarded as an unjustifiable invasion, and by every principle of honor and the duties of citizenship he was bound to defend her with heart and hand against all odds. Being a thorough master of the art of war, he at once comprehended the situation and promptly adopted measures to provide for it. The governor's call for men met with a prompt response from all parts of the State, and Lee proceeded vigorously with the work of organization. Companies were rapidly raised and equipped as well as circumstances would admit, and formed into regiments which were sent to the front for the occupation of important points, where they were brigaded and formed into divisions. There was no scarcity of men, but much difficulty was experienced in obtaining arms and equipments for the gallant volunteers. The limited supply of arms possessed by the State was soon exhausted, and it became necessary to supply deficiencies by collecting all the private arms that could be found; so the sporting rifle and fowling-piece were necessarily substituted for the musket, while in the absence of the sabre the cavalry was armed with the lance fabricated by the artisans of the country. Lee was not content with simply providing for the present emergency, but caused steps to be rapidly taken for the manufacture of cannon and for providing ammunition and small-arms for the future use of the army. Notwithstanding the enormous difficulties to be surmounted, the Virginia forces ere long rose to the proportions of a grand army.

Among the inconveniences with which the commanding general had then to contend was one which meets every person in a position of importance—that of solicitation to provide places of trust and emolument for relatives and friends on considerations of family ties and affectionate interest rather than of devotion to the public good. How he met demands of this kind the following letter will serve to show, as also to indicate the sentiments which then ruled in his mind. It is dated immediately after he assumed command of the Virginia troops:

"RICHMOND, 25 April, 1861.

"MY DEAR ———: I have received your letter of 23d. I am sorry your nephew has left his college and become a soldier. It is necessary that persons on my staff should have a knowledge of their duties and an experience of the wants of the service to enable me to attend to other matters. It would otherwise give me great pleasure to take your nephew. I shall remember him if anything can be done. I am much obliged to you for Dr. M——'s letter. Express to him my gratitude for his sentiments, and tell him that no earthly act could give me so much pleasure as to restore peace to my country. But I fear it is now out of the power of man, and in God alone must be our trust. I think our policy should be purely on the defensive —to resist aggression and allow time to allay the passions and permit Reason to resume her sway. Virginia has to-day, I understand, joined the Confederate States. Her policy will doubtless, therefore, be shaped by united counsels. I cannot say what it will be, but trust that a merciful Providence will not dash us from the height to which his smiles have raised us. I wanted to say many things to you before I left home, but the event was rendered so imperatively speedy that I could not.

"May God preserve you and yours! Very truly,

"R. E. LEE."

Having proved his great powers of organization and administration, General Lee soon exhibited his remarkable skill as a tactician and strategist. Being well acquainted with the topography of Virginia, which was obviously destined to become a grand theatre of war, he skilfully availed himself of this knowledge for the approaching campaign. In order to show how this was accomplished, it is necessary in advance to describe the topography of a large portion of Virginia, so far as to delineate the natural features which were destined to influence military operations, such as mountains, rivers, valleys, peninsulas, and swamps, and also roads.

The Potomac, which formed a part of the eastern boundary, served as a primary base for the armies of invasion, and, taken in connection with the Chesapeake and with Hampton Roads, afforded an easy line of communication between this base and the army operating in the country contiguous to those waters. The interior rivers, such as the Rappahannock and the Rapidan, furnished good defensive lines and convenient intermediate bases for aggressive operations; and the York and the James became important auxiliaries to the armies that operated on the peninsula lying between those rivers. The Dismal Swamp, the Blue Ridge, and the successive ridges of the Alleghany Mountains were adapted to serve, in the hands of an able general, as powerful barriers and impenetrable masks for secret or delicate manœuvring. The railroads and the principal turnpikes also bore an important part in giving character and direction to military operations. The grand theatre of war may be divided into five strategic divisions, which are distinctly marked out by the natural features of the country. First comes Western Virginia, lying between the Alleghany Mountains and the Ohio River; next in order is the Valley of Virginia; then the area embraced by the Blue Ridge and the Rappahannock; then the peninsulas between that river, the York, and the James, and the country south of the James, including Petersburg; and lastly, the peninsula formed by the James and the Appomattox.

Western Virginia being separated from the main theatre of war by mountain-barriers, and bordered on two sides by hostile territory, was difficult to defend. The Shenandoah Valley, being a wealthy region and well calculated for flank or turning movements, became a favorite field of operations, while the other strategical divisions afforded fine fields for attack and defence and for manœuvring.

About the last of May, General Lee had organized, equipped, and sent to the field more than 30,000 men, and various regiments were in a forward state of preparation. At that time the Confederate authorities held his military capacity in such high estimation as to retain him at Richmond, which had then become the seat of government, as acting commander-in-chief of the Confederate forces until his services were urgently demanded elsewhere.

During the month of June the Federal plan of operations

became obvious and the Confederate line of defence developed. It was thought by the Washington authorities that the capture of Richmond would be the most speedy way to master the revolution. Therefore the United States put forth its strength for that purpose, and Richmond became the object of future operations. A defensive line was established by the Confederate military authorities, the left of which nestled among the mountains of Western Virginia, while its right rested on the Dismal Swamp, the line embracing the Shenandoah Valley, the Orange and Alexandria and the Manassas Gap railroads, the lower Potomac, Yorktown, and Norfolk. At the same time the Federal forces occupied an exterior line extending from the Ohio River to Fortress Monroe, and including a part of the Baltimore and Ohio Railroad, the Potomac, the Chesapeake Bay, and Hampton Roads.

The effective Confederate force in Virginia by the last of June amounted to about 65,000 men, distributed as follows: 5000 in Western Virginia, under General Robert Garnett; 15,000 in the Shenandoah Valley, under General J. E. Johnston; 20,000 at Manassas and Bull Run, commanded by General Beauregard; about 8000 at Acquia Creek and on the lower Potomac, under General T. H. Holmes; while the remainder were comprised within the commands of Magruder at Yorktown and Huger at Norfolk.

At the same time, the Federal forces at Fortress Monroe, under Butler; at Washington, under McDowell; at Williamsport, under Patterson; and on the border of Western Virginia, under McClellan, aggregated at least 100,000 men.

Although it was well known that the Federals had selected Richmond for their objective point, their real line of operation was still in obscurity. There was at Washington a diversity of opinion regarding the plan to be adopted: some proposed to establish the base of operations at Fortress Monroe, and then to proceed up the Peninsula by way of Yorktown and Williamsburg; others recommended the assumption of a base at some convenient point on the Rappahannock, whence an advance might be made by the shortest line to Richmond.

But the majority favored the line of the Orange and Alexandria Railroad as far as Manassas Junction, and thence south-ward by Fredericksburg. This line was ultimately taken, for the reason that Washington would not be left uncovered while the army was forcing its way toward Richmond.

The advantages of the several lines of operations suggested will appear during the progress of this narrative. About the 1st of June a collision occurred between a part of the forces of Magruder and Butler on the Peninsula, and early in July Gar-nett was defeated in North-western Virginia by McClellan. These affairs were initiatory to the more serious conflict at Manassas.

It may be said at this point that whilst there will necessarily be in this work much in which the subject of the memoir is not directly concerned, many scenes and incidents in which he did not personally appear, it should not be forgotten that it was his master mind and hand that first collected and prepared and set in motion from the smallest and most discouraging beginnings the means of defence that afterward became so mighty.

As to the actual extent of these means of defence at the period of secession, some interesting information may be ob-tained from the statements of General Josiah Gorgas, the able chief of ordnance of the Confederate States. He remarks that when he assumed his place as chief of ordnance he found in all the arsenals within the Confederacy only 15,000 rifles and 120,000 inferior muskets, with some old flint muskets at Rich-mond and Hall's rifles and carbines at Baton Rouge. There was no powder, except small quantities at Baton Rouge and at Mount Vernon, Ala., relics of the Mexican War. There was very little artillery, and no cavalry arms or equipments. It is but just to this able officer to state that his services in managing the ordnance department were invaluable to the Confederacy. He strenuously objected to the project of destroying the cotton and tobacco, and advised their use to purchase arms and muni-tions by aid of blockade-runners. It may be said that there was scarcely ever a demand on him which he was not prepared to meet, and that, in the words of General J. E. Johnston, "He created the ordnance department out of nothing."

The Federal preparations by the 1st of July were near completion. At that time General McClellan with a large force advanced into West Virginia, while General Patterson entered the Shenandoah Valley at the head of twenty-five thousand men. General McDowell was at Washington with a splendidly-appointed army, ready to cross the Potomac at that point.

On the 8th of July, McClellan attacked and defeated a small Confederate force in West Virginia, killing its gallant commander, General Robert Garnett. Patterson had in the mean time advanced toward Martinsburg, meeting with but little opposition. From that place he slowly advanced, while General Joseph E. Johnston retired toward the vicinity of Winchester.

While these operations were in progress in the Valley and West Virginia, Generals McDowell and Beauregard were preparing for the real contest on the line of the Orange and Alexandria Railroad. By referring to the map of Virginia it will be perceived that the position of Manassas is one of considerable strategic importance. The intersection of the Manassas Gap and the Orange and Alexandria railroads and the convergence of several common roads make it a place of easy concentration. The Warrenton and Leesburg turnpikes, the roads to Fredericksburg, and the important passes of the Blue Ridge were of great military importance, while the Manassas Gap Railroad afforded a rapid line of communication between the Valley and the position at Manassas. The occupation of this position by a large Confederate force doubtless confirmed the Federals in the adoption of that route for their advance upon Richmond; for to have taken either the route of the Peninsula or the one by way of the Rappahannock before having dislodged this force would have endangered the safety of Washington. The Federals' plan of operation being developed, General Beauregard prepared to receive their attack. For that purpose he occupied a range of low hills about a mile in the rear of, and nearly parallel to, Bull Run, a small stream four miles east of Manassas Junction. His right rested on the Occoquan, his centre on the Orange and Alexandria

Railroad, and his left on the Warrenton turnpike. This turn-pike, continuing nearly parallel with the railroad, crosses Bull Run by a stone bridge of a single span of about thirty feet. This stream, flowing between steep banks, offers a formidable obstruction to an army advancing in battle array. It was strongly picketed with infantry from the stone bridge down, covering the entire Confederate front. For some distance above the bridge the stream was only lightly picketed with cavalry. Beauregard, impressed with the belief that the Federals would direct their main effort against his right wing in order to force it back and turn his position on that flank, with the view of cutting off his communication with Richmond, directed his chief attention to that part of his line. For the greater security of this position, and for increased facility in gaining information, he established strong outposts at Fairfax Court-house and Centreville, points a few miles east of Bull Run.

By the middle of July, McDowell was ready for the intended movement with the best appointed army that had ever been seen in America. It had been created under the fostering care of the President and under the eye of the veteran Scott. It therefore lacked nothing its critical commander could suggest in the way of equipments and means for transportation and supplies. On the 16th of July this proud army entered Virginia, confident of a triumphant march to Richmond. On the 17th, General McDowell drove in the Confederate outposts at Centreville and Fairfax Court-house, and on the 18th appeared in force before the Confederate lines on Bull Run. An active skirmish ensued, under cover of which the Federal commander made a critical reconnoissance. Finding that the Confederate centre and right were too formidable to admit of an encouraging hope of success, he abandoned the preconceived plan of forcing the right and withdrew his forces to Centreville, where he intended to operate by the road from Sudley Ford to Manassas, which was discovered to have been undefended by General Beauregard in his anxiety concerning his right.

A battle being now inevitable, Generals Johnston and Holmes were directed to reinforce Beauregard. Such was the condition of affairs on the 18th of July. On the 19th and 20th the Fed-

eral army remained inactive except in making partial reconnoissances. This unlooked-for delay enabled General T. H.
Holmes to reach the vicinity of Manassas with his command,
consisting of 1265 infantry, six pieces of light artillery, and
one company of cavalry, 90 men. General J. E. Johnston also
arrived about noon on the 20th inst. with a portion of Bee's
and Bartow's brigades, numbering 2732 infantry, 300 cavalry
under Stuart, and Imboden's and Pendleton's batteries, to
which were afterward added Barksdale's Mississippi regiment,
which had arrived from Lynchburg, and Hampton's Legion
of 600 men. Jackson's brigade, 2611 strong, had reached
Manassas Junction the evening previous, as had the Seventh
and Eighth Georgia regiments.

Early in the morning of the 21st, McDowell, contrary to the
expectations of the Confederates, had crossed Bull Run at
Sudley's Ford, and nearly gained their left before he was discovered. At this critical moment he was gallantly attacked by
Colonel N. G. Evans with a small brigade, and held in check
until Generals Bee, Bartow, and Hampton could put their troops
in position. Leaving a force to oppose Evans, McDowell continued to advance and attack General Bee. A brilliant conflict
ensued, in which Bartow's regiment and Hampton's Legion
participated. At length these troops were forced back until
supported by the brigades of Cocke and Jackson. The interposition of Jackson enabled Bee to re-form his brigade and
continue the conflict.* The positions of the other part of the
army being remote, reinforcements could not be readily sent to
those engaged. Notwithstanding the great odds against them,
these troops maintained their ground, until about the middle
of the afternoon they were suddenly reinforced by Kirby Smith's
brigade, which had been detained by a railroad accident. Smith
attacked vigorously on the flank of the Federals, who, being thus

---

* It is to this event we owe a title that has become famous in history, that of *Stonewall Jackson.* Bee approached Jackson, and pointed to the shattered columns that
were huddled together in the woods, exclaiming, "General, they are beating us back."—
"Sir, we'll give them the bayonet," replied Jackson. Bee, rushing back to his troops,
rallied them with the words, "There is Jackson *standing like a stone wall;* let us determine to die here, and we will conquer." In a few moments afterward Bee fell mortally
wounded, holding in his hand the sword which South Carolina had presented him.

unexpectedly assailed at the moment when victory seemed in their grasp, paused, wavered, and then gave way. Being now pressed in front and flank, they fell into confusion; then a panic ensued, and the whole army became a disorganized mass, rush‹ ing wildly toward Washington. There was never a more complete victory, but it was dearly bought at the price of Bee, Bartow, and many other gallant soldiers.

Pending the battle, Richmond was greatly agitated. The pale faces of the women and the anxious looks of the men plainly bespoke intense anxiety. The telegraph-office was con‹ stantly surrounded by dense crowds eager to catch every item of news from the field of battle. At one time the despatch would state an advantage gained by the Confederates; then a gleam of joy would pervade the crowd and the good news would be proclaimed by an exultant shout. At another time it would tell that the Federals were gaining ground, when anxiety and doubt would dispel the previous joy, and the crowd would sink into gloomy silence and dark forebodings. As the day wore on several hours elapsed without news. The suspense was then agonizing. Conjecture suggested the most disastrous results, and at last rumor whispered that Johnston and Beauregard had been defeated, the telegraph had been seized, and McDowell was in full march upon Richmond. These groundless rumors filled the city with consternation, but about four o'clock they were succeeded by the intelligence that the enemy was giving away, and that Bee, Jackson, and others had held the field against all odds until the opportune arrival of Kirby Smith caused the defeat of the Federal army. A little later another telegram announced a glorious victory for the Confederates— that Johnston and Beauregard were masters of the field, and that McDowell had been routed and his entire army was in rapid flight for Washington. This news created a reaction of feeling beyond description. The people were lifted from the depths of despair to the height of joy, and the city was filled with the wildest exultation. This, however, was soon moderated by the recollection that the sweetness of victory must necessarily be followed by the bitterness of grief.

After the battle followed tidings of the casualties. First

came news that Bee and Bartow were slain, and Jackson and Smith were wounded. Then followed the long lists of killed and wounded, composed of those less conspicuous in the army, but not less dearly loved at home. The perusal of these lists soon spread mourning throughout the land, and the natural respect for the bereaved checked all further demonstration of victory. Scenes of terror and grief such as those above described yield sad evidence to the fact that the miseries of war are by no means confined to the camp and field, but are yet more keenly felt at home.

Some of the principal features of the Federal plan of the campaign were that McDowell with a powerful central army should advance on the Orange and Alexandria Railroad, crush Beauregard at Manassas, and proceed by the most favorable route to Richmond, while Butler from Fortress Monroe threatened the Confederate forces on the Peninsula, and Patterson occupied Johnston in the Valley. In case the latter should retire beyond the Blue Ridge, Patterson was to promptly reinforce McDowell. Johnston, however, skilfully eluded his adversary, and by rapid movements over the Manassas Gap Railroad joined Beauregard on the eve of battle with the greater part of his forces, leaving his antagonist in ignorance of his movements until it was too late for him to execute the latter part of his instructions. Therefore McDowell had to contend single-handed with the combined forces of Johnston and Beauregard. The rapid concentration of the Confederate forces and the splendid victory at Manassas are conclusive evidences of the masterly combination that led to those results.

Soon after the battle of Manassas, Lee, Johnston, and Beauregard were created generals, and General Lee was assigned to the command of the department of West Virginia.

The signal defeat of McDowell, which was so complete as to paralyze the Federal plan of operations for months, has been the subject of much discussion, and the search for its causes has been productive of numerous theories, from which we shall select that of Mr. Stephens in his *War between the States*. He says:

"Great as was the skill of Generals Johnston and Beauregard

in the disposition and movements of their squadrons, that of McDowell was also very great. His whole plan of operations from the beginning to the end showed military genius of the highest order. The result, therefore, did not so much depend upon the superior skill of the commanders on the Confederate side as upon the high objects and motives with which they, as well as those under them, were inspired. Johnston and Beauregard were both often in the thickest of the fight, leading in person, with colors in hand, on to the charge regiments whose officers had fallen. They and those who followed them . . . . were animated by the sentiments uttered by Mr. Davis in his message at Montgomery and received the day before at Richmond.

"The struggle with them was not for power, dominion, or dignity, nor for fame, but to resist palpable and dangerous assumptions of power and to repel wanton aggressions upon long-established rights. They fought for those principles and institutions of self-government which were the priceless heritage of their ancestors.

"On the other side, thousands of those who were sent on this expedition set out not only with reluctance, but with the consciousness that the whole movement was wrong. They had volunteered for no such purpose. They had tendered their services with the sole view of defending the capital. It was under the impression and belief, so extensively created at the North, that the Confederates intended to take Washington, that much the greater portion of this immense army had with very patriotic motives rushed to the rescue. Their object was to defend their own rights against an expected assault, and not to make aggressions upon the rights of others."

The period at which we have now arrived is that in which A. L. Long, the writer of this work, first entered into personal relations with General Lee—relations which ere long became intimate and were destined to continue throughout the war. Arriving in Richmond shortly before the battle of Manassas, he, in company with Colonels Loring and Stevenson and Lieutenant Deshler, all of whom had resigned their commissions in the United States army, waited upon General Lee to offer their services to the Confederacy. Loring and Stevenson, being old acquaintances of the general and superior in rank to their two companions, naturally received his attention first. This gave the writer an opportunity of observing his personal appearance and surroundings. The impression received it will be of interest to describe after we have detailed the incidents of the interview.

Having ended his interview with Loring and Stevenson, the general addressed himself to Deshler and Long. His words were few, but directly to the point. After a few commonplace remarks he informed Long that he had been appointed major and chief of artillery of the Army of North-western Virginia; that Colonel Loring had been created brigadier-general and assigned to its command, and that Long should report to him for further orders. Stevenson received the appointment of colonel and assistant adjutant-general for the Army of North-western Virginia. Deshler was made captain of artillery and assigned to the same army. When this interview was about concluded, General Lee remarked that it was necessary to strike the enemy in North-western Virginia without delay, and asked Loring when he would be ready to set out for his command. Loring replied that two or three days would be necessary for his preparation.

In this, Major Long's first interview with General Lee, he was struck with the ease and grace of his bearing and his courteous and mild but decided manner; and the high opinion he then formed of him was fully sustained in the intimate relations which afterward existed between them. Though at that time he had attained the age of fifty-four years, his erect and muscular frame, firm step, and the animated expression of his eye made him appear much younger. He exhibited no external signs of his rank, his dress being a plain suit of gray. His office was simply furnished with plain desks and chairs. There were no handsomely-dressed aides-de-camp or staff officers filling the anteroom. There was not even a sentinel to mark the military headquarters. His only attendants were Captain Walter Taylor—afterward Colonel Taylor—adjutant-general of the Army of Northern Virginia, and two or three clerks.

General Lee was remarkable for his rapid despatch of business and ready appreciation of character—qualities which are indispensable to a commander-in-chief. Having been appointed, as has been stated, major-general and commander-in-chief of the Virginia forces a few days after the secession of that State, he entered with alacrity upon the arduous duty of forming an army from new levies. Such was his wonderful talent for organization that in the space of two months he was able to equip for the field sixty regiments of infantry and cavalry, besides numerous batteries of artillery, making an aggregate of nearly 50,000 men. Nor was equipment for service the whole of the duty performed. The valiant behavior of these new troops not long afterward on the field of Manassas showed that the essential of drill had by no means been neglected, and that, though inferior to their antagonists in equipment, they were their superiors in most of the qualities which go to the making of effective soldiery. They formed the germ and rudiment of that gallant Army of Northern Virginia which was to prove its mettle on many a hard-fought field, and under the lead of its great commander to win a glory from which its final fate can in no just sense detract.

CHAPTER VII.

THE WEST VIRGINIA CAMPAIGN.

General Garnett Defeated.—De Lagnel's Adventure.—Loring's Operations.—General Lee takes Command.—The Cheat Mountain Ambush.—Its Failure.—Letter to Governor Letcher.—Movements on the Kanawha.—West Virginia Abandoned.— Description of Traveller.

BEFORE proceeding to describe the operations in North-western Virginia it will be necessary to glance at the condition of that section and the previous military operations that had been carried on within its limits. This section of Virginia did not cordially coincide in the ordinance of secession that had been passed by the State Convention, inasmuch as a considerable part of its inhabitants were opposed to secession, or, in other words, were Unionists. A large number, however, of its most influential citizens were ardent Southern supporters, and there was also an intermediate class, indifferent to politics, which was ready to join the party which might prove the strongest; besides, it soon became apparent that the Baltimore and Ohio Railroad was destined to exercise an important influence on military movements; therefore this section became an object of interest to both sides. At first, the Confederate colonel Porterfield was sent with a few companies to operate on the Baltimore and Ohio Railroad, but this force was too small and illy provided with the essentials for service, so that it could effect nothing. Shortly afterward General Robert Garnett was sent by the Confederate authorities to seize the Baltimore and Ohio Railroad and to confirm the North-western Virginians in their allegiance to the State. Garnett, with a force of about 5000 men, reached the railroad in June and occupied Laurel Hill. About the same time General McClellan crossed the Ohio into North-western Virginia with the view of gaining the adherence of its inhabitants to the Federal Government

114

and to protect the Baltimore and Ohio Railroad. Having a greatly superior force, he made it his first object to attack Garnett before that general could be reinforced (Colonel Pegram with a considerable detachment being defeated by General Rosecrans with a part of McClellan's force), and Garnett was obliged to retreat in order to save the rest of his little army. McClellan pursued, and, overtaking the rear-guard at Carrack's Ford, a skirmish ensued, in which Garnett was killed.

The adjutant-general, Captain Corley, assisted by other members of Garnett's staff, safely continued the retreat, and placed the remnant of the army where it could rest and recruit. An adventure may be related in connection with Garnett's defeat which exhibited great courage, endurance, and address. De Lagnel was an old army officer, and commanded the artillery of Pegram's detachment. When attacked by Rosecrans at Rich Mountain he fought his guns with great gallantry and effect; his men behaved well until the enemy began to close upon them; they then fled, leaving De Lagnel almost alone. Undaunted by the desertion of his men, he served a gun himself until disabled by a severe wound. Then, amid the confusion of a defeat, he escaped to a laurel-thicket near by, in which he concealed himself until the enemy had disappeared. He then found shelter under the roof of a friendly mountaineer. His kind host and hostess concealed and attended him until his wound was healed and his strength restored. He then determined to join the Confederate forces, which had again entered North-western Virginia, but to do so it was necessary to pass through the Federal lines. To accomplish this, he concluded to assume the character of a mountaineer, being supplied by his host with a herder's garb with the exception of shoes. Then, with a well-filled wallet over his shoulder and a staff in his hand, he bade adieu to his kind friends and launched forth into the mountains. After wandering among them for several days he fell in with the Federal pickets. On being questioned by them, he so well sustained the character he had assumed that all the pickets were easily passed until he reached the last outpost that separated him from his friends. Here he was more strictly examined than he had hitherto been, but by his wit fully sustained the character he had adopted, and was told to continue his way; but just as he was about to depart one of the guards observed his boots, which, though soiled and worn, still exhibited signs of a fashionable make. Upon this the examination was renewed, and with all his ingenuity he could not escape detection; his boots had betrayed him. These traitors were drawn off, and in the leg of one the name of "De Lagnel" was found, and he was at once recognized as the officer whose disappearance at Rich Mountain had led to so much inquiry. He was sent as prisoner of war to the Federal headquarters, where he was courteously received. (It may be here remarked that General McClellan was always distinguished for courtesy and kindness to those whom the chances of war placed in his power.)

The defeat of General Garnett left McClellan in undisputed possession of all North-western Virginia. In order to secure his acquisition, he strongly occupied some of the principal mountain-passes and took other measures for its permanent occupation. A few days later the total defeat of McDowell at Bull Run considerably changed the order of things. McClellan was called to take the command of the Army of the Potomac, and the greater part of his force was withdrawn, leaving only a few thousand men to hold North-western Virginia. The result of McClellan's success in that quarter proved to be of much greater importance than was at first apprehended, by disheartening its loyal inhabitants and encouraging the doubtful or indifferent to give their adhesion to the Federal Government. The Confederate authorities, being aware of the importance of Western Virginia at that time both in a political and military point of view, determined to send there a force sufficiently strong to reoccupy and retain possession of it. There had been assembled in the neighborhood of Staunton five or six thousand men for the purpose of reinforcing General Garnett. These troops were ordered to advance on the 15th of July, under the command of General Henry R. Jackson, on the Parkersburg turnpike, to re-enter Western Virginia, and to occupy some convenient position until the remainder of the forces intended to operate in that quarter should arrive. Loring, whom we have seen assigned to the command of the Army of North-western Virginia, was an officer of considerable reputation. He had served with distinction in the Mexican War, had subsequently become colonel of a regiment of mounted rifles, and for several years prior to his resignation had commanded the department of New Mexico, where he acquired an experience in mountain-service. His appointment therefore gave general satisfaction. His staff was composed chiefly of experienced officers—Colonel Carter Stevens, adjutant-general; Major A. L. Long, chief of artillery; Captain Corley, chief quartermaster; Captain Cole, chief commissary; Lieutenant Matthews, aide-de-camp, and Colonel Starke, volunteer aide-de-camp—and as the country was full of enthusiasm on account of the recent victory at Manassas, he was about to enter upon his new field of operations under the most favorable auspices.

General Loring, accompanied by his staff, left Richmond on the 22d of July, the day after the battle of Manassas. On the 24th he arrived at Monterey, a small village about sixty miles west of Staunton, where he found Jackson, who informed him that on arriving at the Greenbrier River he had found Cheat Mountain Pass so strongly occupied by Federals that he deemed it unadvisable to attempt to carry it by a direct attack. So he retired, leaving Colonel Edward Johnson, with the Twelfth Georgia regiment and Anderson's battery, to occupy the Alleghany Mountain Pass, and, posting Rust's Arkansas regiment and Baldwin's Virginia regiment in convenient supporting distance of Johnson, he established himself at Monterey, with Fulkerson's and Scott's Virginia regiments, the First Georgia regiment (Colonel Ramsey's), Major Jackson's cavalry, and Shoemaker's battery. Having heard of a pass about forty miles west, near Huntersville, by which Cheat Mountain might be turned, he sent Colonel Gilham with his own Virginia regiment and Colonel Lee's Sixth North Carolina regiment, being a force of about 2000 men, to occupy this pass, and had ordered the remaining troops intended for the Army of North-western Virginia to proceed direct from Staunton to Huntersville. This was the condition of affairs when General Loring arrived at Monterey and assumed command. He remained several days

in the neighborhood of Monterey, examining the condition of
the troops and reconnoitering the position of the enemy on
Cheat Mountain.   Cheat Mountain Pass is a narrow gap near
the top of the mountain whose natural strength had been
greatly increased by the art of engineers since its occupation
by the Federals.   It was approachable from the east only by
the Parkersburg turnpike, which, ascending the rugged side
of the mountain, enters this narrow defile and winds its way
through it for nearly a mile before it begins the western
descent.

The Federals, finding this pass unoccupied, and foreseeing the
importance the Parkersburg turnpike would be to the Confederates in their attempt to reoccupy West Virginia, seized it and
fortified it, and now held it with a force of about 2500 men.
The remainder of the Federal force was in the vicinity of Beverly, a village a few miles west of Cheat River.   General
Loring, having satisfied himself that a direct attack on Cheat
Mountain Pass was impracticable, and that there was no force
of the enemy near the west base of Cheat Mountain except that
of Beverly, determined to take command of the force which
had been ordered to rendezvous at Huntersville and advance
by the pass that Colonel Gilham had been directed to occupy
to the rear of the enemy's position on Cheat Mountain.
He therefore directed Jackson to advance his whole force,
which at this time amounted to 6000 men, to the Greenbrier
River, and hold himself in readiness to co-operate when the
advance was made from Huntersville, and then proceeded to
that place to make arrangements for the proposed movement.   When Loring arrived at Huntersville, about the
1st of August, he found already there Maney's, Hatten's,
and Savage's Tennessee regiments, Campbell's Virginia regiment, a battalion of Virginia regulars, 400 strong, commanded
by Colonel Munford, Major W. H. F. Lee's squadron of cavalry, and Marye's and Stanley's batteries of artillery.   Colonel
Gilham was at Valley Mountain Pass, fifteen miles west of
Huntersville, with two regiments, and two other regiments,
Burke's Virginia and a Georgia regiment, were *en route* from
Staunton.   The force of Loring on the Huntersville line

amounted in round numbers to 8500 effective men. The general's staff were particularly active in their efforts to prepare for a speedy advance. Colonel Stevenson, adjutant-general, and Captains Corley and Cole, chief quartermaster and commissary, being experienced officers, rendered valuable service in organizing the troops and in collecting transportation and supplies. Major A. L. Long, in addition to his duties as chief of artillery, had assigned him those of inspector-general. The troops were well armed and equipped, all of them were accustomed to the use of arms, and many were expert marksmen, and a large proportion had received military instruction in the various volunteer companies of which they had been members. The troops were in fine spirits, and desired nothing more than to be led against the enemy. It was obvious to all those about the general that the success of the proposed movement depended upon its speedy execution. It was impossible that the occupation of Valley Mountain by a force as large as that of Gilham could escape the observation of the Federals, and its position would expose the design of the Confederates. Delay would enable the Federals to seize all the important passes on the route, and fortify them so strongly that they would effectually arrest the advance of any force. Yet, notwithstanding the great value of time in the execution of the movement contemplated by General Loring, he seemed to regard the formation of a depot of supplies at Huntersville and the organization of a supply-train as a matter of first importance. He appeared to overlook the fact that the line from Huntersville to Beverly, only forty miles long, was to be only temporary—for so soon as Cheat Mountain Pass was opened he would receive his supplies from Staunton over the Parkersburg turnpike— and also that the country along his line abounded in beef and grain.

While Loring is preparing to advance we will take a view of affairs in other quarters. After the withdrawal of McClellan, General Rosecrans was assigned to the command of the department of Western Virginia. At the same time a large portion of the troops in that department were withdrawn for the defence of the capital. The Federal force in Western Virginia at the

time Loring assumed command of the Army of North-western
Virginia was only about six or seven thousand men, about half
of which, under the command of General Reynolds, occupied
the Cheat Mountain Pass. The other portion, commanded by
General Cox, was designed for operations on the line of the
Kanawha. General Rosecrans was one of the most energetic
and skilful of the Federal commanders. As soon as he found
himself in command of the department of Western Virginia he
set about increasing his force and strengthening his position.
Taking advantage of the political disaffection among the Western Virginians, he obtained many recruits, which, with recruits
from other quarters, rapidly increased his force. The Confederate authorities in the mean time, being informed of the
advance of General Cox to the Kanawha, sent a force of about
5000 men to oppose him under the command of General Wise,
and appointed General Robert E. Lee to the command of the
department of Western Virginia. He had displayed such remarkable administrative ability in the organization of the Virginia troops that he was retained at the head of the Confederate
military bureau till the time of his appointment to the command
of this department. Although aware of the difficulties to be
met with in a mountainous country like Western Virginia, he
unflinchingly accepted this new command, and entered upon
his arduous task with no other feelings than those for the good
of his country. When Lee arrived at Huntersville, he found
General Loring busily engaged in forming his dépôt of supplies
and organizing his transportation-train. Several days had
already elapsed, and several days more would be necessary
before he could complete his preparations for an advance. The
arrival of Lee at Huntersville as commander of the department
took Loring by surprise. Having been his superior in rank in
the old army, he could not suppress a feeling of jealousy. Lee
was accompanied by his aides-de-camp, Colonel John A. Washington and Captain Walter H. Taylor. After remaining several days at Huntersville without gaining any positive information from Loring in regard to the time of his probable
advance, he proceeded to join Colonel Gilham at Valley Mountain. He took with him Major Lee's cavalry, not as an escort,

but for the purpose of scouting and reconnoitering. It had now been eight or ten days since Gilham had first arrived at Valley Mountain Pass. At that time he learned from the inhabitants and his scouts that the road to Beverly was unoccupied. But within the last day or two a force of the Federals had advanced within less than a mile of his front, and then retired. Lee at once busied himself about gaining information respecting the position of the enemy. He soon learned that the Federals had taken possession of a strong pass ten miles in front of Valley Mountain, and were actively engaged in fortifying it. When Loring arrived, about the 12th of August, the Federals had been reinforced, and this position had been so greatly strengthened that General Lee deemed it unadvisable to attempt a direct attack, so the only course now to be pursued was to gain the Federal flank or rear.

General Lee, as we already know, had been distinguished in the Mexican War as a reconnoitering officer, and Scott had been mainly indebted to his bold reconnoissances for the brilliant success of his Mexican campaigns. Rank and age had not impaired the qualities that had formerly rendered him so distinguished. He brought them with him to the mountains of Virginia. There was not a day when it was possible for him to be out that the general, with either Colonel Washington or Captain Taylor, might not be seen crossing the mountains, climbing over rocks and crags, to get a view of the Federal position. Ever mindful of the safety of his men, he would never spare himself toil or fatigue when seeking the means to prevent unnecessary loss of life. By way of illustrating his boldness as a reconnoitering officer, an anecdote may be related as told by Captain Preston, adjutant of the Forty-eighth Virginia regiment (Colonel Campbell's). The regiment being on picket, he, seeing three men on an elevated point about half a mile in advance of the line of pickets, and believing them to be Federals, asked his colonel to let him capture them. Permission being obtained, he selected two men from a number of volunteers who had offered to accompany him, and set forth to capture the Federal scouts. Dashing through the brushwood and over the rocks, he suddenly burst upon the unsuspecting trio, when lo! to his amazement, General Lee stood before him!

To add to the difficulties of a campaign in the mountains, the rainy season set in: it began to rain about the middle of August, and continued to do so without much cessation for six weeks; in the mean time, the narrow mountain-roads became saturated and softened, so that the passage of heavy trains of wagons soon rendered them almost impassable: while the wet weather lasted any movement was simply impossible. The troops, being new and unaccustomed to camp-life, began to suffer from all the camp-diseases. Typhoid fever, measles, and home-sickness began to spread among them, so that in the course of a few weeks nearly one-third of the army was rendered *hors de combat* by sickness. Amid this accumulation of difficulties Lee preserved his equanimity and cheerfulness; his chief aim now was to ameliorate as much as possible the sufferings of his men. During this period of inactivity he exerted himself to find a practicable route leading to the rear of Cheat Mountain Pass, the route by which Loring had proposed to reach it being now effectually closed. The possession of the pass was of great importance to the Confederates, as the Parkersburg turnpike was the principal line over which operations could be successfully carried on in North-western Virginia. Individual scouts were employed, both from among the well-affected inhabitants and the enterprising young soldiers of the army: Lieutenant Lewis Randolph, of the Virginia State regulars, was particularly distinguished for the boldness of his reconnoissances. Early in September, General Jackson reported to Loring that Colonel Rust, Third Arkansas regiment, had made a reconnoissance to the rear of Cheat Mountain Pass, and had discovered a route, though difficult, by which infantry could be led. Soon after Colonel Rust reported in person, and informed General Lee of the practicability of reaching the rear of the enemy's position on Cheat Mountain, from which a favorable attack could be made, and requested the general, in case his information was favorably considered, to permit him to lead the attacking column, to consist of his regiment and such other troops as the general might designate. Another route was in the mean time discovered, leading along the western side of Cheat Mountain, by which troops could be conducted to a point on the Parkersburg turnpike about two miles below the Federal position in the pass. This being the information that General Lee had been most desirous of obtaining, he determined to attack the enemy without further delay. The opposing forces were at this time about equal in numbers. Loring's force was now 6000, Jackson's about 5000 strong. Reynolds's force had been increased to about 11,000 men; of these, 2000 were on Cheat Mountain, and about 5000 in position on the Lewisburg road in front of Loring. The remainder of Reynolds's force was held in reserve near the junction of the Parkersburg turnpike and the Lewisburg road.

Lee determined to attack on the morning of the 12th of September. The plan was that Colonel Rust should gain the rear of the Federal position by early dawn and begin the attack. General Anderson, with two Tennessee regiments from Loring's command, was to support him, while Jackson was to make a diversion in front. Cheat Mountain Pass being carried, Jackson with his whole force was to sweep down the mountain and fall upon the rear of the other Federal position; General Donaldson with two regiments was to gain a favorable position for attacking the enemy on the Lewisburg road in flank or rear; and Loring was to advance by the main road on the Federal front. In case of failure Anderson and Donaldson were to rejoin Loring, and Rust was to find his way back to Jackson. The troops gained their designated positions with remarkable promptness and accuracy in point of time, considering the distance and the difficulties to be overcome. Colonel Rust's attack on Cheat Mountain was to be the signal for the general advance of all the troops. It was anxiously expected from early dawn throughout the day. On every side was continuously heard, "What has become of Rust?" "Why don't he attack?" "Rust must have lost his way." The Tennesseeans under Anderson became so impatient that they requested to be led to the attack without waiting for Rust, but Anderson thought that he must be governed by the letter of his instructions and declined granting the request of his men. Thus we see a plan that offered every prospect of success come to naught by the failure of a subordinate officer to equal the expectations of his commander. Anderson and Donaldson, finding that their situation was becoming critical, being liable to discovery and being between two superior forces, rejoined Loring on the 13th. On the same day Colonel Rust reported in person his operations, which amounted to this: He had heard nothing of Anderson; he passed the day watching the Federals, who were in a state of unconscious security, and then retired, his presence not having been suspected. When Rust rendered his report, General Lee, perceiving the deep mortification he felt at the great blunder he had committed, permitted him to rejoin his regiment. A council of war was then held, in which it was decided that the position of the Federals was too strong to be attacked in front with any reasonable prospect of success, and that a flank attack was now out of the question, inasmuch as the Federals had been aroused by the discovery of the danger which had so recently threatened them. The troops were therefore ordered to resume their former positions. During the operations just related there had been but little skirmishing, and the Confederate loss had been slight. One circumstance, however, occurred which cast a gloom over the whole army. Colonel J. A. Washington while making a reconnoissance fell into an ambuscade and was killed. He had by his soldierly qualities and high gentlemanly bearing gained the esteem of all. Too much praise cannot be bestowed upon the troops for their courage and patient endurance in this campaign, and Colonels Burke, Gilliam, Campbell, Lee, Munford, Maney, Hatten, and Savage were worthy of the gallant fellows that it had fallen to their lot to command.

The failure of this well-devised operation was due to one of those errors of judgment to which all warlike movements are liable, and through which many a neatly-laid scheme has come to naught. The system of operations had been clearly defined in General Loring's order of September 8th, but the unavoidable difficulty in producing concert of action between divided troops, and the hesitation of each commander to act on his own responsibility, stood in the way of success, and caused an inglorious withdrawal of the ambushed forces, from whom such a very different result was reasonably expected.

In this connection may be given General Lee's stirring appeal to the patriotism of the troops, issued at the same time with General Loring's special order to the commanders of the columns of attack :

"HEADQUARTERS, VALLEY MOUNTAIN,
"September 8, 1861.

"The forward movement announced to the Army of the North-west in Special Order No. 28, from its headquarters, of this date, gives the general commanding the opportunity of exhorting the troops to keep steadily in view the great principles for which they contend, and to manifest to the world their determination to maintain them. The eyes of the country, are upon you. The safety of your homes and the lives of all you hold dear depend upon your courage and exertions. Let each man resolve to be victorious, and that the right of self-government, liberty, and peace shall in him find a defender. The progress of this army must be forward.

"R. E. LEE,
"*General commanding.*"

We here append a letter from General Lee to Governor Letcher bearing upon this campaign, which has been so variously criticised and generally misunderstood:

"VALLEY MOUNTAIN, Sept. 17, 1861.

"MY DEAR GOVERNOR: I received your very kind note of the 5th inst. just as I was about to accompany General Loring's command on an expedition to the enemy's works in front, or I would have before thanked you for the interest you take in my welfare and your too flattering expressions of my ability. Indeed, you overrate me much, and I feel humbled when I weigh myself by your standard. I am, however, very grateful for your confidence, and I can answer for my sincerity in the earnest endeavor I make to advance the cause I have so much at heart, though conscious of the slow progress I make.

" I was very sanguine of taking the enemy's works on last Thursday morning. I had considered the subject well. With great effort the troops intended for the surprise had reached their destination, having traversed twenty miles of steep, rugged mountain-paths, and the last day through a terrible storm, which lasted all night, and in which they had to stand drenched to the skin in the cold rain. Still, their spirits were good. When morning broke I could see the enemy's tents on Valley River at the point on the Huttonsville road just below me. It was a tempting sight. We waited for the attack on Cheat Mountain, which was to be the signal, till 10 A.M.; the men were cleaning their unserviceable arms. But the signal did not come. All chance for surprise was gone. The provisions of the men had been destroyed the preceding day by the storm. They had nothing to eat that morning, could not hold out another day, and were obliged to be withdrawn. The party sent to Cheat Mountain to take that in the rear had also to be withdrawn. The attack to come off from the east side failed from the difficulties in the way; the opportunity was lost and our plan discovered.

" It is a grievous disappointment to me, I assure you. But for the rain-storm I have no doubt it would have succeeded. This, governor, is for your own eye. Please do not speak of it; we must try again. Our greatest loss is the death of my dear friend Colonel Washington. He and my son were reconnoitering the front of the enemy. They came unawares upon a concealed party, who fired upon them within twenty yards, and the colonel fell pierced by three balls. My son's horse received three shots, but he escaped on the colonel's horse. His zeal for the cause to which he had devoted himself carried him, I fear, too far.

" We took some seventy prisoners and killed some twenty-five or thirty of the enemy. Our loss was small besides what I have mentioned. Our greatest difficulty is the roads. It has been raining in these mountains about six weeks. It is impossible to get along. It is that which has paralyzed all our efforts.

"With sincere thanks for your good wishes,

"I am very truly yours,

"R. E. LEE.

"His Excellency Gov. JOHN LETCHER."

We will now examine into the condition of affairs on the line of the Kanawha.

General Wise entered the Kanawha Valley in August. General Cox was then near Charleston. After some manœuvring, Wise fell back to the junction of the New River and the Gauley, where he was joined by General Floyd, whose force now numbered between eight and ten thousand men. Being uncertain whether Cox would advance up the New River line or upon that of the Gauley, he posted a force under Wise on the New River line, while he occupied a favorable position on the Gauley. At Carnifex Ferry, Floyd and Wise were in easy supporting distance of each other, but there was no cordiality between them. About the 15th of September, General Floyd, seeing that it was the evident intention of Rosecrans to attack him, ordered Wise to his support; which order Wise failed to obey, and Floyd was left to receive alone the attack of a greatly superior force, which, however, he succeeded in repulsing with considerable loss, but, being still unsupported by Wise, he was obliged to retire. Among the casualties on the side of the Confederates, Floyd had received a painful wound in the arm. Wise having finally joined Floyd, they fell back to a position on the James River and Kanawha turnpike, near the Hawk's Nest.

About the last of September, General Rosecrans, having reinforced Cox, took command in person and advanced on the James River and Kanawha turnpike, gradually pushing back Floyd and Wise in the direction of Lewisburg, it being his intention to turn the Confederate position on Valley Mountain and the Greenbrier River. Such was the condition of affairs on the line of the Kanawha at the close of the Valley Mountain campaign. Lee, perceiving that the operations on the Kanawha were not progressing favorably, determined to take control of affairs in that quarter himself. He therefore directed Loring to detach Gilliam with his own regiment (the battalion of State regulars) and a section of artillery to occupy Valley Mountain Pass, and proceeded with the remainder of his force to reinforce General Floyd. General Lee arrived at Meadow Bluff about the 7th of October, where he found Floyd. Meadow Bluff is a small village near the eastern base of Sewell Mountain. Floyd had proposed making a stand there, but Wise had halted on the top of the mountain, five miles in rear, where he had determined to fight. The hostility that had previously existed between the two generals had not been diminished by the affair of Carnifex Ferry; the arrival of General Lee was therefore fortunate, as it most probably prevented a disaster, since Rosecrans was advancing, and would have been able to strike both Wise and Floyd in detail. Lee found Wise occupying the eastern crest of Sewell Mountain. Being satisfied with the position, he determined to hold it and give battle to Rosecrans if he persisted in advancing. So he ordered Floyd to return and support Wise. Lee had barely time to complete his arrangements when Rosecrans appeared on the opposite crest.

Each army now occupied a mountain-crest nearly parallel, separated by a gap or depression forming a notch in the mountain about a mile wide, over which it was difficult to pass except by the James River and Kanawha turnpike, which crosses it. Both positions were naturally very strong. The Confederate force being greatly inferior to that of the Federals, and Rosecrans having assumed the offensive, Lee naturally expected to be attacked before Loring could come up; he therefore actively employed his skill as an engineer in adding to the natural strength of his position. Rosecrans, discovering the formidable preparations of the Confederates, prudently forbore to attack them. The arrival of Loring on the 9th placed General Lee's force almost on an equality with that of the Federals.

The force of Lee now amounted to about 15,000 men. The troops were in fine spirits and anxious to be led to the attack, but the general, ever mindful of the safety of his men, restrained their ardor. On one occasion, when several of his commanders were urging an attack, he remarked: "I know, gentlemen, you could carry the enemy's lines, but we cannot spare the brave men who would lose their lives in doing it. If Rosecrans does not attack us, we will find a way to reach him that will not cost us so dearly." After waiting several days for General Rosecrans to attack, he began to make preparations for a flank movement to gain Rosecrans's rear, who no longer manifested a disposition to continue the aggressive. Floyd and others who had a good knowledge of the routes in the vicinity of Sewell Mountain reported to Lee a practicable route for artillery and infantry leading about ten miles to the rear of the Federal position. Upon this information he conceived the plan of sending a column of 5000 men by this route at night, to fall at dawn upon the Federals' rear, while a strong demonstration was being made in front. Had this plan been executed, it would most likely have been successful, but Rosecrans escaped the trap by a night retreat. Great was the disappointment of the troops when they discovered that the Federals had retired and the prospect of a battle had vanished.

As soon as the retreat of the Federals was discovered pursuit was ordered, but Lee soon perceived that it would be impossible to overtake Rosecrans and bring him to a successful engagement in the rough, mountainous country through which he was retreating; and, not wishing to harass his troops unnecessarily, he ordered them to return to their several positions, and Rosecrans was allowed to pursue his retreat unmolested to the Kanawha Valley. Lee knew that with the bravery of his troops and the strength of his position he could repel any attack that the Federals could make, while, on the other hand, if he attacked them in their position the result, even if successful, would be attended with great loss. He therefore determined to give Rosecrans every opportunity to attack before taking the offensive himself, which, as we have seen, Rosecrans prevented by abandoning his own plans and retreating.

The season was now so far advanced that it was impossible to continue active operations in Western Virginia. Snow had already fallen and the roads had become almost impassable.

Lee therefore deemed it necessary to withdraw the troops from Sewell Mountain. About the 1st of November the different columns were sent to their various destinations.

The campaign had been pronounced a failure. The press and the public were clamorous against him. No one stopped to inquire the cause or examine into the difficulties that surrounded him. Upon him alone were heaped the impracticability of mountains, the hostility of the elements, and the want of harmony of subordinate commanders. The difficulties to be encountered in Western Virginia were so great and the chances of success so doubtful that the Confederate authorities abandoned the idea of its further occupation. Therefore the greater part of the troops that had been serving in Western Virginia were ordered where their services would be more available, and Lee was assigned to the command of the department of South Carolina, Georgia, and Florida.

While the operations on Big Sewell were in progress Reynolds made a descent from Cheat Mountain and attacked the Confederate position on the Greenbrier. This attack was promptly met by General H. R. Jackson, and repulsed with considerable loss. Soon after his return to Huntersville, General Loring was instructed to report to General T. J. Jackson (Stonewall Jackson), then commanding in the Shenandoah Valley, to participate in a contemplated winter campaign. About the same time Major Long received orders from the War Office to report to General Lee in the department of South Carolina, Georgia, and Florida.

The inactivity of the forces on the Potomac that succeeded the battle of Manassas had a powerful influence on the campaign in Western Virginia, as it permitted the Federals to collect a force sufficiently powerful to render insurmountable difficulties which, under the most favorable circumstances, were exceedingly embarrassing. Had the Confederates made an advance across the Potomac and boldly threatened Washington in August or September, the nervous fear which then possessed the Federal authorities for the safety of that city would have caused them to draw forces from all quarters to defend their capital. The pressure on Lee in Western Virginia would have

GENERAL LEE ON HIS HORSE, TRAVELER.

thus been relieved, and it is within the scope of military probability that he would have regained all that had been lost in
that section, and have taken measures for its future preservation and the permanent occupation of the Baltimore and Ohio
Railroad, which became of such immense importance to the
Federal Government as the connecting-link between the Western States and the Eastern theatre of war.

In connection with this West Virginia campaign we may
revert to another matter of considerable interest, that relating
to Lee's favorite horse "Traveller," a noble animal which
attained almost as much celebrity in the Army of Northern
Virginia as the gallant form which he bore through so many
fields of battle. He was purchased during this campaign, and
served his master royally throughout the whole duration of the
war and for many years afterward. We are fortunately able to
give a history and description of this celebrated charger from
Lee himself. It was dictated to his daughter Agnes, with cor-
rections in his own handwriting, apparently in response to some
artist who had asked for a description of the animal. The enthusiasm with which the general speaks of his companion of
so many days of peril and hardship shows the spirit of a true
horseman and a nature capable of kindly affection and companionship for every creature with which he came into intimate
relations:

"If I was an artist like you, I would draw a true picture of
'Traveller,' representing his fine proportions, muscular figure,
deep chest and short back, strong haunches, flat legs, small
head, broad forehead, delicate ears, quick eye, small feet, and
black mane and tail. Such a picture would inspire a poet,
whose genius could then depict his worth and describe his endurance of toil, hunger, thirst, heat, cold, and the dangers and
suffering through which he has passed. He could dilate upon
his sagacity and affection and his invariable response to every
wish of his rider. He might even imagine his thoughts through
the long night-marches and days of battle through which he has
passed. But I am no artist, and can only say he is a *Confederate gray.* I purchased him in the mountains of Virginia in the
autumn of 1861, and he has been my patient follower ever since

—to Georgia, the Carolinas, and back to Virginia. He carried me through the seven days' battle around Richmond, the Second Manassas, at Sharpsburg, Fredericksburg, the last day at Chancellorsville, to Pennsylvania, at Gettysburg, and back to the Rappahannock. From the commencement of the campaign in 1864 at Orange till its close around Petersburg the saddle was scarcely off his back, as he passed through the fire of the Wilderness, Spottsylvania, Cold Harbor, and across the James River. He was almost in daily requisition in the winter of 1864–65 on the long line of defences from the Chickahominy north of Richmond and Hatcher's Run south of the Appomattox. In the campaign of 1865 he bore me from Petersburg to the final days at Appomattox Court-house.

"You must know the comfort he is to me in my present retirement. He is well supplied with equipments. Two sets have been sent to him from England, one from the ladies of Baltimore, and one was made for him in Richmond; but I think his favorite is the American saddle from St. Louis.* Of all his companions in toil, 'Richmond,' 'Brown Roan,' 'Ajax,' and quiet 'Lucy Long,' he is the only one that retained his vigor to the last.† The first two expired under their onerous burden, and the last two failed. You can, I am sure, from what I have said, paint his portrait."

To General Lee's description of his noble horse may be added some few further particulars of his appearance and history. He was sixteen hands high, of a dark iron-gray color, and when purchased about five years old. He was strong and active, but perfectly docile, and as calm as his master under fire. General Lee had always a strong affection for him, which he manifested

---

* This saddle has its story, which is worth relating. When Colonel Lee resigned from the United States army and repaired to Richmond to offer his services to his native State, his baggage, which had just reached New York, was seized by the authorities. Among his effects was a saddle of peculiar form which he preferred to all others. He immediately wrote to St. Louis, to the maker, desiring to have another like it if he was willing to take the risk of receiving his pay. The saddle was at once sent, and the soldier did not let the busy occupation of war make him forget to send the full price to the maker through a safe channel. He rode this saddle all through the war and throughout his after-life.

† The horse ridden by Lee in the Mexican War was named "Grace Darling."

on many occasions. Six years after the war " Traveller " had become almost milk-white, having grown hoary with age and honors. He died very soon after the decease of his master, his death arising from lockjaw caused by his treading on a nail which penetrated his foot and could not be withdrawn.

CHAPTER VIII.

THE SOUTH COAST DEFENCES.

General Lee in Charleston.—A Great Conflagration.—Topography of the Coast.—Its Defences.—General Lee's Engineering Operations.—His Mode of Life.—Ordered back to Richmond.

HAVING received orders to report to General Lee on the South Atlantic coast, the writer arrived in Charleston on the eve of the great fire that laid half of that beautiful city in ruins. The fire-alarm was heard by him on his way to the Mills House, but as fires are of frequent occurrence in cities, he gave little heed to it, as the conflagration seemed small and at a great distance from the hotel. General Lee had arrived a little before from his headquarters at Coosawhatchie. Soon after the arrival of Major Long he reported to Lee, who was in the hotel-parlor with Captains Taylor and Ives and some others. After a short conversation all separated for the night, little thinking that they would soon be compelled to seek safety in flight. Before retiring they observed that the fire had increased in volume, but it was not yet of sufficient magnitude to cause uneasiness. About eleven o'clock the general had Major Long called, who found him viewing the fire from the parlor window. To their amazement, it had acquired the proportions of a conflagration enveloping a quarter of the city. General Lee remarked that as the fire seemed beyond control and was advancing toward the hotel, it would be necessary to prepare to leave at a moment's notice. Mrs. Long was informed how matters stood, and in a few minutes was ready and repaired to the parlor, where she found Mrs. Washington, the wife of Captain Washington of General Lee's staff. By this time many of the guests of the hotel had assembled in the parlor, commenting anxiously on the terrible prospect. In order to get a better view of the desolating scene, General Lee, Major Long,

134

and some others assembled on the roof of the hotel, which towered far above the adjacent houses. From this position a scene of awful sublimity met the eye: more than one-third of the city appeared a sea of fire, shooting up columns of flame that seemed to mingle with the stars. From King street eastward to the river, extending back more than a mile, stores and dwellings, churches and public buildings, were enveloped in one common blaze, which was marching steadily and rapidly across the city. The mind was held fascinated by the fierce rage of the devouring element, until the thought was turned upon the helpless victims that crowded the streets as far as the eye could reach bending beneath the household goods that had been rescued from destruction, and struggling with might and main to gain a place of safety. Wagons, carts, and all kinds of vehicles loaded with every conceivable article were pressing women and children in dense masses to the sidewalks, and sometimes the combustible articles with which the carts and wagons were loaded became ignited by the sparks that swept from time to time along the streets, thus increasing the confusion that reigned among the bewildered multitude. Turning from the human misery below to the increasing fury of the conflagration, the question arose, Why has the demon of destruction been permitted to rage an unopposed destroyer of the Queen City of the South Atlantic, transforming her matchless beauty to hideous ruin? The reservoir, which was supplied by the water of the bay, had been drained by the receding tide, and the fire companies had been depleted by the demands of war; consequently, the city became a helpless victim.

The fire had by twelve o'clock reached the immediate vicinity of the hotel, and the flames were lapping themselves about the opposite houses. Just as the party was about to descend from its post of observation a body of soldiers appeared, headed by General Ripley (these were the troops brought by their gallant leader from Sullivan's Island to rescue the city). Now the flames were about to meet their first real opposition, and the hotel, whose huge bulk covered an important district, claimed especial attention. On returning to the parlor the ladies were found with bundles and babies ready to decamp.

It was indeed time to move, for the hotel had become a scene of great confusion, and the heat from without was oppressive, while the only remaining chance of escape was by a back stairway through the cellar. General Lee took one baby in his arms and Major Long took another, they being preceded by a guide with a lantern to light the way. Mrs. Long and Mrs. Washington, accompanied by Taylor and Ives, brought up the rear. On emerging from the cellar the group were met by the glare and heat of the burning buildings on the opposite side of the street. An omnibus was a few yards distant, into which all hurried, and were driven off amid a shower of sparks and cinders to the house of Mr. Alston on the Battery, which, in the absence of the family, was kindly put at General Lee's disposal by young Mr. Alston, who had remained in the city. The fire was subdued during the night, and the morning revealed a hideous ruin extending from the Ashley to the Cooper River, and bearing fearful testimony to the magnitude of the conflagration. The hotel was saved, and after order was restored its comfortable quarters were resumed. But the scene without was entirely changed: the superb edifices of the previous day had been converted into smoking beams and tottering walls, and the happy people of the day before were mournful spectators of the desolation that surrounded them. In this impressive manner Major Long was introduced to a companionship with General Lee which was destined to last throughout the war.

The defences of the coast, embracing numerous vital points, chiefly occupied General Lee's attention during his period of service in this southern department. The character of the work to be done and the method in which he performed it here call for description.

The line of coast extending from the entrance of Chesapeake Bay to the mouth of the Rio Grande presents innumerable bays, inlets, and harbors, into which vessels could run either for predatory incursions or with the intention of actual invasion. The Federals having the command of the sea, it was certain that they would take advantage of this open condition of the coast to employ their naval force as soon as it could be collected, not only to enforce the blockade which had been declared, but also for making inroads along our unprotected ocean border. That the system of defence adopted may be understood it is necessary to describe a little in detail the topography of the coast.

On the coast of North Carolina are Albemarle and Pamlico Sounds, penetrating far into the interior. Farther south, Cape Fear River connects with the ocean by two channels, the south-west channel being then defended by a small enclosed fort and a water battery. On the coast of South Carolina are Georgetown and Charleston harbors. A succession of islands extends along the coast of South Carolina and Georgia, separated from the main land by a channel which is navigable for vessels of moderate draught from Charleston to Fernandina, Florida. There are fewer assailable points on the Gulf than on the Atlantic. Pensacola, Mobile, and the mouths of the Mississippi were defended by works that had hitherto been regarded as sufficiently strong to repulse any naval attack that might be made upon them. Immediately after the bombardment and capture of Fort Sumter the work of seacoast defence was begun, and carried forward as rapidly as the limited means of the Confederacy would permit. Roanoke Island and other points on Albemarle and Pamlico Sounds were fortified. Batteries were established at the south-east entrance of Cape Fear River, and the works on the south-west entrance of that river were strengthened. Defences were constructed at Georgetown and at all assailable points on the north-east coast of South Carolina. The works of Charleston harbor were greatly strengthened by earthworks and floating batteries. The defences from Charleston down the coast of South Carolina and Georgia were confined chiefly to the islands and salient points bearing upon the channels leading inland. Defensive works were erected at all important points along the coast. Many of the defences, being injudiciously located and hastily erected, offered but little resistance to the enemy when attacked. These defects were not surprising when we take into consideration the inexperience of the engineers and the long line of seacoast to be defended. As soon as a sufficient naval force had been collected by the

Federals, an expedition under the command of General Butler was sent to the coast of North Carolina, and captured several important points. A second expedition, under Admiral
Dupont and General T. W. Sherman, was sent to make a descent on the coast of South Carolina.   On the 27th of November, Dupont attacked the batteries that were designed to defend
Port Royal harbor, and almost without resistance carried them
and gained possession of Port Royal.   This is the best harbor
in South Carolina, and is the strategic key to all the South
Atlantic coast.   Later, Burnside captured Roanoke Island and
established himself in Eastern North Carolina without resistance. The rapid fall of Roanoke Island and Port Royal struck
consternation into the hearts of the inhabitants along the entire
coast. The capture of Port Royal gave the Federals the entire
possession of Beaufort Island, which afforded a secure place of
arms for the troops, while the harbor gave a safe anchorage for
the fleet.   Beaufort Island almost fills a deep indenture in the
main shore, from which it is separated for the greater part of
its extent by a narrow channel which is navigable throughout.
Its northern extremity extends to within a few miles of the
Charleston and Savannah Railroad.   The main road from Port
Royal to Pocotaligo crosses the channel at this point. The
evacuation of Hilton Head, on the south-western extremity of
Beaufort Island, followed the capture of Port Royal.   This
exposed Savannah, only about twenty-five miles distant, to an
attack from that direction.   At the same time, the Federals
having command of Helena Bay, Charleston was liable to be
assailed from North Edisto or Stono Inlet, and the railroad
could have been reached without opposition by the road from
Port Royal to Pocotaligo.

Such was the state of affairs when General Lee reached
Charleston, in the early part of November, 1861, to assume
the command of the department of South Carolina, Georgia,
and Florida. His vigorous mind at once comprehended the
essential features of the situation, and with his accustomed
energy he prepared to overcome the many difficulties that presented themselves. Directing fortifications to be constructed
on the Stono, the Edisto, and the Combahee, he fixed his head-

quarters at Coosawhatchie, the point most threatened, and directed defences to be erected opposite Hilton Head and on the Broad and Salcatchie to cover Savannah. These were the points requiring immediate attention. He superintended in person the works overlooking the approach to the railroad from Port Royal, and soon infused into his troops a part of his own energy. The works he had planned rose with magical rapidity. A few days after his arrival at Coosawhatchie, Dupont and Sherman sent their first reconnoissance in that direction, which was met and repulsed by shot from the newly-erected batteries; and now, whether the Federals advanced toward the railroad or turned in the direction of Charleston or Savannah, they were arrested by the Confederate batteries. The people, seeing the Federals repulsed at every point, regained their confidence, and with it their energy.

We may, at this point, introduce a letter addressed to two of his daughters shortly after his journey South, as it gives, in his own words, his opinion of the preceding state of the coast defences, together with some interesting matter relating to his home life:

"SAVANNAH, 22 Nov., 1861.

" MY DARLING DAUGHTERS: I wish I could see you, be with you, and never again part from you. God only can give me that happiness. I pray for it night and day. But my prayers, I know, are not worthy to be heard. . . . . I am much pleased at your description of Stratford and your visit there. It is endeared to me by many recollections, and it has always been the desire of my life to be able to purchase it. Now that we have no other home, and the one we so loved has been for ever desecrated, that desire is stronger with me than ever. The horse-chestnut you mention in the garden was planted by my mother. I am sorry the vault is so dilapidated. You do not mention the spring, one of the objects of my earliest recollections. How my heart goes back to those happy days ! . . . . This is my second visit to Savannah. I have been down the coast as far as Amelia Island to examine the defences. They are poor indeed, and I have laid off work to employ our people a month.

I hope our enemy will be polite enough to wait for us. It is difficult to get our people to realize their position. . . . .

"Your devoted father,

"R. E. LEE."

The most important points being now secured against immediate attack, the general proceeded to organize a system of seacoast defence different from that which had previously been adopted. He withdrew the troops and material from those works which had been established on the islands and salient points, which he could not defend, to a strong interior line, where the effect of the Federal naval force would be neutralized. After a careful reconnoissance of the coast he designated such points as he considered it necessary to fortify. The most important positions on this extensive line were Georgetown, Charleston, Pocotaligo, Coosawhatchie, and Savannah. Coosawhatchie, being central, could communicate with either Charleston or Savannah in two or three hours by railroad, so in case of an attack they could support each other. The positions between Coosawhatchie and Savannah, and those between Charleston and Coosawhatchie, could be reinforced from the positions contiguous to them. There was thus a defensive relation throughout the entire line.

At this time there was great want of guns suitable for seacoast defence. Those in use had been on the coast for more than thirty years, and were of too light a calibre to cope with the powerful ordnance that had been introduced into the Federal navy. It was therefore desirable to arm the batteries now constructed with heavy guns. The ordnance department being prepared to cast guns of the heaviest calibre, requisitions were made for eight- and ten-inch columbiads for the batteries bordering on the channels that would be entered by gunboats. The heavy smooth-bore guns were preferred to the rifle cannons for fixed batteries, as experiments had shown that the crushing effect of the solid round shot was more destructive than the small breach and deeper penetration of the rifle-bolts. The difference of range was not important, as beyond a certain distance the aim could not be accurate. By the last of December many batteries had been completed and other works were being rapidly constructed. When the new year of 1862 opened there was a greater feeling of security among the people of South Carolina and Georgia than had been felt for several months.

The information received from every quarter led to the belief that the Federal Government was making preparations for a powerful attack upon either Charleston or Savannah. In anticipation of this attack every effort was made to strengthen these places. General Ripley, who commanded at Charleston, and General Lawton, the commander at Savannah, ably seconded Lee in the execution of his plans, while Generals Evans, Drayton, and Mercer assisted him at other points. The ordnance department, under the direction of its energetic chief, Colonel Gorgas, filled with wonderful promptitude the various demands made upon it. This greatly facilitated the completion of the defences.

The Federal troops on Beaufort Island were inactive during the months of December, January, and February, and the fleet was in the offing blockading Charleston and Savannah. About the 1st of March the Federal gunboats entered the Savannah River by way of the channel leading from Hilton Head. The small Confederate fleet was too weak to engage them, so they retained undisputed possession of the river. They then established batteries to intercept the communication between Fort Pulaski and the city of Savannah. This fort commands the entrance to the Savannah River, twelve miles below the city.

A few days after getting possession of the river the Federals landed a force under General Q. A. Gillmore on the opposite side of the fort. General Gillmore, having completed his batteries, opened fire about the 1st of April. Having no hope of succor, Fort Pulaski, after striking a blow for honor, surrendered with about 500 men.

The house at Coosawhatchie selected by General Lee for headquarters was of just sufficient capacity for himself and military family, which consisted of Captain Thornton Washington, adjutant-general, Captains Walter H. Taylor and Manigault, aides-de-camp, Captain Ives, engineer officer, Captain Walker, cavalry officer, and Major A. L. Long, chief of artil-

lery. Though not habitually present, may be added Captain
Stephen Elliot, whose perfect knowledge of the coast enabled
him to render the most valuable service. The general was as
unpretending in the interior arrangement of his quarters as
were his exterior surroundings. His simple camp-equipage
and that of his staff comprised the entire furniture of the
house. The table-service consisted of a neat set of tin-ware,
plates, dishes, and cups made to fit into each other for convenience in packing. The bill of fare corresponded in frugality
to the plainness of the furniture. The general occupied the
head of his table, and always seasoned the meal with his good-
humor and pleasant jests, often at the expense of some member
of the staff who seemed to miss the luxuries of the table more
than himself.

The extensive line of operations that demanded his attention
caused Lee to be almost constantly on the move, first at one
place, and then at another, where important work was in progress. It was remarkable how his quiet, confident manner
stimulated the men to exertion whenever he came among
them. On these occasions he more forcibly impressed one
with the magnetic influence of the power of genius over in-
feriors than in any man the writer of this memoir ever saw.

When inspecting the defences of Charleston harbor the mind
of the writer naturally was carried back to the time of his first
acquaintance with Fort Moultrie. At that time the political
harmony of the country was agitated by a ripple of discontent
which was soon dispelled, and Charleston was permitted ten
years of uninterrupted prosperity. Then she stood in her
wealth, beauty, and commercial importance queen among the
cities of the Southern Atlantic. Now war had closed her spacious harbor and the flames had consumed her wealth and destroyed her beauty. Though oppressed by misfortune, she still
proudly bore her crest, determined to preserve her honor un-
tarnished to the close of her existence.

It was only necessary to perfect the defences on James and
John's Islands to entirely secure Charleston from attack sea-
ward. This being done, this city was enabled, with the skill
of the engineer and the bravery of the troops under the direc-

tion of Generals G. T. Beauregard, Sam Jones, and others, to sustain, considering the power of the engines brought against her, one of the most remarkable sieges on record.

About the middle of March, Lee was directed to proceed to Richmond. By that time he had established a strong interior line of defence extending from Winyaw Bay to the mouth of St. Mary's River. This line, being bravely and skilfully defended, proved to be an impenetrable barrier to the combined efforts of the land and naval forces of the enemy constantly employed on the coast, until it was carried by Sherman in his unopposed march through Georgia and South Carolina. In order that the importance of this series of defensive works may be understood, it is necessary to know what it accomplished. It protected the most valuable agricultural section of the Confederacy, ensured the safety of Charleston and Savannah, and covered the principal line of communication between the Mississippi and the Potomac. Besides these important results it produced a desirable effect by diffusing among the inhabitants a sense of security they had not felt for many months.

When Lee took his departure the command devolved upon General Pemberton, a brave and experienced officer. He was well acquainted with the plan of operation adopted, and was therefore able to advance successfully the works that necessarily remained incomplete. Major Long remained on duty with Pemberton until May, when he received orders to report to General Lee in Richmond. At that time a general depression was felt throughout the Confederacy, caused by the results following the battle of Shiloh, the death of General Albert Sidney Johnston, the fall of New Orleans, and the tremendous losses occasioned by the evacuation of Yorktown and Norfolk.

The Southern campaign of General Lee which we have just described presents a remarkable example of a successful opposition of science and art to mere physical power. With surprising strategic ability he selected the important points of a long and difficult line, and with equal tactical skill adopted measures for their defence. The infantry was disposed for mutual support, while the artillery, in groups of a few guns, was placed in batteries at intervals, so as to cover extensive districts, and at the same time to be able to bring a heavy concentric fire on intermediate points. This combination was the most effective that could have been devised to prevent the incursion of gunboats.

We may also observe that there is a striking contrast between the vigor and energy displayed on the one side and the supineness manifested on the other. The Federal commander, instead of making after his easy capture of Port Royal a rapid movement toward the railroad at Pocotaligo and Charleston by the Edisto, or toward Savannah by way of Hilton Head—in either of which movements he would at that time have met with little or no opposition—contented himself with gathering the harvest of cotton found on Beaufort Island and providing a refuge for the fugitive slaves from the neighboring plantations; thus giving a petty financial enterprise and a negro sentimentality precedence over military operations of the highest importance; while his active opponent erected, unmolested, an insurmountable barrier to his future advance.

CHAPTER IX.

THE PENINSULAR CAMPAIGN.

The Defences of the Peninsula.—Cruise of the Merrimac.—Siege of Yorktown by McClellan's Army.—General Johnston's Plan of Operations.—It is not Accepted.—Retreat of the Confederate Army.—Battle of Williamsburg.—Surrender of Norfolk.—The Federal Fleet Repulsed.—Battle of Seven Pines.—General Lee takes Command.

BEFORE proceeding with this narrative it may be well to review previous operations, especially those that had taken place on the Peninsula and about Norfolk. To gain a clear idea of them a description of the peninsula embraced by the York and James rivers, Hampton Roads, and Chesapeake Bay is necessary. Its principal natural features are—the Chickahominy, a stream of considerable length; the Warwick, an estuary of the James which rises in the neighborhood of Yorktown; and the primeval forest, interspersed with farms and plantations. Its surface is generally level, except along the Chickahominy and the James, where it is diversified by low ranges of hills. The strip between the Warwick and Hampton Roads is marshy and easily inundated. Old Point, Hampton Roads, Yorktown, Williamsburg, Newport News, and Sewell's Point are also included in its topography. Norfolk, situated on the Elizabeth River a few miles from its junction with Hampton Roads, is surrounded by a flat, sandy country, bordered on the south by the Dismal Swamp, and terminated on the north and east by Hampton Roads and Chesapeake Bay. The town of Portsmouth and Gosport navy-yard lie on the Elizabeth River, directly opposite.

The first act of the governor of Virginia upon the secession of the State was to seize the Gosport navy-yard and provide for the security of the James and York rivers. This measure was of the highest importance, as the safety of the capital and

of an important portion of the State depended on their security.
The vessels of war captured in Norfolk harbor and the immense
quantity of naval stores found at the navy-yard were of incalculable value to the Confederacy.   The defences of Norfolk
and the mouth of the James River were assigned to General
Huger, while those of Yorktown and the Peninsula were entrusted to General Magruder. These officers had obtained high
distinction in the United States army, and the zeal and energy
they exhibited in the new work to which they had been
assigned fully entitled them to the highest confidence of the
Confederacy.

The Federals, at the same time, were also active in their
preparations on the Peninsula. General Butler appeared almost
simultaneously with Huger and Magruder at the head of large
forces, for the double purpose of defending Fortress Monroe
from Confederate attack and of operating either against Norfolk or Yorktown as circumstances might suggest.   On the
8th of June, 1861, Butler sent a strong reconnoitering party
toward Yorktown. This force was met at Big Bethel Church,
a few miles from the village of Hampton, by Colonel D. H.
Hill, with a detachment of infantry, supported by Colonel
G. W. Randolph's battalion of artillery, and was repulsed with
heavy loss. This was the first conflict of arms since the fall of
Fort Sumter, and, although small in point of numbers, its moral
effect was considerable by inspiring the Confederates with confidence, while it had a depressing influence upon the Federals.

After this affair the Federals made no other demonstration
on the Peninsula until the ensuing spring. During the interim
Magruder and Huger applied themselves with skill and industry
to the completion of the defences of their respective positions,
while the naval department was active in its preparations at
the Gosport navy-yard.   Magruder first occupied himself in
securing the command of the York River by the erection of
strong batteries at Yorktown and Gloucester Point, where the
river is less than a mile wide; then he completed his land-
defences to the Warwick near its head, subsequently extending
them down that river to its mouth.   The strip of land between
the Warwick and the James, being marshy, could be easily

rendered difficult, if not impracticable, for military movements by inundation, for which purpose dams had been built on the Warwick. General Huger, on his part, protected Norfolk on the land side by a system of defences extending from the Dismal Swamp to the Elizabeth River, and secured that river and the mouth of the James by strong batteries, the most important of which were those on Crany Island and Sewell's Point. Being connected by a part of the James, the works of Magruder and Huger formed a continuous defensive line from the Dismal Swamp to Yorktown, of such strength that its reduction could only be accomplished by the tedious process of a siege, and could be turned only on the right by way of Albemarle Sound, and on the left by the Rappahannock River. In either case, through their possession of an interior line, the Confederates could have easily anticipated such a movement. Referring to the part of this line traversing the Peninsula, General Magruder says:

"Deeming it of vital importance to hold Yorktown on the York River, and Mulberry Island on the James River, and to keep the enemy in check by an intervening line until the authorities might take such steps as should be held necessary to meet a serious advance of the enemy in the Peninsula, I felt compelled to dispose my forces in such a manner as to accomplish these objects with the least possible risk under the circumstances of great hazard which surrounded the little army I commanded. I had prepared, as my real line of defence, positions in advance at Harwood's and Young's mills. Both flanks of this line were defended by boggy and difficult streams and swamps. In addition, the left flank, reaching to the York River, was defended by elaborate fortifications at Ship's Point, connected by a broken line of redoubts crossing the heads of the various ravines which empty into the York River and Wormley's Creek, and terminating at Fort Grafton nearly in front of Yorktown. The right flank was defended by the fortifications at the mouth of the Warwick River and at Mulberry Island Point, and the redoubts extending from the Warwick to the James River. Intervening between the two hills was a wooded country about two miles in extent. This wooded line, forming the centre, needed the defence of infantry in sufficient force to prevent any attempt on the part of the enemy to break through it. In my opinion, this advanced line with its flank defences might have been held by 20,000 troops. With 25,000 I do not believe it could have been broken by any force the enemy could have brought against it."

On examining the theatre of operations embracing Norfolk and Yorktown, it will be observed that those places bear a defensive relation to each other, so that the fall of one would necessarily involve the evacuation or capture of the other. While the military authorities at Washington were discussing the several lines of operation of which Richmond was the objective point, that by way of Norfolk was suggested; but as the Peninsula presented not only a shorter line, but also fewer difficulties than the Norfolk one, it was adopted as the field of operation. McClellan in answer to the question, "During the early part of last winter could not a force of 30,000 or 40,000 men have been concentrated suddenly at Fortress Monroe, and Norfolk captured and the Merrimac destroyed without incurring any great hazard to us?" said, "Such a thing was possible, but would have been difficult, and I do not think it would have promoted the general objects of the war. I looked upon the fall of Norfolk as a necessary consequence of a movement upon Richmond." Question: "Would not the destruction of the Merrimac have been a great point gained, and have rendered the move upon Richmond, by way of the James or York River, very much more safe?" Answer: "As things turned out, yes. But I do not think the importance of the Merrimac was appreciated until she came out. I remember very well that the Navy Department thought that the Congress and the Cumberland were capable of taking care of the Merrimac. The question of taking Norfolk after the Merrimac made its appearance and destroyed the Congress and Cumberland was seriously discussed. The conclusion arrived at was, that it was better not to depart from the direct movement upon Richmond under all the circumstances of the case." *

* See "McClellan's Testimony before the Congressional Committee on the Conduct of the War," vol. i. p. 425.

By the 1st of March, 1862, the famous iron-clad Merrimac was ready for service, and other vessels of similar character were rapidly approaching completion. The Merrimac on the 8th of March made her first cruise, in which she encountered a part of the Federal fleet in Hampton Roads and destroyed two first-class frigates. On the 9th she attacked the Monitor, the especial boast of the Federals, and, while inflicting considerable damage on this antagonist, sustained herself but little injury. The Confederate authorities at this time believed that with the Merrimac and the other vessels of war, when completed, the tide-water section of Virginia would be secure, both by land and water, against the attack of the land and naval forces of the enemy.

We will now turn our attention to the operations on the Potomac. After the battle of Manassas, General Johnston continued to direct military affairs on the Potomac and in the Shenandoah Valley. There were, however, no operations of a general character during the fall and winter. The occupation of Centreville, the defeat of the Federals at Ball's Bluff by General Evans, and the expedition against Romney led by General T. J. Jackson were the principal events that occurred during that period.

The main body of the army went into winter quarters at Centreville, and that position was strongly fortified. The proximity of General Johnston was looked upon with an anxious eye at Washington, where his force was exaggerated to more than double its real strength.

When General McClellan entered upon the defence of the Federal capital, about the end of July, 1861, he found himself surrounded with difficulties of no ordinary character. The army which afterward became so distinguished as the Army of the Potomac consisted of about 50,000 men, mostly fugitives from the late field of Manassas who had returned to their colors. McClellan was therefore obliged to shoulder at once the onerous task of reorganizing, recruiting, and disciplining the army while at the same time he provided for the completion of the exterior defences of the city. In each of these duties he displayed great administrative abilities. He also manifested in

the course of his labors much firmness and self-control in resisting newspaper taunts and the impatience of the Federal
authorities, which urged him to the field before his arrangements were complete. He could not, however, be turned from
his purpose of perfecting his army and the defences of Washington in all their details before he advanced. This, through
patient labor, he accomplished by the opening of spring,
1862, when he was in condition to leave Washington in security and enter the field at the head of an army of 150,000
men, perfect in all its appointments, in addition to a large
reserve force organized for the defence of the capital during
his absence.

Though Johnston's force did not then much exceed 40,000
men, the Federal mind was still deluded with the belief that
it was much greater, and McClellan was confident that he
would have to encounter at Centreville and Manassas a force
of at least 80,000 men strongly intrenched. General Johnston,
perceiving that this delusion would be speedily dissipated by a
collision with an army numerically four times greater than his
own, prepared to evacuate Centreville and Manassas at the moment McClellan should commence his advance. This looked-for
event occurred on the 8th of March, 1862, whereupon Johnston
retired behind the Rappahannock.

General McClellan, on finding Centreville and Manassas
evacuated and the railroad bridge over the Rappahannock
destroyed, prepared for an immediate transfer of his army to
the Peninsula by way of the Potomac. The greater part of
his army having arrived, he appeared in front of Magruder on
the 4th of April with the main body of his forces, accompanied
by a powerful siege-train of Parrot guns and mortars.

Before his arrival at this locality McClellan was ignorant of
the defences on the Warwick, and had been misled by his map
in regard to the topography of the contiguous country; therefore he made a careful personal examination of the works on
the Warwick previous to deciding on a plan of attack. His
reconnoissance convinced him that Magruder's position could
not be carried by assault, and he determined to reduce it by
regular approaches. For that purpose he promptly commenced

the erection of his primary batteries beyond the effective range of Magruder's guns—one and a half miles.

The Peninsula having become the principal theatre of war in Virginia, and Magruder's force, of less than 11,000 strong, being now inadequate for its defence, General Johnston was directed to send thither all his available troops and assume in person the command of that important field of operation. By the 20th of April all of the designated reinforcements had arrived. We shall here give a brief summary of the opposing armies:

The Federals had on the Peninsula, under the immediate command of General McClellan, 115,000 men; in the Valley and on the line of the Orange and Alexandria Railroad, 30,000 men, commanded by Generals Banks and Shields; and on the Potomac, a reserve of 40,000, under General McDowell—making an aggregate of 185,000 men.

Opposed to this force the Confederates had on the Peninsula 53,000 men, under the immediate command of General Johnston, with Ewell and Jackson on the upper Rappahannock; in the Valley, something over 16,000 men; and 18,000 at Norfolk, commanded by Huger—making a total of 90,000 men. These numbers will not differ materially from the statements given by the opposing generals. There was also a small local force at Richmond, and a much larger one of a similar character in and about Washington. Besides the Federal land-forces there was a powerful naval force in Hampton Roads, opposed by a small Confederate one in Norfolk harbor, consisting of the Merrimac and a few river gunboats.

At this time General J. E. Johnston bore the highest military reputation in the Confederacy, since by his manœuvring with Patterson in the Valley, his splendid success at Manassas, and his masterly retreat from Centreville he had acquired a world-wide renown. Before entering upon his new command he presented to the President a plan of operations entirely different from that which had been previously adopted. It, however, involved the risk of such great sacrifices that it was disapproved of by Mr. Davis and his military advisers, General Randolph, Secretary of War, and General Lee.

Johnston, regarding Magruder's line on the Peninsula indefensible, thus explains his plan: "Instead of only delaying the Federal army in its approach, I proposed that it should be encountered in front of Richmond by one quite as numerous, formed by uniting there all the available forces of the Confederacy in North Carolina, South Carolina, and Georgia, with those at Norfolk, those on the Peninsula, and those near Richmond, including Smith's and Longstreet's divisions, which had recently arrived. The great army thus formed, surprising that of the United States by an attack when it was expecting to besiege Richmond, would be almost certain to win; and the enemy, defeated a hundred miles from Fort Monroe, their place of refuge, could scarcely escape destruction. Such a victory would decide not only the campaign, but the war, while the present plan could produce no decisive results.

"The President, who had listened with apparent interest, replied that the question was so important that he would hear it fully discussed before making his decision, and desired the writer of this work [General Johnston] to meet General Randolph (Secretary of War) and General Lee in his office at an appointed time for the purpose: upon advice, Mr. Davis authorized the invitation of Major-generals Smith and Longstreet to the conference."

In the mean time General Johnston proceeded to Yorktown, and after a personal examination of Magruder's position returned to Richmond with his opinion in regard to its strength unchanged. General Johnston continues: "The conference began more than an hour before noon by my describing, at the President's request, General Magruder's defensive arrangements, as I had previously done to him, and representing that General McClellan's probable design of molesting our batteries at Gloucester Point and Yorktown, and turning our position by transporting his army up the river, could not be prevented, so that the adoption of a new plan was necessary. . . . .

"In the discussion that followed General Randolph, who had been a naval officer, objected to the plan proposed because it included at least the temporary abandonment of Norfolk, which would involve the probable loss of the materials for

Union troops entering line near Yorktown, May, 1862, and finding
"Dummy" Soldiers and "Quaker" Guns.

many vessels of war contained in the navy-yard there. Lee opposed it because he thought that the withdrawal from South Carolina and Georgia of any considerable number of troops would expose the important seaports of Charleston and Savannah to the danger of capture. He thought, too, .that the Peninsula had excellent fields of battle for a small army contending with a great one, and that we should for that reason make the contest with McClellan's army there. Longstreet, owing to his deafness, took little part in the conference.

" The writer of these pages maintained that all to be accomplished, by any success attainable on the Peninsula, would be to delay the enemy two or three weeks in his march to Richmond, for the reasons already given, and that success would soon give us back everything temporarily abandoned to achieve it, and would be decisive of the war as well as of the campaign.

" The President decided in favor of the opinion of General Lee, and ordered General Johnston to take command of the Army of the Peninsula, adding the departments of Norfolk and the Peninsula to that of Northern Virginia."*

General Johnston further relates : " I assumed my new command on the 17th. The arrival of Smith's and Longstreet's divisions had increased the army on the Peninsula to about 53,000 men, including 3000 sick. It was opposed to 133,000 Federal soldiers. Magruder's division formed the Confederate right, Longstreet's the centre, D. H. Hill's the left, and Smith's the reserve. The field-works at Gloucester Point and Yorktown on the left flank, and Mulberry Point on the right, were occupied by 8000 men. In this position we had nothing to do but to finish the works begun between Yorktown and the head of the inundations, and observe the enemy's operations. They were limited to a little skirmishing at long range and daily cannonading, generally directed at Magruder's left or Longstreet's right, and the construction of a long line of batteries in front of Yorktown and beyond the range of our old-fashioned ship-guns. These batteries, our scouts reported, were of about one hundred of the heaviest Parrot guns and above thirty mortars. A battery on the shore three miles (pilot's

* See Johnston's *Narrative of Military Operations,* pp. 113-116.

distance) below Yorktown received the first guns mounted. Shots of the first volley, fired to get the range of the Confederate works, fell in the camp of the reserve, a mile and a half beyond the village. . . . . Finding on the 27th that the Federal batteries would be ready for action in five or six days, the War Department was informed of the fact, and of the intention to abandon Yorktown and the Warwick before the fire of that artillery should be opened upon our troops. The suggestion made in the conference in the President's office was also repeated—to form a powerful army near Richmond of all the available forces of the Confederacy, and to fall upon McClellan's army when it should come within reach. Major-general Huger was instructed at the same time to prepare to evacuate Norfolk, and Captain S. S. Lee, commanding the navy-yard at Gosport, to remove to a place of safety as much of the valuable property it contained as he could.''

Learning that the Federal batteries would be ready for action on the 4th of May, General Johnston evacuated Yorktown and its defences on the night of the 3d, and retired with his whole army toward Richmond. Since Magruder's position was never put to the test, the difference of opinion respecting it must be reconciled by speculative criticism. The next morning McClellan found himself again baffled by his wily antagonist, and saw the batteries he had so carefully constructed doomed to silence. General McClellan on the morning of the 4th of May took possession of Yorktown and instituted a vigorous pursuit of Johnston's retreating columns.

The rear-guard, under Longstreet, being overtaken at Williamsburg, was compelled to halt and offer battle to check the rapid advance of the enemy. General Johnston was also obliged to turn back D. H. Hill's division to support his rear-guard. The greater part of the forenoon of the 5th was occupied in skirmishing, but in the afternoon a spirited combat ensued between the Confederate rear-guard under General Longstreet and the Federal advance under General Sumner, which continued until terminated by night.

In this affair Hill and Early on the part of the Confederates, and Hooker, Hancock, and Kearny on that of the Federals, were conspicuously prominent. Both sides claimed the victory, but the result was that Johnston gained the time he required to extricate his trains, which had been retarded by the bad condition of the roads, while the Federals were left masters of the field by the withdrawal of the Confederate rear-guard. Without any other interruption worthy of note Johnston continued his retreat to the Chickahominy.

The movements here described were immediately followed by the surrender of Norfolk in accordance with the suggestion of General Johnston. Though the yielding of this important place with its highly valuable navy-yard was strongly opposed by members of the Cabinet at Richmond, yet the impossibility of holding it after the retreat of the army from the Peninsula became evident, and it was ordered to be abandoned. In accordance therewith, General Huger destroyed the dockyards and removed the stores, and on the 10th of May evacuated the place, withdrawing its garrison to Richmond. On the next day a Federal force from Fortress Monroe, under the command of General Wool, occupied the town.

Hopes were entertained of saving the Merrimac, a vessel which had done such noble service for the Confederacy, and caused such serious disaster to the Federal navy. But it was quickly perceived that its draught of water was too great to permit it to ascend the James River to Richmond, and there was no alternative but its destruction. It was therefore blown up by order of its commander, Commodore Tatnall.

The inevitable result of the loss of the Merrimac was the opening of the James River to the Federal gunboats, which was at once taken advantage of by a fleet composed of the Monitor, Galena, Aroostook, Port Royal, and Naugatuck, under Commodore Rogers. This fleet ascended the stream to within twelve miles of Richmond, where it was arrested by the fire of Fort Darling on Drewry's Bluff. A four hours' engagement took place, which resulted in the withdrawal of the fleet, considerably the worse for the vigorous play of the Confederate battery.

Yet, despite this check to the approach to Richmond by water through the repulse of a strong fleet of gunboats by a fortification of no great strength, it was evident that the evacuation of the defences at the mouth of the James, with the loss of the Merrimac, would greatly embarrass the future defence of Richmond. McClellan slowly continued his pursuit of Johnston by the principal roads and the York River. The ascent of the James River by the Federal gunboats obliged General Johnston to cross the Chickahominy in order to defend Richmond against their attack, as well as to protect it from the advance of McClellan.

About the 20th, Johnston took a position near Richmond covering the roads leading to the lower James and the Peninsula. His right rested on the James near Drewry's Bluff, the scene of the engagement with the gunboats, and his left on the Chickahominy a little above New Bridge. The force withdrawn from Yorktown, having experienced some loss on its retreat, now amounted to about 50,000 men. In addition to these General Johnston embraced in his command the troops under Huger at Petersburg, Anderson at Fredericksburg, and Branch near Hanover C. H., making an aggregate of about 22,000 men. His active force, therefore, at this time was 70,000 men. He also included in his command the force under General Jackson of between 15,000 and 20,000, then operating in the Valley of Virginia. The Federal army of the Peninsula at this time exceeded 100,000 men, divided into five corps d'armée, two of which, commanded by Heintzelman and Keyes, crossed the Chickahominy on the 23d, and advanced to the Fair Oaks Station on the York River Railroad.

On the 24th Casey's division of Keyes' corps was advanced to Seven Pines, a mile and a half in advance of Fair Oaks, when it took a position across the Williamsburg road and covered it by earth-works and batteries. The other division of Keyes' corps was in position to support Casey, and Heintzelman's corps was stationed on the railroad near Fair Oaks Station. When Johnston discovered that a portion of the Federal army had crossed the Chickahominy, he ordered Huger to Richmond and Anderson to join Branch at Hanover C. H. Branch was attacked and roughly handled by a part of

Porter's corps on the 27th, but being opportunely joined by Anderson he was able to maintain his position, and the Federals fell back to Mechanicsville. Anderson and Branch were then ordered to Meadow Bridge, opposite that place. General D. H. Hill was ordered, on the 30th, to make a reconnoissance of the Federal position at Seven Pines. This duty was assigned to the brigades of Rodes and Garland. The former advanced by the Charles City road and the latter by the Williamsburg road.

The Federal position was soon developed and reported to General Johnston. An attack was ordered to be made the next morning. The divisions of Longstreet and D. H. Hill were to be formed in two lines across and at right angles to the Williamsburg road. Huger's division was to move to the right of Longstreet, and Hill to the Charles City road opposite the left flank of the Federal position, and then to co-operate with Longstreet in the attack. The division of G. W. Smith on the left moved by the Nine Mile road to its junction with the New Bridge road, there to act either in opposing reinforcements that might be sent across the Chickahominy during the engagement, or on the right flank of the Federal force about to be attacked, as circumstances might suggest. Magruder's division formed the reserve. The division commanded by A. P. Hill occupied the position in front of Mechanicsville. The cavalry constituted the extreme left of the Confederate line. As soon as the troops had gained their designated positions Longstreet was to attack in front, and the troops on his right and left were to support him.

On the afternoon and night of the 30th a heavy fall of rain caused the water of the Chickahominy to rise so high that it was rendered impassable. The corps of Keyes and Heintzelman were thus isolated from the other Federal corps. This intervention of the elements afforded the Confederates an opportunity of giving the Federals an effective blow, which, however, was not taken advantage of as promptly as might have been expected. Considerable delay occurred by the failure of the troops to get into position. Longstreet, after impatiently awaiting the arrival of Huger until nearly two o'clock in the afternoon, determined to attack without further delay. He therefore advanced his own and D. H. Hill's divisions, and attacked the first position of the Federals, which was gallantly carried in the face of a terrible fire of artillery and musketry. The Federals were forced back upon their supports, which in turn were compelled to yield to the impetuous assault of the Confederates and were borne back to Fair Oaks Station, where, being confronted by the corps of Heintzelman, then fresh, the divisions of Longstreet and Hill were obliged to pause. All that was now required for the complete destruction of two Federal corps was the prompt co-operation of Smith's division, which had remained inactive during the attack of Longstreet from two until four o'clock. When this division did advance it was too late to accomplish what might have been easily done a short time before, for the waters of the Chickahominy had sufficiently subsided during the day to admit of the passage of the other corps of the enemy. This delay gave the Federals time to send over reinforcements.

When the battle of Seven Pines had begun General McClellan ordered General Sumner to hold his corps in readiness to support the troops on the south side of the Chickahominy. That officer, in order to prevent delay, placed his corps under arms and moved the heads of his columns to the river. This promptness on the part of General Sumner enabled him to reach the field in time to meet Smith's division as it advanced to attack the troops of Heintzelman and Keyes in flank, and a sharp engagement ensued which lasted till nightfall without decisive result.

In the movements here detailed and the severe engagement with which they closed Lee took no active part, his position continuing that of military adviser of the President without command in the field. This inactivity, however, was by no means to his taste, and on the 30th he sent the writer (Colonel Long) on a visit to Johnston to tell him that he would be glad to participate in the battle. He had no desire to interfere with his command, but simply wished to aid him on the field to the best of his ability and in any manner in which his services would be of most value. General Johnston expressed gratification at this message, and the hope that General Lee would ride out to the field, with the desire that he would send him all the reinforcements he could.

On the morning of the 31st, before nine o'clock, General Lee and President Davis rode out to General Smith's headquarters on the Nine Mile road, where they joined General Johnston. They remained there for some time during the progress of the battle, in which, however, General Lee took no part. At the close of the day's fight a serious event took place, which was destined to greatly change the aspect of affairs and bring into active service the great commander, whose remarkable abilities had hitherto been confined to secondary details of the service, and who had yet been given no proper opportunity to display his genius on the field.

The event in question was the wounding of Johnston, who received a severe hurt at the close of the day's fight, and was carried from the field, disabled for the time from any active service. The command devolved upon General G. W. Smith, the officer next in rank.

The battle closed with nightfall, the contending forces remaining upon the field in the positions they had occupied at the cessation of the engagement.

On the next morning there was a partial renewal of the battle between a portion of the contending forces. This lasted until about eleven o'clock, when the fighting closed on both sides without any important results.

On this day (June 1st), however, occurred the notable circumstance to which we have above alluded, as it withdrew General Lee from his partial retirement and placed him in a position in which his extraordinary military genius gained the first opportunity for its full display. Shortly after the wounding of Johnston a decision was reached by President Davis, which he communicated at an early hour of the next morning to Smith, to the effect that Lee had been assigned to the command of the Army of Northern Virginia. This decision was expected by and agreeable to General Smith, who was sick, and in an unfit condition to take command of the army. Immediately after being relieved, indeed, he retired from the service, which he did not re-enter till a subsequent period, when he had recovered from his disability.

At a later hour of the same day Lee repaired in person to Smith's headquarters and relieved him of the command of the army. It was a vital incident, and one fraught with momentous consequences. From that time the motto of the Army of Northern Virginia was "Forward!" under the control of its valiant and skilful commander, who was destined to lead it to victory on many a hard-fought field, and finally, when its reduction in numbers forced it into a defensive attitude, to withstand for months its overwhelming foe, and never submit until only a meagre and starving fragment of that gallant army remained, too few and too exhausted to yield any glory in their conquest to the victorious enemy.

CHAPTER X.

THE SEVEN DAYS' FIGHT.

Recapitulation.—Lee Takes Command.—Selects and Fortifies his Position.—Extracts from Long's Notebook.—Lee Decides to Attack the Enemy.—Dispositions for the Assault.—Battle of Gaines's Mill.—Federal Defeat.—McClellan's Retreat.—Frazier's Farm.—Malvern Hill.—The Federals reach Harrison's Landing.

HITHERTO, in our detail of the opening events of the Civil War, the name of General Lee has scarcely appeared, his position, while of great importance, being one to keep him from public prominence. From this time forward he becomes the central figure of the war, and in order to properly appreciate the circumstances attending this change of conditions it is necessary to briefly recapitulate a portion of the preceding chapter.

In the winter of 1862 the Confederate Congress created the office of "military adviser to the President," with the view of lightening the arduous duties which devolved upon him as commander-in-chief of the Confederate forces. Lee was selected to fill this position, and about the 13th of March, 1862, he entered upon his duties. The staff allowed him consisted of a military secretary with the rank of colonel and four aides with the rank of major. General Lee offered to Major A. L. Long the position of military secretary, and selected for his aides-de-camp Majors Randolph Talcott, Walter H. Taylor, Charles S. Venable, and Charles Marshall. When the writer reported for duty, about the middle of May, he found the general actively engaged in superintending the erection of defences on the James River near Richmond. The battery and obstructions at Drewry's Bluff were so advanced that the great alarm that had been felt for the safety of the city upon the evacuation of Norfolk began to subside, as there was no longer the fear of an immediate attack. The Federal gunboats had entered the

James, and on the 15th the battery at Drewry's Bluff was attacked by the enemy's fleet, consisting of the iron-clads Galena and Naugatuck, a monitor, and two gunboats. These vessels were skilfully handled and gallantly fought. The Galena approached within four hundred yards of the battery, and then opened a spirited fire with her powerful guns; the Naugatuck and monitor closely supported her, while the gunboats delivered their fire at a longer range. After a hotly-contested conflict the fleet was repulsed with heavy loss. The Galena was so severely damaged as to be rendered unfit for future service, while the other vessels were more or less injured; the battery sustained but slight damage. This defeat of the gunboats by an incomplete earthwork of only five guns for the first time caused a just value to be placed on defences of that character, which thenceforth became a conspicuous element in defensive operations.

At this time the safety of Richmond was entirely due to the skill and energy of General Lee, for upon the evacuation of Norfolk the James was left entirely open from its mouth to Richmond, and the hastily-constructed defence at Drewry's Bluff was the only barrier interposed between that city and a hostile fleet. After crossing the Chickahominy, about the 20th, General J. E. Johnston assumed the defence of Richmond. He attacked the enemy at Seven Pines on the 31st of May, and was severely wounded, as we have seen, near the close of the action. That event was immediately followed by the appointment of Lee to the command of the Army of Northern Virginia. Though regretting the cause that led to his assignment to the command of the army, he was pleased to be released from the duties of the office for those of the field, which were far better suited to his active and energetic disposition. He carried with him to the field the same personal staff that had been allowed him in Richmond.

On the afternoon of the 1st of June, General G. W. Smith, on whom the command of the army had devolved when General Johnston was wounded, resigned his command to General Lee, and shortly after retired on account of bad health. It soon appeared that there was considerable depression in the army, the natural consequence of the incidents of war. As some of the officers were apprehensive that the army would not be able to maintain its position should it be attacked, Lee thought it advisable to assemble his principal officers for deliberation on its condition at an early period.

In reference to this point, Mr. Davis, in his *Rise and Fall of the Confederacy*, chap. xxiii., vol. ii., says: "The day after General Lee assumed command I was riding out to the army, when I saw at a house on my left a number of horses, and among them one I recognized as belonging to him. I dismounted and entered the house, where I found him in consultation with a number of his general officers. The tone of the conversation was quite despondent, and one especially pointed out the inevitable consequence of the enemy's advance by throwing out bayoux and constructing successive parallels." Farther on he refers to a want of co-operation that existed among the different divisions during the battle of Fair Oaks and Seven Pines, which was productive of natural distrust that might have resulted in serious demoralization had it not been speedily corrected. The council met, as had been previously ordered, on the Nine Mile road, near the house which had been occupied by Smith as his headquarters.

The principal officers of the army were present, and were almost unanimous in the opinion that the line then occupied should be abandoned for one nearer Richmond which was considered more defensible.

The line in question was that which had been adopted by Johnston prior to the occupation in force of the south bank of the Chickahominy by the enemy, and was the strongest the country presented; but now the dispirited condition of our troops and the occupation in force by the enemy of the south side of the river caused the most prominent Confederate officers to doubt their ability to hold it, and consequently they urged its evacuation and withdrawal to a position nearer Richmond. Lee thus found himself in a situation of great embarrassment. He did not then possess the fame he was destined soon to acquire. He was also unknown to that army, and lacked its confidence. Under these disadvantages he was obliged to assume the re-

sponsibility of maintaining a position pronounced untenable by
his principal officers, or of hazarding the safety of Richmond
by a withdrawal of his forces that would inevitably result in a
forced occupation of the outer defences of the capital and its
complete investiture by the enemy, which would have ensured
the speedy capture of the city.   Lee, who had long been accustomed, to rely upon himself, quickly decided on the course
to be adopted.   It was evident that the present position of the
army must be maintained or that Richmond must be abandoned
to the enemy, and the loss of Richmond at this time would
have been of incalculable injury to the Confederate cause.   He
therefore, in opposition to the opinion of his subordinates,
determined to hold the position in which he found the army ;
but before making known his determination he made a careful
reconnoissance of the whole position, and then declared his
intention of holding it, ordering it to be immediately fortified
in the most effective manner.

General Lee then reorganized his forces and established a
strong defensive line.   He selected, with slight alterations, the
position then occupied by his troops.   This line extended
from Chaffin's Bluff, on the James River, crossing the river
road about four miles, and the Darby Town, Charles City, Williamsburg, and Nine Mile roads, about five miles from Richmond to a point on the Chickahominy a little above New
Bridge, and then continued up that stream to Meadow Bridge.
The army consisted of six divisions.   Longstreet's division
formed the right, while those of Huger, D. H. Hill, Magruder,
Whiting, and A. P. Hill, in the order named, extended to the
left.   The division of A. P. Hill constituted the left of the
Confederate position.   The greater part of Stuart's cavalry
was on the left, picketing on the Rappahannock and having
a small force in observation at Fredericksburg.   The duty of
constructing a fortified line was apportioned among the divisions, each commander being responsible for the defence in his
own front.   Very soon a continuous line of breastworks appeared, and as these arose the spirits of the men revived and
the sullen silence with which their labor began gave place to
jokes and laughter.   Those who had entered upon the work

with reluctance now felt recompensed by the sense of safety it gave them. The defences daily increased until they were sufficiently strong to resist any attack that was likely to be made upon them. In the mean time the stragglers and convalescents began to return, and the army gradually increased. Lee daily appeared upon the lines, and after a few days his presence inspired the troops with confidence and enthusiasm. McClellan established his headquarters on the south side of the Chickahominy about the same time that Lee assumed the command of the Army of Northern Virginia. The Federal army, after deducting the casualties of the late battle, amounted to about 100,000 men for duty; 75,000 of this force were on the south side of the Chickahominy, the remainder on the north of that stream, extending as high up as Mechanicsville. From this position a junction would be easily formed with McDowell's corps of 40,000 men, which, although a part of McClellan's forces, was persistently held in the neighborhood of Fredericksburg as a covering force for Washington.

The writer is fortunately able to add some personal details of General Lee's actions and mode of life during this period, from a notebook which he then began and kept up throughout the war, and which has been of great value to him in securing accuracy of statement during the preparation of this work. Though it is not his purpose to quote directly from this notebook as a rule, yet a selection from its opening pages, which are particularly full of descriptive detail, may be of interest and value, as placing the new commander upon his first entry into an important field of active service in the Civil War more directly before the reader. He therefore here subjoins the entries for several days, beginning with June 3d, the date of the opening entry:

"*June 3d.*—The day has been a very busy one. The general went to the lines early in the morning, and did not return until afternoon. The work was in rapid progress all along the line. The men appeared in better spirits than the day before, and seemed to be interested in their work. When he arrived on General Toombs's part of the line he found that general had been true to his word; he had 'no picks nor spades,' but he was having logs piled up for his defence. General Lee laughed at this freak of Toombs's, and remarked, 'Colonel Long, when General Toombs gains a little more experience he will be convinced that *earth* is a better protection against can- non-balls than logs.' The general continued: 'There is a great difference between mercenary armies and volunteer armies, and consequently there must be a difference in the mode of disci- pline. The volunteer army is more easily disciplined by en- couraging a patriotic spirit than by a strict enforcement of the Articles of War.' We hear from the Federal newspapers and our spies that McClellan is prevented from advancing by the softness of the ground and his belief that he has a greatly superior force in his front. If he continues to wait two days longer, we will not thank him for his forbearance.

"*June 4th.*—The general did not go out to-day, being occu- pied with office-work. He had double duty upon him—the reorganization of the army and the providing for the defence of its position. Our headquarters are very comfortable. The front room on the house floor is the adjutant-general's office. The general's private office is in rear of this. There all the confidential business of the army is transacted, the general's usual attendant being his military secretary or some other member of his personal staff. In the front room the general business of the army is transacted by the adjutant-general and his assistants. General Lee and his household mess together. The mess arrangements are not very ostentatious. Our meals are served and despatched without any very great ceremony. The general is always pleasant at meals, and frequently hurls a pleasant jest at some member of his staff. Captain P. Mason is the assistant adjutant-general: he had been previously at- tached to General Johnston's staff. We were visited to-day by several high officials from Richmond. Their visit was more from curiosity than any special business. The general bears interruption with great equanimity.

"*June 5th.*—The general was on the lines early to-day. The work has progressed very satisfactorily, and the confidence of the men increases as the work advances. The general made a partial reconnoissance of the Federal position. This embraces

a front of about four miles, the right resting on the Chickahominy a little below New Bridge, and the left on the White
Oak Swamp.   Our line extends from Chaffin's Bluff to a point
a little above Mechanicsville, a distance of about twelve miles.
Our main force, however, confronts that of General McClellan
lying south of the Chickahominy.

"*June 6th.*—The general visited that portion of the line
to-day occupied by Huger, Longstreet, and D. H. Hill.   The
troops were in good spirits, and their confidence in General
Lee is rapidly increasing.   The defences are now so far advanced that they will offer a formidable resistance to an open
attack.   General McClellan has not yet shown any disposition
to advance.   He has two balloons out to-day.   Our troops are,
however, so well sheltered by the timber that his balloon reconnoissances will avail him but little.   While the works are
advancing, General Lee does not forget the discipline of his
army.   This he entrusts mainly to his division and brigade
commanders, all of whom are men of ability, and some of
them men of considerable military experience.   General Lee
is no martinet, but he requires his subordinates to strictly
enforce the rules of discipline.   Among the major-generals
are Longstreet, Magruder, D. H. Hill, and A. P. Hill.   These
have already been distinguished for gallantry and ability.
Among his brigadiers are Pickett, Wilcox, D. R. Jones, Hood,
and Field.   These officers have also acquired considerable
reputation, and, having been graduates of West Point and
members of the old army, are well qualified to instruct and
discipline their troops.

"*June 7th.*—The general did not visit the lines to-day, but
sent Colonel Long to inspect that portion of the line in the
neighborhood of Mechanicsville.   A. P. Hill's division occupied that portion of the line.   Hill's defences are as well
advanced as those of any part of the line.   His troops are in
fine condition.   He designates his division 'the Light Division.'   Hill is every inch a soldier, and is destined to make his
mark.   This afternoon Mr. Davis visited headquarters.   The
relations between General Lee and Mr. Davis are very friendly.
The general is ever willing to receive the suggestions of the

President, while the President exhibits the greatest confidence in General Lee's experience and ability, and does not hamper him with executive interference.

"*June 8th, Sunday.*—Divine service held in the different brigades of the army. General Lee attended service at one of the right-wing brigades, attended by some of his staff. Visited the lines. . . . .

"*June 16th.*—General Lee, accompanied by Colonel Long, made a reconnoissance of the Federal position on the north side of the Chickahominy. There was then, on that side of the line, a Federal force of about 25,000 men, commanded by General Fitz John Porter. The main body of this force occupied a position near Mr. Gaines's house, and one division, five or six thousand strong, was posted at Mechanicsville. During this reconnoissance General Lee turned to the writer and remarked, 'Now, Colonel Long, how can we get at those people?' This mode of designating the enemy was common with him.

"The Chickahominy between New Bridge and Mechanicsville is narrow, and to facilitate its passage could be easily bridged. Fitz John Porter's position was sufficiently exposed to invite attack, and, the force at Fredericksburg having been withdrawn, General Lee determined to assume the aggressive. This determination, however, was communicated only to his military family until he had fully matured his plan of operation, which he then submitted to Mr. Davis in a personal interview."

Lee's headquarters at this time were on the Nine Mile road, a position which gave him a good oversight of the army and brought all portions of the lines within easy reach. Yet the batteries, rifle-pits, and earthworks which had been erected with so much labor under his personal supervision were destined to have no further utility than that already adverted to—the infusion of confidence into the previously dispirited army. It was not the purpose of the commanding general to remain upon the defensive and await the slow but sure advances of the enemy. He, on the contrary, formed the bolder decision of hurling the force under his command against the serried battalions of the foe, as indicated in the last-quoted extract from the notebook.

When McClellan crossed the Chickahominy it was thought he would advance immediately upon Richmond. This expectation was disappointed, however, for instead of advancing he began to fortify his position. The right wing rested on the Chickahominy a little below New Bridge, and the left extended to the White Oak Swamp, embracing a front of about four miles, nearly parallel with that of the Confederates. The opposing lines were separated by an interval but little exceeding a mile, but each was obscured from the other's view by the intervening forest. The picket-lines were often within close musket-range of each other. At first there was a good deal of picket-skirmishing, but this was soon discontinued by mutual consent, and a lively exchange of newspapers, coffee, and tobacco succeeded it. The strength of the Confederate force was always greatly over-estimated by McClellan, and his frequent and urgent calls for reinforcements exposed his want of confidence in his own strength. General Lee knowing this uneasy, insecure feeling of his antagonist, and McDowell's force, which had always been a thorn in his side, being about this time withdrawn from Fredericksburg for the support of Banks and Shields in the Valley, prepared, as we have said, to assume the offensive. He conceived the bold plan of crossing the Chickahominy, and, attacking the Federal right wing, to force it back and seize McClellan's line of communication with his base of operations. This plan being successfully executed, the Federal general would be compelled to save his army as best he could by retreat. Preparatory to the execution of this plan General J. E. B. Stuart was ordered to make a reconnoissance in the rear of the Federal position. This officer, with a force of about 1000 cavalry, executed his instructions with great boldness and success. He made the entire circuit of the Federal army and gained much important information.

This movement, indeed, was so skilful and brilliant that it has been classed among the most daring cavalry raids ever made. In addition to the information gained he captured many prisoners and destroyed Federal stores to the value of seven million dollars; and all this with the loss of but a single man, the lamented Captain Latane, who fell while leading a successful charge against a superior force of the enemy.   He finally recrossed the Chickahominy, almost in the face of the enemy, with the same intrepidity he had shown at every step of his progress, and with a prestige of daring and success that for years clung to his banner and gained him the reputation of being the most dashing and brilliant cavalry leader of the war.

His design being confirmed by Stuart's successful reconnoissance, Lee proceeded to organize a force requisite for the accomplishment of his proposed enterprise.   The troops that could be conveniently spared from North Carolina, South Carolina, and Georgia were ordered to Richmond.   By the 20th of June, Major-general T. H. Holmes, with 6000 men from North Carolina; Brigadier-general Ripley, with 6000 from South Carolina; and Brigadier-general Lawton, with 5000 from Georgia, had arrived in Richmond.   At the same time General Jackson was ordered to withdraw secretly from the Valley and proceed with such expedition as would enable him to reach Hanover Junction by the afternoon of the 25th of June.   In order to mask his designs from the Federals, Lee directed Whiting's division and Lawton's brigade to proceed to Staunton, apparently with the view of reinforcing Jackson, but really under orders to return immediately and join that general on the 25th at Hanover Junction.   This movement further strengthened McClellan in his opinion of Lee's vastly superior force, and completely blinded him in regard to the real intentions of that general.

General Lee determined to attack the Federal right wing on the morning of the 26th of June.   Jackson was directed to move to Atlee's Station on the Central Railroad.   A. P. Hill was directed to cross the Chickahominy at Meadow Bridge as soon as Jackson arrived in supporting distance, attack the Federals at Mechanicsville, and drive them from that place, so that the bridge on the Richmond and Mechanicsville road might be open for the advance of the other troops; Longstreet and D. H. Hill were ordered to move their divisions as near as practicable to the Mechanicsville bridge without discovering them-

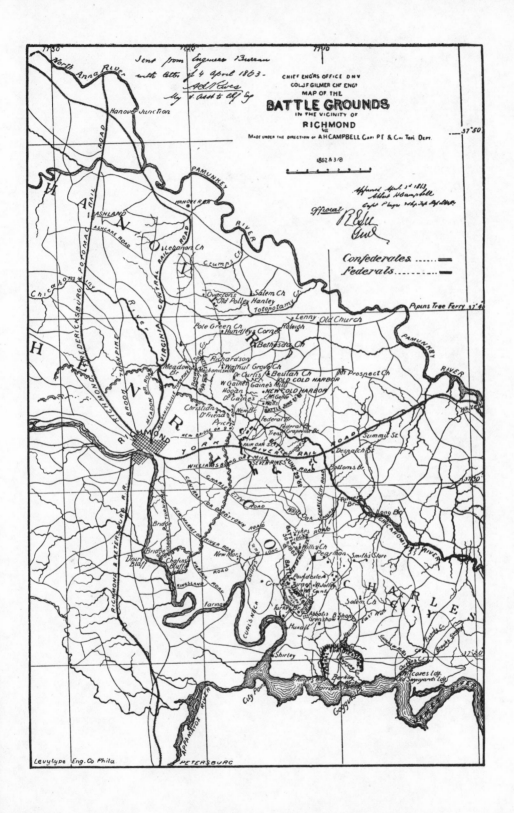

selves to the observation of the Federals ; while Magruder, Huger, and Holmes held the lines that were now completed, with instructions to watch closely the movements of the enemy in their front and act as circumstances might suggest. The effective force of the Army of Northern Virginia, including that brought by Jackson from the valley, as shown by the field returns of June 24th or 25th, amounted to a little more than 81,000 men : 30,000 of these were left in observation under Magruder, while Lee led 50,000 to the attack of the Federal force north of the Chickahominy, which amounted to about 25,000 men, commanded by Fitz John Porter. One division of this force, about 6000 or 7000 strong, under the command of General J. F. Reynolds, occupied Mechanicsville at the extreme right of the Federal position. The main body, under the immediate command of Porter, was posted near Cold Harbor or Gaines's Mill, about six miles below Mechanicsville, and connected by bridges with the main body of the Federal army south of the Chickahominy.

Jackson, having bivouacked at Ashton on the night of the 25th, and his men being fatigued by previous long marches, did not reach his designated position in line of battle until the afternoon of the 26th. This delay was very embarrassing to Lee, and greatly increased the difficulty of executing his plan of operations, as it exposed his design to the enemy and allowed him time to prepare for the approaching storm. General A. P. Hill, on the arrival of Jackson—about four o'clock— crossed the Chickahominy and made a spirited attack on the Federal force at Mechanicsville and compelled it to retire to a position which had been previously prepared beyond the Beaver Dam, a small stream about one mile south-east of the village. The way being now open, the divisions of Longstreet and D. H. Hill began to cross the Chickahominy. Ripley's brigade, which was the first to cross, was ordered to support A. P. Hill in his attempt to dislodge the Federals from their new position. Failing in their first attempt to dislodge them, the approach of night prevented any other being made to carry their position. Reynolds, finding his position would be turned, retired during the night to Gaines's Mill. On the morning of the 27th, Lee formed his army into three columns. The division of A. P. Hill, forming the centre, moved by the main road from Mechanicsville to Gaines's Mill; Longstreet moved by a road between this and the Chickahominy; while Jackson and D. H. Hill moved by a road to the left which intersected the Mechanicsville road a mile and a half beyond Gaines's Mill or Cold Harbor. Stuart with his cavalry covered the left flank of the army as it advanced. The guide, having received indefinite instructions from Jackson, led his column by a road that intersected with the Mechanicsville road before reaching Gaines's Mill. This brought the head of Jackson's column against Hill's troops. Jackson, being obliged to countermarch in order to gain the right road, caused a delay of several hours in the operations of General Lee and materially affected his plan of attack. It was his intention that when Jackson reached the Mechanicsville road he should form his troops in order of battle and attack the Federal right, while A. P. Hill attacked the centre and Longstreet the left.

The Federal position near Gaines's Mill was a plateau bounded on the north-west side by a bluff eighty or ninety feet in elevation, which, curving to the north and east, gradually diminished into a gentle slope. The plateau was bounded on its north side by a stream flowing along its base, whose banks gradually widened and deepened until, when reaching the bluff, they had gained the width of eight or ten and the depth of five or six feet, thus forming a natural ditch. Three lines of breastworks, rising one above the other, had been constructed upon the base of the bluff, and its crest was crowned with artillery. Three lines of Federal infantry occupied the bluff, and one line extended along the north-east crest for more than a mile, and batteries of artillery were in position in rear of the infantry. The Federal position was very strong, and to carry it required the greatest bravery and resolution on the part of the assailants. McClellan, being now aware of Lee's real design, reinforced Porter, increasing his force to about 40,000 men. When the columns of Hill and Longstreet had arrived in easy attacking-distance, General Lee caused them to halt in order to give Jackson time to gain his position. Waiting until

one o'clock, Lee ordered Longstreet and A. P. Hill to commence the attack. The Confederate skirmishers advanced and
drove in the Federal pickets. While the column of Longstreet
advanced by the road to Dr. Gaines's house, and that of Hill
by the main Mechanicsville road, the Federal position was hidden from Hill by the intervening woods. Deploying several regiments to support his skirmishers, he pushed them through the
woods. Very soon the Federal line was developed by a heavy
fire of musketry. Hill's column then deployed and advanced
to the attack on the Federal centre.

When Longstreet arrived at Gaines's house he was in full
view of the Federal left. Taking advantage of an intervening
ridge, the crest of which was parallel with and about three
hundred yards from the Federal lines, he deployed his troops
under its cover. Hearing Hill's attack, Longstreet approached
to gain the Federal left. His first line on reaching the crest of
the ridge was met by a storm of shot and shell; without faltering it swept down the slope toward the Federal position in the
face of a terrible fire of artillery and musketry until arrested
by the wide and steep banks of the stream at the foot. Being
unable to cross it, this line was obliged to fall back. These
troops, although much cut up, re-formed for a second attack.
Several Confederate batteries were served with considerable
effect in covering the advance of the infantry. D. H. Hill, on
reaching the scene of action, took position on the left of A. P.
Hill and engaged the enemy. The battle having become general, General Lee sent several staff officers to bring up Jackson's
troops to the support of Hill and Longstreet. Whiting's division and Lawton's brigade were the first to arrive. Whiting was
directed to fill the interval between Longstreet and A. P. Hill,
and Lawton was sent to the left of D. H. Hill to engage the
Federal right. Generals Ewell, Elzey, and Winder, as they
arrived, were sent to the support of the Hills, and one brigade
was sent to the support of Longstreet. Jackson led in person
the remainder of his troops against the Federal right. The
battle had raged with great fury for more than two hours, and
the Federal lines seemed as unshaken as when it first began.
The Confederates had been repulsed in several attempts to force

them. The day was now drawing to a close, and Lee decided
to end the conflict by a charge of the whole line. The word
"Charge!" as it passed along the line, was responded to by a
wild shout and an irresistible rush on the Federal position.
The Texas brigade, led by the gallant Hood, was the first to
penetrate the Federal works. It was immediately followed by
other regiments, and in a few minutes the whole position was
carried and the plateau was covered with a mass of fugitives.
The Federals were in full flight, pursued by the Confederates,
who delivered deadly volleys at every step.

While General Lee was attacking Porter's position at Gaines's
Mill, Magruder made a spirited demonstration against that of
McClellan on the south side of the Chickahominy. This
double attack served to bewilder McClellan, and caused him
to withhold reinforcements that would otherwise have been
sent to Porter. This battle is considered by many as the most
stubbornly-contested battle of the war. It is true that the
troops on both sides displayed great valor and determination, and proved themselves worthy of the nation to which
they belonged. Porter deserves much credit for the skilful
selection of his position and the gallant manner in which he
defended it. The victory was complete. When night closed
the Confederates were in undisputed possession of the field.
The next morning Lee directed Stuart with his cavalry, supported by Ewell's division of infantry, to seize the York River
Railroad. McClellan was thus cut off from his base of supplies, and reduced to the necessity of retreating by one of two
routes—the one by the Peninsula, the other by the James River,
under the cover of the gunboats. He chose the latter as the
shortest and easiest.

General Lee remained on the 28th on the north side of the
Chickahominy in observation of McClellan's movements. Instructions were sent at the same time to Magruder to keep a
vigilant watch on the Federals and without delay report any
movement that might be discovered. These instructions were
not as faithfully executed as they should have been, for the
retreat of the Federals had commenced on the morning of the
28th, and was not discovered until the morning of the 29th,

when the Federal lines were found by two engineer officers, Captains Meade and Johnston, to be abandoned, although the Confederate pickets were in many places less than half a mile from the Federal lines.

The safe retreat of McClellan to the James is mainly due to the advantage thus gained. When General Lee on the morning of the 29th found that the Federal army was in retreat he ordered an immediate pursuit. All of the troops on the north of the Chickahominy, with the exception of the divisions of Ewell and Jackson, and Stuart's cavalry, which were to remain in observation lest the Federals might change their line of retreat, were ordered to recross that stream with the view of overtaking the retreating columns. General Lee on recrossing the Chickahominy found Magruder, Huger, and Holmes preparing to pursue the retreating Federal army. At twelve o'clock the pursuit was commenced, and about three Magruder came upon Sumner's corps, which was in position near Savage's Station. General Heintzelman having retired, Sumner's and Franklin's corps had to receive Magruder's attack unsupported. Sumner held his position with great obstinacy until night ended the conflict. This determined stand enabled the Federal army to make a safe passage of the White Oak Swamp. In the afternoon of the 29th, Jackson was directed to cross the Chickahominy and relieve Magruder in the pursuit. Lee directed the other divisions of his army to march by several roads leading in the direction of McClellan's line of retreat, with the view of striking his column in the flank while Jackson pressed him in the rear. About three o'clock on the 30th, Lee, with the divisions of Longstreet and A. P. Hill, struck the Federal column at Frazier's Farm, and a fierce combat ensued which was closely contested until night. Contrary to his expectations, he was not supported in this attack by Generals Jackson and Huger, consequently McClellan again escaped and continued his retreat during the night to Malvern Hill.

The delay on the part of General Jackson was very unusual. The explanation of his delay on this occasion was that, being greatly exhausted by long marches and battles for more than a week, he sought a short repose. His staff, out of mistaken regard for their general, permitted him to sleep far beyond the time he had allowed himself. When he awoke he was greatly chagrined at the loss of time that had occurred, the damage of which he was unable to repair. Though General Lee accomplished all that was at first proposed, yet had the parts assigned to some of his subordinates been performed with the exactness that was naturally expected, the results of his operations would have been far greater than those shown in the sequel.

On the morning of the 1st of July it was discovered that McClellan had occupied in force the strong position of Malvern Hill, while his powerful artillery swept every approach, and the shot of the gunboats fell beyond the Confederate lines. After a careful reconnoissance of McClellan's position, Lee determined to attack his left. His first line, composed of the divisions of Magruder, D. H. Hill, and Jackson, was advanced under cover of the wood near the base of the hill. Magruder was ordered to attack the Federal left, while Hill and Jackson threatened their centre and right. The attack was delayed until near sundown, when Magruder made a most gallant assault. By dint of hard fighting his troops gained the crest of the hill and forced back the Federal left, but were in turn driven back. The firing continued along the line until ten o'clock. The Confederates lay upon their arms where the battle closed, ready to resume the fight as soon as the daylight should appear.

Under the cover of the night McClellan secretly retired, his retreat being facilitated by a heavy fall of rain, which deadened the sound of his withdrawal. The Confederates the next morning, groping through the dense fog, came upon the abandoned lines. This was the first information they had of the retreat. McClellan had now gained the protection of the Federal gunboats; therefore Lee did not immediately pursue, but ordered a day's rest, which the troops greatly needed. McClellan continued his retreat to Harrison's Landing on the James River, where he took up a position. Lee advanced the next day to that neighborhood and after a careful reconnoissance of the Federal lines deemed it inadvisable to attack, and, as there was no probability of the Army of the Potomac speedily resuming operations, he returned to his former camp near Richmond to rest, recruit, and reorganize his army.

While in the vicinity of Harrison's Landing the attack of Colonel J. Thompson Brown's artillery upon the Federal gunboats afforded a brilliant episode to the last scene of the military drama that had just been acted.

The loss sustained by both armies during the recent operations was considerable; that, however, caused by exhaustion and illness probably equalled the casualties of actual battle. The number of Confederate killed and wounded amounted to about 10,000, whilst the Federal loss exceeded this. Reviewing the operations that have just been described, we cannot fail to observe the important results achieved by the skill and energy of an able commander. On the 1st of June, General Lee assumed the command of an army that did not exceed 50,000 men. With this force he erected defences to withstand any attack that might be made against them, and besides in less than a month increased his army to 80,000 men, without giving up one foot of territory and without endangering either public or private property. He also raised its discipline and spirit to such a height that he was enabled to take the offensive and force his adversary, notwithstanding his superiority of numbers and the finely-appointed state of his army, to abandon a base of operations that had occupied almost the exclusive attention of his Government for more than a year, incurring in doing so a heavy loss of material.

McClellan, after establishing himself at Harrison's Landing, called for large reinforcements to enable him to resume active operations. It was decided to order Burnside from North Carolina to reinforce the Army of the Potomac. When Lee regained his former camp near Richmond he immediately set about reorganizing his army. His victory over McClellan had filled the Confederacy with joy, and the men who had left the army a short time before broken down and depressed returned full of spirit and energy.

Before the end of July the Army of Northern Virginia, with the addition of one or two brigades from South Carolina and Georgia, numbered about 70,000 effective men. This army,

having to a great extent supplied itself by captures from the
Federal army, was better armed and equipped than it had previously been.

Lee had formed it into two corps, giving one to Longstreet
and the other to Jackson, officers who had proved themselves
fully worthy of the important commands conferred upon them.
As they have borne a most distinguished part in the events
which form the subject of this narrative, it is proper that a
sketch of them should be given. They were both graduates
of the national Military Academy, and each on receiving his
diploma entered on a military career.

Longstreet was Jackson's senior, having graduated at West
Point in 1842, while Jackson did not complete his academic
labors until four years later. These chieftains, whose career
seemed to be united by destiny, were entirely dissimilar in
person and character. Longstreet in his younger days possessed
a figure remarkable for manly beauty, which in maturer years,
though much expanded, was still commanding and graceful,
and his person was further rendered agreeable by a social and
genial manner. To his superior physical qualities was added
mental ability of considerable scope. On the other hand,
though physically and mentally inferior to Longstreet, Jackson possessed an iron mind, with a determination and perse-
verance that enabled him to accomplish great results. He did
not have the genial and attractive manner of his distinguished
contemporary, but exhibited a quiet reserve, amounting almost
to austerity, which, being taken in connection with his strict
observance of the faith of the Covenanter, might warrant the
idea of finding his counterpart among the Ironsides of Cromwell. The breaking out of the war with Mexico in 1846
afforded the youthful aspirants to military renown a rich harvest of fame, and in the brilliant campaign of General Scott
in the Valley of Mexico, Jackson as lieutenant of artillery and
Longstreet on the staff of General Garland gathered abundant
laurels, and at the close of the war each received from the Government as a reward of merit the brevet rank of major.

After the restoration of peace, finding the inactivity of gar-
rison-life distasteful to him, Jackson resigned his commission

in the army and accepted a professorship in the Virginia Military Institute, which he filled with honor until the civil rupture between the States. Longstreet in the mean time remained in the army, where he had conferred on him the position of paymaster, with the full rank of major.

At the commencement of the war between the States both Longstreet and Jackson tendered their services to their native States, and as we progress with our narrative it will be seen to what distinction each rose in defence of the Southern Confederacy.

It would be unjust to General Lee to pass unnoticed some of the criticisms that have been made on the foregoing campaign by General Dick Taylor in his sprightly work, *Destruction and Reconstruction.* Among some of his random remarks we find one to the following effect: "General Lee was without maps or efficient guides, and was himself and staff unacquainted with the topography of his field of operations, which materially resulted in blunders on the part of his subordinate commanders."

Mr. Davis reiterated the above assertion in his *History of the Confederacy*, vol. ii. chap. xxiv., pp. 142, 144: "It is an extraordinary fact that, though the capital had been threatened by an attack from the seaboard on the right, though our army had retreated from Yorktown up the Chickahominy, and after encamping there for a time had crossed the river and moved up to Richmond, yet when, at the close of the battles around Richmond, McClellan retreated and was pursued toward the James River, we had no maps of the country in which we were operating; our generals were ignorant of the roads, and their guides knew little more than the way from their homes to Richmond. . . . .

"It was after a personal and hazardous reconnoissance that General Lee assigned General Holmes to his last position; and when I remonstrated with General Lee, whom I met returning from his reconnoissance, on account of the exposure to which he had subjected himself, he said he could not get the required information, and therefore had gone himself."

The blame implied in these remarks in reference to the want

of maps should be placed where it properly belongs—with the war-directing authority at Richmond. It is from the topographical bureaus of governments that the geographical and topographical knowledge requisite for a campaign should be obtained; and in the present instance neither Johnston nor Lee had opportunities to cause reconnoissances and surveys to be made, which were necessary for the construction of maps.

The statement in regard to Lee's want of knowledge of the topography of his field of operations and the inferiority of his guides is incorrect. The blunders complained of were more the result of inattention to orders and want of proper energy on the part of a few subordinate commanders than of lack of knowledge of the country. For years Lee had been accustomed to traverse the country between the White House and Richmond, and from Richmond to the different estates of his friends on the lower James. He was therefore well acquainted with the country on both sides of the Chickahominy, and it was natural that he should apply his previous information to his present purposes. The inhabitants of that region supplied efficient guides, and his staff officers had been employed in making themselves acquainted with the roads and natural features of the country over which the army was likely to operate. Moreover, a few days before his attack on McClellan, Stuart was sent on a reconnoissance to the rear of the Federal army to acquire information that might be useful in carrying out his plan of attack, and during the battle Baker's regiment of cavalry was kept in the vicinity of Malvern Hill to observe the enemy.

Just before the battle of Frazier's Farm, Mr. Davis with his staff arrived at the position then occupied by General Lee; almost immediately thereafter the enemy's batteries opened a lively fire, sending a shower of shells into startling proximity. Lee then, accompanied by several of his staff, proceeded to make a personal observation of the field of battle; which practice had been and continued to be his custom. After satisfying himself of the condition of affairs, he proceeded to join Longstreet at his field headquarters, where he found Mr. Davis, when the conversation referred to above took place. Mr. Davis clearly misunderstood General Lee's remark in regard to his lack of information, since he could but have expressed a desire to satisfy himself by personal observation, and not have professed ignorance of the general features of the locality occupied by the armies.

(The map accompanying this chapter is a copy of the official map used by General Lee during this campaign. It was filed with his report of these operations in the War Department, C. S. A., by the special direction of General Lee.)

CHAPTER XI.

POPE OUTGENERALLED.

The New Federal Commander.—Lee's March Northward.—Pope's Retreat.—Jackson's Flanking Movement.—Capture of the Stores at Manassas.—Lee's Narrow Escape.— A Lady in Distress.—Thoroughfare Gap.—Longstreet's Corps joins Jackson.—Second Battle of Manassas.—Pope's Defeat.—Telegrams.

THE short and disastrous campaign of Pope affords a striking commentary on the timid policy that characterized the Federal Government in its prosecution of the war, as had been previously illustrated by the injudicious interference of Mr. Lincoln with military operations in the field, and his obvious want of confidence in General McClellan. This was manifested by withholding from him McDowell's corps of 40,000 men, whose co-operation was calculated on in the advance upon Richmond, and subsequently by allowing his fears for the safety of Washington to neutralize a powerful force in the Valley of Virginia, which might have, by timely co-operation, given a different turn to the Richmond campaign. Besides executive interference, military operations were further embarrassed by the introduction of an inquisitorial tribunal known as the "Congressional Committee on the Conduct of the War."

It was through this engine of mischief that the popular curiosity of the North was feasted with news from the seat of war, by which feuds were bred in the army, and which became the source from which the Confederates were supplied with the most important information, thus paving the way for those disastrous blows which fell upon the Federal arms. Pope in his interviews so dazzled with his brilliant plan of operations the authorities who, from their seat in Washington, directed military affairs that they dislocated the plan of McClellan, withdrew the Army of the Potomac from its position on the James, and threw the whole of that army into Pope's scheme of victory. He tells President Lincoln, General Halleck, and the Secretary of War at the White House, and repeats to the Congressional Committee at the Capitol, that with McClellan's army, 200,000 strong, he could not only dissipate every danger that threatened the capital, but could make a victorious march to New Orleans. Great, then, must have been the disappointment at Washington, after such glorious prospects, on witnessing the precipitate retreat of the Federal army on which such high hopes had been centred. Pope's chastisement should also serve to admonish the future military tyro to mask his ignorance by curbing his arrogance when thrown by a credulous government into a position far beyond his capacity.

As there was no probability of McClellan's immediately resuming active operations against Richmond, Lee determined, by assuming the offensive and threatening the Federal capital, to force him to make an entire change in his plan of campaign. With that view he despatched Jackson with three divisions of infantry and a proportionate amount of artillery to the neighborhood of Gordonsville, while remaining himself at Richmond with Longstreet's corps, D. H. Hill's and Anderson's divisions of infantry, and Stuart's cavalry in observation of McClellan, who was now slowly recovering from the stunning effect of his defeat. Having learned through the newspapers and other sources that there was a conflict of opinion between General McClellan and Mr. Lincoln in regard to future operations, and knowing the Federal President's anxiety concerning the safety of his capital, Lee rightly concluded that any movement in that direction would cause McClellan's opinion to be overruled and the Army of the Potomac to be withdrawn from the James for the defence of Washington.

There had not been as yet any understanding between the belligerents in regard to the treatment and exchange of prisoners. It was now very desirable that some plan on this subject should be established. General Dix on the part of the Federals and General D. H. Hill on that of the Confederates were commissioned to form a plan for the exchange of prisoners. They met and framed a cartel on very liberal principles, which was agreed to by both Governments. The exchange of prisoners began under it, but was discontinued later by the Federal Government. About the 1st of August, the advance of the Federal army having reached Culpeper Court-house, Jackson moved to the Rapidan and took a position in the vicinity of Orange Court-house. Being there joined by two small brigades of cavalry, commanded by W. E. Jones and Beverly Robertson, his strength was increased to about 20,000 men. The forces under Banks, Fremont, and McDowell, amounting to 50,000 men, were formed into an army, the command of which was given to General Pope, who, in assuming the command, introduced himself in a very bombastic order, in which he announced his intention of conducting the war on very different principles from those that had been previously adopted.

In his pseudo-Napoleonic order to his soldiers he said: " I constantly hear of taking strong positions and holding them —of lines of retreat and bases of supplies," and enjoined them to dismiss all such ideas as unworthy of soldiers commanded by one who had been used to see only "the backs of his enemies." His headquarters were to be "in the saddle," and he had come from the West, "from an army *whose business it has been to seek the adversary, and to beat him when found*—whose policy has been attack, and not defence." Before the Committee on the Conduct of the War he grandiloquently declared that he meant to "lie off on the flanks of the rebels," and that with an army equal to McClellan's he would promise to march straight from Washington to New Orleans. We need scarcely say that before he was many days older this vain-glorious boaster found that there were obstacles in the way of his projected march, that the intrenchments around Washington were a safer place than his "headquarters in the saddle," and that "lines of retreat and bases of supplies" were very good things in an emergency.

By reference to the map of Virginia the principal points mentioned in this narrative may be observed. About the time that Jackson reached the Rapidan, Pope arrived at Culpeper Court-house, and extended his advance corps toward the Rapidan. The Federal cavalry finding the Rapidan occupied by the Confederates, the leading corps took up a position along a range of low hills near Cedar Mountain, about four miles west of Culpeper Court-house. Having learned that a part of the Federal force had not arrived there, Jackson determined to attack Pope before his army could be united. He therefore secretly recrossed the Rapidan, and by a rapid movement on the 9th of August gained the position near Cedar Mountain before the Federals were aware of his design. The battle was hotly contested for several hours, when the Federals were defeated and driven back to Culpeper Court-house. Jackson held the field until he had secured the fruit of his victory and buried the dead. He then recrossed the Rapidan. Among the gallant soldiers who fell in this engagement none were more deeply regretted than General Charles S. Winder, in tribute to whose memory I cannot do more than refer to the order of General Jackson announcing his death. McClellan had remained quiet at Harrison's Landing during the month of July, resting and recruiting his army. At the same time he made a requisition upon the Government for a reinforcement of 50,000 men to enable him to resume his advance upon Richmond. President Lincoln declined furnishing him this reinforcement upon the ground that he had not so large a force available for that purpose.

About the last of July, General Halleck, commander-in-chief of the Federal army, visited the Army of the Potomac, which at that time numbered 90,000 effective men. At a council of the principal officers of the army it was found that a majority was opposed to renewing the advance upon Richmond, while McClellan and two or three of his most experienced officers were in favor of it. Halleck therefore promised McClellan a reinforcement of 20,000 men to enable him to carry out his plan, that being the largest force that could be then furnished for that purpose. The Federal authorities at Washington were not cordial in their support of McClellan's plan of operations. They were in favor of changing the base of operations from the James to the Potomac River, to operate with Pope on the Rapidan. The advance of Jackson to Gordonsville, above mentioned, and his subsequent advance upon the position of General Pope near Culpeper Court-house, caused

the Federal authorities to determine upon the immediate withdrawal of the Army of the Potomac from the James.

The circumstances here detailed very considerably modified
the military situation, and enabled General Lee to act with a
skill and boldness which was destined to astonish and alarm
the Federal authorities quite as much as his notable defeat of
McClellan had done.   He divined, with the intuition of genius,
that his presence and that of his army could be spared from the
immediate vicinity of Richmond, and might be able to teach
General Pope that the road to New Orleans was "a hard road
to travel."   Preliminary to future operations he sent forward
Longstreet's corps to join Jackson in the vicinity of Gordonsville, and about the middle of August proceeded in person to
assume the direction of affairs in that quarter.

On reaching the locality of the projected movements he
found Jackson occupying the line of the Rapidan, while Longstreet's force was encamped in the neighborhood of Gordonsville.   The army, including Stuart's cavalry, at this time
amounted to 65,000 effective men, while the opposing army of
Pope numbered 50,000, and occupied a position between Culpeper Court-house and the Rapidan.

Lee at once determined to assume the offensive, and with
that purpose in view he moved his whole army below Orange
Court-house to a position south of Clark's Mountain, where he
could avail himself of the fords of the Rapidan on the flanks
of the Federal army.   He reached this position on August
17th, the movement having been effected, under cover of the
forest, without the knowledge of General Pope.

The absence of Stuart's cavalry delayed the army in this
position till the morning of the 20th, and enabled Pope—who,
through an unlucky accident, became aware of the movement
of his shrewd adversary—to beat a hasty retreat.   The cavalry
had been employed in observation on the lower Rappahannock
and the York rivers, and were thus, unfortunately, not available at the moment when their presence would have been of
the most essential service.

On the 18th, Lee and his staff ascended Clark's Mountain,
and reconnoitered the Federal position.   In plain view before

General Stuart's Narrow Escape at Vediersville.   Page 187.

them lay Pope's army, stretched out in fancied security, and to all appearance in utter ignorance of the vicinity of a powerful foe. It was evident from that elevated position that the two armies were about equally distant from Culpeper Court-house, and that the Confederate force was in a position to gain the Federal rear. The absence of the cavalry, however, prevented an immediate advance, and Lee retained his position till the next day, satisfied that the enemy was still in ignorance of his danger. On the afternoon of the 19th the signal-station on the top of the mountain notified the Confederate commander that a change had occurred in the situation of affairs. The enemy had evidently taken the alarm. There was a bustle in the camp that indicated a move, as if Pope had suddenly learned the peril of his position and was preparing for a hasty flight toward the Rappahannock.

As it afterward appeared, Pope had learned of Lee's vicinity through the capture of Lieutenant Fitzhugh of Stuart's staff, on whom had been found a letter revealing the fact of the movement of the Confederate army. On gaining this important and somewhat startling information, he had immediately given orders to break camp and retreat in all haste to the line of the Rappahannock. During this interval General Stuart himself had run a serious risk of capture. The main body of the cavalry, under Fitz Lee, failing to make their appearance at the point where Stuart awaited them, he had become impatient, and advanced with some members of his staff to meet them. On the night of the 17th he occupied a house at Vediersville, intending to continue his search for the cavalry the next morning. At an early hour of that morning a squadron of Federal cavalry which was out reconnoitering suddenly made its appearance in front of the house which sheltered the Confederate general. The surprise was complete, but, fortunately, the Federals did not dream of the valuable prize within their reach. Ere they were able to grasp the situation Stuart had become aroused and apprised of his imminent peril. He instantly sprang up, and without hat or haversack rushed for the rear door of the house. There he sprang on his horse without heed of saddle or accoutrements and rode hastily into the woods, followed by those members of his staff who had accompanied him. The Federals learned only too late of the valuable prize which had slipped through their fingers, and had to content themselves with the hat and haversack of the dashing leader of the Confederate cavalry.

The retreating Federal army was followed by Lee in rapid pursuit, but it had crossed the Rappahannock by the time he reached the vicinity of that stream. Pope on crossing the river took up a position on the left bank, his left covering Rappahannock Station, his right extending in the direction of Warrenton Springs. Lee confronted him on the right bank of the river. The two armies remained thus opposed two or three days, during which nothing occurred except some unimportant skirmishing between the cavalry and the outposts.

When it became known at Washington that Pope had been compelled to retreat and recross the Rappahannock, the Federal authorities made every effort to rapidly reinforce him by troops drawn from the Army of the Potomac and from Burnside's force, which had been withdrawn from North Carolina. General Lee, in order to retard the forwarding of troops and supplies to the Federal army, ordered Stuart to turn Pope's right, gain his rear, inflict as much damage as he could upon the Orange and Alexandria Railroad, and gain information of the enemy's movements. Stuart, in compliance with his instructions, crossed the Rappahannock late in the afternoon of the 21st, a few miles above Warrenton Springs, with a brigade of cavalry, and, screening his movement by the mountain-spurs and intervening forests, he proceeded toward the village of Warrenton, passing that place after nightfall, and advanced direct upon Catlett's Station on the railroad. Arriving in the midst of a violent storm, he surprised and captured the Federal encampment at that place, which he found to contain General Pope's headquarters. He secured Pope's letter-book and papers with many other valuable articles.

On account of the heavy fall of rain the timbers of the railroad bridge at Catlett's were so saturated with water that Stuart was unable to burn it, and, being pressed for time, he failed to greatly damage the railroad. He returned, bringing with him

his valuable booty, without the loss of a man. By the capture
of Pope's papers Lee gained an accurate knowledge of the
situation of the Federal army. Acting on it, he ordered Jackson to advance his corps to Jeffersonton and secure the bridge
over the Rappahannock at Warrenton Springs. Jackson moved
up the river, leaving his train to follow under the escort of
Trimble's brigade. The Federals, being tempted by the appearance of a large train in their vicinity, sent a strong detachment to intercept it. Trimble, reinforced by Hood's brigade
of Longstreet's corps, met this detachment, and after a fierce
combat drove it back with heavy loss. Jackson, on arriving at
Jeffersonton in the afternoon of the 22d, found that the bridge
on the Warrenton turnpike had been destroyed by the Federals.
The river being low, he succeeded in sending Early's brigade
with one of Lawton's Georgia regiments across the river·on an
old mill-dam to act as a corps of observation. During the
night the river was made impassable by heavy rains. The
next day, the Federals beginning to appear in great force,
Early with great dexterity took a position in a wood adjacent
to the river, so as to effectually conceal his lack of strength.
The river having fallen during the day, he recrossed at night
without loss. The Federals burned the railroad bridge of Rappahannock Station, and moved their left higher up the river.
On the 23d, Lee ordered Longstreet's corps to follow Jackson
and mass in the vicinity of Jeffersonton. The headquarters of
the army was also moved to that place. In the afternoon a
demonstration was made by a part of the artillery of Jackson's
corps on the Federal position at Warrenton Springs, to create a
diversion in favor of Early, which provoked a spirited reply
from the Federal batteries.

General Longstreet made a feint on the position of Warren-.
ton on the morning of the 24th, under cover of which Jackson's corps was withdrawn from the front to the vicinity of the
road from Jeffersonton to the upper fords of the Rappahannock.
Jackson was then directed to make preparation to turn the
Federal position and seize their communications about Manassas Junction. Longstreet continued his cannonade at intervals
throughout the day, to which the Federals replied with increas-

ing vigor, showing that Pope was massing his army in Lee's front.

It was the object of Lee to hold Pope in his present position by deluding him with the belief that it was his intention to force a passage of the river at that point, until Jackson by a flank movement could gain his rear. Longstreet, on the morning of the 25th, resumed his cannonade with increased energy, and at the same time made a display of infantry above and below the bridge. Jackson then moved up the river to a ford eight miles above; crossing at that point and turning eastward, by a rapid march he reached the vicinity of Salem. Having made a march of twenty-five miles, he bivouacked for the night. Stuart's cavalry covered his right flank, the movement being masked by the natural features of the country. The next morning at dawn the march was resumed by the route through Thoroughfare Gap.

The cavalry, moving well to the right, passed around the west end of Bull Run Mountain and joined the infantry at the village of Gainesville, a few miles from the Orange and Alexandria Railroad. Pressing forward, still keeping the cavalry well to the right, Jackson struck the railroad at Bristoe Station late in the afternoon, where he captured two empty trains going east. After dark he sent a detachment under Stuart to secure Manassas Junction, the main dépôt of supplies of the Federal army. The cavalry moved upon the flanks of this position, while the infantry, commanded by Trimble, assaulted the works in front and carried them with insignificant loss, capturing two batteries of light artillery with their horses and a detachment of 300 men, besides an immense amount of army supplies. The next morning, after effectually destroying the railroad at Bristoe, Jackson left Ewell with his division and a part of Stuart's cavalry to retard the Federals if they should advance in that direction, and moved his main body to Manassas, where he allowed his troops a few hours to refresh themselves upon the abundant stores that had been captured. About twelve o'clock the sound of artillery in the direction of Bristoe announced the Federal advance. Not having transportation to remove the captured supplies, Jackson directed his men to take what they can carry off, and ordered the rest to be destroyed.

General Ewell, having repulsed the advance of two Federal columns, rejoined Jackson at Manassas. The destruction of the captured stores having been completed, Jackson retired with his whole force to Bull Run and took a position for the night, a part of his troops resting on the battle-field of the previous year. Pope, on hearing of the interruption of his communications, sent a force to get information of the extent of the damage that had been done to the railroad. Upon learning that Jackson was in his rear, he immediately abandoned his position on the Rappahannock and proceeded with all despatch to intercept him before he could be reinforced by Lee. His advance having been arrested on the 27th by Ewell, he did not proceed beyond Bristoe that day. Lee on the 26th withdrew Longstreet's corps from its position in front of Warrenton Springs, covering the withdrawal by a small rear-guard and artillery, and directed it to follow Jackson by the route he had taken the day before. The trains were ordered to move by the same route and to keep closed on Longstreet's corps.

On the evening of this day Longstreet, accompanied by Lee and his staff, reached the vicinity of the small village of Orleans, where the corps bivouacked for the night. We may at this point, as a break to the uniformity of the war-narrative, introduce some personal details concerning General Lee, and particularly those in relation to a very narrow escape which he made from capture by a squadron of Federal cavalry. His peril was quite as great as had been that of Stuart a few days before, while the danger of disaster to the Confederate cause was tenfold greater. This incident has never yet been told, and we may be pardoned for pausing in our narrative to relate it.

On the evening in question Mrs. Marshall, a hospitable lady residing in the vicinity of Orleans, invited Generals Lee and Longstreet to partake of a repast which she had prepared for them on hearing of their approach. After enjoying the meal, whose abundance was in pleasant contrast to their usual scanty camp-fare, they passed an agreeable evening with the ladies.

Lee threw off the stern bearing of the soldier and assumed that of the genial cavalier, while Longstreet laid aside his ordinary reticence and made himself very entertaining. At the conclusion of the evening's entertainment the guests informed their hostess that they must be astir very early the next morning, as the march would be resumed by the dawn of day.

Yet, early as they were, their hospitable hostess was up before them, and to their surprise when ready to depart they found a sumptuous breakfast awaiting them. After partaking of this the whole party bade adieu to Mrs. Marshall and her household, and took their places at the head of the advancing column just as day began to dawn. On approaching the neighborhood of Salem the general and his staff found themselves at some distance in advance of the column, having ridden briskly onward in the fresh morning air. At this moment a quartermaster, who had luckily been still farther in advance, came dashing back at full speed and in a high state of excitement, calling out loudly as he approached, "The Federal cavalry are upon you!" Almost at the same instant the head of a galloping squadron was seen moving briskly toward them and only a few hundred yards distant.

It was a moment of imminent peril, and one that needed quick decision and skilful action. The general was accompanied only by his staff and couriers, some ten or twelve men in all. But these were men who were fully ready to devote their lives or liberties to the safety of their great commander. They instantly formed across the road and impulsively bade Lee to retire, promising to retard the enemy until he had gained a safe distance. The Federal cavalry, seeing this line of horsemen, which occupied the full width of the road, and presuming that it was the head of a considerable troop, halted, gazed upon it for a moment, and then wheeled and rode off in the opposite direction.

The quick action of the staff alone saved General Lee from capture. Had they been seen by the opposing squadron before they formed in line the Confederate commander and his staff would undoubtedly have been captured. Or if a bold dash had been made by the Federal squadron, Lee could scarcely have escaped. This incident is the more worthy of relation as it was the only case during the war in which the Confederate leader was in imminent danger of capture.

In this connection may be mentioned another incident which occurred on the same morning. A patriotic lady who resided in the vicinity of Salem, and who was naturally desirous to greet the great general as he passed, rode out for this purpose, in company with her daughters, in their family carriage, which was drawn by a pair of handsome and spirited horses. Unfortunately for her, she was met by the body of Federal cavalry just spoken of, who, without ceremony and despite entreaties, dispossessed her of her magnificent bays, and left the dejected lady and her daughters sitting helpless in their carriage in the middle of the road. When General Lee rode up to the spot he found the distressed party in a house by the wayside, in which they had taken refuge. With his usual gallantry and courtesy he dismounted and strove to cheer up the unfortunate lady, expressing his deep sympathy with her mishap, and regretting his inability to relieve her from her difficulty by supplying her with another pair of horses. Since the war the lady has frequently repeated this anecdote, and, though glad of the opportunity it gave her for an interview with the famous warrior, she has never become quite reconciled to the price which she paid for it—the loss of her favorite bays.

The corps bivouacked for the night in the vicinity of Salem. On the morning of the succeeding day, the 27th, a messenger appeared bringing the important and cheering news of the success of Jackson at Bristoe and Manassas. These tidings were received with enthusiasm by the soldiers, who, animated with high hopes of victory, pressed on with the greatest energy, and that evening reached the plains a few miles west of Thoroughfare Gap, in the Bull Run Mountains, through which Jackson's column had passed a few days previously.

Thoroughfare Gap was reached about noon of the 28th. It was quickly found to be occupied by a Federal force. Some slight attempt was made to dislodge the enemy, but without success, as their position proved too strong, and it seemed as if the movement of the Confederate army in that direction was destined to be seriously interfered with. Meanwhile, nothing further had been heard from Jackson, and there was a natural anxiety in regard to his position and possible peril. Unless the mountains could speedily be passed by Longstreet's corps the force under Jackson might be assailed by the whole of Pope's army, and very severely dealt with.

Under these critical circumstances General Lee made every effort to find some available route over the mountains, sending reconnoissances to right and left in search of a practicable pass. Some of the officers ascended the mountain during the evening, and perceived from its summit a large force which lay in front of the Gap. Meanwhile, the sound of cannonading was audible from the other side of the range, and it was evident that an engagement was taking place. The moment was a critical one, and the most phlegmatic commander might have been pardoned for yielding to excitement under such circumstances; yet Lee preserved his usual equanimity, and permitted his face to show no indication of the anxiety which he must have felt. That he was lost in deep reflection as he surveyed the mountain-pass in front was evident, yet neither in looks nor words did he show that he was not fully master of himself and of the occasion. And the absence of any overmastering anxiety was shown in another manner. Mr. Robison, a gentleman who lived near the Gap, invited Lee and his staff to take dinner with him; and this meal was partaken of with as good an appetite and with as much geniality of manner as if the occasion was an ordinary one, not a moment in which victory or ruin hung trembling in the balance.

Fortunately, circumstances favored the Confederate cause. One of the reconnoitering parties found a woodchopper, who told them of an old road over the mountain to which he could guide them, and which might be practicable for infantry. Hood was at once directed to make an effort to lead his division across the mountain by this route. This he succeeded in doing, and the head of his column reached the other side of the range by morning. Another route had also been discovered by which Wilcox was enabled to turn the Gap.

In the mean time, Pope himself had been playing into the

hands of his adversary. He had ordered McDowell to retire from the Gap and join him to aid in the anticipated crushing of Jackson. McDowell did so, leaving Rickett's division to hold the Gap. In evident ignorance of the vicinity of Longstreet's corps, this force was also withdrawn during the night, and on the morning of the 29th Lee found the Gap unoccupied, and at once marched through at the head of Longstreet's column. On reaching Gainesville, three miles beyond the Gap, he found Stuart, who informed him of Jackson's situation. The division was at once marched into position on Jackson's right.

Pope had unknowingly favored the advance of the Confederate commander. His removal of McDowell from his position had been a tactical error of such magnitude that it could not well be retrieved. The object of the movement had been to surround Jackson at Manassas Junction, upon which place the several corps of the army were marching by various routes. Pope wrote in his order to McDowell, "If you will march promptly and rapidly at the earliest dawn upon Manassas Junction, we shall bag the whole crowd." The scheme was a good one, but for two unconsidered contingencies. Had Jackson awaited the enemy at Manassas Junction, he would have found himself in a trap. But he did not choose to do so. When the van of the Federal columns reached the Junction, they found that the bird had flown. And Longstreet's corps, which might have been prevented from passing the Bull Run range, had been given free opportunity to cross to the aid of Jackson, who on the night of the 27th and morning of the 28th left the Junction and made a rapid march to the westward. The error was a fatal one to the hopes of the boasting Western general.

The cannonade at the Gap on the 28th had informed Jackson of Lee's proximity. He at once took a position north of the Warrenton turnpike, his left resting on Bull Run, near Sudley Church, and his right extending toward Gainesville. The distance of this position from the Warrenton road varied from one to two miles, the greater part of the left embracing a railroad cut, while the centre and right occupied a commanding ridge. In this position Jackson could easily unite with Lee on his passing Thoroughfare Gap, or, failing in that and being hard pressed, he could retire by the east end of Bull Run Mountain and unite with Lee on the north side of that mountain. The divisions of Ewell and Taliaferro formed the right and centre of Jackson's line of battle, while that of A. P. Hill constituted his left. Jackson had barely completed his arrangements when a heavy column of Federal infantry (King's division of McDowell's corps) appeared on the Warrenton turnpike. In order to delay its advance several batteries were placed in position, which by a well-directed fire caused them to halt; at the same time Jackson ordered Taliaferro to deploy one brigade across the Warrenton turnpike, holding his other brigades in reserve. Ewell was directed to support him. About three o'clock the Federals bore down in heavy force upon Ewell and Taliaferro, who maintained their positions with admirable firmness, repelling attack after attack until night. The loss on both sides was considerable. Among the wounded on the side of the Confederates were Generals Taliaferro and Ewell, the latter seriously, having to lose his leg.

Jackson, with barely 20,000 men, now found himself confronted by the greater part of the Federal army. Any commander with less firmness would have sought safety in retreat. But having heard the Confederate guns at Thoroughfare Gap, he knew that Lee would join him the next day. Therefore he determined to hold his position at all hazards.

By the morning of the 29th, as we have already described, Hood's division had reached the south side of the mountain, and early in the day was joined by the remainder of Longstreet's corps by way of the open Gap.

While these important movements were in progress, Pope had resumed his attack upon Jackson, and was pressing him with his whole force, hoping to crush him before he could be relieved by Lee. On the arrival of Lee, Pope discontinued his attack, and retired to the position which the year before had been the scene of the famous battle of Bull Run, or Manassas. Lee then took a position opposite, with Longstreet's corps occupying a lower range of hills extending across and at right angles to the Warrenton turnpike, while Jackson occupied the line of railroad before mentioned, which, slightly deviating from the general direction of Longstreet's position, formed with it an obtuse crotchet, opening toward the enemy. An elevated ridge connecting Jackson's right with Longstreet's left, forming the centre of the Confederate position, was strongly occupied with artillery to fill the interval between Longstreet and Jackson. The hills on the right, were crowned by the Washington Artillery, commanded by Colonel Walton. The remainder of the artillery was distributed at prominent points throughout the line, while Stuart's cavalry covered its flanks and observed the movements of the enemy. Since Pope's retreat from Culpeper Court-house he had been frequently reinforced by detachments from the armies of McClellan and Burnside. The greater part of those armies having now joined him, and the remainder being in supporting-distance, his arrogance revived, and, being sure of an easy victory, he sent the most sanguine despatches to the authorities at Washington. In preparation for battle he took a position embracing a succession of low ridges, nearly parallel to, and about a mile from, the line assumed by Lee. About midway between the two armies lay a narrow valley, through which meandered a small brook, whose low murmurs seemed to invite the weary soldier to slake his thirst with its cool and limpid waters. The afternoon of the 29th was principally occupied in preparation. Longstreet's corps, on the right, was formed in two lines. Jackson, on the left, having been considerably reduced by rapid marching and hard fighting, could present only a single line with a small reserve.

On the morning of the 30th an ominous silence pervaded both armies. Each seemed to be taking the measure of its antagonist. Lee saw threatening him the armies of Pope, McClellan, and Burnside, whose combined strength exceeded 150,000 men, while his own army was less than 60,000 strong. Notwithstanding this disparity of numbers, the presence of Lee, Jackson, and Longstreet inspired the troops with confidence far exceeding their numerical strength. About eight o'clock the Federal batteries opened a lively cannonade upon the Confederate centre, which was responded to with spirit by the battalions of Colonel Stephen D. Lee and Major Shoemaker. This practice having continued for an hour, both sides relapsed into silence. This was the prelude to the approaching contest. Between twelve and one o'clock the cannonade was resumed in earnest. The thunder of cannon shook the hills, while shot and shell, shrieking and hissing, filled the air, and the sulphurous smoke, settling in black clouds along the intervening valley, hung like a pall over the heavy columns of infantry which rushed into the "jaws of death." Pope, having directed his principal attack upon the Confederate left, advanced his infantry in powerful force against Jackson, whose single line behind the friendly shelter of railroad cuts and embankments received this mighty array with tremendous volleys of musketry, hurling back line after line, only to be replaced by fresh assailants. Each moment the conflict became closer and more deadly. At times the roar of musketry gave place to the clash of bayonets, and at one point, after the Confederates had exhausted their ammunition, the assailants were repelled with stones which had been thrown up from a neighboring excavation. At the critical moment when the fate of Jackson's corps was trembling in the balance, Colonel Lee dashed with his artillery into a position that enfiladed the Federal right wing and hurled upon it a storm of shot and shell. At the same moment Longstreet's infantry rushed like a tempest against Pope's left, driving everything before it. This assault was irresistible, and speedily decided the fortune of the day. Pope's left wing gave way before it at every point, and his right, being assailed in flank and threatened in rear, relaxed its efforts and began to retire.

The Confederates, seeing the enemy in retreat, pursued with a shout that rose above the din of battle, and pressed him with such vigor that he soon fell into disorder and broke into rapid flight toward Bull Run. The pursuit was continued until arrested by the cover of night. After the storm of battle the field presented a scene of dreadful carnage. Thirty thousand men *hors de combat*, wrecks of batteries and the mangled carcasses of horses, gave proof of the desperate character of the conflict. Pope left upon the field 15,000 killed, wounded, and prisoners, while his army was greatly reduced by stragglers, who, imbued with the sentiment, "He who fights and runs away will live to fight another day," sought refuge far beyond the range of battle. The Confederate loss was also heavy, the killed and wounded being numbered at between 7000 and 8000. Beside the heavy losses in *personnel* sustained by the Federals, a large amount of valuable property fell into the hands of the victor, the most important of which was twenty-five thousand stand of small-arms and twenty-three pieces of artillery; also a large amount of medical stores was subsequently taken at Centreville.

Pope retired to Centreville, where he was opportunely joined by Generals Sumner and Franklin with 25,000 fresh troops, upon which Pope endeavored to rally his army.

General Lee, being well aware that powerful reinforcements from McClellan's and Burnside's armies and from other sources had been ordered to join Pope, did not deem it advisable to immediately pursue the retreating enemy, but prudently paused to ascertain what force he had to contend with before renewing the conflict. After the close of the battle Colonel Long made a personal reconnoissance of the whole field and reported to Lee. Wishing to strike the enemy another blow before he could recover from the effects of his repulse, Lee by rapid movement turned Centreville on the 1st of September, and took a position on the Little River turnpike, between Chantilly and Ox Hill, with the view of intercepting his retreat to Washington. This movement was covered by Robertson's cavalry, while Stuart advanced to Germantown, a small village a few miles east of Ox Hill, where he discovered the Federal army in retreat. After a sharp attack Stuart was obliged to retire before a superior force. About dusk A. P. Hill's division encountered a large detachment of the enemy at Ox Hill. A brief but sanguinary combat ensued, whose dramatic effect was greatly heightened by a furious thunderstorm, which burst upon the combatants almost simultaneously with the clash of arms. A singular opportunity was thus presented for contrasting the warring of the elements with the strife of man, and of comparing the acts of man with the power of Omnipotence. It was seen how greatly peals of thunder and vivid lightning, intensified by the darkness of night, enfeebled the flash and roar of musketry and cannon. The combatants being separated by night and storm, Hill's division occupied the field, while the Federals resumed the retreat. In this engagement they numbered among their slain two distinguished officers (Generals Kearny and Stephens), whose loss was regretted by friends in both armies. Pope made good his retreat during the night, and we once more see the fugitives from Manassas seeking a refuge within the defences of Washington.

Since Pope, on assuming the command of the Army of the Potomac, expressed his disregard for lines of communication and plans of operation, declaring that his headquarters should always be found in the saddle, it may be interesting to know the effect the advantage taken by Lee of this novelty in the art of war had upon the Federal authorities in Washington. I shall therefore introduce some of the correspondence between President Lincoln, McClellan, Halleck, and Pope:

"August 29, 1862—2.30 P. M.

"What news from direction of Manassas Junction? What generally?

"A. LINCOLN."

"August 29, 1862—2.45 P. M.

"The last news I received from direction of Manassas was from stragglers, to the effect that the enemy was evacuating Centreville and retiring toward Thoroughfare Gap. This is by no means reliable.

"I am clear that one of two courses should be adopted: First, to concentrate all our available forces to open communication with Pope; second, to leave Pope to get out of his scrape, and at once use all our means to make the capital perfectly safe. No middle course will now answer. Tell me what you wish me to do, and I will do all in my power to accomplish it. I wish to know what my orders and authority are. I ask for nothing, but will obey whatever orders you give. I only ask a prompt decision, that I may at once give the necessary orders. It will not do to delay longer.

"GEO. B. McCLELLAN,
"*Major-general.*"

"August 29, 1862.

"Yours of to-day just received. I think your first alternative—to wit, to concentrate all our available forces to open communication with Pope—is the right one. But I wish not to control. That I now leave to General Halleck, aided by your counsels.

"A. LINCOLN."

"August 29, 1862.

"I think you had better place Sumner's corps, as it arrives, near the fortifications, and particularly at the Chain Bridge. The principal thing to be feared now is a cavalry raid into this city, especially in the night-time. Use Cox's and Tyler's brigades and the new troops for the same object, if you need them. Porter writes to Burnside from Bristoe, 9.30 P. M. yesterday, that Pope's forces were then moving on Manassas, and that Burnside would soon hear of them by way of Alexandria.

"General Cullum has gone to Harper's Ferry, and I have only a single regular officer for duty in the office. Please send some of your officers to-day to see that every precaution is taken at the forks against a raid; also at the bridges.

"H. W. HALLECK,
"*General-in-chief.*"

"August 30, 1862.

"Franklin's and all of Sumner's corps should be pushed forward with all possible despatch. They must use their legs and make forced marches. Time now is everything. Send some sharp-shooters on train to Bull Run. The bridges and property are threatened by bands of Prince William cavalry. Give Colonel Haupt all the assistance you can. The sharp-shooters on top of cars can assist in unloading trains.

"H. W. HALLECK,
"*General-in-chief.*"

"August 30, 1862.

"Sumner's corps was fully in motion by 2.30 P. M., and Franklin's was past Fairfax at 10 A. M., moving forward as rapidly as possible. I have sent the last cavalryman I have to the front; also every other soldier in my command, except a small camp-guard. The firing in front has been extremely heavy for the last hour.

"GEO. B. McCLELLAN,
"*Major-general.*"

"CENTREVILLE, August 31, 1862.

"Our troops are all here and in position, though much used up and worn out. I think it would perhaps have been greatly better if Sumner and Franklin had been here three or four days ago; but you may rely upon our giving them as desperate a fight as I can force our men to stand up to. I should like to know whether you feel secure about Washington should this army be destroyed. I shall fight it as long as a man will stand up to the work. You must judge what is to be done, having in view the safety of the capital. The enemy is already pushing a cavalry reconnoissance in our front at Cub Run—whether in advance of an attack to-day I don't know yet.

"I send you this that you may know our position and my purpose.

"JNO. POPE,
"*Major-general.*"

CHAPTER XII.

ADVANCE INTO MARYLAND.

Purpose of the Invasion of Maryland.—The Army Moves North.—Condition and Spirit of the Troops.—Proclamation Issued.—Jackson Advances on Harper's Ferry.—Its Capture.—McClellan at Frederick.—Lee's Army Order Found.—Position of Confederate Army.—Battle of Boonsboro' Gap.—Federal Success.—Lee's Stand at Sharpsburg.—McClellan Attacks.—The Battle.—Its Results.—Anecdotes of Lee.

BEFORE proceeding with the operations of the Army of Northern Virginia, it is necessary to refer briefly to a portion of the political history of the Confederacy bearing on military affairs.

At the commencement of hostilities the Confederate Government determined to conduct the war purely on defensive principles. In view of the immense superiority of the North over the South in all the essentials for creating armies and the prosecution of war, this was the true policy to be adopted. It must be remembered, however, that a strictly non-aggressive system does not always ensure the best defence; for it frequently happens that a judicious departure from the defensive to bold and energetic offensive measures is productive of the most desirable results, and that it is far better to govern the course of events than to passively yield to its control. At an early period of the war a favorable opportunity occurred for applying the principle above mentioned.

The occasion here referred to is that of the battle of Manassas, in July, 1861, when the defeat of McDowell's army left the Federal capital defenceless. At that time a prompt and vigorous advance of the Confederate army upon Washington City would very probably have resulted in its capture, and a penetration into Maryland would have gained the adherence of that State to the Confederacy. This course, however, was rejected—partly on the ground that the capture of Washington would firmly unite the political parties of the North and obliterate the hope of a speedy termination of the war, and partly for the reason that the military preparation for an advance was incomplete. This latter objection could have been easily overcome by an energetic commander with the cordial support of the Government. And subsequent events clearly proved that an erroneous conception dictated the timid policy that was pursued.

It is now obvious that the capture of Washington and an invasion of Maryland in 1861 could not have more firmly united the political parties of the North than the mortifying defeat of the army at Manassas had done. Moreover, the year that had since elapsed had been so industriously improved by the Federal Government that the defences of Washington were now complete and the political bonds of Maryland were firmly riveted.

With the view of shedding additional light on this period of the history of the war, we shall here introduce a scrap of personal information. On the 2d of September succeeding Pope's defeat, Colonel Long wrote from the dictation of General Lee to President Davis in substance as follows: As Virginia was free from invaders, the Federal army being within the defences of Washington, shattered and dispirited by defeat, and as the passage of the Potomac could now be effected without opposition, the present was deemed a proper moment, with His Excellency's approbation, to penetrate into Maryland. The presence of the victorious army could not fail to alarm the Federal authorities and make them draw forces from every quarter for the defence of their capital, thus relieving the Confederacy from pressure and—for a time, at least—from the exhaustion incident to invasion. The presence of a powerful army would also revive the hopes of the Marylanders, allow them a free exercise of their sympathies, and give them an opportunity of rallying to the aid of their Southern friends. Above all, the position of the army, should it again be crowned with victory, would be most favorable for seizing and making the best use of the advantages which such an event would produce. In conclusion, a few remarks were made in regard to the condition of the army.

In anticipation of the President's concurrence, General Lee immediately began the preparation for the invasion of Maryland. On the 3d he put the army in motion, and on the 4th took a position between Leesburg and the contiguous fords of the Potomac. The inhabitants of this section of country, having been crushed by the heel of oppression, were now transported with the cheering prospect of liberty. The presence of the army whose movements they had anxiously and proudly watched filled them with unbounded joy. Their doors were thrown open and their stores were spread out in hospitable profusion to welcome their honored guest. Leesburg, being on the border, had at an early period fallen into the hands of the enemy. All of the men who were able had joined the army, and many of those who were unfit for service had retired within the Confederate lines to escape the miseries of the Northern prison; so that the women and children had been left almost alone. Now all these gladly returned to their homes, and tender greetings on every side penetrated to the deepest recesses of the heart and made them thank God that misery and woe had been replaced by happiness and joy.

The strength of the Confederate army at this time, including D. H. Hill's division, did not exceed 45,000 effective men; yet, though it had been greatly reduced in numbers during the campaign through which it had just passed, its spirit was raised by the victories it had achieved. Its numerical diminution was not so much the result of casualties in battle as that of losses incident to long and rapid marches with insufficient supplies of food and the want of shoes. It frequently happened that the only food of the soldiers was the green corn and fruit gathered from the fields and orchards adjacent to the line of march, and often the bravest men were seen with lacerated feet painfully striving to keep pace with their comrades, until, worn out with pain and fatigue, they were obliged to yield and wait to be taken up by the ambulances or wagons, to be carried where their wants could be supplied.

The invasion of Maryland being determined on, the army was stripped of all incumbrances, and, from fear that the soldiers might be induced to retaliate on the defenceless inhabit-

ants for outrages committed by the Federal troops upon the
people of the South, stringent orders were issued against straggling and plundering.   These orders were strictly enforced
throughout the campaign.   Lee's earnestness in this particular
will be shown later in the chapter.

General Lee at the beginning of this march was suffering
from a painful hurt which to some extent disabled him throughout the Maryland campaign.   On the day after the second
battle of Manassas he was standing near the stone bridge, surrounded by a group of officers, when a squadron of Federal
cavalry suddenly appeared on the brow of a neighboring hill.
A movement of excitement in the group followed, with the
effect of frightening the general's horse.   The animal gave a
quick start, and his master, who was standing beside him with
his arm in the bridle, was flung violently to the ground with
such force as to break some of the bones of his right hand.
This disabled him so that he was unable to ride during the
greater part of the campaign.

The army was at this time in anything but a presentable
condition.   The long marches, hard fighting, and excessive
hardships they had gone through since leaving Richmond had
by no means improved the appearance of the men, and, in the
words of General Jones, who commanded Jackson's old "Stonewall" division, "never had the army been so ragged, dirty,
and ill provided for as on.this march."   Yet never were the
men in better spirits.   They crossed the river to the music of
the popular air, "Maryland, my Maryland," while their hearts
beat high with hopes of new victories to be won in that far
North from which the hosts of their invaders had come, and
with desire to wrest their sister-State of Maryland from the
iron grasp of the foe.   The Marylanders in the ranks felt a
natural sentiment of exultation at the cheering prospect of
relieving their native commonwealth from what was to them
a hateful bondage, while the Virginians—many of whom now
looked for the first time on that noble stream which formed the
northern boundary of the Confederacy—were filled with joyful
expectations of "conquering a peace," perhaps in the fields of
Pennsylvania, or at least of making the North suffer in its

own homes some of the horrors of war which it had freely inflicted upon the South.

The passage of the Potomac was successfully accomplished on the 5th. The infantry, artillery, and trains crossed at White's and Cheek's fords, the cavalry having previously crossed with instructions to seize important points and cover the movements of the army. From the Potomac, General Lee advanced to Frederick, at which place he arrived on the 6th and established himself behind the Monocacy. He at the same time seized the Baltimore and Ohio Railroad, and the principal roads to Baltimore, Washington, Harper's Ferry, and the upper Potomac. From this important position radiated several lines upon which he could operate. Those toward Harper's Ferry, Baltimore, and Pennsylvania were unoccupied, while that in the direction of Washington was held by the Federal army. As the principal object of the present advance into Maryland was to create a diversion in her favor in order that if so disposed she might array herself beside her sister Southern States, General Lee determined to remain at Frederick a sufficient time to allow the Marylanders to rally to his support.

At the commencement of hostilities many brave Marylanders had flocked to the Confederacy, and there were soon seen in the Southern ranks Elzey, G. H. Steuart, Bradley, Johnson, McLean, Marshall, Andrews, and a host of others of a like noble and generous spirit. Many of these gallant gentlemen were now with the army, anxious to assist in rescuing their State from the Federal authority.

On the 7th, General Lee issued the following proclamation.

"HEADQUARTERS ARMY N. VA.,
Near Frederick Town, 8th September, 1862.

"TO THE PEOPLE OF MARYLAND:

"It is right that you should know the purpose that has brought the army under my command within the limits of your State, so far as that purpose concerns yourselves.

"The people of the Confederate States have long watched with the deepest sympathy the wrongs and outrages that have been inflicted upon the citizens of a Commonwealth allied to the States of the South by the strongest social, political, and commercial ties.

"They have seen with profound indignation their sister-State deprived of every right and reduced to the condition of a conquered province.

"Under the pretence of supporting the Constitution, but in violation of its most valuable provisions, your citizens have been arrested and imprisoned upon no charge and contrary to all forms of law; the faithful and manly protest against this outrage made by the venerable and illustrious Marylander to whom in better days no citizen appealed for right in vain was treated with scorn and contempt; the government of your chief city has been usurped by armed strangers; your legislature has been dissolved by the unlawful arrest of its members; freedom of the press and of speech has been suppressed; words have been declared offences by an arbitrary decree of the Federal executive, and citizens ordered to be tried by a military commission for what they may dare to speak.

"Believing that the people of Maryland possessed a spirit too lofty to submit to such a government, the people of the South have long wished to aid you in throwing off this foreign yoke, to enable you again to enjoy the inalienable rights of freemen and restore independence and sovereignty to your State.

"In obedience to this wish our army has come among you, and is prepared to assist you with the power of its arms in regaining the rights of which you have been despoiled.

"This, citizens of Maryland, is our mission, so far as you are concerned.

"No constraint upon your free will is intended ; no intimidation will be allowed.

"Within the limits of this army at least, Marylanders shall once more enjoy their ancient freedom of thought and speech.

"We know no enemies among you, and will protect all, of every opinion.

"It is for you to decide your destiny freely and without constraint.

"This army will respect your choice, whatever it may be;

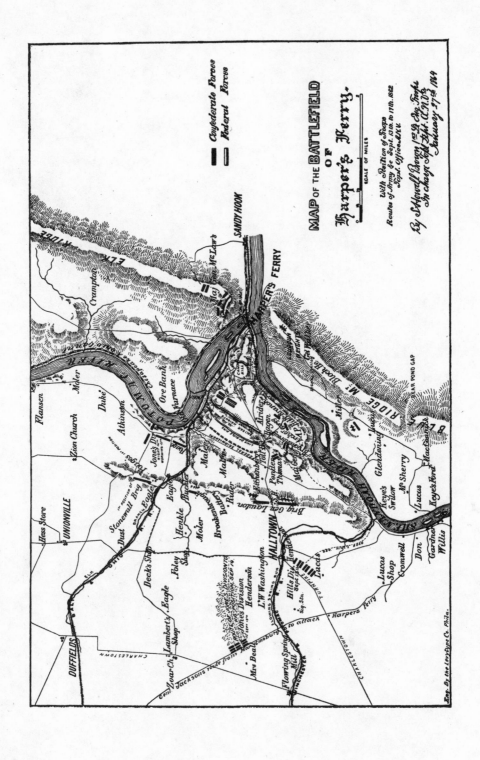

MAP of the BATTLEFIELD
OF
Harper's Ferry.

With Position of Troops
Routes of Army &c. Sept. 13th. to 17th. 1862
Topd. Office. A.N.Va.

SCALE OF MILES

By *S. Howell Brown* 1st Lt. Eng. Troops
In charge Topd. Office A.N.Va.
January 27th 1864

Confederate Forces
Federal Forces

SANDY HOOK

HARPER'S FERRY

Maj. McLar's

Crampton

ELK RIDGE

SHORT MT.

Flansen

Zion Church

Miler

Duke

Atkinson

Ore Bank

Furnace

Hess Store

UNIONVILLE

Stonewall Brig. Dust

Jones D.

Eagles

Eagle

Henkle Shop

Moler

Brodenbaugh Battery

Rider

Malet

Maj.

Kirtley

Tull

Hugen

McGee

Maj.

Poindexter Thomas

Brig Gen Laudon

Glendering

McSherry

Keyes Swilow

Lucius

Don.

Gardner

KeyesFord

Willis

BEAR POND GAP

MT. Dick Heb

MD.

RIDGE

Potomac River

Shenandoah River

DUFFIELDS

CHARLESTOWN

Deck's Shop

Foley Shop

Jones Durosan

Lambert's Eagle Shop

L.W. Washington

Henderson

HALLTOWN

Hills D. Kendal

Gen. Jacksons route from Martinsburg to attack Harpers Ferry

Mrs Beall

Flowing Spring

Lucas Shop

Cronwell

CHARLESTOWN

TURNPIKE

Eng. By the Levytype Co. Phila.

and, while the Southern people will rejoice to welcome you to your natural position among them, they will only welcome you when you come of your own free will.

"R. E. LEE,
"General commanding."

This was coldly received, and it soon became evident that the expectation of hearty co-operation from Maryland was fallacious. The Marylanders as a people sympathized with the Confederates, but stood aloof because they did not wish to see their State become the theatre of war.

It was not without surprise that General Lee discovered, upon reaching Frederick, that Harper's Ferry was still garrisoned. He had expected on entering Maryland that it would be at once abandoned, as it should have been had ordinary military principles been observed. Its continued occupation subjected its defenders to imminent danger of capture. Yet, through a military error, its occupation was unfavorable to the success of the Confederate movement, particularly if there was any idea entertained by General Lee of invading Pennsylvania. It would not do to leave this strongly-fortified post, on the direct line of communication of the army, in possession of the enemy; yet to reduce it needed a separation and retardation of the army that seriously interfered with the projected movements, and might have resulted adversely to the Southern cause but for the rapidity of Jackson's marches and the errors of Colonel Miles, the commander of the garrison. This will appear when we come to describe the subsequent events.

Yet, whatever might be the effect, its reduction was absolutely necessary ere any further operations of importance could be undertaken. Nor could the whole army be judiciously used for this purpose. Not only is it extremely unusual for a commander to use his whole force for a service which can be performed by a detachment, but in this case it would have necessitated a recrossing of the Potomac, with the strong probability that McClellan would take sure measures to prevent a return of the army into Maryland.

This service, had the claims of senior rank been alone

considered, should have been intrusted to Longstreet; but it was given to Jackson on account of his superior qualifications for duty of this character, Longstreet making no objection. Jackson was therefore directed to move his corps on the morning of the 10th by way of Williamsport to Martinsburg, to capture or disperse the Federal force at that place, and then proceed to Harper's Ferry and take steps for its immediate reduction. At the same time, Major-general McLaws was ordered to move with his and Anderson's divisions by the most direct route upon Maryland Heights, to seize that important position and co-operate with Jackson in his attack on Harper's Ferry. Brigadier-general Walker was instructed to recross the Potomac with his division and occupy Loudoun Heights for. the same purpose. The several movements were executed with wonderful celerity and precision.

Jackson on leaving Frederick marched with great rapidity by way of Middletown, Boonsboro', and Williamsport, near which latter place he forded the Potomac on the 11th and entered Virginia. Here he disposed his forces so as to prevent an escape of the garrison of Harper's Ferry in this direction and marched upon that place, the rear of which he reached on the 13th. On his approach General White evacuated Martinsburg and retired with its garrison to Harper's Ferry. On reaching Bolivar Heights, Jackson found that Walker was already in position on Loudoun Heights, and that McLaws had reached the foot of Maryland Heights, the key to Harper's Ferry, since it is the loftiest of the three heights by which that place is surrounded, and is sufficiently near to reach it even by musketry. Harper's Ferry, in fact, is a mere trap for its garrison, since it lies open to cannonade from the three heights named; so that the occupation of these renders it completely untenable.

Colonel Miles had posted a small force under Colonel Ford on Maryland Heights, retaining the bulk of his troops in Harper's Ferry. Instead of removing his whole command to the heights, which military prudence plainly dictated, and which his subordinates strongly recommended, he insisted upon a literal obedience to General Halleck's orders to hold Harper's

Ferry to the last extremity. In fact, Maryland Heights was quickly abandoned altogether, Ford but feebly resisting McLaws and retiring before his advance, first spiking his guns and hurling them down the steep declivity. This retreat left Maryland Heights open to occupation by the assailing force, and it was not long ere McLaws had succeeded in dragging some guns to the summit of the rugged ridge and placing them in position to command the garrison below. Jackson and Walker were already in position, and, by the morning of the 14th, Harper's Ferry was completely invested. During the day the summits of the other hills were crowned with artillery, which was ready to open fire by dawn of the 15th.

There was never a more complete trap than that into which the doomed garrison had suffered itself to fall. Escape and resistance were alike impossible. Maryland Heights might easily have been held until McClellan came up had the whole garrison defended it, but its abandonment was a fatal movement. They lay at the bottom of a funnel-shaped opening commanded by a plunging fire from three directions and within reach of volleys of musketry from Maryland Heights. Two hours of cannonade sufficed to prove this, and at the end of that time Colonel Miles raised the white flag of surrender. The signal was not immediately perceived by the Confederates, who continued their fire, one of the shots killing the Federal commander. The force surrendered numbered between 11,000 and 12,000 men, while there fell into Jackson's hands 73 pieces of artillery, 13,000 stand of arms, 200 wagons, and a large quantity of military stores.

Pending the reduction of Harper's Ferry, General Lee moved by easy marches with two divisions of Longstreet's corps to the neighborhood of Hagerstown, leaving D. H. Hill with his division and a detachment of cavalry to serve as rear-guard, with instructions to hold the Boonsboro' pass of South Mountain. By taking a position between Williamsport and Hagerstown a junction could be easily effected with the troops operating against Harper's Ferry, and on the reduction of that place Lee would have a secure line of communication through the Valley of Virginia, which would enable him to advance into

Pennsylvania or to assume such other line of operation as circumstances might suggest.

Since the advance of the Confederate army into Maryland no considerable Federal force had appeared, and as yet only some unimportant cavalry affairs had occurred.   After the evacuation of Virginia the Army of the Potomac had been augmented by the addition of the Army of Virginia and that of General Burnside, giving it an effective strength of about 90,000 men.   This force was assigned to the command of General McClellan for active operations, and was put in motion about the 6th of September.

Although it was known in Washington that Lee had crossed the Potomac, McClellan was checked in his movements by General Halleck, who was still apprehensive that the ubiquitous Jackson or Stuart might suddenly appear before the city of Washington.

When it became known that Lee had left Frederick and was advancing toward Hagerstown, McClellan advanced with greater confidence, and an attempt was made to relieve Harper's Ferry.   Franklin was sent to force his way through Crampton's Pass, in the South Mountain range.   This pass was defended by Mumford's cavalry, supported by a part of McLaws's division, under General Cobb, who had been sent back with three brigades under orders to hold Crampton's Pass until Harper's Ferry had surrendered, "even if he lost his last man in doing it."   This pass is in the rear of, and but five miles from, Maryland Heights, and its occupation by the Federals would have seriously imperilled the Confederate operations.   It was gallantly defended against the strong force of assailants, and, though Franklin succeeded in forcing his way through by the morning of the 15th, he was too late: Miles was already on the point of surrender.   McLaws at once withdrew his force from Maryland Heights, with the exception of one regiment, and formed a line of battle across Pleasant Valley to resist the threatening corps.   The surrender of the garrison immediately afterward left him a free line of retreat.   He crossed the Potomac at the Ferry, and moved by way of Shepherdstown to rejoin Lee at Sharpsburg.   The Confederates had in this enterprise met with the most complete and gratifying success.

The Federal army, moving with great caution and deliberation, reached Frederick on the 12th. Here occurred one of those untoward events which have so often changed the course of wars, and which in this instance completely modified the character of the campaign. A copy of General Lee's order directing the movements of the army accidentally fell into the hands of McClellan, who, being thus accurately informed of the position of the forces of his opponent, at once determined to abandon his cautious policy and boldly assume the offensive. He therefore pressed forward with the view of forcing the South Mountain passes, held by Hill, and of intruding himself between the wings of the Confederate army, with the hope of being able to crush them in detail before they could reunite.

The order in question, addressed to D. H. Hill, was found by a soldier after the Confederate evacuation of Frederick, and was quickly in McClellan's possession. Hill has been blamed for unpardonable carelessness in losing it; yet, as the original order was still in his possession after the war, it is evident that the one found must have been a copy. The mystery is made clear by Colonel Venable, one of General Lee's staff-officers, in the following remark: "This is very easily explained. One copy was sent directly to Hill from headquarters. General Jackson sent him a copy, as he regarded Hill in his command. It is Jackson's copy, in his own handwriting, which General Hill has. The other was undoubtedly left carelessly by some one at Hill's headquarters." However that be, its possession by McClellan immediately reversed the character of his movements, which were changed from snail-like slowness to energetic rapidity. In his own words, "Upon learning the contents of this order, I at once gave orders for a vigorous pursuit."

The detachment by General Lee of a large portion of his army for the reduction of Harper's Ferry was made with the reasonable assurance that that object could be effected and a junction formed before General McClellan would be in position to press him. Though this expectation proved well based, yet it was imperilled by the unforeseen event above mentioned.

The rapid movements to which the finding of Lee's order gave rise brought the leading corps of the Federal army in front of Hill's position upon South Mountain on the afternoon of the 13th. This mountain is intersected by three passes in front of Boonsboro'. The main, or central, pass is traversed by the Frederick and Boonsboro' turnpike; the second, three-fourths of a mile south-east of the first, is crossed by the old Sharpsburg turnpike; the third is an obscure pass behind the elevated crest, about a quarter of a mile north-west of the turnpike.

General Hill's right occupied the south-east pass, and his left held the central. The centre was posted on a narrow mountain-road connecting the right and left. The pass on the left was watched by a small cavalry force. The position of Hill was strong, as it was only assailable by the pike on the left and the road on the right and along the rugged mountain-sides.

Early on the morning of the 14th, General McClellan advanced to the attack, directing his principal efforts against the south-east pass. Hill maintained his position with his usual firmness and intrepidity, and his troops exhibited the same gallantry that had characterized them on various fields.

At this time the position of the several corps of the Confederate army was the following: Jackson was at Harper's Ferry, about fifteen miles from Sharpsburg; Longstreet, at Hagerstown, a somewhat greater distance to the north of Sharpsburg; and D. H. Hill, at Boonsboro' Gap, eastward of these positions; while McClellan's whole force, with the exception of the detachment sent toward Harper's Ferry, lay east of the Gap. Had the Gap been left undefended, as it has been recently suggested it should have been, there would have been nothing to hinder McClellan from inserting his army between the two sections of the Confederate forces and attacking them in detail. The occupation of Sharpsburg by the enemy would have placed Lee in a difficult and dangerous position. Had he retired across the Potomac, as it has been suggested was his proper course to pursue, it would have been a virtual abandonment of his trains and artillery, which were then extended along the road between Hagerstown and Sharpsburg, and could have been reached by McClellan with his cavalry in an hour or two from Boonsboro'.

The battle of Boonsboro' was therefore necessary to the security of the army; and when, on the night of the 13th, Lee received information of the rapid advance of McClellan, he at once took steps for the effective reinforcement of General Hill. Longstreet's corps was put in motion for this purpose early in the morning of the 14th, and, fortunately, arrived at the Gap in time to prevent Hill's brave men from being overwhelmed by the superior numbers of the enemy.

This timely reinforcement secured the Confederate position. McClellan, finding that his efforts against the centre and right were unavailing, at length discontinued them, with the intention of renewing the conflict at a more assailable point. The contest during the morning had been severe and the loss on each side considerable. On the side of the Confederates, the chief loss fell on the brigade of Brigadier-general Garland. This brigade numbered among its slain its gallant commander, who fell while bravely opposing a fierce attack on South-east Pass.

When General Lee reached Boonsboro' with Longstreet's corps, he sent forward Colonel Long, Major Venable, and other members of his staff, to learn the condition of affairs in front. The pass on the left proved to be unoccupied, and a heavy Federal force was tending in that direction. In anticipation of an attack from this quarter, Hood's division was deployed across the turnpike and Rodes's was posted on the ridge overlooking the unoccupied pass, with Evans's brigade connecting his right with Hood's left. There was a small field in front of Evans and Hood, while Rodes was masked by the timber on the side of the mountain. About three o'clock the battle was renewed by McClellan, who with great energy directed his main attack against Rodes. This was successfully resisted until nightfall, when Rodes's troops gave way before the assault of a superior force. The possession of the ground that had been held by Rodes gave the Federals the command of the central pass, but they could not immediately avail themselves of their success, on account of the intervening darkness.

The Confederate position was now untenable, and its evacuation became necessary. The withdrawal of the rear-guard was assigned to General Rodes, the successful execution of the movement being in a great measure due to the sagacity and boldness of Major Green Peyton, adjutant-general of Rodes's division.

At ten o'clock the next morning the Confederate army was safely in position at Sharpsburg.

At Boonsboro', McClellan had displayed more than usual pertinacity in his attacks upon the Confederate position; yet these were met by the troops of Longstreet and Hill with a firmness worthy of the veterans of Manassas and the Chickahominy. Although Lee had been forced into an unexpected battle when his army was divided, he baffled McClellan in his designs by retarding him so as to gain time for the reduction of Harper's Ferry and to place himself where he could be easily joined by Jackson.

On the morning of the 15th, Harper's Ferry was surrendered, and about noon General Lee received the report of its capture. Two courses now presented themselves to the general, each of which involved results of the highest importance. He might either retire across the Potomac and form a junction, in the neighborhood of Shepherdstown, with the forces that had been employed in the reduction of Harper's Ferry, or maintain his position at Sharpsburg and give battle to a superior force. By pursuing the former course the object of the campaign would be abandoned and the hope of co-operation from Maryland for ever relinquished. The latter, although hazardous, if successful would be productive of results more than commensurate with the risk attending its execution. Having a sympathy for the Marylanders, to whom he had offered his services, and a confidence in the bravery of his troops and the strength of his position, he adopted the latter course, and prepared to receive the attack of General McClellan.

Jackson's troops were hurried from Harper's Ferry and a strong defensive position was carefully selected. It embraced the heights fringing the right bank of the Antietam east and south-east of the village of Sharpsburg and a range of hills stretching north-west to the Potomac. Lee's right and centre were protected by stone fences and ledges of rock, and his left

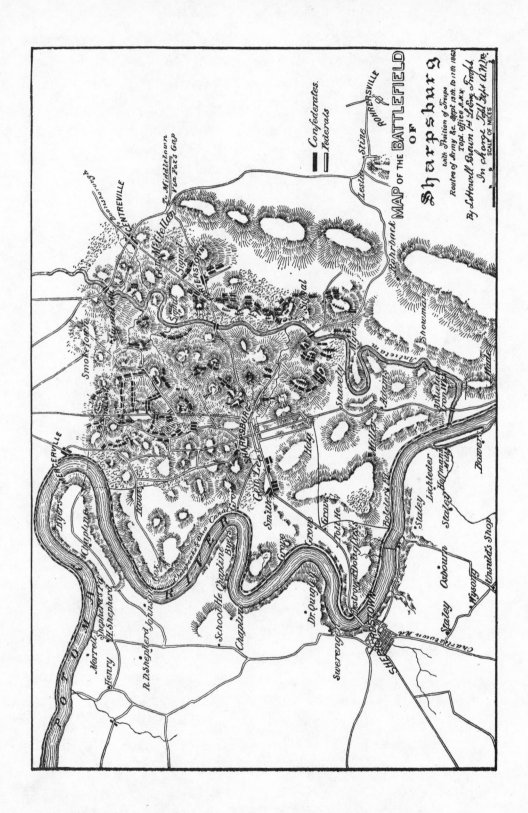

MAP OF THE BATTLEFIELD
OF
Sharpsburg
with Position of Troops
Routes of Army &c. Sept 13th to 17th 1862
TOP. office A.M.V.
By Lt Horvell Bugum 1st Lt.Eng Trofs &
In charge Topl Dep A.N.Va.
SCALE OF MILES

Confederates.
Federals

was principally covered by a wood. The right and centre were occupied by Longstreet's corps, D. H. Hill's division, and Lee's, Walton's, and Garnett's artillery, while Jackson's corps and Stuart's cavalry occupied the left. The Federal forces having been much shattered by the battle of the 14th, McClellan did not resume his advance until late on the morning of the 15th, and did not appear before Sharpsburg until afternoon.

He employed the following day chiefly in preparations for the battle. The corps of Hooker, Mansfield, Sumner, and Franklin, constituting his right, were massed opposite the Confederate left. The hills east of the Antietam which formed the centre of the Federal position were crowned by a powerful artillery, and Burnside's corps, which occupied the left, confronted the Confederate right. Porter's corps formed the reserve, while the cavalry operated on the flanks. Late in the afternoon Mansfield and Hooker crossed the Antietam opposite Longstreet's left. Some preliminary skirmishing closed the day. Both armies now lay on their arms, conscious that the next day would be marked by the most desperate battle that had yet been witnessed in the country. The Confederates, who had never known defeat, confident in themselves, confident in the strength of their position, and confident in their glorious leader, although less in numbers than their opponents by more than one-half, never doubted that victory would again rest on their tattered banners. The Federals, on their part, burning to obliterate the marks of defeat they had lately borne, were impatient for the approaching struggle. The Federal force present on the field amounted to 90,000 men; that of the Confederates, including the division of A. P. Hill, then at Harper's Ferry in charge of prisoners and captured property, amounted to 40,000.

At dawn on the 17th the corps of Mansfield and Hooker advanced to the attack; they were met by the divisions of Anderson and Hood with their usual vigor. Being greatly outnumbered, these divisions were reinforced by Evans's brigade and the division of D. H. Hill. The contest continued close and determined for more than an hour, when the Federals began to give way. They were hotly pressed. Hooker was wounded,

Mansfield was killed, and their corps were irretrievably shattered when relieved by the fresh corps of Sumner and Franklin. The Confederates, who had advanced more than a mile, were gradually borne back to their original position. McClellan now directed his chief attack upon Lee's left, with the hope of forcing it back, so that he might penetrate between it and the river and take the Confederate position in reverse. This attack was received by Jackson's corps with intrepidity. The veterans under Early, Trimble, Lawton, and Starke gallantly held their ground against large odds. At an opportune moment the Confederate line was reinforced by the division of McLaws and Walker. The entire Confederate force, except D. R. Jones's division, on the right, was now engaged.

The roar of musketry and the thunder of artillery proclaimed the deadly conflict that raged. These deafening sounds of battle continued until about twelve o'clock, when they began to abate, and about one they ceased. The Federals had been repulsed at every point, and four corps were so much broken by loss and fatigue that they were unable to renew the contest.

After the battle had concluded on the left General Burnside prepared to assault the Confederate right with 20,000 fresh troops. He had remained inactive during the forenoon; but when the attack on the Confederate left had failed, he proceeded to force the passage of the Antietam at the bridge southeast of Sharpsburg, on the Pleasant Valley road, and at the ford below. These points were gallantly maintained by Toombs's brigade of Jones's division until about four o'clock, when they were carried. General Burnside then crossed the Antietam and formed his troops under the bluff.

At five o'clock he advanced, and, quickly dispersing the small division of D. R. Jones, gained the crest of the ridge south of the town. At that moment the division of A. P. Hill, 4500 strong, just arrived from Harper's Ferry, was on the road which traverses its western slope. Seeing the Federal line on its flank, the division faced to the right, and, taking advantage of the stone fence that bordered the road, delivered such destructive volleys that the Federals were forced to retire as suddenly as they had appeared. Sharply followed by Hill and raked by the artillery, Burnside was forced to recross the Antietam. Just as the sun disappeared in the west the last of Burnside's corps gained the eastern side. Thus closed the battle of Sharpsburg. The Federal troops fought well and did honor to their gallant leaders, but, being compelled to attack a strong position defended by men who had been justly characterized as the finest soldiers of the age, they failed to obtain the mastery of the field. The casualties on both sides were heavy; the numbers have never been accurately stated. On the side of the Federals were Mansfield killed, Major-general Hooker wounded, and a number of other distinguished officers killed or wounded; on the side of the Confederates, Brigadier-general Starke was killed and Brigadiers Lawton, Ripley, and G. B. Anderson were wounded, and a number of others were put *hors de combat.* Anderson afterward died of his wound.

Among the cases of individual gallantry, one of the most conspicuous was that of General Longstreet, with Majors Fairfax and Sorrell and Captain Latrobe of his staff, who, on observing a large Federal force approaching an unoccupied portion of his line, served with such effect two pieces of artillery that had been left without cannoneers that the Federals were arrested in their advance and speedily forced to retire beyond the range of the guns.

During the night General Lee prepared for the renewal of the battle the next day. A part of his line was withdrawn to the range of hills west of the town, which gave him a very strong and much better field than that of the previous day. He remained in his new position during the 18th, prepared for battle; but General McClellan, perceiving that his troops had been greatly disorganized by the battle of the previous day, declined resuming the attack until the arrival of 15,000 fresh troops that were hastening to his support.

Foreseeing that no important results could be achieved by a second battle with McClellan's augmented forces, and being unwilling to sacrifice unnecessarily his gallant men, Lee withdrew during the night to the south side of the Potomac, and on the 19th took a position a few miles west of Shepherdstown.

When McClellan learned, on the morning of the 19th, that the Confederate position had been evacuated, he ordered an immediate pursuit, which, however, proved unavailing, as the Confederate rear-guard was disappearing in the defile leading from the ford below Shepherdstown when the Federal advance appeared on the opposite heights. A few batteries were then put into position, and a harmless cannonade commenced, which was kept up in a desultory manner during the greater part of the day. Late in the afternoon a large detachment approached the ford, and about nightfall dislodged General Pendleton, who had been charged with its defence, and effected a crossing without serious opposition. This occurrence was reported about midnight to General Lee, who immediately despatched orders to Jackson to take steps to arrest the Federal advance. The division of A. P. Hill, moving with rapidity, reached the mouth of the defile leading to the river just as the Federal detachment was debouching from it, and attacked this force with such impetuosity that it was compelled to retire with heavy loss across the Potomac. McClellan made no further attempt to continue offensive operations for several weeks, this interval being passed in the neighborhood of Sharpsburg in resting and reorganizing his forces. This campaign, especially the battle of Sharpsburg, has been the subject of much discussion, in which the Northern writers generally claim for the Federal arms a complete victory ; but the historian of the Army of the Potomac, with greater impartiality, acknowledges Antietam (or Sharpsburg) to have been a drawn battle. This admission is corroborated by the evidence of General McClellan in his testimony before the Congressional Committee on the Conduct of the War, since he admitted that his losses on the 17th had been so heavy, and that his forces were so greatly disorganized on the morning of the 18th, that, although General Lee still maintained a defiant attitude, he was unable to resume the attack. Swinton, however, claims for the Army of the Potomac a political victory, with apparent justice ; but in reality his claim is without foundation, for Lee was politically defeated before the occurrence of a collision with McClellan by his failure to induce the Marylanders to rally in any considerable force to his standard; and even when McClellan, by accident, became aware of the disposition of his forces and his intentions, he was establishing a line of communication that would enable him to engage his opponent with no other hope of political results than such as would naturally arise from a victory, whether gained north or south of the Potomac. The severe chastisement that had been inflicted on the Army of the Potomac is evident from the long prostration it exhibited, notwithstanding the facility with which it received reinforcements and supplies.

As a relief to the tale of war and bloodshed through which this chapter has carried us, we may relate some incidents of the battle of Sharpsburg of a lighter and more personal character. Lee's position during the engagement was on a hill to the east of Sharpsburg, which gave him an oversight of the whole field. While standing here conversing with Longstreet and attended by some members of his staff, D. H. Hill rode up on an errand to the general. He was admonished to dismount, as his conspicuous appearance might draw the fire of the enemy. He declined to do so, however, as he was in great haste to deliver an important communication. A minute afterward a puff of smoke was seen to rise from a distant Federal battery, and a shell came whirling toward the group. It had been well aimed, and, though a little too low for the horseman, was in the direct line for his horse. It passed very near General Lee, who was standing by the horse's head talking with Hill, and, striking the animal's fore legs, took them both off below the knee. The poor brute fell on his knees, and remained in that position, with his back at an awkward slant, while his startled rider was making ineffectual efforts to dismount. He threw his legs in the usual manner over the cantle of the saddle, but in his haste found it impossible to get off his horse, while the ludicrous spectacle which he presented brought a roar of laughter from the persons present. "Try it the other way," suggested Longstreet. "Throw your legs over the pommel and see if you cannot get off that way." Hill obeyed the suggestion, and finally succeeded in dismounting. He was good-natured enough to take part in the merriment which his adventure had excited.   The shell, however, had not yet finished its death-dealing work.   It went on and fell into a Confederate regiment behind a hill, where it killed several men.

Another anecdote of the Sharpsburg engagement is of interest as descriptive of an instance of General Lee's losing his temper—a circumstance which happened only twice, to my knowledge, during my long acquaintance with him.   He was not wanting in temper, but was, on the contrary, a man of decided character and strong passions; yet he had such complete control of himself that few men ever knew him to deviate from his habitual calm dignity of mien.   On the occasion here alluded to Lee was riding along a little in rear of the lines, when he came across a soldier who had stolen and killed a pig, which he was surreptitiously conveying to his quarters. Positive orders having been given against pillage of every kind, this flagrant disregard of his commands threw the general into a hot passion.   Though usually greatly disinclined to capital punishment, he determined to make an example of this skulking pilferer, and ordered the man to be arrested and taken back to Jackson with directions to have him shot.   Jackson, on receiving the culprit, could not quite see the utility of his execution, when men were already scarce, and it struck him that it would answer the purpose quite as well to put the fellow in the front ranks of the army at the most threatened point and let the enemy perform the work assigned to him.   He accordingly did so, placing him where his chance of being shot was a most excellent one.   The fellow, though fond of surreptitious pork, was not wanting in courage, and behaved gallantly. He redeemed his credit by his bravery, and came through the thick of the fight unscathed.   If a commonplace witticism be not out of order here, it may be said that, though he lost his pig, he "saved his bacon."

While on the subject of Lee's self-command it may be of interest to quote some incidents from Colonel Taylor's *Four Years with General Lee* as illustrative of his strong power over his feelings even on the most trying occasions:

"Tidings reached General Lee soon after his return to Virginia (from Maryland) of the serious illness of one of his daughters, the darling of his flock. For several days apprehensions were entertained that the next intelligence would be of her death. One morning the mail was received, and the private letters were distributed, as was the custom, but no one knew whether any home-news had been received by the general. At the usual hour he summoned me to his presence to know if there were any matters of army routine upon which his judgment and action were desired. The papers containing a few such cases were presented to him; he reviewed and gave his orders in regard to them. I then left him, but for some cause returned in a few moments, and with my accustomed freedom entered his tent without announcement or ceremony, when I was startled and shocked to see him overcome with grief, an open letter in his hands. That letter contained the sad intelligence of his daughter's death. . . . .

" His army demanded his first thought and care; to his men, to their needs, he must first attend, and then he could surrender himself to his private, personal affairs. Who can tell with what anguish of soul he endeavored to control himself and to maintain a calm exterior, and who can estimate the immense effort necessary to still the heart filled to overflowing with tenderest emotions and to give attention to the important trusts committed to him, before permitting the more selfish indulgence of private meditation, grief, and prayer? 'Duty first' was the rule of his life, and his every thought, word, and action was made to square with duty's inexorable demands."

There is another anecdote told by Colonel Taylor bearing upon the same trait of character and his consideration for the feelings of others, with which this chapter may be closed:

" He had a great dislike to reviewing army communications; this was so thoroughly appreciated by me that I would never present a paper for his action unless it was of decided importance and of a nature to demand his judgment and decision. On one occasion, when an audience had not been asked of him for several days, it became necessary to have one. The few papers requiring his action were submitted. He was not in a very pleasant humor; something irritated him, and he manifested his ill-humor by a little nervous twist or jerk of the neck and head peculiar to himself, accompanied by some harshness of manner. This was perceived by me, and I hastily concluded that my efforts to save him annoyance were not appreciated. In disposing of some cases of a vexatious character matters reached a climax; he became really worried, and, forgetting what was due to my superior, I petulantly threw the paper down at my side and gave evident signs of anger. Then, in a perfectly calm and measured tone of voice, he said, 'Colonel Taylor, when I lose my temper don't you let it make you angry.'"

Most men in his position would have dealt more severely with the petulance of a subordinate, and not have administered this quiet and considerate rebuke by indicating that the loss of temper was not directed toward him and gave him no warrant for a display of anger.

CHAPTER XIII.

FREDERICKSBURG.

AFTER remaining a few days in the neighborhood of Shepherdstown, General Lee gradually withdrew to a position between Bunker Hill and Winchester. Notwithstanding he had failed, from accidental causes, to accomplish the chief object of the invasion of Maryland, the expedition was not wholly without beneficial results, since it relieved Virginia from the presence of the enemy and gave her an opportunity to recover in a measure from the exhausting effect of war, while the spirit and confidence of the troops were not impaired by the unexpected termination of the campaign.

In order to explain the achievements of this campaign, I shall here insert General Lee's address to his troops a few days after its termination:

"HEADQUARTERS ARMY OF NORTHERN VIRGINIA,
October 2, 1862.

"In reviewing the achievements of the army during the present campaign, the commanding general cannot withhold the expression of his admiration of the indomitable courage it has displayed in battle and its cheerful endurance of privation and hardships on the march.

"Since your great victories around Richmond you have defeated the enemy at Cedar Mountain, expelled him from the Rappahannock, and after a conflict of three days utterly repulsed him on the plains of Manassas and forced him to take shelter within the fortifications around his capital.   Without halting for repose, you crossed the Potomac, stormed the heights of Harper's Ferry, made prisoners of more than 11,600 men, and captured upward of seventy pieces of artillery, all their small-arms, and other munitions of war.   While one corps of the army was thus engaged the other ensured its success by arresting at Boonsboro' the combined armies of the enemy, advancing under their favorite general to the relief of their beleaguered comrades.

"On the field of Sharpsburg, with less than one-third his numbers, you resisted from daylight until dark the whole army of the enemy, and repulsed every attack along his entire front of more than four miles in extent.

"The whole of the following day you stood prepared to resume the conflict on the same ground, and retired next morning without molestation across the Potomac.

"Two attempts subsequently made by the enemy to follow you across the river have resulted in his complete discomfiture and his being driven back with loss.   Achievements such as these demanded much valor and patriotism.   History records fewer examples of greater fortitude and endurance than this army has exhibited, and I am commissioned by the President to thank you in the name of the Confederate States for the undying fame you have won for their arms.

"Much as you have done, much more remains to be accomplished.   The enemy again threatens us with invasion, and to your tried valor and patriotism the country looks with confidence for deliverance and safety.   Your past exploits give assurance that this confidence is not misplaced.
                    "R. E. LEE,
                "*General Commanding.*"

The inactivity of General McClellan allowed General Lee several weeks of uninterrupted repose.   During that interval the guardianship of the Potomac was confided to the cavalry and horse-artillery.   While thus employed General Stuart made a swoop into Pennsylvania, captured a thousand horses, and after making the entire circuit of the Federal army recrossed the Potomac with only the loss of three missing and three wounded. This achievement drew from Mr. Lincoln a very sarcastic criticism on his own cavalry, which, however, was not wholly merited, for it was no sooner learned that Stuart had crossed the border than Pleasonton made the most rapid pursuit that was ever performed by the Federal cavalry; but he arrived just in time to see the prey safe beyond the Potomac.

Throughout the late campaign the duty of selecting a place for headquarters usually devolved upon the writer. The general would say, "Colonel Long has a good eye for locality: let him find a place for the camp." It was not always so easy to find a desirable situation, but, as the general was easily satisfied, the difficulties of the task were greatly lightened. Only once, to my recollection, did he object to the selection made for headquarters; this was on reaching the neighborhood of Winchester. The army had preceded the general and taken possession of every desirable camping-place. After a long and fatiguing search a farm-house was discovered, surrounded by a large shady yard. The occupants of the house with great satisfaction gave permission for the establishment of General Lee not only in the yard, but insisted on his occupying a part of the house. Everything being satisfactorily settled, the wagons were ordered up, but just as their unloading began the general rode up and flatly refused to occupy either yard or house. No one expected him to violate his custom by occupying the house, but it was thought he would not object to a temporary occupation of the yard. Being vexed at having to look for another place for headquarters, I ordered the wagons into a field almost entirely covered with massive stones. The boulders were so large and thick that it was difficult to find space for the tents. The only redeeming feature the location possessed was a small stream of good water. When the tents were pitched, the general looked around with a smile of satisfaction, and said, "This is better than the yard. We will not now disturb those good people."

While occupying this camp we were visited by several distinguished British officers—among them, Colonel Garnet Wolseley, who has since become prominent in history. Subsequently, one of the number published the following account of General Lee and his surroundings:

"In visiting the headquarters of the Confederate generals, but particularly those of General Lee, any one accustomed to see European armies in the field, cannot fail to be struck with the great absence of all the pomp and circumstance of war in and around their encampments.

"Lee's headquarters consisted of about seven or eight pole-tents, pitched, with their backs to a stake-fence, upon a piece of ground so rocky that it was unpleasant to ride over it, its only recommendation being a little stream of good water which flowed close by the general's tent. In front of the tents were some three or four army-wagons, drawn up without any regularity, and a number of horses turned loose about the field. The servants—who were, of course, slaves—and the mounted soldiers called couriers, who always accompany each general of division in the field, were unprovided with tents, and slept in or under the wagons. Wagons, tents, and some of the horses were marked 'U. S.,' showing that part of that huge debt in the North has gone to furnishing even the Confederate generals with camp-equipments. No guard or sentries were to be seen in the vicinity, no crowd of aides-de-camp loitering about, making themselves agreeable to visitors and endeavoring to save their generals from receiving those who had no particular business. A large farm-house stands close by, which in any other army would have been the general's residence *pro tem.;* but, as no liberties are allowed to be taken with personal property in Lee's army, he is particular in setting a good example himself. His staff are crowded together, two or three in a tent; none are allowed to carry more baggage than a small box each, and his own kit is but very little larger. Every one who approaches him does so with marked respect, although there is none of that bowing and flourishing of forage-caps which occurs in the presence of European generals; and, while all honor him and place implicit faith in his courage and ability, those with whom he is most intimate feel for him the affection of sons to a father. Old General Scott was correct in saying that when Lee joined the Southern cause it was worth as much as the accession of 20,000 men to the 'rebels.' Since then every injury that it was possible to inflict the Northerners have heaped upon him. Notwithstanding all these personal losses, however, when speaking of the Yankees he neither evinced any bitterness of feeling nor gave utterance to a single violent expression, but alluded to many of his former friends and companions among them in the kindest terms. He spoke as a man proud of the victories won by his country and confident of ultimate success under the blessing of the Almighty, whom he glorified for past successes, and whose aid he invoked for all future operations.''

Notwithstanding the ruggedness of this encampment, it proved unusually lively. Besides the foreign friends, we had numerous visitors from the army, also ladies and gentlemen from Winchester and the neighborhood, all of whom had some remark to make upon the rocky situation of our camp. This the general seemed to enjoy, as it gave him an opportunity of making a jest at the expense of Colonel Long, whom he accused of having set him down there among the rocks in revenge for his refusing to occupy the yard. Although there were no habitual drinkers on the general's staff, an occasional demijohn would find its way to headquarters. While at this place one of the officers received a present of a jug of fine old rye. Soon after its advent General J. E. B. Stuart, with Sweeney and his banjo, arrived—not on account, however, of the jug, but, as was his wont, to give us a serenade. The bright camp-fire was surrounded by a merry party, and a lively concert commenced. After a while the general came out, and, observing the jug perched on a boulder, asked with a merry smile, ''Gentlemen, am I to thank General Stuart or the jug for this fine music?''

By this time the men had come to know their leader. The brilliant campaigns through which he had led them had inspired them with love and confidence, and whenever he appeared among them his approach was announced by ''Here comes Mars' Robert!'' and he would be immediately saluted with the well-known Confederate yell, which called forth in other quarters the exclamation, ''There goes Mars' Robert— ole Jackson, or an ole hare.''

At this time a strong religious sentiment prevailed in the army, and every evening from the various camps might be heard the sound of devotional exercises. General Lee encouraged this sentiment by attending services whenever circumstances permitted.

While indulging in the sweets of repose the army was gradually increased, principally by the return of absentees, until the middle of October, when its effective strength amounted to about 60,000 men. Its efficiency had been much improved by the activity and energy of Colonel Corley, chief quartermaster, and Colonel Cole, chief commissary. These officers displayed great ability in furnishing the necessary requirements of the army in the field. Colonels Chilton, Murray, Henry Peyton, Captains Mason and Latham, of the adjutant- and inspector-general's department, contributed greatly to its high state of discipline, and General Lee made in his report honorable mention of his personal staff.

The cavalry, at this time between 3000 and 4000 strong, was distinguished as the finest corps of modern cavalry, and Stuart had justly become celebrated as a cavalry commander. His brigadiers, the two Lees, W. E. Jones, Robertson, Munford, Hampton, Lomax, and a host of others of less rank, were officers who would have graced the brightest days of chivalry, and the rank and file were composed of the best material of the South.

Stuart was unequalled as an outpost officer. Throughout a line of fifty miles his eye and hand were everywhere present; his pickets and scouts never slept; the movements of the enemy were immediately discovered, and promptly reported to the commander-in-chief.

When McClellan crossed the Potomac, Stuart withdrew his cavalry to a line embracing Bunker's Hill and Smithfield, extending on the right to the Shenandoah and on the left to the eastern base of North Mountain. The connection between this line of outposts and that east of the Blue Ridge was by the way of Snicker's Gap and Berryville. The Federal army by the 15th of October had been concentrated in the neighborhood of Harper's Ferry. The opposing armies were now only

separated by their outposts, between which spirited encoun
ters frequently occurred.

The repose of a month had greatly improved in every way
the Confederate army; it had reached a high state of efficiency,
and General Lee was fully prepared to meet General McClellan
whenever he might think fit to advance to attack him in his
position before Winchester. When McClellan resumed active
operations two plans presented themselves. One was to bring
Lee to an engagement in the Shenandoah Valley; the other,
to pass south of the Blue Ridge into Loudoun, Fauquier, and
Culpeper, thus penetrating between the Confederate army and
Richmond, its base of supplies. The first presented the disadvantage of attacking a formidable opponent in position, while
retreat was hazardous by the proximity of two large and difficult rivers, the Shenandoah and Potomac. The other offered
a wider scope for the operations of large armies, and in case of
defeat, as on previous occasions, the protection of the defences
about Washington could easily be gained. McClellan adopted
the latter plan, and on the 23d of October commenced the passage of the Potomac south of Harper's Ferry, and by the 1st
of November his army had entered Loudoun and was slowly extending into Fauquier. He occupied the line of the Manassas
Gap Railroad on the 5th, and at the same time the Federal outposts were extended to the neighborhood of Warrenton. When
McClellan had crossed the Potomac and the direction of his
advance was ascertained, Lee moved Longstreet's corps and
the greater part of the cavalry to a position near Culpeper
Court-house and established his outposts along the right
bank of the Rappahannock.

Jackson's corps was detained in the Valley until the Federal
plans should be more fully developed. The delay that followed
the battle of Sharpsburg and the deliberate manner in which
McClellan resumed active operations did not accord with the
impetuous character of the authorities of Washington, and were
productive of a voluminous correspondence with Mr. Lincoln
and General Halleck, in which the President and commander-
in-chief exhibited marked disapprobation, which culminated
in the removal of McClellan. That this step was injudicious

at that time was clearly demonstrated by the subsequent disasters that befell .the army.

General McClellan had been in command of the Army of the Potomac more than a year. He had been assigned to its command when it was broken and dispirited by defeat, and had brought it up to a high state of efficiency. In the Peninsular campaign, in the spring of 1862, he accomplished more in two months than any subsequent commander of the Army of the Potomac did in a much greater period. The results of the capture of Yorktown and Norfolk, the destruction of the Merrimac, and the possession of the York and the James rivers were not at the time fully appreciated. They, however, ultimately led to the fall of Richmond and the defeat and capture of the Army of Northern Virginia, and, had not his plans been frustrated by the Federal Executive by withholding at the important moment the co-operation of McDowell's corps of 40,000 men, then at Fredericksburg, this series of operations might have been followed by the capture of Richmond and stamped as one of the most brilliant campaigns on record. After a successful campaign, having reorganized and raised his army in point of numbers and equipment to the highest state of military excellence, and having just entered upon a new field of operation with every element of success that the foresight of a commander could give, General McClellan was relieved from command and placed in retirement. The impression created at the time was that this step was a military necessity, but the course afterward displayed by the radical party would naturally lead to the inference that the removal of McClellan originated from political jealousy. His great personal popularity and his influence with the Democratic party, enhanced by military fame, would have made him a formidable political aspirant.

A great diversity of opinion exists as to the military capacity of McClellan, and he has been both unduly praised and censured by his friends and foes. That his slowness and caution were elements on which the opposing general might safely count must be admitted, but that he had a high degree of military ability cannot be denied. His skill in planning movements was certainly admirable, but their effect was in more than one instance lost by over-slowness in their execution. In this connection it will be of interest to give General Lee's own opinion concerning McClellan's ability, as related by a relative of the general, who had it from her father, an old gentleman of eighty years:

"One thing I remember hearing him say. He asked General Lee which in his opinion was the ablest of the Union generals; to which the latter answered, bringing his hand down on the table with an emphatic energy, 'McClellan, by all odds!'"

This opinion, however, could but have referred to his skill as a tactician, as it is unquestionable that Lee availed himself of McClellan's over-caution and essayed perilous movements which he could not have safely ventured in the presence of a more active opponent.

It was with surprise that the Confederate officers who knew the distinguished merit of Sumner, Sedgwick, Meade, and others learned that Burnside had been elevated above them, and General Burnside himself with diffidence accepted the high honor that had been conferred upon him. Mr. Lincoln, accompanied by General Halleck, visited the headquarters of the army near Warrenton, where a plan of operations was adopted. A rapid advance upon Richmond by the way of Fredericksburg was advised. It was supposed from the position of General Lee's forces that by gaining a march or two upon him Richmond might be reached and captured before that general could relieve it. All that prevented the immediate execution of this plan was the want of a pontoon-train, which was necessary for the passage of the Rappahannock.

Having arranged to his satisfaction with General Halleck and Mr. Lincoln in regard to a prompt compliance with his requisitions for pontoons and supplies for the army, General Burnside, about the 15th of November, put the Army of the Potomac in motion, and on the 17th, Sumner's corps reached Fredericksburg. This energetic officer would probably have immediately crossed the Rappahannock by the fords above the town, and thus have saved much delay. He was, however, restrained by Burnside, who directed him to await the arrival of the pontoons. At this time the river in the neighborhood of Fredericksburg was held simply by a small picket-force, and could have been forded without much difficulty. General Lee, having penetrated the designs of the Federal commander, prepared to oppose them. About the 18th he sent reinforcements to Fredericksburg with instructions to retard, as far as practicable, the Federal forces in the passage of the Rappahannock, and at the same time he sent orders to Jackson to join him as speedily as possible.

Upon the supposition that Burnside would cross the Rappahannock before he could form a junction of his forces, Lee proposed to take a position behind the North Anna with part of Longstreet's corps, the force then about Richmond, and such other troops as might be drawn from other points, while, with Jackson's and the remainder of Longstreet's corps united, he moved in such a manner as might enable him to fall upon the flank and rear of the Federal army when it attempted the passage of that river. But when it was ascertained that Burnside was prevented from immediately crossing the Rappahannock by a delay in the arrival of his pontoons, Lee determined to move Longstreet's corps immediately to Fredericksburg and take possession of the heights opposite those occupied by the Federal force, as these heights afforded a stronger defensive line than the North Anna.

In execution of this determination Longstreet's corps left the vicinity of Culpeper Court-house on the 24th, crossed the Rapidan at Raccoon Ford, and, proceeding by the Wilderness road, reached Fredericksburg the next day. In the mean time, Jackson was rapidly approaching from the Valley. The Army of the Potomac had been a week before Fredericksburg and the pontoons had not yet arrived, and what might have been effected a few days before without opposition could now be accomplished only by force. Even after passing the river Burnside would be obliged to remove from his path a formidable opponent before he could continue his advance upon the city of Richmond.

On arriving at Fredericksburg, General Lee caused the heights south of the river to be occupied by artillery and in-

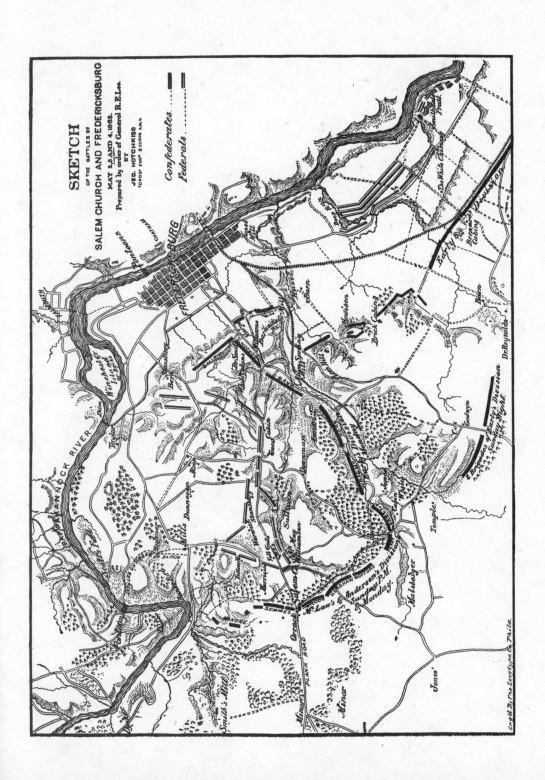

SKETCH
OF THE BATTLES OF
SALEM CHURCH AND FREDERICKSBURG
MAY 3,3,AND 4,1863.
Prepared by order of General R.E.Lee.
BY
JED. HOTCHKISS
TOPOG'. ENG'R CORPS A.N.V.

Confederates . . . .
Federals . . . .

fantry from Banks's Ford, four miles above, to the Massaponax, five miles below the city, while the cavalry extended up the river beyond the United States Ford and down as far as Port Royal. The prominent points were crowned with artillery covered by epaulments, and in the intervals were constructed breastworks for the protection of infantry. The heights closely fringe the river from Banks's Ford to Falmouth; thence they recede, leaving a low ground, which gradually increases in width to about two miles; then the hills again abut upon the river a little below the mouth of the Massaponax, and, extending nearly parallel to that stream, abruptly terminate in broad, low grounds. These low grounds are traversed by the main road to Bowling Green and are intersected by several small streams. The most important of these is Deep Run, which empties into the Rappahannock a little more than a mile above the mouth of the Massaponax. That portion of the road embraced between Deep Run and the Massaponax is enclosed by embankments sufficiently high and thick to afford good covers for troops. We have here endeavored to describe some of the principal features of the Confederate position at Fredericksburg, that the plan of battle may be more clearly understood.

Jackson's corps on its arrival at the end of November was posted a few miles south of the Massaponax, in the neighborhood of Guinea Station on the Richmond and Fredericksburg Railroad. From this position he could easily support Longstreet, or, in case Burnside attempted a passage of the Rappahannock between the Massaponax and Port Royal, he would be ready to intercept him. After much delay the pontoon-train reached Fredericksburg. But then the position of Lee presented a formidable obstacle to the passage of the river at that point.

General Burnside thereupon caused careful reconnoissances to be made both above and below, with the view of finding a more favorable point for crossing. But he invariably found wherever he appeared the forces of General Lee ready to oppose him. Finding no part of the river more suitable or less guarded than that about Fredericksburg, Burnside determined to effect a crossing at that place. Two points were selected—one opposite the town, and the other two miles below, near the mouth of Deep Run—and early on the morning of the 11th of December the work was begun under cover of a dense fog. A bridge was laid at the mouth of Deep Run, and Franklin's grand division passed over without opposition. In front of Fredericksburg, however, the case was different. The gallant Barksdale with his brigade of Mississippians, to whom the defence of the town had been assigned, repelled every attempt to construct the bridges until the afternoon, when the powerful artillery of the Federal army was massed and a cannonade from one hundred and eighty guns was opened upon the devoted town, under cover of which troops crossed in boats under the direction of General Hunt, chief of artillery. Then Barksdale, fighting, retired step by step until he gained the cover of the road embankment at the foot of Marye's Heights, which he held until relieved by fresh troops. Burnside having developed his plan of attack, Lee concentrated his forces preparatory for battle. His right rested on the Massaponax, and his left on the Rappahannock at the dam in the vicinity of Falmouth. Jackson's corps, in three lines, occupied the space between the Massaponax and Deep Run, while Longstreet's corps, with artillery, occupied the remainder of the position. The flanks were covered by Stuart's cavalry and horse artillery. It was here for the first time that the Confederate artillery was systematically massed for battle. On his arrival at Fredericksburg, General Lee assigned to Colonel Long the duty of verifying and selecting positions for the artillery, in which he was assisted by Majors Venable and Talcott and Captain Sam Johnson. On the day of battle two hundred pieces of artillery were in position, and so arranged that at least fifty pieces could be brought to bear on any threatened point, and on Fredericksburg and Deep Run, the points of attack, a hundred guns could be concentrated. The artillery on Longstreet's front was commanded by Colonels Alexander, Walton, and Cabell, and that on Jackson's by Colonels Brown and Walker. The horse artillery was commanded by Major Pelham. These officers on all occasions served with marked ability. General Pendleton, chief of artillery, exercised special control of the reserve artillery.

As Jackson's corps had been extended some distance down the Rappahannock, it was not until the night of the 11th that its concentration was completed. On the morning of the 12th of December, General Lee's entire force was in position, prepared to receive the Federal attack. The strength of the opposing armies, as on previous occasions, was disproportionate. The effective strength of the Army of Northern Virginia was about 60,000, of which about 52,000 were infantry, 4000 artillery with 250 guns, and the cavalry composed the remainder. That of the Army of the Potomac exceeded 100,000 men and 300 pieces of artillery. 90,000 men had crossed the river—40,000 of Sumner's grand division at Fredericksburg, and Franklin's grand division of 50,000 men at Deep Run. From this disposition of forces it was apparent that General Burnside designed a simultaneous attack upon the Confederate right and centre. Jackson's first line, composed of two brigades of A. P. Hill's division, held the railroad; a second line, consisting of artillery and the other brigades of Hill's division, occupied the heights immediately overlooking the railroad; and the reserves, commanded by D. H. Hill, were in convenient supporting-distance. In the centre the most conspicuous feature was Marye's Heights, behind the town of Fredericksburg and separated from it by an open space of several hundreds yards in width. The telegraph road passing between the base of the heights and a strong embankment was occupied by two brigades—Cobb's and Kershaw's of Longstreet's corps —while the crest was crowned by a powerful artillery covered by a continuous line of earthworks. A reserve of two brigades, commanded by Brigadier-general Ransom, occupied the reverse slope of the heights. [These troops did good service during the battle.] On the hills behind were grouped batteries so disposed that the heights in front could be raked with shot and shell in case they were carried by the Federals.

On the morning of the 13th of December, as the fog slowly lifted, a scene was unfolded which in point of grandeur has seldom been witnessed. The Stafford Heights, from Falmouth to the Massaponax, were crowned with thickly-grouped batteries of artillery, while the shores of the Rappahannock were cov-

ered with dark masses of troops in battle array. Opposite the
Confederate right the attacking force, in two lines, began to
advance. Simultaneously the heights were wreathed in smoke
and the thunder of artillery announced the commencement of
battle. When the attacking column had become disengaged
from the embankments of the river-road, Stuart's horse artillery on the right and the artillery of Jackson's corps in front
opened a destructive fire, which checked it for a brief space,
until its own batteries could be placed in position to occupy
the opposing artillery. It then moved steadily onward, and
quickly dislodged the first Confederate line from the railroad,
and disappeared in the wood that concealed the greater part
of the second line. A deadly conflict ensued, which, although
hidden by the forest, was proclaimed by the terrific clash of
musketry. Very soon the troops that had advanced so gallantly were seen to retire. At first a straggling few and then
large masses came rushing out, followed by long lines of gray
veterans, who dealt death at every step. General Meade, from
the want of support after his gallant achievement, was compelled to witness the present deplorable condition of his corps.
Forty thousand of Franklin's grand division, remaining idly
by, had beheld the defeat of their brave comrades without extending a helping hand. This apathy of Franklin was at the
time regarded by the Confederates as remarkable.

During the attack on the right preparations were in progress
to assail the Confederate centre. Dense masses of troops, which
had been previously concentrated in and about Fredericksburg,
were now formed in columns of attack to be led against Marye's
Heights. About noon the attack commenced. Column after
column advanced to the assault, to be hurled back with terrible
slaughter. Attack after attack was hopelessly renewed until
the stoutest heart quailed at the dreadful carnage that ensued.
Seeing his repeated efforts unavailing, General Burnside ordered a discontinuance of the conflict. The Confederates on the
next day expected the battle to be renewed with greater vigor
than had been displayed on the day before, but the Federals
maintained a sullen silence, and at night recrossed the Rappahannock. The next morning the spectator could hardly be-

lieve his senses on beholding the great Federal army that had on the day previous lined the southern shore of the Rappahannock now covering the heights of Stafford, bereft of that martial spirit it had exhibited a few days before. The dispirited condition of the Federal army was not so much the consequence of losses in battle as the effect of the want of co-operation and the fruitless results of misdirected valor.

The appointment of General Burnside to the command of the Army of the Potomac had proved a mistake—more, however, from the combination of circumstances against him than from lack of conduct on his part. His successes in North Carolina had given him prominence, while his soldierly bearing and fine appearance evidently had their influence with Mr. Lincoln in the selection of him as commander-in-chief of the Army of the Potomac, while neglecting the superior claims of several others, two of whom—Generals Hooker and Franklin—could never forget their sense of superiority sufficiently to render him cordial co-operation. Bourrienne gives us a maxim of Bonaparte that "two great generals in the same army are sure to make a bad one." This maxim particularly applied in the present instance to the Army of the Potomac, where its truth was fully verified.

The losses sustained, as stated by General Burnside, amounted to about 10,000, among whom was General Bayard, a young officer of great merit, whose loss was sincerely felt in the army as well as by a large circle of acquaintances. The Confederate loss was numerically much less than that sustained by the enemy. The Confederates, however, numbered among their slain Brigadier-generals Gregg and Cobb, and among their mortally wounded Colonel Coleman of the artillery. The fall of these noble and gallant spirits was deeply deplored by the army.

In preparation for this battle General Lee had established his field headquarters on a spur of the ridge on which he had located his line of battle. From this position he had a commanding view of the adjacent valley, the Rappahannock from Fredericksburg to Massaponax, and the Stafford Heights beyond. This spur has since been known as Lee's Hill. On the day of battle Longstreet had his headquarters at the same place, so that Lee was able to keep his hand on the rein of his "old war-horse" and to direct him where to apply his strength.

After the battle of Fredericksburg, General Lee retained his headquarters, established previous to the battle, at a point on the road midway between Fredericksburg and Hamilton Crossing, selected on account of its accessibility. Although there was a vacant house near which he could have occupied, he preferred, as in the instance we have recently given, to remain in camp, thus giving an example of endurance of hardship that might prove useful to his troops. The headquarters did not present a very imposing appearance. It consisted of four or five wall tents and three or four common tents, situated on the edge of an old pine field, and not far from a fine grove of forest trees, from which was obtained an abundant supply of excellent wood, while the branches of the old field-pine served to fortify the tents against the cold of winter and to make shelter for the horses. Though outwardly the winter quarters presented rather a dismal aspect, yet within cheerfulness prevailed. Notwithstanding the responsibility of his position and the difficulties that surrounded him, General Lee usually maintained a cheerful mien toward his staff, and at times indulged his humor for a practical joke in a manner which would have surprised an outsider who saw only the grave and dignified side of his character. As a companion-piece to the demijohn story previously told, we may give another in which General Lee was the active agent. On one occasion a demijohn was observed to be carried into his tent, which excited in the minds of those who beheld it visions of good wine or brandy. (The general well knew that several of his staff enjoyed a glass of wine, or even something stronger.) About twelve o'clock he walked out of his tent, and with a twinkle in his eye remarked, "Perhaps you gentlemen would like a glass of something?" All assenting, he directed Bryan, the steward of the mess, to carry the demijohn to the mess-tent and arrange cups for the gentlemen. They followed him with pleasant anticipations of the unexpected treat. The general ordered the cork to be drawn and the cups filled. The disappointment of the expectants and Lee's enjoyment may be better imagined than described when the contents proved to be buttermilk. On another occasion he was much amused at the dissatisfaction expressed one morning at breakfast by a member of his staff at the tough biscuits, and at another's remarking, "You ought not to mind that; they will stick by you all the longer." It was a time when great scarcity of provisions prevailed throughout the army, and all were glad to get even a little fried bacon and tough biscuits, with cold water for a beverage: sugar and coffee were unknown luxuries.

We were frequently visited by distinguished personages from Richmond and elsewhere. Among those deserving of especial mention were Colonel Freemantle of the British army and Captain Scheibert of the Prussian engineers. Scheibert remained with us for some time; he was present at the battle of Chancellorsville, and accompanied us to Gettysburg, where Colonel Freemantle was also present. Both of these officers were highly esteemed at headquarters.

Having for some time been reduced to very meagre fare, we were rejoiced to receive a present of a lot of chickens. One of the hens so distinguished herself as to be worthy of a place in history. Bryan, the steward of General Lee's mess, having discovered that she daily contributed an egg, spared her life. She proved to be a very discriminating hen, for she selected the general's tent to make her daily deposit. Instinct seemed to teach her that he was fond of fowls and domestic animals. Every day she would walk to and fro in front of his tent, and when all was quiet walk in, find a place under his bed, and deposit her egg; then walk out with a gratified cackle. Appreciating her partiality for him, he would leave his tent-door open for her to come in. This she kept up daily for weeks, Bryan always securing her contributions for the general's breakfast. She chose a roosting-place in the baggage-wagon, and on breaking up camp to meet Hooker at Chancellorsville, Bryan found room in the wagon for the hen. During the battle she seemed too much disturbed to lay, but as soon as the engagement was over she fell at once into her regular routine. She accompanied the army to Gettysburg. One night, when preparing for retreat, with the wagon loaded and everything ready, the question was raised, "Where is the hen?" By that time everybody knew her and took an interest in her; search was made in every direction, even General Lee joining in it. She was found at last perched on the wagon, where she had taken her place of her own accord. She accompanied the army in all its marches and countermarches for more than a year, and finally came to rather an unsentimental end. In the winter of 1864, General Lee's headquarters was near Orange Court-house. The hen had become rather fat and lazy, and on one occasion, when the general had a distinguished visitor to dine with him, Bryan, finding it extremely difficult to procure material for a dinner, very inhumanly killed the hen, unknown to any of the staff. At the dinner the general was very much surprised to see so fine a fowl; all enjoyed it, not dreaming of the great sacrifice made upon the altar of hospitality. When she was missed and inquiry made, Bryan had to acknowledge that he had killed her in order to provide something for the gentlemen's dinner.

Several highly interesting letters written by General Lee to his wife and daughters at the period considered in the present chapter have been kindly handed to the writer with permission to publish them. As they possess both a personal and public significance, with some amusing comments upon army matters, he takes pleasure in laying them before the reader. General Lee's devotion to his family, his religious faith, and his sense of humor are all here strongly displayed. No better introduction can be offered than a sentence from a letter written by Miss Mildred Lee in reference to these letters: In them "one has glimpses of a great war raging mercilessly, while the chief actor sits down, to the sound of shot and cannon, and pours out his heart in affection to his 'little daughters.'"

From a letter to his daughter Mildred, written on Christmas, 1862, we make the following extract:

"I cannot tell you how I long to see you when a little quiet occurs. My thoughts revert to you, your sisters and mother; my heart aches for our reunion. Your brothers I see occasionally. This morning Fitzhugh rode by with his young aide-de-camp (Rob) at the head of his brigade, on his way up the Rappahannock. You must study hard, gain knowledge, and learn your duty to God and your neighbor: that is the great object of life. I have no news, confined constantly to camp and my thoughts occupied with its necessities and duties. I am, however, happy in the knowledge that General Burnside and his army will not eat their promised Xmas dinner in Richmond to-day."

On the succeeding day he writes as follows to his daughter Agnes:

".CAMP FREDERICKSBURG, 26th December, 1862.

"MY PRECIOUS LITTLE AGNES: I have not heard of you for a long time. I wish you were with me, for, always solitary, I am sometimes weary, and long for the reunion of my family once again. But I will not speak of myself, but of you. . . . . I have only seen the ladies in this vicinity when flying from the enemy, and it caused me acute grief to witness their exposure and suffering. But a more noble spirit was never displayed anywhere. The faces of old and young were wreathed with smiles and glowed with happiness at their sacrifices for the good of their country. Many have lost *everything*. What the fire and shells of the enemy spared their pillagers destroyed. But God will shelter them, I know. So much heroism will not be unregarded. I can only hold oral communication with your sister, and have forbidden the scouts to bring any writing, and have taken back some that I had given them for her. If caught it would compromise them. They only convey messages. I learn in that way she is well. . . . .

"Your devoted father,

"R. E. LEE.

"To AGNES LEE."

We add two other letters, one written to his daughter Agnes, and one to Mrs. Lee:

"CAMP FREDERICKSBURG, 6th February, 1863.

"TO AGNES LEE: I read yesterday, my precious daughter, your letter, and grieved very much when last in Richmond at not seeing you. My movements are so uncertain that I cannot be relied on for anything. The only place I am to be found is in camp, and I am so cross now that I am not worth seeing anywhere. Here you will have to take me with the three stools— the snow, the rain, and the mud. The storm of the last twenty-four hours has added to our stock of all, and we are now in a floating condition. But the sun and wind will carry all off in time, and then we shall appreciate our relief. Our horses and mules suffer the most. They have to bear the cold and rain, tug through the mud, and suffer all the time with hunger. The roads are wretched, almost impassable. I heard of Mag lately. One of our scouts brought me a card of Margaret Stuart's, with a pair of gauntlets directed to 'Cousin Robert.' . . . . I have no news. General Hooker is obliged to do something: I do not know what it will be. He is playing the Chinese game, trying what frightening will do. He runs out his guns, starts his wagons and troops up and down the river, and creates an excitement generally. Our men look on in wonder, give a cheer, and all again subsides *in statu quo ante bellum.* I wish you were here with me to-day. You would have to sit by this little stove, look out at the rain, and keep yourself dry. But here come, in all their wet, the adjutant-generals with the papers. I must stop and go to work. See how kind God is: we have plenty to do in good weather and bad. . . . .

"Your devoted father,

"R. E. LEE."

Extract from Letter to Mrs. Lee.

"CAMP FREDERICKSBURG, 23d February, 1863.

"The weather now is very hard upon our poor bushmen. This morning the whole country is covered with a mantle of snow fully a foot deep. It was nearly up to my knees as I stepped out this morning, and our poor horses were enveloped. We have dug them out and opened our avenues a little, but it will be terrible and the roads impassable. No cars from Richmond yesterday. I fear our short rations for man and horse will have to be curtailed. Our enemies have their troubles too. They are very strong immediately in front, but have withdrawn their troops above and below us back toward Acquia Creek. I owe Mr. F. J. Hooker no thanks for keeping me here. He ought to have made up his mind long ago what to do.—*24th.* The cars have arrived, and brought me a young French officer full of vivacity, and ardent for service with me. I think the appearance of things will cool him. If they do not, the night will, for he brought no blankets.

"R. E. LEE."

CHAPTER XIV.

CHANCELLORSVILLE.

Conscript Act passed.—Deficiency of Army Stores.—Lee's Position.—Hooker succeeds Burnside.—Federal Advance.—Description of Chancellorsville.—Lee's Movements. —The Federals Driven Back.—Last Interview of Lee and Jackson.—The Flank Movement.—The Federal Defeat.—Jackson Wounded.—The Battle of the 3d.— Hooker Withdraws.—Sedgwick's Advance.—He is Defeated and Recrosses the River.—Results of the Battle.—Life and Character of Jackson.—Reorganization of the Army.—Financial Difficulties of the Government.

THE Army of Northern Virginia in the winter of 1862–63 began to feel seriously the want of judicious legislation. There had neither been formed an adequate plan for recruiting the army, nor had a reliable financial system been adopted. When the country was full of enthusiasm the ranks of the army were filled by voluntary enlistment, but when the novelty of war disappeared and the depreciating value of the pay of the soldier was seen, this mode could no longer be relied on, and it became necessary to resort to conscription. This measure, being regarded by many as too despotic for a republic, was taken hold of with reluctance, but after much delay and fruitless discussion Congress in 1862 passed a conscript act as the only means that could be devised for the preservation of the army.

Having neglected at the beginning of the war to take advantage of the abundant resources of the country to establish a firm financial basis upon which the pecuniary demands of the country could safely rest, the Confederate legislators were obliged, in order to meet the demand upon the treasury, to resort to a system of inflation, without providing for a corresponding reflux of the fiscal tide to the treasury; consequently, each new issue was followed by a proportionate decline in the value of the currency.

Besides the want of money and men, the Army of Northern

246

Virginia was deficient in clothing, shoes, blankets, tents, provisions; in fact, everything needful was wanted except arms and ammunition. The abundant supplies with which the country teemed at the beginning of the war, instead of being collected and preserved for future use, were allowed to be dissipated, and in less than two years one of the most fruitful countries known was reduced to the condition of being barely able to afford a scanty subsistence for armies whose effective strength did not exceed 200,000 men. Besides the inclemency of the season, scant clothing, and short rations, the proximity of the Federal army required them to be always prepared for battle.

At this time the necessities of the army were greatly relieved by voluntary contributions from patriotic citizens throughout the country. The embarrassments of General Lee were further increased by having to fill the ranks of the army, which were becoming diminished by discharges from the expiration of the term of enlistment. In order to relieve the drain upon the scanty commissariat, Longstreet was sent with two divisions to the district south of Petersburg, where provisions were still abundant, with a view of subsisting these troops, while they collected the surplus supplies to be sent to the troops in other quarters. This detachment reduced the Confederate army to barely 40,000 men, while the Federal force exceeded 100,000.

After this reduction General Lee conceived the design of adopting a position more remote from the Federal lines than the one he then occupied, where his army might enjoy greater repose than it could in its position about Fredericksburg, and where he would have greater scope to manœuvre when the enemy should advance, and be better able to secure the fruit of any advantage he might gain in battle. With this aim he directed Colonel Long and Colonel Venable of his staff to make a careful examination of the country contiguous to the North Anna River, from the neighborhood of Hanover Junction to a point twenty-five or thirty miles above that place, to ascertain the character of the south bank of that stream as a defensive position. These officers, after making the examination as directed, reported adversely to the North Anna. As no position could be found which afforded greater advantages than

the one he then occupied, Lee continued to hold the line of
the Rappahannock, and busied himself in preparation for the
ensuing campaign.

Many of the troops whose term of enlistment had expired,
from motives of patriotism and devotion to their commander,
and others who had honorably served, rather than be subjected
to conscription, voluntarily re-enlisted for the war upon receiving a short furlough to visit their homes. By these reductions
the army was at one time reduced to a little above 30,000 men.
By the exercise of his influence and authority General Lee
caused the ranks of his army to be rapidly filled, so that by the
last of April it numbered, exclusive of the two divisions of
Longstreet, then absent, 45,000 men of all arms.*

The appointment of Hooker to the command of the Army
of the Potomac was a surprise to General Lee, who had no
great respect for the military ability of his new opponent in a
position of such importance. Swinton thus comments on the
condition of the Army of the Potomac and the appointment of
Hooker to the supreme command:

"Notwithstanding the untoward fortunes the Army of the
Potomac had suffered, it could hardly be said to be really demoralized, for its heart was still in the war; it never failed to
respond to any demand made upon it; and it was ever ready to
renew its courage at the first ray of hope. Such a day-spring
came with the appointment of General Hooker to the chief
command, and under his influence the tone of the army under-
went a change that would appear astonishing had not its elastic
vitality been so often proved. Hooker's measures of reform
were judicious: he cut away the roots of many evils; stopped
desertion and its causes; did away with the nuisance of the
'grand-division' organization ; infused vitality through the
staff and administrative service; gave distinctive badges to the
different corps; instituted a system of furloughs; consolidated
the cavalry under able leaders, and soon enabled it not only to

---

* Colonel Taylor, in his *Four Years with General Lee,* places the Confederate force
on the 31st of March at 57,000; he makes no allowance, however, for changes that might
have occurred during April, nor for detachments serving elsewhere, but borne upon the
the returns of the Army of Northern Virginia.

stand upon an equality with, but to assert its superiority over, the Virginia horsemen of Stuart. These things proved General Hooker to be an able administrative officer, but they did not prove him to be a competent commander for a great army, and whatever anticipation might be formed touching this had to be drawn from his previous career as a corps commander, in which he had won the reputation of being what is called a 'dashing' officer, and carried the sobriquet of 'Fighting Joe.'

"The new commander judiciously resolved to defer all grand military operations during the wet season, and the first three months after he assumed command were well spent in rehabilitating the army. The ranks were filled up by the return of absentees; the discipline and instruction of the troops were energetically continued; and the close of April found the Army of the Potomac in a high degree of efficiency in all arms. It numbered 120,000 men (infantry and artillery), with a body of 12,000 well-equipped cavalry and a powerful artillery force of above 400 guns. It was divided into seven corps—the First corps under General Reynolds; the Second under General Couch; the Third under General Sickles; the Fifth under General Meade; the Sixth under General Sedgwick; the Eleventh under General Howard; and the Twelfth under General Slocum."

During his period of preparation Hooker very properly resisted that spirit of impatience that had characterized Mr. Lincoln in his intercourse with the previous commanders of the Army of the Potomac, and only gratified once that "up-and-be-doing" spirit that prevailed in Washington by indulging General Averill in a cavalry combat with General Fitz Lee, who guarded the upper fords of the Rappahannock. Being now fully prepared for active operations, Hooker determined to take the initiative by moving on the left of his opponent's position. By careful study of Lee's position he correctly concluded that his left was his most vulnerable point.

In order to mask his real design he sent forward a force of 10,000 cavalry under General Stoneman to operate upon Lee's lines of communication with Richmond, and sent Sedgwick with a force of 30,000 men still further to mask his movement.

Stoneman crossed the Rappahannock at Kelly's Ford on the 29th, and Sedgwick appeared on the 28th on the heights below Fredericksburg. These preparatory measures having been taken, Hooker proceeded to the execution of his plan. Swinton, after a picturesque description of the passage of the Rappahannock and the Rapidan, tells us "that on the afternoon of the 30th of April four corps of the Federal army had gained the position of Chancellorsville, where Hooker at the same time established his headquarters."

Chancellorsville is situated ten miles south-west of Fredericksburg. It is not, as its name implies, a town or village, but simply a farm-house with its usual appendages, situated at the edge of a small field surrounded by a dense thicket of second growth, which sprang up after the primeval forest had been cut to furnish fuel to a neighboring furnace. This thicket extends for miles in every direction, and its wild aspect very properly suggests its name, The Wilderness. The intersection of several important roads gives it the semblance of strategic importance, while in reality a more unfavorable place for military operations could not well be found.

Hooker, however, seemed well pleased with his acquisition, for on reaching Chancellorsville on Thursday night he issued an order to the troops in which he announced that "the enemy must either ingloriously fly or come out from behind his defences and give us battle on our own ground, where certain destruction awaits him." This boast, we are told, so much in the style of Hooker, was amplified by the whole tenor of his conversation. "The Confederate army," said he, "is now the legitimate property of the Army of the Potomac. They may as well pack up their haversacks and make for Richmond, and I shall be after them," etc.

General Lee was fully aware of the preparations that were being made by his adversary, but calmly awaited the complete development of his plans before exerting his strength to oppose him. The presence of the enemy during the winter had made it necessary to maintain a defensive line of about twenty-five miles, the right being in the vicinity of Port Royal, while the left extended to the neighborhood of the United States Ford.

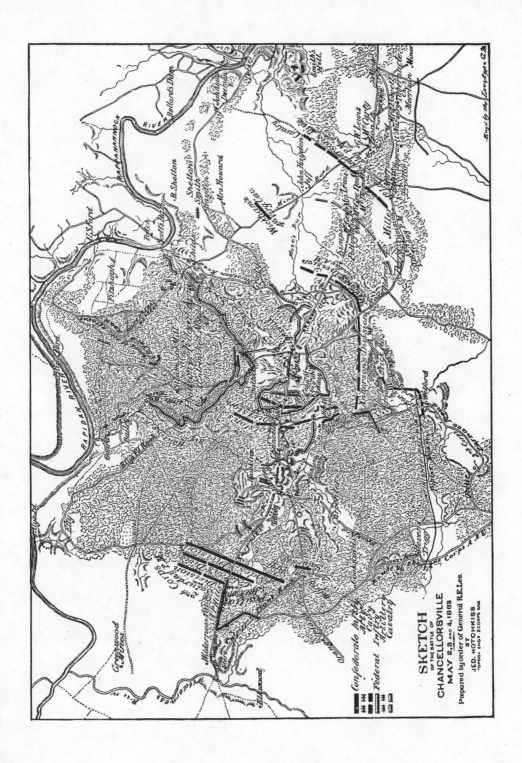

SKETCH
OF THE BATTLE OF
CHANCELLORSVILLE
MAY 2,3 AND 4, 1863
Prepared by order of General R.E.Lee.
BY
JED. HOTCHKISS
TOPOG. ENGT. 2D CORPS. ANV.

This line was occupied by six divisions: Anderson's on the left, and McLaws's between Fredericksburg and the Massaponax, while the four divisions of Jackson's corps occupied the space below the Massaponax. This line had been greatly attenuated by the removal of Longstreet's two divisions of 15,000 men.

Lee's whole cavalry force consisted of two brigades—Fitz Lee's and W. H. F. Lee's—under the immediate command of Stuart, and was mainly employed in guarding the fords of the upper Rappahannock. Hooker had no sooner commenced his movement than it was reported by Stuart to General Lee, and Sedgwick's appearance on the 28th came under his own observation. Perceiving that the time for action had arrived, Lee ordered Jackson to concentrate his whole corps in the immediate vicinity of Fredericksburg.

Early on the morning of the 29th, Sedgwick crossed the Rappahannock below the mouth of Deep Run, but made no other aggressive movement on that day or the day following. On the night of the 30th, Lee was informed of Hooker's arrival at Chancellorsville. He had been previously informed of Stoneman's movements against his line of operations by General Stuart, and was now satisfied that the main attack of the enemy would come from the direction of Chancellorsville. Therefore on the morning of the 1st of May he made the necessary preparations to meet it. Accompanied by his staff, he took a position on a height where one of his batteries overlooked the Rappahannock. He there observed carefully the position of Sedgwick while waiting for information from the direction of Chancellorsville. Jackson was present, while his troops occupied the telegraph road. As far as the eye could reach these men with their bright muskets and tarnished uniforms were distributed in picturesque groups, lightly chatting and laughing, and awaiting the order to march.

Very soon the sound of cannon indicated that the work had begun. At the same time couriers arrived from Stuart and Anderson informing the general that the enemy were advancing on the old turnpike, the plank road, and on the river roads, and asking for reinforcements. McLaws was immediately ordered to the support of Anderson, and shortly after Jackson was ordered to follow with three of his divisions, leaving Early with his division, Barksdale's brigade, and the reserve artillery under General Pendleton—a force of about 9000 men and 45 pieces of artillery—in observation of Sedgwick. When Jackson joined McLaws and Anderson a lively skirmish was in progress, in which he immediately participated. When General Lee arrived he found the Federals were being driven back to Chancellorsville. At the close of the afternoon they had retired within their lines.

General Lee occupied the ridge about three-quarters of a mile south-east and south of Chancellorsville. The opposing armies were hidden from each other by the intervening thicket of brushwood. By a close examination it was discovered that the Federal position was protected by two strong lines of breastworks, one fronting east and the other south. The brushwood had been cleared off for a space of a hundred yards, thus giving an unobstructed field for musketry, while the roads were commanded by artillery. Toward the north and west the position was open. It was obvious that the Federal position was too formidable to be attacked in front with any hope of success; therefore Lee proceeded to devise a plan by which the position of Hooker might be turned and a point of attack gained from which no danger was apprehended by the Federal commander.

General Lee was informed that the Rev. Mr. Lacy, a chaplain in Jackson's corps, was familiar with the country about Chancellorsville. Mr. Lacy informed the general that he had been the pastor of a church near Chancellorsville, and was well acquainted with all the roads in that neighborhood, and that troops could be conducted to a designated point beyond Chancellorsville by a road sufficiently remote from the Federal position to prevent discovery. With this information Lee determined to turn the Federal position and assail it from a point where an attack was unexpected. The execution of a movement so much in accordance with his genius and inclination was assigned to General Jackson, Captain Carter acting as guide.

The above statement is made from personal knowledge of

the writer, gained on the ground at the time; still, since some of Jackson's biographers have allowed their partiality for him so far to outstrip their knowledge of facts as to claim for him the origin of that movement, I will introduce, in corroboration of my statement, the following letter from General Lee published in the address of General Fitzhugh Lee before the Southern Historical Society:

"LEXINGTON, VA., October 28, 1867.

"DR. A. T. BLEDSOE, Office *Southern Review*, Baltimore, Maryland.

"MY DEAR SIR: In reply to your inquiry, I must acknowledge that I have not read the article on Chancellorsville in the last number of the *Southern Review*, nor have I read any of the books published on either side since the termination of hostilities. I have as yet felt no desire to revive any recollections of those events, and have been satisfied with the knowledge I possessed of what transpired. I have, however, learned from others that the various authors of the life of Jackson award to him the credit of the success gained by the Army of Northern Virginia when he was present, and describe the movements of his corps or command as independent of the general plan of operations and undertaken at his own suggestion and upon his own responsibility. I have the greatest reluctance to do anything that might be considered detracting from his well-deserved fame, for I believe no one was more convinced of his worth or appreciated him more highly than myself; yet your knowledge of military affairs, if you have none of the events themselves, will teach you that this could not have been so. Every movement of an army must be well considered and properly ordered, and every one who knew General Jackson must know that he was too good a soldier to violate this fundamental principle. In the operations around Chancellorsville I overtook General Jackson, who had been placed in command of the advance as the skirmishers of the approaching armies met, advanced with the troops to the Federal line of defences, and was on the field until their whole army recrossed the Rappahannock. There is no question as to who was responsible for the operations of the Confederates, or to whom any failure would have been charged.

"What I have said is for your own information. With my best wishes for the success of the *Southern Review* and for your own welfare, in both of which I take a lively interest,

"I am, with great respect, your friend and servant,

"R. E. Lee."

The last interview between Lee and Jackson, during which this important movement was decided upon, was an occasion of great historical interest, in regard to which the writer is fortunately able to add some information from his own knowledge of the circumstances, and that of other members of General Lee's staff. He has been favored by Major T. M. R. Talcott with certain important details of this event, conveyed in a private letter, from which the following extract is made:

"My recollections of the night before the battle of Chancellorsville are briefly as follows:

"About sunset General Jackson sent word to General Lee (by me) that his advance was checked and that the enemy was in force at Chancellorsville. This brought General Lee to the front, and General Jackson met him in the south-east angle of the Chancellorsville and Catharine Forge roads.

"General Lee asked General Jackson whether he had ascertained the position and strength of the enemy on our left, to which General Jackson replied by stating the result of an attack made by Stuart's cavalry near Catharine Forge about dusk. The position of the enemy immediately in front was then discussed, and Captain Boswell and myself were sent to make a moonlight reconnoissance, the result of which was reported about 10 P. M., and was not favorable to an attack in front.

"At this time Generals Lee and Jackson were together, and Lee, who had a map before him, asked Jackson, 'How can we get at these people?' To which Jackson replied, in effect, 'You know best. Show me what to do, and we will try to do it.' General Lee looked thoughtfully at the map; then indicated on it and explained the movement he desired General Jackson to make, and closed by saying, 'General Stuart will cover your movement with his cavalry.' General Jackson listened attentively, and his face lighted up with a smile while General Lee was speaking. Then rising and touching his cap, he said, 'My troops will move at four o'clock.'"

Having, in the manner here described, settled upon their plan of operations for the ensuing day, the two generals, accompanied by their staff officers, repaired to a neighboring pine-thicket, where an open space, well sheltered by overhanging boughs, afforded the party a good bivouac. The day having been a fatiguing one, they lost little time in preparing for the night's repose. Each selected his ground for a bed, spread his saddle-blanket, substituted his saddle for a pillow and his overcoat for covering, and was soon in a happy state of oblivion.

At dawn on the morning of the 2d, Jackson's corps, 22,000 strong, was in motion, and while it was making one of the most famous flank movements on record, General Lee, with the divisions of Anderson and McLaws, with 20 pieces of artillery, a force not exceeding 12,000 men, occupied the position he had assumed the previous evening, and General Hooker, with 90,000 men, lay behind his breastworks awaiting the Confederate attack. Having in the forenoon seen a part of Jackson's ammunition-train, Hooker believed that Lee was retreating, and sent two divisions of Sickles's corps and Pleasonton's cavalry to gain information. This movement was promptly arrested by Colonel Thompson Brown with his battalion of artillery, supported by Jackson's rear-guard. Sickles's and Pleasonton's cavalry lingered about Catharine Furnace in a state of uncertainty until recalled by Jackson's attack on the right of the Federal position.

After making a circuitous march of fifteen miles, Jackson reached a point on the Orange Court-house road three miles in the rear of Chancellorsville. Had Hooker possessed a handful of cavalry equal in spirit to the "Virginia horsemen" under W. H. F. Lee that neutralized Stoneman's ten thousand, he might have escaped the peril that now awaited him. On the arrival of Jackson on the plank road, Fitz Lee, who had covered his movement with his brigade of cavalry, conducted him to a position from which he obtained a view of the enemy, which disclosed the following scene:

"Below and but a few hundred yards distant ran the Federal line of battle. There was the line of defence, with abatis in front and long lines of stacked arms in rear. Two cannons were visible in the part of the line seen. The soldiers were in groups in the rear, laughing, chatting, and smoking, probably engaged here and there in games of cards and other amusements indulged in while feeling safe and comfortable, awaiting orders. In the rear of them were other parties driving up and butchering beeves."

Returning from this point of observation, Jackson proceeded to make his dispositions of attack, which by six o'clock were completed. The divisions of Rodes and Colston were formed at right angles to the old turnpike, the division of Rodes being in advance, and the division of A. P. Hill, in column on the road, formed the reserve.

Howard's corps was first assailed. This corps, being surprised, was panic-stricken and fled precipitately, and in its flight communicated the panic to the troops through which it passed. Jackson's forces followed, routing line after line, until arrested by the close of day. The rout of the Federal army was fast becoming general, and it was only saved from entire defeat by the interposition of night. When compelled to halt Jackson remarked that with one more hour of daylight he could have completed the destruction of the Federal army.

This, the most famous of all Jackson's brilliant achievements, closed his military career. After his troops had halted, and while the lines were being adjusted, he rode forward with several of his staff to reconnoitre the Federal position. It was then after nine o'clock at night. The moon faintly illuminated the scene, but floating clouds dimmed its light. The battle had ceased, and deep silence reigned over what recently had been the scene of war's fiercest turmoil. The reconnoitering party rode several hundred yards in advance of the lines, and halted to listen for any sounds that might come from the direction of the enemy, when suddenly a volley was poured into them from the right of the road. They had been mistaken for Federal scouts by the Confederate infantry. Some of the party fell, and Jackson wheeled his horse in the wood in dread of a renewal of the fire.

This movement proved an unfortunate one. It brought him directly in front of, and not twenty paces from, a portion of his own men, who had been warned against a possible attack from the Federal cavalry. A volley saluted him, with the unfortunate effect of wounding him in three places—two bullets striking his left arm, and one his right hand. At this moment his left hand held the bridle, while his right was held erect, perhaps to protect his face from boughs, yet seemingly with the peculiar gesture which he frequently used in battle. When the bullets struck him his wounded hand dropped, but he instantly seized the bridle with his bleeding right hand, while the frightened horse wheeled and darted through the wood. As he did so the limb of a pine tree struck Jackson in the face, hurled off his cap, and nearly flung him to the ground. Retaining his seat with difficulty, he reached the road and his own lines, where he was assisted to dismount by Captain Wilbourn, one of his staff officers, who laid him at the foot of a tree.

He was soon afterward supported to the rear by his officers, and, becoming so weak as to be unable to walk, was placed in a litter and borne from the field. His last order, as he was being carried back, was given to General Pender, who had expressed doubts of being able to hold his position. The eyes of the wounded hero flashed as he energetically replied, "You *must* hold your ground, General Pender! You *must* hold your ground, sir!"

The discharge of musketry provoked a terrible response from the Federal batteries, which swept the ground as Jackson was being borne from the field. During this movement one of the bearers stumbled and let fall his end of the litter. A groan of agony came from the wounded man, and in the moonlight his face looked deathly pale. On being asked, however, if he was much hurt, he replied, "No, my friend; don't trouble yourself about me."

There is an incident of considerable interest in relation to the wounding of General Jackson which has never yet been told, yet is worthy of being put on record as one of those remarkable coincidences which have so often happened in the lives of great men.   On the morning of May 2d, Jackson was the first to rise from the bivouac above described, and, observing a staff officer (General W. N. Pendleton) without cover, he spread over him his own overcoat.   The morning being chilly, he drew near a small fire that had been kindled by a courier, and the writer, who soon after sought the same place, found him seated on a cracker-box.   He complained of the cold, and, as the cooks were preparing breakfast, I managed to procure him a cup of hot coffee, which by good fortune our cook was able to provide.

While we were still talking the general's sword, which was leaning against a tree, without *apparent* cause fell with a clank to the ground.   I picked it up and handed it to him.   He thanked me and buckled it on.   It was now about dawn, the troops were on the march, and our bivouac was all astir.   After a few words with General Lee he mounted his horse and rode off.   This was the last meeting of Lee and Jackson.

I have spoken of the falling of Jackson's sword because it strongly impressed me at the time as an omen of evil—an indefinable superstition such as sometimes affects persons on the falling of a picture or mirror.   This feeling haunted me the whole day, and when the tidings of Jackson's wound reached my ears it was without surprise that I heard this unfortunate confirmation of the superstitious fears with which I had been so oppressed.

After the fall of Jackson the command fell to General Stuart, who was co-operating with him, and was the senior officer present, General A. P. Hill having been wounded at the same time with Jackson.   About midnight Lee received from Stuart the report both of Jackson's wound and his success.   Instructions were sent to Stuart to continue what had been so successfully begun, and Anderson was directed to support him, while McLaws threatened Hooker's right.

Early on the morning of the 3d the attack was resumed by the Confederates with great vigor.   Hooker, taking advantage of the night, had restored order in his army and strengthened his position; his troops regained courage and contested the field with great stubbornness until ten o'clock, when they yielded at every point and rapidly retreated before the impetuous assaults of Rodes, Heth, Pender, Doles, Archer, and other gallant leaders within a strong line of defences which had been previously constructed to cover the road to the United States Ford, their line of communication with the north side of the Rappahannock. When Stuart assumed the direction of affairs on the night of the 2d the command of the cavalry devolved on Fitz Lee, who operated with vigor on the flanks of the enemy during the continuance of the operations about Chancellorsville.

General Lee's part in this battle of the 3d can be best described in the words of Colonel Charles Marshall, in his eloquent address at the Soldiers' Memorial Meeting in Baltimore:

"General Lee accompanied the troops in person, and as they emerged from the fierce combat they had waged in 'the depths of that tangled wilderness,' driving the superior forces of the enemy before them across the open ground, he rode into their midst. The scene is one that can never be effaced from the minds of those that witnessed it. The troops were pressing forward with all the ardor and enthusiasm of combat. The white smoke of musketry fringed the front of the line of battle, while the artillery on the hills in the rear of the infantry shook the earth with its thunder and filled the air with the wild shrieks of the shells that plunged into the masses of the retreating foe. To add greater horror and sublimity to the scene, the Chancellorsville house and the woods surrounding it were wrapped in flames. In the midst of this awful scene General Lee, mounted upon that horse which we all remember so well, rode to the front of his advancing battalions. His presence was the signal for one of those uncontrollable outbursts of enthusiasm which none can appreciate who have not witnessed them.

"The fierce soldiers, with their faces blackened with the smoke of battle, the wounded, crawling with feeble limbs from the fury of the devouring flames, all seemed possessed with a common impulse. One long, unbroken cheer, in which the feeble cry of those who lay helpless on the earth blended with the strong voices of those who still fought, rose high above the roar of battle and hailed the presence of the victorious chief. He sat in the full realization of all that soldiers dream of—triumph; and as I looked on him in the complete fruition of the success which his genius, courage, and confidence in his army had won, I thought that it must have been from some such scene that men in ancient days ascended to the dignity of the gods.

"His first care was for the wounded of both armies, and he was among the foremost at the burning mansion, where some of them lay. But at that moment, when the transports of his victorious troops were drowning the roar of battle with acclamations, a note was brought to him from General Jackson. It was brought to General Lee as he sat on his horse near the Chancellorsville house, and, unable to open it with his gauntleted hands, he passed it to me with directions to read it to him. The note made no mention of the wound which General Jackson had received, but congratulated General Lee upon the great victory.

"I shall never forget the look of pain and anguish that passed over his face as he listened. With a voice broken with emotion he bade me say to General Jackson that the victory was his, and that the congratulations were due to him. I do not know how others may regard this incident, but for myself, as I gave expression to the thoughts of his exalted mind, I forgot the genius that won the day in my reverence for the generosity that refused its glory."

The troops being much fatigued and having accomplished all that could have been expected of them, Lee caused a suspension of further operations in order that they might rest and refresh themselves preparatory for the final blow. While the operations above described were in progress at Chancellorsville, General Early by skilful manœuvring had detained Sedgwick at Fredericksburg until the 3d, when that general, by a determined advance, forced back Early, carried Marye's Heights, and proceeded toward Chancellorsville. The condition of affairs was communicated to General Lee during the forenoon.

Wilcox's brigade, then at Banks's Ford, was ordered to intercept Sedgwick and retard his advance, while McLaws's division was ordered to support him. Wilcox on reaching Salem Church, six miles from Chancellorsville, encountered the Federal advance, and after a sharp conflict he repulsed it with loss.

The success of Wilcox delayed Sedgwick until Anderson and McLaws could come up. The premeditated attack on Hooker being thus interrupted, Lee on the forenoon of the 4th repaired to the neighborhood of Fredericksburg. A combined attack was then directed to be made by Early on the rear, while McLaws and Anderson bore down upon the front. The battle was hotly contested during the afternoon, in which the forces of Sedgwick were defeated, and were only saved from destruction by a night-passage across the Rappahannock at Banks's Ford. On the 5th, Lee collected his forces at Chancellorsville to give the *coup de grâce* to Hooker, but that general, under cover of a dark and stormy night, effected his retreat beyond the Rappahannock at the United States Ford.

The losses sustained at Chancellorsville and Fredericksburg were estimated at the time at 20,000 killed and wounded, and among the wounded was General Hooker, besides a large number of prisoners. Swinton places Hooker's loss at Chancellorsville at 17,000; Sedgwick's loss at Fredericksburg must have considerably increased that number. The loss sustained by the Confederates was proportionately as great as that of the Federals. The casualties reported were about 9000. After expressing his praise and admiration for the heroic conduct of his troops, and after mentioning the names of a large number of line officers whose zeal and gallantry entitled them to special notice, General Lee thus concludes his report:

"The loss of the enemy in the battle of Chancellorsville and the other engagements was severe. His dead and a large number of wounded were left on the field. About 5000 prisoners exclusive of the wounded were taken, and 13 pieces of artillery, 19,500 stands of arms, 17 colors, and a large quantity of ammunition fell into our hands. To the members of my staff I am greatly indebted for assistance in observing the movements of the enemy, posting troops, and conveying orders.   On so extended and varied a field all were called into requisition and all evinced the greatest energy and zeal.   The medical director of the army, Surgeon Guild, with the officers of his department, were untiring in their attention to the wounded.   Lieutenant-colonel Corley, chief quartermaster, took charge of the disposition and safety of the trains of the army.   Lieutenant-colonel Cole, chief commissary of subsistence, and Lieutenant-colonel Baldwin, chief of ordnance, were everywhere on the field attending to the wants of their departments;   General Chilton, chief of staff, Lieutenant-colonel Murray, Major Peyton, and Captain Young, of the adjutant- and inspector-general's department, were active in seeing to the execution of orders; Lieutenant-colonel Proctor Smith and Captain Johnston of the Engineers in reconnoitering the enemy and constructing batteries; Colonel Long in posting troops and artillery; Majors Taylor, Talcott, Marshall, and Venable were engaged night and day in watching the operations, carrying orders, etc.

"Respectfully submitted,   R. E. Lee, *General.*

"Note.—Notwithstanding the unfavorable character of the country for the use of artillery, Colonels Brown, Carter, and Hardaway succeeded in placing thirty or forty guns in position to be used with effect on parts of the enemy's position, especially that in the vicinity of the Chancellor house."

On the 7th, General Lee ordered his troops to resume their former position about Fredericksburg.   A few days after the sad intelligence of the death of Lieutenant-general Jackson reached the army.   The estimation in which that distinguished officer was held will be best explained by the general orders of the commander-in-chief announcing his death to the army:

"Headquarters Army of Northern Virginia,
"General Orders No. 61.   May 11, 1863.

"With deep regret the commanding general announces to the army the death of Lieutenant-general T. J. Jackson, who expired on the 10th instant at a quarter past 3 P. M.   The daring, skill, and energy of this great and good soldier by the decree of an all-wise Providence are now lost us.   But while we mourn his death we feel that his spirit still lives, and will inspire the whole army with his indomitable courage and unshaken confidence in God as our hope and strength. Let his name be a watchword to his corps, who have followed him to victory on so many fields. Let his officers and soldiers emulate his invincible determination to do everything in the defence of our beloved country.

"R. E. LEE, *General.*"

It is but just to pause at this point in our narrative, and append some remarks upon the appearance and character of the remarkable man whose striking history ends with the field of Chancellorsville and with the achievement of a victory in which he was the chief instrument, under the skilful control of the great Confederate leader.

The writer first knew Jackson as a young man, then an officer in the First Artillery. Shortly after that time he retired from the army and became a professor in the Virginia Military Institute, which he left to join the army of the Confederacy. I next saw him in Richmond when on a brief visit to Lee to consult in regard to the projected movement against McClellan. He seemed then in much better health than before he left the United States army, but presented the same tall, gaunt, awkward figure and the rusty gray dress and still rustier gray forage-cap by which he was distinguished from the spruce young officers under him. There was nothing of a very striking character in his personal appearance. He had a good face, but one that promised no unusual powers. Yet in the excitement of battle his countenance would light up and his form appear to expand, a peculiar animation seeming to infuse itself through his whole person. At the battle of Gaines's Mill, where I next saw him, he was very poorly mounted on an old sorrel horse, and in his rusty suit was anything but a striking figure. And yet as he put himself at the head of his last regiment and advanced with his face lit up with the enthusiasm of war, he looked truly heroic and appeared a man made by Nature to lead armies to victory.

I saw him frequently afterward during the progress of the

war, and in the march against Harper's Ferry I wrote off the order for the movement. The conversation in regard to it between Lee and Jackson took place in my presence, and I well remember not only his strong approval of it, but also the earnest energy with which he undertook the enterprise. He at that time seemed improved in health, and was more animated than usual in manner. It was in the camp near Winchester, however, that Jackson presented his most attractive appearance. General Stuart had made him a present of a new uniform, and a handsome horse in place of his old raw-boned sorrel. It was with some difficulty that he was induced to part with his ancient attire in favor of this new and showy dress, and it is doubtful if he was ever quite comfortable in it.

He was a very reticent man, and ordinarily seemed absorbed in his own thoughts, while he displayed some marked peculiarities of manner. One of these was a strange habit of stopping and throwing up his hands, as if in supplication to the Invisible. In religion he was a strict Presbyterian of the sternest creed, and very attentive to religious observances. He not only believed in predestination, but had a strong belief in his personal safety—a presentiment that he would never fall by the hands of the enemy that seemed singularly warranted by the result. The men under his command were to a considerable extent of his own faith. In this he presented a parallel with Cromwell, whom, indeed, he resembled in character.

Jackson was very hospitable in disposition and welcomed warmly any guest to his tent or his table. The writer has often partaken of his hospitality, and found him ever an agreeable and generous host. As for himself, he was very abstemious. He had been at one period of his life a decided dyspeptic, and was always obliged to be very careful of his diet.

In this work the greater part of his military history has been included, yet no description has been given of that notable Valley campaign in which he so greatly astounded his adversaries, and to which he owes so much of his reputation as a brilliant tactician and a commander of extraordinary powers. This campaign formed no part of the military history of General Lee, and it is but alluded to here as a fitting close to this tribute to the most remarkable, and one of the most able, of the great champions developed during our Civil War.

After the return of the victorious army to its old quarters at Fredericksburg the remainder of May was consumed in recruiting and reorganizing. The infantry was formed into three corps of three divisions each. The First corps was commanded by Longstreet, the Second by Ewell, and the Third by A. P. Hill. Each of these officers had been elevated to the rank of lieutenant-general. The organization of the cavalry remained unchanged, but that of the artillery demanded the special attention of the commander-in-chief. The artillery of the army consisted of about sixty batteries of light artillery and of six batteries of horse artillery, whose *personnel* was unsurpassed by any troops in the army, though they were imperfectly organized. General Lee, having determined to improve the efficiency of his artillery, directed a plan to be drafted for its more perfect organization. The plan presented and adopted was to group the artillery of the army into battalions of four batteries each. The artillery of the line was thus formed into fifteen battalions, besides the battalion of horse artillery. To each battalion was assigned a lieutenant-colonel and major, and two or three battalions constituted the command of a colonel. The whole light artillery of the army was separated into three divisions, each of which was commanded by a chief with the rank of brigadier-general. One of these divisions was assigned to each corps of infantry. The chiefs of the corps of artillery reported and received orders direct from the corps commanders, and the chief of artillery of the army reported direct to the commander-in-chief. This organization proved entirely successful, and the Confederate artillery became famous in the later campaigns.

By the 1st of June the reconstruction and equipment of the army was completed, and the Army of Northern Virginia appeared the best disciplined, the most high-spirited, and enthusiastic army on the continent. It consisted of 52,000 infantry, 250 pieces of artillery, and 9000 cavalry, making an aggregate force of 65,000 men. The successful campaign which this army had recently passed through inspired it with almost invincible ardor. This splendid result had been accomplished by the almost unaided efforts of General Lee.*

The financial condition of the country became worse almost daily, without any effectual efforts being made to arrest the continual decline in the value of money and give a healthy tone to the currency. Almost all external resources had been cut off, and now the only course to be adopted to improve the currency was the resort to direct taxation. At this time the real estate and the personal wealth of the country afforded an ample basis for the establishment of a currency reliable and sufficient for the general demand. But this resource was neglected, and the finances of the country came to naught. The want of money was severely felt by the army, and many of the best soldiers were only retained by the assurance of the patriotic citizens that their families should be provided for. To add to the embarrassment of the army, it was confined to one line of operations—the defence of Richmond. Both the State and Confederate Governments demanded with Quixotic persistency the defence of a place that had been rendered almost untenable since the Federals had gained the possession of the James and York rivers. The general had been heard to say that Richmond was the millstone that was dragging down the army.

* The rapid increase of the army after the battle of Chancellorsville was mainly due to the return of Longstreet's two divisions and the cavalry brigades of Hampton, Robertson, and Jones, which had been detached from the army during the fall and winter.

CHAPTER XV.

GETTYSBURG.

A New Plan of Operations Discussed.—The Army Advances.—Through Shenandoah Valley to the Potomac.—The Federals March North.—Hooker Superseded by Meade.—The Army in Pennsylvania.—General Order.—Both Armies Move upon Gettysburg.—The Battle of July 1st.—An Assault Ordered for the Next Morning.—Criticism of the Count of Paris.—Topography.—Stuart's Movement.—Lee's Anxiety at the Delay.—An Opportunity Lost.—Position of Sickles's Corps.—A Dash for Little Round Top.—The Texans Repulsed.—The Fight at the Peach Orchard.—Federal Repulse.—Ewell's Assault.—The Battle of the 3d.—An Attack Ordered on the Centre.—Pickett's Charge.—Failure of the Assault.—Colonel Taylor's Testimony.—Lee's Letter to Pickett.—After the Battle.—Retreat to the Potomac.—Advance of the Federal Army.—Lee Crosses the Potomac.—Subsequent Movements.—Venable's Anecdote.—Story of a Federal Soldier.

BY the first of June General Lee had completed his arrangements for the ensuing campaign. The army, though numerically less than it was when he commenced his operations against McClellan on the Chickahominy, had been by its recent victories imbued with a confidence that greatly increased its efficiency. Its spirit was now high, and it was anxious to grapple again its powerful foe, which still lingered on the Stafford Heights.

The object of the campaign being the defence of Richmond, General Lee could either continue on the defensive and oppose the Federal advance as he had recently done, or he might assume the offensive and by bold manœuvring oblige the Federal army to recede from its present line of operations to protect its capital or oppose the invasion of Maryland or Pennsylvania. The advance upon Richmond would thus be frustrated, and the attack upon that city delayed, at least for a time. The dispirited condition of the Federal army since its late defeat, and the high tone of that of the Confederates, induced the adoption of the latter plan.

This decision was reached by General Lee near the close of

May and after the completion of the reorganization of the army which followed the battle of Chancellorsville. Before the movement began his plans of operation were fully matured, and with such precision that the exact locality at which a conflict with the enemy was expected to take place was indicated on his map. This locality was the town of Gettysburg, the scene of the subsequent great battle.

At the period mentioned he called the writer into his tent, headquarters being then near Fredericksburg. On entering I found that he had a map spread on the table before him, which he seemed to have been earnestly consulting. He advised me of his designed plan of operations, which we discussed together and commented upon the probable result. He traced on the map the proposed route of the army and its destination in Pennsylvania, while in his quietly effective manner he made clear to me his plans for the campaign. He first proposed, in furtherance of his design, to manœuvre the army in such a way as to draw Hooker from the Rappahannock. At this point in the conversation I suggested that it might be advantageous to bring Hooker to an engagement somewhere in the vicinity of the old battlefield of Manassas. To this idea General Lee objected, and stated as his reason for opposing it that no results of decisive value to the Confederate States could come from a victory in that locality. The Federal army, if defeated, would fall back to the defences of Washington, as on previous occasions, where it could reorganize in safety and again take the field in full force.

In his view, the best course would be to invade Pennsylvania, penetrating this State in the direction of Chambersburg, York, or Gettysburg. He might be forced to give battle at one or the other of these places as circumstances might suggest, but, in his view, the vicinity of Gettysburg was much the best point, as it was less distant from his base on the Potomac, and was so situated that by holding the passes of the South Mountain he would be able to keep open his line of communication. York, being some twenty-five miles farther from the mountains, was a less desirable locality.

In this plan he had a decided object. There was in his

mind no thought of reaching Philadelphia, as was subsequently feared in the North. Yet he was satisfied that the Federal army, if defeated in a pitched battle, would be seriously disorganized and forced to retreat across the Susquehanna—an event which would give him control of Maryland and Western Pennsylvania, and probably of West Virginia, while it would very likely cause the fall of Washington City and the flight of the Federal Government. Moreover, an important diversion would be made in favor of the Western department, where the affairs of the Confederacy were on the decline. These highly important results, which would in all probability follow a successful battle, fully warranted, in his opinion, the hazard of an invasion of the North.

The plan which he thus indicated was already fully matured in his own mind, and the whole line of movement was laid down on the map. He alluded to the several strategic points in Maryland, but did not think it would be advisable to make any stand in that State, for the same reason as before given. This interview took place about two weeks before the movement began. The proposed scheme of operations was submitted to President Davis in a personal interview, and fully approved by him.

General Lee entertained the reasonable expectation that with his powerful cavalry he would be able to obtain all necessary supplies in Pennsylvania. It was his intention to subsist his soldiers on the country of the enemy, and he knew that the fertile Cumberland Valley could supply an army of any size. He had strong confidence of success in this movement, relying greatly on the high spirit of his army and the depressed condition of Hooker's forces. Everything, indeed, seemed to promise success, and the joyful animation with which the men marched North after the movement actually began and the destination of the army was communicated to them appeared a true presage of victory.

Since the battle of Chancellorsville, although the Federal army had been increased to its former dimensions, it still retained a spiritless attitude. As yet no future plan of operations had been developed. It was just to conclude that General

Hooker would not again advance on his present line, and that a change of base was in contemplation, and as the James and York presented the most propitious lines, it was probable that the Army of the Potomac, if left uninterrupted, would move in that direction. But the arrival of the advance of the Confederate army early in June at Culpeper Court-house excited the apprehensions of the Federal authorities for the safety of their capital, and forced them to entertain new ideas as to the destination of the Army of the Potomac.

On the 2d of June, Ewell's corps, preceded by the cavalry, was sent forward to Culpeper Court-house. A day or two after, Longstreet, accompanied by the commander-in-chief, followed Ewell, while Hill remained at Fredericksburg to observe the movements of Hooker. By the 8th of June the main body of the Confederate army was concentrated in the neighborhood of Culpeper and the Federal army was in motion for the upper Rappahannock.

Early on the morning of the 9th, Pleasonton's cavalry crossed the Rappahannock and attacked Stuart in his position south of that river. A fierce engagement ensued, in which the Confederate cavalry was roughly handled, but finally, with the assistance of Rodes's division of infantry, the Federals were repulsed and forced to cross the Rappahannock.

Having learned by this encounter that Lee was in force at Culpeper, Hooker hastened the concentration of his forces in the neighborhood of Rappahannock Station. On the 10th, Ewell was advanced toward the Shenandoah Valley, both for the purpose of expelling from that section a considerable Federal force, and to create an impression of a flank movement with the view of interrupting Hooker's communications. Having not yet recovered from the shock he had received at Chancellorsville, and having before him the picture of Pope's disaster of the previous year, Hooker suddenly withdrew from the Rappahannock and retired to the vicinity of Manassas and Centreville, where he assumed a defensive attitude for the protection of Washington.

Thus by a series of bold strategic movements General Lee removed the enemy from his path and accomplished the most difficult step in his plan of operations without opposition. The extension of his line from Fredericksburg to Winchester in the face of an enemy of more than double his numerical strength would ordinarily be considered an act of unpardonable rashness, but on the present occasion, being aware of the dispirited condition of the Federal army and the dread of disaster to Washington, Lee felt safe in undertaking this movement.

General Ewell on the 14th defeated Milroy at Winchester, and after expelling him from the Valley took a position on the Baltimore and Ohio Railroad between Martinsburg and Harper's Ferry. Hill, as soon as the enemy disappeared from his front, withdrew from Fredericksburg and proceeded to close upon the main body of the army.

On the 15th, Longstreet was put in motion for the Valley, and Hill was directed to follow a day later, while Stuart was left east of the Blue Ridge with instructions to observe closely the movements of the enemy.

General Lee arrived with Longstreet's corps at Berryville on the 18th, where he remained two or three days perfecting his preparations for the invasion of Pennsylvania. About the 21st he continued his advance in two columns: the one, composed of the corps of Ewell and Hill, was directed to Shepherdstown, and the other, consisting of Longstreet's corps and the supply-train, proceeded to Williamsport. Ewell crossed the Potomac on the 23d, followed by Hill on the 24th, while its passage was effected by Longstreet and the trains on the 25th at Williamsport.

As Lee's plan of operations unfolded itself, Hooker advanced to the Potomac and took possession of the fords in the neighborhood of Leesburg. When he learned that Lee had entered Maryland he immediately crossed the river and advanced to Frederick. A controversy then occurred between Halleck and himself, which resulted in his removal on the 27th and the placing of General Meade in command of the Army of the Potomac.

Previous to the passage of the Potomac, General Stuart was instructed to make the movements of the cavalry correspond with those of the Federal army, so that he might be in position to observe and report all important information. In the performance of this duty Stuart had never failed, and probably his great confidence in him made Lee less specific in his instructions than he would otherwise have been. But on this occasion, either from the misapprehension of instructions or the love of the éclat of a bold raid, Stuart, instead of maintaining his appropriate position between the armies, placed himself on the right flank of the enemy, where his communication with Lee was effectually severed. This greatly embarrassed the movements of General Lee, and eventually forced him to an engagement under disadvantageous circumstances.

Immediately on completing the passage of the Potomac, Lee resumed his advance, directing Ewell to Carlisle, while he proceeded with Longstreet and Hill to Chambersburg. Ewell sent Early to York by way of Gettysburg, and then moved with the rest of his corps, accompanied by Jenkins's cavalry, to Carlisle. These places were occupied without opposition. Longstreet and Hill reached Chambersburg on the 26th, when they were halted to wait tidings of Stuart and to gain information of the movements of the enemy. Such was the disposition of the Confederate army during the latter part of June.

On the day succeeding his arrival at Chambersburg, General Lee issued the following order to his army, which breathes the same highly commendable spirit as that issued on the occasion of the advance into Maryland:

> "HEADQUARTERS ARMY OF NORTHERN VIRGINIA,
> "CHAMBERSBURG, Pa., June 27, 1863.

"GENERAL ORDER NO. 73.

"The commanding general has observed with marked satisfaction the conduct of the troops on the march, and confidently anticipates results commensurate with the high spirit they have manifested. No troops could have displayed greater fortitude or better performed the arduous marches of the past ten days. Their conduct in other respects has, with few exceptions, been in keeping with their character as soldiers, and entitles them to approbation and praise.

"There have, however, been instances of forgetfulness on

the part of some that they have in keeping the yet unsullied reputation of the army, and that the duties exacted of us by civilization and Christianity are not less obligatory in the country of the enemy than in our own. The commanding general considers that no greater disgrace could befall the army, and through it our whole people, than the perpetration of the barbarous outrages upon the innocent and defenceless and the wanton destruction of private property that have marked the course of the enemy in our own country. Such proceedings not only disgrace the perpetrators and all connected with them, but are subversive of the discipline and efficiency of the army and destructive of the ends of our present movements. It must be remembered that we make war only on armed men, and that we cannot take vengeance for the wrongs our people have suffered without lowering ourselves in the eyes of all whose abhorrence has been excited by the atrocities of our enemy, and offending against Him to whom vengeance belongeth, without whose favor and support our efforts must all prove in vain.

"The commanding general therefore earnestly exhorts the troops to abstain, with most scrupulous care, from unnecessary or wanton injury to private property, and he enjoins upon all officers to arrest and bring to summary punishment all who shall in any way offend against the orders on this subject.

"R. E. LEE,
"*General.*"

To the strict observance of the above order Colonel Freemantle, of the British army, thus testifies: "I saw no straggling into the houses, nor were any of the inhabitants disturbed or annoyed by the soldiers. . . . . I went into Chambersburg again, and witnessed the singular good behavior of the troops toward the citizens. . . . . To one who has seen, as I have, the ravages of the Northern troops in Southern towns this forbearance seems most commendable and surprising."

Colonel Freemantle was also on the field of Gettysburg, and behaved most handsomely on the repulse of Pickett's division. Speaking of that affair, he says: "General Lee and his officers were fully impressed with a sense of the situation, yet there was much less noise, fuss, or confusion of orders than at an ordinary field-day. The men, as they were rallied in the wood, were brought up in detachments and lay down quietly and coolly in the positions assigned them.''

By referring to the map of Pennsylvania it will be seen that Chambersburg, Carlisle, and York are nearly equidistant from Gettysburg, each being about twenty-five miles distant from that place. When General Lee arrived at Chambersburg he had received no intelligence from Stuart for several days, consequently he had no information of the movements of the Army of the Potomac, and the continued want of intelligence for several days longer greatly embarrassed him.

Lee first learned of the appointment of General Meade to the command of the Federal army on the 28th of June. He was surprised to hear of such a change of commanders being made at that critical stage of affairs. The change itself he considered advantageous to the Federal cause, as he had always held Meade in much higher estimation as a commander than Hooker. But he was of the opinion that the difficulties which would beset Meade in taking command of an army in the midst of a campaign would more than counterbalance his superiority as a general over the previous commander. , He was therefore rather satisfied than otherwise by the change. The army at large was in no sense discomposed in learning that General Lee was opposed to a new adversary. They had known the same thing to happen on several previous occasions with rather loss than gain to the Federal cause, and the news tended to add to their hopes of success. They had little fear that any of the generals of the Army of the Potomac would prove a match for their own admired and almost worshipped leader.

On reaching Chambersburg, General Lee, not having heard from Stuart, was under the impression that the Federal army had not yet crossed the Potomac. It was not until the night of the 28th that he learned that the enemy had reached Frederick. This important information was brought by a scout from Hood's Texas brigade.

On receiving this news Lee immediately ordered the advance of Robertson's and W. E. Jones's divisions of cavalry, which

Stuart had left to guard the passes of the Blue Ridge. This cavalry, however, did not arrive in time to be of any service in the movements preceding the battle.

The rapid advance of General Meade was unexpected, and exhibited a celerity that had not hitherto been displayed by the Federal army. A speedy concentration of the Confederate army was now necessary. Before dawn on the morning of the 29th orders were despatched requiring the immediate junction of the army, and on the 30th the Confederate forces were in motion toward Gettysburg. At the same time General Meade was pressing forward for that place.

This movement of the Confederate army began with the advance of A. P. Hill's corps, which bivouacked near Greenville on the night of the 29th, and reached Cashtown during the next day. Orders had been sent to Ewell to recall his advanced divisions and concentrate in the same locality. Longstreet's corps followed on the 30th, accompanied by headquarters, and encamped that night near the western base of South Mountain, in the neighborhood of the Stevens furnace. On July 1st he advanced to Cashtown, a locality about six miles from Gettysburg.

While Lee and his staff were ascending South Mountain firing was heard from the direction of Gettysburg. This caused Lee some little uneasiness. The unfortunate absence of the cavalry prevented him from knowing the position and movements of the enemy, and it was impossible to estimate the true condition of affairs in his front. He was at first persuaded that the firing indicated a cavalry affair of minor importance, but by the time Cashtown was reached the sound had become heavy and continuous, and indicated a severe engagement.

General Lee now exhibited a degree of anxiety and impatience, and expressed regret at the absence of the cavalry. He said that he had been kept in the dark ever since crossing the Potomac, and intimated that Stuart's disappearance had materially hampered the movements and disorganized the plans of the campaign.

In a short time, however, his suspense was relieved by a message from A. P. Hill, who reported that he was engaged with two corps of the enemy, and requested reinforcements. Anderson's division, which had just reached Cashtown, was at once pushed forward to his support, and General Lee with his staff quickly followed.

The situation in front at that time was as follows: During the forenoon of July 1st the two leading corps of the Federal army, commanded by General Reynolds, had arrived at Gettysburg; at the same time the heads of Hill's and Ewell's corps were rapidly approaching. About ten o'clock, General Heth of Hill's corps encountered a part of Buford's cavalry, which had been thrown forward on the Chambersburg road to a small stream called Willoughby Run, three miles from Gettysburg. Having driven back Buford, Heth engaged Wadsworth's division of the First corps, which was soon reinforced by other divisions of that corps, while Heth was supported by Pender's division of Hill's corps. The advance of the Eleventh corps (Howard's) and the arrival of Rodes's and Early's divisions of Ewell's corps, increased the proportions of the combat, which quickly became animated and continued with spirit until about four o'clock in the afternoon, when the Federal corps were totally defeated and driven from the field with very heavy loss. General Reynolds was killed, and his two corps were seriously reduced in numbers and greatly disorganized. The Confederate loss was much smaller than that of the enemy; nevertheless, the fall of many gallant soldiers was to be regretted. Among the wounded was the gallant General Heth, whose command suffered severely.

Near the close of the action General Lee reached the field. Anderson's division came up soon afterward, and about the same time Longstreet arrived in advance of his corps, which was a few miles behind. As the troops were evidently very much fatigued, and somewhat disorganized by rapid marching and hard fighting, it seemed inadvisable to immediately pursue the advantage which had been gained, particularly as the retreating forces of the enemy were known to have been reinforced, and to have taken a defensive position about a mile south of the town.

This subject occupied Lee's attention upon perceiving the

situation of affairs and the victory gained by his advance forces, and he entered into a conversation with Longstreet, in the presence of the writer, concerning the relative positions of the two armies and the movements it was advisable to make. Longstreet gave it as his opinion that the best plan would be to turn Meade's left flank and force him back to the neighborhood of Pipeclay Creek. To this General Lee objected, and pronounced it impracticable under the circumstances.

At the conclusion of the conversation Colonel Long was directed to make a reconnoissance of the Federal position on Cemetery Ridge, to which strong line the retreating troops had retired. This he did, and found that the ridge was occupied in considerable force. On this fact being reported to General Lee, he decided to make no farther advance that evening, but to wait till morning before attempting to follow up his advantage. This decision the worn-out condition of his men and the strength of the position held by the enemy rendered advisable. He turned to Longstreet and Hill, who were present, and said, "Gentlemen, we will attack the enemy in the morning as early as practicable." In the conversation that succeeded he directed them to make the necessary preparations and be ready for prompt action the next day. Longstreet's corps was at that time near Cashtown, but bivouacked for the night on Willoughby's Creek, about four miles from the battlefield.

I will here add that Gettysburg affords a good example of the difficulties to be encountered and the uncertainty of being able to harmonize the various elements of armies when the field of operations is extensive. This battle was precipitated by the absence of information which could only be obtained by an active cavalry force. General Lee had previously considered the possibility of engaging the enemy in the vicinity of Gettysburg, but the time and position were to have been of his own selection. This could have been easily effected had not the cavalry been severed from its proper place with the army.

At a later hour in the evening than that of the events above mentioned the writer had a further conversation with General Lee, which is of sufficient interest to be here narrated. We were then together at the bivouac, under the trees of an apple orchard.

The general, as if he had been thinking over his plans and orders, turned to me with the remark, "Colonel Long, do you think we had better attack without the cavalry? If we do so, we will not, if successful, be able to reap the fruits of victory."

"In my opinion," I replied, "it would be best not to wait for Stuart. It is uncertain where he is or when he will arrive. At present only two or three corps of the enemy's army are up, and it seems best to attack them before they can be greatly strengthened by reinforcements. The cavalry had better be left to take care of itself."

General Lee evidently agreed with me in this opinion. Much as he had been annoyed and his movements hampered by Stu-·art's absence, the condition of affairs was such that but one judicious course was open. An attack in force on the enemy before he could concentrate his army was very promising of success, and it was with this purpose fully determined upon in the general's mind that the events of that day ended for the Confederate army.

At this stage of the campaign the Count of Paris alludes to the tactics and strategy of General Lee in a tone of criticism which calls for some rejoinder on our part. He remarks:

"He has four alternatives to select from: He has the choice to retire into the gaps of the South Mountain, in order to compel Meade to come after him; or to wait steadily in his present positions for the attack of the Federals; or, again, to manœuvre in order to dislodge them from those they occupy by menacing their communications by the right or left; or, finally, to storm these positions in front, in the hope of carrying them by main force. The best plan would undoubtedly have been the first, because, by preserving the strategic offensive, Lee would thus secure all the advantages of the tactical defensive."

Could the count have seen the actual field of operation and have known the circumstances that governed General Lee, he would probably have taken a different view of his actions.

It must be borne in mind that in entering Pennsylvania without his cavalry General Lee was unable to accumulate supplies.

In fact, the subsistence of his army mainly depended on the provisions that could be collected in the vicinity of his line of march by detachments of infantry mounted on artillery- and wagon-horses. Therefore, if Lee had adopted the count's preferred plan of operation and occupied one of the passes of South Mountain, he would have placed his army in a trap that would have, in the absence of a miracle, resulted in its destruction; for Meade with his superior forces could have enclosed him without supplies or the means of obtaining them. Lee would thus have been reduced to the alternative of laying down his arms or of cutting his way out with great sacrifice of life and the loss of his artillery and transportation.

The above objection is also applicable to the count's second plan, with the addition that General Lee's line was too much extended to admit of a successful defence against General Meade's superior force. In answer to the count's third plan, it is only necessary to say that the proximity of the two armies and the absence of cavalry on the part of the Confederates rendered manœuvring impracticable. The fourth is the only one that admitted of the hope of success, and was the one adopted by General Lee.

That the battle may be more clearly described it is necessary to present some of the principal topographical features of the neighborhood of Gettysburg. The town of Gettysburg, nestling in a small valley, is surrounded by numerous low ridges making various angles with each other. The most important of them is the one situated about a mile south-west, known as Cemetery Ridge. It is terminated by two conical mounds about four miles apart. The one to the south is designated the Round Top. The one to the north is called Culp's Hill.

Immediately after the defeat of the First and Eleventh corps Cemetery Ridge was selected as the Federal position. Nearer the town is a second ridge, nearly parallel to, and about a thousand yards west of, the Cemetery Ridge. This ridge during the battle formed the Confederate centre. From its southern extremity springs obliquely a spur extending almost on a line with the Round Top. This naturally formed the Confederate right. East of the town the valley is traversed by a small stream, beyond which rises abruptly a commanding ridge which was occupied by the Confederate left. The more distant view is bounded by South Mountain and its projecting spurs.

As we have said so much in regard to the absence of the cavalry and the difficulties thence arising, it is proper at this point to explain its cause. Stuart's passage of the Potomac at a point eastward of that where the Federal crossing was made was intended, as has been said, as a feint, with the view of creating a diversion in favor of General Lee by arousing fears of danger to Washington, to the vicinity of which city the cavalry advanced. However, the movement proved a highly unfortunate one, and was followed by irretrievable disaster; for Stuart had no sooner entered Maryland than his return was barred by the intrusion of a large Federal force between him and the river, and he was thus obliged to make a wide circuit through Maryland and Pennsylvania before he could resume his proper place with the army. This occupied him seven or eight days, and it was the 2d of July before he rejoined the army at Gettysburg in a very reduced condition, for many of his men had been dismounted, and the horses of those who remained in the saddle were much jaded by long and rapid marches. Notwithstanding the bad plight of his cavalry, Stuart, with his usual promptitude, placed it on the flanks of the army, where its presence was much needed. On the 3d it engaged the enemy's cavalry in frequent skirmishes and several fierce encounters, in one of which General Hampton was severely wounded.

The divisions of Robertson and Jones, which had been ordered up from the passes of the Blue Ridge, did not reach the army in time to take part in the battles of the 1st and 2d, and were too late to be of any service in preliminary reconnoissances. In consequence of these facts, General Lee in the whole of this campaign was deprived of the use of that portion of his force which has been truly named "the eye of the army," since without it all movements are made in the dark and the army is forced to grope its way forward.

At an early hour on the morning of the 2d the writer (Colonel Long) was directed to examine and verify the position of the Confederate artillery. He accordingly examined the whole line from right to left, and gave the necessary instructions for its effective service. As the morning advanced surprise began to be felt at the delay in commencing the attack on the right, which had been ordered to take place at an early hour. The object was to dislodge the Federal force, that had retreated after its defeat to the position known as Cemetery Ridge, before it could be reinforced to any considerable extent. By so doing Lee hoped to be able to defeat the Federal army in detail before it could be concentrated. Ewell was directed to take a position opposite the eastern termination of Cemetery Ridge, while Hill occupied the ridge parallel to it; and Longstreet, whose corps had bivouacked four miles in the rear, was to move early the next morning and assail the Federal left, while Ewell was to favor his attack by an assault upon the Federal right. Hill was to hold himself in readiness to throw his strength where it would have the greatest effect.

After completing the duties assigned him, Colonel Long returned to join General Lee, whom he met at Ewell's headquarters about 9 A. M. As it appeared, the general had been waiting there for some time, expecting at every moment to hear of the opening of the attack on the right, and by no means satisfied with the delay. After giving General Ewell instructions as to his part in the coming engagement, he proceeded to reconnoitre Cemetery Ridge in person. He at once saw the importance of an immediate commencement of the assault, as it was evident that the enemy was gradually strengthening his position by fresh arrivals of troops, and that the advantage in numbers and readiness which the Confederate army possessed was rapidly disappearing.

Lee's impatience increased after this reconnoissance, and he proceeded in search of Longstreet, remarking, in a tone of uneasiness, "What *can* detain Longstreet? He ought to be in position now." This was about 10 A. M.

After going some distance he received a message that Longstreet was advancing. This appeared to relieve his anxiety, and he proceeded to the point where he expected the arrival of the corps. Here he waited for some time, during which interval he observed that the enemy had occupied the Peach Orchard, which formed a portion of the ground that was to have been occupied by Longstreet. This was that advance movement of Sickles's command which has given rise to so much controversy among Federal historians.

General Lee, on perceiving this, again expressed his impatience in words and renewed his search for Longstreet. It was now about 1 o'clock P. M. After going some distance to the rear, he discovered Hood's division at a halt, while McLaws was yet at some distance on the Fairfield road, having taken a wrong direction. Longstreet was present, and with General Lee exerted himself to correct the error, but before the corps could be brought into its designated position it was four o'clock. The hope that had been entertained of taking the enemy at a disadvantage and defeating him in detail no longer existed. The whole of the Federal force, except Sedgwick's corps, was strongly posted on Cemetery Ridge. Sedgwick, whose corps had made a march of thirty-five miles in twenty hours, had reached the field, though his men were too much exhausted by the length and rapidity of their march to be of immediate service. Yet the opportunity which the early morning had presented was lost. The entire Army of the Potomac was before us !

General Longstreet has published an explanation of the causes of this unfortunate, if not fatal, delay in the arrival of his troops, yet it cannot be said that the reason which he gives is entirely satisfactory. He says that on the 1st of July the march of his corps had been greatly delayed by the occupation of the road by a division of the Second corps and its wagon-trains. Yet his whole force, except Law's brigade, had reached a position within four miles of Gettysburg by midnight. On the next day, "Fearing that my force was too weak to venture to make an attack, I delayed until General Law's brigade joined its division. As soon after his arrival as we could make our preparations the movement began. Engineers sent out by the commanding general and myself guided us by a road which would have completely disclosed the move. Some delay ensued in seeking a more concealed route.

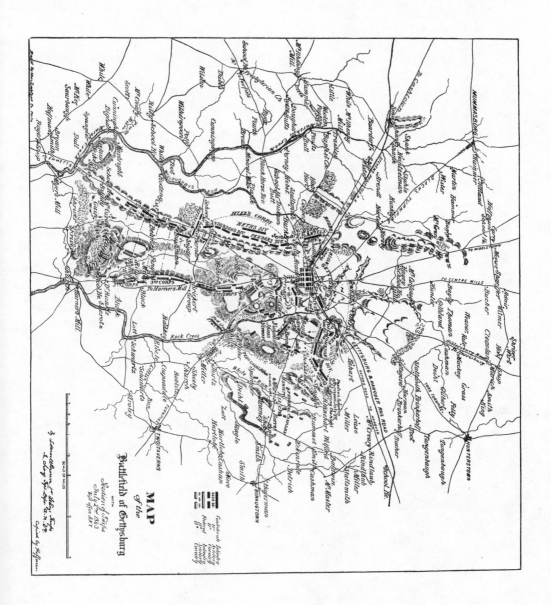

MAP
of the
Battlefield of Gettysburg

WITH
Positions of Troops
July 2nd 1863
9½ o'clock A.M.

McLaws's division got into position opposite the enemy's left about 4 P. M. Hood's division was moved on farther to our right, and got into position, partially enveloping the enemy's left.''

This explanation, as we have said, is not satisfactory. Longstreet, as he admits, had received instructions from Lee to move *with that portion of his command which was up*, to gain the Emmettsburg road. These orders he took the responsibility of postponing on account of the absence of one brigade of his command, so that, instead of being in readiness to attack in the early morning, it was four o'clock in the afternoon when his troops reached the field.

He now found the position which had been laid out for him occupied by Sickles's corps of the Federal army, which had pushed forward considerably in advance of the line of Cemetery Ridge and taken position on the lower ridge along which ran the Emmettsburg road. Cemetery Ridge at this portion of its extent is ill defined, and the movement of Sickles to occupy the advanced position was not without tactical warrant. Yet it was faulty, from the fact that his line, to gain a defensive position for its left flank, had to be bent at a considerable angle at the advanced point known as the "Peach Orchard." General Humphreys's division occupied the road, while Birney's division held the salient point at the Peach Orchard, and was stretched back through low ground of woods and wheatfields toward Round Top, near which the left flank rested in a rocky ravine.

The weak point in this line was the salient at the Peach Orchard, which formed the key of Sickles's position; and on this, when the columns of Longstreet's corps moved to the attack at 4. 30 P. M., the greatest vigor of the assault felt. The first assault, however, was made by Hood's division, which attacked the left wing of Sickles's corps, extending from the Peach Orchard to the vicinity of the two elevations known as Round Top and Little Round Top.

Through an interval which lay between Sickles's left and the foot of Round Top, Hood's extreme right thrust itself unperceived by the Federals, and made a dash for Little Round Top,

which, through some strange oversight, was at this moment
quite unoccupied by any portion of Meade's army.   The elevation known by this name is a bold spur of the loftier height
called Round Top.   It is very rough and rugged, covered with
massive boulders, and rendered difficult of ascent by its steep-
ness and its outcropping granite ledges.   Yet it was the key-
point of that whole section of the battlefield, and had Hood
dreamed of its being unoccupied, pushed a powerful force in
that direction, and seized the commanding summit, the victory
would have been in his grasp, since the possession of this point
would not only have placed Sickles's corps in a highly perilous position, but have enabled him to take the entire line in
reverse.

It was at this critical moment that the Federals discovered
their error and hastened to amend it.   The prompt energy of
a single officer, General Warren, chief engineer of the army,
rescued Meade's army from imminent peril.   He had reached
Little Round Top at the point of time in which Hood's men
penetrated the undefended space between Sickles's left and
Round Top, and just as the signal-officers who occupied the
summit were folding up their flags preparatory to leaving the
dangerous situation.   Directing them to continue waving their
flags, Warren hastened away in search of some available force
to hold the hill, and, meeting a division of Sykes's corps which
was marching to the support of Sickles's command, he detached
from it Vincent's brigade, which he hurried to the threatened
summit.   A battery also, with great difficulty, was dragged
and lifted to the top of the rugged hill.

It was a desperate rush from both sides for the possession of
the important point, and the Federal brigade reached the crest
just as the gallant Texans of Hood's division were swarming
up the rocky slope with shouts of triumph.   There ensued a
desperate struggle for the contested summit.   A severe volley
from the Federals met Hood's men full in the face as they
climbed the steep acclivity.   The fight quickly became a hand-
to-hand conflict, in which levelled bayonet and clubbed musket
did their share in the work of death.   For half an hour the
contest continued.   But the advantage of the Federals in their

possession of the summit was not to be overcome, and, though the brave Texans stubbornly held the rocky glen at the foot of the hill, and worked their way up the ravine between the two elevations, they were eventually forced back by the Federals, though not without causing heavy loss to the latter. The error which had been made by the Federals was immediately retrieved by the reinforcement of Vincent's brigade, while Round Top was occupied at a later hour in the evening.

While this desperate struggle was in progress the assault on Sickles's corps was vigorously pressed by McLaws's division, particularly at the salient in the Peach Orchard, which was evidently the weak point of the line. The Federal resistance was stubborn, and reinforcements were hurried up to the imperilled point; yet the Confederate onslaught proved irresistible, pushing the line back to a wheatfield in the rear of the Peach Orchard, and eventually breaking it and hurling the enemy in disordered flight toward the high grounds in the rear.

This success rendered the Federal position untenable. The flanks of the broken line were exposed right and left, and, though reinforcements were in rapid succession hurried to the front, the whole line was gradually forced back toward Cemetery Ridge, leaving the hotly-contested field strewn with thousands of dead and wounded. Thus, after a severe conflict for several hours, Longstreet had gained the position which he could have occupied earlier in the day without opposition. His advantage had not been gained without heavy loss, and, though the Confederates had gained the base of Cemetery Ridge, its crest was crowned with troops and artillery too strongly placed to be driven out by Longstreet's men in their exhausted condition.

A desperate effort to carry the ridge was made, but it proved unsuccessful, and the battle on that part of the line ended without a decisive result. It had been contested with great determination, and the loss on both sides had been heavy, but the Confederate success had consisted in driving the Federals out of an intrinsically weak position, while the strong defensive line of Cemetery Ridge remained intact in their hands. Whether the result would have been different had the original

assault been made on this line is a question which it is impossible now to answer, and the advantage or disadvantage of
Sickles's advance movement cannot be determined except
from the standpoint of military strategy.

During Longstreet's assault on the right Hill's corps had
made strong demonstrations against the Federal centre, but
Ewell's demonstration on the left, which was ordered to be
made at the same time, was delayed, and the corps only got
fairly to work about sunset. The assault was maintained with
great spirit by the divisions of Early and Edward Johnson
until after dark. Early carried Cemetery Ridge, but was
forced to relinquish it by superior numbers. The left of Ewell's corps penetrated the breastworks on the extreme right of
the Federal line, and this position was held during the night.
The ill-success of Early's movement was due to lack of support, the columns on his right failing to reach the contested
point until after he had been forced to relinquish the position
he had gained on the crest and retire to his original ground.

In the words of Colonel Taylor, ''The whole affair was dis-
jointed. There was an utter absence of accord in the movements
of the several commands, and no decisive results attended the
operations of the second day.'' This discordance was one of
the unfortunate contingencies to which every battle is subject,
and is in no sense chargeable to General Lee, whose plan had
been skilfully laid, and had it been carried out in strict accordance with his instructions would probably have led to a very
different result. On both sides the disregard by corps commanders of the express intentions of their superiors had
changed the conditions of the battle. Sickles's advance beyond the position designed to be held by General Meade had
exposed his corps to repulse and heavy loss, which possibly
might have been avoided had he held the line of Cemetery
Ridge, while Longstreet's assumption of the responsibility of
delaying the assault ordered certainly had a most important
influence on the result of the battle.

The dawn of the 3d of July found the two armies in the
position in which the battle of the preceding day had ended.
Though Cemetery Ridge remained intact in the hands of the

Federals, yet the engagement had resulted at every point in an advantage to the Confederates. Longstreet had cleared his front of the enemy, and occupied the ground from which they had been driven. Ewell's left held the breastworks on Culp's Hill on the extreme right of the Federal line. Meade's army was known to have sustained heavy losses. There was, in consequence, good reason to believe that a renewed assault might prove successful. Ewell's position of advantage, if held, would enable him to take the Federal line in reverse, while an advance in force from Longstreet's position offered excellent promise of success. General Lee therefore determined to renew the assault.

Longstreet, in accordance with this decision, was reinforced, and ordered to assail the heights in his front on the morning of the 3d, while Ewell was directed to make a simultaneous assault on the enemy's right. Longstreet's dispositions, however, were not completed as early as those of Ewell, and the battle opened on the left before the columns on the right were ready to move. Johnson, whose men held the captured breastworks, had been considerably reinforced during the night, and was on the point of resuming the attack when the Federals opened on him at four o'clock with a heavy fire of artillery which had been placed in position under cover of the darkness. An infantry assault in force followed, and, though Ewell's men held their ground with their usual stubbornness, and maintained their position for four hours, they were finally forced to yield the captured breastworks and retire before the superior force of the enemy.

This change in the condition of affairs rendered necessary a reconsideration of the military problem, and induced General Lee, after making a reconnoissance of the enemy's position, to change his plan of assault. Cemetery Ridge, from Round Top to Culp's Hill, was at every point strongly occupied by Federal infantry and artillery, and was evidently a very formidable position. There was, however, a weak point upon which an attack could be made with a reasonable prospect of success. This was where the ridge, sloping westward, formed the depression through which the Emmettsburg road passes. Perceiving that by forcing the Federal lines at that point and turning toward Cemetery Hill the right would be taken in flank and the remainder would be neutralized, as its fire would be as destructive to friend as foe, and considering that the losses of the Federal army in the two preceding days must weaken its cohesion and consequently diminish its power of resistance, General Lee determined to attack at that point, and the execution of it was assigned to Longstreet, while instructions were given to Hill and Ewell to support him, and a hundred and forty-five guns were massed to cover the advance of the attacking column.

The decision here indicated was reached at a conference held during the morning on the field in front of and within cannon-range of Round Top, there being present Generals Lee, Longstreet, A. P. Hill, and H. Heth, Colonel A. L. Long, and Major C. S. Venable. The plan of attack was discussed, and it was decided that General Pickett should lead the assaulting column, to be supported by the divisions of McLaws and Hood and such other force as A. P. Hill could spare from his command. The only objection offered was by General Longstreet, who remarked that the guns on Round Top might be brought to bear on his right. This objection was answered by Colonel Long, who said that the guns on Round Top could be suppressed by our batteries. This point being settled, the attack was ordered, and General Longstreet was directed to carry it out.

Pickett's division was fresh, having taken no part in the previous day's fight, and to these veterans was given the post of honor in the coming affray, which promised to be a desperate and terrible one.

About twelve o'clock the preparations for the attack were completed and the signal for battle was given, which was immediately followed by the concentrated fire of all the Confederate artillery on Cemetery Hill, which was promptly responded to by the powerful Federal batteries. Then ensued one of the most tremendous artillery engagements ever witnessed on an open field: the hills shook and quivered beneath the thunder of two hundred and twenty-five guns as if they were about to be torn and rent by some powerful convulsion. In the words of General Hancock in reference to the performance of the opposing batteries, "Their artillery fire was the most terrific cannonade I ever witnessed, and the most prolonged— . . . . one possibly hardly ever paralleled."

For more than an hour this fierce artillery conflict continued, when the Federal guns began to slacken their fire under the heavy blows of the Confederate batteries, and ere long sank into silence—an example which was quickly followed by the Confederates.

A deathlike stillness then reigned over the field, and each army remained in breathless expectation of something yet to come still more dreadful. · In a few moments the attacking column, consisting of Pickett's division, supported on the left by that of Heth commanded by Pettigrew, and on the right by Wilcox's brigade of Anderson's division, appeared from behind a ridge, and, sweeping over its crest, descended into the depression that separated the two armies. The enemy for a moment seemed lost in admiration of this gallant array as it advanced with the steadiness and precision of a review. Their batteries then opened upon it a spasmodic fire, as if recovering from a stunning blow. The force that moved to the attack numbered about 15,000 men. It had a terrible duty to perform. The distance which it was obliged to traverse was more than half a mile in width, and this an open plain in full front of the enemy, who thickly crowded the crest of the ridge, and within easy range of their artillery.

But the tempest of fire which burst upon the devoted column quickly reduced its strength. The troops of Heth's division, decimated by the storm of deadly hail which tore through their ranks, faltered and fell back in disorder before the withering volleys of the Federal musketry. This compelled Pender's division, which had marched out to support the movement, to fall back, while Wilcox, on perceiving that the attack had failed, fell back, after severe loss, leaving Pickett's men to continue the charge alone. The other supports, Hood's and McLaws's divisions, which had been expected to advance in support of the charging column, did not move, and were too remote to offer any assistance. The consequence was that Pickett was left entirely unsupported.

Yet the gallant Virginians marched steadily forward, through the storm of shot and shell that burst upon their devoted ranks, with a gallantry that has never been surpassed. As they approached the ridge their lines were torn by incessant volleys of musketry as by a deadly hail. Yet with unfaltering courage the brave fellows broke into the double-quick, and with an irresistible charge burst into the Federal lines and drove everything before them toward the crest of **Cemetery Hill**, leaping the breastworks and planting their standards on the captured guns with shouts of victory.

The success which General Lee had hoped and expected was gained, but it was a dearly-bought and short-lived one. His plan had gone astray through the failure of the supporting columns. Now was the time that they should have come to the aid of their victorious comrades; but, alas! Heth's division, which had behaved with the greatest gallantry two days before, had not been able to face the terrible fire of the Federal lines, while the other supports were too remote to afford timely relief. The victory which seemed within the grasp of the Confederate army was lost as soon as won. On every side the enemy closed in on Pickett's brigades, concentrating on them the fire of every gun in that part of their lines. It was impossible to long withstand this terrific fusillade. The band of heroes broke and fell back, leaving the greater part of their number dead or wounded upon the field or captive in the hands of their foes.

In justice to Heth's division it must be remembered that on the 1st it was the first to attack the enemy, and maintain an unequal contest until it was reinforced by General Pender with his gallant North Carolinians, and a little later by two divisions of Ewell's corps, and that it continued to oppose the enemy with great gallantry to the close of the action, and suffered heavily both in officers and men, which greatly impaired on the 3d its usual firmness. The brigades of Pender's division had been heavily engaged both on the 1st and 2d, and on the 3d the brigades of Lane and Scales behaved with distinguished gallantry under General Trimble. Wilcox's brigade had gallantly supported Longstreet's attack on the afternoon of the 2d, and on the 3d was prevented by difficulties of the ground from keeping pace with the attacking column; and when it was seen that Pickett's attack had failed, it fell back in good order after having sustained heavy loss. All must admit that the troops from the different States were equally distinguished for valor and patriotism.

The Confederates lost in this attack about 4000 men, the most of whom were in Pickett's division. No troops could have behaved better than those of the Army of Northern Virginia on witnessing Pickett's repulse. The officers of every grade on that part of the field exerted themselves with the utmost coolness in preserving order and in endeavoring to re-form the broken ranks, and the men so promptly obeyed the call to rally that their thin ranks were soon restored to order and the whole line was again established. The army was not discouraged or dispirited, and its sole wish was for an opportunity to efface the mortification of its first serious repulse. The desire was general that Meade should assume the offensive and in his turn make an attack, and no doubt was felt of the ability to give him a yet hotter reception than that which Pickett had received. But Meade found his army so much shattered and discouraged by his recent losses that he deemed it inadvisable to attempt to follow up his success.

That this view is correct is proved by the following passage from Mr. William Swinton's *History of the Army of the Potomac.* Mr. Swinton says: "I have become convinced from the testimony of General Longstreet himself that attack would have resulted disastrously. 'I had,' said that officer to the writer, 'Hood and McLaws, who had not been engaged; I had a heavy force of artillery; I should have liked nothing better than to have been attacked, and have no doubt that I should have given those who tried as bad a reception as Pickett received.'"

Mr. Swinton further informs us that besides the heavy loss it had sustained by Pickett's attack, the Army of the Potomac was thrown into much confusion by the intermingling of the troops of different divisions and corps. Among the wounded were Major-generals Hancock and Gibbon, two of its most prominent officers. The same writer also informs us that the aggregate loss of the Army of the Potomac during the three days' battle was 23,000 men. Among the officers killed was Major-general J. F. Reynolds, whose gentlemanly bearing and soldierly qualities were unsurpassed in any other officer of either army. In view of this heavy loss, while admitting that General Lee was defeated, it must be acknowledged that General Meade was so much crippled that he could not reap any advantage of victory.

The attack of Pickett's division on the 3d has been more criticised, and is still less understood, than any other act of the Gettysburg drama. General Longstreet did not enter into the spirit of it, and consequently did not support it with his wonted vigor. It has been characterized as rash and objectless, on the order of the "charge of the Light Brigade." Nevertheless, it was not ordered without mature consideration and on grounds that presented fair prospects of success. By extending his left wing west of the Emmettsburg road, Meade weakened his position by presenting a weak centre, which being penetrated, his wings would be isolated and paralyzed, so far as regarded supporting each other. A glance at a correct sketch of the Federal position on the 3d will sufficiently corroborate this remark, and had Pickett's division been promptly supported when it burst through Meade's centre, a more positive proof would have been given, for his right wing would have been overwhelmed before the left could have disengaged itself from woods and mountains and come to its relief.

Pickett's charge has been made the subject of so much discussion, and General Lee's intentions in ordering it have been so misunderstood, that it is deemed proper to here offer, in corroboration of what has been said above, the testimony of one who was thoroughly conversant with all the facts. Colonel Walter H. Taylor, adjutant-general on the staff of General Lee, in *Southern Historical Society Papers*, vol. iv. p. 83, states as follows: "Later, General Lee rode over to General Ewell's front and conferred as to future movements. He wanted to follow up the success gained—thought that with Johnson's division, then up, that General Ewell could go forward at dawn next day. Ewell, Early, and Rodes thought it best to await Longstreet's arrival and make the main attack on the enemy's left. This was determined on. Longstreet was then about four miles off, with two of his divisions. He was expected early on the morning of the 2d. Orders were sent him to move up to gain the Emmettsburg road. He did not reach the field early, and his dispositions were not completed for attack until four o'clock in the afternoon. In his report General Longstreet says he received orders to move with the portion of his command that was then up, to gain the Emmettsburg road on the enemy's left, but, fearing that he was too weak to attack, he delayed until one of his brigades (Law's) joined its division, and that he began the movement as soon after its arrival as his preparations would admit. It seemed impossible to get the co-operation of the commanders along the line. When Longstreet did attack, he did it in handsome style—drove the enemy and captured prisoners, artillery, and other trophies. So far, we had succeeded in every encounter with the enemy. It was thought that a continuance of the attack as made by Longstreet offered promise of success. He was ordered to renew the fight early on the 3d; Ewell, who was to co-operate, ordered Johnson to attack at an early hour, anticipating that Longstreet would do the same. Longstreet delayed. He found that a force of the enemy occupying high ground on their left would take his troops in reverse as they advanced. Longstreet was then visited by General Lee, and they conferred as to the mode of attack. It was determined to adhere to the plan proposed, and to strengthen him for the movement he was to be reinforced by Heth's division and two brigades of Pender's of Hill's corps. With his three divisions which were to attack Longstreet made his dispositions, and General Lee went to the centre to observe movements. The attack was not made as designed: Pickett's division, Heth's division, and two brigades of Pender's division advanced. Hood and McLaws were not moved forward. There were nine divisions in the army; seven were quiet, while two assailed the fortified line of the enemy. A. P. Hill had orders to be prepared to assist Longstreet further if necessary. Anderson, who commanded one of Hill's divisions and was in readiness to respond to Longstreet's call, made his dispositions to advance, but General Longstreet told him it was of no use—the attack had failed. Had Hood and McLaws followed or supported Pickett, and Pettigrew and Anderson been advanced, the design of the commanding general would have been carried out: the world would not be so at a loss to understand what was designed by throwing forward, unsupported, against the enemy's stronghold so small a portion of our army. Had General Lee known what was to happen, doubtless he would have manœuvred to force General Meade away from his strong position by threatening his communications with the East, as suggested by ——; but he felt strong enough to carry the enemy's lines, and I believe success would have crowned his plan had it been faithfully carried out.''

The author can add his testimony to that of Colonel Taylor. The original intention of General Lee was that Pickett's attack should be supported by the divisions of McLaws and Hood,* and General Longstreet was so ordered. This order was given verbally by General Lee in the presence of Colonel Long and Major Venable of his staff and other officers of the army.

It is to be regretted that we have no report from the gallant General Pickett in regard to this celebrated charge. It has, however, recently been developed that Pickett did make a very full report, which he forwarded to General Lee. The report severely criticised the failure to furnish him with the supporting force which had been ordered ; and Lee, with his usual magnanimity, and in his great desire for harmony between the officers of his army, returned the report to Pickett, requesting him to withdraw it and to substitute in its stead a report embracing merely the casualties of his command ; to which Pickett assented and destroyed his first report.

The following is a copy of General Lee's letter to General Pickett in which he made this request :

---

* "As they were ordered by General Lee, for I heard him give the orders when arranging the fight, and called his attention to it long afterward, when there was discussion about it. He said, 'I know it! I know it!'   C. S. VENABLE."

"GENERAL G. E. PICKETT, *commanding General:*

"You and your men have crowned yourselves with glory, but we have the enemy to fight, and must carefully, at this critical moment, guard against dissensions which the reflections in your report will create. I will therefore suggest that you destroy both copy and original, substituting one confined to casualties merely.

"I hope all will yet be well.

"I am, with respect, your obedient servant,

"R. E. LEE,
" *General.*"

But one course remained open for General Lee. Retreat was necessary. After the failure of the attack he had withdrawn Ewell to Seminary Ridge, a position north-west of the town, covering the Chambersburg and Fairfield roads, which he caused to be rapidly and strongly fortified in anticipation of the assault which this contraction of his line might invite. He had still an army of 50,000 men, unbroken in spirit and quite ready to sustain any attack which might be made upon them. But it was quickly evident that Meade had no intention of making an aggressive movement, and a renewed assault on the part of the Confederates would have been madness. Moreover, the ammunition of the army had been nearly exhausted in the three days' fight, and, in Lee's own words, "the difficulty of procuring supplies rendered it impossible to continue longer where we were." There was danger of the line of communications being cut by the enemy. General Meade had sent a force to reoccupy Harper's Ferry, and a body of Federal cavalry had reached the Potomac near Falling Waters and destroyed the pontoon bridge laid there for the passage of the Confederate army.

Under these circumstances General Lee determined upon a retreat, but not such an immediate or hasty one as would present the appearance of flight. That he had deeply felt the failure of his effort is unquestionable, yet he preserved much of his ordinary calmness of demeanor, and not one word came from his lips to show that he laid blame on any subordinate officer. An incident is told which shows in a clear light his noble spirit.

The repulse of Pickett's column, and the terrible loss it had sustained, were a severe blow to that gallant officer. Overcome by the disaster to his men, he rode up to General Lee, and, almost sobbing, declared that his division had been nearly destroyed. Lee listened with his face full of sympathy, and replied with his usual kindness and consideration, "Never mind, general; all this has been *my* fault. It is *I* who have lost this fight, and you must help me out of it in the best way you can."

In illustration of his feeling concerning this battle we may here quote from a private letter to a lady relative which has been kindly placed at our disposal. After remarking, "I cannot tell how often and much I have thought of you the past winter, how I have grieved over your restraint and ill-usage by our enemies, and how I have regretted my inability to relieve you," he continues:

"I knew that crossing the Potomac would draw them off, and if we could only have been strong enough we should have detained them. But God willed otherwise, and I fear we shall soon have them all back. The army did all it could. I fear I required of it impossibilities. But it responded to the call nobly and cheerfully, and, though it did not win a victory, it conquered a success. We must now prepare for heavier blows and harder work. But my trust is in Him who favors the weak and relieves the oppressed, and my hourly prayer is that He will 'fight for us once again.'"

During the interval between the repulse of Pickett's charge and the night of July 4th no aggressive movement was made by General Meade, and the Army of Northern Virginia was left undisturbed by the enemy. General Lee employed this repose in preparation for his retreat. He caused the dead to be buried and the severely wounded to be carefully provided for, while those whose wounds permitted their removal were placed in ambulances and wagons and moved out on the Chambersburg road. In the afternoon the ambulance- and empty supply-trains, under the escort of Imboden's cavalry, were put in motion on the Chambersburg road, and after passing South Mountain were moved on the direct road to Williamsport.

When it became dark the withdrawal of the army began. First the trains, under protection of Hill's corps, moved out on the Fairfield road ; Longstreet followed Hill ; then came Ewell, bringing up the rear. The movement was so much impeded by soft roads, darkness, and rains that the rear-guard could not be withdrawn until daylight on the morning of the 5th. General Meade did not attempt to harass the retreating columns of Lee until the rear-guard had reached the neighborhood of Fairfield ; then a pursuing column appeared on the neighboring heights, which Early promptly prepared to meet by throwing the rear-guard across its path. After exchanging a few shots the enemy retired, and the retreat was continued without any other molestation than an attack on the ambulance-train by a detachment of the enemy's cavalry and the capture of a few ambulances and wagons loaded with wounded. This mishap was attributable more to the roving character and want of discipline of the escort than to the daring of the enemy.

Without further interruption the trains reached Williamsport on the 6th, where their progress was arrested by a swollen river. Being menaced soon after their arrival by a large body of the enemy's cavalry, 1500 teamsters promptly volunteered, and, being armed with muskets brought from Gettysburg, gallantly defended their trains until reinforced by General Fitz Lee, when the combined force of teamsters and cavalry signally repulsed the enemy. About the same time Stuart encountered Pleasonton near Hagerstown, and after a fierce conflict Pleasonton was obliged to retire behind the Antietam.

The army bivouacked on the night of the 5th in South Mountain Pass, and on the morning of the 6th entered the rich and beautiful Cumberland Valley. The sky had cleared, and the bright sun and beautiful landscape filled the hearts of the stern veterans with pleasure as they passed with measured tread over the smooth and easy-graded roads.

Reaching Williamsport on the 7th, and finding his pontoon bridge destroyed and the Potomac swollen far above the fording-point, General Lee occupied a strong position, covering

Williamsport and Falling Waters, the point where he had left his bridge on advancing into Pennsylvania. As day after day passed without the appearance of the enemy, General Lee was able to complete his defences, so that when Meade arrived in force on the 12th the Army of Northern Virginia was eager to encounter its old antagonist, though double its numerical strength.

"The retreat of Lee, which became definitely known to the Federal commander on the morning of Sunday, July 5th, brought with it the important question of pursuit. Now, there were two lines by which the Confederates might be followed up: the one was a direct pursuit by the same routes over which they had retreated, pressing them down the Cumberland Valley; the other, a flank march by the east side of the South Mountains, defiling by the Boonsboro' passes, with the view to head off the enemy or take him in flank. The former had the advantage of being the shorter line—the distance to the Potomac at Williamsport being in this case about forty miles, and by the latter line nearly eighty. The only disadvantage attending it arose from the fact that the enemy might hold the débouches of the mountains with a rear-guard while making good his escape with his main body and trains. General Meade appears to have been in some doubt as to the proper method of action, but on the morning of the 6th he sent a column in direct pursuit. He ordered Sedgwick's Sixth corps, then the freshest in the army, to follow up the enemy on the Fairfield road, while he despatched a cavalry force to press the retreating Confederates on the Chambersburg road. Sedgwick that evening overtook the rear of the Confederate column, after a pursuit of ten miles, where the Fairfield road breaks through a pass in the South Mountain range. This position was found to be very defensible, but there was no attack, as another course had meanwhile been determined on, and Sedgwick was recalled. Instead of pursuing the Confederates by the direct route over which the retreat had been made, Meade judged it better to make a flank march by Middletown and the lower passes of the South Mountain. To this end, General French, who with 7000 men had since the evacuation of Harper's Ferry been occupying Frederick, was directed to seize these passes in advance and repossess himself of Harper's Ferry. Both of these orders were executed by General French, who also sent out a cavalry force that penetrated as far as Williamsport and destroyed there a pontoon bridge across the Potomac. Then the army was put in motion by the east side of the South Mountains. On July 6th a large part of the army moved from Gettysburg toward Emmettsburg, and the remainder on the following day.

"On July 7th the Federal headquarters were at Frederick. On the 8th they were at Middletown, and nearly all the army was concentrated in the neighborhood of that place and South Mountain. On the 9th the headquarters were at South Mountain House, and the advance of the army at Boonsboro' and Rohrersville. On the 10th they were moved to Antietam Creek, while the left of the line crossed the creek and the right moved up near Funkstown. On the 11th the engineers threw a new bridge over the Antietam Creek, when the left of the line advanced to Fairplay and Jones's Cross-roads, while the right remained nearly stationary. On the 12th, Meade had his forces in front of the position taken up by Lee to cover the passage of the Potomac.

"The above data will suffice to show that the pursuit was conducted with an excessive circumspection, and that Lee, having reached the river six days before, had time to select and fortify a strong position. Indeed, the Confederate army might have effected an unmolested escape into Virginia had it not been for the fact that the great rains had so swollen the Potomac as to make it impassable by the ford at Williamsport, and that the pontoon bridge at Falling Waters had been destroyed by General French. This perilous circumstance compelled Lee to take up a defensive position where he might stand at bay while his communications were being re-established." *

From the fact that Lee was not pursued, and that no effort was made to crush him before he could extricate himself from his perilous situation at Williamsport, it would be just to conclude that the Army of the Potomac was too much crippled to do so, and that Meade's success was mainly due to the want of

* Swinton's *Campaigns of the Army of the Potomac,* pp. 366-368.

prompt co-operation by a portion of the forces of his antagonist, otherwise, as an able general, he would have vigorously followed up his advantage in order to gather the fruits of his victory.

Notwithstanding the Army of the Potomac after its departure from Gettysburg was reinforced to its former numerical strength, General Meade did not attack, but employed the 12th and 13th in fortifying his position. On the other hand, General Lee, now that his bridge was finished and that the river had fallen so as to be fordable for cavalry and empty and lightly-loaded wagons, being unwilling to engage in a battle that could not promise important results, withdrew from his position on the night of the 13th, and retired across the Potomac. The movement was completed during the forenoon of the 14th without interruption, and the broad Potomac rolled between the hostile armies. The only incident that indicated that the retreat had been discovered was the charge of a squadron of Federal cavalry on the rear-guard as it was about to follow the army across the river, the result of which was a slight loss to the Confederates, including the gallant General Pettigrew of North Carolina, who was rapidly rising to distinction. General Lee continued to retire slowly toward Winchester, and shortly after Meade moved down the river to the neighborhood of Harper's Ferry, and late in July entered Virginia east of the Blue Ridge, whereupon Lee withdrew from the Valley and took a position behind the Rapidan about the 1st of August, while General Meade occupied the neighborhood of Culpeper Court-house.

The losses of the army in killed, wounded, and prisoners were heavy, reaching nearly 16,000 men: many of these, however, being slightly wounded, returned to the ranks in time to participate in the ensuing campaign. Amongst the killed were Generals Armistead, Garnett, and Barksdale, gallant soldiers, much beloved by the army; among the wounded were Generals Hood, Heth, and Kemper, and Pender mortally.

The Army of Northern Virginia was distinguished for valor in battle, for discipline and patient endurance on the toilsome marches and in comfortless bivouacs: although depressed by defeat, it did not lose its courage for a moment, nor was its confidence shaken in its great commander.

Having placed the army in position on the Rapidan, and fearing the failure of his campaign in Pennsylvania might have caused the Confederate authorities to lose confidence in him, and feeling unwilling by retaining command of the army to embarrass them in their future plan of operations, General Lee sent his resignation to the President; which was, however, returned by Mr. Davis with every assurance of confidence.

Colonel Venable has related to the author an anecdote of considerable interest as showing the estimable character of General Lee. The incident occurred during the retreat from Gettysburg.

One day in July, 1863, after the battle of Gettysburg, when the Army of Northern Virginia lay on the north bank of the Potomac between Williamsport and Falling Waters, General Lee spoke pretty hotly to Lieutenant-colonel Venable of his staff for making a report of an unsatisfactory condition of things at the Williamsport ford or ferry in too loud a tone of voice. Venable retired to his tent in no pleasant mood. Very soon, however, the general sent him an invitation to come and drink a glass of buttermilk with him. He of course accepted the invitation, but his angry feelings at what he esteemed an unmerited rebuke were only partially soothed by partaking of the friendly glass of the mild but sour beverage with his honored chieftain. On the next night the army recrossed the Potomac. About 3 A. M., after getting through the work of supervision of the crossing of the army-trains at one of the Williamsport fords, which had been assigned to Lieutenant-colonel Baldwin and himself, Venable rode down, in a drizzling rain, to the vicinity of the pontoon bridge at Falling Waters. Having made his report, he threw himself on the ground near by, and soon fell asleep. When he awoke he found General Lee had taken the oil-cloth poncho from his own shoulders and thrown it over him. The hot-tempered aide-de-camp was thoroughly conquered.

We cannot better end this somewhat extended chapter than by presenting the following incident, for whose authenticity we can give no higher authority than the columns of a newspaper, yet which is so consonant with all that the writer knows of the character of General Lee that no better voucher for its complete truth could be offered.   It is a story told by an old "Grand Army" man who has been viewing the panorama of the battle of Gettysburg, and says:

"I was at the battle of Gettysburg myself, and an incident occurred there which largely changed my views of the Southern people.   I had been a most bitter anti-South man, and fought and cursed the Confederates desperately.   I could see nothing good in any of them.   The last day of the fight I was badly wounded.   A ball shattered my left leg.   I lay on the ground not far from Cemetery Ridge, and as General Lee ordered his retreat he and his officers rode near me.   As they came along I recognized him, and, though faint from exposure and loss of blood, I raised up my hands, looked Lee in the face, and shouted as loud as I could, 'Hurrah for the Union!'   The general heard me, looked, stopped his horse, dismounted, and came toward me.   I confess that I at first thought he meant to kill me.   But as he came up he looked down at me with such a sad expression upon his face that all fear left me, and I wondered what he was about.   He extended his hand to me, and grasping mine firmly and looking right into my eyes, said, 'My son, I hope you will soon be well.'

"If I live a thousand years I shall never forget the expression on General Lee's face.   There he was, defeated, retiring from a field that had cost him and his cause almost their last hope, and yet he stopped to say words like those to a wounded soldier of the opposition who had taunted him as he passed by !   As soon as the general had left me I cried myself to sleep there upon the bloody ground."

General Lee and the Wounded Union Soldier.   Page 302.

CHAPTER XVI.

A CAMPAIGN OF STRATEGY.

FOR several weeks both armies remained inactive in the positions they had assumed—Lee on the Rapidan, and Meade in the vicinity of Culpeper Court-house. During that time so many convalescents and other absentees were restored to the ranks that the Army of Northern Virginia, with a small accession from other sources, was raised to a strength of nearly 60,000 men. Since the reorganization of the artillery in May that arm had been greatly increased in efficiency; and as the scope for promotion had been extended, many artillery officers who had been previously confined to the lower grades had now before them a prospect of advancement. About the last of September, Colonel Long of General Lee's staff was promoted to the rank of brigadier-general, and assigned to the command of the artillery of the Second corps. Colonel E. P. Alexander of the artillery of the First, and Colonel Lindsay Walker, chief of that of the Third corps, were a little later promoted to a similar rank to Colonel Long, and a number of other promotions were made in the lower grades. The repose of two months had greatly improved the condition of the Confederate army.

Within the same period two corps had been detached from

the Federal army, and about the same time Longstreet with
two divisions was withdrawn from the Army of Northern Virginia to reinforce General Bragg in Tennessee, and the third
division (Pickett's) was sent to the district south of Petersburg
to arrest raiding-parties of the enemy and collect supplies for
the army.　This reduction brought the opposing forces more
nearly to a numerical equality than had previously been the
case, and the change of conditions in his favor induced Lee
to make an effort to force Meade to an engagement while his
army was reduced in numbers.

There ensued a singular and interesting campaign, in which
manœuvring in great measure took the place of fighting, each
of the commanding generals endeavoring to take the other at
a disadvantage, and each signally failing through the alertness
and skill of his opponent.　It was a game of wits instead of
bullets, and for two months the armies were marched back and
forth over the war-trodden soil of Virginia, ending very much
where they began, the advantages of the game being about
equal on both sides.

In pursuance of his plan of operations, on the 9th of October
Lee crossed the Rapidan, and advanced to the neighborhood
of Madison Court-house, leaving Fitz Lee with his division
of cavalry and a small detachment of infantry to guard the
fords of that stream, while Stuart with Hampton's division
covered the army from the intrusion of the Federal cavalry,
which was at that time picketing Robinson's River.　On the
10th, Stuart encountered Kilpatrick's cavalry in the neighborhood of James City, and after a sharp conflict Kilpatrick withdrew, but still hovered in the vicinity of Stuart during the
remainder of that day and part of the next, without, however, inviting another collision.　From Madison Court-house
Lee directed his course eastward, taking a circuitous route in
order to screen his movements from observation by means of
the forest and intervening mountain-spurs.　Being much retarded by difficult roads, he did not reach his objective point
near Culpeper Court-house until the afternoon of the 11th, too
late to assail the Federal position that day.

Meanwhile, Meade had become aware of the movement of

the Confederate army. His first intimation of this had come from the cavalry engagement between Kilpatrick and Stuart. It becoming clear that Lee's infantry was moving in the rear of the cavalry, and that the Federal right was already turned, Meade quietly withdrew his army from its position at Culpeper, and retired during the night along the line of the Orange and Alexandria Railroad toward the Rappahannock. Pleasonton's cavalry was left to cover the retreat.

Stuart, whom Fitz Lee had joined on the previous evening, pushed forward with his usual energy, and on reaching Culpeper Court-house came upon the enemy's rear-guard, consisting of Kilpatrick's division of cavalry, which occupied the ridges east of the village. As Stuart approached they fell back toward Brandy Station. Stuart pursued with Hampton's division, and a little beyond the station closed on Kilpatrick and forced him to an engagement. On hearing the sound of battle, Fitz Lee came rapidly to the support of Stuart, but at the moment he was about to attack Kilpatrick in flank he discovered Buford on his own flank in order of battle. Affairs had now assumed a most singular attitude, Kilpatrick being between Stuart and Fitz Lee, while Fitz Lee was between Kilpatrick and Buford. Fitz Lee dexterously extricated himself from this perilous situation, while Kilpatrick availed himself of the opportunity to join Buford. Stuart and Pleasonton, being now again face to face with nearly equal force, renewed the conflict on the same ground which had been the scene of an indefinite conclusion several months before—one of the most brilliant cavalry engagements of the war, in which both sides claimed the victory. The advantage of the present affair remained with the Southern cavalry, their opponents retiring before them toward the Rappahannock. That night the Federal army crossed the river and blew up the railroad bridge in their rear.

Thus ended the first move in the game. On the approach of Lee his alert opponent had hastily retired, yet with such skill that nothing of value was left behind. Lee's purpose of bringing the enemy to battle south of the Rappahannock had been foiled by this rapid retreat. It became necessary, if the flanking movement was to be continued, to cross the river and endeavor to reach the Orange and Alexandria Railroad in time to intercept the retreat of the foe. Unluckily, the rapidity of movement which this required was hindered by a lack of provisions. The army was obliged to remain at Culpeper Courthouse nearly all day of the 11th in order to collect supplies.

During this halt an incident occurred which shows an interesting phase of General Lee's character, and which we give in the words of General Hunt:

"Lee, while encamped at Culpeper, was of course cordially received by the people of the town. One of these, a lady who had been somewhat scandalized by the friendly relations between some of her neighbors and the Yankees, took occasion to complain to the general that certain young ladies, then present, had been in the habit of visiting General Sedgwick at his headquarters, which was pitched in the ample grounds of a citizen whose house he had declined to use.

"The young ladies were troubled, for the general looked very grave. But they were soon relieved when he said, 'I know General Sedgwick very well. It is just like him to be so kindly and considerate, and to have his band there to entertain them.—So, young ladies, if the music is good, go and hear it as often as you can, and enjoy yourselves. You will find that General Sedgwick will have none but agreeable gentlemen about him.'"

Early on the morning of the 12th, Lee became aware of the Federal movement. The army was at once put in motion in the direction of Warrenton Springs. The advance and retreat now presented much the character of a race. There is reason to believe that Meade was as willing to accept battle as Lee was to offer it, but neither general had any desire to fight at a disadvantage, and a brisk series of manœuvres for the advantage of position began.

Directing Stuart to follow and retard as much as possible the retreating column of the enemy, Lee advanced by a route nearly parallel with that on which Meade was retreating, with the hope of intercepting him at some point north of the Rappahannock.

Meanwhile, Meade had made a false move in the game which threatened to place him in a dangerous position. On the morning of the 12th he became aware of Lee's halt at Culpeper during the previous day. Conceiving the idea that his own haste had been premature, and that the intended movement of the Confederate general had been completed, he ordered a countermarch of the main body of the army to the south of the Rappahannock, retaining only the Third corps and General Gregg's cavalry division on the north of the stream.

The situation was now a singular one. While Lee was marching rapidly northward to seize Meade's communications, the latter was marching southward to meet Lee at Culpeper. It was an error that might have proved disastrous to the Federal army had not its commander become speedily aware of his mistake.

Gregg's division of cavalry, which had been advanced to watch the passage of the upper Rappahannock at Warrenton Springs, found itself assailed on the afternoon of the 12th by the van-guard of Lee's army, which was crossing the stream at that point. Gregg was severely handled by the Confederate column, and hastened back to apprise Meade of the movement he had discovered.

There was no longer any doubt as to Lee's intention. A courier was at once sent back in all haste to the three Federal corps south of the river to apprise them that the whole Confederate army was in full march upon Warrenton. Reaching them about midnight at their bivouac on the road to Culpeper, the messenger delivered his order, and very soon afterward the camp was broken up and the whole force in a rapid retrograde march toward the stream which they had so recently crossed. On the morning of the 13th the Federal army was again concentrated on the north of the Rappahannock.

Lee, unaware of the division of the Federal army and of the smallness of the force that was opposed to him north of the river, lost the important advantage which might have come from an attack on this single corps had he been advised of its isolated position. He continued his march upon Warrenton, in which location he was beyond the head of Meade's column, and if he could have continued the pursuit on a converging line, he would have reached Bristoe Station in advance of Meade, and could have forced him to a general engagement. But as the army had progressed more rapidly than the supply-trains and the haversacks of the men were empty, it was necessary to halt in order to replenish them.

In the mean time, Stuart was expected to retard the retreat of the enemy as much as possible, and keep General Lee fully informed of his movements. While thus employed he observed a large wagon-train, and, hoping to secure a valuable prize, he pushed forward two brigades for that purpose. It may be remarked that an attack upon the train might have been the most effective way of accomplishing his purpose of retarding the Federal retreat, as Meade would have probably come to the rescue of so important an element in his army. But on approaching the train Stuart found it too strongly guarded to admit a possibility of its capture; he therefore abandoned the enterprise and prepared to regain his former position, when to his chagrin he found himself intercepted by two large bodies of Federal infantry, who were marching north by parallel roads on both sides of his position. His only chance of escape was to conceal his force from observation, which he did with remarkable coolness and address behind a wooded ridge that flanked the enemy's line of retreat. Here he was compelled, by the proximity of the enemy, to remain twelve hours. The position was a perilous one, as the coming of daylight would expose his little force to capture or annihilation. He sent a staff officer, Major A. R. Venable, to ride in the darkness between the two marching columns of the enemy until he could pass around the head of that one between him and the Confederate forces, and report his danger and the movements of the enemy to the commanding general. As this was a long road, he also sent one of his favorite scouts, Goode, to make his way on foot directly through the enemy's columns to General Lee and give him his exact position, with the request that a heavy fire of artillery be opened on the Federal columns at a point near the village of Auburn on their line of retreat, and thus facilitate the escape of his force, which he proposed to effect by simultaneously opening fire on them with his own guns, and then making a dash through with a combined charge of cavalry and artillery. Meantime, General Lee, who had camped near War- renton for the night, hearing nothing from Stuart as to the position and movements of the enemy, became uneasy, and remained awake until a very late hour of the night in order to make preparations and give the necessary orders for the early movement of his army. Goode made his way safely through the Federal columns, and arrived at headquarters about one o'clock in the morning.

For the description of this event above given we are indebted to Colonel Venable, and particularly for the following character- istic anecdote of General Lee, which adds another to the many evidences of his innate nobility of soul:

General Lee, after listening by the camp-fire to Goode's account of Stuart's situation, retired to his tent. The scout, however, being very anxious in regard to General Stuart's danger, began, after the general retired, to explain more fully with the map to an aide-de-camp the relative positions of Stuart's and the enemy's forces, and the exact point where the fire of our artillery would be most effective in promoting his safe retreat from his perilous environment.

General Lee could hear from his tent something of this conversation, but caught from it only that Goode was talking of matters which scouts, as a rule, were permitted to tell only to the commanding general himself. So, coming to the door of his tent, he called out with stern voice that he did not wish his scouts to talk in camp. He spoke very angrily, and stepped back into his tent. Goode fairly trembled. The aide-de-camp, however, went forward to the general's tent and told him that the scout, who was devoted to Stuart and naturally very anx- ious for his safety, was only endeavoring to mark accurately on the map the point at which the diversion of the artillery fire was to be made, and was by no means talking from the mere desire to talk. General Lee came out at once from his tent, commanded his orderly to have supper with hot coffee put on the table for Goode, made him sit in his own camp-chair at the table, stood at the fire near by, and performed all the duties of a hospitable host to the fine fellow. Few generals ever made such thorough amends to a private soldier for an injustice done him in anger.

Immediately afterward, Lee ordered Ewell to the relief of the imperilled cavalry. In the mean time, Lomax with his brigade of cavalry was endeavoring to create a diversion in Stuart's favor. On approaching Auburn, Ewell's advance-guard encountered the enemy's rear-guard and engaged it in a sharp skirmish, which terminated without important results. From his position Stuart heard all night the continuous tramp of the enemy. About daylight a detachment halted opposite his place of concealment to take some refreshments. While the unsuspecting Federals were thus employed Stuart suddenly opened upon them with his artillery, knocking over their coffee-pots and other utensils, as he says in his report, while his sharpshooters poured a rapid fire into the surprised troops. They were as quickly as possible moved to the opposite side of the hill, under cover from this destructive fire. Taking advantage of the confusion he had created, the "rollicksome *sabreur*" wheeled to the left and emerged safely toward Warrenton. He was greeted with cheers by the army, and the whole force was in the best of spirits at their narrow escape from capture or destruction.

Yet the delay thus occasioned was favorable to Meade, who continued his rapid movement toward Manassas. In General Lee's report of these operations no mention is made of this mishap of Stuart, which had such an injurious effect upon them. It is therefore to be inferred that he considered it an excusable accident of war.

On the release of Stuart from his perilous position Ewell and Hill resumed the pursuit. Meade had made the best use of the several unavoidable delays of the Confederate army, and though Hill, who was seeking to intercept the Federal retreat at Bristoe Station, made all haste in his march, he arrived there only in time to meet the rear-guard of Meade's army. He made a prompt attack on the Federal column, which was hastening to pass Broad Run, which the remainder of the army had already crossed. The assault proved unfortunate. General

Warren, who led the Federal rear-guard, quickly posted his men behind the railroad embankment at that point, from which impromptu breastwork he poured a destructive fire upon Hill's advancing troops. General Cooke, who led the charging brigade, was severely wounded, and his command repulsed with the loss of a number of prisoners and five pieces of artillery.

General Warren, having achieved this success, did not wait for a further assault, but hastened across Broad Run and hurried forward to join the main body. By the next morning the Federal army had crossed Bull Run, behind which they were erecting fortifications, their line extending toward the Little River turnpike.

When General Lee reached the position of Hill's repulse, that officer, mortified by his mishap, endeavored to explain the causes of his failure. The general listened in silence, and as they rode over the field strewn with dead bodies replied with sad gravity, "Well, well, general, bury these poor men and let us say no more about it."

The movement had evidently proved a failure. Meade was safe from any further pursuit, with the intrenchments around Washington and Alexandria to fall back upon in the event of a repulse or to retire to if he wished to avoid a battle. Lee felt it expedient to withdraw, and after destroying the railroad from Cub Run to the Rappahannock, he retired on the 18th to the line of that river, leaving the cavalry in the enemy's front.

Stuart did not retreat without giving the enemy a characteristic reminder of his presence. Leaving Fitz Lee near Manassas on the Federal front, he made a rapid détour with Hampton's division, and attacked the Second corps of Meade's army with his men dismounted and acting as sharpshooters. This assault produced some alarm at first, from the natural surmise that the attacking force might be the van-guard of Lee's army. On the advance of the Federal infantry, however, Stuart quickly drew back, and rode off in the direction of Warrenton.

He was followed by a body of Federal cavalry under General Kilpatrick, who came up with him near the village of Buckland on the Warrenton road. Here Stuart, at Fitz Lee's suggestion, executed a shrewd manœuvre. He retired, with Hampton's division, before the Federal cavalry, leaving Fitz Lee on the enemy's left flank. Kilpatrick pushed forward ardently after his retreating adversary, when suddenly the boom of Fitz Lee's artillery gave the prearranged signal. At sound of the guns Stuart wheeled and charged fiercely upon his pursuers. Fitz Lee at the same moment fell upon their flank. This unexpected double attack threw the enemy into confusion, and they retreated with headlong haste, pursued by Stuart at full speed "from within three miles of Warrenton to Buckland." The flight and pursuit was afterward known among the troopers by the humorous title of "the Buckland Races."

Lee remained on the Rappahannock until the railroad track was broken up and the rails removed for a distance extending from Catlett's Station to Culpeper Court-house. Meanwhile, the Federal army had again advanced, rapidly repairing the railroad as they moved forward, and on November 7th reached the Rappahannock. Lee's army was now encamped at Culpeper, with advanced forces near the river. A crossing was quickly effected at Kelly's Ford, and the troops which occupied the rifle-pits at that point were driven off with considerable loss in prisoners. An attack was made at the same time on a Confederate force which was injudiciously posted on the north bank of the river at Rappahannock Station. Here some old Federal intrenchments were occupied by a brigade of Early's division. They were assailed in force by a part of Sedgwick's corps, the works carried, and nearly the whole brigade, with a battery of artillery, captured by the Federals.

The way being thus cleared, Meade threw his whole army across the river and advanced on Culpeper, Lee retiring to his former position on the Rapidan. All the advantages of the campaign had been gained by Meade, and General Lee's well-designed movement had been defeated by untoward circumstances and by the alertness of the enemy. The summer campaign having been one of unusual activity, and the late operations having entailed severe hardships, it was thought advisable to go into winter quarters, particularly as a sharp prelude had already announced the approach of winter and the proper season for active operations seemed to be at an end.

Yet Meade was not of this opinion. He was destined, ere the winter had fully set in, to make a movement which would prove as unsuccessful for him as the one just described had been for his antagonist, and end the year's campaigning with the final advantage in Lee's favor. As a prelude to this movement we may briefly describe the position of Lee's army, upon which the effort of his antagonist was based.

Ewell's corps occupied a position extending from the base of Clark's Mountain to Mine Run, a small tributary of the Rapidan, and covered Mitchell's, Morton's, Raccoon, and Summerville's fords; A. P. Hill's corps extended from Orange Courthouse to Liberty Mills; and Stuart, as usual, protected the front and flanks of the army. Longstreet, as we have seen, had been detached on distant service; and, as numerous furloughs had been granted since the return of the army to the Rapidan, Lee's forces were far below any previous minimum.

Taking this circumstance into consideration, and having failed to satisfy the expectations of the Washington authorities, Meade determined to strike a blow that might accomplish some desirable result. Therefore, about the last of November he advanced his entire force to Germanna Ford, hoping to cross the Rapidan at that point and surprise Lee in his extended winter quarters. The movement seemed hopeful of success could Lee be caught unawares. Meade began his march upon the Rapidan on November 26th, making every effort to ensure secrecy and rapidity. Yet his advance had but fairly begun when the watchful Stuart discovered the movement, and hastened to report it to the Southern commander, who at once instituted measures for the rapid concentration of his army. An order was despatched to A. P. Hill to march to Vediersville, and there form a junction with Ewell, who was directed to retire from the Rapidan and take position behind Mine Run, a small stream which was excellently defended by Nature.

Ewell's corps, which was at hand, was concentrated quickly, while Hill, who had from fifteen to twenty miles to march, was but a few hours later in taking his position. The night of the 26th, during which these hasty movements were taking place, was a severely cold one. Yet General Lee, in his plain uniform and without other protection from the weather, was early in the saddle, and had reached Vediersville, where Stuart was bivouacked, before sunrise. Here, beside an open-air fire, covered only with an army blanket, the cavalry leader lay stretched in slumber. Lee is said to have remarked admiringly, as Stuart rose and advanced to meet him, "What a hardy soldier!" After a short consultation Stuart rode to the front, where he formed his command in face of the advancing foe, and with artillery and dismounted sharpshooters made every effort to obstruct their advance.

Meanwhile, Meade's army was advancing in the lightest marching order. All the trains had been left behind and the men supplied with ten days' rations, that nothing might impede their progress. Yet there were unforeseen causes of delay. The Third corps was three hours late in reaching the Rapidan, detaining the whole army for that time, since Meade was not willing to risk a crossing with less than his whole force. In laying the pontoon bridges they proved too short, causing another delay. Other obstacles arose, so that by the time the river was crossed twenty-four hours had elapsed.

This delay gave Lee all the time he needed. The rugged banks of Mine Run were densely clothed with timber, which the troops as they reached the ground hastily attacked with axes, and dragged the heavy logs to the points to be defended. The breastworks rose as if by magic. Lee rode along the banks of the stream, and with his great engineering skill selected the points to be defended and gave the necessary orders. In a remarkably short space of time an extended line of works was erected, composed of double walls of logs filled in with earth and with a strong abatis in front. The position had suddenly become formidable.

The Federal army had in the mean time been still further delayed. French's corps, marching too far to the right, had fallen in with Johnson's division of Ewell's corps. A sharp brush was the result, and by the time it could extricate itself

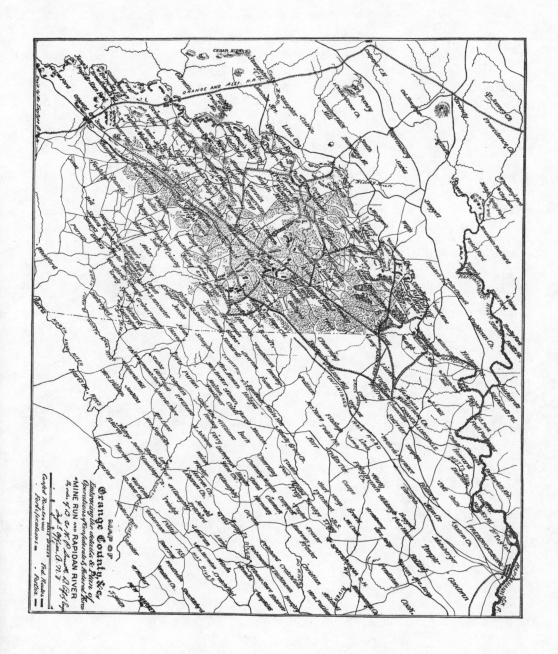

MAP OF
Orange County, &c.
Embracing the details & Plan of
Operations & Explorations for Battles near
"MINE RUN and RAPIDAN RIVER
By order of Gen. R.E. Lee. A.N.V.
By J.S. Offices A.N.V.
Scale
Coupld Routes ====== Fed. Routes =====
Pork directions ==== . Paths.

and open communications with the remainder of the army night had fallen.

It was not until the morning of the 28th that the army made its final advance to Mine Run, where, when Meade arrived hoping to gain an easy victory, he was confronted by a strong line of breastworks garnished with 150 pieces of artillery and backed by 30,000 veterans. The sight surprised him. The remarkable rapidity with which the defences on Mine Run were constructed must be attributed to the natural intelligence of the men, aided by their previous experience in throwing up earthworks around Richmond and Fredericksburg under the eye of General Lee, who, it must be remembered, had long been distinguished as a military engineer.

It was a bitter disappointment to General Meade to find that his well-laid plans had been utterly foiled by the skill and alertness of his antagonist. The next two days were spent in reconnoitering movements, in hope of finding a favorable point of attack. On the 29th, Warren reported favorable conditions for assault on the Confederate right, while Sedgwick discovered what seemed a weak point on its left. Orders for an assault at both points on the next morning were accordingly given, and at the appointed time the artillery of the right and centre opened briskly on the Confederate lines.

But not a sound came from Warren on the left. A new conclusion had been reached in that quarter—a verdict of the men themselves, communicated in a manner of startling significance to their commander. As the hour for the assault arrived it was found that each man had pinned to his blue blouse a scrap of paper with his name written thereon, that he might be recognized by his friends in case of death. This significant indication of the verdict of men whom long experience had made as expert military critics as their officers, was not to be disregarded. Warren, and after him Meade, made a new reconnoissance of the works before them, and the designed assault was pronounced hopeless. Meade declared that the position could not be carried without the loss of 30,000 men. This contingency was too terrible to be entertained. Yet the rations of the men were nearly exhausted, and nothing remained but retreat. This was safely accomplished on the night of the 1st of December, and on the following day the Federal army regained its quarters at Culpeper Court-house. Lee was more surprised at the retreat of Meade than he was by his advance, and his men, who had been in high spirits at the prospect of obliterating the memory of Gettysburg, were sadly disappointed at the loss of the opportunity.

During these operations occurred an incident which has often been told of General Lee. On Sunday, the 28th, while waiting for the expected Federal attack, the general was riding down the lines, attended by General Hill with his staff, when he came upon a group of his men who were holding a prayer-meeting. They were riding briskly, but the general at once halted and listened reverently to the singing of the men. He remained in that attitude until the benediction was pronounced, when he raised his hat, received the blessing, and then continued his ride. It was an impressive scene, and disposed to solemn feelings all who were present.

Finding that the enemy was not inclined to attack, Lee decided to give them a surprise, and to assail their lines on the morning of December 2d. Preparations were made during the night, two divisions being concentrated on the right in readiness to fall on the enemy's left flank, while all other arrangements for a battle were completed. But with the dawning of the next day it was discovered that the camp in front, which the day before had been full of busy life, was silent and empty. Meade's army was in full retreat toward the Rapidan. Pursuit was immediately made. But it was in vain. The light marching equipment of General Meade enabled him to far outstrip his pursuers. So suddenly had he disappeared that the army was astounded. This fact is illustrated in a story told by a staff officer who had been sent with an order to General Hampton.

"In looking for him," he says, "I got far to our right, and in a hollow of the woods found a grand guard of the Eleventh cavalry, with pickets and videttes out, gravely sitting their horses and watching the wood-roads for the advance of an enemy who was then retreating across Ely's Ford."

The pursuit was quickly abandoned as useless, and the army was marched back over a road which was bordered by burning woods, which had been set on fire by the Federal camp-fires. It was an imposing spectacle as the gleaming flames lit up the pathway of the army which was marching between them toward the impregnable post in which it had so recently defied a still more threatening foe.

Thus ended the campaigning of the year 1863, the most eventful year of the war, and one in which, while the army led by General Lee had experienced a variety of fortunes, it had won for itself imperishable fame, and done much to establish for its leader his well-deserved title of "one of the great captains of the world." The year had not closed as propitiously for the Confederate cause as the previous year, and the brilliant success of the army in the spring had been marred by its unsuccessful campaign in Pennsylvania. Although it had not felt itself beaten and its spirit was still unshaken, yet its failure to accomplish what had been expected, together with the fall of Vicksburg and the want of success in the South and West, had a depressing effect. Yet, despite these reverses, the Army of Northern Virginia at all times presented a bold and defiant front, and was ever ready to meet the enemy in battle, with thorough confidence in the ability of its leader and in its own steady valor.

The season was now so far advanced that neither general contemplated the prosecution of further operations during the winter; therefore preparations were commenced for going into winter quarters. While the main body of the Confederate army remained on the Rapidan, the artillery, with the exception of two or three battalions, was sent to the line of the Virginia Central Railroad, for the greater convenience of foraging the horses. The artillery of the Second corps was located at Frederick's Hall, while that of the Third occupied the neighborhood of Cobham Station, a few miles west of Gordonsville.

The prayer-meeting scene which we have described was significant of an unusual phase of army life of which something further may be said. A revival of religion had taken place in the army, and religious gatherings in the woods and in the camp, in which bronzed and war-worn veterans listened devoutly to the exhortations of their pastors and prayed fervently to the God of battles for aid to their country and themselves, became of common occurrence. General Lee took great pleasure in this display of religious emotion. He gave it every encouragement, conversed with the chaplains, and assisted them in their labors to the utmost of his power. He requested their prayers for himself, and exhibited that sincere religious faith which was ever a strong element in his character.

An interval of favorable weather in February caused the Army of the Potomac to exhibit signs of renewed activity; but the prompt appearance of General Lee induced General Meade to return to his winter quarters. The inactivity of winter was not again disturbed until March, when the Federals projected a cavalry expedition for the capture of Richmond by a secret and rapid movement. This expedition was composed of two columns, one of which advanced toward Richmond under Kilpatrick, while the other, commanded by Colonel Dahlgren, proceeded from the neighborhood of Culpeper Courthouse, with instructions to destroy the artillery at Frederick's Hall, form a junction with Kilpatrick, capture Richmond by a *coup de main*, destroy the city, and liberate the prisoners on Belle Isle. Being apprehensive that a cavalry dash might be made on the artillery cantoned about Frederick's Hall, General Long applied for two regiments of infantry in order to secure him against such an attempt. This small force was declined, on the ground that the army was so much depleted that it could with difficulty protect the line. of the Rapidan.

General Long, however, obtained a hundred and twenty-five muskets and accoutrements, which he distributed among four battalions of artillery, and organized in each a small company of sharpshooters. To this precaution may be attributed the safety of the artillery at Frederick's Hall. Dahlgren captured the Confederate pickets at Germanna Ford, crossed the Rapidan, and advanced within a few miles of the artillery cantonment before his approach had been discovered. Long had barely time to make the following disposition: Colonel Braxton was ordered to place one battery in position to command the road on which Dahlgren was advancing, to deploy his sharpshooters as skirmishers, and to withdraw his other batteries to a position near the station; at the same time he directed Brown's battalion to be placed in position to command the approaches below the station. Cutshaw's and Carter's battalions were ordered to a position a little in the rear of Braxton's and Brown's, in order to support them, and sharpshooters were sent to reinforce Brown's battalion.

These dispositions were barely completed before the head of Dahlgren's column came in view of Braxton's battery on the road. Seeing the battle-flag flying above the battery, and catching a glimpse of the bayonets of the sharpshooters, he halted in some surprise, having been led to suppose that the artillery at Frederick's Hall was without an infantry support. Bringing forward a contraband who had been recently captured, Dahlgren inquired whether or not there was infantry posted with the artillery, to which the negro replied, " Yes, massa, plenty of it." Being doubtful whether the negro knew what infantry meant, he asked him how he knew it. "Because," he said, "the infantry had stickers on the ends of their guns." Convinced by the evidence of the negro that the artillery was not unprotected, Dahlgren made a détour to the left, keeping beyond the range of the guns. The only loss sustained was the capture of a court-martial which was in session in a house on the enemy's line of march; whereupon a wag remarked, as the court, prisoners, and witnesses were all present, the trial might go on and the proceedings might be sent to General Long from Point Lookout or Fort Delaware. The court, however, was not reduced to this alternative, as all, with one exception, escaped during the following night.

Kilpatrick, having failed to meet Dahlgren at the appointed time before Richmond, determined not to wait, but to attack at once. He crossed the outer line of defences without resistance, but on reaching the second line he was so warmly received that he was obliged to retire, and with difficulty made good his retreat through the Confederate lines. This lack of co-operation in the Federal forces was due to the fact that Dahlgren put in the responsible position of guide a contraband who showed his fidelity to the Southern cause by misleading him from his proposed line of march, and thus created a delay which prevented his forming a junction with Kilpatrick. We are told that the negro was executed on the alleged charge of treachery. When Dahlgren approached the neighborhood of Richmond he was met by a Confederate force and signally defeated; he himself was killed, and only a remnant of his command escaped destruction.

Colonel Beale of the Ninth Virginia cavalry thus relates the circumstance of Dahlgren's death (*Southern Historical Papers*, April, 1877):

"On reaching the route of the enemy's march, he met a home-guard company under command of Captain Richard Hugh Bagby, with several lieutenants and some privates from other regular regiments, ready to dispute the advance of the enemy. Falling back until a good position was reached, the men were posted and darkness closed in. No advance was expected, and a lieutenant was kept in command on the road. About eleven o'clock the tramp of horses was heard, and when within twenty or thirty paces the officer stationed at this point commanded, 'Halt!' The reply was, 'Disperse, you damned rebels, or I shall charge you.'—'Fire!' ordered the lieutenant, and under it the horsemen retreated rapidly. Their leader had fallen, being instantly killed as his horse wheeled. Deserted by their officers, the men next morning on the flats before the hill hoisted the white flag. Important papers were found on Colonel Dahlgren's person, consisting of an address to the command, the order of attack from the south side of the James upon the city of Richmond, enjoining the release of the prisoners, the killing of the executive officers of the Confederate Government, the burning and sacking of the city, directions where to apply for the materials necessary for setting fire to the city, and an accurate copy of the last field return of our cavalry made to General Stuart, with the location of every regiment. This last was furnished by the Bureau of Instruction at Washington. The rest was accredited to no one. We forwarded all the papers by Pollard's courier to Richmond. After the publication of the papers and the denial of their authenticity, we were interrogated, and ordered to forward the memorandum-book, which was done.''

It is but justice to the memory of Dahlgren to say that no act of cruelty was perpetrated by him throughout this hapless expedition. His soldierly spirit abhorred the duty that had been assigned him.

In the succeeding April, General Lee was directed to inquire, under flag of truce, of General Meade if he or his Government had sanctioned the barbarous orders which had been found on Colonel Dahlgren's person. A reply was received to the effect that neither the Government at Washington nor any of the commanding officers had ordered or approved of the atrocities mentioned. General Kilpatrick stated that the photographic copy of the ''address'' which General Lee had forwarded was a fac-simile of an address which Dahlgren had submitted to him for approval, *except* that it lacked his approval, and that the objectionable passages it contained were not in that which had been submitted to him. General Meade's disclaimer was equally candid and emphatic.

It may be mentioned here that during the period covered by the events of this chapter (in November, 1863) the City Council of Richmond passed a resolution to purchase an elegant mansion for General Lee, to replace his lost mansions of Arlington and the White House, and in token of the esteem in which he was held by the city he had so long defended. General Lee, on hearing of this offer, wrote as follows to the president of the Council:

''I assure you, sir, that no want of appreciation of the honor conferred upon me by this resolution, or insensibility to the kind feelings which prompted it, induces me to ask, as I most respectfully do, that no further proceedings be taken with reference to the subject. The house is not necessary for the use of my family, and my own duties will prevent my residence in Richmond. I should therefore be compelled to decline the generous offer, and I trust that whatever means the City Councils may have to spare for this purpose may be devoted to the relief of the families of our soldiers in the field, who are more in want of assistance, and more deserving of it, than myself.''

CHAPTER XVII.

WILDERNESS, SPOTTSYLVANIA, AND COLD HARBOR.

General Grant in Command of the Army of the Potomac.—Preparations for the Campaign.—New Policy.—The Overland Route Selected.—Passage of the Rapidan.—In "The Wilderness."—Grant Intercepted by Lee.—The Fight on the 5th.—The Federal Error.—Battle of the 6th.—Longstreet's Opportune Arrival.—Statement of Colonel Venable.—Hancock Repulsed.—Longstreet Wounded.—The Woods on Fire.—Graphic Descriptions of the Battle.—March for Spottsylvania Court-house.—Grant Outgeneralled.—Lee in Position.—His Able Strategy.—Battle of May 10th.—Federal Repulse.—Battle of the 12th.—Johnson's Division Captured.—Terrible Conflict.—The Federals Checked.—Deadly Character of the Conflict.—A Tree Cut down by Bullets.—Sheridan's Raid on Richmond.—Death of General Stuart.—March to the North Anna.—Lee's Brilliant Strategy.—Grant's March to the Pamunkey.—Lee on the Totopotomoy.—Battle of Cold Harbor.—Terrible Slaughter in Grant's Army.—The Men Refuse to Charge.—Losses.—Lee's Tactics.—Grant's Change of System.

THE hostile armies having remained opposed to each other for more than six months, and having frequently measured each other's strength with the skill of practised gladiators, were aware that the ensuing campaign would be one of the most formidable character. Therefore, each side made full use of its resources in preparation for the coming struggle. The North replaced the fragmentary principle on which the war had been previously conducted by a system of powerful combinations, the guidance of which was entrusted to a strong and energetic hand.

In March, 1864, General Ulysses S. Grant was appointed lieutenant-general and assigned to the command of all the Federal armies. These were formed into two grand divisions. That of the West was assigned to the command of General Sherman, while that of the East was commanded by General Grant in person. Having established his headquarters with the Army of the Potomac, he applied himself to the study of the military situation in Virginia and of the several lines of

322

operation which appeared worthy of consideration for the future movements of the army. While thus employed he caused the Army of the Potomac to be raised to the imposing strength of 140,000 men, and to be furnished with all the appliances necessary to place it in the highest state of efficiency. At the same time, the Army of the James, that of the Valley, and the Grand Army of the West were put in a condition to afford the most effective co-operation in support of the principal object of the campaign.

In the mean time, General Lee applied himself with his accustomed energy and far-seeing policy to the preparation of his army for the field. By recalling Longstreet from Tennessee and ordering into the ranks the convalescents and the conscripts that had been raised during the winter, and by using every other means at his disposal, he could only raise an effective force of 64,000 men. Notwithstanding this inequality of numbers, the Army of Northern Virginia on the 1st of May awaited with undaunted spirit the opposing host.

In addition to the difference in numbers there was as marked a difference in condition. The Army of the Potomac was well clothed and amply supplied. The Army of Northern Virginia was in ragged clothing and but half fed. For this condition of his troops General Lee was in no sense accountable. He had protested against it in vain: the supplies did not come. But, as on previous occasions of the kind, the soldiers were ready to fight, and were not likely to let lack of provisions affect their valor in the field.

They had before them a severer task than any they had yet experienced. General Grant had proved himself the ablest commander in the Federal army, and had come fresh from victory in the West to measure his strength with the ablest of the Confederate leaders. And their previous ill-success had taught the Federal authorities the useful lesson to leave the direction of military affairs to the commander in the field, and, while supplying him with abundant reinforcements, to cease hampering him with the incessant restrictions to which the preceding commanders had been subjected.

The new Federal general did not fail to properly estimate the magnitude of the task before him, and he equally perceived that his skilled antagonist was not to be overcome by the policy which had hitherto been pursued. For three years a succession of pitched battles had been fought with no decisive result. The two armies still stood face to face—with a marked difference in numbers, it is true, but this was no new circumstance—and its enemies clearly realized that the army of the South was as dangerous as ever and as ready to show its teeth to its foes. General Grant, governed by these considerations, devised a new system of operations, as set forth in his official report. In this he said that his design was "*to hammer continuously* against the armed force of the enemy and his resources, until by *mere attrition*, if by nothing else, there should be nothing left for him but an equal submission with the loyal section of our common country to the Constitution and the laws."

This was a policy that was sure to result in terrible loss to the Federal armies, since it threw Lee on the defensive, and his army had more than once shown a remarkable ability to defend itself against assault. "Lee's army," says a Northern writer of that period, "is an army of veterans: it is an instrument sharpened to a perfect edge. You turn its flanks—well, its flanks are made to be turned. This effects little or nothing. All that we reckon as gained, therefore, is the loss of life inflicted on the enemy." This General Grant thoroughly understood. He knew that there was but one policy by which Lee could be beaten, and estimating, in a somewhat heartless manner, that even if he lost ten men to Lee's one he could better afford the loss, he firmly resolved to pursue the "continual hammering" system until he had utterly worn away the Army of Northern Virginia and left his opponent unsupported by a single regiment of his war-worn veterans.

While fully decided to make an advance in force against Richmond, Grant had two plans of movement to consider—that of transferring his whole army, after leaving a sufficient force for the defence of Washington, to the Peninsula or to the south side of the James River, and that of pursuing the "overland route." He seems to have been at first strongly in favor of the movement by way of the James. While in the West he had strongly urged it as the measure most promising of success. But on taking command of the Army of the Potomac he appears to have changed his views, possibly under that persistent pressure from Washington which his predecessors had so severely felt. However that may be, he determined on the southward movement through Virginia with his main army, while sending General Butler with 30,000 men to operate against Richmond from the James, and Sigel with a considerable force to advance through West Virginia and up the Shenandoah Valley.

Yet as the position of General Lee behind the Rappahannock was too strong to warrant a direct attack, it became necessary to select a line of movement that would turn this position by either the right or the left flank. The experience of General Pope had already demonstrated the dangers attending the line that traversed the upper fords of the Rapidan. Grant was therefore induced to adopt the other line—crossing the Rapidan below Lee's right, and to endeavor to turn that flank of the Confederate army. This line, besides being shorter, possessed the advantage of preserving intact the communication with Washington, while it threatened to sever Lee's connection with Richmond.

The line being decided on and the necessary preparations being completed, General Meade on the 4th of May, under the eye of General Grant, put the Army of the Potomac in motion. The corps of Sedgwick and Warren moved forward on the road to Germanna Ford, while Hancock's corps proceeded to Ely's Ford, each column being preceded by a large force of cavalry. The passage of the river was effected without opposition.

This easy passage of the Rapidan does not seem to have been anticipated by General Grant. In his report he says: "This I regarded as a great success, and it removed from my mind the most serious apprehension I had entertained, that of crossing the river in the face of an active, large, well-appointed, and ably-commanded army." Lee had made no movement to dispute the passage of the stream. He could, had he chosen, have rendered its passage extremely difficult. But perceiving that Grant was making the mistake that had proved so disastrous to Hooker, by plunging with his army into that dense and sombre thicket well named "The Wilderness," he took care to do nothing to obstruct so desirable a result.

On reaching the southern side of the stream, Grant established himself at the intersection of the Germanna and old plank roads and at Chancellorsville. This position embraced the upper part of what is known as the Wilderness of Spottsylvania.

Lee simultaneously ordered the concentration of his forces on Mine Run, a position about four miles north-west of that occupied by Grant. The corps of Ewell and Hill and the artillery of Long and Walker gained their positions on Mine Run during the evening and night of the 4th; Longstreet's corps, which since its arrival from Tennessee had been posted at Gordonsville, distant twenty miles from the point of concentration, was necessarily delayed in reaching the scene of the coming struggle.

There seemed no good reason to believe that General Lee would risk the hazard of a battle in open field, and expose his small force to the danger of being overwhelmed by Grant's enormous army. That he would offer battle somewhere on the road to Richmond was unquestionable, but Grant naturally expected his adversary to select some point strong alike by nature and art, and which must be forced by sheer strength ere the march to Richmond could be resumed. He did not dream that Lee would himself make the attack and force a battle with no other intrenchments than the unyielding ranks of his veteran troops.

Yet Lee had already tried the woods of the Wilderness as a battlefield, and knew its advantages. Its intricacies, which were familiar to him and his generals, were unknown ground to Grant. In them he had already vanquished a large army with half its force. The natural hope of success in baffling his new opponent which this gave him he did not fail to avail himself of, and Grant found himself on his southward march unexpectedly arrested by the presence of the Confederate army in the wilds in which, just a year before, Hooker's confident army had been hurled back in defeat.

The writer spent the night of the 4th at Lee's headquarters, and breakfasted with him the next morning. The general displayed the cheerfulness which he usually exhibited at meals, and indulged in a few pleasant jests at the expense of his staff officers, as was his custom on such occasions. In the course of the conversation that attended the meal he expressed himself surprised that his new adversary had placed himself in the same predicament as "Fighting Joe" had done the previous spring. He hoped the result would be even more disastrous to Grant than that which Hooker had experienced. He was, indeed, in the best of spirits, and expressed much confidence in the result —a confidence which was well founded, for there was much reason to believe that his antagonist would be at his mercy while entangled in these pathless and entangled thickets, in whose intricacies disparity of numbers lost much of its importance.

On the morning of the 5th, Lee's army advanced in two columns, Ewell taking the Orange Court-house and Fredericksburg turnpike, while Hill moved on the plank road. After advancing about three miles, Ewell encountered the enemy's outposts. Jones's brigade and a battery of artillery were then placed in position to cover the further deployment of Ewell's corps. Rodes's division formed in line to the right and at right angles to the road. The divisions of Early and Edward Johnson executed a similar deployment to the left.

Before this movement was finished Jones's brigade was ordered to change its position, and while in the execution of this was suddenly attacked by a heavy Federal force which had advanced unobserved under cover of a dense thicket. Before it could be extricated General Jones, its gallant leader, was killed, with the loss of several hundred of his men, either killed, wounded, or taken prisoner. This was the prelude to a succession of battles.

About four o'clock in the afternoon a collision occurred between the Federal right and the Confederate left. The hostile forces were concealed from view by a wilderness of tangled brushwood until they were within musket-range of each other. Then the Confederates, being in position, were prepared to deliver a staggering volley the moment their antagonists appeared, which was followed up so persistently that the Federals were driven back with heavy loss for nearly a mile. This affair closed the operations on the left.

On the right Hill met the enemy on the plank road and engaged in a heavy conflict. Hancock, who was opposed to him, made desperate efforts to drive him from his position, but in vain. "The assaults," as General Lee wrote, "were heavy and desperate, but every one was repulsed." Night fell, leaving both parties in the position which they held at the beginning of the fight. Neither had advanced or retired, but Hill had held his post and established his connection with Ewell.

The two armies had now assumed a most singular attitude. They had enveloped themselves in a jungle of tangled brushwood so dense that they were invisible to each other at half musket-range, and along the lines of battle in many places objects were not discernible half the length of a battalion. A Northern writer aptly described this region as a "terra incognita." It formerly had been an extensive mining district, from which the timber had been cut to supply fuel for feeding the smelting-furnaces, and since then the young growth had sprung up ten times thicker than the primeval forest. The roads traversing it and the small brooks meandering through it, with a few diminutive clearings, were the only openings in this dismal wilderness.

As soon as General Grant had crossed the Rapidan and enveloped himself in the Wilderness of Spottsylvania, General Lee determined, as above said, to bring his adversary to an engagement in a position whose difficulties neutralized the vastly superior force against him. "Neither General Grant nor General Meade believed that aught but a small force was in front of Warren to mask the Confederate retreat, as it was not deemed possible that Lee, after his defensive line had been turned, could have acted with such boldness as to launch forward his army in an offensive sally. It was therefore at once resolved to brush away or capture this force, but as this determination was formed under a very erroneous apprehension of the actual situation, the means employed were inadequate to the task" (Swinton).

In corroboration of this statement may be quoted a remark ascribed to General Meade in conversation with Warren, Sedgwick, and others on the morning of the 5th: "They have left a division to fool us here, while they concentrate and prepare a position toward the North Anna; and what I want is to prevent those fellows from getting back to Mine Run."

Before nightfall of that day it was discovered that "those fellows" had other objects in view, and were not to be brushed away with a wave of the hand. Grant had become convinced that Lee was advancing upon him in force, and hastened to put his whole army in battle array. His line, crossing the plank road and old turnpike nearly at right angles, extended from Todd's Tavern on Brock road to within a short distance of Germanna Ford, presenting a front of about five miles.

General Lee had accompanied the advance of Hill on the plank road, and witnessed the noble firmness with which the divisions of Heth and Wilcox maintained the conflict against greatly superior odds until relieved by the coming of night. Perceiving that these troops had sustained considerable loss and were greatly fatigued by the exertions of the day, he wished to relieve them by Longstreet's corps, which had bivouacked during the evening about five miles from the field of battle. He therefore sent a message to General Longstreet to hurry him forward.

Notwithstanding the severe conflicts during the day, the troops of both Ewell and Hill maintained their unshaken courage, and lay upon their arms during the night in anticipation of a renewal of the attack.

Early on the following morning Hill's division was assailed with increased vigor, so heavy a pressure being brought to bear upon Heth and Wilcox that they were driven back, and, owing to the difficulties of the country, were thrown into confusion. The failure of Longstreet to appear came near causing a serious disaster to the army. But at this critical moment he arrived and attacked with such vigor that the enemy was driven back and the position regained.

Colonel C. S. Venable of General Lee's staff, in his address before the Southern Historical Society, thus describes this event: "The assertion, made by several writers, that Hill's troops were driven back a mile and a half is a most serious mistake. The right of his line was thrown back several hundred yards, but a portion of his troops still maintained their position. The danger, however, was great, and General Lee sent his trusted adjutant, Colonel W. H. Taylor, back to Parker's Store to get the trains ready for a movement to the rear. He sent an aide also to hasten the march of Longstreet's divisions. These came the last mile and a half at a double-quick, in parallel columns, along the plank road.

" General Longstreet rode forward with that imperturbable coolness which always characterized him in times of perilous action, and began to put them in position on the right and left of the road. His men came to the front of the disordered battle with a steadiness unexampled even among veterans, and with an *élan* that presaged restoration of our position and certain victory. When they arrived the bullets of the enemy on our right flank had begun to sweep the field in the rear of the artillery-pits on the left of the road, where General Lee was giving directions and assisting General Hill in rallying and re-forming his troops.

" It was here that the incident of Lee's charge with Gregg's Texas brigade occurred. The Texans cheered lustily as their line of battle, coming up in splendid style, passed by Wilcox's disordered columns and swept across our artillery-pit and its adjacent breastwork. Much moved by the greeting of these brave men and their magnificent behavior, General Lee spurred his horse through an opening in the trenches and followed close on their line as it moved rapidly forward. The men did not perceive that he was going with them until they had advanced some distance in the charge. When they did recognize him, there came from the entire line as it rushed on the cry, 'Go back, General Lee! go back!' Some historians like to put this in less homely words, but the brave Texans did not pick their phrases: 'We won't go on unless you go back.' A sergeant seized his bridle-rein. . . . .

"Just then I turned his attention to General Longstreet, whom he had been seeking, and who sat on his horse on a knoll to the right of the Texans directing the attack of his divisions. He yielded with evident reluctance to the entreaties of his men, and rode up to Longstreet's position. With the first opportunity I informed General Longstreet of what had just happened, and he with affectionate bluntness urged General Lee to go farther back. I need not say the Texans went forward in their charge and did well their duty. They were eight hundred strong, and lost half their number killed and wounded on that bloody day. The battle was soon restored and the enemy driven to his position of the night before."

Wilcox's and Heth's divisions, to whom Longstreet's arrival and General Lee's presence had done much to restore confidence, were placed in line a short distance to the left of the plank road. Shortly afterward Anderson's division arrived from Orange Court-house. Longstreet now advanced from his own and Anderson's divisions three brigades to operate on the right flank of the enemy, while himself advancing on their front.

Attacked with great vigor by these fresh troops and his right flank rolled up at the same time that a heavy onslaught fell upon his front, Hancock's force was completely defeated, and sent reeling back toward the Brock road, the important highway to the seizure of which Lee's efforts were directed. That this purpose would be achieved seemed highly probable when an unfortunate accident put a stop to the Confederate advance. General Longstreet, who afterward declared that he "thought that he had another Bull Run on them," had ridden forward with his staff in front of his advancing line, when he was fired upon by a portion of his own flanking column, who mistook the party for Federal cavalry. He was struck by a musket-ball, and fell from his horse severely wounded.

This accident—which, as will be seen, bears a striking resemblance to that in which Lee's other great lieutenant, Jackson, was disabled in a previous battle in that same region—threw the lines into disorder and put a stop to the advance. General Lee, as soon as he learned of the accident, hastened to the spot to take command of the corps. But a considerable time elapsed before the divisions were ready for a renewal of the assault, and in the mean time the enemy had recovered from his confusion and had been strongly reinforced.

The battle was renewed about four o'clock in the afternoon, the columns of Longstreet and Hill, now commanded by Lee in person, making a most vigorous assault upon Hancock's men, who now lay intrenched behind a strongly-built breast-work of logs. The battle raged with great fury. The incessant volleys set fire to the woods, as at Chancellorsville, and flames and smoke soon filled the valley in which the contest was raging. The flames ere long caught to the breastworks of the enemy, which were soon a mass of seething fire. The battle went on through smoke and flame, and a portion of the breastworks were carried, though they were not long held. The few who had entered them were quickly driven out by a forward rush of a Federal brigade. With this charge ended the main action of the day.

In this engagement the attack of General Meade was conducted with such vigor by Hancock, Warren, and Burnside that under ordinary circumstances, with his great superiority of force, it would have been successful; but here the difficulties of the country prevented his making systematic combinations, and failure was the consequence.

While the battle was in progress on our right a spirited combat ensued between a part of Ewell's and Sedgwick's corps which terminated without important results. General Grant, being satisfied that any further attempt to dislodge Lee would be fruitless, determined to draw him out by a change of position. Therefore on the 7th he made his preparations to withdraw by night toward Spottsylvania Court-house.

Before ending our account of the battle of the Wilderness it may be of interest to offer some extracts from other writers which present graphic pictures of the singular and terrible character of the conflict. A Northern writer describes the country as covered by "a dense undergrowth of low-limbed and scraggy pines, stiff and bristling chinkapins, scrub oaks, and hazel. It is a region of gloom and the shadow of death.

Fighting in the fire.   Wilderness Campaign 1864.   Page 332.

Manœuvring here was necessarily out of the question, and only Indian tactics told. The troops could only receive direction by a point of the compass, for not only were the lines of battle entirely hidden from the sight of the commander, but no officer could see ten files on each side of him. Artillery was wholly ruled out of use; the massive concentration of three hundred guns stood silent, and only an occasional piece or section could be brought into play in the roadsides. Cavalry was still more useless. But in that horrid thicket there lurked two hundred thousand men, and through it lurid fires played, and, though no array of battle could be seen, there came out of its depths the roll and crackle of musketry like the noisy boiling of some hell-caldron that told the dread story of death.''

A Southern writer describes the struggle in equally vivid language: ''The land was sombre—a land of thicket, undergrowth, jungle, ooze, where men could not see each other twenty yards off, and assault had to be made by the compass. The fights there were not as easy as night-attacks in open country, for at night you can travel by the stars. Death came unseen; regiments stumbled on each other, and sent swift destruction into each other's ranks guided by the crackling of the bushes. It was not war—military manœuvring; science had as little to do with it as sight. Two wild animals were hunting each other; when they heard each other's steps they sprang and grappled. The conqueror advanced or went elsewhere. . . . . Here, in blind wrestle as at midnight, did two hundred thousand men in blue and gray clutch each other—bloodiest and weirdest of encounters. . . . . On the low line of the works, dimly seen in the thickets, rested the muzzles spouting flame; from the depths rose cheers; charges were made and repulsed, the lines scarcely seeing each other; men fell and writhed and died unseen, their bodies lost in the bushes, their death-groans drowned in the steady, continuous, never-ceasing crash.''

During the battle the numerous cavalry of Grant's army, commanded by General Sheridan, was completely neutralized by the topographical difficulties of the country. Becoming impatient of its inaction, a portion of Wilson's division passed the Brock road and advanced a short distance into the open country, where it was met by General Rosser with his brigade, and after a sharp conflict was compelled to retreat into the Wilderness from which it had emerged. The country was equally unfavorable for the use of artillery, which could only be employed along the roads or fired at random in the direction of the sounds of battle. The infantry, being thus deprived of its two powerful auxiliaries, was compelled to grapple single-handed its resolute antagonist. The casualties of both armies during the 5th and 6th were heavy. The Confederates, besides the loss of 7000 men killed and wounded, had to lament the severe wound of General Longstreet, which disabled him during the remainder of the campaign, and the death of Colonel J. Thompson Brown of the artillery and the gallant General Jenkins of South Carolina. The Federal loss was much greater.

During the 7th the battle was not resumed and the day passed in comparative quiet. General Lee waited behind his slight intrenchments for an assault from the Federal army, though keenly on the alert for a possible southward march of Grant's columns. Grant, indeed, designed by a rapid flank movement to seize the important position of Spottsylvania Court-house, fifteen miles south-east of the Wilderness battlefield. But quick as he was, his antagonist proved too active for him.

Having been informed by Stuart on the afternoon of the 7th that the wagon-trains of the Federal army were moving southward, Lee at once divined Grant's intention, and he hastily took the necessary measures to forestall it. He ordered Longstreet's corps, then commanded by General R. H. Anderson, to proceed that night, by a circuitous route a few miles to the right of the left flank of the enemy, to Spottsylvania Court-house, situated on the main route to Richmond. While Anderson was in rapid progress toward that point, the Federal army was advancing in two columns for the same place—the one by the Brock road, and the other by way of Chancellorsville. By reason of the numerous difficulties to be encountered, and the steady opposition of Stuart's men, who behind improvised breastworks harassed the Federal advance at every step, the movement was so much retarded that the advance corps under Warren did not reach the neighborhood of Spottsylvania Court-house until about the middle of the forenoon of the 8th.

The Confederate cavalry, under Fitz Lee, yielded before the strong advance of Warren's leading division. At that opportune moment Anderson reached the field, and as the cavalry gave way the Federals found themselves unexpectedly confronted by a line of infantry and met by a severe musketry fire, which took them so greatly by surprise that they hastily fell back to a position a mile and a half north of the court-house. Lee had again outgeneralled his opponent, and placed his army, which was supposed to be fifteen miles in the rear, squarely across Grant's line of advance to Richmond, prepared to dispute the road with the same energy it had displayed in the Wilderness battle.

The appearance of Longstreet's corps under these conditions naturally astounded the Federals, and forced them to retire in dismayed confusion. Anderson then took his position on a range of hills partly encircling the village on the north and north-east, and distant from it about a mile. The Federal corps, as they slowly arrived, finding Lee in their front, took up a position without attempting to dislodge him. Early, who had been assigned to the command of the Third corps during the temporary illness of Hill, and Ewell with his corps, having been directed to follow Anderson as rapidly as circumstances would permit, arrived late in the afternoon and established themselves in strong positions. Thus General Lee had passed entirely around the Army of the Potomac, and planted himself so firmly across its path to Richmond that he could not be dislodged by the repeated efforts of Grant.

The operations of the last four days furnish a page of military history of striking singularity. General Lee, on finding his position turned, to the surprise of Grant did not retreat, but introduced an exception to the rules of war of startling audacity. On the 5th, at the head of only Ewell's corps and two divisions of Hill's, he boldly advanced and hurled the gage of battle at his antagonist in defiance of his army of 140,000 men; and on the 6th, with less than half his force, inflicted such stunning blows that on the 8th he was able to swing entirely around him and plant himself firmly across his path at Spottsylvania Court-house, completely reversing the positions of the two armies, and bringing Richmond again under the wing of its ever-watchful protector.

This eccentricity of General Lee must have inspired General Grant with the opinion that was expressed of Bonaparte by an Austrian general of the martinettish school, who, on being asked what he thought of the state of the war, replied: "Nothing can be worse on your side. Here you have a youth who absolutely knows nothing of the rules of war. To-day he is in our rear, to-morrow on our flank, next day again in our front. Such gross violations of the principles of the art of war are not to be supported" (Bourrienne).

Before proceeding with our narrative it is important to give a short description of the new field of operations. Spottsylvania Court-house is situated at the junction of the Fredericksburg and Louisa Court-house road with the main road to Richmond. About a mile to the north and north-east is a range of hills that, as above said, had become the Confederate position. To the east of the court-house and parallel to Richmond road is another ridge, about a mile in length, which abruptly terminates near a third ridge of considerable elevation nearly parallel with and about six hundred yards in rear of the Confederate right. To the south and south-west the country is level or moderately undulating. The whole face of the country is diversified by farms and bodies of timber of considerable extent.

The Army of the Potomac being still surrounded by topographical difficulties of such magnitude as to render manœuvring hazardous and difficult, General Grant was obliged to extricate it from a false position by desperate fighting. He therefore formed his plans with that view, and proceeded to execute them with unsurpassed energy. No aggressive operations of importance were projected on the 9th. The opposing hosts during that interval were chiefly occupied in strengthening their positions, to which they applied themselves so diligently that by the close of the day each army was covered by a continuous line of formidable breastworks.

On the morning of the 10th, General Grant formed a powerful combination of the corps of Warren, Burnside, and Hancock with the design of attacking Lee's left centre near the
point of junction of the corps of Longstreet and Ewell. Shortly after 10 A. M. a severe attack was made upon this position,
which was met with great intrepidity and repulsed with severe
loss. At 3 P. M. a second assault was made, which was similarly repulsed with heavy slaughter. These efforts were
preliminary to the main attack, which was ordered for five
o'clock.

Hancock's corps, which had crossed the Po on the preceding
day, and advanced during the morning against the Confederate
lines, had been ordered back to take part in the main assault.
While retiring across the stream it was vigorously assailed,
and both sides lost heavily. During this contest the woods in
the rear of the Federal troops and between them and the river
took fire, and many of the wounded perished in the flames.
With a fierce foe in front and a burning forest in the rear
Hancock's men found themselves in a critical situation, and
were very severely handled in the effort to extricate themselves. On crossing the stream they destroyed the bridges,
and thus checked the Confederate pursuit.

At five o'clock the main assault was made. Hancock's and
Warren's men advanced with great intrepidity against the
strong Confederate works, but were repulsed with terrible
slaughter. After barely sufficient time to reorganize the shattered columns another attack was made. This met with a still
more bloody reception. The Confederate loss in the two assaults was inconsiderable, while from 5000 to 6000 of the
Federal forces lay dead and wounded upon the field.

Throughout the day the divisions of Heth, Field, Kershaw,
and Wilcox, with the artillery of Alexander and Walker, maintained a firmness and displayed a valor that well became veterans of a hundred battles. The Army of the Potomac never
fought with more desperate courage, nor had its ranks ever
been visited with such frightful havoc.

In the afternoon, about five o'clock, the Sixth corps made a
heavy attack on Ewell's left, which was urged with such per-

sistency that the portion of the line held by Doles's brigade was broken, and the exultant assailants rushed through the breach in heavy masses. But this gallant brigade being quickly rallied and promptly supported by the brigades of Daniel, Gordon, and G. H. Steuart, the assailants were forced back with terrible slaughter. After their repulse the Federals discontinued the attack, leaving the ground thickly strewn with killed and wounded. The breach which had been the scene of so sanguinary a struggle was immediately closed and Ewell's line was entirely re-established. On this occasion General Daniel of North Carolina was killed while bravely leading his troops, and Major Watson of the artillery was mortally wounded. The loss of these officers was deeply regretted. In this engagement the Army of Northern Virginia occupied a position of great natural strength and fortified by strong breastworks. For this reason the Confederate loss was very small as compared with that of the Federals, who had essayed an impossible task and had met with a terrible repulse.

During the hottest portion of this engagement, when the Federals were pouring through the broken Confederate lines and disaster seemed imminent, General Lee rode forward and took his position at the head of General Gordon's column, then preparing to charge. Perceiving that it was his intention to lead the charge, Gordon spurred hastily to his side, seized the reins of his horse and excitedly cried,

"General Lee, this is no place for you. Do go to the rear. These are Virginians and Georgians, sir—men who have never failed—and they will not fail now.—Will you, boys? Is it necessary for General Lee to lead this charge?"

"No! no! General Lee to the rear! General Lee to the rear!" cried the men. "We will drive them back if General Lee will only go to the rear."

As Lee retired Gordon put himself at the head of his division and cried out in his ringing voice, "Forward! charge! and remember your promise to General Lee!"

The charge that followed was fierce and telling, and the Federals who had entered the lines were hurled back before the resolute advance of Gordon's gallant men. The works

General Lee to the Rear. Page 338.

were retaken, the Confederate line again established, and an impending disaster converted into a brilliant victory.

During the 11th, General Grant was employed in shifting the positions of his corps preparatory to a new assault upon the Confederate lines. Before daylight on the morning of the 12th his army assailed a portion of the Confederate lines, which was carried, with the capture of several thousand prisoners. It is proper, before describing this affair, to relate the circumstances which led to it. In the afternoon of the 11th, General Lee, having received intelligence that induced him to suspect that Grant was taking another step toward Richmond, directed that the army should be held in readiness to make a night-movement in case his apprehensions were correct. This involved the removal before dark of such artillery as might embarrass or retard a withdrawal from the lines at night. With this view two batteries were withdrawn from an advanced salient on Ewell's front in the dusk of evening with as much caution as possible to prevent observation. Notwithstanding the intended secrecy of the removal of these two batteries, the fact was conveyed, as it was afterward stated, to the enemy that night by a deserter from Johnson's division.

The weakening of the Confederate lines is supposed to have determined the Federal commander to make a night-attack, which General Hancock executed with his accustomed vigor a little before daylight on the 12th. Although the preparations for the attack had been heard by General Johnson, and the artillery had been recalled, the darkness of the night was so intensified by a thick fog that the attacking column was able to advance unobserved, to break through Johnson's line, and to capture his whole division, with about twenty pieces of artillery, almost without a struggle. The artillery that had been left on the line fired only two guns, while the infantry offered little resistance.

This success inaugurated one of the most desperate conflicts that occurred during the war. The long breach made by the capture of Johnson's division admitted the Federals in heavy masses, which were promptly arrested by Ramseur's, Rodes's, and Gordon's infantry and Long's artillery. These troops, stretching across the base of the salient, confined the assailants within its triangular area, while the artillery from the surrounding hills hurled deadly missiles upon them.

For several hours the dense fog, hovering like a black curtain around the combatants, concealed all knowledge of the raging strife excepting as it was proclaimed by the deafening roar of musketry and the thunder of artillery. From four o'clock in the morning until night the battle continued, marked by terrible slaughter. The diminished ranks on each side were constantly refilled with fresh troops. General Lee sent during the day to the assistance of Rodes, on whose front the battle raged, three brigades (McGowan's South Carolina, Perrin's Alabama, and Harris's Mississippi), while the artillery was reinforced by the battalions of Cabell and McIntosh. Hancock was reinforced by the Sixth corps and the two divisions of Warren's corps.

While Hancock's attack was in progress General Grant attempted to create a diversion in his favor by threatening the Confederate position on his right and left, which was, however, promptly repelled by the troops of Early and Anderson. An important diversion was made during the day on the right by Mahone of Hill's corps, which resulted in the capture of several hundred prisoners. At last the persistent attacks of the enemy were obliged to yield to constant repulse and the Federals discontinued the contest.

"Of all the struggles of the war, this was perhaps the fiercest and most deadly. Frequently throughout the conflict so close was the fight that the rival standards were planted on opposite sides of the breastworks. The enemy's most savage sallies were directed to retake the famous salient, which was now become an angle of death and presented a spectacle ghastly and terrible. On the Confederate side of the works lay many corpses of those who had been bayoneted by Hancock's men when they first leaped the intrenchments. To these were constantly added the bravest of those who in the assaults to recapture the position fell at the margin of the works, till the ground was literally covered with piles of dead and the woods in front of the salient were one hideous Golgotha" (Swinton).

As had happened on the 10th, so on this day General Lee rode to the head of a column prepared to charge at a moment when the need of desperate valor was urgent. As on the previous occasion, the men refused to move unless he would retire, calling out, as with one voice, "If you will go back, General Lee, we will do all you desire." It was under such circumstances as this that General Lee, by his readiness to share their dangers, endeared himself to his men. The assertion has been made, however, that he exposed himself purposely, courting death through sheer despair of success. This idea is utterly unfounded. On the occasions mentioned his army was in no more serious danger than it had been twenty times before. His presence and action were necessary to stimulate the men to greater deeds of valor. It had become a question of victory or defeat, and any general may excusably expose himself when the fate of a battle hangs upon a thread. In the writer's experience General Lee never unnecessarily courted danger, though he never cautiously avoided it. It was always his custom to make a personal examination of the movements in progress, as he always wished to avoid any reckless exposure of his men. This habit frequently brought him under the fire of the enemy. But he never had a thought of self-destruction, even in the most desperate situations, and never exposed himself recklessly or unnecessarily, though no consideration of personal safety ever deterred him from the full performance of the duties which necessarily devolve upon a commanding general.

On reviewing the results of the day it was apparent that the Federal success in the morning was more than counterbalanced by subsequent losses in killed and wounded. In this respect there was a great disparity between Lee's and Grant's armies. The Federal losses in killed, wounded, and missing up to the 11th of May, by Grant's own estimate, reached the aggregate of 20,000 men. On the 12th the losses were fully 10,000 more. Other statements make the losses much more considerable. The Confederate losses, though severe, were much less, this being due to the fact that the Confederates were protected by secure breastworks, from behind which they could with comparative safety repel the assailants. At night General

Ewell withdrew to a range of hills a little in rear of his first position, which formed a shorter and stronger line, where he prepared to meet other attacks. But of these there was no immediate danger. The succession of bloody combats which had marked the career of Grant in the Wilderness had by this time so greatly reduced his army that he was obliged to pause and await reinforcements.

A singular incident of the battle of the 12th has often been told, yet is still worth relating. The musketry fire during this engagement had never been exceeded in intensity. From both sides came an incessant, deadly hail of bullets, so continuous and close that every shrub and tree between the lines was pierced and scarred, and one hickory tree, of eighteen inches diameter, was so chipped away by the storm of lead as to be scarcely able to stand. The first gust of wind levelled it to the earth. It was literally cut down by musket-balls. This trunk is now preserved at Washington as a memento of the war.

General Grant remained inactive until about the 18th, when a strong force advanced toward the new line of Lee's army. "When well within range General Long opened upon them with thirty pieces of artillery, which, with the fire of our skirmishers, broke and drove them back with severe loss. We afterward learned that they were two fresh divisions, nearly 10,000 strong, just come up from the rear" (*Ewell's Report*).

On the 19th, General Lee directed Ewell to demonstrate against the enemy in his front, as he believed that he was moving to his right. Finding the Federals in his front to be strongly intrenched, Ewell was compelled to move round their right—a task which proved very difficult, there being many obstacles in the route. This delay gave the enemy, who had perceived his movement, time to prepare to meet him, and on reaching the desired point he found himself assailed by a superior force. He maintained his ground, however, until nightfall, when he retreated and regained his former position, having lost about 900 men in the movement.

During the operations about Spottsylvania Court-house, Sheridan conceived the idea of capturing Richmond by a *coup de main*, and on the 9th proceeded to its execution. Of this movement General Stuart quickly became aware, and with his usual promptitude threw himself in Sheridan's path, and encountered him on the 10th at the Yellow Tavern, a few miles north of Richmond. A severe conflict ensued, in which Stuart fell mortally wounded, and his troops were compelled to retire before the superior numbers of the foe.

This contest between the two ablest cavalry leaders of the war led, in the fall of General Stuart, to a severe disaster to the Confederate cause. "Endowed by nature with a courage that shrank from nothing; active, energetic, of immense physical stamina, which enabled him to endure any amount of fatigue; devoted, heart and soul, to the cause in which he fought, and looking up to the commander of the army with child-like love and admiration,—Stuart could be ill spared at this critical moment, and General Lee was plunged into the deepest melancholy at the intelligence of his death. When it reached him he retired from those around him, and remained for some time communing with his own heart and memory. When one of his staff entered and spoke of Stuart, General Lee said, in a low voice, 'I can scarcely think of him without weeping'" (Cooke).

Sheridan had been so much delayed by Stuart's assault that the small force which had been left for the defence of Richmond had time to reach the works, which were very feebly garrisoned on Sheridan's first approach. He carried the first line, but recoiled from the second, and retired toward the Chickahominy. He subsequently rejoined Grant on the Pamunkey.

About the same time that the Confederate army lost its great cavalry leader—a loss which can only be paralleled with that of Jackson—the Federal army was afflicted with a loss little less felt in the death of General Sedgwick. Always noble as a man and gallant as a soldier, in time of peace his generous heart was as unfailing in friendly sympathy as his valiant spirit in the time of war was ready to call forth the admiration and respect of his companions.

Referring to the operations just related, the historian of the Army of the Potomac says: "Before the lines of Spottsylvania the Army of the Potomac had for twelve days and nights engaged in a fierce wrestle in which it had done all that valor may do to carry a position by nature and art impregnable. In this contest, unparalleled in its continuous fury and swelling to the proportions of a campaign, language is inadequate to convey an impression of the labors, fatigues, and sufferings of the troops, who fought by day only to march by night from point to point of the long line, and renew the fight on the morrow. Above 40,000 men had already fallen in the bloody encounters of the Wilderness and Spottsylvania, and the exhausted army began to lose its spirits. It was with joy, therefore, that it at length turned its back upon the lines of Spottsylvania.''

In no previous operations did the Army of Northern Virginia display higher soldierly qualities. Regardless of numbers, every breach was filled, and with unparalleled stubbornness its lines were maintained. The soldiers of that army not only gratified their countrymen, but by their gallantry and vigor won the admiration of their enemies. Wherever the men in blue appeared they were met by those in gray, and muzzle to muzzle and point to point they measured the foeman's strength.

No further effort was made by Grant on the desperately-fought field of Spottsylvania. Having been reinforced by 40,000 reserves, on the 20th of May he disappeared from the front of Lee's army. As in the Wilderness, he began a movement to turn the impregnable position of Spottsylvania by a flank march.

General Lee, however, with his usual alertness, had his men on the march the instant the movement of his adversary was discovered, and he advanced with such rapidity as to reach Hanover Junction, at the intersection of the Fredericksburg and Richmond and the Central railroads, in advance of Grant. This objective point of the Federal army was occupied by Lee on the 22d. He at once took up a strong position, and when Grant arrived on the 23d it was to find himself again intercepted by his active opponent.

The North Anna River, which here formed the Confederate line of defence, was strongly guarded, and Grant's immediate effort to throw his army across it met with strong resistance.

Warren on the right, indeed, found an unguarded ford, and succeeded in crossing his whole corps without opposition. A severe conflict ensued, which ended in his strongly establishing himself. But Hancock's effort to cross on the left met with considerable opposition, and was not achieved without loss.

On the succeeding day Burnside endeavored to cross at a point intermediate between those adopted by Warren and Hancock. He met with severe loss in the effort, and found the river very strongly guarded. Lee's army, in fact, now occupied a singular position. Its centre touched the stream, while both wings were thrown back at an obtuse angle, facing the corps of Warren and Hancock respectively. To quote again from Swinton: "The game of war seldom presents a more effectual checkmate than was here given by Lee; for after Grant had made the brilliantly successful passage of the North Anna, the Confederate commander, thrusting his centre between the two wings of the Army of the Potomac, put his antagonist at an enormous disadvantage, and compelled him, for the reinforcement of one or the other wing, to make a double passage of the river."

Warren's corps advanced with the view of striking the Central Railroad, a few miles above the junction, but was met by Hill and driven back with loss. The corps that had crossed the river remained several days without manifesting any inclination to advance, and were then withdrawn to the north side of the stream, the movement being performed at night and with the greatest caution and secrecy. General Grant on this occasion did not exhibit his usual pertinacity, but seemed satisfied by observation alone that the Confederate position could not be carried by main strength. He therefore proceeded down the North Anna to the Pamunkey, which he crossed on the 28th. Grant thus explains his withdrawal from before Hanover Junction: "Finding the enemy's position on the North Anna stronger than either of his previous ones, I withdrew on the night of the 26th to the north bank of the North Anna" (Report).

At this time the Federal army, with the reinforcements it had received during its march, numbered 100,000 men, while the Confederate army, whose only reinforcement had been 6000 men under Breckenridge and Pickett, received on the North Anna, did not exceed 40,000 men. According to Colonel Taylor's estimate, the total reinforcements received by Lee from the Wilderness to Cold Harbor numbered 14,400 men, while during the same period Grant was strengthened by more than 50,000 additional men.

In addition to this, all the aids of science and art were brought into use in the Army of the Potomac to an extent impossible to Lee. In Grant's *Memoirs* he gives a detailed account of the perfection of his signal system, by which at every halt of the army telegraphic wires were immediately laid along the whole line, so that in a short time after encamping each corps and division was connected with the others and with headquarters by a telegraphic network, making of the whole extended army a single body under instant control of the brain of the commander through these outstretching iron nerves. Other points of superiority which his unlimited command of resources gave the Federal commander might be named, but the above will suffice to show the disadvantages under which Lee labored, and against which he could only oppose the valor of his men and his own original genius as a commander.

The disparity of numbers between the two armies had prevented Lee from taking advantage of Grant's flank march from Spottsylvania to attack him under the advantageous circumstances which such a movement presents, and forced him to the alternative of seeking to check his advance at strong defensive points. The movement of Grant to the Pamunkey was met by Lee in the same manner as before, by an intercepting march to the line of the Totopotomoy, a small tributary of the Mattapony, where the adjacent hills afford a good defensive position. Lee's purpose in this movement was the following: If he had marched so as to detain Grant on the Pamunkey, the latter would have held command of the James and York rivers, and would have been at liberty to reinforce Butler, who was operating on the James. By this means Butler might have been strengthened sufficiently to crush the Confederate force which was operating against him, and thus have become at liberty to co-operate with Grant against Lee or to capture Richmond before it could be relieved. On the other hand, if Grant could be detained on the line of the Totopotomoy he would be unable to send detachments to Butler unobserved, and Lee, by his closer vicinity to Richmond, would be better able to obtain the co-operation of the troops employed in the defence of that place.

Proceeding on his march from the Pamunkey, Grant found his advance upon Richmond again arrested by Lee, who awaited him, as above said, on the Totopotomoy in the neighborhood of Mechanicsville and Atlee's Station on the Central Railroad. Grant did not at this point attempt to force his opponent from his path, but moved slowly by his left flank toward the Chickahominy, while Lee, by a similar movement to his right, kept pace with him and constantly confronted him at every stage.

Both armies carefully protected themselves with breastworks until a flank of each rested upon the Chickahominy. On the 1st of June, Lee was joined by about 5000 men under Pickett and Hoke, who had been operating against Butler on the south side of the James. This increased his army to 45,000 men. At the same time Butler reinforced Grant with 12,000 men, raising his numerical strength to 112,000.

The old battlefield of Cold Harbor was again occupied by the contending forces, though in an inverse order. The Confederate right now occupied the position that had been previously held by the Federals, and the Federal left held that which had been occupied by the Confederates. This field was about to become the theatre of a second conflict more desperate than the first.

Apparently with the intention of blotting out the memory of the defeat of the Federal arms on the former occasion, General Grant massed the flower of his army for battle. A portion of the Confederate line occupied the edge of a swamp of several hundred yards in length and breadth, enclosed by a low semicircular ridge covered with brushwood. On the previous night the troops assigned to this part of the line, finding the ground wet and miry, withdrew to the encircling ridge, leaving the breastworks to be held by their picket-line. The attacking column quickly carried this part of the line, and advanced through the mud and water until arrested by the deliberate fire of the Confederates.

The battle that succeeded was one of the most desperately contested and murderous engagements of the war. Along the whole Federal line a simultaneous assault was made on the Confederate works, and at every point with the same disastrous result. Rank after rank was swept away until the column of assault was almost annihilated. Attack after attack was made, and men fell in myriads before the murderous fire from the Confederate line. While Hill, Breckenridge, Anderson, and Pickett repulsed Grant's desperate assaults upon the right, Early with Rodes, Gordon, and Ramseur on the left successfully opposed Burnside and Warren. In the brief space of one hour the bloody battle of the 3d of June was over, and 13,000 dead and wounded Federals lay in front of the lines behind which little more than 1000 of the Confederate force had fallen.

A few hours afterward orders were sent to the corps commanders to renew the assault, and transmitted by them through the intermediate channels to the men. Then an event occurred which has seldom been witnessed on a battlefield, yet which testified most emphatically to the silent judgment of the men on the useless slaughter to which they had been subjected. Though the orders to advance were given, not a man stirred. The troops stood silent, but immovable, presenting in this unmistakable protest the verdict of the rank and file against the murderous work decided on by their commanders.

Thus ended Grant's overland campaign, in which his losses aggregated the enormous total of 60,000 men—a greater number than the whole of Lee's army at the beginning of the campaign. Lee's losses, on the contrary, were not more than 20,000. As to the *morale* of the two armies, that of Lee's continued excellent. Their successful defence against their powerful opponent had raised the spirits of the men and their confidence in their general to the highest pitch. On the contrary, the dreadful slaughter to which Grant's army had been subjected produced an inevitable sense of depression in the ranks, and a feeling that they were destined to destruction before the terrible blows of their able antagonist.

It is an error to suppose that in this campaign Lee was afraid to meet his adversary in open field, as has been asserted by Northern writers. He was always ready for action, whether offensive or defensive, under favorable circumstances. "I happen to know," says General Early, "that General Lee had always the greatest anxiety to strike at Grant in the open field." It was the practice of both armies, whenever encamping, to build intrenchments, and it would have been utter folly for Lee to leave his when he found his antagonist willing to attack him behind his breastworks, thus giving him that advantage of a defensive position which the smallness of his army imperatively demanded. Had he advanced against Grant, it would only have been to find the latter behind his works, and the comparative size of the two armies did not warrant this reversal of the conditions of the contest.

At the beginning of the campaign, perceiving that General Grant's *rôle* was fighting and not manœuvring, General Lee restrained his desire for the bold and adventurous offensive and strictly confined himself to the defensive, hoping in the course of events to reduce his opponent sufficiently near a physical equality to warrant his attacking him openly with reasonable hope of success. Believing that object had been accomplished after the battle of Cold Harbor, General Lee was anxious to assume the offensive and attack Grant before his army could recover from the stunning effect of its defeat on that occasion ; but being obliged to send a large detachment from his army to oppose Sigel and Hunter in the Valley, he was compelled to continue on the defensive.

Grant, on his part, had been taught a costly lesson by his many bloody repulses, and after the battle of Cold Harbor changed his whole plan of operations, deciding to endeavor to accomplish by patient siege what he had failed to achieve by the reckless application of force. With this decision began a new chapter in the history of the war, and one of the most remarkable sieges known to history was inaugurated—that in

which the Confederate commander behind the breastworks of
Petersburg for a full year baffled every effort of his powerful
foe, and taught the world that General Lee was as great in
defence as he had already proved himself in offence, and, in
the fullest sense of the phrase, was "every inch a soldier."

In conclusion of this chapter the following extracts from
letters written by General Lee to Miss Margaret Stuart are of
great interest, as showing his feeling in regard to the coming
struggle and his natural sense of uncertainty as to its result.
On the 29th of March, 1864, he writes from "Camp Orange Co.:"

"The indications at present are that we shall have a hard
struggle. General Grant is with the Army of the Potomac.
All the officers' wives, sick, etc. have been sent to Washington. No ingress or egress from the lines is now permitted,
and no papers are allowed to come out. They claim to be
assembling a large force."

On April 28th he writes from the same camp:

"I dislike to send letters within reach of the enemy, as
they might serve, if captured, to bring distress on others.
But you must sometimes cast your thoughts on the Army of
Northern Virginia, and never forget it in your pious prayers.
It is preparing for a great struggle, but I pray and trust that
the great God, Mighty to deliver, will spread over it his
Almighty arm and drive its enemies before it."

A third letter to the same person, which we give in full, is
of considerable interest, as showing General Lee's love of a
pleasant jest, and from the fact that the article named in it
has been placed in the writer's hands for reproduction. Following the letter is an engraving of this historic pincushion:

"Camp Orange Co., 7th Apr., 1864.

"My Dear Cousin Margaret: I send you a pincushion
made on the banks of the Ohio. The sentiment on its face I
trust inspires the action of every man in the Confederacy, whilst
their hearts overflow with the passion inscribed on its reverse.
A soldier's heart, you know, is divided between love and glory.
One goes to Richmond to-day who has his share of both. You

will probably see him. Elevate his desire for the latter, but do not hearken to his words on the former.

"Soliciting your prayers for the safety of the army, the success of our cause, and the restoration of peace to our country,

"I am, with great affection,

"Very truly yours,

"R. E. LEE.

"MISS MARGARET STUART."

CHAPTER XVIII.

EARLY'S VALLEY CAMPAIGN.

Butler on the James.—Beauregard at Petersburg.—Butler Defeated.—Sigel Defeated at Newmarket.—Hunter Succeeds Sigel.—He Defeats and Kills General W. E. Jones. —Sheridan's Cavalry Movement.—Encountered and Defeated by Hampton.—Hunter's March upon Lynchburg.—Early Sent to the Valley.—Hunter Retires through the Mountains.—Early's Plan of Advance to Maryland.—At Sharpsburg.—Defeats Wallace on the Monocacy.—Marches upon Washington.—Federal Alarm.—Early Returns to the Valley.—Battle of Kernstown.—Federal Defeat.—Sheridan Sent to the Valley.—Battle of Winchester.—Early Defeated.—Fight at Fisher's Hill.— Early again Driven Back.—He Surprises and Defeats the Federals at Cedar Creek. —Sheridan Rallies his Army and Gains a Victory.—The Spring Campaign.—Sheridan drives Early from the Valley and forms a Junction with Grant.—Barbarism of the Valley Campaign.

THE collateral operations bearing on the general plan of campaign adopted by General Grant in Virginia now claim attention. While the contest was in progress between Lee and Grant in Spottsylvania and Hanover co-operative columns were in motion in other quarters. Sigel was operating in the Valley; Crook and Averell were advancing in Southwestern Virginia toward the Virginia and Tennessee Railroad; and Butler was ascending the James with a view of operating against Richmond and Petersburg from the south side of that river. On the 5th of May, Butler with his main force, about 30,000 strong, entered the James, and on the 6th landed at City Point and Bermuda Hundred, a point of land at the intersection of the James and Appomattox rivers.

A column was at once sent to capture Petersburg, but on approaching that place it was turned back by a false rumor that the town was strongly occupied by the Confederates, though in fact both Richmond and Petersburg were but feebly defended. Butler fortified his position at Bermuda Hundred by the erection of earthworks extending from the James to the Appomat-

352

tox, and embracing a front of about three miles. While thus engaged he sent a detachment of infantry and cavalry to sever the connection between Richmond and Petersburg by breaking up the railroad, and to make a reconnoissance of the intervening country. This detachment encountered a Confederate force, before which it fell back after inflicting some damage on the railroad.

All of the available force south of James River and that in North and South Carolina were ordered up to oppose Butler. General Beauregard arrived at Petersburg on the 10th of May, and assumed command of the troops assembled there. He immediately took energetic steps to oppose the advance of Butler. On the 16th a battle ensued, in which Butler was defeated and forced to retire within his defences at Bermuda Hundred. It is thought that General Beauregard would have gained a decisive victory had not General Whiting failed to attack as ordered. The prompt action of Beauregard on the Richmond and Petersburg Railroad resulted in the "bottling up" of General Butler until he was called to the north side of the James River to reinforce General Grant before Richmond.

Early in May, General Sigel entered the Valley with a force of 10,000 or 12,000 men, and proceeded to advance toward Staunton. The Valley at that time was occupied only by a small force under General Imboden, which was wholly inadequate for its defence. General Breckenridge was therefore withdrawn from South-western Virginia to oppose Sigel. On the 15th of May, Breckenridge with a force of 3000 men encountered Sigel at Newmarket, and defeated him and compelled him to retire behind Cedar Creek. The cadets of the Virginia Military Institute formed a portion of Breckenridge's division; and behaved with distinguished gallantry. General Breckenridge wished to shield these youths, but they insisted upon being led forward, and were soon in the hottest of the fight, where they maintained themselves with the steadiness of veterans. After the battle of Newmarket, Breckenridge was withdrawn from the Valley to reinforce Lee, as has been before stated, in the neighborhood of Hanover Junction.

In the mean time, Crook and Averell had reached the Virginia and Tennessee Railroad, where they inflicted some damage, but were compelled to retire by a force sent against them by General Sam Jones. They then proceeded to join the main column operating in the Valley.

After the battle of Newmarket, Sigel was relieved by General David Hunter, who was instructed by General Grant to advance upon Staunton, thence to Charlottesville, and on to Lynchburg if circumstances favored that movement.

Breckenridge having been withdrawn, General W. E. Jones was ordered to the Valley to oppose Hunter, who slowly advanced, opposed by Imboden with an almost nominal force. About the 4th of June, Imboden was joined by General Jones in the neighborhood of Harrisonburg with a force of between 3000 and 4000 men, which he had hastily collected in Southwestern Virginia. This force, however, being composed of fragments of regiments and brigades, lacked compactness, and was therefore quite unreliable. Jones, nevertheless, wishing to attack Hunter before he could be joined by Crook and Averell, who were advancing from the opposite direction to Staunton, determined to give him battle without delay.

Although greatly outnumbered, he engaged Hunter near Port Republic, where he was defeated and killed. There were few men in the army of greater bravery and worth, and his loss was deeply felt. After the fall of Jones, McCauslin opposed Hunter with gallantry and vigor, but his small force was no match for the greatly superior force against which he contended.

The affairs in the Valley now began to attract the attention of the commanding generals of both armies. It was evident that if Hunter could succeed in taking Lynchburg and breaking up the canal and Central Railroad, it would only be necessary to tap the Richmond and Danville and the Petersburg and Weldon railroads to complete a line of circumvallation around Richmond and Petersburg.

On the 7th of June, General Grant detached General Sheridan, with a large cavalry force, with instructions to break up the Central Railroad between Richmond and Gordonsville, then proceed to the James River and Kanawha Canal, break that line of communication with Richmond, and then to co-operate with Hunter in his operations against Lynchburg. About the same time General Lee sent General Breckenridge with his division, 2500 strong, to occupy Rockfish Gap of the Blue Ridge to deflect Hunter from Charlottesville and protect the Central Railroad as far as practicable. A few days later General Early was detached by General Lee to oppose Hunter, and take such other steps as in his judgment would tend to create a diversion in favor of Richmond. General Sheridan, in compliance with his instructions, proceeded by a circuitous route to strike the railroad somewhere in the neighborhood of Gordonsville. This movement was, however, discovered by General Hampton, who with a considerable force of cavalry encountered Sheridan on the 12th of June at Travillian's Station. After much severe and varied fighting Sheridan was defeated, and in order to escape was obliged to make a night-retreat. After a difficult and circuitous march he rejoined General Grant south of Richmond. This was one of the most masterly and spirited cavalry engagements of the war.

Hunter, finding Rockfish Gap occupied in force, was unable to comply with that part of his instructions which directed him to Charlottesville. He therefore continued his march up the Valley, with the view of reaching Lynchburg by way of some one of the passes of the Blue Ridge south of the James River. In the neighborhood of Staunton he was joined by Crook and Averell, increasing his force to about 20,000 men, including cavalry and artillery. From Staunton he advanced by way of Lexington and Buchanan, burning and destroying everything that came in his way, leaving a track of desolation rarely witnessed in the course of civilized warfare. He crossed the Blue Ridge in the neighborhood of the Peaks of Otter, and approached Lynchburg by the way of the Lynchburg and Salem turnpike, having been vigorously opposed by McCauslin throughout his line of march.

In compliance with his instructions, General Early, on the 13th of June, withdrew his corps,* consisting of about 8000

---

* The Second corps, formerly commanded by General Ewell, who had been compelled through ill-health to give up operations in the field, and had been placed in command of the defences of Richmond.

infantry and 24 pieces of artillery, from the Army of Northern Virginia and proceeded toward Staunton. The artillery was subsequently increased to 40 guns, and his forces were further augmented by the addition of about 1500 cavalry and 2000 infantry. At Charlottesville, Early received intelligence of the rapid advance of Hunter upon Lynchburg with a force of 20,000 men.

Promptly shifting his objective point, and availing himself of the Orange and Alexandria Railroad, he moved with such rapidity that he reached Lynchburg in time to rescue it. At that time the only force at hand for the defence of Lynchburg was the division of Breckenridge, less than 2000 strong, and a few hundred home-guards, composed of old men and boys whose age exempted them from active service. Hunter, finding himself unexpectedly confronted by Early, relinquished his intended attack upon the city and sought safety in a rapid night-retreat.

The next day Early instituted a vigorous pursuit, which continued with uninterrupted pertinacity until Hunter was overtaken in the neighborhood of Salem, a small town on the Virginia and Tennessee Railroad, where he was encountered and obliged to make a hazardous and disorganizing retreat through the mountains to the Ohio River.

Having at a single blow liberated the Valley, Early determined upon an immediate invasion of Maryland and a bold advance on Washington City. As his instructions were discretionary, he was at liberty to adopt that course, which at the time was both in a political and military point of view the best plan of action that could have been assumed.

The defence of Richmond being the settled policy of the Confederate Government, General Lee had on two occasions assumed the offensive in order to relieve that place from the paralyzing influence of the Federals.

The invasion of Maryland in 1862 and the campaign into Pennsylvania the following year had relieved Richmond of the presence of the enemy for more than a year, but the tide of war had again returned, and that celebrated city was gradually yielding to the powerful embrace of her besiegers, which could only be loosened by a strong diversion in her favor.

This Early undertook with the force at his command after the disposal of Hunter's army. By uniting with his own corps the division of Breckenridge and Ransom's cavalry, Early found himself at the head of about 12,000 men. Though he knew this force to be inadequate to the magnitude of the work in hand, nevertheless he determined to overcome his want of numbers by the rapidity of his movements, thus hoping to acquire a momentum by velocity that would enable him to overcome that produced by the superior weight of his opponents.

After the dispersion of Hunter's forces one day in preparation sufficed Early for the commencement of his advance upon Maryland. His route through the Valley extended over a distance of about two hundred miles, but the road was good, and, although the country had been laid waste a short time before by Hunter, the genial season and fertile soil had already reproduced abundant subsistence for the horses and mules of the expedition, but the greater part of the supplies for the troops were necessarily drawn from Lynchburg and Richmond. To prevent delay, therefore, orders were sent to these places directing supplies to be forwarded to convenient points along the line of march. Staunton was reached on the 27th of June. This was the most suitable point at which to supply the army, and here Early made a short halt to make the necessary arrangements to ensure the uninterrupted continuance of his march. In this he was ably assisted by Colonel Allan, Majors Harman, Rogers, Hawks, and other members of his staff. The beautiful Valley of Virginia everywhere gave evidence of the ravages of war. Throughout the march down the Valley the unsparing hand of Hunter was proclaimed by the charred ruins of its once beautiful and happy homes. At Lexington were seen the cracked and tottering walls of the Virginia Military Institute, the pride of Virginia and the *alma mater* of many of the distinguished sons of the South, and near them appeared the blackened remains of the private residence of Governor Letcher.

When Early reached Winchester he learned that there was a

Federal force at Harper's Ferry and another at Martinsburg which it was necessary to dislodge before attempting the passage of the Potomac; and this was effected by the 4th of July without much opposition, the Federals having withdrawn without awaiting an attack. The way being now clear, the passage of the Potomac was made on the 5th at Shepherdstown, and the army advanced to Sharpsburg.

Since the defeat of Hunter the advance of Early had been so rapid that his design to invade Maryland had not been discovered by the Federal authorities in time to oppose his passage of the Potomac. But his entrance into Maryland being now known, it had produced great consternation as far as Baltimore and Washington. The boldness of this movement caused Early's force to be greatly exaggerated, and rumor soon magnified it to four or five times its real strength. The invasion was considered of such magnitude, and the cities of Washington and Baltimore were thought to be in such imminent danger, that the greatest alacrity was instituted in every direction to collect troops for the defence of those places.

The object of General Early being simply a diversion in favor of the operations about Richmond, he remained a day or two at Sharpsburg in order that the impression created by his invasion might have time to produce its full effect before he exposed his weakness by a further advance. At this time all the troops in the vicinity of Washington had been collected, besides which a large number of quartermaster's employés had been improvised as soldiers, thus making the force at hand exceed 20,000 men, while two corps from the army besieging Richmond and a part of another corps from North Carolina, intended to reinforce that army, had been detached and put in rapid motion for the defence of the capital.

In the face of these odds Early continued his advance into Maryland. At Frederick he found General Wallace, with about 10,000 men, in position to oppose the passage of the Monocacy. Immediate preparations were made to dislodge Wallace and effect a crossing of that stream. Rodes was thrown forward on the Baltimore and Ramseur on the Washington City road, while Gordon and Breckenridge, with a portion of Ransom's cavalry, inclining to the right, moved to the fords a mile or two below the railroad bridge. At the same time the heights contiguous to the river were crowned by Long's artillery (consisting of the guns of Nelson, Braxton, King, and McLaughlin) to cover the movement of the other troops.

When the troops had gained their position the crossing at the lower fords was promptly accomplished, and Breckenridge and Gordon, quickly forming their line of battle, advanced rapidly up the stream toward the Federal position, and, after a short but spirited conflict, defeated Wallace, whose army soon fell into a panic and fled in wild confusion, spreading dismay for miles in every direction by the terrible accounts they gave of the tremendous force Early was leading through the country. The route being now open, Early proceeded by rapid marches to within cannon-shot of the walls of Washing. ton. Since his entrance into Maryland his force had been exaggerated by the inhabitants and the soldiery he had met, until in their terrified imagination it was magnified to 30,000 or 40,000 men.

On his arrival before the Federal capital, the exaggerated rumor of his strength having preceded him, its occupants were variously affected. The Federal authorities and all of their adherents were in a state of consternation, while the Southern sympathizers were full of exultation, for at the time it was thought by many that he would take the city. Had he had 20,000 or 30,000 men, he might have done so with a prospect of holding it and giving a new turn to subsequent military operations. But Early was too prudent and sagacious to attempt an enterprise with a force of 8000 men which if successful could only be of temporary benefit. He was therefore content to remain in observation long enough to give his movement full time to produce its greatest effect, and then withdrew in the face of a large army and recrossed the Potomac without molestation.

This campaign is remarkable for having accomplished more in proportion to the force employed, and for having given less public satisfaction, than any other campaign of the war. The

want of appreciation of it is entirely due to the erroneous opinion that the city of Washington should have been taken; but
this may be passed over as one of the absurdities of public
criticism on the conduct of the war.

By glancing at the operations of Early from the 13th of
June to the last of July, it will be seen that in less than two
months he had marched more than four hundred miles, and
with a force not exceeding 12,000 men had not only defeated,
but entirely dispersed, two Federal armies of an aggregate
strength of more than double his own; had invaded Maryland, and by his bold and rapid movement upon Washington
had created an important diversion in favor of General Lee in
the defence of Richmond; and had re-entered Virginia with a
loss of less than 3000 men. After remaining a short time in
the neighborhood of Leesburg, he returned to the Valley by
way of Snicker's Gap, and about the 17th of July occupied
the neighborhood of Berryville.

Early had no sooner established himself at Berryville than
a considerable force of the enemy appeared on the Shenandoah
near Castleman's Ferry, and partially effected a crossing, but
were promptly driven back with heavy loss, after which they
retired to the neighborhood of Harper's Ferry.

About the same time a large force under General Averell
was reported to be advancing from Martinsburg to Winchester.
Being unwilling to receive an attack in an unfavorable position, Early sent Ramseur with a division and two batteries of
artillery to Winchester to retard Averell, while he withdrew
with the main body of the army and supply-trains by way of
White Post and Newtown to Strasburg.

Ramseur, having encountered the enemy a few miles east
of Winchester, was defeated with a loss of four pieces of artillery, and forced to retire to Newtown, where he rejoined Early.

Averell, being arrested in his pursuit of Ramseur near Newtown, fell back to Kernstown, where he was soon joined by
General Crook with the forces from Harper's Ferry.

From Newtown, Early continued his march to Strasburg
without interruption. On the 23d he was informed of the
junction of Crook and Averell and of their occupation of Kerns-

town ; thereupon it was determined to attack them without delay. The security of the trains having been properly provided for, the army was put in motion early on the morning of the 24th toward the enemy.

About noon a position was gained from which it was observed that the enemy was in possession of the identical ground which had been occupied by Shields when encountered by Stonewall Jackson in March, 1862. The memory of that battle evidently did much to inspire the troops to deeds of valor in the approaching conflict.

Early quickly made his dispositions for battle. The divisions of Breckenridge and Rodes were thrown to the right of the turnpike, and those of Ramseur and Gordon were deployed to its left, the artillery being disposed of so as to cover the advance of the infantry, while the cavalry received instructions to close behind the enemy as soon as defeated.

Perceiving that the left flank of the enemy was exposed, Breckenridge under cover of a wooded hill gained a position from which he bore down upon it, and in gallant style doubled it upon the centre. This success was so vigorously followed up by the other troops that the Federals gave way at all points, and were soon in rapid retreat, which was accelerated by a vigorous pursuit. In this battle the losses on the part of the Confederates were insignificant, while those of the Federals in killed, wounded, and prisoners were considerable. While on the retreat a large number of their wagons and a considerable quantity of their stores were destroyed to prevent capture.

Finding that the enemy had again sought safety behind his defences, Early determined to re-enter Maryland, for the double purpose of covering a retaliatory expedition into Pennsylvania and to keep alive the diversion which had already been made in favor of the defence of Richmond. Therefore, about the 6th of August he crossed the Potomac in two columns— the one at Williamsport, and the other at Shepherdstown—and took a position between Sharpsburg and Hagerstown.

This occupation of Maryland was destined to be of short duration, for since Early's audacity had caused his strength to be so greatly magnified and the importance of his operations so exaggerated, Grant had considered it necessary to largely increase the Army of the Shenandoah, and to supersede Hunter by Phil Sheridan, one of the most energetic of his lieutenants. Being aware of the great increase of force prepared to be brought against him, Early recrossed the Potomac and returned up the Valley, being slowly followed by Sheridan, who had now taken command of the Middle Department.

On reaching Fisher's Hill, a position three miles west of Strasburg, Early halted and offered battle, which Sheridan made a show of accepting until the morning of the 17th, when he was discovered to be retreating toward Winchester. He was immediately pursued by Early, and, being overtaken near Kernstown, a spirited skirmish ensued while he continued to retire. Night coming on, the combatants separated, Early bivouacking in the neighborhood of Winchester, while Sheridan crossed the Opequan.

About this time Lieutenant-general R. H. Anderson joined Early with a division of infantry and a division of cavalry, thus increasing his force to about 12,000 men, while that of Sheridan exceeded 40,000. Notwithstanding the great disparity of numbers, the campaign was characterized by a series of skilful movements and brilliant skirmishes, which resulted on the 19th of September in the battle of Winchester, which had doubtless been hastened to a conclusion by the departure of Anderson from the Valley on the 15th with Kershaw's division for Richmond. Anderson had no sooner turned his back on the mountains than Sheridan threw his whole force against Early at Winchester and defeated him, not so much by force of numbers as by one of those chances of war which sometimes beset the ablest commander; for, after having gallantly contested the field and firmly maintained their position until near the close of the day, a portion of his troops was seized with a panic, which rapidly spread until the greater part of the infantry and cavalry fell into confusion, and troops who had never before turned their backs upon the enemy retired in disorder from the field. The artillery alone remained firm, and covered with distinguished gallantry the retreat of the other troops until a place of safety was gained and order restored, and then retired fighting, step by step, until it extricated itself from overwhelming numbers, leaving heaps of dead to testify to its matchless conduct and power. Sheridan's forces were so shattered that he could not immediately avail himself of the success he had gained, and Early was permitted an uninterrupted retreat to Fisher's Hill.

Notwithstanding his force had been considerably weakened by its late disaster, Early determined to maintain his position on Fisher's Hill. He could not realize that every man was not as stout-hearted as himself, nor that the troops he had so often led to victory were not invincible; and besides his reluctance to abandon the rich and beautiful Valley, there were other and stronger reasons for his decision. It was evident that, if left unopposed in the Valley, Sheridan would immediately concert a plan of co-operation with Grant, either by advancing directly upon Richmond or by operating on its lines of communication with a powerful cavalry force until a junction was formed with him below Petersburg; in which case the important diversion in favor of Lee would have come to naught. Therefore the object of detaining Sheridan with his formidable force in the Valley sufficiently warranted Early, on the soundest military principles, in his determination to oppose him at all hazards.

The defiant attitude assumed by him was the most effective he could have adopted for accomplishing his object, and it created a deception as to his strength that made his opponent cautious, but which was quickly dissipated by a collision. His force at this time was less than 7000 men, while that of Sheridan was greater by at least four to one.

Sheridan's forces, having sufficiently recovered from the effect of the battle, pursued Early, and on the 22d attacked him in his position on Fisher's Hill. The thin Confederate ranks could offer but feeble resistance to the overwhelming force brought against them, and the conflict was consequently of short duration, and, owing to the extent and difficulty of the position, the Confederates sustained considerable loss before they could extricate themselves.

Early then retired up the Valley to a position above Harrisonburg, while Sheridan pursued as far as Newmarket. Both armies then remained inactive for some days, in order to rest and reorganize their forces.

About the 1st of October, Sheridan retraced his steps down the Valley to the neighborhood of Middletown, where he encamped on an elevated plateau behind Cedar Creek. Early, perceiving that his adversary had retired, pursued him to the neighborhood of Strasburg, where he took up a position from which he might be able to attack with advantage. Sheridan had unwittingly occupied a location that gave his adversary admirable advantages and opportunity to execute a surprise.

Early entrusted a considerable force to General Gordon for that purpose. Having made himself familiar with the work in hand, Gordon, on the night of October 18th, proceeded to its execution. Crossing Cedar Creek sufficiently below the Federal pickets to avoid observation, he cautiously proceeded in the direction of the Federal encampments without accident or discovery. A favorable point for the accomplishment of his plans was gained just before daybreak on the 19th. The camp was reached, and in the midst of quiet sleep and peaceful dreams the war-cry and the ringing peals of musketry arose to wake the slumbering warriors and call them to arms. The drums and bugles loudly summoned the soldier to his colors, but there was no ear for those familiar sounds. The crack of the rifle and the shouts of battle were upon the breeze, and no other sounds were heeded by the flying multitude.

Gordon's surprise had been complete, and when the dawn appeared long lines of fugitives were seen rushing madly toward Winchester. Such a rout had not been seen since the famous battle of Bull Run.

The Federals left artillery, baggage, small-arms, camp equipage, clothing, knapsacks, haversacks, canteens—in fact, everything—in their panic. The whole camp was filled with valuable booty, which in the end proved a dangerous temptation to the Confederates, many of whom, instead of following up their brilliant success, left their ranks for plunder.

If an apology for such conduct were ever admissible, it was

so on this occasion, the troops having been so long unaccustomed to the commonest comfort while making long and fatiguing marches and battling against large odds, and being now broken down, ragged, and hungry, they would have been superhuman had they resisted the tempting stores that lay scattered on every hand.

The Federals finding that they were not pursued, when they reached the neighborhood of Newtown their spirits began to revive, the habit of discipline and order assumed its sway, and the shapeless mass of the morning regained the appearance of an army.

Sheridan, having been absent, met his fugitive army a little below Newtown. Order having been restored, he re-formed his troops, and, facing them about, returned to the scene of their late disaster. The Confederates, being unprepared for an attack, were quickly defeated and forced to retire to Fisher's Hill, and from there to Newmarket, where Early maintained a bold front for several weeks. By this return of fortune Sheridan not only recovered all that had been lost in the morning, but acquired considerable captures from the Confederates.

The Confederates then retired to the neighborhood of Staunton, and further operations were suspended on account of the inclemency of the season.

Sheridan then occupied the lower Valley, where he employed himself in completing the work of destruction begun by Hunter. His work of devastation was so complete that he exultingly reported to his superior that a "crow in traversing the Valley would be obliged to carry his rations." Before the spring was open Sheridan was in motion with a cavalry, or rather mounted infantry, force 9000 strong, his objective point being Staunton. The force of Early, having been greatly reduced, was entirely inadequate for an effective resistance. Staunton was therefore evacuated, and Early retired to Waynesboro'. His entire force now consisted of Wharton's division of infantry, six pieces of artillery, and a small body of cavalry, making in all about 1800 men. With this force he took a position to protect an important railroad bridge

over the south branch of the Shenandoah, and at the same
time to cover Rockfish Gap, a pass connecting the Valley
with Eastern Virginia. This pass was doubly important, as
it gave a passage both to the Charlottesville turnpike and
the Central Railroad.

As Sheridan was without artillery and the ground was unfit
for the operations of cavalry, Early could have easily maintained his position with reliable troops; but there was considerable disaffection in Wharton's division. Therefore, without
his knowledge his little army harbored the elements of defeat,
for at the first show of an attack the malcontents threw down
their arms, and, almost without opposition, Sheridan carried
the position, compelling Early with his faithful few to seek
safety in retreat. A number of these, however, were captured
before they could make their escape.

Sheridan, having now removed all opposition, passed through
Rockfish Gap into Eastern Virginia, traversed the interior of
the State, and formed a junction with Grant almost without
interruption.

On reaching Gordonsville, Early collected a handful of men
and threw himself upon the flank and rear of Sheridan, but his
force was too small to make any impression. He was only induced to make this effort by his extreme reluctance to witness
an unopposed march of an enemy through his country.

It has been said that Early, at the head of his faithful band,
hovering like an eagle about the columns of Sheridan, displayed more heroic valor than when at the head of his victorious army in Maryland.

In operations of the character above described long lists of
casualties may naturally be expected, in which the names of
the bravest, noblest, and truest are sure to be found. While it
is impossible for me to make separate mention of these, memory dictates the names of Rodes and Ramseur. From Richmond to the memorable campaign of the Wilderness they bore
a conspicuous part, and their names rose high on the roll of
fame. Rodes fell in the battle of Winchester at the head of
his splendid division, and Ramseur was mortally wounded at
Cedar Creek in his heroic attempt to retrieve the fortune of the

day. Their fall was a noble sacrifice to the cause for which
they fought, and their memory will ever remain green in the
hearts of their countrymen.

The Valley campaign above described was attended with a
series of barbarities happily without parallel in the history of
the war. General Hunter had gone in his depredations far
beyond any warrant in the exigencies of war. The destruction of agricultural products, and even of mills and factories,
might have been defended as a warrantable military measure,
but the burning of private habitations was an instance of pure
vandalism utterly devoid of excuse, and sure to instigate retaliatory measures of the same barbarous character. This retaliation came in the cavalry raid sent by Early into Pennsylvania,
in which the town of Chambersburg was given to the flames.
It is but just to state here, however, that these cruel proceedings were in neither case dictated by the commanding general.
Hunter's operations were unauthorized by General Grant, and
the responsibility for them rests solely upon himself. The
same may be said of Early's reprisal. It was not authorized
by General Lee, and was instigated by the desire to prove that
such outrages could not be committed with impunity.

The subsequent devastation of the Valley by General Sheridan was still more complete than that effected by Hunter,
though the destruction of residences and institutions by the
latter was not repeated. Sheridan says: "The whole country
from the Blue Ridge to the North Mountain has been made
entirely untenable for a rebel army. I have destroyed over
two thousand barns filled with wheat and hay and farming-
implements; over seventy mills filled with flour and wheat;
have driven in front of the army over four thousand head of
stock; and have killed and issued to the troops not less than
three thousand sheep. This destruction embraces the Luray
Valley and the Little Fort Valley, as well as the main Valley."
Such a recital, given in a tone almost of boasting, seems more
like the story of some ruthless warrior of the olden times than
of a modern soldier. Admitting that the destruction of provisions may be defended as an important aid to the defeat of
an enemy, no such excuse can be offered for the burning of

mills and farming-implements. The destruction of the property of private citizens, who are in no sense responsible for, and are taking no part in, a war has always in it the elements of barbarism, and the suffering thereby caused to the defenceless has seldom or never been warranted by the military advantage gained.

CHAPTER XIX.

THE SIEGE OF PETERSBURG.

THE war in Virginia had now been reduced to the attack and defence of Richmond—in other words, to a siege whose termination was only a question of time.

Why the military operations in Virginia should have been contracted to this narrow limit, and the independence of a people struggling for nationality brought to depend upon the defence of a city, may be naturally asked, yet this question cannot be fully answered without casting a reflection upon the judgment of the distinguished patriots who presided over the destiny of the Confederacy. It may, however, be said that, having made Richmond the capital when it was of considerable military importance as the base of a defensive system embracing Yorktown, Norfolk, and the mouth of the James River, it could not, when circumstances changed, be easily abandoned without creating an impression both at home and abroad of national weakness; and, having seen it successfully defended against large odds, it was hoped that the same head and hand would be able to defend it in future peril. Therefore it was decided to employ all the resources of the country in its defence.

369

This decision was not adopted without hope of success; for the brilliant campaigns of Lee, and especially his late gigantic contest with Grant, had inspired such confidence that no military achievement was considered impossible to him and his army. In this connection it must be borne in mind that on an extensive theatre of operations, with free scope for the exercise of his powers, an able general may reasonably hope to satisfy public expectation, but when confined to the defensive in a siege, all that can be expected is to delay the final result. If it should be asked, What was General Lee's opinion in regard to the defence of Richmond? it might be said that he was too thorough a soldier openly to question the wisdom of the Government in forming its plan of operations or to employ less than his utmost ability in his efforts to execute them. The general who places himself in opposition to his government, no matter how weak that government may be, is sure to incur public condemnation and disgrace. A striking example in corroboration of this assertion presents itself in the case of Marshal Bazaine at the close of the late Franco-Prussian War.

Having now to sustain a siege, General Lee applied himself to it with all his energy. His whole soul was given to the gigantic struggle before him, and no labor or hardship deterred him.

The battle of Cold Harbor had taught Grant the inutility and peril of direct assaults upon the Confederate intrenchments. He therefore determined upon siege operations, and about the middle of June he threw a large portion of his army south of the James and extended his line of investment so as to embrace the city of Petersburg. This caused Lee to make a counter-movement in order to cover that place and protect the railroads leading to it. The capture of Petersburg was of primary importance to the Federals, as it would enable them to cut off two lines of communication very necessary for the support of Richmond, and at the same time to greatly contract their line of circumvallation. Therefore its possession was much desired.

As descriptive of the preliminary operations about Petersburg we introduce an extract from the able address of Captain McCabe before the Southern Historical Society:

"Warren with the Fifth corps and Wilson's division of cavalry, seizing the crossing at Long Bridge, made his dispositions to screen the movement.* Hancock's corps, marching past the Fifth, was directed upon Wilcox's landing (on the James); Wright's and Burnside's corps upon Douthard's; while Smith, with four divisions of the Tenth and Eighteenth corps, moved rapidly to White House and embarked for Bermuda Hundred. . . . .

"Smith's command reached Bermuda Hundred, where Grant was in person, on the evening of the 14th, and, being reinforced by Kautz's division of cavalry and Hinks's division of negro infantry, was at once directed to cross the Appomattox at Point of Rocks, where pontoons had been laid, and move rapidly on Petersburg. The passage of the river was effected during the same night, and early on the 15th Smith advanced in three columns, Kautz with his horsemen covering his left. Now, Hancock's entire corps had been ferried to the south side on the night of Smith's arrival at Bermuda Hundred, and might easily have been pushed forward to take part in the assault, but, left in ignorance of the projected *coup de main*, its commander, in obedience to orders, was awaiting rations where he had crossed. Incredible as it may seem, General Meade, the immediate commander of the Army of the Potomac, was left in like ignorance, and General Grant, hurrying back to the north side to push forward reinforcements from the corps of Wright and Burnside, found that the army pontoon-train had been sent to piece out the wagon-train pontoons, which had proved insufficient for the passage of the Chickahominy at Coles's Ferry. Thus nearly a day was gained to the handful of brave men defending the lines of Petersburg, and lost to the Army of the Potomac—a curious instance of the uncertain contingencies of war, reminding the military student, with a difference, of the happy chance which saved Zaragoza in the first siege when Lefèbre Desnouettes, 'missing the road to the bridge, missed that to victory.'

* The crossing of the Chickahominy.

"Smith, pushing forward his columns toward Petersburg early on the morning of the 15th, had scarcely advanced a distance of two miles when he encountered a hasty line of rifle-trenches, held by Graham's light battery and a meagre force of dismounted cavalry, the whole under Dearing, a young brigadier of high and daring spirit and of much experience in war. This position, resolutely held for two hours, was finally carried by the infantry, yet Dearing, retiring slowly with unabashed front, hotly disputing every foot of the advance, so delayed the hostile columns that it was 11 o'clock A. M. before they came upon the heavy line of intrenchments covering the eastern approaches to the town.

"Shortly after that hour Smith moved by the Baxter road upon the works in front of Batteries 6 and 7, but the men of Wise's brigade resisted his repeated assaults with 'unsurpassed stubbornness'—I use the exact language of Beauregard—while the rapid fire of the light batteries completed for the time his discomfiture.

"Smith had been told that the works defending Petersburg were such that 'cavalry could ride over them'—'a representation,' says Mr. Swinton archly, 'not justified by his experience;' and he now proceeded to reconnoitre more carefully what was in his front.

"The old defences of Petersburg consisted of a heavy line of redans connected by powerful rifle-trenches, and were of such extent as to require a garrison of 25,000 men. In the opinion of General Beauregard, this line was in many places faultily located, and especially vulnerable in the quarter of Batteries 5, 6, and 7. Reckoning his heavy gunners and the local militia, Beauregard had for the defence of this extended line on the morning of the 15th but 2200 men of all arms, while Smith confronted him with above 20,000. At 7.30 P. M. the enemy, warned by their heavy losses of the morning against assaulting in column in face of artillery served with such rapidity and precision, advanced at a charging pace in line, and after a spirited contest carried with a rush the whole line of redans from 5 to 9 inclusive.

"Scarcely had the assault ended when Hancock came up

with the Second corps, and, though the ranking officer, with rare generosity—which recalls the chivalric conduct of Sir James Outram to Havelock in front of Lucknow—at once offered his troops to Smith and stood ready to receive the orders of his subordinate.

"The prize was now within his grasp had he boldly advanced—and the moon shining brightly highly favored such enterprise—but Smith, it would seem, though possessed of considerable professional skill, was not endowed with that intuitive sagacity which swiftly discerns the chances of the moment, and, thus halting on the very threshold of decisive victory, contented himself with partial success, and, having relieved his divisions in the captured works with Hancock's troops, waited for the morning.

"Meanwhile, Hoke had arrived on the Confederate side, and Beauregard, having disposed his meagre force upon a new line a short distance in rear of the lost redans, ordered down Bushrod Johnson's three brigades from the Bermuda Hundred front and made such preparation as was possible for the assault of the morrow.

"The situation was indeed critical, for, though the enemy assaulted but feebly the next morning and Johnson's brigades arrived at 10 A. M., there was still such disparity of numbers as might well have shaken the resolution of a less determined commander. Burnside's corps reached the Federal front at noon, and General Meade, having met General Grant on the City Point road, was directed to assume immediate command of the troops and assault as soon as practicable. Thus at 5.30 on the evening of the 16th more than 70,000 troops were launched against the works manned by but 10,000 brave men —a disparity still further increased by the arrival at dusk of Warren's corps, two brigades of which (Miles's and Griffin's) took part in the closing assaults. For three hours the fight raged furiously along the whole line with varying success, nor did the contest subside until after nine o'clock, when it was found that Birney of Hancock's corps had effected a serious lodgment, from which the Confederates in vain attempted to expel him during the night.

"On the same day Pickett's division, despatched by Lee and leading the advance of Anderson's corps, recaptured the lines on the Bermuda Hundred front which Beauregard had been forced to uncover, and which had been immediately seized by Butler's troops.   It is surely sufficient answer to those who represent Lee as even then despondently forecasting the final issue to find him writing next day in great good-humor to Anderson: 'I believe that the men of your corps will carry anything they are put against.   We tried very hard to stop Pickett's men from capturing the breastworks of the enemy, but couldn't do it.''

" Fortunately for the weary Confederates, the enemy attempted no offensive movement until nearly noon of the next day, at which hour the Ninth corps, advancing with spirit, carried a redoubt in its front, together with four pieces of artillery and several hundred prisoners, while Hancock's corps pressed back the Confederates over Hare's Hill—the spot afterward known as Fort Steadman, and made famous by Gordon's sudden and daring stroke.   Later in the day the Ninth corps attacked again, but was driven back with severe loss.

"Then along the whole front occurred a series of assaults and counter-charges creditable to the courage and enterprise of both sides, yet so confused that an attempted narrative would necessarily share that confusion.   Suffice it to say that at dusk the Confederate lines were pierced, and, the troops crowding together in disorder, irreparable disaster seemed imminent, when suddenly in the dim twilight a dark column was descried mounting swiftly from the ravines in rear, and Gracie's gallant Alabamians, springing along the crest with fierce cries, leaped over the works, captured over 1500 prisoners, and drove the enemy pell-mell from the disputed point.   Then the combat broke out afresh, for the enemy, with reason, felt that chance alone had foiled them of decisive success, and, despite the darkness, the fight raged with unabated fury until past midnight. . . . .

" The battle, as we have seen, did not cease until half-past twelve on the night of the 17th, and the evacuation of the town seemed inevitable, when, by a happy accident, an officer of

Burnside's staff, losing his way in the darkness, rode into the Confederate lines bearing a despatch from Burnside to Meade to the effect that the Ninth corps had been very roughly handled and should be promptly reinforced. This despatch had been referred by Meade to Smith for his information, with the request that he at once reinforce Burnside with such troops as could be spared. Scarcely had Beauregard finished reading the captured missive when a courier galloped up with a message from Hoke, stating that he had easily repulsed Smith's assaults and could lend a helping hand elsewhere. But before this, Beauregard, foreseeing the rupture of his lines, as yet too extended for the strength of his command, now materially weakened by recent casualties, had selected a new and shorter line to the rear, and shortly after the combat ceased the troops were ordered to retire upon this new position—a delicate movement, considering the proximity of the enemy, yet executed rapidly and without confusion, for he had caused the line to be marked with white stakes, and required brigade and division staff officers to acquaint themselves with the positions to be occupied by their respective commands. This was the line held until the close of the defence.

"Grant had ordered Meade to assault along the whole front at daylight of the 18th, but when the Federal skirmishers moved forward at that hour it was found that the line so stoutly defended the evening before had been abandoned by the Confederates. This necessitated fresh dispositions, and Meade, having reconnoitred his front, now determined upon assault in column against certain selected points instead of a general attack in line, as originally intended.

"It was noon before the enemy essayed any vigorous attack, but then began a series of swift and furious assaults, continuing at intervals far into the evening, from Martindale on the right, from Hancock and Burnside in the centre, from Warren on the left ; but, though their men advanced with spirit, cheering and at the run, and their officers displayed an astonishing hardihood, several of them rushing up to within thirty yards of the adverse works bearing the colors, yet the huge columns, rent by the plunging fire of the light guns and smitten with a tempest of bullets, recoiled in confusion, and finally fled, leaving their dead and dying on the field along the whole front.

"The men of Anderson's and Hill's corps were now pouring into the Confederate works, division after division, battery after battery, and when night fell those two grim adversaries, the Army of the Potomac and the Army of Northern Virginia, again confronted each other in array of battle, while General Grant had learned that Petersburg, as Napoleon said of Valencia, 'could not be taken by the collar.'

"In these four days of assault, from Wednesday to Saturday inclusive, the enemy confessed to a loss of more than 10,000 men—a fact which attests with appalling eloquence the vigor of the defence.

"Sunday morning, June 19th, dawned with soft and dewy brightness, and the Sabbath's stillness remained unbroken, save when at distant intervals a single gun boomed out from the great salients or the rattling fire of the pickets on the river front fretted for a few brief moments the peaceful air. But it was no day of rest to the contending armies, for the Confederates were actively strengthening their crude position, while the enemy plied pick and spade and axe with such silent vigor that, this comparative quiet reigning for two successive days, there arose, as if by touch of a magician's wand, a vast cordon of redoubts of powerful profile connected by heavy infantry parapets, stretching from the Appomattox to the extreme Federal left—a line of prodigious strength and constructed with amazing skill, destined long to remain, to the military student at least, an enduring monument of the ability of the engineers of the Army of the Potomac.

"This done, General Grant was now free to begin that series of attempts against Lee's communications which, despite repeated disaster, he continued with slight intermission to the end.

"On Tuesday, the 21st, the Second and Sixth corps were put in motion to extend the Federal left—the Second to take position west of the Jerusalem plank road, its right connecting with Warren's left, which rested at that point; the Sixth to extend to the left of the Second, and if possible effect a lodgment on the Weldon Railroad. On the same day Wilson with about 6000 sabres, consisting of his own and Kautz's divisions, was despatched to destroy the Weldon road farther to the south, and thence, by a wide sweep to the west, to cut the Southside and Danville roads. The Second corps, now commanded by Birney —for Hancock's wound, received at Gettysburg, had broken out afresh—succeeded, after some sharp skirmishing with the Confederate cavalry, in taking position to the left of Warren, and the Sixth corps, moving up the same evening, established itself on a line in rear of and parallel to the Second, its left slightly overlapping that corps. But the next morning the Confederate horse showed such a bold front, though 'twas but a scratch force, with cattle like 'walking trestles,' that General Grant determined to suspend the movements to the railroad, and Birney was ordered 'to swing forward the left of the Second corps so as to envelop the right flank of the Confederates.'

"This change of orders led to delay, which Lee, consummate master of that art which teaches that 'offensive movements are the foundation of a good defence,' was swift to improve. Riding to his right, he sent for Mahone, who as civil engineer had surveyed the country and knew every inch of the ground hidden by the tangled chaparral. Few words were wasted. Mahone proposed that he be allowed to take three brigades of Anderson's old division and strike the enemy in flank. Lee assented. Passing his men quickly along a ravine which screened them from the enemy's pickets, Mahone gained a point which he rightly conjectured to be beyond the hostile flank. Here, in an open field fronting the 'Johnson House,' he formed line of battle, the brigades of Saunders and Wright in front, his own brigade, commanded by Colonel Weisiger, supporting the right, while McIntosh of the artillery was directed to move with two guns in the open on the left. Birney, meanwhile, had nearly completed his movement, which was executed without reference to the Sixth corps, and left an ever-widening gap between the two lines, as, 'pivoting on his right division, under Gibbon, he swung forward his left.' Yet Mott's division had come into position on Gibbon's left, and had commenced intrenching, and Barlow was moving up to the left of Mott, when suddenly and swiftly, with a wild yell which rang out shrill and fierce through the gloomy pines, Mahone's men burst upon the flank. A pealing volley, which roared along the whole front, a stream of wasting fire, under which the Federal left fell as one man, and the bronzed veterans swept forward, shrivelling up Barlow's division as lightning shrivels the dead leaves of autumn; then, cleaving a fiery path diagonally across the enemy's front, spreading dismay and destruction, rolled up Mott's division in its turn, and without check, the woods still reverberating with their fierce clamor, stormed and carried Gibbon's intrenchments and seized his guns.

"When night came down the victors returned to the main lines guarding 1742 prisoners, and bearing as trophies a vast quantity of small-arms, four light guns, and eight standards.

"On the same day Wilson with his cavalry struck the Weldon Railroad at Reams Station, destroyed the track for several miles, and then pushed westward to the Southside road. Here, while tearing up the rails at 'Blacks-and-Whites'—having despatched Kautz, meanwhile, to destroy the junction of the Southside and Danville roads at Burkeville—he was sharply assailed by W. H. F. Lee, who had followed him with his division of cavalry, and who now wrested from him the road upon which the raiders were moving. Again and again did Wilson seek to wrest it back, but Lee could not be dislodged. The combat was renewed next day, lasting from midday till dark, but at daylight of the 24th the Federal cavalry withdrew, leaving their killed and wounded on the field. Wilson reached Meherrin Station on the Danville road the same day, and, Kautz having rejoined him, the two columns pushed on rapidly to Staunton River bridge. But the local militia, intrenched at that point, behaved with great firmness, and W. H. F. Lee, boldly attacking, again drove the Federals before him until dark. Wilson now turned to regain the lines in front of Petersburg, but his officers and men were marauding in a fashion which no prudent officer, on such service as his, should ever have allowed, while W. H. F. Lee hung upon his rear with an exasperating tenacity which brought delay and redoubled his difficulties. At every step, indeed, the peril thickened, for Hampton, who had crossed the James, now came to W. H. F. Lee's help with a strong body of horse, and, attacking the enemy on Tuesday evening (June 28th) at Sappony Church, drove him until dark, harassed him the livelong night, turned his left in the morning, and sent him helter-skelter before his horsemen.

"Wilson, fairly bewildered, sought to reach Reams Station, which he believed to be still in possession of the Federals—a determination destined to be attended with irreparable disaster to him, for General Lee had despatched thither two brigades of infantry (Finegan's and Saunders's) under Mahone, and two light batteries (Brander's and 'the Purcell') under Pegram, followed by Fitz Lee, who had just roughly handled Gregg at Nance's Shop, and who now came down at a sharp trot to take part in the tumult. Wilson, reaching his objective, descried ominous clouds of dust rising on the roads by which he had hoped to win safety, but offered, in desperation, a seemingly bold front prepared for battle.

"Informed by a negro, whose knowledge of the country notably expanded at sight of a six-shooter, that there was a 'blind road' leading in rear of Wilson's left, Fitz Lee at once pushed forward with his dusky guide, and, having assured himself by personal reconnoissance of the truth of the information, quickly made his dispositions. Lomax's horsemen, dismounted, were formed across the road, with Wickham's mounted brigade in reserve, the latter being instructed to charge so soon as Lomax had shaken the enemy. In a twinkling, as it seemed, the rattling fire of the carbines told that Lomax was hotly engaged, and on the instant the movement in front began, the infantry under Mahone advancing swiftly across the open field, pouring in a biting volley, Pegram firing rapidly for a few moments, then limbering up and going forward at a gallop to come into battery on a line with the infantry, while Fitz Lee, the Federals rapidly giving ground before his dismounted troopers, called up his mounted squadrons and went in with his rough stroke at a thundering pace on the enemy's left and rear."

The result of this sharp attack was a severe defeat to Wilson, who was forced to retire in great haste, his trains being fired and abandoned, and his artillery and a considerable number of prisoners left in the hands of the Confederate forces. Making all speed, he succeeded in crossing the Nottoway with the pursuing cavalry at his heels, and very well satisfied to escape into the Federal lines with the shattered remnant of his command.

General Grant, having failed in his various attempts to force the Confederate lines, acquiesced in a proposal to supplement the musket and the sabre with the spade and the pick. About the last of June it was proposed to mine and blow up a Confederate salient that was opposite to Burnside's position. At that point the two lines were sufficiently near to warrant such an attempt. The conduct of this mining operation was assigned to the person by whom it had been originally proposed, Lieutenant-colonel Henry Pleasants of the Forty-eighth Pennsylvania, a skilful mining engineer. Pleasants found a suitable point to commence operations about five hundred feet distant from the salient to be blown up. His working-parties were drawn from his own regiment, which contained a number of experienced miners. The work was pushed forward so expeditiously that by the 23d of July the mine was completed, and was charged with 8000 pounds of powder. The tamping was completed and the mine was pronounced ready for explosion by the 28th. It was decided that the mine should be sprung early on the morning of the 30th, and to that end the necessary preparations were made.

General Grant, in order to mask his real design, on the 26th sent Hancock and Sheridan with the Second corps and two divisions of cavalry to the north side of the James River, with instructions to threaten Lee's right, and thus to create the impression that a real attack was to be made in that quarter, while he perfected his arrangements for making the assault on Petersburg upon the explosion of the mine. At this time the Confederate force about Petersburg did not exceed 13,000 men, whilst opposed to this Grant had over 65,000. On the 29th were made the final dispositions for attack.

Hancock was directed on the night of the 29th to return from the north of the James with all secrecy and despatch, and to take part in the assault, while Sheridan was to pass in rear of the army and with his whole cavalry corps operate toward Petersburg from the south and west. On the evening of the 29th, Meade issued his orders of battle. As soon as it was dusk Burnside was to mass his troops in front of the point to be attacked, and form there in columns of assault, taking care to remove the abatis, so that the troops could debouch rapidly, and to have his pioneers equipped for opening passages for the artillery. He was to spring the mine at 3.30 A.M., move rapidly through the breach, and seize the crest of Cemetery Hill, a ridge four hundred yards in rear of the Confederate lines.

Ord was to mass the Eighteenth corps in rear of the Ninth, immediately follow Burnside, and support him on the right. Warren was to reduce the number of men holding his front to the minimum, concentrate heavily on the right of his corps, and support Burnside on the left. Hancock was to mass the Second corps in rear of the trenches at that time held by Ord, and be prepared to support the assault as events might dictate. Engineer officers were detailed to accompany each corps, and the chief engineer was directed to park his pontoon-train at a convenient point, ready to move at a moment's warning.

Meade having assured himself that the Confederates had no second line on Cemetery Hill, as he had formerly supposed and as Duane had positively reported, was now sanguine of success. He made these preparations to meet the contingency of the meagre Confederate force retiring beyond the Appomattox and burning the bridges; in which event he proposed to push immediately across that river to Swift Creek and open up communication with Butler at Bermuda Hundred, before Lee could send any reinforcements from his five divisions north of the James.

The commanders of the white divisions of Burnside's corps decided by lot which division should have the honor of making the assault, the chance favoring Ledlie's division, though, as the sequel shows, it had but little heart for the distinction conferred upon it.

On the morning of the 30th, shortly before the hour appointed for springing the mine, all the columns were in position ready for action. Half-past three arrived, but the silence of the morning was unbroken; minute after minute went by, while a painful suspense pervaded the expectant columns. Time passed on, yet silence continued to reign. The suspense became almost unbearable. The delay could not be understood, and various conjectures flew rapidly among the troops. At last it was discovered that the fuse had gone out within fifty yards of the mine.

All this time the Confederates lay in peaceful slumber, unconscious of the terrible storm that was about to burst upon them. The fuse was relighted, and at about half-past four the flame reached the powder in the mine.

A tremendous explosion instantly followed, and there was hurled into the air an immense column of smoke and earth, which, after rising to a great height, burst into fragments of timber, stone, broken gun-carriages, muskets, and black and mutilated corpses, which quickly returned in a heavy shower upon the earth. Two hundred men were killed by the explosion, and a rent was torn in the Confederate lines 135 feet long, 90 feet wide, and 30 feet deep.

The whole Confederate line was aroused by the explosion. The men in the immediate vicinity of the mine were for some minutes paralyzed by the shock, while those on the more distant portions of the lines remained a while in a state of ignorance and wonder as to what had occurred.

But the troops stationed near the mine soon became conscious of the catastrophe, and, alive to the importance of immediate action, Lieutenant-colonel John Haskell, who commanded the artillery at that point, turned his guns upon the approaches to the breach, and poured such a destructive fire of canister and shell upon them as to render the advance of the enemy extremely difficult. Some time elapsed before the assaulting column could be got in motion, and when it cleared the breastwork it was met by such a storm of shot and shell that it was thrown into confusion, and the men were so demoralized that they hastily sought shelter. Great numbers rushed into the crater of the mine; others hid themselves behind traverses; some even crouched close beneath the Confederate breastworks, and no efforts of their officers could induce them to advance. The delay thus occasioned enabled the Confederates to collect a force sufficient to defend the breach.

General Lee, who had been early apprised of the disaster, sent Colonel Venable of his staff to hasten forward troops from other parts of the line. This energetic officer first found General Mahone, whose division was already under arms, and instructed him to proceed to the threatened point. Mahone rapidly advanced, and on reaching the crater promptly formed a cordon of bayonets and took decisive steps to expel the Federal forces that had effected a lodgment upon the Confederate works. Mahone's forces were rapidly reinforced by other troops, and the fighting now became desperate. The Federals, who had for some time been delayed, pushed forward with great resolution and with the determination to counteract the effects of the blunder that had been made in the first assault. But all their efforts were unavailing, and by ten o'clock they were driven back within their own lines.

The mine, instead of opening the gate to victory, had proved a sepulchre. General Grant lost 5000 men in his attempt to pass the breach. Although the distance between the hostile breastworks was barely a hundred yards, only a few of the Federals succeeded in establishing themselves on the Confederate works. The only advantage to the Federals was in the blowing up of 200 Confederates and the killing and wounding of a few hundreds more. The men thus lost by the Confederates could never be replaced, and to this extent General Grant saw himself a step nearer the end.

Generals Lee and Beauregard were eye-witnesses of the gallant defence of the breach and the signal repulse of the enemy. Colonel Weisiger, whose brigade encircled the crater, repelled the enemy with great determination, and his gallantry won for him the grade of brigadier-general. Captain Girardey, for his gallant conduct, received a similar promotion, while the names of Lieutenant-colonels John Haskell, Pegram, and many others of the artillery obtained prominence in the roll of honor.

Critical remarks in reference to the strategic bearings of this mining operation are perhaps uncalled for. The mine itself proved useless and became a death-trap to its excavators; yet, if we accept the Federal statements, this was a result of bad management after the explosion, and has no necessary bearing on the question of the military value of the undertaking itself. To mine fortified works which cannot be breached or scaled has long been a common expedient in siege operations, but to attack an earthwork by such a method had never before been attempted, and its ill-success on this occasion will probably prevent its being quickly again essayed.

Federal historians and military authorities ascribe the non-success of the enterprise to an unwise withdrawal, at the last moment, of the black troops, who had been carefully drilled for this special service, and their replacement by a brigade of whites, who were very badly led and held back from charging until the Confederates in the vicinity had recovered from their temporary panic and had hastened to the defence of their imperilled lines. Yet this censure of General Ledlie seems hardly just in view of all the circumstances of the case. The crater into which his division plunged was very difficult to pass—much more so than an ordinary earthwork. And the lack of previous training of his men, or of any full comprehension on his part of the character of the work before him, operated as a serious disadvantage. Had men trained to the work been given the advance in the charge, the result might possibly have been very different. It cannot be denied that the Confederate position was for a short time in serious jeopardy, and that had the Federals taken instant and decided advantage of their opportunity they might have gained an important victory. There has seldom been a case in which the old adage, "Delay is dangerous," more fully applied, yet it was one of those cases in which delay is almost unavoidable, and it becomes a question, therefore, whether there was sufficient probability of success to warrant such a dangerous enterprise.

The ultimate effect of the mining operation was beneficial to the Confederate army. We do not here refer to the heavy Federal loss, but to the feeling of security which naturally followed the failure of the assault, and to the greater degree of wariness which succeeded. A second enterprise of the same sort would have had much less chance of success than the first. Yet to guard against a repetition of mining operations by the Federals, General Lee adopted a series of precautionary measures consisting of the excavation of extensive underground works so constructed as to check the enemy should they seek to repeat their subterranean scheme of attack.

In the relation of the events of this siege we have been necessarily confined to military details, and, though fully recognizing that the mind of General Lee controlled the movements of the Confederate army and the wonderful series of defensive works which arose as if by magic under his skilful directions, we do not see him directly concerned in them. Some relation of personal incidents connected with his everyday life is important as a counterpoise to the story of his great military achievements, and we cannot better end this chapter than with some anecdotal matter belonging to this period of his life.

Colonel Thomas H. Carter has furnished the author with several interesting reminiscences never before given to the public, yet so indicative of certain traits of General Lee's character as to make them important additions to our work. In Colonel Carter's words, "They are simple anecdotes, treasured by myself because of their personal relation chiefly, though they illustrate a playful vein of character in General Lee of which many persons may not be aware, and one of them brings out his consideration for others—a characteristic that under no circumstances ever failed him."

In the relation of these incidents we shall let Colonel Carter speak for himself, as we cannot hope to improve on his manner of telling his story:

"In 1864, either during July or August, when General Lee's headquarters were near Petersburg, I had charge of the light artillery north of the James River. The line lay near Deep Bottom, and ran eastwardly by Newmarket toward the Chickahominy River, and I was partially but imperfectly intrenched, with skirmishers well advanced and in pits. One day General Lee rode over from Petersburg, and reached us quite early in the morning, considering the distance he had ridden. My tent was a mile and a half in the rear of the line, in charge of the servants, while I myself slept on the line for fear of an attack by the enemy, then close in front. My cooking utensils were brought up to the line and rations cooked twice daily, and the servant then returned with blankets in the morning to be aired during the day, and with the cooking and eating wares.

"Martin, my servant, a good-tempered, smiling, and most deferential black boy, was quietly walking the gray horse back to camp through the woods after breakfast, pretty well enveloped with blankets, a tray, skillets, tin plates and cans, knives and forks, etc., when General Lee met him. Nothing escaped General Lee's observant eye. Grave, quiet, and taciturn, he saw everything. He pulled up his horse and put Martin through a course of questions, in which he learned his name, to whom he belonged, where he was going, where he had been, and, in short, left not much behind of Martin's limited stock of knowledge.

"All ignorant of this little incident, I advanced to meet the general as he rode up to the line. 'Good-morning, Colonel Carter.'—'Good-morning, general.'—'I expected, colonel, to find the troops in motion.'—'In motion, general? No, sir, there is no movement on foot here—all is quiet,' I said in reply, looking at him with surprise. A merry look in his eye showed me he was joking as he added, 'Well, I met Martin, on the gray, going to the rear with baggage and camp-equipage, and when they go to the rear the troops are usually going to the front.' I explained what he had already heard from Martin, that I slept on the line. 'You are right,' he said, 'to be at your post with your command.'

"Not long after this, while we were stationed at the same place, he rode over from Petersburg, and reached us quite late in the afternoon—too late to return to his headquarters that night. After some conversation about the line and troops he mentioned the necessity of finding quarters for himself and those with him for the night. Apologizing for my inability to make him comfortable and to have him stay with me, for reasons above given, I suggested that he should go to Chaffin's

General Lee and the Sparrow.   Page 387.

Bluff, where he would find houses occupied, I thought, by
Major Dick Taylor (Walter's brother) and Colonel Jack Maury
and others connected with the heavy and stationary artillery.
He replied in his quiet, punctuating way of talking, as if
weighing each word, 'Well, Colonel Carter, if I turn those
gentlemen out of their rooms, where will they sleep?'—'On
the ground,' I replied at once, 'like the rest of the army;'
and I added, what I knew to be literally true, 'They will be
delighted to give up their rooms to you.''—'None of your
blarney, Colonel Carter—none of your blarney, sir,' he replied
with a smile. Though not sure of it, I think he went there,
but I am sure if he went the rooms were given up with *delight.*

"When the infantry was hurrying to the support of Fitz
Lee's cavalry at Spottsylvania Court-house, as each division
arrived it would form into line on the right of its predecessor.
I happened to be near General Lee when a few bullets cut the
limbs and struck the ground near him. Some general—I forget who—said, 'General, this is no place for you; do go away
at once to a safe place.' He replied, with a half-complaining
smile and manner, 'I wish I knew where my place is on the
battlefield: wherever I go some one tells me it is not the place
for me to be.' But he was always deeply touched by these
indications of the devotion of his army and people to him."

An incident somewhat analogous to that just related, but
indicating a different and very noble phase of General Lee's
character, is told by an officer who was present on the occasion. General Lee was visiting a battery on the lines below
Richmond, and the soldiers, inspired by their affection for
him, gathered near him in a group that attracted the enemy's
fire. Turning toward them, he said, in his quiet manner,
"Men, you had better go farther to the rear; they are firing
up here, and you are exposing yourselves to unnecessary
danger."

The men drew back, but General Lee, as if unconscious of
danger to himself, walked across the yard, picked up some
small object from the ground, and placed it upon the limb of
a tree above his head. It was afterward perceived that the
object for which he had thus risked his life was *an unfledged*

sparrow that had fallen from its nest. It was a marked instance of that love for the lower animals and deep feeling for the helpless which he always displayed.

One story further we may relate of a very delicately administered, yet probably very effectual, reproof. On one of his daily visits to the lines at Petersburg, General Lee asked one of his officers who was riding with him if a work he had ordered to be performed was finished. The officer replied, hesitatingly, that it was. Lee then proposed to ride to the spot and inspect it. On arriving there he found that the work had made very little progress since his last visit to it, a week before. The officer in much confusion sought to excuse himself for his negligence, saying that he had ordered it to be completed at once, and had been told that it was finished, but had not himself been there. General Lee simply remarked, "We must give our personal attention to the lines," and rode quietly on. While doing so he began to compliment his companion on the fine charger he rode.

"Yes, sir," replied the general, "he is a splendid animal, and I prize him the more highly because he belongs to my wife and is her favorite riding-horse."

"A magnificent horse indeed," was General Lee's reply, "but I should not think him safe for Mrs. —— to ride. He is entirely too spirited for a lady, and I would urge you by all means to take some of the mettle out of him before you suffer your wife to ride him again. And, by the way, general, I would suggest to you that *the rough paths along these trenches would be admirable ground over which to tame him.*"

It need scarcely be said the rebuked officer did not trust to the reports of subordinates from that time forward, and that he found a new field for the exercise of his horse.

To these reminiscences we may add the following story, told by General Hampton: On one occasion, when headquarters were at Petersburg, General Hampton happened to be there at meal-time, and was invited to dine with General Lee. It was a period in which rations were very short. A small bowl of soup graced the table, far too limited in quantity to go the rounds of the mess. General Lee accordingly divided it with his guest, and, as he looked around the table with a merry twinkle in his eye, quietly remarked, "I am credibly informed that the young men of my staff never eat soup."

As a fitting conclusion to this chapter we append the following letter, written by General Lee to one of his daughters during the Petersburg campaign. An interesting feature of it is its indication of his love for buttermilk as a beverage, of which we have already given several instances:

"CAMP, PETERSBURG, July 5, 1864.

"MY PRECIOUS LIFE: I received this morning, by your brother, your note, and am very glad to hear your mother is better. I sent out immediately to try and find some lemons, but could only procure two—sent to me by a kind lady, Mrs. Kirkland, in Petersburg. These were gathered from her own trees; there are none to be purchased. I found one in my valise, dried up, which I also send, as it may be of some value. I also put up some early apples, which you can roast for your mother, and one pear. This is all the fruit I can get.

"You must go to market every morning and see if you cannot find some fresh fruit for her. There are no lemons to be had here. Tell her lemonade is not as palatable or digestible as buttermilk. Try and get some for her—with ice it is delicious, and very nutritious. I hope she will continue to improve, and be soon well and leave that heated city. It must be roasting now. Tell her I can only think of her and pray for her recovery. I wish I could be with her to nurse her and care for her. I want to see you all very much, but cannot now see the day when we shall be together once more. I think of you, long for you, pray for you: it is all I can do. Think sometimes of your devoted father,

"R. E. LEE."

CHAPTER XX.

THE SIEGE CONTINUED.

Grant's Purpose.—Extension of the Lines.—Difficulties of Lee's Position.—Collateral Operations.—Attack on Fort Fisher.—Its Failure.—Subsequent Successful Assault.—Progress of the Siege.—Loss of the Weldon Railroad.—Federal Repulse at Reams Station.—Butler Takes Fort Harrison.—Later Engagements.—General Lee's Appearance.—His Relations to his Soldiers.—Letter to his Daughter.—Extracts from Colonel Taylor's Note-book.—Anecdote.—Lee's Opinion of War Editors.—Lee Appointed Commander-in-Chief.—Peace Conference.—Its Failure.—President Davis's Address.—Lee's Plan of Action.—Overruled by the Authorities. —The Attack on Fort Steadman.—Its Partial Success and Final Failure.—Grant's Advance.—Battle at White Oak Road.—Cavalry Fight.—The Federals Capture Five Forks.—Their Advance on Petersburg.—Checked by Longstreet.—Death of A. P. Hill.

BEFORE proceeding with the description of the siege operations at Petersburg some remarks concerning the general military situation and the purposes of the opposing commanders are desirable.

Though the objective point of Grant's operations was the city of Richmond, his field of immediate action was the city of Petersburg, twenty-two miles south of the Confederate capital. His purpose in this was to seize and hold the Weldon and Southside railroads, the latter of special importance, since it would open the way to the possession of the Danville Railroad, the main line of communication between Richmond and the South. The possession of these roads would force the evacuation of the capital city and the desertion by the Army of Northern Virginia of the formidable line of defensive works on which had been expended such severe and long-continued labor.

With this object in view, Grant steadily extended his lines southward and westward beyond Petersburg, while Lee with unceasing activity faced him at every point with new earthworks covering the all-important arteries of travel which his powerful antagonist was striving to seize. Eventually, the Confederate line of defence, extending from the Chickahominy to Petersburg, and continued to the Southside Railroad, traversed a distance of thirty-five miles. This extensive line was defended by a force barely exceeding a thousand men to the mile, and often falling below that number, and to maintain it in the face of an enemy outnumbering more than three times the Confederate army unquestionably demanded a remarkable exercise of military genius.

Few men could have borne up against such odds, especially when beset by every difficulty that can embarrass a commander. Lee proved always able to multiply his forces at any threatened point, and was constantly ready to meet attacks, displaying a fertility of resources that surprised both friend and foe. Not once during the campaign had Grant been able to take him unawares, but found him always prepared even for the most covert movements.

After the failure of the mining enterprise direct assaults flagged, and during the remainder of the summer and the autumn the spade took the place of the musket, and both armies employed themselves in constructing new and strengthening old works, Grant gradually extending his left toward the railroads which he desired to capture, and Lee steadily covering these roads by a similar extension of his right.

The monotony of this labor was occasionally relieved by a sortie or lively picket-skirmish, and now and then by a reconnoissance or an outpost affair between the opposing cavalry forces. But these events had no further importance than that of lightening the tedium of the siege. Grant had evidently deferred the doubtful issue of an attack upon his alert opponent, of whose ability in defensive warfare he had already received such disastrous testimony, and he seemed inclined to patiently await the exhaustion of the few remaining resources of his adversary for a final *coup de main*.

We may pause here for a glance at the state of the war in the other regions of the Confederacy. In fact, General Lee was fighting not alone against the army directly confronting him, but against all the military forces of the Northern States wherever situated. Grant's rank as commander-in-chief of the Federal armies enabled him to wield them all in concert for the great aim which he had in view, the defeat of Lee, and throughout the South armies were manœuvring and marching for a single end, that of cutting at all points the strategic lines of the Confederacy, and so isolating the Army of Northern Virginia as to deprive it of all hope of assistance or reinforcement.

General Lee possessed no such comprehensive authority. He was commander of a single army only, and while his advice in relation to the movements of other armies was constantly asked by the Government, it was not always followed. The command-in-chief was eventually given him, it is true, but too late for it to be more than an empty honor. Had he from the beginning of his contest with Grant possessed authoritative control of all the military resources of the Confederacy, the management of the war would certainly have been more efficient, and the armies of the Gulf States must have been handled with better judgment and success than they were under the orders of the civil authorities. The power of resistance of the Confederacy would probably have been protracted, and it is within the limits of possibility that eventual success in the effort to gain independence might have been attained, though at that late stage of the war this had become almost hopeless.

The collateral operations of the forces under Grant's command were the following: Early's success in the Valley had called a large detachment of the Army of the Potomac to that quarter, whose operations we have already considered. Sheridan in the Valley, Sherman and Thomas in Georgia and Tennessee, and the powerful naval force that was blockading the port of Wilmington, formed a cordon which was gradually crushing out the life of the Confederacy.

As Sherman advanced from Chattanooga, Johnston declined to make a counter-advance into Tennessee, as advised by the authorities at Richmond, but gradually retired before him to Atlanta. He was removed from command at this point, and replaced by Hood, who, after an unsuccessful engagement with

Sherman, adopted the Government plan of an advance into Tennessee, where he was seriously defeated by Thomas. The removal of Johnston at that critical juncture—at the very time when, as he affirms, he was about to attack the enemy—was a serious error that could scarcely fail to be followed by disaster.

Sherman was now relieved from all organized opposition, and advanced leisurely to Savannah, and thence northward through South Carolina, leaving a broad track of desolation behind him.

The blockade of Wilmington was conducted for the purpose of closing the final gateway of intercourse between the Confederacy and the outer world, the port through which munitions of war and supplies for the Confederate armies were chiefly obtained. This port had become of such importance that the greatest efforts were made to maintain it, while the Federal authorities made as strenuous efforts to close it to the daring blockade-runners which had so long evaded the utmost vigilance of the blockading fleet.

Its most important defensive work was Fort Fisher, a powerful and admirably situated earthwork commanding the narrow pass which connects Cape Fear River with the ocean. This was garrisoned by about 1000 men under Colonel Lamb, with, usually, a covering force of several thousand men under General Whiting.

General Grant at an early stage of the siege saw the necessity of taking this fort, and during the summer and fall there was prepared a powerful fleet of transports and gunboats under Admiral Porter. General Butler, who was given the command of the land forces, had conceived the idea of exploding a powder-ship near the fort, with the belief that the shock would so shatter its walls as to render it an easy prey to the fleet.

General Grant had no great faith in this new method of reducing a fortress, but he did not object to its being tried; and the expedition eventually set sail, reaching the neighborhood of Fort Fisher on December 15th.

The powder-ship was exploded several days afterward, just before dawn, but with so little effect upon the fort that the garrison did not know what had actually happened, but supposed that an explosion had occurred among the blockading ships in the offing. The failure was followed by a fierce bombardment from the fleet, but the land force did not deem it expedient, after a careful reconnoissance, to make an assault, and the expedition withdrew on December 23d, leaving Fort Fisher but little the worse for the enterprise.

Yet the easy repulse of so formidable an expedition had an unfortunate result. It created a false sense of security that subsequently led to an easy capture of the fort, and the consequent fall of Wilmington, the sole remaining port of the Confederate States. In fact, Grant was so far from being discouraged by the failure of the powder-ship enterprise that he ordered the immediate preparation of another and more formidable expedition. This reached the locality of Fort Fisher about the middle of January, 1865. The column of assault, under the command of General Terry, was immediately landed, and while the fort was assailed by a terrific naval bombardment the troops advanced on it with such vigor that the garrison was compelled to yield after a short but gallant resistance. The fall of Fort Fisher closed the port of Wilmington and threw the Confederacy entirely upon its own resources.

While the operations above described were in progress the siege of Petersburg languished. The large detachments which had been withdrawn from Grant's army, first to oppose Early, and subsequently for the expedition against Wilmington, had so reduced his force as to prevent very vigorous operations against Richmond and Petersburg.

In the mean time, Lee, finding himself too weak to hazard a serious blow, did all he could to preserve his army from the constant attrition that was wearing it away. The only means that now remained open to him for replenishing his army was through conscription, yet the few unwilling recruits obtained in this way were of doubtful utility, since many either deserted to the enemy, bearing with them much important information, or spread dissatisfaction among the tried troops.

We may briefly recapitulate the principal military events that occurred from the period of the mine explosion till the coming of winter. The first of these was an indecisive attack on the Confederate works north of the James. A force under General Hancock was landed at Deep Bottom on the 13th of August. This movement, which comprised two corps of infantry and General Gregg's cavalry division, was made with great secrecy, and was intended to be a surprise. But in this respect it failed, since General Lee penetrated the design of the enemy, reinforced the lines north of the river, and finally succeeded in driving off the assailants, who experienced a loss of 1500 men.

This assault was immediately followed by a movement from the left flank, designed to seize the Weldon Railroad while the Confederate line at that point was weakened in consequence of the reinforcements sent to oppose Hancock. This advance, which was under the leadership of Warren, proved successful in its main object. The Federals met with considerable loss, but they succeeded in taking and holding the railroad. The possession of this road was important to Lee, though not vitally so, and he made a spirited effort to recapture it. An assault was made on Warren's line which turned his left flank and captured 2500 prisoners, among them General Hays. Yet Warren had established himself too firmly to be driven out, and the Weldon road was lost to the Confederate cause.

Grant at once followed up his advantage by sending a powerful force to Reams Station, to which point the road was torn up. This force was attacked on August 25th by A. P. Hill with such vigor that the Federal line was broken and driven back with severe loss. Hancock, who commanded the Federal force, withdrew during the night, leaving behind him, out of a force of 8000 men, 2400 killed, wounded, and missing, 1700 of these being prisoners. The Confederate loss was also severe.

These engagements were followed by a persistent advance of the Federal left, point after point being occupied and the works extended, though at every point the invading columns found themselves faced by strong Confederate earthworks. During these movements there were some sharp encounters, though no action of importance took place.

While these operations on the right were in progress, General Butler crossed to the north of the James on the night of September 8th, and the next morning made a sudden assault on the Confederate earthwork below Chapin's farm known as Fort Harrison, which he captured, with fifteen pieces of artillery. This was the extent of his successes, though he succeeded in holding the fort despite several efforts to dislodge him.

Late in October a turning movement against Petersburg was attempted, a heavy column being thrown across Hatcher's Run on the 27th, which advanced to the vicinity of Burgess's mill on the Boydton road—an avenue which had become of considerable importance to General Lee since the loss of the Weldon Railroad. A severe struggle took place at this point, Lee taking advantage of the opportunity to launch Hill's corps against the isolated force of the enemy, while nearly at the same time Hampton's cavalry division made a vigorous assault upon the Federal left and rear. Hancock was forced back with a loss of 1500 men, his enterprise having proved a complete failure.

This ended the operations on the right of the lines until the opening of the spring campaign, with the exception of a Federal movement begun on the 5th of February with the same purpose as that of the October advance—namely, to turn the Confederate right and seize the Southside Railroad. It met with the same fortune as the preceding operation, the advancing column being assailed in flank and rear by the Confederates and driven back in disorder. The loss in this affair was about 2000 to the Federals and nearly 1000 to the Confederates, who advanced too far and were met by a heavy fire from a Federal intrenchment. At this point fell the brave general John Pegram, one of the most gallant and lamented of the Confederate officers. His loss was the more regretted as he had just before been married, and therefore that he left by his untimely death a widowed bride.

During the period of the autumn and winter campaign General Lee continued in excellent health and bore his many cares with his usual equanimity. He had aged somewhat in appearance since the beginning of the war, but had rather gained than lost in physical vigor from the severe life he had led. His hair had grown gray, but his face had the ruddy hue of health and his eyes were as clear and bright as ever. His dress was always a plain gray uniform, with cavalry boots reaching nearly to his knees, and a broad-brimmed gray felt hat. He seldom wore a weapon, and his only marks of rank were the stars on his collar. Though always abstemious in diet, he seemed able to bear any amount of fatigue, being capable of remaining in his saddle all day and at his desk half the night.

No commander was ever more careful of his men, and never had care for the comfort of an army given rise to greater devotion. He was constantly calling to the attention of the authorities the wants of his soldiers, and making every effort to provide them with food and clothing. The feeling for him was one of love, not of awe or dread. They could approach him with the assurance that they would be received with kindness and consideration, and that any just complaint would receive proper attention. There was no condescension in his manner, but he was ever simple, kind, and sympathetic, and his men, while having unbounded faith in him as a leader, almost worshipped him as a man. These relations of affection and mutual confidence between the army and its commander had much to do with the undaunted bravery displayed by the men, and bore a due share in the many victories they gained.

Nor was his attention solely given to the cares of camp and field. His warm affection for his wife and children never for a moment ceased, and his letters to them breathe the spirit of the quiet father of a family, not of the great warrior engaged in deadly fray. Seldom has a general busied in the details of a mighty war written home a letter so full of wise fatherly counsel and deep affection as may be found in the one which we append, from General Lee to one of his daughters:

"Camp, Petersburg, 6th November, 1864.

"My Precious Life: This is the first day I have had leisure to answer your letter. I enjoyed it very much at the time of its reception, and have enjoyed it since. But I have often thought of you in the mean time, and have seen you besides. Indeed, I may say you are never out of my thoughts. I hope you think of me often, and if you could know how earnestly I desire your true happiness, how ardently I pray you may be directed to every good and saved from every evil, you would as sincerely strive for its accomplishment. Now in your youth you must be careful to discipline your thoughts, words, and actions. Habituate yourself to useful employment, regular improvement, and to the benefit of all those around you.

"You have had some opportunity of learning the rudiments of your education—not as good as I should have desired, but I am much cheered by the belief that you availed yourself of it—and I think you are now prepared by diligence and study to learn whatever you desire. Do not allow yourself to forget what you have spent so much time and labor in acquiring, but increase it every day by extended application. I hope you will embrace in your studies all useful acquisitions.

"I was so much pleased to hear that while at 'Bremo' you passed much of your time in reading and music: all accomplishments will enable you to give pleasure, and thus exert a wholesome influence. Never neglect the means of making yourself useful in the world.

"I think you will not have to complain of Rob again for neglecting your schoolmates. He has equipped himself with a new uniform from top to toe, and with a new and handsome horse is cultivating a marvellous beard and preparing for conquest.

"I went down on the lines to the right Friday, beyond Rowanty Creek, and pitched my camp within six miles of Fitzhugh's that night. Rob came up and spent the night with me, and Fitzhugh appeared early in the morning. They rode with me till late that day. I visited the battlefield in that quarter, and General Hampton in describing it said there had not been during the war a more spirited charge than Fitzhugh's division made that day up the Boydton plank road, driving cavalry and infantry before him, in which he was stopped by night. I did not know before that his horse had been shot under him.

"Give a great deal of love to your dear mother, and kiss your sisters for me. Tell them they must keep well, not talk too much, and go to bed early.

"Ever your devoted father,

"R. E. LEE."

We may add some anecdotes of his life during this period, ere we proceed with the record of historical events. Colonel Taylor, in his *Four Years with General Lee*, gives some interesting extracts from his note-book, from which we select the following characteristic incident:

"PETERSBURG, VA., November 7, 1864.—On leaving the north side the general left it to me to select an abiding-place for our party here. I, of course, selected a place where I thought he would be comfortable, although I firmly believe he concluded that I was thinking more of myself than of him. I took possession of a vacant house, and had his room prepared with a cheerful fire, and everything made as cozy as possible. It was entirely too pleasant for him, for he is never so uncomfortable as when comfortable. A day or two after our arrival he informed me that he desired to visit the cavalry lines, and thought it best to move our camp down. So we packed up bag and baggage, books and records, and moved to a point about eight miles distant, pitched our tents, and concluded that we were fixed for some days at least. The next morning, however, the general concluded that we had better return. So back I came to Petersburg, and, as I could find no better place—nor a *worse* one that was suitable—I returned to the house we had vacated, where we are now comfortably established. This is the first time we have been quartered in a house."

Another note of Colonel Taylor's, dated November 27th, will serve as a companion-piece to the foregoing:

"While General Lee was at Richmond, I concluded to move headquarters, as a party that proposed to occupy the house as soon as we should vacate had given a gentle hint by sending to inquire when General Lee would leave the house. The only other house available was one two miles from the city, kindly offered by the owner, Mr. Turnbull. So here we are at 'Edge Hill.' I am finely fixed in the parlor with piano, sofas, rocking-chairs, and pictures—capital surroundings for a winter campaign. After locating the general and my associates of the staff, I concluded that I would have to occupy one of the miserable little back rooms, but the gentleman of the house suggested that I should take the parlor. I think that the general was pleased with his room, and on entering mine he remarked, 'Ah, you are finely fixed. Couldn't you find any other room?' —'No,' I replied, 'but *this will do;* I can make myself tolerably comfortable here.' He was struck dumb with amazement at my impudence, and soon vanished.''

From Jones's *Personal Reminiscences of General Lee* we extract the following amusing anecdote:

"While at winter quarters at Petersburg a party of officers were one night busily engaged in discussing at the same time a mathematical problem and the contents of a stone jug which was garnished by two tin cups. In the midst of this General Lee came in to make some inquiry. He got the information he wanted, gave a solution of the problem, and went out, the officers expressing to each other the hope that the general had not noticed the jug and cups. The next day one of the officers in the presence of the others was relating to General Lee a very strange dream he had the night before. The general listened with apparent interest to the narrative, and quietly rejoined: 'That is not at all remarkable. When young gentlemen discuss at midnight mathematical problems the unknown quantities of which are a stone jug and two tin cups, they may expect to have strange dreams.' ''

His opinion of newspaper generals, those talented editors who have no difficulty in wielding armies and winning victories from editorial rooms, was satirically expressed in a conversation with the Hon. B. H. Hill during this period of the war.

"We made a great mistake, Mr. Hill, in the beginning of our struggle," said General Lee in his quietly humorous manner, "and I fear, in spite of all we can do, it will prove to be a fatal mistake."

"What mistake is that, general?"

"Why, sir, in the beginning we appointed all our worst generals to command the armies, and all our best generals to edit the newspapers. As you know, I have planned some campaigns and quite a number of battles. I have given the work all the care and thought I could, and sometimes, when my plans were completed, as far as I could see they seemed to be perfect. But when I have fought them through I have discovered defects, and occasionally wondered I did not see some of the defects in advance. When it was all over I found by reading a newspaper that these best editor-generals saw all the defects plainly from the start. Unfortunately, they did not communicate their knowledge to me until it was too late."

Pausing for a moment, he resumed, with his beautiful, grave expression:

"I have no ambition but to serve the Confederacy and do all I can to win our independence. I am willing to serve in any capacity to which the authorities may assign me. I have done the best I could in the field, and have not succeeded as I should wish. I am willing to yield my place to these best generals, and I will do my best for the cause in editing a newspaper."

On another occasion he remarked in the same connection, "Even as poor a soldier as I am can generally discover mistakes *after it is all over*. But if I could only induce these wise gentlemen, who see them so clearly *beforehand*, to communicate with me in advance, instead of waiting till the evil has come upon us—to let me know that *they knew all the time*—it would be far better for my reputation and, what is of more consequence, far better for the cause."

During this period two events occurred which are worthy of notice. One of these was the appointment of General Lee, on February 6, 1865, as commander-in-chief of all the Confederate armies. Had this appointment been made two years earlier, it is probable that a different state of affairs would have existed; but at that late date it was merely an empty title, since the Confederate armies had become, with the exception of the Army of Northern Virginia, nearly dissipated, and no opportunity remained for the profitable exercise of his extended power.

The other incident was the arrival in Richmond of Mr.
Francis Blair, a distinguished citizen of the United States
and a confidential friend of Mr. Lincoln.   Although this
visit was entirely unofficial in its character, it proved to be
the origin of a peace commission which was soon after accredited to meet Mr. Lincoln and his Secretary of State, Mr.
Seward, at Fortress Monroe.   The interview took place in
February, on board a United States vessel then lying in
Hampton Roads.

The commission consisted of Mr. A. H. Stephens, Vice-President of the Confederacy, and Messrs. Hunter and Campbell,
two of the most distinguished Southern statesmen.   The meeting was without formality, and assumed more the appearance
of a private interview than of a diplomatic conference.

Mr. Blair, on his visit to President Davis, suggested that the
Monroe doctrine, a favorite principle in American politics, might
be made the means of allaying the existing hostility and bringing about a reunion of the States, especially as the usurpation
of the Mexican Government by Maximilian under the patron-
age of France afforded a sufficient pretext for the enforcement
of that doctrine.   Six months earlier this plausible solution of
the American difficulties might have met with favorable consideration; but now it was too late for the introduction of such
a scheme, as the sequel proved.   When this point was touched
upon by Mr. Stephens, it was coldly received by Mr. Lincoln,
whose ultimatum was unconditional surrender.   As the powers
of the Confederate commission did not involve such an alternative, the conference came to an end.

When the Confederate commissioners returned to Richmond
and reported the ill-success of their mission, a sense of disappointment was felt throughout the land.   This was succeeded by
an indignant determination to carry on the contest to the bitter
end.   The event called forth from President Davis an address
of the greatest eloquence and inspired by the highest spirit of
patriotism.   This notable oration rekindled the expiring enthusiasm of the Confederates and nerved their arms to renewed
efforts in the maintenance of a now almost desperate cause.
So great was the feeling raised by his inspiring words that

if General Lee could at that time have taken the field and drawn Grant high up the country among the hills and moun-tain-spurs, whose friendly aid he knew so well how to apply, the Confederate power might have longer remained unbroken and honorable terms of peace have been obtained.

General Lee had actually taken steps to adopt a plan that offered the only hope of success, but this was overruled. The soundest advice in the land was disregarded, and it was decided that the Confederacy should live or die at Richmond. Lee knew well that there could be but one end to a continuance of the siege, and this opinion he freely expressed to General Long in a conversation held with him the day before the surrender. It had been his wish to withdraw his forces and take up a line behind the Staunton River. In this position he could have greatly harassed and hampered Grant, who would have found it difficult to perform any effective offensive operations with a line of communications one hundred and fifty miles long to defend. Thus situated, he might have prolonged the war almost indefinitely. The mountains in his rear would have given him an opportunity to retreat into Tennessee if neces-sary, or to move south by way of Danville, with little or no danger of interception. At the same time, he could readily have drawn to his aid all the detachments from West Virginia, North and South Carolina, and the other States, which com-bined would have given him a very respectable army. When his actual retreat took place his intention was that here indi-cated, but at that time his depletion in numbers and the advan-tageous position of his opponents so greatly increased the difficulties of the movement as to render it almost hopeless.

A continued defence of Richmond in accordance with the plan of the civil authorities offered but one chance of success. If Lee could have been rapidly reinforced by 25,000 men, he would have been able to assume the offensive, and might have pushed Grant into the swamps of the Chickahominy, as he had served McClellan on a previous occasion. Yet it was impos-sible to obtain such a reinforcement. With a force of barely 35,000 men he had from June until March maintained with matchless skill a line of thirty-five miles in extent against a force of more than four times that number. But as the spring opened it became daily more apparent that human power and endurance could do no more, and that a forced evacuation of the beleaguered cities was near at hand.

In anticipation of that event General Lee caused the removal of all his surplus material to Amelia Court-house. This point was suitable as a rallying-place for the army on the occurrence of an event which to all observing minds appeared inevitable. Notwithstanding the hopelessness of the contest, nothing was omitted that the genius of the general could devise or the energy and devotion of the troops accomplish.

While Lee was quietly making these preparations in anticipation of an event which was evidently near at hand, and which, if he had been guided by his own counsel, he would have hastened instead of delaying until forcibly driven to it, Grant had begun the concentration of his forces in order to complete his interior cordon or line of investment.

His circle of external investment was now complete, and every line of communication with the more distant portions of the Confederacy was effectually cut off. By the last of March, Sheridan had joined him with his forces from the Valley, while Sherman was moving slowly through South Carolina toward Virginia and Thomas was preparing to advance on the East Tennessee and the Virginia and Tennessee railroads. The next step in the progress of the siege was the seizure of the communications between Petersburg and the South.

While his adversary was thus active, Lee was not idle. He had formed a plan to surprise the enemy's centre by a night-attack, which if successful would have given him possession of a commanding position in the enemy's rear and control of the military railroad to City Point—a very important part of Grant's communications. Lee's full purpose in this movement has been variously surmised by historians. If it was to favor his retreat, as some conclude, it was well devised, since success would have forced Grant to withdraw his left to protect his base of supplies, and thus have left Lee an open road of withdrawal. If it was designed to improve his own position and check the Federal operations against his right, it was equally well devised, since it might have led to the capture or destruction of Grant's left wing. It was one of those military movements whose purpose is left in abeyance, the future policy of the commander being dependent upon his measure of success and the change in the situation thereby occasioned. Whatever the design in General Lee's mind, the ill-success of the effort rendered it abortive.

The portion of the enemy's line selected for the point of attack lay opposite General Gordon's front, and within about two hundred yards of it, the opposing works being here very close together. Gordon was assigned to the command of the attacking column, whose movement was directed against Fort Steadman, a strong earthwork near the south bank of the Appomattox. The ground in front of the fort was obstructed by abatis, but it was hoped these difficulties could be overcome by a movement under cover of the darkness and the fort reached unobserved.

The column of attack was drawn up before dawn on the morning of March 25th. It consisted of some 3000 or 4000 men, but a considerable force was held in reserve to follow up the attack if successful.

In the early dawn the Confederate column moved noiselessly out into the intervening space and passed swiftly forward, unnoticed by the Federals, whose guards displayed little vigilance. A few minutes sufficed to reach the front of the opposing works, and the surprised garrison of Fort Steadman arose to find their stronghold in the possession of their foes.

All this had been the work of very few minutes, at the end of which time all of the garrison who were not prisoners were flying in a panic from the fort. The guns of the redoubt were at once turned on the neighboring works, and several batteries to the right and left were cleared of their defenders and occupied by Gordon's brave stormers.

Now was the time for the supporting column to advance. Had it done so rapidly, the advantage could have been sustained, and by a seizure of the hill in the rear of Fort Steadman the Federal army would have been cut in two at its centre. For some reason which has never been made very clear this advance was not made.   One of those unfortunate failures in combination which have caused the loss of so many battles here occurred, and the well-devised plan of the Confederate commander came to naught through dereliction of duty, misconception of orders, or whatever may have been the cause of the fatal delay.

Gordon with his small force was left to bear the whole brunt of the Federal assault which quickly fell upon him.   Fort Hascall, to the left of Fort Steadman, opened upon it a terrific fire, under cover of which a heavy column of infantry advanced, and something like the scene which followed the mine explosion ensued.   A considerable portion of the assailing column was unable to withdraw and remained prisoners in the hands of the Federals, while many lay dead and wounded about the recaptured works.   Thus through misconception or mismanagement this promising assault failed, and an early retreat became the only alternative remaining to General Lee.

This unsuccessful effort was quickly followed by a vigorous advance on the part of Grant, who concentrated his principal force south and west of Petersburg with the view of assailing the Confederate right.   Early on the morning of March 29th the corps of Warren and Humphreys broke camp and moved toward Lee's intrenchments on the extreme right, while Sheridan, with the cavalry, made a wider sweep and occupied Dinwiddie Court-house, six miles south-west of the point reached by the infantry.

Yet, swiftly and secretly as this movement was made, it did not escape Lee's vigilant eye.   He quickly divined where the blow was to fall, and, leaving the works north of the James under Longstreet and those at Petersburg under Gordon but weakly garrisoned, he removed the remainder of his army, consisting of about 15,000 infantry and 2000 cavalry, into the works along the White Oak road.

Here, on the morning of the 31st, Lee made the flank attack which he had so often attempted with success against the Federal columns.   Not waiting for the assault, he boldly took the initiative, and fell upon their exposed flank while they were entangled in the intricacies of a swampy forest.   So sudden and heavy was the blow that the divisions encountered hastily gave way. But upon meeting the main body of the Federal troops he found it so thickly massed and well posted as to render an assault hopeless. He therefore fell back to his works.

On the same day Sheridan advanced toward Five Forks. Before reaching that point, however, he was encountered by the Confederate cavalry under the chief command of General Fitz Lee, supported by the infantry under Pickett. A severe combat ensued, in which Sheridan was driven back to Dinwiddie Court-house with considerable loss.

On the 1st of April, Sheridan was reinforced by two corps of infantry, and with this powerful aid he renewed his attack upon Five Forks, which place was carried late in the evening and the Confederates driven back.

General Lee, perceiving that his forces were too weak to combat successfully with the enemy, ordered Longstreet on the afternoon of the 1st to bring his corps with all speed from before Richmond to Petersburg, with the object of supporting his right wing.

Early on the morning of the 2d the Federals renewed the attack, breaking the lines of the Confederates and forcing them from their position. The Federals then took possession of the Southside Railroad with little opposition, while the Confederates fell back toward Petersburg, followed by the victorious enemy. The pursuit was continued until it was arrested by the guns from two redoubts, Forts Alexander and Gregg, which with great gallantry held the enemy in check until Longstreet came up and interposed his corps, effectually arresting the further advance of the Federal columns.

In the conflict here described fell many gallant warriors, chief among them Lieutenant-general A. P. Hill, who was slain while endeavoring to reach Heth's division, which had been ordered to support Pickett on the right. No man had been more distinguished throughout the war for chivalric bearing than this brave soldier. On every field where appeared the Army of Northern Virginia he had borne a conspicuous part, and now in the last battle of that noble army he found a hero's grave.

With the advantage here gained by the Federal army Lee's position at Petersburg became untenable, and nothing remained but a retreat, either to the fortifications about Richmond or to the mountain-region to the west.   The description of the course adopted by General Lee and the subsequent events of the war will form the subject of our next chapter.

CHAPTER XXI.

FROM PETERSBURG TO APPOMATTOX.

The Last Day at Petersburg.—The Evacuation.—Richmond on Fire.—The Army in Retreat.—The Federals in Richmond.—Grant in Pursuit.—At Amelia Court-house. —The Food-train Missing.—Perilous State of the Army.—Lee's Demeanor.—The Federals at Hand.—Skirmishing.—Capture of Ewell's Corps.—Rations at Farmville.—Engagements with the Pursuers.—Reminiscence of Colonel Jones.—General Wise in his War-paint.—A Delegation to Lee from the Officers.—General Pendleton Describes the Interview.—The Retreat Continued.—Correspondence between Lee and Grant.—Loss of the Stores at Appomattox.—Preparation for Battle.—The Advance on the 9th.—The Final Assault.—Colonel Venable's Relation.—The Flag of Truce.—Lee's "Apple Tree."—Meeting of Lee and Grant.— Their Conversation.—Terms of Surrender.—Lee Greeted by his Army.—Extracts from Letter to Davis.—The Number of Effective Men.—The Army Disbanded.— Lee and Meade.—General Hunter Interviewed.—Lee Returns to Richmond.—At Home.

THE success of the Federal army in breaking the lines of Petersburg had rendered the retreat of the Confederate force imperative. An effort to hold Richmond with every line of communication with the South broken or in imminent danger would have been madness. But by abandoning his works and concentrating his army, which still amounted to about 30,000 men, General Lee might retire to some natural stronghold in the interior, where the defensible features of the country would enable him to oppose Grant's formidable host until he could rally strength to strike an effective blow.

This course was at once decided upon, and early on the morning of the 2d of April, Lee sent a despatch to the Government authorities at Richmond informing them of the disastrous situation of affairs and of the necessity of his evacuating Petersburg that night. Orders were also sent to the forces north of the James to move at once and join him, while all the preparations necessary for the evacuation of Richmond, both as the seat of Government and as a military post, were expeditiously made.

There was, indeed, no time to be lost. The Federal forces were at every point pressing forward upon the Petersburg lines. Fort Gregg had fallen, and the city was strongly threatened. A battery on a hill near General Lee's headquarters was attacked by an infantry force, and had to be withdrawn to save it from capture. Lee mounted his horse and rode back, surrounded by his staff, toward his inner line of defence. His composure was remarkable, considering the situation, and it was in his habitually quiet tone that he said to a member of his staff, "This is a bad business, colonel."

To another officer he remarked, "Well, colonel, it has happened as I told them at Richmond it would : the line has been stretched until it has broken."

As he continued to ride slowly back toward Petersburg the group drew the fire of the Federal artillery, and shells began to burst around them, an officer's horse being killed and other damage done. With his usual undisturbed demeanor under fire, he continued to ride slowly onward until he had entered the line of earthworks immediately surrounding the city, where he was greeted with shouts of welcome by the ragged but unflinching defenders. Orders were given to hold this line, if possible, until night. Fortunately, General Grant did not press his attack, and time was given the Confederates to complete their preparations for withdrawal.

Along the north bank of the Appomattox moved the long lines of artillery and dark columns of infantry through the gloom of the night, over the roads leading to Amelia Courthouse. By midnight the evacuation was completed, and a death-like silence reigned in the breastworks which for nine months had been "clothed in thunder," and whose deadly blows had kept at bay a foe of threefold strength.

As the troops moved noiselessly onward in the darkness that just precedes the dawn a bright light like a broad flash of lightning illumined the heavens for an instant; then followed a tremendous explosion. "The magazine at Fort Drewry is blown up," ran in whispers through the ranks, and again silence reigned. Once more the sky was overspread by a lurid light, but not so fleeting as before. It was now the conflagration of Richmond that lighted the night-march of the soldiers, and many a stout heart was wrung with anguish at the fate of the city and its defenceless inhabitants. The burning of public property of little value had given rise to a destructive fire that laid in ashes nearly one-third of the devoted city.

The columns from Petersburg and its vicinity reached Chesterfield Court-house soon after daylight. Here a brief halt was ordered for the rest and refreshment of the troops, after which the retreat was resumed with renewed strength. A sense of relief seemed to pervade the ranks at their release from the lines where they had watched and worked for more than nine weary months. Once more in the open field, they were invigorated with hope, and felt better able to cope with their powerful adversary.

The April woods were budding round them, the odors of spring were in the air, the green fields and the broad prospect of woods and hills formed an inspiriting contrast to the close earthworks behind which they had so long lain, and as they marched along the unobstructed roads memories of the many victories to which they had formerly been led arose to nerve their arms and make them feel that while they had the same noble chieftain at their head they were still the equal of the foe. Thoughts like these lightened the weary march and gave new spirit to the ragged and hungry but undaunted men.

The retreat of Lee's army did not long remain unknown to the Federals. The explosion of the magazine at Fort Drewry and the conflagration of Richmond apprised them of the fact, and they lost no time in taking possession of the abandoned works and entering the defenceless cities.

On the morning of the 3d of April the mayor of Richmond surrendered the city to the Federal commander in its vicinity, and General Weitzel took immediate possession. He at once proceeded to enforce order and took measures to arrest the conflagration, while with great humanity he endeavored to relieve the distressed citizens. After four years of courageous sacrifice and patriotic devotion the city of Richmond was compelled to yield to the decree of fate and bow her proud crest to the victor. But she felt no shame or disgrace, for her defence had been bold and chivalrous, and in the hour of her adversity her majestic fortitude drew from her conquerors respect and admiration.

As soon as Grant became aware of Lee's line of retreat he pushed forward his whole available force, numbering 70,000 or 80,000 men, in order to intercept him on the line of the Richmond and Danville Railroad. Sheridan's cavalry formed the van of the pursuing column, and was closely followed by the artillery and infantry. Lee pressed on as rapidly as possible to Amelia Court-house, where he had ordered supplies to be deposited for the use of his troops on their arrival. This forethought was highly necessary in consequence of the scanty supply of rations provided at the commencement of the retreat.

The hope of finding a supply of food at this point, which had done much to buoy up the spirits of the men, was destined to be cruelly dispelled. Through an unfortunate error or misapprehension of orders the provision-train had been taken on to Richmond without unloading its stores at Amelia Court-house, and its much-needed food disappeared during the excitement and confusion of the capital city. As a result, on reaching that point not a single ration was found to be provided for the hungry troops.

It was a terrible blow alike to the men and to their general. A reaction from hope to despair came upon the brave soldiers who had so far borne up under the most depressing difficulties, while on General Lee's face came a deeper shadow than it had yet worn. He saw his well-devised plan imperilled by a circumstance beyond his control. The necessity of speed if he would achieve the aim which he had in his mind was opposed by the absolute need of halting and collecting food for his impoverished troops. Grant was pursuing him with all haste. The only chance remaining to the Army of Northern Virginia was to reach the hill-country without delay. Yet here it was detained by the error of a railroad official, while the precious minutes and hours moved remorselessly by.

By the morning of the 5th the whole army had reached the place of general rendezvous. Bitter was its disappointment to learn that no food was to be had save such scanty quantities as might be collected by the foraging-parties that had immediately been sent out, and that a distance of fifty miles lay between it and adequate supplies. Yet no murmur came from the lips of the men to the ear of their commander, and on the evening of that unfortunate day they resumed their weary march in silence and composure. Some small amount of food had been brought in by the foragers, greatly inadequate for the wants of the soldiers, yet aiding them to somewhat alleviate the pangs of hunger. A handful of corn was now a feast to the weary veterans as they trudged onward through the April night.

General Lee had never appeared more grandly heroic than on this occasion. All eyes were raised to him for a deliverance which no human power seemed able to give. He alone was expected to provide food for the starving army and rescue it from the attacks of a powerful and eager enemy. Under the accumulation of difficulties his courage seemed to expand, and wherever he appeared his presence inspired the weak and weary with renewed energy to continue the toilsome march.

During these trying scenes his countenance wore its habitual calm, grave expression. Those who watched his face to catch a glimpse of what was passing in his mind could gather thence no trace of his inner sentiments. Only once during the retreat was he perceived to lose the most complete self-control. On inquiring at Farmville why a certain bridge had not been burned, he spoke of the blunder with a warmth and impatience which served to show how great a repression he ordinarily exercised over his feelings.

The progress of the retreat during the night was slow and tedious, the route for the most part lying through farms and over farm-lands, whose condition frequently demanded the aid of the pioneers to construct and repair bridges and causeways for the artillery and wagons, the teams of which by this time had become weak and jaded. The country roads were miry from the spring rains, the streams were swollen, and the numerous wagons which were necessary to transport the munitions of war from Richmond to a new line of defence served to retard the retreat and permit the Federals to rapidly gain upon the slowly-marching columns.

Sheridan's cavalry was already upon the flank of the Confederate army, and the infantry was following with all speed. On the morning of the 6th a wagon-train fell into the hands of Sheridan's troopers, but this was recaptured by the Confederates. During the forenoon of that day the pursuing columns thickened and frequent skirmishes delayed the march. These delays enabled the Federals to accumulate in such force that it became necessary for Lee to halt his advance in order to arrest their attack till his column could close up, and the trains and such artillery as was not needed for action could reach a point of safety.

This object was accomplished early in the afternoon. Ewell's, the rearmost corps in the army, closed upon those in front at a position on Sailor's Creek, a small tributary of the Appomattox River. While the troops were moving to their destination, and the trains had passed, General Gordon, who commanded the rear-guard, observing a considerable Federal force moving around the Confederate rear, apparently with the intention of turning it, sent notice of this movement to the troops in front, and then proceeded by a near route to a suitable position on the line of retreat.

Ewell, unfortunately, either failed to receive Gordon's message or his troops were so worn out with hunger and fatigue as to be dilatory in complying with orders. As a consequence his corps was surrounded by the pursuing columns and captured with but little opposition. About the same time the divisions of Anderson, Pickett, and Bushrod Johnson were almost broken up, about 10,000 men in all being captured. The remainder of the army continued its retreat during the night of the 6th, and reached Farmville early on the morning of the 7th, where the troops obtained two days' rations, the first regular supplies they had received during the retreat. At Farmville a short halt was made to allow the men to rest and cook their provisions.

The effective portion of the Army of Northern Virginia did not now exceed 10,000 men. This great reduction had been caused by the disaster of the previous day at Sailor's Creek, by desertions on the retreat, and by an exhaustion which obliged many to leave the ranks. Those who still remained by their colors were veterans whose courage never failed, and who were yet ready to face any odds.

The heads of the Federal columns beginning to appear about eleven o'clock, the Confederates resumed their retreat. The teams of the wagons and artillery were weak, being travel-worn and suffering from lack of forage. Their progress, therefore, was necessarily slow, and as the troops were obliged to move in conformity with the artillery and trains, the Federal cavalry closed upon the retreating army. In the afternoon it became necessary to make dispositions to retard the rapid advance of the enemy. Mahone's division, with a few batteries, was thrown out for that purpose, and a spirited conflict ensued in which the Federals were checked. Other attempts were made during the afternoon to retard or arrest the Confederate columns, which in every instance were repulsed. In one of these encounters General Fitz Lee engaged General Gregg, captured the general, and repulsed his division of cavalry. This occurrence was a source of great pleasure to General Lee, who remarked to his son, General W. H. F. Lee, "Keep your command together and in good spirits, general: don't let it think of surrender. I will get you out of this."

As to General Lee's personal bearing during the events of this retreat, an interesting incident has been furnished by Colonel Thomas G. Jones of Montgomery, Ala., then on General Gordon's staff. He remarks:

"It was noticed that General Lee exposed himself unsparingly to fire. He sat for some time on his iron-gray close beside a section of Chamberlayne's battery, which on the brow of the hill was shelling the advancing enemy, and gazed intently through his glass at the movements of the approaching foe. Receiving a report from a staff officer, General Lee told him he had ridden up on the wrong side of the hill and unnecessarily exposed himself. When the officer remarked that he was ashamed to try to shelter himself when his commander was so exposed, General Lee remarked rather sharply,

'It is my duty to be here. I must see. Go back the way I told you, sir.'

"Forgetful of his own safety at such a time, he cared more for the life of the lowest of his command than for his own."

Colonel Jones's anecdote may be supplemented with one of an amusing character which occurred in the presence of the writer. The event in question, of which General Wise was the hero, took place on the morning preceding the surrender. The general had made his morning ablutions, in the absence of the requisites of a civilized toilet, in a mud-hole in the road, the water of which was deeply tinged with the prevailing red clay of that country. Towels were as scarce as basins, and in the lack of any better method he permitted the water to dry upon his face. The consequence was that his countenance displayed a very decided coating of red clay.

Unaware of the appearance which he presented, mirrors having been left behind with the other impedimenta of civilization, Wise, with his blanket thrown around him and presenting a not inapt resemblance to an Indian chief, walked up to where General Lee was standing in the midst of a group of officers. Despite the gravity of the situation, Lee's face broke into a humorous smile on perceiving the ludicrous appearance of the unconscious officer.

"Good-morning, General Wise," he remarked in a tone of merry pleasantry. "I perceive that you, at any rate, have not given up the contest, as you are in your war-paint this morning."

The laugh that followed at the expense of General Wise was heartily joined in by himself when he discovered its cause and learned what an amusing spectacle he presented in his paint and blanket.

An event occurred on the 7th which must not be omitted from this narrative. Perceiving the difficulties that surrounded the army, and believing its extrication hopeless, a number of the principal officers, from a feeling of affection and sympathy for the commander-in-chief, and with a wish to lighten his responsibility and soften the pain of defeat, volunteered to inform him that in their opinion the struggle had reached a point where further resistance was hopeless, and that the contest should be terminated and negotiations opened for a surrender of the army. The delivery of this opinion was confided to General Pendleton, who by his character and devotion to General Lee was well qualified for such an office. The names of Longstreet and some others who did not coincide in opinion with their associates did not appear in the list presented by Pendleton. The interview that succeeded is thus described by General Pendleton :

"General Lee was lying on the ground. No others heard the conversation between him and myself. He received my communication with the reply, 'Oh no, I trust it has not come to that;' and added, 'General, we have yet too many bold men to think of laying down our arms. The enemy do not fight with spirit, while our boys still do. Besides, if I were to say a word to the Federal commander he would regard it as such a confession of weakness as to make it the condition of demanding unconditional surrender—a proposal to which I will never listen. . . . . I have never believed we could, against the gigantic combination for our subjugation, make good in the long run our independence unless foreign powers should, directly or indirectly, assist us. . . . . But such considerations really made with me no difference. We had, I was satisfied, sacred principles to maintain and rights to defend, for which we were in duty bound to do our best, even if we perished in the endeavor.'

"Such were, as nearly as I can recall them, the exact words of General Lee on that most critical occasion. You see in them the soul of the man. What his conscience dictated and his judgment decided, there his heart was."

Desperate as the situation had become, and irretrievable as it seemed hourly growing, General Lee could not forego the hope of breaking through the net that was rapidly enclosing him and of forming a junction with Johnston. In the event of success in this he felt confident of being able to manœuvre with Grant at least until favorable terms of peace could be obtained.

A crisis was now at hand. Should Lee obtain the necessary

supplies at Appomattox Court-house, he would push on to the Staunton River and maintain himself behind that stream until a junction could be made with Johnston. If, however, supplies should fail him, the surrender and dissolution of the army were inevitable. On the 8th the retreat, being uninterrupted, progressed more expeditiously than on the previous day. Yet, though the Federals did not press the Confederate flank and rear as on the day before, a heavy column of cavalry advanced upon Appomattox Station, where the supplies for the Confederate army had been deposited.

On the preceding day a correspondence had begun between the two commanding generals, opening in the following note sent by General Grant to General Lee:

> "HEADQUARTERS ARMIES OF THE U. S.,
> "5 P. M., April 7, 1865.

"GENERAL R. E. LEE, COMMANDING C. S. A.,

"GENERAL: The results of the last week must convince you of the hopelessness of further resistance on the part of the Army of Northern Virginia in this struggle. I feel that it is so, and regard it as my duty to shift from myself the responsibility of any further effusion of blood, by asking of you the surrender of that portion of the Confederate Southern army known as the Army of Northern Virginia.

> "Very respectfully,
> "Your obedient servant,
> "U. S. GRANT,
> "*Lieutenant-general commanding Armies of the U. S.*"

To which General Lee replied:

> "APRIL 7, 1865.

"GENERAL: I have received your note of this day. Though not entertaining the opinion you express on the hopelessness of further resistance on the part of the Army of Northern Virginia, I reciprocate your desire to avoid useless effusion of blood, and therefore, before considering your proposition, ask the terms you will offer on condition of its surrender.

> "R. E. LEE,
> "*General.*

"LIEUTENANT-GENERAL U. S. GRANT, *commanding the Armies of the United States.*"

On the succeeding day General Grant returned the following reply :

"APRIL 8, 1865.

"To GENERAL R. E. LEE, COMMANDING C. S. A.,

"GENERAL: Your note of the last evening, in reply to
mine of the same date, asking the condition on which I will
accept the surrender of the Army of Northern Virginia, is
just received.   In reply I would say that peace being my great
desire, there is but one condition I would insist upon—namely,
that the men and officers surrendered shall be disqualified for
taking up arms again against the Government of the United
States until properly exchanged.   I will meet you, or will
designate officers to meet any officers you might name for the
same purpose, at any point agreeable to you, for the purpose
of arranging definitely the terms upon which the surrender
of the Army of Northern Virginia will be received.

"U. S. GRANT,
"*Lieutenant-general.*"

General Lee immediately responded :

"APRIL 8, 1865.

"GENERAL : I received at a late hour your note of to-day.
In mine of yesterday I did not intend to propose the surrender
of the Army of Northern Virginia, but to ask the terms of
your proposition.   To be frank, I do not think the emergency
has arisen to call for the surrender of this army, but as the
restoration of peace should be the sole object of all, I desired
to know whether your proposals would lead to that end.   I
cannot therefore meet you with a view to surrender the Army
of Northern Virginia, but as far as your proposal may affect
the Confederate States forces under my command and tend
to the restoration of peace, I should be pleased to meet you
at ten A. M. to-morrow on the old stage-road to Richmond,
between the picket-lines of the two armies.

"R. E. LEE,
General.

"LIEUTENANT-GENERAL GRANT."

When Lee in the afternoon reached the neighborhood of
Appomattox Court-house, he was met by the intelligence of

the capture of the stores placed for his army at the station two miles beyond. Notwithstanding this overwhelming news, he determined to make one more effort to force himself through the Federal toils that encompassed him. Therefore he made preparations for battle, but under circumstances more desperate than had hitherto befallen the Army of Northern Virginia. The remnant of that noble army, now reduced to 10,000 effective men, was marshalled to cut its way through a host 75,000 strong; but, notwithstanding the stupendous odds, there was not in that little band a heart that quailed or a hand that trembled; there was not one of them who would not willingly have laid down his life in the cause they had so long maintained, and for the noble chief who had so often led them to victory.

On the evening of that day the last council of the leaders of the Army of Northern Virginia was held around a bivouac-fire in the woods, there being present Generals Lee, Longstreet, Gordon, and Fitz Lee. This conference ended in a determination to make a renewed effort on the following morning to break through the impediments in front, of which there was still a possibility if only cavalry should be found and no heavy force of infantry had reached that point.

At three o'clock on the morning of the 9th of April the Confederates moved silently forward. The advance under Gordon, reaching the heights a little beyond the court-house at dawn, found that the route was obstructed by a large force of Federal cavalry. Gordon then deployed the Second corps, now less than 2000 strong and supported by thirty pieces of artillery under General Long, with Fitz Lee's cavalry on the flank.

This artillery consisted of parts of the commands of Colonel Carter, Lieutenant-colonels Poague and Duke Johnson, and Major Stark, and the guns were served with the usual skill and gallantry. A well-directed fire from the artillery and an attack from the cavalry quickly dislodged the force in front. Gordon then advanced, but was arrested by a greatly superior force of the enemy's infantry, whereupon he informed General Lee that a powerful reinforcement was necessary to enable him to continue his advance.

Lee being unable to grant that request, but one course remained. A flag of truce was sent to General Grant requesting a suspension of hostilities for the arrangement of preliminaries of surrender. Then an order to cease firing passed along the lines. This order, on being received by General Long, was sent by him, through Major Southall and other members of his staff, to the different batteries to direct them to discontinue firing. General Long then proceeded to the court-house.

On reaching that point he discovered that the order had not been carried to a battery that occupied the hill immediately above the village, which continued to fire rapidly at an advancing line of Federal infantry. He at once rode in person to the battery and gave the order to the captain to cease firing and to withdraw his battery to a point east of the town, where the artillery was ordered to be parked. These were the last shots fired by the Army of Northern Virginia.

Colonel C. S. Venable of General Lee's staff graphically tells what took place at headquarters on that eventful morning. His story is of great interest, as showing how reluctantly yet how nobly the heroic commander submitted to the inevitable after having till the last minute, like a lion at bay, faced the overwhelming force of his opponent:

"At three o'clock on the morning of that fatal day General Lee rode forward, still hoping that we might break through the countless hordes of the enemy who hemmed us in. Halting a short distance in rear of our van-guard, he sent me on to General Gordon to ask him if he could break through the enemy. I found General Gordon and General Fitz Lee on their front line in the dim light of the morning arranging an attack. Gordon's reply to the message (I give the expressive phrase of the gallant Georgian) was this: 'Tell General Lee I have fought my corps to a frazzle, and I fear I can do nothing unless I am heavily supported by Longstreet's corps.'

"When I bore this message back to General Lee he said, 'Then there is nothing left me but to go and see General Grant,* and I would rather die a thousand deaths.'

---

* Field's and Mahone's divisions of Longstreet's corps, staunch in the midst of all our disasters, were holding Meade back in our rear, and could not be spared for the attack.

" Convulsed with passionate grief, many were the wild words which we spoke as we stood around him. Said one, 'Oh, general, what will history say of the surrender of the army in the field ?'

" He replied, 'Yes, I know they will say hard things of us: they will not understand how we were overwhelmed by numbers. But that is not the question, colonel: the question is, Is it right to surrender this army? If it is right, then *I* will take *all* the responsibility.' "

The artillery had been withdrawn from the heights, as above stated, and parked in the small valley east of the village, while the infantry, who were formed on the left, stacked arms and silently waited the result of the interview between the opposing commanders.

The flag of truce was sent out from General Gordon's lines. Grant had not yet come up, and while waiting for his arrival General Lee seated himself upon some rails which Colonel Talcott of the Engineers had fixed at the foot of an apple tree for his convenience. This tree was half a mile distant from the point where the meeting of Lee and Grant took place, yet widespread currency has been given to the story that the surrender took place under its shade, and " apple-tree " jewelry has been profusely distributed from the orchard in which it grew.

About 11 o'clock General Lee, accompanied only by Colonel Marshall of his staff, proceeded to the village to meet General Grant, who had now arrived. The meeting between the two renowned generals took place at the house of a Mr. McLean at Appomattox Court-house, to which mansion, after exchanging courteous salutations, they repaired to settle the terms on which the surrender of the Army of Northern Virginia should be concluded.

A conversation here took place which General Grant, as he himself tells us, led to various subjects divergent from the immediate purpose of the meeting, talking of old army matters and comparing recollections with General Lee. As he says, the conversation grew so pleasant that he almost forgot the object of the meeting.

General Lee was obliged more than once to remind him of

this object, and it was some time before the terms of the surrender were written out. The written instrument of surrender covered the following points: Duplicate rolls of all the officers and men were to be made, and the officers to sign paroles for themselves and their men, all agreeing not to bear arms against the United States unless regularly exchanged. The arms, artillery, and public property were to be turned over to an officer appointed to receive them, the officers retaining their side-arms and private horses and baggage. In addition to this, General Grant permitted every man of the Confederate army who claimed to own a horse or mule to retain it for farming purposes, General Lee remarking that this would have a happy effect. As for the surrender by General Lee of his sword, a report of which has been widely circulated, General Grant disposes of it in the following words: "The much-talked of surrendering of Lee's sword and my handing it back, this and much more that has been said about it is the purest romance."

After completion of these measures General Lee remarked that his men were badly in need of food, that they had been living for several days on parched corn exclusively, and requested rations and forage for 25,000 men. These rations were granted out of the car-loads of Confederate provisions which had been stopped by the Federal cavalry. As for forage, Grant remarked that he was himself depending upon the country for that. The negotiations completed, General Lee left the house, mounted his horse, and rode back to headquarters.

It is impossible to describe the anguish of the troops when it was known that the surrender of the army was inevitable. Of all their trials, this was the greatest and hardest to endure. There was no consciousness of shame; each heart could boast with honest pride that its duty had been done to the end, and that still unsullied remained its honor. When, after his interview with Grant, General Lee again appeared, a shout of welcome instinctively ran through the army. But instantly recollecting the sad occasion that brought him before them, their shouts sank into silence, every hat was raised, and the bronzed faces of the thousands of grim warriors were bathed with tears.

As he rode slowly along the lines hundreds of his devoted veterans pressed around the noble chief, trying to take his hand, touch his person, or even lay a hand upon his horse, thus exhibiting for him their great affection. The general then, with head bare and tears flowing freely down his manly cheeks, bade adieu to the army. In a few words he told the brave men who had been so true in arms to return to their homes and become worthy citizens.

Thus closed the career of the noble Army of Northern Virginia.

At this point some extracts from General Lee's final report to President Davis, announcing the surrender, may be of interest. The report will be found in full in the Appendix:

"HIS EXCELLENCY JEFFERSON DAVIS,

"MR. PRESIDENT: It is with pain that I announce to Your Excellency the surrender of the Army of Northern Virginia. . . . . Upon arriving at Amelia Court-house on the morning of the 4th with the advance of the army, ... and not finding the supplies ordered to be placed there, nearly twenty-four hours were lost in endeavoring to collect in the country subsistence for men and horses. This delay was fatal and could not be retrieved. . . . . On the morning of the 9th . . . . there were 7892 organized infantry with arms, with an average of seventy-five rounds of ammunition per man. . . . . I have no accurate report of the cavalry, but believe it did not exceed 2100 effective men. The enemy was more than five times our numbers. If we could have forced our way one day longer, it would have been at a great sacrifice of life, and at its end I do not see how a surrender could have been avoided. The supplies ordered to Pamplin's Station from Lynchburg could not reach us, and the men, deprived of food and sleep for many days, were worn-out and exhausted.

"With great respect, your obedient servant,
"R. E. LEE,
"*General.*"

It will be noticed that a large seeming discrepancy exists

between the 10,000 men here mentioned as effective, and the 28,231 men and officers paroled. It will also be observed that General Lee asked for rations for 25,000 men. This difference is easily explainable. Of effective infantry, with arms and in fighting condition, there were less than 8000, and about 2000 cavalry. The remainder of the paroled men were composed of unarmed stragglers who had come up since the halt of the army, and of extra-duty and detailed men of every description, the sum of whom very greatly swelled the aggregate present, while adding nothing to the fighting capacity of the army.

During the proceedings above described not a sound of exultation arose from the Army of the Potomac, and when it was seen how small was the number that had so long opposed their proud array, the honest and brave men of the Union army accorded the meed of honor where honor was due.

Three days after the surrender the Army of Northern Virginia had dispersed in every direction, and three weeks later the veterans of a hundred battles had changed the musket and the sword for the implements of husbandry. It is worthy of remark that never before was there an army disbanded with less disorder. Thousands of soldiers were set adrift on the world without a penny in their pockets to enable them to reach their homes. Yet none of the scenes of riot that often follow the disbanding of armies marked their course.

The surrender of the Army of Northern Virginia was the closing scene in the drama of war and bloodshed whose successive acts reached from Manassas to the heights of Appomattox Court-house. The terrible struggle between Grant and Lee had occupied nearly a year, from their meeting in deadly conflict at the Wilderness on the 4th of May, 1864, to the last scene on the 9th of April, 1865. During that period Lee had most thoroughly proved his soldiership and destroyed of the army opposed to him a number considerably exceeding his whole force, while not until the process of attrition had reduced his army to a mere handful of half-starved and utterly worn-out men did he yield to the overwhelming force which closed from him every avenue of retreat.

This fact was impressed upon the writer by a conversation

that took place between General Lee and General Meade on the afternoon of the day of the surrender. Meade had made a friendly visit to Lee at his headquarters, and in the course of the conversation remarked, "Now that the war may be considered over, I hope you will not deem it improper for me to ask, for my personal information, the strength of your army during the operations about Richmond and Petersburg."

General Lee replied: "At no time did my force exceed 35,000 men; often it was less."

With a look of surprise Meade answered, "General, you amaze me! We always estimated your force at about 70,000 men."

This conversation was repeated to the writer by General Lee immediately after his visitor had withdrawn.

An amusing portion of the conversation between Meade and Lee has been published by General de Chanal, a French officer, who was present. He states that during the interview Lee turned to Meade, who had been an associate with him as an officer of Engineers in the "old army," and said pleasantly, "Meade, years are telling on you: your hair is getting quite gray."

"Ah, General Lee," was Meade's prompt reply, "it is not the work of years: *you* are responsible for my gray hairs."

General Hunt also had an interview with Lee on that day, which he describes in the following language:

"At Appomattox I spent half an hour with General Lee in his tent. He looked, of course, weary and careworn, but in this supreme hour was the same self-possessed, dignified gentleman that I had always known him. After a time General Wise came in, and in a few minutes I took my leave, asking General Lee how General Long was and where I would find him. He answered, 'Long will be very glad to see you, but you will find him much changed in appearance; he has suffered much from neuralgia of the face. He is now with General Longstreet's corps.'

"He then described the place to me, but General Wilcox, coming in, offered to ride with me to General Long's camp, where I spent the afternoon. Long had been a lieutenant in my battery before the war, and we were old friends. This was the last time that I saw General Lee—a truly great man, as great in adversity as in prosperity.''

Shortly after the surrender General Lee returned to Richmond, riding slowly from the scene on his iron-gray, ''Traveller,'' who had borne him so nobly through all the years of the war. His parting with his soldiers was pathetic, and everywhere on his road to Richmond he received tokens of admiration and respect from both friend and foe.

His soldierly habits remained unchanged. At one house where he stopped for the night he declined the comfortable bed that had been prepared for him, but slept upon his blanket, which he had spread on the floor. Stopping at the house of his brother, Charles Carter Lee, in Powhatan, he spent the evening in conversation, but at bedtime, despite the fact that rain was falling, he took up his quarters in his well-worn tent, in which he had spent the greater part of the time during the last year's campaign.

On reaching Richmond the party passed sadly through a portion of the city which had been destroyed by the conflagration, and which exhibited a distressing scene of blackened ruins. He was quickly recognized, and the inhabitants flocked out in multitudes to meet him, cheering and waving hats and handkerchiefs. General Lee, to whom this ovation could not have been agreeable, simply raised his hat in reply to the greetings of the citizens, and rode on to his house in Franklin street. The closing of its doors upon his retiring form was the final scene in that long drama of war in which he had for years been the central figure. He had returned to that private family life for which his soul had yearned even in the most active years of the war, and had become once more, what he had always desired to be, a peaceful citizen of a peaceful land.

CHAPTER XXII.

GENERAL LEE AS A SOLDIER.

Early Military Labors.—Engineering and Organizing Abilities.—Breadth of View.—Skill as a Strategist and Tactician.—Diversity of Methods.—Influence over his Men.—Ability in Defence; in Attack.—Comparison with Other Soldiers of the War; with Celebrated Generals.—Lee as a Man.—His Guiding Principle.—Lack of Ambition.—Sense of Justice.—Firmness in Decision.—His Spirit Reflected in the Army.—Final Summary.

WITH the surrender of the Army of Northern Virginia, General Lee's military career ended. My intimate relations with him continued to the close of his life.

I frequently visited him at his home in Lexington, Va., and saw him in the discharge of his duties as a college president, but before laying aside my pen it is proper that I should attempt some estimate of him as a soldier and a man.

General Lee was both by nature and by education a great soldier. By diligent study under the most favorable conditions, and by long and varied experience, he became a master of the science of war in all its branches. In early life he was especially distinguished as an engineer. All the important points from the coast of Georgia to New York bear witness to his engineering skill, and his name will be identified with the Rip Raps, Fort Carroll, and the defences of New York harbor until those granite structures crumble into dust.

Perhaps even more important than his work on the Atlantic coast was that on the Mississippi and Des Moines rapids, of which General Meigs, U. S. A., has kindly furnished for this volume a highly interesting account.

The Mexican War opened to him a wider field, and the quick eye of General Scott discovered in the young captain of Engineers "a man of all kinds of merit."

On assuming command in Virginia in April, 1861, General

428

Lee at once showed his talents for adminstration and organization. He found the country almost destitute of the essentials
of war, and, as if by magic, he created and equipped an army.
His very ability as an organizer made many doubt whether he
could be great in other directions, and it was only after successful trial that they were willing to recognize his wonderful
versatility.

It was with surprise that they saw him showing himself
equal to all the demands made upon him as the commander
of a great army in the field. As they looked on, their surprise changed to admiration; the glory of the engineer and
organizer was first dimmed, and then eclipsed, by that of the
strategist and tactician.

The great soldier is something more than a fighter of battles. He must have a breadth of view sufficient to take in
widely-separated movements and to form great and far-reach-
ing combinations. That General Lee had this breadth of
view, this subtle intuition, which constitutes the very flower of
military genius, is shown by the whole history of the war. The
reader will recall how, when he was contemplating an attack
on McClellan on the Chickahominy, he sent Jackson to make
a vigorous movement in the Valley. He nicely calculated the
moral effect of that movement. He intended it to alarm the
authorities at Washington—to hold McDowell in position near
the Federal capital, and thus prevent his joining in the coming battle.

The Pennsylvania campaign had a wider outlook: it was
charged with great possibilities. The defeat of Meade's army
in Pennsylvania might be expected to be much more than the
simple defeat of that one army. Its effect would be felt on
the Mississippi; Grant's army would be needed in the East;
the siege of Vicksburg would be raised, and Pemberton's
army released for active service. What else might follow it
was easy to conjecture. Lee fought, and knew that he fought,
for a great stake. That he did not succeed and that the movement came too late, even if it had been successful, to affect the
result at Vicksburg, detracts nothing from the brilliancy of the
conception. The one pertinent thing is that the Confederate

general saw that by a single bold and successful stroke it might be possible virtually to end the war and secure the independence of the Southern Confederacy. That success was possible is shown by the narrow chance by which it failed. It has been well said that when the Confederate charge at Cemetery Ridge for a while seemed successful, the Muse of History took up her pen to record the birth of a new nation.

Breadth of plan is often neutralized by neglect of details. General Lee did not make that mistake. Before a battle he neglected nothing that might be needful either for attack or defence; in the battle he was quick to see and prompt to meet emergencies. He knew his men, rank and file—what they could do, and how far he might trust them. He was careful to know the ground on which he was to operate, and also to seize and use every advantage of position: he made a league with rivers and mountains and mountain-passes. He studied his adversary, knew his peculiarities, and adapted himself to them. His own methods no one could foresee; he varied them with every change in the commanders opposed to him. He had one method with McClellan, another with Pope, another with Hooker, and yet another with Grant. But for a knowledge of his own resources, of the field, and of his adversary some of his movements might have been rash. As it was, they were wisely bold. Because he was so attentive to details, and guarded so rigidly against the accidents of battle, he was sometimes supposed to be over-cautious; because he sometimes attacked greatly superior numbers or divided his forces, he was often thought over-bold. The truth is, that there was in him that harmonious blending of caution and boldness without which a general must often either rashly expose himself to defeat or lose an opportunity for victory.

Whatever other qualities a man may have, he cannot be a great soldier unless he has the power to win the confidence and inspire the enthusiasm of his men. General Lee had this power; few men have had it in a higher degree. No privation or suffering or disaster could shake the confidence of his men in him. In the darkest hour the sight of his form or the mention of his name stirred the hearts of his veterans. They spoke of him with an affection and pride that have not been dimmed by the lapse of years.

It is sometimes said that while General Lee was without a peer in defence, he was not so great in attack. That he was great in defence is witnessed by the series of combats from the Wilderness to Cold Harbor. Hardly anything in the history of warfare, ancient or modern, equals the skill and adroitness with which he met and repulsed Grant's obstinate and persevering assaults. But, on the other hand, in the second battle of Manassas and at Chancellorsville he was the aggressor; he went to seek the enemy. And even in those cases in which he was resisting the enemy's advance he often struck a blow in preference to waiting to receive one.

But perhaps the readiest way to fix Lee's position and to realize his greatness would be to compare him with others. It is significant that in attempting to do this no one ever thinks of comparing him with any but men of the first rank. Among the distinguished soldiers on the Confederate side his position was peculiar. He came from the old army with a brilliant reputation, and during the war he occupied the most prominent and responsible position. It is no injustice either to the living or the dead to say that by common consent he holds the first place among Southern soldiers.

Among the dead heroes of the war Albert Sidney Johnston challenges admiring attention. He had great qualities; anything that skill, courage, and a lofty, unselfish character might accomplish seemed possible to him; but he died at Shiloh. Jackson was Lee's most trusted lieutenant, and deserved all the confidence that his commander reposed in him. In the sphere of his operations he had no superior, nor can it be known that he would not have shown himself equal to a greater sphere. All honor to that brave, true soldier! but it would not be proper to compare him with his chief. There was no rivalry between them living; let there be none now that they are dead. There was A. P. Hill, a modest man, always ready; one of the finest soldiers in the army: he had the best division when he had a division, and one of the best corps when he had a corps. Lee and Jackson agreed in their admiration of Hill, and both mentioned him in the delirium of death; but no one thinks of comparing him with Lee.

There is a sort of infallibility in an undivided popular judgment, and the whole South looked to Lee as its greatest man. So impressed was Grant with the devotion of the Southern people to Lee that after the surrender at Appomattox he sought his influence, being convinced that if he should advise the surrender of all the Southern armies, the advice would be followed with alacrity. And in his report of the operations of the Army of the Potomac in 1864–65 he attributes it to General Lee's example that, as he says, "the armies lately under his leadership are at their homes, desiring peace and quiet, and their arms are in the hands of our ordnance officers."

Nothing is more characteristic of General Lee, or reveals more clearly his simple moral grandeur, than the fact that when no more could be accomplished by arms he used his influence to promote peace and good feeling toward the people against whom he had been waging war.

Of the great soldiers opposed to General Lee, some may have equalled him in single qualities, none in the combination of qualities. They were great in some directions; he in many. Let it not be forgotten that his was a long and varied career, and that he was distinguished in every part of it. He was called on to do many things, and he did them all in a masterly way.

In judging him account must be taken not only of what he did in the war between the States, but also of what he did before the Mexican War, in the Mexican War, and after the Mexican War, and in the last years of his life. When all these things are considered, and when we take into the account his perfect acquaintance with his art, his organizing power, his skill in combining, his wisdom in planning, his boldness and vigor in execution, his power to awaken enthusiasm and to lead men, we must place him first among the great soldiers of both armies. The time has not yet come to compare him with soldiers of the past and of other lands. They show great in the haze of time and distance, but the time will come when by the suffrages of all he will take his place among the greatest of those who have marshalled armies to battle.

We turn now from Lee as a soldier to Lee as a man; and here it is difficult to find suitable words in which to speak of him. In a private conversation a gentleman once said to an officer who had been intimately associated with him, "Most men have their weak point. What was General Lee's?" After a thoughtful pause, the answer was, "I really do not know." This answer may be taken for that of the great majority of those who knew him personally or who have studied his character. He was singularly free from the faults which so often mar the character of great men. He was without envy, jealousy, or suspicion, self-seeking, or covetousness; there was nothing about him to diminish or chill the respect which all men felt for him. General Grant speaks of him as "a large, austere man, difficult of approach to his subordinates." "Austere" is not the word to use in speaking of him. I should rather say that he was clothed with a natural dignity which could either repel or invite as occasion might require. He could pass with perfect ease from familiar, cheerful conversation to earnest conference, and from earnest conference to authoritative command. He had a pleasant humor, could see the ludicrous side of things, and could enjoy an anecdote or a joke. But even in his lightest moods he was still the cultivated gentleman, having that just degree of reserve that suited his high and responsible position.

His character was perfectly simple; there were in it no folds or sinuosities. It was simple because guided by a single principle. It is common to say that this principle was duty. This is not the whole truth. Duty is faithfulness to obligation, and is measured by obligation. That which moulded General Lee's life was something more than duty. It was a fine soldierly instinct that made him feel that it was his business to devote his life and powers to the accomplishment of high impersonal ends. Duty is the highest conception of Roman stoicism; it was the ambition of the Christian soldier to serve. General Grant interpreted him correctly when he said, "I knew there was no use to urge him to anything against his ideas of right."

If there are any who blame him for resigning his position
in the United States army and taking part with the South,
they must at the same time acknowledge that he was influenced by no unworthy motive.   What he did involved sacrifice
of feeling, of position, and of interest: he might have had the
highest place in the old army; he had but to consent to take
it.   A man of smaller mould might have been dazzled and
attracted by the prospect of leading a successful revolution and
establishing a new nation, but in all my association with him
I saw no indication that any feeling of personal ambition was
present with him.   If he had such feeling it was checked by a
consciousness of the great interests confided to him.

As he appeared to me, so he appeared to others.   When the
Confederate capital was transferred from Montgomery to Richmond, the Virginia forces, of which he was commander-in-
chief, were incorporated in the Confederate army.   He then
lost his independent command.   While the transfer was yet
in contemplation the Confederate authorities were anxious to
know whether an apparent lowering of his rank would offend
or make him less zealous in the service of the Confederacy.
When Mr. Stephens, the Confederate Vice-President, mentioned the matter to him, he promptly said, "Mr. Stephens,
I am willing to serve anywhere where I can be useful."

It was in perfect accord with his character that he was no
stickler for rank or position.   In the early part of the war the
positions held by him were not such as to attract public attention; the duties assigned to him, while very important, were
not of a showy kind.   Others were winning distinction in the
field and rising into prominence, while he was in the background.   No great laurels could be won in the mountains of
West Virginia or in strengthening the coast defences of South
Carolina and Georgia.   In the estimation of the general public
his reputation was suffering; it was said that his former distinction had been too easily won.   During this time he uttered
no word of complaint, and gave no intimation that he felt
himself in any way wronged or overlooked.   One might wonder whether this sweetness of spirit, this calmness, this cheerful content, did not spring from a consciousness of power and

assured belief that he had only to bide his time; but a close acquaintance with the workings of his mind convinced me that it was rather from a single-hearted desire to be useful, and the conviction that the best way to be useful was to work contentedly and to the best of his ability in the place assigned him.

It was his constant feeling that he was living and working to an end that constituted the source of General Lee's magnanimity and put him far above any petty jealousy. He looked at everything as unrelated to himself, and only as it affected the cause he was serving. This is shown in his treatment of his subordinates. He had no favorites, no unworthy partialities. On one occasion he spoke highly of an officer and remarked that he ought to be promoted. Some surprise was expressed at this, and it was said that that particular officer had sometimes spoken disparagingly of him. "I cannot help that," said the general; "he is a good soldier, and would be useful in a higher position." As he judged of the work of others, so he judged of his own. A victory gave him pleasure only as it contributed to the end he had in view, an honorable peace and the happiness of his country. It was for this cause that even his greatest victories produced in him no exaltation of spirits: he saw the end yet far off. He even thought more of what might have been done than of what was actually accomplished. In the same way a reverse gave him pain, not as a private but as a public calamity. He was the ruling spirit of his army. His campaigns and battles were his own.

He frequently consulted others that his own judgment might be informed, not that he might lean on their judgment or advice. It was because he felt himself so completely the commander of his army that he sometimes assumed the responsibility of the failure of movements which a less strong and generous spirit would have made his subordinates bear.

There was no hesitation or vacillation about him. When he had once formed a plan the orders for its execution were positive, decisive, and final. The army which he so long commanded is a witness for him. He imbued it with his own spirit; it reflected his energy and devotion. Such an army, so responsive to orders, so rapid in movement, so sturdy and prompt in action, so often victorious, sometimes checked but never defeated, so patient in the endurance of hardships, yielding at last rather to the friction of battle and the pressure of hunger than to the power of the enemy, gives indication that its commander was gifted with that imperial quality, the power to command.

As I recall the past, and the four years of the war come back and move in silent procession before me, I can easily forget that more than twenty years have passed away since I selected for General Lee the spot at Appomattox where his tent was pitched for the last time. His image stands out clearly before me, but it is unnecessary to describe his personal appearance. The majesty of his form will endure in marble and bronze, while his memory will pass down the ages as representing all that is greatest in military art, as well as what is truest, bravest, and noblest in human life—a soldier who never failed in duty, a man who feared and trusted God and served his generation.

> " Vanquished,
> He was yet a victor.
> To honor virtue is to honor him;
> To reverence wisdom is to do him reverence.
> In life he was a model for all who live;
> In death
> He left a heritage to all.
> One such example is worth more to earth
> Than the stained triumphs of ten thousand Cæsars."

CHAPTER XXIII.

PRESIDENT OF WASHINGTON COLLEGE.

AFTER the Army of Northern Virginia had surrendered at Appomattox Court-house, General Lee, as has been described in a previous chapter, joined his family at Richmond, where they had continued to reside. His disposition of mind was averse to a public reception. He hoped to re-enter his domestic portals unobserved, and to enjoy in quiet and privacy the reunion with the objects of his love. But it was impossible to prevent the heralding of his coming. Upon his approach to the city he found the whole population gathered to testify its devotion. As he passed through crowded streets Union veterans pressed Confederate soldiers in the throng, eager to catch a glimpse of the great soldier. Upon every hand manifestations of respect in ways of silent sincerity were shown him, and men of the Federal army vied in the universal tribute. The crowd attended him to the very threshold of his residence, and there drew back in quiet defer-ence as he withdrew into the sacred privacy of home.

An eye-witness who was at the time a guest of General Lee recounts an incident illustrative of the respect and affection which pervaded the city. One morning an Irishman who had gone through the war in the Federal ranks appeared at

437

the door with a basket well filled with provisions, and insisted upon seeing General Lee. The servant protested and offered to carry a message, but Pat was not to be put off. The general, hearing the altercation, came from an adjoining room, and was greeted with profuse terms of admiration: "Sure, sir, you are a great soldier, and it's I that know it. I've been fighting against you all these years, and many a hard knock we've had. But, general, I honor you for it; and now they tell me you are poor and in want, and I've brought this basket and beg you to take it from a soldier." The general, touched by this spirit of sympathy, thanked him most kindly, and said, "My man, I am not in need, but if you will carry your basket to the hospital you will find some poor fellow glad to be remembered by so generous a foe."

There was a continuous stream of callers at the residence. Officers of both armies were received with the cordiality and courtesy which were innate. Frankness and chivalry, marks of the true soldier, characterized his reception of men who had held rank in the Federal army. His sword was sheathed, and no rancor or petty animosity existed in his mind to embitter the amenities of social·intercourse. "For his own people he had words of sympathy, and always advised moderation and quiet acquiescence ·in the conditions of defeat."

The assassination of President Lincoln renewed the storm of passionate hatred against the South. The imprisonment of Mr. Davis and the bitter appeals voiced by the Northern press for his execution created grave apprehensions in the minds of friends as to General Lee's safety, and in the warmth of their devotion they urged him to find a secure retreat in the mountains, where they would be ready to devote their lives as a sacrifice for his protection.

This solicitude was shared throughout the South. An incident is related which shows that it rendered even those who were shattered in fortune oblivious of their own condition and generous of their remaining estate. Two Confederate soldiers in tattered garments and with bodies emaciated by prison confinement called upon General Lee. They told him that they were the delegates "of sixty other fellows around the corner who are too ragged to come themselves." They tendered their loved general a home in the mountains, promising him a comfortable house and a good farm. "We hear," they said, "that Underwood intends having you indicted for treason and rebellion. But there is a defile near the farm we offer, and there the whole Federal army can be defied."

This heartfelt exhibition of fealty brought tears to General Lee's eyes, but he resolutely refused to accept the proffer, and reasoned with his devoted callers against the propriety of urging him to accept the life of a fugitive. He finally substituted for their ragged suits some clothing of his own, and the representatives of the assembly "around the corner" departed with elated spirits. There were almost daily episodes typical of this single-hearted adherence.

But his residence at Richmond grew irksome. There could be no seclusion. The rest and quiet for which he so longed were disturbed by continuous attentions, which could not have been repressed without some degree of discourtesy. Mrs. Lee was almost a confirmed invalid, and for her declining health the devoted husband felt deep anxiety. His longing at this time is best expressed in a passage from a letter to General Long :

"I am looking for some little quiet house in the woods where I can procure shelter and my daily bread if permitted by the victor. I wish to get Mrs. Lee out of the city as soon as practicable."

A friend enabled him to realize his wish by offering him a country-house near Cartersville in Cumberland county. Thither he soon removed, but he was not destined long to enjoy the pleasures of retirement. Into this abode of peace and quiet business propositions, friendly proffers, and even tenders of pecuniary assistance, followed him. An English nobleman desired him to accept a mansion and an estate commensurate with his individual merits and the greatness of an historic family. But he would not desert his native State. She lay prostrate through the devastations of war; it would take years of devotion to her interests to bring her back to her former condition, and one of the noblest of her sons could suffer no beguilement to lead him away from her distress. He responded, "I must abide her fortunes and share her fate."

Before leaving Richmond, General Lee wrote to General Grant the appended letter, which forcibly corroborates the fact of his entire acceptance of the situation and his desire to comply with all the terms of the surrender:

"RICHMOND, VA., April 25, 1865.

"LIEUTENANT-GENERAL U. S. GRANT, COMMANDING THE ARMIES OF THE UNITED STATES,

"GENERAL: I have awaited your arrival in Richmond to propose that the men and officers of the Army of Northern Virginia, captured or surrendered on the 2d and 6th of April, or since that time, may be granted the same terms as given to those surrendered by me on the 9th. I see no benefit that will result by retaining them in prison, but, on the contrary, think good may be accomplished by returning them to their homes. Indeed, if all now held as prisoners of war were liberated in the same manner, I think it would be advantageous. Should there, however, be objections to this course, I would ask that exceptions be made in favor of the invalid officers and men, and that they be allowed to return to their homes on parole. I call your attention particularly to General Ewell, the members of the reserves, local-defence troops, naval battalion, etc. The local troops were not performing military duty, and the naval battalion fell in the line of march of the army for subsistence and protection.

"Understanding that you may not reach Richmond for some days, I take the liberty to forward this application for your consideration.

"Very respectfully,
"Your obedient servant,
"R. E. LEE."

In the partial seclusion of his country retreat General Lee gave serious attention to plans for improving his personal resources. His fortune had disappeared in the years of warfare, and the future maintenance of his family became a question of primary importance. Offers of money, of land, of corporation stock to secure the mere endorsement of his name, still poured in upon him. But there was no proposition as yet that involved compensation in direct return for his individual labor. Yet nothing less honorable than this could be acceptable to him. Gratuities, however richly merited in return for his sacrifices, he could not consent to receive. Labor and wages constituted in his mind the sole solution of the problem of gaining a livelihood.

During this interval of expectancy General Lee conceived the idea of collecting material upon which he might base an authentic history of his various campaigns. The value of such a work in the series of war histories would have been incalculable. The military education, equipoise of mind, and attributes of charity and truth combined in the author must have won a generous welcome for his production from candid students of the war. In furtherance of this project General Lee sent out to many officers a circular, of which we subjoin a copy of that received by General Ewell:

"Near Cartersville, Cumberland Co., Va.,
"July 31, 1867.

"General: I am desirous that the bravery and devotion of the Army of Northern Virginia be correctly transmitted to posterity. This is the only tribute that can be paid to the worth of its noble officers and soldiers. And I am anxious to collect the necessary information for the history of its campaigns, including the operations in the Valley of Western Virginia, from its organization to its final surrender.

"I have copies of my reports of the battles, commencing with those around Richmond, to the close of the Pennsylvania campaign, but no report of the campaign in 1864 and of the operations of the winter of 1864–65 to the 1st of April, 1865, has been written, and the corps and division reports for that period, which had been sent to headquarters before the abandonment of the lines before Petersburg, with all the records, returns, maps, plans, etc., were destroyed the day before the army reached Appomattox Court-house. My letter-books, public and confidential, were also destroyed, and the regular returns transmitted to the adjutant-general at Richmond have been burned also.

"Should you have reports of the operations of your command within the period specified (from 1st of May, 1864, to 1st of April, 1865), or should you be able to renew them, I will be greatly obliged to you to send them to me. Should you be able to procure reports of other commanders, returns of the effective strength of the army at any of the battles from the first Manassas to the 1st of April, 1865, or copies of my official orders, letters, etc., you will confer a favor by sending them to me.

"Very respectfully and truly yours,

"R. E. LEE."

This endeavor to supply the missing records of the war met with persistent embarrassment. His application to the War Department at Washington for the privilege of copying such official documents as might aid him in the preparation of his volume was refused, for at that time the archives of the Confederacy were an undigested mass and preserved in secret alcoves. The spirit of historical research had not yet successfully combated the prejudices of strife, and the records of the Confederacy were regarded as trophies rather than as rich historical material.

When General Lee's intention of writing his military history became known, it excited the liveliest interest among army instructors and commandants of military establishments in foreign countries. An officer of the German army desired the privilege of translating it into the language of his country. The obstacles, however, that lay in the way of this cherished work proved insurmountable. The project, as conceived by General Lee, had not been to rear a memorial to his own military genius, but to vindicate and set forth the valor of his soldiers. He relinquished the work with less reluctance because he felt that its truths and indispensable facts must expose certain persons to severe censure.

Shortly after the close of the war a trust was conferred upon

General Lee which became his life-work, and in the honorable execution of which he continued until his lamented death. He was elected by the Board of Trustees of Washington College, at Lexington, president of that institution on August 4, 1865. The formal notification of the Board's action came to him as a complete surprise. Before the meeting of the trustees, Hon. Bolivar Christian of Staunton, a member of the Board, had endeavored to discover if General Lee would be willing to accept so arduous an office, but General Lee's answer was delayed in the mails until after Colonel Christian had left Staunton to attend the meeting of the trustees. That answer so decidedly remonstrated against the intended proposal of his name for the position that knowledge of its contents might have influenced Colonel Christian to withdraw the proposition.

But before its reception the presidency had been conferred by unanimous vote upon General Lee. The rector of the Board, Hon. John W. Brockenbrough, was selected to convey to him the notification of his election. It was two weeks before a formal reply was made to the tender, and then in a characteristic letter General Lee without reservation discussed the embarrassments and exactions of the proffered place, and with marked self-abnegation considered the possible detriment to the historic school that his installation as its president might bring. He wrote the trustees thus:

"POWHATAN COUNTY, August 24, 1865.

"GENTLEMEN: I have delayed for some days replying to your letter of the 5th inst., informing me of my election by the Board of Trustees to the presidency of Washington College, from a desire to give the subject due consideration. Fully impressed with the responsibilities of the office, I have feared that I should be unable to discharge its duties to the satisfaction of the trustees or to the benefit of the country. The proper education of youth requires not only great ability, but, I fear, more strength than I now possess, for I do not feel able to undergo the labor of conducting classes in regular courses of instruction: I could not therefore undertake more than the general administration and supervision of the institution.

"There is another subject which has caused me serious reflection, and is, I think, worthy of the consideration of the Board. Being excluded from the terms of amnesty in the proclamation of the President of the United States of·the 29th of May last, and an object of censure to a portion of the country, I have thought it probable that my occupation of the position of president might draw upon the college a feeling of hostility, and I should therefore cause injury to an institution which it would be my highest desire to advance.

"I think it the duty of every citizen, in the present condition of the country, to do all in his power to aid in the restoration of peace and harmony, and in no way to oppose the policy of the State or General Government directed to that object. It is particularly incumbent on those charged with the instruction of the young to set them an example of submission to authority, and I could not consent to be the cause of animadversion upon the college.

"Should you, however, take a different view, and think that my services in the position tendered to me by the Board will be advantageous to the college and country, I will yield to your judgment and accept it, otherwise I must most respectfully decline the office.

"Begging you to express to the trustees of the college my heartfelt gratitude for the honor conferred upon me, and requesting you to accept my cordial thanks for the kind manner in which you have communicated their decision,

"I am, gentlemen, with great respect,

"Your most obedient servant,

"R. E. LEE.

" Messrs. JOHN W. BROCKENBROUGH, Rector; S. McD. REID, ALFRED LEYBURN, HORATIO THOMPSON, D. D., BOLIVAR CHRISTIAN, T. J. KIRKPATRICK, } *Committee.*"

The Board of Trustees immediately assured General Lee that his apprehensions of damage to the college, as resultant from his assumption of the presidency, were groundless, and again pressed upon him an acceptance of the place. His installation occurred October 2, 1865, the oath of office being administered by Rev. W. S. White in the presence of the trustees, faculty, and students. A new impetus was at once given to this venerable college, which had suffered greatly in the war. Its funds no longer furnished a reliable income, and even their actual value was yet a problem of the future. The campus had been despoiled by military marauders, who carried their spoliation to the libraries and laboratory of the college. But four professors and forty students were at the institution when General Lee undertook the exacting task of restoring it to its former prosperity and reputation.

Not only was the material destruction within the buildings a serious embarrassment, but far greater was the obstacle to any rehabilitation that the reduced circumstances of the people presented. Washington College had enjoyed a long career. It was the earliest classical school established in the Shenandoah Valley. It was originally instituted in 1749, and won so excellent a reputation that General Washington determined to give it permanency. The legislature had presented him with shares in the "Old James River Company," but to their acceptance he had attached the condition that he be allowed to appropriate them "to some public purpose in the upper part of the State, such as the education of the poor, particularly of such as have fallen in the defence of their country." In pursuance of this condition he gave to what became Washington College one hundred of these valuable shares. It was a magnificent endowment, and the academy, which previously had been peripatetic, became from that time a permanent college.

General Lee gave himself with unrestrained ardor to the labor of improving the impoverished college. In this laudable purpose the trustees heartily co-operated with him, and were inspired by the hope and zeal exhibited by the new president. His first attention was devoted to the better equipment of the scientific departments. Apparatus for the laboratory was purchased. The library was replenished. The dismantled buildings were reconstructed or repaired. Three new chairs were instituted—Physics, Mathematics, and Modern Languages— with a subordinate classification of correlated studies which embraced Engineering, Astronomy, and English Philology. He also suggested chairs of the English Language and of

Applied Chemistry, and wished to add a School of Commerce. The Lexington Law School was, just before his death, embraced within the collegiate jurisdiction.

While General Lee thus added to the curriculum the above-named modern and practical studies, he in no sense opposed the study of the classical languages. He fully recognized their utility as a means of refinement, of mental discipline, and of the acquirement of a copious vocabulary. In devoting his energies to the institution of modern branches of study he was but supplying manifest defects in the existing course. Yet he was innately inclined toward the practical in education. In writing to General John B. Gordon he declares: "The thorough education of all classes of the people is the most efficacious means, in my opinion, of promoting the prosperity of the South; and the material interests of the citizens, as well as their moral and intellectual culture, depend upon its establishment. The text-books of our schools, therefore, should not only be clear, systematic, and scientific, but they should be acceptable to parents and pupils in order to enlist the minds of all in the subjects."

One most important innovation introduced by General Lee was the system of elective studies. The compulsory curriculum was discarded, and the student permitted to select the branches he could pursue with the most benefit or with more direct influence upon his future avocation. The only limitation imposed was that the choice of studies should embrace sufficient to fully employ the student's time.

The mode of discipline introduced merits extended notice. It was a departure from the time-sanctioned tyrannical control exercised by the heads of schools. No espionage was practised—that system which lessens self-respect by placing it beneath the ban of suspicion, or which works yet greater harm by substituting for frankness and openness avoidance and concealment.

He became personally acquainted with each student, and so accurate was his remembrance of their names that when, on one occasion, a name was read from the college-rolls that was unfamiliar to him, he required it to be read again, and repeated the name with a marked emphasis on each syllable, adding in a tone of self-reproach, "I have no recollection of a student of that name. It is very strange that I have forgotten him. I thought I knew every one in the college. How long has he been here?" He would not be satisfied until an investigation showed that the student had recently entered and during his absence, so that he had never seen him.

It was his constant desire to cultivate the individual sense of honor of those under him, and to erect no factitious barriers of rank between faculty and students. The respect exacted from the latter was the natural reverence due to superior age and experience. A pride in good order was inspired, and obedience to the rules and the conduct of gentlemen were natural corollaries. He did not assert military discipline, as might have been expected from his West Point career, but recognized the fact that the students were to be fitted for the avocations of civil life, and that the rigor of military methods was not here desirable. His own manner was dignified, and there was a formal presence suggestive of army leadership, yet in his mode of college government no trace of the habits of the soldier appeared.

He won the confidence of students, and their affections soon went out toward him. With their instincts of honor always uppermost, their self-respect carefully preserved, and their pride in the institution fostered, discipline was apparently relaxed, while in fact it was precise and effective. Seldom was there a breach of decorum. The students honored and loved the president, and sedulously avoided transgressions that would cause him pain. He fully appreciated the natural waywardness of youth, and while he was firm in endeavors to repress it, he was never so uncharitable as to act summarily against a student and affix the stigma of expulsion upon a young career. He preferred to acquaint the parent with the course being pursued by the son; and when it was manifest that collegiate life could no longer prove beneficial, a quiet withdrawal by parental request was the honorable subterfuge adopted.

He tolerated no drones in the college classes. While never

prying into the private conduct of students, he judged almost infallibly of the probable profit that they were receiving from their studies, and how far responsive their manhood was to the refined surroundings of college life. If it were plain that they did not assimilate the elements of the intellectual atmosphere, a note to parent or guardian frankly gave the evidences of the fact. The common and unfortunate deception of parents as to the progress of their sons was impossible to one of his upright character.

General Lee let nothing requisite to the due government of the college or the advancement of the individual students escape his attention. He weekly examined the reports of absences and failures in recitation, and retained clearly in his memory the standing of each student. The exactness of his memory in these particulars was indeed remarkable, and several interesting illustrations of this fact are upon record. On a visitor inquiring how a certain student was getting on, General Lee replied, in that tone of grave satire in which he occasionally indulged, "He is a quiet, orderly young man, but seems very careful *not to injure the health of his father's son.* He got last month only forty on his Greek, thirty-five on his Mathematics, forty-seven on his Latin, and fifty on his English; which is a very low standing, as one hundred is our maximum. Now, I do not want our young men to really injure their health, *but I wish them to come as near it as possible.*"

On another occasion, when a certain name was called, General Lee remarked, "I am sorry to see that he has fallen back so far in his Mathematics."—"You are mistaken, general," said the professor; "he is one of the very best men in my class."—"He only got fifty-four last month," was the reply. On looking at the report, it was found that there had been a mistake in the copying, and that General Lee was correct according to the record.

During the earlier years of his incumbency the presence of emancipated slaves was naturally a disturbing element. The young Southerner had not adjusted his views to the new status of the colored race, and in the flush of freedom many of the negro population were arrogant and exasperating. General

Lee anxiously devoted his attention to the situation, and sought sternly to suppress all interference of the students with the negroes. Information was at one time brought to him that the students had deliberately organized to disturb a public meeting of colored people at Lexington. He at once posted the subjoined order upon the bulletin-board in the college hall:

"WASHINGTON COLLEGE,
"November 20, 1868.

"It has been reported to the faculty of Washington College that some of the students have threatened to disturb a public meeting of the colored people of Lexington, to be held at the fair-grounds this evening, the 20th instant.

"It is not believed that the students of this college, who have heretofore conducted themselves in such an exemplary manner, would do anything to disturb the public peace or bring discredit on themselves or the institution to which they belong; but it is feared that some, prompted by curiosity or a desire to witness the proceedings, may be present. The president therefore requests all students to abstain from attending this and all similar meetings, and thinks it only necessary to call their attention to the advantages of attending strictly, as heretofore, to their important duties at the college, and of, in no way, interfering with the business of others. From past experience they may feel certain that should any disturbance occur, efforts will be made to fix the blame on Washington College. It therefore behooves every student to keep away from all such assemblies.

"Respectfully,

"R. E. LEE,
"*President of Washington College.*"

If the disturbance had ever been planned, this appeal from the president effectually prevented it. There is more than reasonable doubt, however, of the existence of any such design among the students. In the Reconstruction era there were circulated many false reports of collisions between the races and unjust treatment of colored people, that political advantage might result. General Lee understood the motive for these aspersions of his students, and saw how readily his presence in the college could be made to lend plausibility to stories of acts of bitterness and hatred. But the majesty of truth came to be vindicated by his calm and sustained conduct. Every word and act of his exerted an influence tending to heal up sectional animosities, to force compliance with the governmental policy, and to inculcate all the indispensable qualities of good citizenship.

This method of appeal to the students was irresistible. It was a happy substitute for the former mode of prescribing penalties after the commission of acts of folly. He successfully appealed to the honor and self-respect of the students as sufficient monitors against any excess in their college hilarity and pranks which might destroy the quiet and rest of peaceful citizens. During his presidency few instances occurred within that community of those students' sports so familiar and annoying in college towns.

In strict conformity with this demand for order and quiet General Lee shortened the Christmas recess. The college exercises had customarily been suspended at Christmas-time for ten days, but the delay in their return to the institution generally disarranged the orderly life of the students. The interval permitted great temptations to beset those who did not avail themselves of it to visit their homes. Released from all restraints of study and attendance, they were easily susceptible to the irregular habits which mark the season of good-will. In order to overcome this relaxation of discipline, the new president did away with the Christmas vacation, and in its place suspended academic exercises for three days "to enable the students to join in the rites and services appropriate to the occasion." He added, "While enjoying these privileges with grateful hearts, all are urged to do or countenance nothing which may disturb the peace, harmony, and happiness that should pervade a Christian community."

One striking feature of President Lee's collegiate incumbency was the religious spirit which animated the institution. He had been from childhood a member of the Church of his ancestors, the Protestant Episcopal. But his religion had a

genuine catholicity of character. The dogmas of sects were
less to him than the essential and universal truths of spiritual
faith. Therefore, when the new chapel he had planned was
completed under his supervision the pastors of four congrega-
tions, at his invitation, officiated at the devotional exercises.
Each student could thus attend worship in conformity with his
own views or in compliance with parental choice. Upon these
chapel devotions General Lee was an unfailing attendant, and
his religious sincerity had a marked influence upon all about
him.

He fostered the organization of a Young Men's Christian
Association among the students, making liberal contributions
to its fund and donating to it a specially-collected library. In
his reports to the Board of Trustees he gave detailed mention
of this society, and dwelt upon the religious influence it exerted. Upon the matriculation of a new student his religious
faith was inquired into, and it was sought at once to bring him
in close relations with the pastor of the Church of his belief.
Nothing better illustrated General Lee's theory of collegiate
training than did this tender solicitude for the spiritual welfare and culture of his students. He had a loftier idea of
education than that comprised in the laborious task of the text-
book. His view of a true education embraced the moral expansion of mind and soul, the implanting of high principles of
manhood and of a delicate sense of honor, and he often expressed himself as feeling that his duty would be ill done were
not his students led to become consistent Christians. His own
life exemplified his teachings. A member of a church (not
his own), who had known him intimately for years, said that
"his lips were never soiled by a profane or obscene word, and
that when the provocation was great for a display of angry
feelings, it was his course to use the 'soft answer which turn-
eth away wrath.'"

In no spirit of undue eulogy it may be said that General Lee
was the ideal college president. There have been many others
who stand forth more prominent in educational annals—some
noted for the accumulation of pedantry, others for deep and valuable research in special fields of learning of benefit to man-

kind, and still others for polemical ability; but few have presented that happy combination of qualities which makes the working president. It is not our intention to ascribe remarkable learning to General Lee, though no one without injustice can depreciate his broad culture. But as an executive officer, patiently and indefatigably giving personal attention to details and achieving well-rounded results, the meed of praise should be unstinted.

He occupied the presidency not to enjoy a sinecure at the mere outlay of his great reputation. He was an actual, steadfast laborer with a well-defined plan to consummate, and his zeal never flagged. No grander duty was ever conceived and heroically self-imposed than that of educating the Southern youth into a spirit of loyalty to the new conditions and the transformation of the social fabric which had resulted from the war, and only through a peaceful obedience to which could the future peace and harmony of the country be assured. It was this sense of obligation which prompted General Lee to accept the college presidency, and its unremitting impulses can be traced in systematical action throughout his career at Washington College. There was a preconceived policy which had a consecutive and consistent execution.

The affectionate regard entertained for General Lee by the college faculty and his many friends in the South was shown in numerous manifestations. General Ewell contributed to the college endowment five hundred dollars, with the expressed condition that it should be applied to increasing the president's salary. But General Lee treated this generous offer as he had many similar ones. The friendly motive which prompted the contribution was appreciated, but he argued that he already received more than his services were worth. He reviewed in a tone of personal distress the pressing needs of the college—its lack of apparatus, its inefficient library—and alluded wistfully to what a liberal endowment would accomplish, for "we must look to the rising generation for the restoration of the country."

In the last winter of his life General Lee's failing health excited alarm among his colleagues, and he was urged to find relaxation from the sustained tension of his duties in a Southern trip. He was reluctant to do so, since his absence would impose additional labors upon the members of the faculty, but he was at length induced to yield. While he was absent the Board of Trustees appropriated money for building him a handsome residence and settling an annuity of three thousand dollars upon his family. This gift, however, he peremptorily declined. The residence was erected under his watchful eye, its cost being far reduced below the estimates. But he persistently declined to consider it as his property, and was punctilious in his reference to it as "the President's House." He wrote to the Board: "Though fully sensible of the kindness of the Board, and justly appreciating the manner in which they sought to administer to my relief, I am unwilling that my family should become a tax to the college, but desire all its funds should be devoted to the purposes of education. I know that my wishes on this subject are equally shared by my wife. I feel full assurance that in case a competency should not be left to my wife, her children would never suffer her to want." However, after General Lee's death the trustees endeavored to secure Mrs. Lee's acceptance of a deed to the mansion and the annuity. Imbued with her husband's spirit, she declined.

There is something highly attractive in the spectacle of this great man, who had occupied so prominent a position in the eyes of the world, and whom thousands would have been glad to honor and enrich, refusing all gratuities and all adulation, and settling down in a quiet country town to perform the duties of a noble but arduous profession, without a shadow of discontent or gloom, and with nothing in his demeanor to show that he had not spent his life in the teaching and management of youth. The remarkable ability which he displayed in this new field of duty goes to show that he was a man of varied intellectual powers, and one who, if he had not been thrown by chance into the life of a soldier, could not have failed to make his mark in any profession he might have undertaken.

Such limitations as he had were certainly not unknown to himself, and he was not the man to accept any position whose duties he did not feel competent to perform under the impulse of the honor or emolument which he might thereby attain. This fact is clearly brought out in a conversation related by Hon. B. H. Hill which took place during the last years of the war. Meeting him on the streets of Richmond, Mr. Hill said, "General, I wish you would give us your opinion as to the propriety of changing the seat of Government and going farther south."

"That is a political question, Mr. Hill, and you politicians must determine it. I shall endeavor to take care of the army, and you must make the laws and control the Government."

"Ah, general," said Mr. Hill, "but you will have to change that rule, and form and express political opinions, for if we establish our independence the people will make you Mr. Davis's successor."

"Never, sir," he replied with a firm dignity that belonged only to Lee: "that I will never permit. Whatever talents I may possess (and they are but limited) are military talents. My education and training are military. I think the military and civil talents are distinct if not different, and full duty in either sphere is about as much as one man can qualify himself to perform. I shall not do the people the injustice to accept high civil office with whose questions it has not been my business to become familiar."

"Well, but, general, history does not sustain your view. Cæsar and Frederick of Prussia and Bonaparte were great statesmen as well as great generals."

"And great tyrants," he promptly responded. "I speak of the proper rule in republics, where, I think, we should have neither military statesmen nor political generals."

"But Washington was both, and yet not a tyrant."

With a beautiful smile he responded, "Washington was an exception to all rule, and there was none like him."

This evidence of self-knowledge and this exhibition of self-abnegation were in keeping with the character of the man, and afford a lesson which few men in General Lee's position have taught. In his whole life he exhibited an ambition not for self, but for the discharge of what he conscientiously deemed his duty; and no allurements or emoluments of place or profit could seduce him from his firmly-fixed convictions.   The truly wise and patriotic man is he who, like General Lee, has fully gauged his powers, and who will not let thirst for honor or love of power lead him to accept an office whose duties he has been unfitted by nature and education to properly perform.

CHAPTER XXIV.

HOME AND SOCIETY LIFE.

Correspondence.—Requested to Enter Public Life.—Advice to Soldiers.—Declines Publicity.—Offer of Lucrative Situations.—Private Testimonials.—Character of Lee's Letters.—Social Intercourse.—Love of Children.—Anecdotes.—Ride to the Peaks of Otter.—Incident.—Home Life.—Farming Advice.—Letter to G. W. C. Lee.—Letter to his Daughter.—A Visitor's Description.—Hospitality.—A Pleasant Dinner.—Tomato-canning.—Another Visit.—War Relics.—An Accident.—The Saddle-blanket.

DURING the period covered by the preceding chapter General Lee lived a non-official as well as an official life. He was a citizen of Lexington—or perhaps we should say a citizen of the world—as well as a college president. And it is his life as a citizen which we have next to review. That he took pleasure in this new phase of existence he himself testifies: "For my own part, I much enjoy the charms of civil life, and find too late that I have wasted the best years of my existence." It could indeed hardly have been otherwise with one of his ardent family affection, and who had for so many years been deprived of the peaceful enjoyments of home life and social intercourse.

His correspondence in relation to matters distinct from his collegiate position was extensive and varied. Several applications were made to him for material by persons who desired to write his biography. To each he answered that whatever his life possessed of interest was connected with public events, the chronicles of which were at easy command. He writes to a lady: "I know of nothing good I could tell you of myself, and I fear I should not like to say any evil."

There is cumulative evidence throughout his letters of his unalterable purpose to aid in the regeneration of the South and to devote his tireless energies to restoring the unity of the nation. He writes General Beauregard a letter, the appended

456

extract from which breathes a noble spirit of patriotism, and to the candid mind must be conclusive testimony of General Lee's loyalty to the Government:

"I think the South requires the aid of her sons now more than at any period of her history. As you ask my purpose, I will state that I have no thought of abandoning her unless compelled to do so. After the surrender of the Southern armies in April the revolution in the opinions and feelings of the people seemed so complete, and the return of the Southern States into the Union of all the States so inevitable, that it became, in my opinion, the duty of every citizen, the contest being virtually ended, to cease opposition and place himself in a position to serve the country. I therefore, upon the promulgation of the proclamation of President Johnson of 29th of May, which indicated his policy in the restoration of peace, determined to comply with its requirements, and applied on the 13th of June to be embraced within its provisions. I have not heard the result of my application. Since then I have been elected to the presidency of Washington College, and have entered upon the duties of the office in the hope of being of some service to the noble youth of our country.

"I need not tell you that true patriotism sometimes requires of men to act exactly contrary at one period to that which it does at another, and the motive which impels them, the desire to do right, is precisely the same. The circumstances which govern their actions change, and their conduct must conform to the new order of things. History is full of illustrations of this: Washington himself is an example of this. At one time he fought against the French, under Braddock, in the service of the king of Great Britain; at another, he fought with the French at Yorktown, under the orders of the Continental Congress of America, against him. He has not been branded by the world with reproach for this, but his course has been applauded."

Again, he answers the query of a friend in New Orleans as to the propriety of taking the amnesty oath in this loyal strain: "If you intend to reside in this country, and wish to do your part in the restoration of your State and in the Government of the country, which I think it the duty of every citizen to do, I know of no objection to your taking the amnesty oath which I have seen."

In 1867 there was a ruling desire in the minds of leading men of Virginia that General Lee should accept the nomination for governor of the State. Hon. Robert Ould communicated this wish to him, but political ambition was not burning in his breast. The welfare of Virginia was the crucial test to which he submitted the proffered honor, and the result seemed to compel his judgment to conclude against its acceptance. He candidly confessed that his feelings also induced him to prefer private life, which was more suitable to his condition, and in which he believed he could better advance the interests of the State. He saw that it was no time to indulge in personal or political considerations, and that high office could not be properly bestowed as a reward for supposed former services. He confided to Mr. Ould, for his private information, that he believed that his election "would be used by the dominant party to excite hostility toward the State and to injure the people in the eyes of the country." In conclusion he said: "I therefore cannot consent to become the instrument of bringing distress upon those whose prosperity and happiness are so dear to me. If my disfranchisement and privation of civil rights would secure to the citizens of the State the enjoyment of civil liberty and equal rights under the Constitution, I would willingly accept them in their stead."

General Jubal A. Early had formed the design of writing a narrative of his operations before leaving the Army of Northern Virginia, and the project was submitted for approval to General Lee. In commending it he added: "I would recommend, however, that, while giving facts which you think necessary for your own vindication, you omit all epithets or remarks calculated to excite bitterness or animosity between different sections of the country."

One could easily augment the testimony of his sincere regard for his native State, for a reinauguration of an era of good feeling and for the lifting up of the prostrate South. Just before his removal to Lexington he received numerous requests for advice from soldiers who were being tempted by the vision of a new life in the Franco-Mexican empire. There is an evident reluctance to chill the ardor of emigrants beguiled by the Maximilian decree of encouragement, but he cannot refrain from declaring that "although prospects may not now be cheering, I have entertained the opinion that, unless prevented by circumstances or necessity, it would be better for them and the country for them to remain at their homes and share the fate of their respective States."

To Governor Letcher he writes more explicitly: "The interests of the State are therefore the same as those of the United States. Its prosperity will rise or fall with the welfare of the country. The duty of its citizens, then, appears to me too plain to admit of doubt. All should unite in honest efforts to obliterate the effects of war and to restore the blessings of peace. They should remain, if possible, in the country, promote harmony and good feeling, qualify themselves to vote, and elect to the State and general legislatures wise and patriotic men who will devote their abilities to the interests of the country and the healing of all dissensions. I have invariably recommended this course since the cessation of hostilities, and have endeavored to practise it myself."

General Lee shrank from appearing upon the public rostrum, and abstained even from attendance at meetings where his presence could be tortured into any interpretation hostile to peaceful submission. Hence he refused an invitation in April, 1867, to lecture before the Peabody Institute of New York. The declination must have been an additional sacrifice, for he was a known friend of the great philanthropist. In 1869, however, he yielded to a request for his photograph, which was placed among those of the "friends" of Mr. Peabody at the institute in Peabody, Mass. When the death of that noble benefactor occurred he penned a touching tribute to his memory.

While at Lexington repeated endeavors were made to allure him from college duties into business enterprises in which the promise of wealth was more flattering. His salary was but $3000 per annum. The presidency of the Southern Life Insurance Company, with the salary of $10,000, was tendered him, but he wrote General John B. Gordon: "It would be a great pleasure to me to be associated with you, Hampton, B. H. Hill, and the other good men whose names I see on your list of directors, but I feel that I ought not to abandon the position I hold at Washington College at this time or as long as I can be of service to it." Just before his death he did accept the presidency of the Valley Railroad Company. His acquiescence was obtained by the forcible presentation of the advantages which would accrue to Washington College from the construction of the road.

Constant private testimonials of esteem and remembrance were sent to the old soldier. While, as has already been shown, he persistently refused proffers of pecuniary aid, and was unwilling that any funds should be diverted from the college endowment, yet he was never churlish in declining small tokens whose value was more suggestive than intrinsic. His notes acknowledging the receipts of the gifts are models of the epistolary art. A hat is sent from Baltimore, a saddle and a dressing-gown from a Southern Relief fair, a beaver robe from far-away Wyoming; an English Bible comes from distinguished members of Parliament; a translation of the *Iliad* is sent to him, and he writes to its author that it has furnished him his evening's recreation.

Throughout that final period of his life his correspondence was occupied with official matters, domestic interchanges of parental love and sympathy in family bereavements, patriotic appeals to let the issues of the war sink into oblivion, and with those minor notes of friendly intercourse which so help to exhibit the real man. No one can peruse the letters of General Lee, placed in chronological sequence, without being impressed with the nobility of character which is infused into every sentence. They occupy a lofty plane, yet one that is not above the earth. Throughout them one finds the spirit of practical wisdom. There is not here the ecstasy of the saint nor the vapory imagination of the transcendentalist. A man of the world, trained in its rudest and most material shocks, writes, but ennobling virtues guide the pen.

In this epistolary collection may be found evidence of the

keen interest felt by General Lee in the adjudication of the question involving the confiscation of the Arlington estate. As the executor of the will of G. W. P. Custis he was alive to the duties of the trust. He did not survive the tedious litigation which eventually resulted in a decree by the United States Supreme Court of comparative compensation for the estate.

It remains to investigate the relations which existed between him and the people of Lexington, and to draw back with careful hand the curtain from the sacred shrine of his domestic life. The same personal devotion which went out to him from the hearts of his soldiery was displayed by the residents of the college town. Their intercourse was of the most cordial and agreeable character. The negroes manifested for him on all occasions the most profound respect. When he approached, either walking or mounted on his famous horse Traveller, they would stop, bow politely, and stand until he had passed. He never failed to acknowledge their salutes with kind and dignified courtesy.

All the children knew and loved him, and felt no hesitation in approaching. A pleasant incident is related of Virginia Lee Letcher, his god-daughter, and her baby-sister, Fannie. Jennie had been followed by her persistent sister down the road, and all the coaxing and commanding of the six-year-old failed to make the younger turn home and leave her to continue her walk without company. Fannie had sat down by the roadside to pout, when General Lee came riding along. Jennie at once appealed to him: "General Lee, won't you make this child go home to her mother?" The general immediately rode over to the refractory child, leaned over from his saddle, and drew her up into his lap. There she sat in royal contentment, and was thus grandly escorted home. When Mrs. Letcher inquired of Jennie why she had given General Lee so much trouble, she received the naïve reply: "I couldn't make Fan go home, and I thought he could do anything." This delicious episode is yet remembered among Lexington people, though the veracious chronicler may have to pause in doubt between the introduction of the horseback ride and the variorum account which makes the occurrence pedestrian.

There was a child at Lexington who was accustomed to clamber up by the side of General Lee at the college-chapel exercises, and who was so kindly treated that whenever he saw his distinguished friend he straightway assumed a position beside him. At the college commencement the little fellow glided from his mother's side and quietly stole up to the platform. Soon he was nestled at the feet of the dignified president and resting his head confidingly upon the knees of his chosen patron. General Lee tenderly remained without moving, preferring to suffer from the constrained position rather than disturb the innocent slumberer. The youth has grown up into the Rev. Mr. Jones, a Baptist minister.

Circus-day was an event to the children of Lexington. They flocked around General Lee, and he was their escort by wholesale. He sat in the midst of them upon the boards of the tent, and it would have been difficult to estimate the relative amounts of enjoyment derived by him and his little guests.

In 1867, in company with his daughter Mildred, he rode on horseback to the Peaks of Otter, fifty miles from Lexington. At a ferry on the route the boatman chanced to be an old soldier. When the usual charge was tendered the rough mountaineer's eyes filled with tears, and he shook his head while saying, "I could not take pay from you, Master Robert: I have followed you in many a battle."

As father and daughter rode on a sudden shower came down upon them, and they galloped up to a log hut by the roadside, and without ceremony sought shelter. The poor woman of the house did not view the intrusion with cordiality. Her floors were scrupulously clean and every footprint was an offence. On the wall were suspended rudely-colored portraits of Lee, Jackson, and Davis. When the storm abated the general stepped out to bring up the horses. In his momentary absence Miss Mildred gently intimated that the unceremonious caller was the original of one of the portraits. The woman was transfixed with astonishment, and, throwing up her hands, exclaimed, "Lord bless my soul! That I should have lived to have General Lee in my house!" When the general returned her gratitude knew no bounds, and every

General Lee and the Ferryman. Page 462.

attention was lavished upon the travellers. The opportunity of this long ride was taken to visit Mr. Buford, in whose house Mrs. Lee had found refuge on several occasions during the war.

General Lee's domestic life was noble in its purity, admirable in its loving indulgences and devotion, and happy in all the family pleasures that rule in refined homes. When one reflects upon the military qualities which won him rank as a ruler of men, his quiet home life, rich in all the affections, stands in admirable though striking antithesis; and yet the contrast disappears when his whole consistent career is passed in review. As a son his attachment to his mother knew no bounds. His affection for his wife was, if possible, even stronger. In social and domestic intercourse he was not the cold and austere man he appeared in the crisis of battle. No man more enjoyed quiet humor. In the home circle he was genial, captivating, and as unaffected in his ways as a child. He entered heartily into all the domestic rounds of amusement, and contributed by many little inventions to the enjoyment of guests. His children were fond of pets, and he indulged all their innocent propensities.

His wife had become a confirmed invalid, and to her he gave devoted attention. He spent much of his leisure time in her company, cheering her spirits by his conversation while he wheeled her invalid chair about.

A few of his family letters will disclose the mutual ties of affection and confidence which bound the members together. In October, 1867, he writes R. E. Lee, Jr.: "I am clear for your marriage, if you select a good wife. Otherwise, you had better remain as you are for a time. An improvident or uncongenial woman is worse than the *minks*."*

With what fatherly solicitude he watched over and counselled his children is admirably shown by this farmer's letter he pens his son in the spring of 1868:

"I am sorry to learn from your letter of the 1st that the winter has been so hard on your wheat. I hope, however, the present good weather is shedding its influence upon it, and

* The chief pest of the Virginia farmer is the *mink*.

that it will turn out better than it promises. You must take a lesson from the past season. What you do cultivate, do well. Improve and prepare your land in the best manner. Your labor will be less and your profits more. Your flat lands were always uncertain in wet winters. The uplands were more sure. . . . . .

"A farmer's motto should be ' Toil and trust.' I am glad you have got your lime and sown oats and clover. Do you use the drill or sow broadcast? I rode out the other day to Mr. A. C——'s, and went into the field where he was ploughing. I took great pleasure in following his ploughs around the circuit. He had four in operation. Three of them were held by his former comrades in the army, who are regularly employed by him, and much, he says, to his satisfaction and profit. People have got to work now. It is creditable to them to do so—their bodies and their minds are benefited by it, and those who can and will, will be advanced by it."

A letter to his eldest son, G. W. Custis Lee, written at an earlier period of his life, is so full of aphoristic wisdom and breathes such a high sense of duty and honor that we cannot refrain from introducing an extract from it here:

"You must study to be frank with the world: frankness is the child of honesty and courage. Say just what you mean to do on every occasion, and take it for granted you mean to do right. If a friend asks a favor, you should grant it if it is reasonable; if not, tell him plainly why you cannot: you will wrong him and wrong yourself by equivocation of any kind. Never do a wrong thing to make a friend or keep one; the man who requires you to do so is dearly purchased at a sacrifice. Deal kindly but firmly with all your classmates; you will find it the policy which wears best. Above all, do not appear to others what you are not. If you have any fault to find with any one, tell him, not others, of what you complain; there is no more dangerous experiment than that of undertaking to be one thing before a man's face and another behind his back. We should live, act, and say nothing to the injury of any one. It is not only better as a matter of principle, but it is the path of peace and honor.

"In regard to duty, let me, in conclusion of this hasty letter, inform you that nearly a hundred years ago there was a day of remarkable gloom and darkness, still known as 'the Dark Day' —a day when the light of the sun was slowly extinguished as if by an eclipse. The legislature of Connecticut was in session, and as its members saw the unexpected and unaccountable darkness coming on they shared in the general awe and terror. It was supposed by many that the Last Day, the day of judgment, had come. Some one, in the consternation of the hour, moved an adjournment. Then there arose an old Puritan legislator, Davenport of Stamford, and said that if the Last Day had come he desired to be found at his place doing his duty, and therefore moved that candles be brought in, so that the House could proceed with its duty. There was quietness in that man's mind—the quietness of heavenly wisdom and inflexible willingness to obey present duty. Duty, then, is the sublimest word in our language. Do your duty in all things, like the old Puritan. You cannot do more—you should never wish to do less. Never let me and your mother wear one gray hair for any lack of duty on your part."

In the light which letters like these shed around the man the perfect domesticity of his nature appears. All the tests of son, husband, and father he endures. He thus guides a daughter's mind:

"LEXINGTON, 21st Dec., 1867.

"MY DEAREST LIFE: I was glad to learn through your letter that you were well and happy. I was pleased to find, too, that while enjoying the kindness of your friends we were not forgotten. Experience will teach you that, notwithstanding all appearances to the contrary, you will never receive such love as is felt for you by your father and mother: *that* lives through absence, difficulties, and times. I hope you will find time to read and improve your mind. Read history and works of truth—not novels and romances. Get correct views of life, and learn to see the world in its true light.

"We are getting on in the usual way. Agnes takes good care of us, and is always thoughtful and attentive. It is very cold.   The ground is covered with six inches of snow, and the mountains, as far as the eye can reach, elevate their white crests as monuments of winter.   I must leave to your sisters a description of all the gayeties, and also an account of the 'Reading Club.'   As far as I can judge, it is a great institution for the discussion of apples and chestnuts, but is quite innocent of the pleasures of literature.

"Our feline companions are flourishing.   Young Baxter is growing in gracefulness and favor, and gives cat-like evidences of future worth.   He indulges in the fashionable color of 'moonlight on the lake '—apparently a dingy hue of the kitchen— and is strictly aristocratic in appearance and conduct.   Tom, surnamed the 'Nipper' from the manner in which he slaughters our enemies the rats and mice, is admired for his gravity and sobriety, as well as his strict attention to the pursuits of his race.   They both feel your absence sorely.   Traveller and Custis are both well, and pursue their usual dignified gait and habits, not led away by the frivolous entertainments of lectures and concerts. . . . .

"Think always of your father, who loves you dearly.
                                                "R. E. LEE."

The genial humor of this fatherly letter was a marked feature of General Lee's character.   The relaxation from the dignity of outer life, mistaken for austerity by so many, is thus happily illustrated in the inner home circle.

A further insight into his character, as it was exemplified within the precincts of his home, is afforded by a visit so admirably recounted in the unaffected description of the lady visitor herself that we give it without abridgment:

"In the summer of 1866, General Lee and his family went for some weeks to the Rockbridge Baths, leaving the house and garden in charge of their excellent servant Caroline, who had come with them from Powhatan county.   The vegetables were very abundant and fine, and Mrs. Lee greatly desired to have the tomatoes canned and made into catsup.   As Caroline was not willing to undertake the work alone, Mrs. Lee asked me to spend a day in overlooking and directing the operation;

which I was glad to do. At the time appointed I went over to the house, expecting to spend a quiet but busy and pleasant day. The kettle was boiling, the tomatoes in great quantities ready for paring, and the cans standing ready to be filled. Several hours passed, and by half-past twelve good progress had been made toward filling some eight or ten half-gallon cans. Suddenly a step was heard on the porch upon which the kitchen opened, and before we could turn round General Lee walked in. He had ridden up from the baths to attend to some important letters, and, knowing that the house was closed except on that side, had come in that way.

"He greeted us both most kindly, but was much surprised to see me in the kitchen. When he learned how matters stood, he became anxious to know what preparations had been made for dinner for me. Some broiled ham and eggs, with bread and butter, were what Caroline had suggested, and with these I would have been more than satisfied; but the general would not hear of so simple a bill of fare. He ordered coffee, and asked if some fruit or cake could not be found. Neither of these dainties being on hand, and I assuring him that the dinner provided was ample if he could find satisfaction in it, he agreed that we should dine together. When the table was laid neither knives, forks, nor spoons could be found, everything having been carefully locked up and the keys put away.

"His large camp-chest, used during the Mexican War and also during the four years of our war, stood in the dining-room, and when the fruitless search was over the general asked if I would object to the use of the knives, forks, and spoons which for so many years had been kept there and used by him. I assured him the meal would be vastly more enjoyable with these than with any others; and when he had let me inspect the chest, he handling and explaining everything, we sat down at the table. He was as charming and as anxious to consult my comfort and pleasure as if I had been a queen. When the dishes were removed he fancied that the dinner was scarcely sufficient for one who, he thought, had been occupied, and would be constantly during the afternoon; so he insisted upon searching the pantry for something in the way of sweetmeats, and soon found two jars, from one of which he produced some dried ginger, and from the other some delicious peach chips. No amount of begging could induce him to taste either, and I enjoyed the little dessert more than I can tell as he sat by chatting brightly and cutting the ginger in bits for me, while Caroline leisurely ate her own dinner and made ready for our afternoon's work.

"We sat in the parlor, the general reading and commenting on some of the many letters which daily came to him. Some amused him very much, and others he was very grave over. One, I remember, was from a lady asking him to find and send her a little Confederate orphan girl. She was to be of a certain age, a certain size, beautiful, a blonde, of gentle birth, interesting, with no vices, no oddities, and never to be molested by her relatives! Another was from the head of a convent in Wheeling offering to educate some ten or twelve Confederate orphan girls free of all charge, but upon condition that they became Romanists. This, I recollect, he said he could not agree to.

"When Caroline came to call me he made me promise not to overtax my strength and to rest before returning home. Several times during the evening he came into the kitchen to superintend, as he laughingly said, but really to see that I was not doing more than my share of the work; and nobody could have been more interested than he was in the proper seasoning for tomato catsup. When the tops had been soldered on the cans by the tinner, and Caroline had promised to put them safely away, I left her to put the corks in the bottles of catsup, and went into Mrs. Lee's room to rest a short time. The general came from his little study and insisted upon my going there to sit, as I did not care to lie down, and, putting aside his writing, he talked as he had done at dinner, in his own beautiful, genial way, making me feel perfectly at home.

"I remember his taking up a picture of his birthplace and telling me some little anecdotes of his boyhood. When I arose to come away he thanked me, and showed as much concern lest I should be over-fatigued by my day's work as if I had done something extraordinary. The remembrance of this day spent with General Lee in his own house has been, and ever will be, greatly treasured by me, and there are many people who will, I feel sure, enjoy this little glimpse of the great soldier at home. Unfortunately, the tomatoes upon which we had bestowed ,so much care were never used by the family. Caroline put the cans into an unlocked safe on the back porch, and that very night they were all stolen. The catsup proved very nice.

"About two years after this I went over one morning in July with a young friend from Baltimore to call on Mrs. Lee. As we entered the house we could see through the back door several suits of uniform, blue and gray, with one or two Mexican blankets, hanging upon a line in the yard. We were taken into Mrs. Lee's room, and finding the general there I asked if the moths had got into his trunks. He replied that they had, and everything was being aired and inspected. He left the room a moment, and when he returned he brought a most beautiful Mexican blanket, woven in imitation of the Mexican flag and the gift of the women of the city of Mexico. This he prized most highly. After admiring and examining it carefully, we comforted him by the assurance that it was uninjured. Mrs. Lee asked him to show my friend some of the beautiful gifts received by him during the war, and which were then lying about his room. He took us into his study, where we saw, among other things, some beautiful gauntlets sent from England, and which had never been worn. On the table was a splendid sword in its scabbard. This I drew out, and, finding on one or both sides an inscription in French, asked for some explanation. He simply said it was sent from France, but was too fine for use, and then he put it aside, not wishing us to see how beautiful and laudatory the inscription was. He then took up another sword, plain and dull in appearance as compared with the other. This he showed with great pride. It was the sword presented to General Washington during or after the Revolutionary War, afterward given to the Patent Office by Mr. Custis, and after the Mexican War presented to General (Colonel) Lee by another Congress. This he kept with him during our war.

"With some little difficulty we induced him to give the

history of a handsome pair of silver spurs sent from Maryland, also of a beautiful yellow silk scarf worn once or twice on grand reviews. While he was busy with Miss B——, I espied on a small trunk, under a pile of clothes, a blue cloth saddle-blanket with some lettering in gold braid in the corners. Going over to it, I carefully drew it out, thereby turning completely over on the floor the clean clothes. His keen eyes immediately saw the mischief done, and with the exclamation, 'Oh, my clean clothes!' he stepped across the room and rescued the freshly-laundried garments. I was much confused and dismayed by my great awkwardness, but he most courteously and kindly assured me that they were unsoiled, at the same time placing them on the bed. The saddle-blanket proved to be a gorgeous affair, made and sent by some kind lady with the request that he would use it. This he had never done. In each corner were the words in rich gold thread, 'Honor to the brave!' He told us he had sent her word that until these were picked out he had no more right to use it than the poorest private who faithfully did his duty."

All the sentiments embalmed in his home letters, and all the memories of his home life cherished by his friends, combine to tell to the world the manner of man General Lee was in the society of his wife and children. Artless, sympathetic, solicitous, devoted, indulgent, fond of teasing, are descriptive terms whose accuracy must appear to all in the side-lights thrown upon the private circle.

CHAPTER XXV.

DEATH AND MEMORIAL CEREMONIES.

General Lee's Failing Health.—The Fatal Attack.—His Death.—Colonel Johnston's
Testimony.—Mrs. Lee's Description of the Final Illness.—Effect of the News upon
the South.—Procession to the Chapel.—Religious Observances.—The Funeral Ceremonies.—Great Meeting at Richmond.—Extracts from Addresses of Jefferson Davis,
General Gordon, and Colonel Withers.—Testimony of Reverdy Johnson.—Letter
from General Scott.—General Preston's Remarks.—The Lee Memorial Association.
—The Valentine Recumbent Statue.—Ceremonies of its Reception.—Description
of Statue and Chamber.—General Lee as a Christian.—His Feeling toward the
North.—Selected Thoughts.—A Captain Rebuked.

IN the last year of General Lee's life his friends experienced
many fluctuations of hope and despair respecting his health.
In the arduous campaign of 1863 he had contracted a severe
sore throat, the sequence of which was rheumatism of the heart-
sac. The malady was intermittent, and so infrequently did he
complain that few ever thought that his constitution was impaired. But in October, 1869, he was attacked by inflamma-
tion of the heart-sac, associated with rheumatism of the body.
His friends persuaded him in the early spring of 1870 to spend
six weeks in Florida and Georgia. He returned with more
elated spirits, for his reception among old friends had been so
cordial as to exorcise depression, though his ailment was not
eradicated. Shortly afterward, feeling the steady advances of
the disease, he began to express the belief that he had but a
short time to remain upon this earth, and wished to resign from
the presidency of the college, being conscious that his strength
was inadequate to the performance of its duties. To this the
faculty would not consent. His mere presence exerted an influence that could not be otherwise supplied.

In the summer he remained a few weeks at the Virginia Hot
Springs, and was somewhat benefited. When the fall session

began he evinced an energy in the discharge of his college duties that deluded many into the fond hope that a new lease of life had been vouchsafed him. There was a manifestation of interest in affairs and an elation which are so often but the indications of an approaching end. The college year had continued only a few days when pleasing hope and all the exhilaration that was infused through the academic halls departed.

Upon Wednesday morning, September 28, 1870, General Lee was promptly at his desk, and gave his correspondence and other official matters the usual attention. After dinner, at four o'clock, there was a meeting of the vestry of Grace (Episcopal) Church, which he attended. A steady rain was falling and the air was quite chilly. (This rain poured down for several days and caused a flood that is yet remembered for its unusual destruction.) He presided at the meeting, sitting in the cold and damp church with only his military cloak loosely wrapped about him. The discussion over the rebuilding of the church and the increase of the rector's salary was protracted until after seven o'clock. One of his acts at this meeting was characteristic of him. When a deficit was announced as still existing in the subscriptions for the minister's salary, General Lee promptly assumed payment of the balance, though it was beyond any proportionate amount justly due from him.

Tea was waiting for him when he returned home. He approached the table, and stood as if to invoke grace. His family watched in terrible anxiety the mute lips and the look that came upon his face. He could not speak. Quietly he sat down in his chair. His expression told that he comprehended the functional failure. There was no paralysis of sensation or motion, no swoon, yet his weakness was marked. Drs. H. T. Barton and R. L. Madison were called in and administered the usual restoratives. When carried to his bed he gave silent indication of his resignation to the summons. He was treated for venous congestion, and the remedies appeared to produce favorable results. But there was no buoyancy of hope in the watchers by his side, and no expectation of recovery in his own mind. He knew he had been mortally stricken, and his own composed waiting for the end was too firm in its decision to be influenced by momentary symptoms of improvement.

The seeming rally from the initial shock grew perceptibly greater until October 10th. But on the afternoon of that day his pulse became accelerated and his hurried breathing betokened a serious relapse. At midnight a chill of exhaustion supervened, and the intelligence of his critical condition was broken to his family. Through the next day he rapidly sank, and his dissolution was felt to be imminent at any hour. A few moments after nine on the morning of the 12th he calmly breathed his last.

Colonel William Preston Johnston, who watched almost constantly at his bedside, has thus eloquently and touchingly portrayed the sad scenes attendant upon his death:

"General Lee's closing hours were consonant with his noble and disciplined life. Never was more beautifully displayed how a long and severe education of mind and character enables the soul to pass with equal step through this supreme ordeal—never did the habits and qualities of a lifetime, solemnly gathered into a few last sad hours, more grandly maintain themselves amid the gloom and shadow of approaching death. The reticence, the self-contained composure, the obedience to proper authority, the magnanimity, and the Christian meekness that marked all his actions still preserved their sway, in spite of the inroads of disease and the creeping lethargy that weighed down his faculties.

"As the old hero lay in the darkened room or with the lamp and hearth-fire casting shadows upon his calm, noble front, all the massive grandeur of his form and face and brow remained, and death seemed to lose its terrors and to borrow a grace and dignity in sublime keeping with the life that was ebbing away. The great mind sank to its last repose almost with the equal poise of health. The few broken utterances that evinced at times a wandering intellect were spoken under the influence of the remedies administered; but as long as consciousness lasted there was evidence that all the high controlling influences of his whole life still ruled; and even when stupor was laying its cold hand on the intellectual perceptions, the moral

nature, with its complete orb of duties and affections, still
asserted itself. A Southern poet has celebrated in song those
last significant words, 'Strike the tent!' and a thousand voices
were raised to give meaning to the uncertain sound when the
dying man said, with emphasis, 'Tell Hill he *must* come up.'
These sentences serve to show most touchingly through what
fields the imagination was passing; but generally his words,
though few, were coherent, and for the most part his silence
was unbroken."

His widow, in a letter to an intimate friend, told the sad
story of his last hours, and dwelt with sustaining trust upon
their perfect Christian sublimity: "My husband came in. We
had been waiting tea for him, and I remarked, 'You have kept
us waiting a long time. Where have you been?' He did not
reply, but stood up as if to say grace. Yet no word proceeded
from his lips, and he sat down in his chair perfectly upright
and with a sublime air of resignation on his countenance,
and did not attempt a reply to our inquiries. That look was
never to be forgotten, and I have no doubt he felt that his hour
had come; for, though he submitted to the doctors, who were
immediately summoned, and who had not even reached their
homes from the same vestry-meeting, yet his whole demeanor
during his illness showed one who had taken leave of earth.
He never smiled, and rarely attempted to speak, except in his
dreams, and then he wandered to those dreadful battlefields.
Once, when Agnes urged him to take some medicine, which
he always did with reluctance, he looked at her and said, 'It is
no use.' But afterward he took it. When he became so much
better the doctor said, 'You must soon get out and ride your
favorite gray.' He shook his head most emphatically and
looked upward. He slept a great deal, but knew us all,
greeted us with a kindly pressure of the hand, and loved to
have us around him. For the last forty-eight hours he seemed
quite insensible of our presence. He breathed more heavily,
and at last gently sank to rest with one deep-drawn sigh. And
oh, what a glorious rest was in store for him!"

The death of General Lee was solemnly proclaimed to the
residents of Lexington by the tolling of bells. With common

accord all business was suspended. Tokens of mourning appeared on all buildings. The schools were closed and the college exercises ceased. The grief manifested by the people was profound. The little children whom he had cherished, and who had entertained for him a reverential love, wept over the absence of one whose death in the full measure of its bereavement they scarce understood. Women were affected to tears, and strong men turned aside to repress their emotion. It was a personal loss to them. In the Southern States his death was deplored as a calamity. Citizens, societies, and all associations of men met in some manner of assemblage and recorded their sense of the sad event. Resolutions of condolence and respect were adopted. Legislatures paused in their proceedings to add to the tokens of grief. All professions, all callings in mercantile life, were represented in the tributes. Rarely has sorrow been so universal, and seldom has genuine affection entered so deeply into the mourning over the death of a public benefactor.

On the 14th of October the remains of the deceased hero were conveyed to the college chapel, where they lay in state until the hour of the final obsequies upon the next day. The procession which moved from the residence was formed under Prof. J. J. White as chief marshal, with assistants appointed by the students. The escort of honor was composed of Confederate soldiers. Following this guard and preceding the hearse came the clergy. The pall-bearers were twelve, representing the trustees, faculty, and students of Washington College, the authorities of the Virginia Military Institute, the soldiers of the Confederate army, and the citizens of the college town. Just in the rear of the hearse two old soldiers led Traveller, the celebrated war-horse, crape emblems appearing upon saddle and bridle. Then followed in the long cortége the college authorities, students, and citizens. When the casket was rested upon the dais within the chapel the procession filed slowly past, and each member looked for the last time upon the uncovered features of the dead. The body was attired in simple black. About the coffin rested floral emblems, the profuse tributes of loving hearts. Until the hour of interment upon Saturday a student guard of honor paced with sentinel care about the dais.

Before the conveyance of the remains to the chapel, funeral exercises had been held of a simple character. Citizens and students made up the saddened congregation which gathered within the chapel-walls. Rev. Dr. Pendleton read from Psalm 27 : 8–11 and 28–40, and made application of its teachings to the life and death of General Lee. The minister was rarely endowed for his·sorrowful mission. For forty-five years he had been associated with Lee as fellow-student, comrade-in-arms, and pastor. He spoke with the full equipment of knowledge and the devotion of friendship, and his tribute to the undeviating rectitude, the consistency of Christian character, that ruled the life-career of the distinguished dead was the eloquent utterance of heartfelt truths. In the beautiful and apposite words of the psalm, "The law of God was in his heart; therefore did none of his steps slide;" "Mark the perfect man and behold the upright, for the end of that man is peace." Dr. White, the pastor of Stonewall Jackson, and Rev. John William Jones, a chaplain in the Army of Northern Virginia, and intimately connected with General Lee, also made brief remarks upon the eminent qualities of the dead.

The day of the funeral found the sky unclouded. The air was bracing. The roads were almost unfit for travel, the effects of the recent freshet not having disappeared. But sorrowing people braved the discomforts. The Virginia Legislature sent a delegation, and various towns in the Commonwealth were represented. It had been determined to make the funeral rites and observances rigorously plain, for the wishes of the deceased, though they had not been expressed in words, were felt by all to be opposed to display. The whole manner of General Lee had given unerring evidence of his desire in this respect, and plainness was in perfect keeping with his lack of ostentation. All the ceremonies were marked by simple dignity.

The procession was formed at ten o'clock on Saturday morning on the college campus. The escort of honor was composed of officers and soldiers of the Confederate army. It moved solemnly onward through the streets of Lexington, being joined at various points by the visiting delegations. The band of the Virginia Military Institute played a solemn dirge, bells tolled, and minute-guns were fired. But there was no attempt at display. No flag was to be seen in the long column. Buildings were festooned with black, and above them the flags were at half-staff. The Virginia Military Institute was notably draped with the emblems of grief. When the procession reached the chapel upon its return, the students and cadets, numbering about six hundred and fifty, marched through the chapel, past the remains, making their exit at an opposite doorway. The procession then filed into the church. Within the space allotted for the members of General Lee's family there sat also his attending physicians, Drs. Barton and Madison, and Colonels W. H. Taylor and C. S. Venable, who had been members of his staff. Upon the platform were seated the clergy and the faculties of the college and the institute.

No sermon was preached. With exquisite voice Rev. Dr. Pendleton read the burial service of the Episcopal Church. At its conclusion the casket was removed to the brick vault prepared for it within the college-chapel area. The top of the vault was level with the floor of the library. Upon its marble capping was the inscription,

"ROBERT EDWARD LEE,

Born January 19, 1807;

Died October 12, 1870."

The concluding services were conducted by the chaplain from the bank on the southern side of the chapel, in front of the vault. The hymn,

"How firm a foundation, ye saints of the Lord,"

was sung by the assemblage after the coffin had been lowered into the vault. Thus in all simplicity were conducted the obsequies of the distinguished dead. There was not the pageantry of rank nor the formal and ostentatious accompaniments of less sincere sorrow. In all that great congregation each individual was present to testify the personal sorrow felt for one whose greatness had never obliterated those qualities which, with admiration, win also affection.

There were meetings of Confederate soldiers throughout the South—at New Orleans, Mobile, Savannah, Memphis, in other cities, and in many towns—to express the universal regret felt at the untimely demise of the great warrior. At Richmond, on November 3d, a monster assemblage of his old soldiers gathered in obedience to a call from General Jubal A. Early, the senior in rank of all the officers of the Army of Northern Virginia. There was no distinction of rank observed in the invitation to this meeting. It included officers and privates of the army surrendered at Appomattox, men of other Confederate armies, and all the survivors of the navy. The immediate object was to secure concerted action in reference to the memorial association already inaugurated at Lexington.

Those who responded to this call were fully representative of military ranks. General and private mingled in committee, all rank forgotten and levelled in the common sorrow. General Early was temporary chairman. The ex-President of the Confederacy, Jefferson Davis, was made the president. He was greeted with every manifestation of respect when he came forward to address the meeting. One extract may possess interest as bearing upon the single point of the relations subsisting between General Lee and Mr. Davis during the protracted struggle:

"Robert E. Lee was my associate and friend in the Military Academy, and we were friends until the hour of his death. We were associates and friends when he was a soldier and I a Congressman, and associates and friends when he led the armies of the Confederacy and I held a civil office, and therefore I may claim to speak as one who knew him. In the many sad scenes and perilous circumstances through which we passed together our conferences were frequent and full, yet never was there an occasion on which there was not entire harmony of purpose and accordance as to means. If ever there was difference of opinion, it was dissipated by discussion, and harmony was the result. I repeat, we never disagreed, and I may add that I never in my life saw in him the slightest tendency to self-seeking. It was not his to make a record, it was not his to shift blame to other shoulders; but it was his, with an eye fixed upon the welfare of his country, never faltering, to follow the line of duty to the end. His was the heart that braved every difficulty: his was the mind that wrought victory out of defeat.''

Tributes were paid to the dead chieftain by General John S. Preston of South Carolina, General John B. Gordon of Georgia, Colonel Charles Marshall of Virginia, Ex-Governor Henry A. Wise of Virginia, Colonel Wm. Preston Johnston (son of Albert Sidney Johnston), and Ex-Senator Robert E. Withers of Virginia.

General Gordon's address was marked for its felicity of expression and affectionate warmth. He thus alluded in eloquent terms to one characteristic of General Lee:

"General Lee is known to the world only as a military man, but it is easy to divine from his history how mindful of all just authority, how observant of all constitutional restrictions, would have been his career as a civilian. When, near the conclusion of the war, darkness was thickening about the falling fortunes of the Confederacy, when its very life was in the sword of Lee, it was my proud privilege to note with special admiration the modest demeanor, the manly decorum, and the respectful homage which marked all his intercourse with the constituted authorities of his country. Clothed with all power, he hid its every symbol behind a genial modesty, and refused to exert it save in obedience to law. And even in his triumphant entry into the territory of the enemy, so regardful was he of civilized warfare that the observance of his general orders as to private property and private rights left the line of his march marked and marred by no devastated fields, charred ruins, or desolated homes.''

Colonel Withers dwelt upon the mutual affection which controlled the hearts of General Lee and his men. "And why was this the predominant sentiment of his soldiery?" he asked. "The answer is obvious: Because he loved his men. His military achievements may have been rivalled, possibly surpassed, by other great commanders. Alexander, Marlborough, Wellington, Napoleon, each and all excited the admiration, enjoyed

the confidence, and aroused the enthusiasm of their soldiers;
but none of these were loved as Lee was loved. They considered their soldiers as mere machines prepared to perform a
certain part in the great drama of the battlefield. They regarded not the question of human life as a controlling element
in their calculations: with unmoved eye and unquickened pulse
they hurled their solid columns against the very face of destruction without reck or care for the destruction of life involved.

"But General Lee never forgot that his men were fellow-
beings as well as soldiers. He cared for them with parental
solicitude, nor ever relaxed in his efforts to promote their comfort and protect their lives. A striking exemplification of this
trait can be found in the fact that it was his constant habit to
turn over to the sick and wounded soldiers in the hospital such
delicate viands as the partiality of friends furnished for his personal consumption, preferring for himself the plain fare of the
camp that his sick soldiers might enjoy the unwonted luxuries.
These facts were well known throughout the army, and hence
his soldiery, though often ragged and emaciated, though suffering from privations and cold and nakedness, never faltered in
their devotion nor abated one tittle of their love for him. They
knew it was not his fault."

Colonel Charles S. Venable also paid a glowing tribute. The
resolutions presented by him were cordially approved by the
great meeting.

At a memorial meeting held in Baltimore, Hon. Reverdy
Johnson joined in the general eulogy of the dead hero, with
whom it had been his good fortune to be personally acquainted
for many years. General Scott had more than once remarked
in the presence of the speaker that his success in Mexico was
largely due to the skill, valor, and undaunted energy of Robert
E. Lee, and had stated his purpose to recommend him as his
successor in the chief command of the army. Much as Scott
regretted Lee's resignation in 1861, he never failed to say that
he was convinced that Lee had taken that step from an imperative sense of duty. The veteran general was somewhat con-
soled by the reflection that in the conduct of the war he would
have as his opponent a soldier worthy of every man's esteem,

and one who would never deviate from the strictest rules of civilized warfare. Mr. Johnson looked upon Robert E. Lee as worthy of all praise, peerless among men, and without an equal as a soldier. During the speaker's residence in England as representative of the United States at the court of Great Britain he had heard with delight the praise of Lee's character and ability from eminent soldiers and statesmen of that country. As one instance he referred to the praises bestowed upon the army order of June 26, 1863, issued during the campaign in Pennsylvania, in which Lee told his men not to forget that the honor of the army required them to observe the same humanity in the country of the enemy as in their own.

As confirmatory of the statement of General Scott's opinion of Lee may be consulted the following letter:

> "HEADQUARTERS OF THE ARMY,
> May 8, 1857.

"HON. J. B. FLOYD, SECRETARY OF WAR,

"SIR: I beg to ask that one of the vacant second lieutenantcies be given to W. H. F. Lee, son of Brevet Colonel R. E. Lee, at present on duty against the Comanches. I make this application mainly on the extraordinary merits of the father, the very best soldier that I ever saw in the field. But the son is himself a very remarkable youth, now about twenty, of a fine stature and constitution, a good linguist, a good mathematician, and about to graduate at Harvard University. He is also honorable and amiable, like his father, and dying to enter the army. I do not ask this commission as a favor, though if I had influence I should be happy to exert it in this case. My application is in the name of national justice, in part payment (and but a small part) of the debt due to the invaluable services of Colonel Lee.

"I have the honor to be, with high respect,
"Your obedient servant,
"WINFIELD SCOTT."

In addition to what has been said upon the subject of General Scott's high appreciation of Lee as a soldier, we cannot desist from giving one further testimony to the same effect in consideration of the value of Scott's opinion in this particular and his excellent opportunities of knowing Lee's character and ability. In his memorial address at Louisville, General Preston related a conversation he had held with General Scott long before the Civil War, in which the latter declared that Lee was the greatest living soldier in America, and added with emphasis, "I tell you that if I were on my death-bed to-morrow, and the President of the United States should tell me that a great battle was to be fought for the liberty or slavery of the country, and he asked my judgment as to the ability of a commander, I would say with my dying breath, 'Let it be Robert E. Lee.'"

The meeting at Richmond on November 3d and 4th resulted in the formation of the Association of the Army of Northern Virginia, and the memorial resolutions authorized the erection of a monument at Richmond. That worthy purpose has not yet been performed, though the subscriptions have reached almost the amount of $100.000.

Immediately after the funeral, however, the soldiers present met at Lexington and took the initial steps toward marking the resting-place of the departed general by an appropriate monument. That their purpose might be the better achieved, an act of incorporation was obtained from the Virginia Legislature in January, 1871, for "The Lee Memorial Association." General John C. Breckenridge of Kentucky, the last Secretary of War of the Confederate States, was the president. After the name of Washington College had been changed to that of Washington and Lee University, the executive committee determined to locate the mausoleum at Lexington and to attach it to the college chapel. The association confided the statuary-work to the distinguished Virginia sculptor Edward V. Valentine, who in the spring of 1870 had modelled a bust of General Lee, the execution of which had been highly commended. His model for the proposed sarcophagus was readily accepted, Mrs. Lee having expressed a preference for his design. It was a recumbent figure after the school of Rauch's figure of Louise of Prussia in the mausoleum at Charlottenburg. The construction of the mausoleum was completed under the supervision of J. Crawford Neilson of Baltimore, who gave his services as a labor of love and a tribute to the memory of Lee.

The exquisite production of Valentine was completed in his studio at Richmond. Its transportation from that city to Lexington in April, 1875, was made in itself to constitute an event in the series of honors which the people seemed ever anxious to pay to the memory of Lee. A student escort of honor accompanied it, and it was conveyed and received with appropriate ceremonies. A procession marched with it to the dépôt at Richmond through the inclemency of a storm. The engine which conveyed the chiselled block of marble was draped. Along the route there was continued exhibition of reverential remembrance. On reaching the university grounds the statue was presented by Mr. J. T. E. Thornhill of the escort, and accepted on behalf of the Lee Memorial Association by Governor Letcher. General Preston followed in a beautiful address as the representative of Washington and Lee University. The cornerstone of the mausoleum was laid November 29, 1878, General Joseph E. Johnston and Hon. J. Randolph Tucker conducting the ceremonies.

The mausoleum rests upon a crypt of heavy masonry containing repositories for a score of burial-caskets, it being intended as a vault for all the Lee family. The exterior is ordinary brick. The interior or monumental chamber is divided by an anteroom from the chapel.

The beautiful creation in marble was unveiled June 28, 1883, with imposing ceremonies and in the presence of an immense assemblage. A touching episode preliminary to the unveiling was the march of the procession to the cemetery and the laying of immortelles upon the graves of distinguished Confederate dead, while at the head of Stonewall Jackson's grave was placed a bronze memorial tablet. The oration of the day was delivered by John W. Daniel, the present United States Senator elect. It elicited praise for its wonderful eloquence from the press of the whole country, but words could not portray the manner in which the auditors were affected by its inspired utterances. Father Ryan recited his famous poem, "The Sword of Lee." Then the multitude repaired to the chapel, and within the mausoleum Miss Julia Jackson, the daughter of General "Stonewall" Jackson, drew back the curtain from the exquisite marble figure.

Virginians entertain a feeling of pride not only that a memorial statue has been inaugurated to their honored chief, but also that this charming work of art is due to the hand of a native sculptor. The figure is of flawless white marble. General Lee is represented in uniform as sleeping upon a soldier's couch. One hand is upon his bosom and touches gently the drapery of his couch; the other lies by his side, resting upon his sword. The features and form are perfect. It is the majesty of repose, tranquil and graceful. The floor of the chamber in which it rests is tessellated in marble and tiles. The walls are of gray marble panels inserted in the dark pressed brick. There are receptacles for medallions in the walls, and upon one already placed is inscribed the name of Robert E. Lee, with the dates of his birth and death. The panels of the sarcophagus bear on one side the Lee coat of arms, and upon the other the armorial bearings of Virginia. The legend upon the panel at the foot repeats the name and dates: at the head a simple cross is carved.

In consonance with the funeral scenes to which this chapter has been devoted we may now allude particularly to General Lee's lofty conception of Christianity and his high ideal of religious duty. Upon his confirmation as a member of the Church, Bishop Johns said to him, "If you will be as faithful a soldier of the cross as you have been of your country, when your warfare is over I shall covet your crown."

He had chastened his spirit with the divine rod of forbearance. Forgiveness was a noble attribute. When a minister once denounced the North in terms of excessive bitterness, General Lee followed him to the door and said, "Doctor, there is a good old book which I read and you preach from which says, 'Love your enemies, bless them that curse you, do good to them that hate you, and pray for them which despitefully use you.' Do you think your remarks this evening were quite in the spirit of that teaching?" And he added, "I have fought against the people of the North because I believed they were

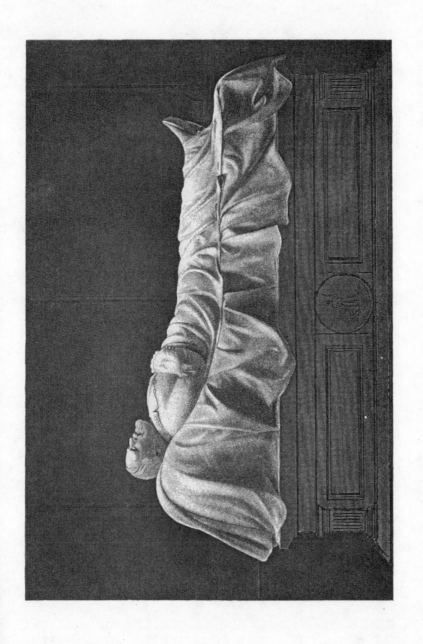

THE RECUMBENT STATUE.

BY VALENTINE

PLACED OVER THE TOMB OF GEN⁺ LEE AT LEXINGTON, VA.

Eng⁺ by H.B.Halls Sons, New York.

seeking to wrest from the South her dearest rights, but I have never cherished toward them bitter or vindictive feelings, and have never seen the day when I did not pray for them.''

Soon after the harsh Reconstruction acts had been passed, against honorable protest and argument even within the dominant circles of Congressional government, some Confederate friends in the presence of General Lee burst forth in strains of invective against the unrelenting spirit which presided over the enactment of such statutes. General Lee took from the table some manuscript pages of his father's *Life*, which he was then editing, and read these lines :

> "Learn from yon Orient shell to love thy foe,
> And store with pearls the hand that brings thee **woe**;
> Free, like yon rock, from base, vindictive pride,
> Emblaze with gems the wrist that rends thy side.
> Mark where yon tree rewards the stony shower
> With fruit nectarious or the balmy flower;
> All Nature cries aloud, Shall men do less
> Than love the smiter and the railer bless ?"

"These lines," said he, "were written in Arabia and by a Mohammedan, the poet of Shiraz, the immortal Hafiz; and ought not we, who profess to be governed by the principles of Christianity, to rise at least to the standard of this Mohammedan poet and learn to forgive our enemies ?''

General Lee had the habit of writing on small slips of paper on his desk such thoughts as might occur to him. From a number of these a few may be selected:

"Honesty in its widest sense is always admirable. The trite saying that 'Honesty is the best policy' has met with the just criticism that honesty is not policy. This seems to be true. The real honest man is honest from conviction of what is right, not from policy.''

"Those who oppose our purposes are not always to be regarded as our enemies. We usually think and act from our immediate surroundings. (See *Macaulay on Machiavelli*.)"

"The better rule is to judge our adversaries from their standpoint, not from ours.''

"God disposes. This ought to satisfy us.''

"Fame which does not result from good actions and achieve-ments for the good of the whole people is not to be desired. Nero had fame (or rather notoriety). Who envies him?"

"No man can be so important in the world that he needs not the good-will and approval of others."

"'Charity should begin at home.' So says ——. No, charity should have no beginning or ending."

The tolerance of General Lee for the religious faith of oth-ers was frequently illustrated. A Jewish soldier applied to his captain for permission to attend certain ceremonies at the synagogue at Richmond. The captain indorsed the request: "Disapproved: if such applications were granted the whole army would turn Jews or Shaking Quakers." When the docu-ment reached General Lee he wrote on it, "Approved, and respectfully returned to Captain ——, with the advice that he should always respect the religious views and feelings of others."

The Christian character of General Lee was one in which the tenderness, forgiveness, philanthropy, and purity of the real disciple of the true Christ conception were the ruling impulses, and not the haughty, austere self-satisfaction or the unrelenting, exacting creed of those who consider themselves the elect.

CHAPTER XXVI.

THE WORLD'S ESTIMATE.

Summary of Lee's Career.—His Character as a Soldier; as an Instructor.—Newspaper Comments.—The New York *World, Herald,* and *Citizen.*—Halifax *Morning Chronicle.*—Statement of Alexander H. Stephens.—Lee's Noble Aspect.—He Consents to Give up his Command.—Sent to West Virginia.—General Starke's Narration.—Chief of Staff to Mr. Davis.—Engineering Duty in the South.—Commander of the Army of Northern Virginia.—Roll-call of his Battles.—Swinton's Comment on the Army.—Resignation Correspondence.—Tribute of Philip Stanhope Worsley.—Concluding Poem.

THE biography of Robert E. Lee, the man whom future ages will undoubtedly name as the greatest military genius of the nineteenth century, has been given in the foregoing pages in all its stirring details, ending with a description of the well-merited honors which were paid to his memory after his death. This work has been a labor of love, and its termination is approached with regret, since we can never again hope to find so worthy a subject for our pen. Yet before bringing our work to an end there seem necessary some brief remarks upon the world's estimate of the dead hero, and a rapid review of his career and character as a fitting conclusion to the story of the great events of his life.

That the tone of this work has been eulogistic is freely admitted; yet it is not the eulogy of undue partiality, but that tribute of honor and respect which the honest writer involuntarily pays to the memory of a great man—one whom, like Washington, we may designate as "first in war, first in peace, and first in the hearts of his countrymen." Throughout his whole life this greatness was at every point evinced. As a boy his tenderness of demeanor to his invalid mother displayed the filial sentiment in a degree that has never been surpassed. As a West Point cadet indications of his future eminence as a soldier and a man became evident to his friends and associates. Never in his earlier

army career did he desire to evade the most irksome or monot-
onous duty.   He married happily, and in the long years of
home felicity no German ideal of domesticity transcends the
reality of his family relations.   He is affectionate, solicitous,
devoted.   The clouds of war lower over him, and in the
tumultuous doubts and dangers that assail men he follows
unhesitatingly, unfalteringly, the beacon of duty.   Allurements of rank and avoidance of disaster cannot beguile him
from heeding the dictates of his cherished principles.   Once
decided upon a course of action consistent with his beliefs
and ideas of right, there is no thought of recantation.   He
becomes without restraint and with earnest enthusiasm the
Confederate leader.   No greater wrong could be done his
memory, no more cruel perversion of the truth be made, than
to claim that during the civil strife duty and principle were
contending in Robert E. Lee's breast, and that duty merely
dominated.   The exact student of his loyal expressions and
of his avowed construction of the Federal Union will readily
discover the reconciliation between his acts and views.   He
fought against what to him was armed aggression upon the
constitutional rights of the South vouchsafed to it and to
the North by the inviolable prescriptions of the organic law
of the Union.

In that calamitous contest his genius and his prowess have
compelled the plaudits of the world.   His generalship was an
exhibition of military genius in which the whole nation feels a
lofty pride.   To remarkable powers as a leader he added those
qualities of self-abnegation, of moral grandeur, and of humane
solicitude which constitute the true ideal of manliness, and
the aggregate was a great military character, to find whose
equal we would need to select the noblest attributes from
many of the historic generals of the world.

When the convulsions of war subsided and peace spread
her broad wings over a reunited land, Robert E. Lee nobly
assumed a civic trust, and in the faithful execution of its
duties added still another laurel to his wreath of honor.   Sub-
missive to the decision of events, he sheathed his sword and
embraced the new career of instructing youth in the culture

and discipline which alone make worthy citizens. Yielding at last to the strain of years of physical exposure and mental anxiety, the hero with sublime resignation gave back his being to the great Creator, soothed by that unfaltering trust which had so long ennobled his life.

Such was, in brief, the career of Robert E. Lee—a noble career, in which intellectual and moral worth struggled for pre-eminence, or, rather, combining in harmonious relations in his well-rounded nature, made up a man who has had few peers upon the face of the earth.

As to the voluminous testimonials to his worth which flowed in from a thousand quarters upon the news of his death, we have no space to give them more than a brief reference, with some few extracts from their more striking remarks. The newspaper press of the North was full of praises of the deceased warrior, while from Europe came with no uncertain sound the eulogistic tones of those best fitted to judge of military ability and manly dignity and eminence.

The New York *World* speaks of his "strategic resources, inexhaustible patience, and calm determination," and says that "if the testimony of all honorable men who contended against the great Southern general agrees with the verdict of all competent foreign critics in awarding to him a place among the most eminent soldiers of history, the concord is not less absolute of all who knew the man in the private and personal aspects of his life as to his gentleness, his love of justice, his truth, and his elevation of soul."

From the long eulogium of the New York *Herald* we extract the following notably truthful passages:

"Never had mother a nobler son. In him the military genius of America was developed to a greater extent than ever before. In him all that was pure and lofty in mind and purpose found lodgment. Dignified without presumption, affable without familiarity, he united all those charms of manner which made him the idol of his friends and of his soldiers, and won for him the respect and admiration of the world. Even as in the days of his triumph glory did not intoxicate, so when the dark clouds swept over him adversity did not depress. From the hour that he surrendered his sword at Appomattox to the fatal autumn morning [of his death] he passed among men, noble in his quiet, simple dignity, displaying neither bitterness nor regret over the irrevocable past. He conquered us in misfortune by the grand manner in which he sustained himself, even as he dazzled us by his genius when the tramp of his soldiers resounded through the valleys of Virginia.

". . . . In person General Lee was a notably handsome man. He was tall of stature and admirably proportioned; his features were regular and most amiable in appearance; and in his manners he was courteous and dignified. In social life he was much admired. As a slaveholder he was beloved by his slaves for his kindness and consideration toward them. General Lee was also noted for his piety. He was an Episcopalian, and was a regular attendant at church. Having a perfect command over his temper, he was never seen angry, and his most intimate friends never heard him utter an oath. Indeed, it is doubtful if there are many men of the present generation who unite so many virtues and so few vices in each of themselves as did General Lee. He came nearer the ideal of a soldier and Christian general than any man we can think of, for he was a greater soldier than Havelock, and equally as devout a Christian. In his death our country has lost a son of whom she might well be proud, and of whose services she might have stood in need had he lived a few years longer, for we are certain that, had occasion required it, General Lee would have given to the United States the benefit of all his great talents."

John Mitchell, the Irish patriot, thus wrote of him in the New York *Citizen:*

"The highest head, the noblest and grandest character of our continent, the most conscientious, humane, and faithful soldier, the most chivalrous gentleman in this world, the best, the most superb sample of the American warrior, has fallen like a mighty tree in the forest; and men wonder, after the first shock of the news, to find that there is such a gap, such a blank in the world."

The Halifax *Morning Chronicle* in a lengthy review said of him:

"In every particular he possessed the requisites of a true soldier. He was brave; his whole military record and his lifelong scorn of danger alike bear testimony to his bravery. He was wise; his great successes against great odds and his almost constant anticipation of the enemy's movements were proofs of his wisdom. He was skilful; his forced marches and unexpected victories assert his skill. He was patient and unyielding; his weary struggle against the mighty armies of the North and his stern defence of Richmond will for ever preserve the memory of his patience and resolution. He was gentle and just; the soldiers who fought under him and who came alive out of the great fight, remembering and cherishing the memory of the man, can one and all testify to his gentleness and his justice. Above all, he was faithful; when he gave up his sword there was no man in his own ranks or in those of the enemy that doubted his faith or believed that he had not done all that mortal could do for the cause for which he had made such a noble struggle."

Alexander H. Stephens, the Vice-President of the Confederate States, who was brought into intimate contact with General Lee at many times during his eventful career, has left a biographical sketch, as yet unpublished, from which we extract some highly interesting passages. He first saw Robert E. Lee at the time of his entry into the service of Virginia as major-general of the State forces, when he replied to the address of the president of the convention in the brief but eloquent oration which has been given in its appropriate place in this work. Mr. Stephens was then in Richmond with the purpose of inducing Virginia to enter the Confederacy which had been formed by the more southern range of States, and to undo, so far as General Lee was concerned, the work which had been that morning performed. He alludes to Lee in the following eloquent words:

"As he stood there, fresh and ruddy as a David from the sheepfold, in the prime of his manly beauty and the embodiment of a line of heroic and patriotic fathers and worthy mothers, it was thus I first saw Robert E. Lee. I had preconceived ideas of the rough soldier with no time for the graces of life and by companionship almost compelled to the vices of his profession. I did not know then that he used no stimulants, was free even from the use of tobacco, and that he was absolutely stainless in his private life. I did not know then, as I do now, that he had been a model youth and young man ; but I had before me the most manly man and entire gentleman I ever saw.

"That this seeming modesty was genuine, that this worth in which his compatriots believed was real, that his character was unselfish, I was to know as the shades of evening fell upon that day and he sat in my room at the Ballard House, at my request, to listen to my proposal that he resign, without any compensation or promise thereof, the very honor and rank he had that same morning received. . . . .

"General Lee heard me quietly, understood the situation at once, and saw that he alone stood between the Confederacy and his State. The members of the convention had seen at once that Lee was left out of the proposed compact that was to make Virginia one of the Confederate States, and I knew that one word, or even a look of dissatisfaction, from him would terminate the negotiations with which I was entrusted. North Carolina would act with Virginia, and either the Border States would protect our lines or the battle-field be moved at once down to South Carolina and the borders of Georgia.

"General Lee did not hesitate for one moment, and, while he saw that it would make matters worse to throw up his commission, he declared that no personal ambition or emolument should be considered or stand in the way. I had admired him in the morning, but I took his hand that night at parting with feelings of respect and almost reverence never yet effaced. I met him at times later, and he was always the same Christian gentleman.

"Virginia became one of us and the battlefield, as all men know, and General Lee took subordinate positions which for a time placed him nearly out of sight. The magnitude of his sacrifice of the position of commander-in-chief of the Union army—if Mr. Blair is right in saying it was offered him—is already appreciated. But the greatness of his self-abnegation in the surrender of the sword of Virginia will not yet be seen unless I show what it at once involved. It is not the man on the battlefield I wish to draw, but a higher thing than a mere sword-flourisher—personal character.

"Nominally, General Lee lost nothing, but practically, for the time being, he lost everything. The Government moved to Richmond, and Mr. Davis directed General Lee to retain his command of the Virginia troops, which was really to make him recruiting- and drill-inspector. . . . .

"General Lee with his Virginians was given special charge of West Virginia, not then a State. His lieutenant, General Garnett, was killed at Cheat River, and the Confederates lost a thousand prisoners, with artillery and baggage, by a blunder. General Wise did little better; so of General Henry R. Jackson; and Lee, when he went personally, found that when he had surrounded the forces of General Reynolds at Elk Water nothing was to be made by the frightful loss of life of an attack while General Rosecrans held an impregnable position on Cheat Mountain, and the campaign simply ended with a good look at the enemy and a feeling of his future foe, McClellan."

Before proceeding with Mr. Stephens's narrative we may introduce at this point a conversation related by General Starke, who was with Lee in West Virginia, and conversant with the widely-entertained opinion that the failure of that campaign stamped him as a greatly over-estimated man and one incompetent to hold an important command. In the conversation referred to General Starke turned the subject under discussion to the Sewell Mountain campaign, saying that as it was now all over he would like to know why General Lee did not fight Rosecrans, as the forces were about equal and the Confederates were ready and anxious for a fight, and felt certain of a victory. General Lee's answer was, in substance, that the men were in good spirits, and would doubtless have done their duty, but that a battle then would have been without substantial results; that the Confederates were seventy miles from the railroad, their base of supplies; that the ordinary road was almost im-

passable, and that it would have been difficult to procure
two days' supplies of provisions; that if he had fought
and won the battle, and Rosecrans had retreated, he would
have been compelled to fall back at last to the source of
supplies.

"But," said General Starke, "your reputation was suffering, the press was denouncing you, your own State was losing
confidence in you, and the army needed a victory to add to its
enthusiasm."

At the remark a smile lighted up the sad face of General
Lee, and his reply was worthy of him: "I could not afford to
sacrifice the lives of five or six hundred of my people to silence
public clamor."

Mr. Stephens summarizes the succeeding military perform-
ances of General Lee as follows:

"Again he had a barren though difficult honor thrust upon
him. On March 13, 1862, General Order No. 14 recited that
'General Robert E. Lee is assigned to duty at the seat of Government, and, under the direction of the President, is charged
with the conduct of military operations in the army of the
Confederacy.' He did much to improve the army as the
chief of staff of Mr. Davis and nominal head of the army,
but soon asked to be relieved from responsibility with no
power. A Congressional act creating the office of commanding general for him had been vetoed by Mr. Davis as
unconstitutional.

"The Confederate Government had adopted the plan of
Austria at the period when Napoleon the First so nearly wiped
her off the map of Europe, and endeavored to 'cover everything' with the armies. The army at Centreville was little
more than a mob clamoring for leave of absence, and with
seldom a day's rations ahead, and General Lee was sent to
repair the disasters of Hilton Head and Beaufort, S. C., by
the impossible task of engineering sufficient fortifications for
a thousand miles of mingled seacoast and inland swamps. I
remember seeing him in Savannah, conspicuous by the blue
uniform which he was the last of the Confederates to put off,
scarcely noticed among the gay uniforms of the new volunteers,

and the least likely of all men to become the first character in the war for States Rights.

"Toward sundown at the battle of Seven Pines, Virginia, on the 31st of May, 1862, General Joseph E. Johnston fell severely wounded. . . . . The time of General Lee had come at last. His appointment by Mr. Davis was very unpopular, as the South had little confidence in him, and even Virginians doubted their old idol. Yet from that time I need only to call the roll of his battles: Richmond relieved, Manassas (the second), Harper's Ferry, Sharpsburg, Fredericksburg, Chancellorsville—where Stonewall Jackson fell—Winchester and Gettysburg, Spottsylvania, Cold Harbor, Petersburg, and Lynchburg. He is identified for ever with that Army of Northern Virginia of which Mr. Swinton says, 'Who that ever looked upon it can forget that army of tattered uniforms and bright muskets—that body of incomparable infantry which for four years carried the revolt upon its bayonets, opposing a constant front to the mighty concentration of power brought against it; which, receiving terrible blows, did not fail to give the like; and which, vital in all its parts, died only with its annihilation?'

"What I had seen General Lee to be at first—child-like in simplicity and unselfish in his character—he remained, unspoiled by praise and by success. While he was always the dignified Virginia gentleman, and never free or familiar with any one, he won the hearts of his men as entirely as ever did Napoleon or Washington."

In addition to the foregoing evidences of General Lee's character, and of the estimation in which he was held by all those associated with him or acquainted with his ability as a soldier and his innate nobility of nature, may be given the following letters, which form an important portion of the secret history of the war. On page 301 of this work the statement is made that on the return of the army to the Rapidan after the battle of Gettysburg, General Lee resigned the command of the army, which resignation, however, was not accepted by Mr. Davis. The correspondence in relation to this resignation is of great interest and value, and is here given:

"CAMP ORANGE, August 8, 1863.

"MR. PRESIDENT: Your letters of the 28th July and 2d August have been received, and I have waited for a leisure hour to reply, but I fear that will never come. I am extremely obliged to you for the attention given to the wants of this army and the efforts made to supply them. Our absentees are returning, and I hope the earnest and beautiful appeal made to the country in your proclamation may stir up the whole people, and that they may see their duty and perform it. Nothing is wanted but that their fortitude should equal their bravery to ensure the success of our cause. We must expect reverses, even defeats. They are sent to teach us wisdom and prudence, to call forth greater energies, and to prevent our falling into greater disasters. Our people have only to be true and united, to bear manfully the misfortunes incident to war, and all will come right in the end. I know how prone we are to censure, and how ready to blame others for the non-fulfilment of our expectations. This is unbecoming in a generous people, and I grieve to see its expression. The general remedy for the want of success in a military commander is his removal. This is natural, and in many instances proper. For, no matter what may be the ability of the officer, if he loses the confidence of his troops disaster must sooner or later ensue.

"I have been prompted by these reflections more than once since my return from Pennsylvania to propose to Your Excellency the propriety of selecting another commander for this army. I have seen and heard of expressions of discontent in the public journals at the result of the expedition. I do not know how far this feeling extends in the army. My brother-officers have been too kind to report it, and so far the troops have been too generous to exhibit it. It is fair, however, to suppose that it does exist, and success is so necessary to us that nothing should be risked to secure it. I therefore, in all sincerity, request Your Excellency to take measures to supply my place. I do this with the more earnestness because no one is more aware than myself of my inability for the duties of my position. I cannot even accomplish what I myself desire. How can I fulfil the expectations of others?

"In addition, I sensibly feel the growing failure of my bodily strength. I have not yet recovered from the attack I experienced the past spring. I am becoming more and more incapable of exertion, and am thus prevented from making the personal examinations and giving the personal supervision to the operations in the field which I feel to be necessary. I am so dull that in making use of the eyes of others I am frequently misled. Everything, therefore, points to the advantages to be derived from a new commander, and I the more anxiously urge the matter upon Your Excellency from my belief that a younger and abler man than myself can readily be obtained. I know that he will have as gallant and brave an army as ever existed to second his efforts, and it would be the happiest day of my life to see at its head a worthy leader —one that could accomplish more than I could perform, and all that I have wished. I hope Your Excellency will attribute my request to the true reason, the desire to serve my country and to do all in my power to ensure the success of her righteous cause.

"I have no complaints to make of any one but myself. I have received nothing but kindness from those above me, and the most considerate attention from my comrades and companions-in-arms. To Your Excellency I am specially indebted for uniform kindness and consideration. You have done everything in your power to aid me in the work committed to my charge, without omitting anything to promote the general welfare.

"I pray that your efforts may at length be crowned with success, and that you may long live to enjoy the thanks of a grateful people. With sentiments of great esteem,

"I am very respectfully and truly yours,

"R. E. LEE,
" *General.*

" HIS EXCELLENCY JEFFERSON DAVIS, *President Confederate States.*"

President Davis replied as follows:

"RICHMOND, VA., August 11, 1863.

"GENERAL R. E. LEE, COMMANDING ARMY OF NORTHERN
      VIRGINIA:

"Yours of the 8th instant has just been received. I am
glad that you concur so entirely with me as to the wants of
our country in this trying hour, and am happy to add that
after the first depression consequent upon our disasters in the
West indications have appeared that our people will exhibit
that fortitude which we agree in believing is alone needful
to secure ultimate success. It well became Sydney Johnston,
when overwhelmed by a senseless clamor, to admit the rule
that success is the test of merit, and yet there has been nothing which I have found to require a greater effort of patience
than to bear the criticisms of the ignorant, who pronounce
everything a failure which does not equal their expectations
or desires, and can see no good result which is not in the line
of their own imaginings. I admit the propriety of your con-
clusions that an officer who loses the confidence of his troops
should have his position changed, whatever may be his ability; but when I read the sentence I was not at all prepared
for the application you were about to make. Expressions of
discontent in the public journals furnish but little evidence
of the sentiment of the army. I wish it were otherwise, even
though all the abuse of myself should be accepted as the
results of honest observation. Were you capable of stooping
to it, you could easily surround yourself with those who would
fill the press with your laudations and seek to exalt you for
what you had not done, rather than detract from the achievements which will make you and your army the subject of history
and objects of the world's admiration for generations to come.

"I am truly sorry to know that you still feel the effects of
the illness you suffered last spring, and can readily understand
the embarrassments you experience in using the eyes of others, having been so much accustomed to make your own reconnoissances. Practice will, however, do much to relieve that
embarrassment, and the minute knowledge of the country
which you have acquired will render you less dependent for
topographical information.

"But suppose, my dear friend, that I were to admit, with all their implications, the points which you present, where am I to find that new commander who is to possess the greater ability which you believe to be required? I do not doubt the readiness with which you would give way to one who could accomplish all that you have wished, and you will do me the justice to believe that if Providence should kindly offer such a person for our use, I would not hesitate to avail [myself] of his services.

"My sight is not sufficiently penetrating to discover such hidden merit, if it exists, and I have but used to you the language of sober earnestness when I have impressed upon you the propriety of avoiding all unnecessary exposure to danger, because I felt our country could not bear to lose you. To ask me to substitute you by some one in my judgment more fit to command, or who would possess more of the confidence of the army or of the reflecting men of the country, is to demand an impossibility.

"It only remains for me to hope that you will take all possible care of yourself, that your health and strength may be entirely restored, and that the Lord will preserve you for the important duties devolved upon you in the struggle of our suffering country for the independence which we have engaged in war to maintain.

"As ever, very respectfully and truly,
"JEFFERSON DAVIS."

We might add to this interesting correspondence an indefinite series of testimonials bearing upon the character of Robert E. Lee, gathering appreciative tributes from numerous sources and adducing the flattering criticisms upon his career of those most competent to judge throughout the world. Yet there seems no necessity for extending our remarks upon this subject. The character of the great soldier and worthy citizen speaks for itself in the foregoing pages, and every one can form his own opinion from the life-story we have told. That this opinion must be an exalted one, alike with military authorities and with the general public, there can be no question, since all must admit that the biography of a nobler man and an abler soldier was never written.

In conclusion may be transcribed the beautiful tribute to General Lee by Philip Stanhope Worsley, Fellow of Corpus Christi College, Oxford, England, accompanying a presented copy of his translation of the *Iliad*:

"To GENERAL R. E. LEE—the most stainless of living commanders, and, except in fortune, the greatest—this volume is presented with the writer's earnest sympathy and respectful admiration.

> "The grand old bard that never dies,
>   Receive him in our English tongue:
> I send thee, but with weeping eyes,
>   The story that he sung.
>
> "Thy Troy is fallen, thy dear land
>   Is marred beneath the spoiler's heel:
> I cannot trust my trembling hand
>   To write the things I feel.
>
> "Ah, realm of tombs! but let her bear
>   This blazon to the last of times:
> No nation rose so white and fair,
>   Or fell so pure of crimes.
>
> "The widow's moan, the orphan's wail
>   Come round thee, yet in truth be strong:
> Eternal right, though all else fail,
>   Can never be made wrong.
>
> "An angel's heart, an angel's mouth,
>   Not Homer's, could alone for me
> Hymn well the great Confederate South,
>   Virginia first, and *Lee!*"

APPENDIX.

GENERAL R. E. LEE.
COMMANDS.
1861.

April 23.—Assumed command of military and naval forces of Virginia.

May 7.—Ordered to assume command of all forces from other States tendering their services to Virginia.

May 10.—Assigned command of Confederate States forces.

May 14.—Appointed brigadier-general C. S. A.

June 14.—General Confederate States Army.

Aug. 3.—Commanding forces in Army of the North-west.

Oct. 20.—Same command.

Nov. 5.—Assigned command of Department of South Carolina, Georgia, and Florida.

1862.

March 13.—Assigned to duty at Richmond, and charged with military operations of armies of the Confederacy.

June 1.—Assumed command of Army and Department of Northern Virginia, and kept it until close of the war.

1865.

Jan. 31.—General-in-Chief Confederate States armies.

Feb. 6.—Assigned command of all armies of the Confederate States.

April 9.—Surrendered Army of Northern Virginia to General U. S. Grant, U. S. A.

GENERAL R. E. LEE'S STAFF.

ALEXANDER, E. PORTER, Lieutenant-colonel, Chief of Ordnance Nov., 1862, from June 1, 1862.

BALDWIN, BRISCOE G., Lieutenant-colonel, Chief of Ordnance Nov., 1862, Sept., 1863, April 9, 1865.

BROOKE, JOHN M., Lieutenant Virginia Navy, Acting A. D. C. May 4-8, 1861.

CHILTON, R. H., Colonel, A. A. General June, 1862, July 31, Aug. 31, 1863; Brigadier-general, A. and I. General, Dec., 1863.

COLE, ROBERT G., Lieutenant-colonel, Chief Commissary of Subsistence June, 1862–April 9, 1865.

COOKE, GILES B., Major, A. A. General Nov. 4, 1864.

CORLEY, JAMES L., Lieutenant-colonel, Chief Quartermaster June, 1862–April, 1865.

CRENSHAW, JOSEPH R., Major, Acting Commissary-general April 29, 1861.

DEAS, GEORGE, Major, A. A. General, Chief of Staff June 15, 1861; Lieutenant-colonel, A. A. General July 4, 1861 (Virginia State Forces).

GARNETT, R. S., Colonel, A. A. General April 26, 1861; Colonel, A. A. General May 7, 1861 (Virginia State Forces).

GILL, WILLIAM G., Lieutenant-colonel, P. A. C. S., Ordnance Officer Nov. 1, 1861.

GUILD, LAFAYETTE, Surgeon, Medical Director Nov. 26, 1862, March 6, Aug. 31, 1863, April 9, 1865.

HARVIE, EDWIN J., Lieutenant-colonel, Inspector-general June, 1862.

HETH, HENRY, Lieutenant-colonel, Acting Q. M. General Virginia State Forces April 29, 1861; promoted Brigadier-general Jan. 6, 1862; Major-general May 24, 1863.

IVES, JOSEPH C., Captain C. S. A., Chief Engineer Nov. 6, 1861.

JOHNSON, S. K., Captain, Engineer Officer Nov., 1862–Sept., 1863.

LAY, GEORGE W., Colonel, A. I. General March 6, 1863.

LONG, ARMISTEAD L., Major, Chief of Artillery Department S. C., Ga., and Fla. Nov., 1861; Colonel, Military Secretary April 21, 1862–Sept., 1863; promoted Brigadier-general of Artillery Sept. 21, 1863.

MANIGAULT, JOSEPH, Vol. A. D. C. Nov., 1861.

MARSHALL, CHARLES, Major, A. D. C. Aug., 1862; Major, A. D. C. March, Aug., 1863; Lieutenant-colonel, A. A. General Nov. 4, 1864–April, 1865.

MASON, A. P., Captain, A. A. General Aug., 1862, March 6, 1863.

MURRAY, E., Lieutenant-colonel, A. A. General July 31–Sept., 1863, Nov. 4, 1864.

PAGE, THOMAS J., Lieutenant Virginia Navy, Acting A. D. C. May 3, 1861.

PENDLETON, W. N., Brigadier-general, Chief of Artillery Mar. 6–Aug. 31, 1863–1865.

PEYTON, HENRY E., Major, A. A. General Nov., 1862; Lieutenant-colonel July 31–Nov. 4, 1864.

RICHARDSON, W. H., Captain, A. A. General May 11, 1861.

SMITH, F. W., Captain, Military Secretary May 27, 1861.

SMITH, WILLIAM PROCTOR, Lieutenant-colonel, Chief of Engineers July 31–Sept., 1863.

TALCOTT, T. M. R., Major, A. D. C. Nov., 1862, July 31–Aug., 1863.

TAYLOR, WALTER H., Captain C. S. A., A. D. C. Nov. 8, 1861–March 27, 1862; Major, A. D. C. Aug., 1862, July 31, Aug. 31, 1863; Lieutenant-colonel, A. A. General Nov. 4, 1864–1865.

VENABLE, CHARLES S., Major, A. D. C. July 31–Aug. 31, 1863; Lieutenant-colonel, A. A. General Nov. 4, 1864–April, 1865.

WASHINGTON, JOHN A., Captain, A. D. C. May 6, 1861.

WASHINGTON, THORNTON A., Captain, A. A. General Nov. 6, 1861.

YOUNG, H. E., Captain, A. A. General July–Sept., 1863; Major, A. A. General Nov. 4, 1864.

OFFICIAL REPORTS

OF THE

OPERATIONS OF THE ARMY OF NORTHERN VIRGINIA,

MADE BY GENERAL R. E. LEE

TO THE WAR DEPARTMENT AT RICHMOND.

REPORT OF THE OPERATIONS AGAINST GENERAL POPE, IN- CLUDING THE SECOND BATTLE OF MANASSAS, AUGUST 13, TO SEPTEMBER 1, 1862.

HEADQUARTERS ARMY OF NORTHERN VIRGINIA,
June 8, 1863.

GENERAL S. COOPER, ADJUTANT- AND INSPECTOR-GENERAL, RICHMOND, VA.,

GENERAL : I have the honor to transmit herewith the report of the operations of this army from the time it crossed the Rappahannock, through the battle of Manassas. Many of the sub-reports of these operations I have been obliged to retain because they contain the narrative in part of the later operations of the campaign. Of these operations succeeding the battle of Manassas I have not yet made a report, as I have not yet received full reports from Jackson's corps. I am, with great respect, your obedient servant,

R. E. LEE,
General.

The victory at Cedar Run effectually checked the progress of the enemy for the time, but it soon became apparent that his army was being largely increased. The corps of Major-general Burnside from North Carolina, which had reached Fredericksburg, was reported to have moved up the Rappahannock a few days after the battle to unite with General Pope, and a part of General McClellan's army was believed to have left Westover for the same purpose. It therefore seemed that active operations on the James were no longer contemplated, and that the most effectual way to relieve Richmond from any danger of attack from that quarter would be to reinforce General Jackson and advance upon General Pope.

Accordingly, on August 13th, Major-general Longstreet with his divisions, and the two brigades under General Hood, were ordered to proceed to Gordonsville. At the same time General Stuart was directed to move with the main body of his cavalry to that point, leaving a sufficient force to observe the enemy still remaining in Fredericksburg and to guard the railroad. General R. H. Anderson was also directed to leave his position on James River and follow Longstreet.

On the 16th the troops began to move from the vicinity of Gordonsville toward the Rapidan, on the north side of which, extending along the Orange and Alexandria Railroad in the direction of Culpeper Court-house, the Federal army lay in force. It was determined with the cavalry to destroy the railroad bridge over the Rappahannock in rear of the enemy, while Longstreet and Jackson crossed the Rapidan and attacked his left flank. The movement, as explained in the accompanying order, was appointed for August 18th, but, the necessary preparations not having been completed, its execution was postponed to the 20th. In the interval the enemy, being apprised of our design, hastily retired beyond the Rappahannock. General Longstreet crossed the Rapidan at Raccoon Ford, and, preceded by Fitzhugh Lee's cavalry brigade, arrived early in the afternoon near Kelly's Ford, on the Rappahannock, where Lee had a sharp and successful skirmish with the rear-guard of the enemy, who held the north side of the river in strong force. Jackson passed the Rapidan at Somerville Ford and moved toward Brandy Station, Robertson's brigade of cavalry, accompanied by General Stuart in person, leading the advance. Near Brandy Station a large body of the enemy's cavalry was encountered, which was gallantly attacked and driven across the Rappahannock by Robertson's command.

General Jackson halted for the night near Stevensburg, and on the morning of the 21st moved upon Beverly Ford, on the Rappahannock. The Fifth Virginia cavalry, under Colonel Rosser, was sent forward by General Stuart to seize the north bank of the river at this point, and gallantly accomplished the object, capturing a number of prisoners and arms. General Stuart subsequently arrived, and, being furnished by General Jackson with a section of artillery, maintained his position for several hours, skirmishing warmly with the enemy. General Robertson, who had crossed the river above Beverly Ford, reported that the enemy was advancing in large force upon the position held by General Stuart, and, as it had been determined in the mean time not to attempt the passage of the river at that point with the army, that officer withdrew to the south side. The enemy soon afterward appeared in great strength upon the opposite bank, and an animated fire was kept up during the rest of the day between his artillery and the batteries attached to Jackson's leading division, under Brigadier-general Taliaferro.

As our positions on the south bank of the Rappahannock were commanded by those of the enemy, who guarded all the fords, it was determined to seek a more favorable place to cross higher up the river, and thus gain the enemy's right. Accordingly, General Longstreet was directed to leave Kelly's Ford on the 21st and take position in front of the enemy in the vicinity of Beverly Ford and the Orange and Alexandria Railroad bridge, then held by Jackson, in order to mask the movement of the latter, who was instructed to ascend the river.

On the 22d, Jackson crossed Hazel River at Welford's Mill and proceeded up the Rappahannock, leaving Trimble's brigade near Freeman's Ford to protect his trains. In the afternoon Longstreet sent General Hood, with his own and Whiting's brigade, under Colonel Law, to relieve Trimble. Hood had just reached the position when he and Trimble were attacked by a considerable force which had crossed at Freeman's Ford. After a short but spirited engagement the enemy was driven precipitately over the river with heavy loss. General Jackson arrived at the Warrenton Springs Ford in the afternoon, and immediately began to cross his troops to the north side, occupying the springs and the adjacent heights. He was interrupted by a heavy rain, which caused the river to rise so rapidly that the ford soon became impassable for infantry and artillery. Under these circumstances it was deemed advisable to withdraw the troops who had reached the opposite side, and they recrossed during the night of the 23d on a temporary bridge constructed for the purpose. General Stuart, who had been directed to cut the railroad in rear of General Pope's army, crossed the Rappahannock on the morning of the 22d about six miles above the springs with parts of Lee's and Robertson's brigades. Passing through Warrenton, he reached Catlett's Station at night, but was prevented from destroying the railroad bridge at that point by the same storm that had arrested Jackson's movements. He captured more than 300 prisoners, including a number of officers. Becoming apprehensive of the effect of the rain upon the streams which separated him from the main body of the army, he retired after firing the enemy's camp, and recrossed the Rappahannock at Warrenton Springs.

On the 23d, General Longstreet directed Colonel Walton, with part of the Washington Artillery and other batteries of his command, to drive back a force of the enemy that had crossed to the south bank of the Rappahannock near the railroad bridge upon the withdrawal of General Jackson on the previous day. Fire was opened about sunrise, and continued with great vigor for several hours, the enemy being compelled to withdraw with loss. Some of the batteries of Colonel S. D. Lee's battalion were ordered to aid those of Colonel Walton, and under their united fire the enemy was forced to abandon his position on the north side of the river, burning in his retreat the railroad bridge and the neighboring dwellings. The rise of the river, rendering the lower fords impassable, enabled the enemy to concentrate his main body opposite General Jackson, and on the 24th, Longstreet was ordered to proceed to his support. Although retarded by the swollen condition of Hazel Run and other tributaries of the Rappahannock, he reached Jeffersonton in the afternoon. General Jackson's command lay between that place and the [Warrenton] Springs Ford, and a warm cannonade was progressing between the batteries of General A. P. Hill's division and those of the enemy. The enemy was massed between Warrenton and the springs, and guarded the fords of the Rappahannock as far above as Waterloo. The army of General McClellan had left Westover. Part of [it] had already marched to join General Pope, and it was reported that the rest would soon follow. The captured correspondence of General Pope confirmed this information, and also disclosed the fact that the greater part of the army of General Cox had been withdrawn from the Kanawha Valley for the same purpose. Two brigades of D. H. Hill's division, under General Ripley, had already been ordered from Richmond, and the remainder, under General D. H. Hill in person, with the division of General McLaws, two brigades under General Walker, and Hampton's cavalry brigade, were now directed to join this army, and were approaching. In pursuance of the plan of operations determined upon, Jackson was directed on the 25th to cross above Waterloo and move around the enemy's right, so as to strike the Orange and Alexandria Railroad in his rear. Longstreet, in the mean time, was to divert his attention by threatening him in front, and to follow Jackson as soon as the latter should be sufficiently advanced.

BATTLE OF MANASSAS.

General Jackson crossed the Rappahannock at Hinson's Mill, about four miles above Waterloo, and, passing through Orleans, encamped on the night of the 25th near Salem after a long and fatiguing march. The next morning, continuing his route with his accustomed vigor and celerity, he passed the Bull Run Mountains at Thoroughfare Gap, and, proceeding by way of Gainesville, reached the railroad at Bristoe Station after sunset. At Gainesville he was joined by General Stuart with the brigades of Robertson and Fitzhugh Lee, who continued with him during the rest of his operations, vigilantly and effectually guarding both his flanks. General Jackson was now between the large army of General Pope and the Federal capital. Thus far, no considerable force of the enemy had been encountered, and he did not appear to be aware of his situation. Upon arriving at Bristoe the greater part of the guard at that point fled. Two trains of cars coming from the direction of Warrenton were captured and a few prisoners were taken. Notwithstanding the darkness of the night and the long and arduous march of the day, General Jackson determined to lose no time in capturing the dépôt of the enemy at Manassas Junction, about seven miles distant on the road to Alexandria. General Trimble volunteered to proceed at once to that place with the Twenty-first North Carolina and the Twenty-first Georgia regiments. The offer was accepted, and, to render success more certain, General Jackson directed General Stuart to accompany the expedition with part of his cavalry, and, as ranking officer, to assume the command. Upon arriving near the junction General Stuart sent Colonel Wickham with his regiment, the Fourth Virginia cavalry, to get in rear of the enemy, who opened with musketry and artillery upon our troops as they approached. The darkness of the night and ignorance of the enemy's numbers and position made it necessary to move cautiously, but about midnight the place was taken with little difficulty, those that defended it being captured or dispersed. Eight pieces of artillery, with their horses, ammunition, and equipments, were taken. More than 300 prisoners, 175 horses besides those belonging to the artillery, 200 new tents, and immense quantities of commissary and quartermaster's stores fell into our hands. General Jackson left Ewell's division, with the Fifth Virginia cavalry, under Colonel Rosser, at Bristoe Station, and with the rest of his command proceeded to the Junction, where he arrived early in the morning. Soon afterward a considerable force of the enemy, under Brigadier-general Taylor, approached from the direction of Alexandria, and pushed forward boldly to recapture the stores that had been lost. After a sharp engagement the enemy was routed and driven back, leaving his killed and wounded on the field, General Taylor himself being mortally wounded during the pursuit. The troops remained at Manassas Junction during the rest of the day, supplying themselves with everything they required from the captured stores.

In the afternoon the enemy advanced upon General Ewell at Bristoe from the direction of Warrenton Junction. They were attacked by three regiments and the batteries of Ewell's division, and two columns of not less than a brigade each were broken and repulsed. Their places were soon supplied by fresh troops, and it was apparent that the Federal commander had now become aware of the situation of affairs, and had turned upon General Jackson with his whole force. In pursuance of instructions to that effect, General Ewell, upon perceiving the strength of the enemy, withdrew his command, part of which was at the time engaged, and rejoined General Jackson at Manassas Junction, having first destroyed the railroad bridge over Broad Run. The enemy halted at Bristoe. General Jackson's force being much inferior to that of General Pope, it became necessary for him to withdraw from Manassas and take a position west of the turnpike road from Warrenton to Alexandria, where he could more readily unite with the approaching column of Longstreet. Having fully supplied the wants of his troops, he was compelled, for want of transportation, to destroy the rest of the captured property. This was done during the night of the 27th, and 50,000 pounds of bacon, 1000 barrels of corned beef, 2000 barrels of salt pork, and 2000 barrels of flour, besides other property of great value, were burned. Taliaferro's division moved during the night by the road to Sudley, and, crossing the turnpike near Groveton, halted on the west side near the battlefield of July 21, 1861, where it was joined on the 28th by the divisions of Hill and Ewell. Perceiving during the afternoon that the enemy, approaching from the direction of Warrenton, was moving down the turnpike toward Alexandria, thus exposing his left flank, General Jackson advanced to attack him. A fierce and sanguinary conflict ensued, which continued until about 9 P. M., when the enemy slowly fell back and left us in possession of the field. The loss on both sides was heavy, and among our wounded were Major-general Ewell and Brigadier-general Taliaferro, the former severely.

The next morning, the 29th, the enemy had taken a position to interpose his army between General Jackson and Alexandria, and about 10 A. M. opened with artillery upon the right of Jackson's line. The troops of the latter were disposed in rear of Groveton, along the line of the unfinished branch of the Manassas Gap Railroad, and extended from a point a short distance west of the turnpike toward Sudley Mill; Jackson's division, under Brigadier-general Starke, being on the right; Ewell's, under General Lawton, in the centre; and A. P. Hill's on the left. The Federal army was evidently concentrating upon Jackson with the design of overwhelming him before the arrival of Longstreet. The latter officer left his position opposite Warrenton Springs on the 26th, being relieved by General R. H. Anderson's division, and marched to join Jackson. He crossed at Hinson's Mill in the afternoon, and encamped near Orleans that night. The next day he reached the White Plains, his march being retarded by the want of cavalry to ascertain the meaning of certain movements of the enemy from the direction of Warrenton which seemed to menace the right flank of his column.

On the 28th, arriving at Thoroughfare Gap, he found the enemy prepared to dispute his progress. General D. R. Jones's division, being ordered to force the passage of the mountain, quickly dislodged the enemy's sharpshooters from the trees and rocks and advanced into the gorge. The enemy held the eastern extremity of the pass in large force and directed a heavy fire of artillery upon the road leading through it and upon the sides of the mountain. The ground occupied by Jones afforded no opportunity for the employment of artillery. Hood, with two brigades, and Wilcox, with three, were ordered to turn the enemy's right, the former moving over the mountain by a narrow path to the left of the pass, and the latter farther to the north by Hopewell Gap. Before these troops reached their destinations the enemy advanced and attacked Jones's left under Brigadier-general G. T. Anderson. Being vigorously repulsed, he withdrew to his position at the eastern end of the gap, from which he kept up an active fire of artillery until dark, and then retreated.

Generals Jones and Wilcox bivouacked that night east of the mountain, and on the morning of the 29th the whole command resumed the march, the sound of cannon at Manassas announcing that Jackson was already engaged. Longstreet entered the turnpike near Gainesville, and, moving down toward Groveton, the head of his column came upon the field in rear of the enemy's left, which had already opened with artillery upon Jackson's right, as previously described. He immediately placed some of his batteries in position, but before he could complete his dispositions to attack the enemy withdrew—not, however, without loss from our artillery. Longstreet took position on the right of Jackson, Hood's two brigades, supported by Evans, being deployed across the turnpike and at right angles to it. These troops were supported on the left by three brigades under General Wilcox, and by a like force on the right under General Kemper. D. R. Jones's division formed the extreme right of the line, resting on the Manassas Gap Railroad. The cavalry guarded our right and left flanks, that on the right being under General Stuart in person. After the arrival of Longstreet the enemy changed his position and began to concentrate opposite Jackson's left, opening a brisk artillery fire, which was responded to with effect by some of General A. P. Hill's batteries. Colonel Walton placed a part of his artillery upon a commanding position between the lines of Generals Jackson and Longstreet, by order of the latter, and engaged the enemy vigorously for several hours. Soon afterward General Stuart reported the approach of a large force from the direction of Bristoe Station, threatening Longstreet's right. The brigades under General Wilcox were sent to reinforce General Jones, but no serious attack was made, and after firing a few shots the enemy withdrew. While this demonstration was being made on our right a large force advanced to assail the left of Jackson's position, occupied by the division of General A. P. Hill. The attack was received by his troops with their accustomed steadiness, and the battle raged with great fury. The enemy was repeatedly repulsed, but again pressed on to the attack with fresh troops. Once he succeeded in penetrating an interval between General Gregg's brigade, on the extreme left, and that of General Thomas, but was quickly driven back with great slaughter by the Fourteenth South Carolina regiment, then in reserve, and the Forty-ninth Georgia of Thomas's brigade. The contest was close and obstinate, the combatants sometimes delivering their fire at ten paces. General Gregg, who was most exposed, was reinforced by Hays's brigade, under Colonel Forno, and successfully and gallantly resisted the attacks of the enemy until, the ammunition of his brigade being exhausted and all his field officers but two killed or wounded, it was relieved, after several hours of severe fighting, by Early's brigade and the Eighth Louisiana regiment. General Early drove the enemy back with heavy loss and pursued about two hundred yards beyond the line of battle, when he was recalled to the position on the railroad, where Thomas, Pender, and Archer had firmly held their ground against every attack. While the battle was raging on Jackson's left, General Longstreet ordered Hood and Evans to advance, but before the order could be obeyed Hood was himself attacked, and his command at once became warmly engaged. General Wilcox was recalled from the right and ordered to advance on Hood's left, and one of Kemper's brigades, under Colonel Hunton, moved forward on his right.   The enemy was repulsed by Hood after a severe contest, and fell back, closely followed by our troops.   The battle continued until 9 P. M., the enemy retreating until he reached a strong position, which he held with a large force.   The darkness of the night put a stop to the engagement, and our troops remained in their advanced position until early next morning, when they were withdrawn to their first line.   One piece of artillery, several stands of colors, and a number of prisoners were captured.

Our loss was severe in this engagement.   Brigadier-generals Field and Trimble and Colonel Forno, commanding Hays's brigade, were severely wounded, and several other valuable officers killed or disabled, whose names are mentioned in the accompanying reports.

On the morning of the 30th the enemy again advanced, and skirmishing began along the line.   The troops of Jackson and Longstreet maintained their positions of the previous day.   Fitzhugh Lee, with three regiments of his cavalry, was posted on Jackson's left, and R. H. Anderson's division, which arrived during the forenoon, was held in reserve near the turnpike.   The batteries of Colonel S. D. Lee took the position occupied the day before by Colonel Walton, and engaged the enemy actively until noon, when firing ceased and all was quiet for several hours.   About 3 P. M. the enemy, having massed his troops in front of General Jackson, advanced against his position in strong force.   His front line pushed forward until engaged at close quarters by Jackson's troops, when its progress was checked, and a fierce and bloody struggle ensued.   A second and third line of great strength moved up to support the first, but in doing so came within easy range of a position a little in advance of Longstreet's left.   He immediately ordered up two batteries, and, two others being thrown forward about the same time by Colonel S. D. Lee, under their well-directed and destructive fire the supporting lines were broken and fell back in confusion.   Their repeated efforts to rally were unavailing, and Jackson's troops, being thus relieved from the pressure of overwhelming numbers, began to press steadily forward, driving the enemy before them.   He retreated in confusion, suffering severely from our artillery, which advanced as he retired.   General Longstreet, anticipating the order for a general advance, now threw his whole command against the Federal centre and left.   Hood's two brigades, closely followed by Evans's, led the attack.   R. H. Anderson's division came gallantly to the support of Hood, while the three brigades under Wilcox moved forward on his left, and those of Kemper on his right.   D. R. Jones advanced on the extreme right, and the whole line swept steadily on, driving the enemy with great carnage from each successive position until 10 P. M., when darkness put an end to the battle and the pursuit.   During the latter part of the engagement General Wilcox, with his own brigade, was ordered to the right, where the resistance of the enemy was most obstinate, and rendered efficient assistance to the troops engaged on that part of the line.

His other two brigades, maintaining their position in line, acted with General Jackson's command. The obscurity of night and the uncertainty of the fords of Bull Run rendered it necessary to suspend operations until morning, when the cavalry, being pushed forward, discovered that the enemy had escaped to the strong position of Centreville, about four miles beyond Bull Run. The prevalence of a heavy rain, which began during the night, threatened to render Bull Run impassable and impeded our movements. Longstreet remained on the battlefield to engage the attention of the enemy and cover the burial of the dead and the removal of the wounded, while Jackson proceeded by Sudley Ford to the Little River turnpike to turn the enemy's right and intercept his retreat to Washington. Jackson's progress was retarded by the inclemency of the weather and the fatigue of his troops, who, in addition to their arduous marches, had fought three severe engagements in as many days. He reached Little River turnpike in the evening, and the next day, September 1st, advanced by that road toward Fairfax Court-house.

The enemy, in the mean time, was falling back rapidly toward Washington, and had thrown out a strong force to Germantown, on the Little River turnpike, to cover his line of retreat from Centreville. The advance of Jackson's column encountered the enemy at Ox Hill, near Germantown, about 5 P. M. Line of battle was at once formed, and two brigades of A. P. Hill's division (those of Branch and Field, under Colonel Brockenbrough) were thrown forward to attack the enemy and ascertain his strength and position. A cold and drenching rain-storm drove in the faces of our troops as they advanced and gallantly engaged the enemy. They were subsequently supported by the brigades of Gregg, Thomas, and Pender, also of Hill's division, which, with part of Ewell's, became engaged. The conflict was obstinately maintained by the enemy until dark, when he retreated, having lost two general officers, one of whom, Major-general Kearny, was left dead on the field.

Longstreet's command arrived after the action was over, and the next morning it was found that the enemy had conducted his retreat so rapidly that the attempt to intercept him was abandoned. The proximity of the fortifications around Alexandria and Washington rendered further pursuit useless, and our army rested during the 2d near Chantilly, the enemy being followed only by the cavalry, who continued to harass him until he reached the shelter of his intrenchments.

In the series of engagements on the plains of Manassas more than 7000 prisoners were taken, in addition to about 2000 wounded left in our hands. Thirty pieces of artillery, upwards of 20,000 stands of small-arms, numerous colors, and a large amount of stores, besides those taken by General Jackson at Manassas Junction, were captured.

The history of the achievements of the army from the time it advanced from Gordonsville leaves nothing to be said in commendation of the courage, fortitude, and good conduct of both officers and men. The accompanying reports of the medical director will show the number of our killed and wounded. Among them will be found the names of many valuable and distinguished officers, who bravely and faithfully discharged their duty, and, with the gallant soldiers who fell with them, have nobly deserved the love and gratitude of their countrymen. The reports of the several commanding officers must necessarily be referred to for the names of those whose services were most conspicuous. The list is too long for enumeration here. During all these operations the cavalry under General Stuart, consisting of the brigades of Generals Robertson and Fitzhugh Lee, rendered most important and valuable service. It guarded the flanks of the army, protected its trains, and gave information of the enemy's movements. Besides engaging the cavalry of the enemy on several occasions with uniform success, a detachment under the gallant and lamented Major Patrick, assisted by the Stuart Horse Artillery under Major Pelham, effectually protected General Jackson's trains against a body of the enemy who penetrated to his rear on the 29th before the arrival of General Longstreet. Toward the close of the action on the 30th, General Robertson, with the Second Virginia regiment under Colonel Munford, supported by the Seventh and Twelfth, made a brilliant charge upon a brigade of the enemy's cavalry, Colonel Munford leading with great gallantry, and completely routed it. Many of the enemy were killed and wounded, more than 300 prisoners were captured, and the remainder pursued beyond Bull Run. The reports of General Stuart and the officers under his command, as well as that of General Jackson, are referred to for more complete details of these and other services of the cavalry.

Respectfully submitted,

R. E. LEE,
General.

Organization of the Army of Northern Virginia, GENERAL R. E. LEE *commanding, during the Battles of August 28 to September 1, 1862.**

RIGHT WING, OR LONGSTREET'S CORPS.
MAJOR-GENERAL JAMES LONGSTREET.

ANDERSON'S DIVISION.
Major-general R. H. Anderson.

Armistead's Brigade.	*Mahone's Brigade.*	*Wright's Brigade.*
Brig.-gen. L. A. Armistead.	Brig.-gen. W. Mahone.	Brig.-gen. A. R. Wright.
9th Virginia.	6th Virginia.	3d Georgia.
14th Virginia.	12th Virginia.	22d Georgia.
38th Virginia.	16th Virginia.	44th Georgia.
53d Virginia.	41st Virginia.	48th Georgia.
57th Virginia.	49th Virginia.	
5th Virginia Battalion (?).		

* Based upon organization of July 23, 1862, subsequent orders of assignment and transfers, and the reports.

JONES'S DIVISION.

Brigadier-general D. R. Jones.

Toombs's Brigade.	*Drayton's Brigade.*	*Jones's Brigade*
Col. H. L. Benning. Brig.-gen. R. Toombs.	Brig.-gen. T. F. Drayton.	Col. Geo. T. Anderson
2d Georgia. 15th Georgia. 17th Georgia. 20th Georgia.	50th Georgia. 51st Georgia. 15th South Carolina. Phillips' Georgia Legion.	1st Georgia (Regulars). 7th Georgia. 8th Georgia. 9th Georgia. 11th Georgia.

WILCOX'S DIVISION.

Brigadier-general C. M. Wilcox.

Wilcox's Brigade.	*Pryor's Brigade.*	*Featherston's Brigade.*
Brig.-gen. C. M. Wilcox.	Brig.-gen. R. A. Pryor.	Brig.-gen. W. S. Featherston Colonel Carnot Posey.
8th Alabama. 9th Alabama. 10th Alabama. 11th Alabama. Anderson's Va. Bat. (Thomas's Artillery).	14th Alabama. 5th Florida. 8th Florida. 3d Virginia.	12th Mississippi. 16th Mississippi. 19th Mississippi. 2d Mississippi Battalion. Chapman's Va. Bat. (Dixie Artillery).

HOOD'S DIVISION.

Brigadier-general John B. Hood.

Hood's Brigade.	*Whiting's Brigade.*
Brig.-gen. John B. Hood.	Col. E. M. Law.
18th Georgia. Hampton's S. C. Legion. 1st Texas. 4th Texas. 5th Texas.	4th Alabama. 2d Mississippi. 11th Mississippi. 6th North Carolina.

Artillery.

Maj. B. W. Frobel.

Bachman's South Carolina Battery.
Garden's South Carolina Battery.
Reilly's North Carolina Battery.

KEMPER'S DIVISION.

Brigadier-general James L. Kemper.

Kemper's Brigade.	*Jenkins's Brigade.*	*Pickett's Brigade.*
Col. M. D. Corse.	Brig.-gen. M. Jenkins. Col. Joseph Walker.	Col. Eppa Hunton.
1st Virginia. 7th Virginia. 11th Virginia. 17th Virginia. 24th Virginia.	1st South Carolina (Volunteers). 2d South Carolina Rifles. 5th South Carolina. 6th South Carolina. 4th S. C. Battalion (?). Palmetto (S. C.) Sharpshooters.	8th Virginia. 18th Virginia. 19th Virginia. 28th Virginia. 56th Virginia.

Evans's Brigade.*

Brig.-gen. N. G. Evans.
Col. P. F. Stevens.

17th South Carolina.
18th South Carolina.
22d South Carolina.
23d South Carolina.
Holcombe (South Carolina) Legion.
Boyce's S. C. Bat. (Macbeth Artillery).

ARTILLERY OF THE RIGHT WING.

Washington (La.) Artillery.

Col. J. B. Walton.

Eshleman's 4th Company.
Miller's 3d Company.
Richardson's 2d Company.
Squires' 1st Company.

Lee's Battalion.

Col. S. D. Lee.

Eubank's Virginia Battery.
Grimes' Virginia Battery.
Jordan's Va. Bat. (Bedford Artillery).
Parker's Virginia Battery.
Rhett's South Carolina Battery.
Taylor's Virginia Battery.

MISCELLANEOUS BATTERIES.

Huger's Virginia Battery. †
Leake's Virginia Battery. ‡
Maurin's Louisiana Battery (Donaldsonville Artillery). ‡
Moorman's Virginia Battery. †
Rogers's Virginia Battery (Loudoun Artillery). ‡
Stribling's Virginia Battery (Fauquier Artillery). ‡

LEFT WING, OR JACKSON'S CORPS.

MAJOR-GENERAL T. J. JACKSON.

JACKSON'S DIVISION.

Brigadier-general W. B. Taliaferro.
Brigadier-general W. E. Starke.

First Brigade.

Col. W. S. H. Baylor.
Col. A. J. Grigsby.

2d Virginia.
4th Virginia.
5th Virginia.
27th Virginia.
33d Virginia.

Second Brigade.

Col. Bradley T. Johnson.

21st Virginia.
42d Virginia.
48th Virginia.
1st Virginia Battalion.

Third Brigade.

Col. A. G. Taliaferro.

47th Alabama.
48th Alabama.
10th Virginia.
23d Virginia.
37th Virginia.

Fourth Brigade.

Brig.-gen. W. E. Starke.
Col. Leroy A. Stafford.

1st Louisiana.
2d Louisiana.
9th Louisiana.
10th Louisiana.
15th Louisiana.
Coppens's Louisiana Battalion.

Artillery.

Maj. L. M. Shumaker.

Brockenbrough's Maryland Battery.
Carpenter's Virginia Battery.
Caskil's Virginia Battery (Hampden Artillery).
Poague's Virginia Battery (Rockbridge Artillery).
Raine's Virginia Battery (Lee Artillery).
Wooding's Virginia Battery (Danville Artillery).

* An independent brigade. On August 30th, Evans commanded Hood's division as well as his own brigade.
† Attached to Anderson's division, but not mentioned in the reports.
‡ Mentioned in the reports, but assignments not indicated.

HILL'S LIGHT DIVISION.
Major-general Ambrose P. Hill.

Branch's Brigade.

Brig.-gen. L. O'B. Branch.

7th North Carolina.
18th North Carolina.
28th North Carolina.
33d North Carolina.
37th North Carolina.

Gregg's Brigade.

Brig.-gen. Maxcy Gregg.

1st South Carolina.
1st South Carolina Rifles.
12th South Carolina.
13th South Carolina.
14th South Carolina.

Field's Brigade.

Brig.-gen. C. W. Field.
Col. J. M. Brockenbrough.

40th Virginia.
47th Virginia.
55th Virginia.
2d Virginia Battalion.

Pender's Brigade.

Brig.-gen. W. D. Pender.

16th North Carolina.
22d North Carolina.
34th North Carolina.
38th North Carolina.

Archer's Brigade.

Brig.-gen. J. J. Archer.

5th Alabama Battalion.
19th Georgia.*
1st Tennessee (Prov. Army).
7th Tennessee.
14th Tennessee.

Thomas's Brigade.

Brig.-gen. E. L. Thomas.

14th Georgia.
19th Georgia.*
35th Georgia.
45th Georgia.
49th Georgia.

Artillery.

Lieut.-col. R. L. Walker.

Braxton's Virginia Battery (Fredericksburg Artillery).
Crenshaw's Virginia Battery.
Davidson's Virginia Battery (Letcher Artillery).
Latham's North Carolina Battery (Branch Artillery).
McIntosh's South Carolina Battery (Pee Dee Artillery).
Pegram's Virginia Battery (Purcell Artillery).

EWELL'S DIVISION.

Major-general R. S. Ewell.
Brigadier-general A. R. Lawton.

Lawton's Brigade.

Brig.-gen. A. R. Lawton.
Colonel M. Douglass.

13th Georgia.
26th Georgia.
31st Georgia.
38th Georgia.
60th Georgia.
61st Georgia.

Early's Brigade.

Brig.-gen. J. A. Early.

13th Virginia.
25th Virginia.
31st Virginia.
44th Virginia.
49th Virginia.
52d Virginia.
58th Virginia.

Hays's Brigade.

Brig.-gen. Harry T. Hays.
Colonel Henry Forno.
Colonel H. B. Strong.

5th Louisiana.
6th Louisiana.
7th Louisiana.
8th Louisiana.

Trimble's Brigade.

Brig.-gen. I. R. Trimble.
Captain W. F. Brown.

15th Alabama.
12th Georgia.
21st Georgia.
21st North Carolina.

Artillery.

Balthis's Va. Battery (Staunton Artillery).
Brown's Md. Battery (Chesapeake Artillery).
D'Aquin's Battery (Louisiana Guard Artillery).
Dement's Maryland Battery.
Latimer's Va. Battery (Courtney Artillery).

* In Archer's brigade August 9th, according to his report of Cedar Run or Slaughter Mountain, and in Thomas's brigade August 30th, according to Surgeon Guild's report of casualties.

Cavalry.

MAJOR-GENERAL J. E. B. STUART.

*Hampton's Brigade.**   *Lee's Brigade.*

Brig.-gen. Wade Hampton.   Brig.-gen. F. Lee.

1st North Carolina.	1st Virginia.
2d North Carolina.	3d Virginia.
10th Virginia.	4th Virginia.
Cobb's Georgia Legion.	5th Virginia.
Jeff Davis Legion.	9th Virginia.

Robertson's Brigade.

Brig.-gen. B. H. Robertson.   *Artillery.*

2d Virginia.   Hart's South Carolina Battery.
6th Virginia.   Pelham's Virginia Battery.
7th Virginia.
12th Virginia.
17th Virginia Battalion.

Artillery.†

1st Virginia Regiment.   *Sumpter (Georgia) Battalion.*

Col. J. T. Brown.   Lieut.-col. A. S. Cutts.

Coke's Va. Battery (Williamsburg Artillery).   Blackshear's Battery (D).
Dance's Va. Battery (Powhatan Artillery).   Lane's Battery (C).
Hupp's Va. Battery (Salem Artillery).   Patterson's Battery (B).
Macon's Battery (Richmond Fayette Artillery).   Ross's Battery (A).
Smith's Battery (3d Co. Richmond Howitzers).
Watson's Battery (2d Co. Richmond Howitzers).

MISCELLANEOUS BATTERIES.

Ancell's Va. Battery (Fluvanna Art.).   Milledge's Georgia Battery.
Cutshaw's Virginia Battery. ‡   Page's (R. C. M.) Va. Bat. (Morris Art.).
Fleet's Va. Battery (Middlesex Art). ‡   Peyton's Va. Battery (Orange Artillery).
Huckstep's Virginia Battery.   Rice's Virginia Battery. ‡
Johnson's Virginia Battery. ‡   Turner's Virginia Battery.

HEADQUARTERS ALEXANDRIA AND LEESBURG ROAD,
Near Dranesville, September 3, 1862.

HIS EXCELLENCY PRESIDENT DAVIS,

MR. PRESIDENT : The present seems to be the most propitious time since the commencement of the war for the Confederate army to enter Maryland. The two grand armies of the United States that have been operating in Virginia, though now united, are much weakened and demoralized. Their new levies, of which I understand 60,000 men have already been posted in Washington, are not yet organized, and will take some time to prepare for the field. If it is ever desired to give material aid to Maryland and afford her an opportunity of

---

   * On detached service until September 2d.
   † The following artillery organizations were in the Army of Northern Virginia July 23 and October 4, 1862, but with the exceptions noted they do not appear in the reports of the battles of Manassas Plains.
   ‡ Mentioned in the reports, but assignments not indicated.

throwing off the oppression to which she is now subject, this would seem the most favorable.

After the enemy had disappeared from the vicinity of Fairfax Court-house and taken the road to Alexandria and Washington, I did not think it would be advantageous to follow him farther. I had no intention of attacking him in his fortifications, and am not prepared to invest them. If I possessed the necessary munitions, I should be unable to supply provisions for the troops. I therefore determined, while threatening the approaches to Washington, to draw the troops into Loudoun, where forage and some provisions can be obtained, menace their possession of the Shenandoah Valley, and, if found practicable, to cross into Maryland. The purpose, if discovered, will have the effect of carrying the enemy north of the Potomac, and if prevented will not result in much evil.

The army is not properly equipped for an invasion of an enemy's territory. It lacks much of the material of war, is feeble in transportation, the animals being much reduced, and the men are poorly provided with clothes, and in thousands of instances are destitute of shoes. Still, we cannot afford to be idle, and, though weaker than our opponents in men and military equipments, must endeavor to harass if we cannot destroy them. I am aware that the movement is attended with much risk, yet I do not consider success impossible, and shall endeavor to guard it from loss. As long as the army of the enemy are employed on this frontier I have no fears for the safety of Richmond, yet I earnestly recommend that advantage be taken of this period of comparative safety to place its defence, both by land and water, in the most perfect condition. A respectable force can be collected to defend its approaches by land, and the steamer Richmond, I hope, is now ready to clear the river of hostile vessels.

Should General Bragg find it impracticable to operate to advantage on his present frontier, his army, after leaving sufficient garrisons, could be advantageously employed in opposing the overwhelming numbers which it seems to be the intention of the enemy now to concentrate in Virginia.

I have already been told by prisoners that some of Buell's cavalry have been joined to General Pope's army, and have reason to believe that the whole of McClellan's, the larger portion of Burnside's and Cox's, and a portion of Hunter's are united to it.

What occasions me most concern is the fear of getting out of ammunition. I beg you will instruct the ordnance department to spare no pains in manufacturing a sufficient amount of the best kind, and to be particular, in preparing that for the artillery, to provide three times as much of the long-range ammunition as of that for smooth-bore or short-range guns. The points to which I desire the ammunition to be forwarded will be made known to the department in time. If the quartermaster's department can furnish any shoes, it would be the greatest relief. We have entered upon September, and the nights are becoming cool.

I have the honor to be, with high respect, your obedient servant,

R. E. LEE,
General.

HEADQUARTERS,
Leesburg, Va., September 4, 1862.

HIS EXCELLENCY PRESIDENT DAVIS,

MR. PRESIDENT: I am extremely indebted to Your Excellency for your letter of the 30th ultimo, and the letter from Washington which you enclosed to me. You will already have learned all that I have ascertained subsequently of the movements of McClellan's army, a large part, if not the whole, of which participated in the battle of Saturday last, as I have good reason to believe.

Since my last communication to you, with reference to the movements which I propose to make with this army, I am more fully persuaded of the benefit that will result from an expedition into Maryland, and I shall proceed to make the movement at once unless you should signify your disapprobation. The only two subjects that give me any uneasiness are my supplies of ammunition and subsistence. Of the former I have enough for present use, and must await results before deciding to what point I will have additional supplies forwarded. Of subsistence, I am taking measures to obtain all that this region will afford ; but to be able to obtain supplies to advantage in Maryland I think it important to have the services of some one known to and acquainted with the resources of the country. I wish, therefore, that if ex-Governor Lowe can make it convenient he will come to me at once, as I have already requested by telegram. As I contemplate entering a part of the State with which Governor Lowe is well acquainted, I think he could be of much service to me in many ways. Should the results of the expedition justify it, I propose to enter Pennsylvania, unless you should deem it unadvisable upon political or other grounds.

As to the movements of the enemy, my latest intelligence shows that the army of Pope is concentrating around Washington and Alexandria in their fortifications. Citizens of this county report that Winchester has been evacuated, which is confirmed by the Baltimore *Sun* of this morning, containing extracts from the Washington *Star* of yesterday. This will still further relieve our country, and, I think, leaves the Valley entirely free. They will concentrate behind the Potomac.

I have the honor to be, with high respect, your obedient servant.

R. E. LEE.
General.

HEADQUARTERS ARMY OF NORTHERN VIRGINIA,
Leesburg, Va., September 4, 1862.

GENERAL ORDERS No. 102.

I. It is ordered and earnestly enjoined upon all commanders to reduce their transportation to a mere sufficiency to transport cooking-utensils and the absolute necessaries of a regiment. All animals not actually employed for artillery, cavalry, or draught purposes will be left in charge of Lieutenant-colonel Corley, chief quartermaster Army of Northern Virginia, to be recruited, the use of public animals, captured or otherwise, except for this service, being positively prohibited. Division, brigade, and regimental commanders, and officers in charge of artillery battalions, will give special attention to this matter. Batteries will select the best horses for use, turning over all others. Those batteries with horses too much reduced for service will be, men and horses, temporarily transferred by General Pendleton to other batteries, the guns and unserviceable horses being sent to the rear, the ammunition being turned in to reserve ordnance train. All cannoneers are positively prohibited from riding on the ammunition-chests or guns.

II. This army is about to engage in most important operations, where any excesses committed will exasperate the people, lead to disastrous results, and enlist the populace on the side of the Federal forces in hostility to our own. Quartermasters and commissaries will make all arrangements for purchase of supplies needed by our army, to be issued to the respective commands upon proper requisitions, thereby removing all excuse for depredations.

III. A provost-guard under direction of Brigadier-general L. A. Armistead will follow in rear of the army, arrest stragglers, and punish summarily all depredators and keep the men with their commands. Commanders of brigades will cause rear-guards to be placed under charge of efficient officers in rear of their brigades, to prevent the men from leaving the ranks, right, left, front, or rear, this officer being held by brigade commanders to a strict accountability for proper performance of this duty.

IV. Stragglers are usually those who desert their comrades in peril. Such characters are better absent from the army on such momentous occasions as those about to be entered upon. They will, as bringing discredit upon our cause, as useless members of the service, and as especially deserving odium, come under the special attention of the provost-marshal and be considered as unworthy members of an army which has immortalized itself in the recent glorious and successful engagements against the enemy, and will be brought before a military commission to receive the punishment due to their misconduct. The gallant soldiers who have so nobly sustained our cause by heroism in battle will assist the commanding general in securing success by aiding their officers in checking the desire for straggling among their comrades.

By order of General R. E. Lee.   R. H. CHILTON,
Assistant Adjutant-general.

HEADQUARTERS ARMY OF NORTHERN VIRGINIA,
Leesburg, Va., September 5, 1862.

HIS EXCELLENCY PRESIDENT DAVIS, RICHMOND, VA.,

MR. PRESIDENT: As I have already had the honor to inform you, this army is about entering Maryland with a view of affording the people of that State an opportunity of liberating themselves. Whatever success may attend that effort, I hope, at any rate, to annoy and harass the enemy. The army being transferred to this section, the road to Richmond through Warrenton has been abandoned as far back as Culpeper Court-house, and all trains are directed to proceed by way of Luray and Front Royal from Culpeper Court-house to Winchester. I desire that everything coming from Richmond may take that route, or any nearer one turning off before reaching Culpeper Court-house. Notwithstanding the abandonment of the line, as above mentioned, I deem it important that as soon as the bridge over the Rapidan shall be completed, that over the Rappahannock should be constructed as soon as possible, and I have requested the president of the road to have timber prepared for that purpose. My reason for desiring that this bridge shall be repaired is that in the event of falling back it is my intention to take a position about Warrenton, where, should the enemy attempt an advance on Richmond, I should be on his flank; or should he attack me, I should have a favorable country to operate in, and, bridges being repaired, should be in full communication with Richmond.

* * * * * * * * * * * *

We shall supply ourselves with provisions and forage in the country in which we operate, but ammunition must be sent from Richmond. I hope that the Secretary of War will see that the ordnance department provides ample supplies of all kinds. In forwarding the ammunition it can be sent in the way above designated for the other trains, or it can be sent to Staunton, and thence by the Valley road to Winchester, which will be my dépôt. It is not yet certain that the enemy have evacuated the Valley, but there are reports to that effect, and I have no doubt that they will leave that section as soon as they learn of the movement across the Potomac. Any officer, however, proceeding toward Winchester with a train will, of course, not move without first ascertaining that the way is clear. I am now more desirous that my suggestion as to General Loring's movements shall be carried into effect as soon as possible, so that with the least delay he may move to the lower end of the Valley, about Martinsburg, and guard the approach in that direction. He should first drive the enemy from the Kanawha Valley, if he can, and afterward, or if he finds he cannot accomplish that result, I wish him to move by way of Romney toward Martinsburg and take position in that vicinity.

I have the honor to be, with high respect, your obedient servant,

R. E. LEE,
General.

HEADQUARTERS,
Two Miles from Fredericktown, Md., September 7, 1862.

HIS EXCELLENCY PRESIDENT DAVIS,

MR. PRESIDENT: I have the honor to inform you that all the divisions of the army have crossed the Potomac, unless it may be General Walker's, from whom I have had no report since his arrival at Leesburg on the evening of the 5th instant. They occupy the line of the Monocacy.

I find there is plenty of provisions and forage in this country, and the community have received us with kindness. There may be some embarrassment in paying for necessaries for the army, as it is probable that many individuals will hesitate to receive Confederate currency. I shall endeavor in all cases to purchase what is wanted, and if unable to pay upon the spot will give certificates of indebtedness of the Confederate States for future adjustment. It is very desirable that the chief quartermaster and commissary should be provided with funds, and that some general arrangement should be made for liquidating the debts that may be incurred to the satisfaction of the people of Maryland, in order that they may willingly furnish us what is wanted. I shall endeavor to purchase horses, clothing, shoes, and medical stores for our present use, and you will see the facility that would arise from being provided with the means of paying for them. I hope it may be convenient for ex-Governor Lowe, or some prominent citizen of Maryland, to join me, with a view of expediting these and other arrangements necessary to the success of our army in this State. Notwithstanding individual expressions of kindness that have been given, and the general sympathy in the success of the Confederate States, situated as Maryland is I do not anticipate any general rising of the people in our behalf. Some additions to our ranks will no doubt be received, and I hope to procure subsistence for our troops.

As yet we have had no encounter with the enemy on this side of the river, except a detachment of cavalry at Poolesville, which resulted in slight loss on both sides, 31 of the enemy being captured. As far as I can learn, the enemy are in their intrenchments around Washington. General Banks, with his division, has advanced to Darnestown. The Shenandoah Valley has been evacuated, and their stores, etc. at Winchester are stated to have been destroyed.

I have the honor to be, with high respect, your obedient servant,

R. E. LEE,
General.

HEADQUARTERS,
Two Miles from Fredericktown, Md., September 7, 1862.

HIS EXCELLENCY PRESIDENT DAVIS,

MR. PRESIDENT: I find that the discipline of the army—which, from the manner of its organization, the necessity of bringing it into immediate service, its constant occupation and hard duty, was naturally defective—has not been improved by the forced marches and hard service it has lately undergone. I need not say to you that the material of which it is composed is the best in the world, and if properly disciplined and instructed would be able successfully to resist any force that could be brought against it. Nothing can surpass the gallantry and intelligence of the main body, but there are individuals who from their backwardness in duty, tardiness of movement, and neglect of orders do it no credit. These, if possible, should be removed from its rolls if they cannot be improved by correction.

Owing to the constitution of our courts-martial, great delay and difficulty occur in correcting daily evils. We require more promptness and certainty of punishment. One of the greatest evils, from which many minor ones proceed, is the habit of straggling from the ranks. The higher officers feel as I do, and I believe have done all in their power to stop it. It has become a habit difficult to correct. With some—the sick and feeble—it results from necessity, but with the greater number from design. These latter do not wish to be with their regiments, nor to share in their hardships and glories. They are the cowards of the army, desert their comrades in times of danger, and fill the houses of the charitable and hospitable in the march. I know of no better way of correcting this great evil than by the appointment of a military commission of men known to the country, and having its confidence and support, to accompany the army constantly, with a provost-marshal and guard to execute promptly its decisions.

If, in addition, a proper inspector-general, with sufficient rank and standing, with assistants, could be appointed to see to the execution of orders and to fix the responsibility of acts, great benefits and saving to the service would be secured. I know there is no law for carrying out these suggestions, but beg to call your attention to the subject, and ask, if this plan does not meet with your approval, that in your better judgment you will devise some other; for I assure you some remedy is necessary, especially now, when the army is in a State whose citizens it is our purpose to conciliate and bring with us. Every outrage upon their feelings and property should be checked.

I am, with high respect, your obedient servant,

R. E. LEE,
General.

RICHMOND, VA.,
September 7 [?], 1862.

GENERAL R. E. LEE, COMMANDING, ETC.,

SIR: It is deemed proper that you should, in accordance with established usage, announce by proclamation to the people of Maryland the motives and purposes of your presence among them at the head of an invading army, and you are instructed in such proclamation to make known—

1st. That the Confederate Government is waging this war solely for self-defence; that it has no design of conquest or any other purpose than to secure peace and the abandonment by the United States of their pretensions to govern a people who have never been their subjects, and who prefer self-government to a union with them.

2d. That this Government, at the very moment of its inauguration, sent commissioners to Washington to treat for a peaceful adjustment of all differences, but that these commissioners were not received, nor even allowed to communicate the object of their mission, and that on a subsequent occasion a communication from the President of the Confederacy to President Lincoln remained without answer, although a reply was promised by General Scott, into whose hands the communication was delivered.

3d. That among the pretexts urged for continuance of the war is the assertion that the Confederate Government desires to deprive the United States of the free navigation of the Western rivers, although the truth is that the Confederate Congress by public act, prior to the commencement of the war, enacted that "the peaceful navigation of the Mississippi River is hereby declared free to the citizens of any of the States upon its boundaries or upon the borders of its navigable tributaries"—a declaration to which this Government has always been, and is still, ready to adhere.

4th. That now, at a juncture when our arms have been successful, we restrict ourselves to the same just and moderate demand that we made at the darkest period of our reverses—the simple demand that the people of the United States should cease to war upon us and permit us to pursue our own path to happiness, while they in peace pursue theirs.

5th. That we are debarred from the renewal of formal proposals for peace by having no reason to expect that they would be received with the respect mutually due by nations in their intercourse, whether in peace or in war.

6th. That under these circumstances we are driven to protect our own country by transferring the seat of war to that of an enemy who pursues us with a relentless and apparently aimless hostility; that our fields have been laid waste, our people killed, many homes made desolate, and that rapine and murder have ravaged our frontiers; that the sacred right of self-defence demands that if such a war is to continue its consequences shall fall on those who persist in their refusal to make peace.

7th. That the Confederate army, therefore, comes to occupy the territory of their enemies, and to make it the theatre of hostilities; that with the people themselves rests the power to put an end to this invasion of their homes, for, if unable to prevail on the Government of the United States to conclude a general peace, their own State Government, in the exercise of its sovereignty, can secure immunity from the desolating effects of warfare on the soil of the State by a separate treaty of peace, which this Government will ever be ready to conclude on the most just and liberal basis.

8th. That the responsibility thus rests on the people of ———— of continuing an unjust and oppressive warfare upon the Confederate States—a warfare which can never end in any other manner than that now proposed. With them is the option of preserving the blessings of peace by the simple abandonment of the design of subjugating a people over whom no right of dominion has ever been conferred either by God or man.

JEFFERSON DAVIS.

———

HEADQUARTERS,
August 19, 1863.

GENERAL S. COOPER, ADJT.- AND INSP.-GEN., RICHMOND, VA.,

GENERAL: I have the honor to forward a report of the capture of Harper's Ferry and the operations of the army in Maryland (1862). The official reports of Lieutenant-general Jackson and the officers of his corps have only been recently received, which prevented its earlier transmittal. This finishes the reports of the operations of the campaign of 1862. They were designed to form a continuous narrative, though, for reasons given, were written at intervals. May I ask you to cause the several reports to be united, and to append the tabular statements accompanying each? Should this be inconvenient, if you could return the reports to me, I would have them properly arranged.

With great respect, your obedient servant,

R. E. LEE,
General.

———

REPORT OF THE CAPTURE OF HARPER'S FERRY AND OPERATIONS IN MARYLAND.

The enemy having retired to the protection of the fortifications around Washington and Alexandria, the army marched on September 3d toward Leesburg. The armies of Generals McClellan and Pope had now been brought back to the point from which they set out on the campaigns of the spring and summer. The objects of those campaigns had been frustrated and the designs of the enemy on the coast of North Carolina and in West Virginia thwarted by the withdrawal of the main body of his forces from those regions. North-eastern Virginia was freed from the presence of Federal soldiers up to the intrenchments of Washington, and soon after the arrival of the army at Leesburg information was received that the troops which had occupied Winchester had retired to Harper's Ferry and Martinsburg. The war was thus transferred from the interior to the frontier, and the supplies of rich and productive districts made accessible to our army. To prolong a state of affairs in every way desirable, and not to permit the season for active operations to pass without endeavoring to inflict further injury upon the enemy, the best course appeared to be the transfer of the army into Maryland. Although not properly equipped for invasion, lacking much of the material of war and feeble in transportation, the troops poorly provided with clothing and thousands of them destitute of shoes, it was yet believed to be strong enough to detain the enemy upon the northern frontier until the approach of winter should render his advance into Virginia difficult, if not impracticable. The condition of Maryland encouraged the belief that the presence of our army, however inferior to that of the enemy, would induce the Washington Government to retain all of its available force to provide against contingencies which its course toward the people of that State gave it reason to apprehend. At the same time, it was hoped that military success might afford us an opportunity to aid the citizens of Maryland in any efforts they might be disposed to make to recover their liberties. The difficulties that surrounded them were fully appreciated, and we expected to derive more assistance in the attainment of our object from the just fears of the Washington Government than from any active demonstration on the part of the people, unless success should enable us to give them assurance of continued protection.

Influenced by these considerations, the army was put in motion, D. H. Hill's division, which had joined us on the 2d, being in advance, and between September 4th and 7th crossed the Potomac at the fords near Leesburg and encamped in the vicinity of Fredericktown.

It was decided to cross the Potomac east of the Blue Ridge, in order, by threatening Washington and Baltimore, to cause the enemy to withdraw from the south bank, where his presence endangered our communications and the safety of those engaged in the removal of our wounded and the captured property from the late battlefields. Having accomplished this result, it was proposed to move the army into Western Maryland, establish our communications with Richmond through the Shenandoah Valley, and by threatening Pennsylvania induce the enemy to follow, and thus draw him from his base of supplies.

It had been supposed that the advance upon Fredericktown would lead to the evacuation of Martinsburg and Harper's Ferry, thus opening the line of communication through the Valley. This not having occurred, it became necessary to dislodge the enemy from those positions before concentrating the army west of the mountains. To accomplish this with the least delay, General Jackson was directed to proceed with his command to Martinsburg, and, after driving the enemy from that place, to move down the south side of the Potomac upon Harper's Ferry. General McLaws, with his own and R. H. Anderson's division, was ordered to seize Maryland Heights, on the north side of the Potomac, opposite Harper's Ferry, and Brigadier-general Walker to take possession of Loudoun Heights, on the east side of the Shenandoah where it unites with the Potomac.   These several commands were directed, after reducing Harper's Ferry and clearing the Valley of the enemy, to join the rest of the army at Boonsboro' or Hagerstown.

The march of these troops began on the 10th, and at the same time the remainder of Longstreet's command and the division of D. H. Hill crossed the South Mountain and moved toward Boonsboro'.   General Stuart, with the cavalry, remained east of the mountains to observe the enemy and retard his advance.

A report having been received that a Federal force was approaching Hagerstown from the direction of Chambersburg, Longstreet continued his march to the former place in order to secure the road leading thence to Williamsport, and also to prevent the removal of stores which were said to be in Hagerstown. He arrived at that place on the 11th, General Hill halting near Boonsboro' to prevent the enemy at Harper's Ferry from escaping through Pleasant Valley, and at the same time to support the cavalry.   The advance of the Federal army was so slow at the time we left Fredericktown as to justify the belief that the reduction of Harper's Ferry would be accomplished and our troops concentrated before they would be called upon to meet it.   In that event it had not been intended to oppose its passage through the South Mountain, as it was desired to engage it as far as possible from its base.

General Jackson marched very rapidly, and, crossing the Potomac near Williamsport on the 11th, sent A. P. Hill's division directly to Martinsburg, and disposed the rest of his command to cut off the retreat of the enemy westward.   On his approach the Federal troops evacuated Martinsburg, retiring to Harper's Ferry on the night of the 11th, and Jackson entered the former place on the 12th, capturing some prisoners and abandoned stores.   In the forenoon of the following day his leading division, under General A. P. Hill, came in sight of the enemy strongly intrenched on Bolivar Heights, in rear of Harper's Ferry.   Before beginning the attack General Jackson proceeded to put himself in communication with the co-operating forces under Generals McLaws and Walker, from the former of whom he was separated by the Potomac, and from the latter by the Shenandoah.   General Walker took possession of Loudoun Heights on the 13th, and the next day was in readiness to open upon Harper's Ferry.   General McLaws encountered more opposition.   He entered Pleasant Valley on the 11th.   On the 12th he directed General Kershaw, with his own and Barksdale's brigade, to ascend the ridge whose southern extremity is known as Maryland Heights, and attack the enemy, who occupied that position with infantry and artillery, protected by intrenchments.   He disposed the rest of his command to hold the roads leading from Harper's Ferry eastward through Weverton and northward from Sandy Hook, guarding the pass in his rear, through which he had entered Pleasant Valley, with the brigades of Semmes and Mahone. Owing to the rugged nature of the ground on which Kershaw had to operate and the want of roads, he was compelled to use infantry alone. Driving in the advance parties of the enemy on the summit of the ridge on the 12th, he assailed the works the next day. After a spirited contest they were carried, the troops engaged in their defence spiking their heavy guns and retreating to Harper's Ferry. By 4.30 P. M. Kershaw was in possession of Maryland Heights. On the 14th a road for artillery was cut along the ridge, and at 2 P. M. four guns opened upon the enemy on the opposite side of the river, and the investment of Harper's Ferry was complete.

In the mean time events transpired in another quarter which threatened to interfere with the reduction of the place. A copy of the order directing the movement of the army from Fredericktown had fallen into the hands of General McClellan, and disclosed to him the dispositions of our forces. He immediately began to push forward rapidly, and on the afternoon of the 13th was reported approaching the pass in South Mountain on the Boonsboro' and Fredericktown road. The cavalry under General Stuart fell back before him, materially impeding his progress by its gallant resistance and gaining time for preparations to oppose his advance. By penetrating the mountain at this point he would reach the rear of McLaws and be enabled to relieve the garrison at Harper's Ferry. To prevent this, General D. H. Hill was directed to guard the Boonsboro' Gap, and Longstreet ordered to march from Hagerstown to his support.

On the 13th, General Hill sent back the brigades of Garland and Colquitt to hold the pass, but, subsequently ascertaining that the enemy was near in heavy force, he ordered up the rest of his division.

Early on the 14th a large body of the enemy attempted to force its way to the rear of the position held by Hill by a road south of the Boonsboro' and Fredericktown turnpike. The attack was repulsed by Garland's brigade after a severe conflict, in which that brave and accomplished young officer was killed. The remainder of the division arriving shortly afterward, Colquitt's brigade was disposed across the turnpike road; that of C. B. Anderson, supported by Ripley, was placed on the right; and Rodes's occupied an important position on the left. Garland's brigade, which had suffered heavily in the first attack, was withdrawn, and the defence of the road occupied by it entrusted to Colonel Rosser of the Fifth Virginia cavalry, who reported to General Hill with his regiment and some artillery. The small command of General Hill repelled the repeated assaults of the Federal army and held it in check for five hours. Several attacks on the centre were gallantly repulsed by Colquitt's brigade, and Rodes maintained his position against heavy odds with the utmost tenacity. Longstreet, leaving one brigade at Hagerstown, had hurried to the assistance of Hill, and reached the scene of action between 3 and 4 P. M. His troops, much exhausted by a long, rapid march and the heat of the day, were disposed on both sides of the turnpike. General D. R. Jones, with three of his brigades —those of Pickett (under General Garnett), Kemper, and Jenkins (under Colonel Walker)—together with Evans's brigade, was posted along the mountain on the left; General Hood, with his own and Whiting's brigade (under Colonel Law), Drayton's, and D. R. Jones's (under Colonel G. T. Anderson), on the right. Batteries had been placed by General Hill in such positions as could be found, but the ground was unfavorable for the use of artillery. The battle continued with great animation until night. On the south of the turnpike the enemy was driven back some distance, and his attack on the centre repulsed with loss. His great superiority of numbers enabled him to extend beyond both of our flanks. By this means he succeeded in reaching the summit of the mountain beyond our left, and, pressing upon us heavily from that direction, gradually forced our troops back after an obstinate resistance. Darkness put an end to the contest.

The effort to force the passage of the mountains had failed, but it was manifest that without reinforcements we could not hazard a renewal of the engagement, as the enemy could easily turn either flank. Information was also received that another large body of Federal troops had during the afternoon forced their way through Crampton's Gap, only five miles in rear of McLaws. Under these circumstances it was determined to retire to Sharpsburg, where we would be upon the flank and rear of the enemy should he move against McLaws, and where we could more readily unite with the rest of the army. This movement was efficiently and skilfully covered by the cavalry brigade of General Fitzhugh Lee, and was accomplished without interruption by the enemy, who did not appear on the west side of the pass at Boonsboro' until about 8 A. M. on the following morning. The resistance that had been offered to the enemy at Boonsboro' secured sufficient time to enable General Jackson to complete the reduction of Harper's Ferry.

On the afternoon of the 14th, when he found that the troops of Walker and McLaws were in position to co-operate in the attack, he ordered General A. P. Hill to turn the enemy's left flank and enter Harper's Ferry. Ewell's division (under General Lawton) was ordered to support Hill, while Winder's brigade of Jackson's division (under Colonel Grigsby), with a battery of artillery, made a demonstration on the enemy's right near the Potomac. The rest of the division was held in reserve. The cavalry under Major Massie was placed on the extreme left to prevent the escape of the enemy. Colonel Grigsby succeeded in getting possession of an eminence on the left, upon which two batteries were advantageously posted. General A. P. Hill, observing a hill on the enemy's extreme left occupied by infantry without artillery, and protected only by an abatis of felled timber, directed General Pender with his own brigade and those of [General] Archer and Colonel Brockenbrough to seize the crest, which was done with slight resistance. At the same time he ordered Generals

Branch and Gregg to march along the Shenandoah, and, taking advantage of the ravines intersecting its steep banks, to establish themselves on the plain to the left and rear of the enemy's works. This was accomplished during the night. Lieutenant-colonel Walker, chief of artillery of A. P. Hill's division, placed several batteries on the eminence taken by General Pender, and under the directions of Colonel Crutchfield, General Jackson's chief of artillery, ten guns belonging to Ewell's division were posted on the east side of the Shenandoah, so as to enfilade the enemy's intrenchments on Bolivar Heights and take his nearest and most formidable works in reverse. General McLaws in the mean time made his preparations to prevent the force which had penetrated at Crampton's Gap from coming to the relief of the garrison. This pass had been defended by the brigade of General Cobb, supported by those of Semmes and Mahone; but, unable to oppose successfully the superior numbers brought against them, they had been compelled to retire with loss. The enemy halted at the gap, and during the night General McLaws formed his command in line of battle across Pleasant Valley about a mile and a half below Crampton's [Gap], leaving one regiment to support the artillery on Maryland Heights and two brigades on each of the roads from Harper's Ferry.

The attack on the garrison began at dawn. A rapid and vigorous fire was opened from the batteries of General Jackson and those on Maryland and Loudoun Heights. In about two hours the garrison, consisting of more than 11,000 men, surrendered; 73 pieces of artillery, about 13,000 small-arms, and a large quantity of military stores fell into our hands. Leaving General A. P. Hill to receive the surrender of the Federal troops and secure the captured property, General Jackson with his two other divisions set out at once for Sharpsburg, ordering Generals McLaws and Walker to follow without delay. Official information of the fall of Harper's Ferry and the approach of General Jackson was received soon after the commands of Longstreet and D. H. Hill reached Sharpsburg on the morning of the 15th, and reanimated the courage of the troops. General Jackson arrived early on the 16th, and General Walker came up in the afternoon. The presence of the enemy at Crampton's Gap embarrassed the movements of General McLaws. He retained the position taken during the night of the 14th to oppose an advance toward Harper's Ferry until the capitulation of that place, when, finding the enemy indisposed to attack, he gradually withdrew his command toward the Potomac. Deeming the roads to Sharpsburg on the north side of the river impracticable, he resolved to cross at Harper's Ferry and march by way of Shepherdstown. Owing to the condition of his troops and other circumstances his progress was slow, and he did not reach the battlefield at Sharpsburg until some time after the engagement of the 17th began. The commands of Longstreet and D. H. Hill on their arrival at Sharpsburg were placed in position along the range of hills between the town and the Antietam, nearly parallel to the course of that stream, Longstreet on the right of the road to Boonsboro', and Hill on the left. The advance of the enemy was delayed by the brave opposition he encountered from Fitzhugh Lee's cavalry, and he did not appear on the opposite side of the Antietam until about 2 P. M. During the afternoon the batteries on each side were slightly engaged.

On the 16th the artillery fire became warmer, and continued throughout the day. The enemy crossed the Antietam beyond the reach of our batteries and menaced our left. In anticipation of this movement Hood's two brigades had been transferred from the right and posted between D. H. Hill and the Hagerstown road. General Jackson was now directed to take position on Hood's left, and formed his line with his right resting upon the Hagerstown road and his left extending toward the Potomac, protected by General Stuart with the cavalry and horse artillery. General Walker with his two brigades was stationed on Longstreet's right. As evening approached the enemy opened more vigorously with his artillery, and bore down heavily with his infantry upon Hood, but the attack was gallantly repulsed. At 10 P. M. Hood's troops were relieved by the brigades of Lawton and Trimble of Ewell's division, commanded by General Lawton. Jackson's own division, under General J. R. Jones, was on Lawton's left, supported by the remaining brigades of Ewell.

At early dawn on the 17th the enemy's artillery opened vigorously from both sides of the Antietam, the heaviest fire being directed against our left. Under cover of this fire a large force of infantry attacked General Jackson. They were met by his troops with the utmost resolution, and for several hours the conflict raged with great fury and alternate success. General J. R. Jones was compelled to leave the field, and the command of Jackson's division devolved on General Starke. The troops advanced with great spirit, and the enemy's lines were repeatedly broken and forced to retire. Fresh troops, however, soon replaced those that were beaten, and Jackson's men were in turn compelled to fall back. The brave General Starke was killed, General Lawton was wounded, and nearly all the field officers, with a large proportion of the men, killed or disabled. Our troops slowly yielded to overwhelming numbers and fell back, obstinately disputing the progress of the enemy. Hood returned to the field and relieved the brigades of Trimble, Lawton, and Hays, which had suffered severely. General Early, who succeeded General Lawton in the command of Ewell's division, was ordered by General Jackson to move with his brigade to take the place of Jackson's division, most of which was withdrawn, its ammunition being nearly exhausted and its numbers much reduced. A small part of the division, under Colonels Grigsby and Stafford, united with Early's brigade, as did portions of the brigades of Trimble, Lawton, and Hays. The battle now raged with great violence, the small commands under Hood and Early holding their ground against many times their own numbers of the enemy and under a tremendous fire of artillery. Hood was reinforced by the brigades of Ripley, Colquitt, and Garland (under Colonel McRae) of D. H. Hill's division, and afterward by D. R. Jones's brigade under Colonel G. T. Anderson. The enemy's lines were broken and forced back, but fresh numbers advanced to their support, and they began to gain ground. The desperate resistance they encountered, however, delayed their progress until the troops of General McLaws arrived and those of General Walker could be brought from the right. Hood's brigade, greatly diminished in numbers, withdrew to replenish their ammunition, their supply being entirely exhausted. They were relieved by Walker's command, which immediately attacked the enemy vigorously, driving him back with great slaughter. Colonel Manning, commanding Walker's brigade, pursued until he was stopped by a strong fence, behind which was posted a large force of infantry with several batteries. The gallant colonel was severely wounded, and his brigade retired to the line on which the rest of Walker's command had halted.

Upon the arrival of the reinforcements under General McLaws, General Early attacked with great resolution the large force opposed to him. McLaws advanced at the same time, and the enemy were driven back in confusion, closely followed by our troops beyond the position occupied at the beginning of the engagement. The enemy renewed the assault on our left several times, but was repulsed with loss. He finally ceased to advance his infantry, and for several hours kept up a furious fire from his numerous batteries, under which our troops held their position with great coolness and courage. The attack on our left was speedily followed by one in heavy force on the centre. This was met by part of Walker's division and the brigades of G. B. Anderson and Rodes of D. H. Hill's command, assisted by a few pieces of artillery. The enemy was repulsed, and retired behind the crest of a hill, from which he kept up a desultory fire. General R. H. Anderson's division came to Hill's support and formed in rear of his line. At this time, by a mistake of orders, General Rodes's brigade was withdrawn from its position during the temporary absence of that officer at another part of the field. The enemy immediately pressed through the gap thus created, and G. B. Anderson's brigade was broken and retired, General Anderson himself being mortally wounded. Major-general R. H. Anderson and Brigadier-general Wright were also wounded and borne from the field.

The heavy masses of the enemy again moved forward, being opposed only by four pieces of artillery, supported by a few hundred men belonging to different brigades, rallied by General D. H. Hill and other officers, and parts of Walker's and R. H. Anderson's commands, Colonel Cooke, with the Twenty-seventh North Carolina regiment of Walker's brigade, standing boldly in line without a cartridge. The firm front presented by this small force and the well-directed fire of the artillery under Captain Miller of the Washington Artillery, and of Captain Boyce's South Carolina battery, checked the progress of the enemy, and in about an hour and a half he retired. Another attack was made soon afterward a little farther to the right, but was repulsed by Miller's guns, which continued to hold the ground until the close of the engagement, supported by a part of R. H. Anderson's troops.

While the attack on the centre and left was in progress the enemy made repeated efforts to force the passage of the bridge over the Antietam opposite the right wing of General Longstreet, commanded by Brigadier-general D. R. Jones. This bridge was defended by General Toombs with two regiments of his brigade (the Second and Twentieth Georgia) and the batteries of General Jones. General Toombs's small command repulsed five different assaults made by a greatly superior force, and maintained its position with distinguished gallantry. In the afternoon the enemy began to extend his line as if to cross the Antietam below the bridge, and at 4 P. M. Toombs's regiments retired from the position they had so bravely held. The enemy immediately crossed the bridge in large numbers and advanced against General Jones, who held the crest with less than two thousand men. After a determined and brave resistance he was forced to give way and the enemy gained the summit.

General A. P. Hill had arrived from Harper's Ferry, having left that place at 7.30 A. M. He was now ordered to reinforce General Jones, and moved to his support with the brigades of Archer, Branch, Gregg, and Pender, the last of whom was placed on the right of the line, and the other three advanced and attacked the enemy, now flushed with success. Hill's batteries were thrown forward, and united their fire with those of General Jones, and one of General D. H. Hill's also opened with good effect from the left of the Boonsboro' road. The progress of the enemy was immediately arrested and his lines began to waver. At this moment General Jones ordered Toombs to charge the flank, while Archer, supported by Branch and Gregg, moved upon the front of the Federal line. The enemy made a brief resistance, then broke, and retreated in confusion toward the Antietam, pursued by the troops of Hill and Jones, until he reached the protection of his batteries on the opposite side of the river. In this attack the brave and lamented Brigadier-general L. O'B. Branch was killed while gallantly leading his brigade.

It was now nearly dark, and the enemy had massed a number of batteries to sweep the approaches to the Antietam, on the opposite side of which the corps of General Porter, which had [not?] been engaged, now appeared to dispute our advance. Our troops were much exhausted and greatly reduced in numbers by fatigue and the casualties of battle. Under these circumstances it was deemed injudicious to push our advantage farther in the face of fresh troops of the enemy much exceeding the number of our own. These were accordingly recalled and formed on the line originally held by General Jones. While the attack on our centre was progressing General Jackson had been directed to endeavor to turn the enemy's right, but found it extending nearly to the Potomac, and so strongly defended with artillery that the attempt had to be abandoned. The repulse on the right ended the engagement, and after a protracted and sanguinary conflict every effort of the enemy to dislodge us from our position had been defeated with severe loss.

The arduous service in which our troops had been engaged, their great privations of rest and food, and the long marches without shoes over mountain-roads, had greatly reduced our ranks before the action began. These causes had compelled thousands of brave men to absent themselves, and many more had done so from unworthy motives. This great battle was fought by less than 40,000 men on our side, all of whom had undergone the greatest labors and hardships in the field and on the march. Nothing could surpass the determined valor with which they met the large army of the enemy, fully supplied and equipped as it was, and the result reflects the highest credit on the officers and men engaged. Our artillery, though much inferior to that of the enemy in the number of guns and weight of metal, rendered most efficient and gallant service throughout the day, and contributed greatly to the repulse of the attacks on every part of the line. General Stuart with the cavalry and horse artillery performed the duty entrusted to him of guarding our left wing with great energy and courage, and rendered valuable assistance in defeating the attack on that part of our line.

On the 18th we occupied the position of the preceding day except in the centre, where our line was drawn in about two hundred yards. Our ranks were increased by the arrival of troops which had not been engaged the day before, and, though still too weak to assume the offensive, we awaited without apprehension the renewal of the attack. The day passed without any demonstration on the part of the enemy, who, from the reports received, was expecting the arrival of reinforcements. As we could not look for a material increase in strength, and the enemy's force could be largely and rapidly augmented, it was not thought prudent to wait until he should be ready again to offer battle. During the night of the 18th the army was accordingly withdrawn to the south side of the Potomac, crossing near Shepherdstown without loss or molestation.

The enemy advanced the next morning, but was held in check by General Fitzhugh Lee with his cavalry, who covered our movement with boldness and success. General Stuart, with the main body, crossed the Potomac above Shepherdstown and moved up the river. The next day he recrossed at Williamsport, and took position to operate upon the right and rear of the enemy should he attempt to follow us. After the army had safely reached the Virginia shore with such of the wounded as could be removed and all its trains, General Porter's corps, with a number of batteries and some cavalry, appeared on the opposite side. General Pendleton was left to guard the ford with the reserve artillery and about 600 infantry. That night the enemy crossed the river above General Pendleton's position, and, his infantry support giving way, four of his guns were taken. A considerable force took position on the right bank under cover of their artillery on the commanding hills on the opposite side. The next morning General A. P. Hill was ordered to return with his division and dislodge them. Advancing under a heavy fire of artillery, the three brigades of Gregg, Pender, and Archer attacked the enemy vigorously and drove him over the river with heavy loss.

The condition of our troops now demanded repose, and the army marched to the Opequan, near Martinsburg, where it remained several days, and then moved to the vicinity of Bunker Hill and Winchester. The enemy seemed to be concentrating in and near Harper's Ferry, but made no forward movement. During this time the Baltimore and Ohio Railroad was destroyed for several miles, and that from Winchester to Harper's Ferry broken up to within a short distance of the latter place, in order to render the occupation of the Valley by the enemy after our withdrawal more difficult.

On October 8th, General Stuart was ordered to cross the Potomac above Williamsport with 1200 or 1500 cavalry and endeavor to ascertain the position and designs of the enemy. He was directed, if practicable, to enter Pennsylvania and do all in his power to impede and embarrass the military operations of the enemy. This order was executed with skill, address, and courage. General Stuart passed through Maryland, occupied Chambersburg, and destroyed a large amount of public property, making the entire circuit of General McClellan's army. He recrossed the Potomac below Harper's Ferry without loss. The enemy soon after crossed the Potomac east of the Blue Ridge and advanced southward, seizing the passes of the mountains as he progressed. General Jackson's corps was ordered to take position on the road between Berryville and Charlestown, to be prepared to oppose an advance from Harper's Ferry or a movement into the Shenandoah Valley from the east side of the mountains, while at the same time he would threaten the flank of the enemy should he continue his march along the eastern base of the Blue Ridge. One division of Longstreet's corps was sent to the vicinity of Upperville to observe the enemy's movements in front.

About the last of October the Federal army began to incline eastwardly from the mountains, moving in the direction of Warrenton. As soon as this intention developed itself Longstreet's corps was moved across the Blue Ridge, and about November 3d to position at Culpeper Court-house, while Jackson advanced one of his divisions to the east side of the Blue Ridge. The enemy gradually concentrated about Warrenton, his cavalry being thrown forward beyond the Rappahannock in the direction of Culpeper Court-house, and occasionally skirmishing with our own, which was closely observing his movements. This situation of affairs continued without material change until about the middle of November, when the movements began which resulted in the winter campaign on the lower Rappahannock.

The accompanying return of the medical director will show the extent of our losses in the engagements mentioned. The reports of the different commanding officers must, of necessity, be referred to for the details of these operations.

I desire to call the attention of the Department to the names of those brave officers and men who are particularly mentioned for courage and good conduct by their commanders. The limits of this report will not permit me to do more than renew the expression of my admiration for the valor that shrank from no peril and the fortitude that endured every privation without a murmur. I must also refer to the report of General Stuart for the particulars of the services rendered by the cavalry, besides those to which I have alluded. Its vigilance, activity, and courage were conspicuous, and to its assistance is due, in a great measure, the success of some of the most important and delicate operations of the campaign.

Respectfully submitted, R. E. LEE,
General.

HEADQUARTERS ARMY OF NORTHERN VIRGINIA,
October 2, 1862.

GENERAL : The enemy's cavalry, under General Pleasonton, with six pieces of artillery, drove back our pickets yesterday in front of Shepherdstown. The Ninth Virginia cavalry, which was on picket, repulsed the enemy several times by vigorous charges, disputing the ground step by step back to the main body. By the time his artillery reached him, Colonel W. H. F. Lee, who was in command of the brigade, was obliged to place it on the west bank of the Opequan, on the flank of the enemy as he approached Martinsburg. General Hampton's brigade had retired through Martinsburg on the Tuscarora road, when General Stuart arrived and made dispositions to attack. Lee's brigade was advanced immediately and Hampton's ordered forward. The enemy retired at the approach of Lee along the Shepherdstown road, and was driven across the Potomac by the cavalry with severe loss, and darkness alone prevented it from being a signal victory. His rear was overtaken and put to flight, our cavalry charging in gallant style under a severe fire of artillery, routing squadron after squadron, killing a number, wounding more, and capturing several. He was driven through Shepherdstown and crossed the river after dark, in no case standing a hand-to-hand conflict, but relying upon his artillery and carbines at long range for protection. I regret that we lost one lieutenant and several privates.

I am, most respectfully, your obedient servant,

R. E. LEE,
General.

GENERAL S. COOPER,
Adjutant- and Inspector-general C. S. A, Richmond, Va.

HEADQUARTERS ARMY OF NORTHERN VIRGINIA,
October 14, 1862.

SIR : The expedition under General Stuart to Pennsylvania, which crossed the Potomac on the evening of the 9th instant at McCoy's Ford, above Williamsport, will reach their camp to-day. They proceeded through Mercersburg to Chambersburg, where they obtained from the United States storehouses such supplies as they needed, but were unable to destroy the railroad bridge over the Conacocheague in consequence of its being of iron. The shops, etc. of the company were, however, destroyed. Thence he proceeded to Emmittsburg, through Liberty, New Market, Hyattsville, Barnesville, to White's Ford, below the mouth of the Monocacy, making a complete circuit of the enemy's position. On approaching the Potomac he was opposed by the enemy's cavalry under General Stoneman, but drove him back, and put to flight the infantry stationed on the bluff at White's Ford to guard the passage.

His expedition was eminently successful, and accomplished without other loss than the wounding of one man. He obtained many remounts for his cavalry and artillery, and deserves much credit for his prudence and enterprise.

From the information he was able to obtain I am inclined to believe that General McClellan has detached no part of his army eastward, but, on the contrary, has been receiving reinforcements. His main army is posted west of the Blue Ridge range, and stretches from Hagerstown to Rockville, the centre resting at Harper's Ferry, with detachments guarding the river. They have a large force repairing the Chesapeake and Ohio Canal, and I should judge, from all I can learn, that the operation of the Baltimore and Ohio [Rail] road from Harper's Ferry west is viewed by them as an object of great importance, and that efforts will be made to repair it. I am breaking up the Harper's Ferry and Winchester [Rail] road to increase the obstacles to their advance up the Shenandoah Valley. The iron would be very useful to the roads farther south, and the flat iron might be used for Government purposes, but I have no means of sending it away.

I have the honor to be your obedient servant,

R. E. LEE,
General.

HON. G. W. RANDOLPH,
Secretary of War, Richmond, Va.

Abstract from Return of the Army of Northern Virginia, GEN-
ERAL R. E. LEE *commanding, for Sept. 22, 1862, during Campaign at Manassas and Antietam, Aug. 28–30 and Sept., 1862.*

COMMAND.	Present for duty.		Aggregate present.
	Officers.	Men.	
Longstreet's Corps.			
General staff	11	. .	11
McLaws's division	269	3,659	4,018
Jones's division	350	3,460	4,403
Anderson's division	389	4,935	6,298
Walker's division	221	3,207	3,871
Hood's division	255	2,592	2,847
Evans's brigade	40	516	556
Lee's and Walton's battalions of artillery	39	632	677
Total	1,574	19,001	22,681
Jackson's Corps.			
D. H. Hill's division	332	4,739	5,821
A. P. Hill's division	342	4,435	5,468
R. S. Ewell's division	298	3,144	4,066
Jackson's own division	186	2,367	3,484
Total	1,158	14,685	18,839
Grand total	2,732	33,686	41,520

Note on original return: "This return is very imperfect, the cavalry and reserve artillery not being reported."

*Abstract from Return of Tri-monthly Report of Ewell's Divis-
ion,* MAJ.-GEN. R. S. EWELL *commanding, for Sept. 22, 1862.*

COMMAND.	Present for duty.		Aggregate present.	Aggregate present and absent.	Aggregate last return.	Remarks.
	Officers.	Men.				
Early's brigade, Gen. J. A. Early . .	124	905	1,221	4,035	4,082	Rolls of several com-panies of 7th Virginia regiment lost.
Fourth (Lawton's) Brigade, Colonel John H. Lamar commanding . .	45	682	804	. .	. .	"Absent" not given by reason of absence of company officers.
Seventh (Trimble's) Brigade, Col. James A. Walker commanding . .	60	781	941	2,759	2,950	
First Louisiana (Hays's) Brigade, Brig.-gen. H. T. Hays command-ing	59	634	936	. .	4,127	"Absent" in 7th Lou-isiana regiment not reported.
Total	288	3,002	3,902			

Station, camp near Martinsburg, Va.

HEADQUARTERS,
Near Fredericktown, Md., September 8, 1862.

HIS EXCELLENCY JEFFERSON DAVIS, PRESIDENT OF THE CONFEDERATE STATES, RICHMOND, VA.,

MR. PRESIDENT: The present position of affairs, in my opinion, places it in the power of the Government of the Confederate States to propose with propriety to that of the United States the recognition of our independence. For more than a year both sections of the country have been devastated by hostilities which have brought sorrow and suffering upon thousands of homes without advancing the objects which our enemies proposed to themselves in beginning the contest. Such a proposition, coming from us at this time, could in no way be regarded as suing for peace, but, being made when it is in our power to inflict injury upon our adversary, would show conclusively to the world that our sole object is the establishment of our independence and the attainment of an honorable peace. The rejection of this offer would prove to the country that the responsibility of the continuance of the war does not rest upon us, but that the party in power in the United States elect to prosecute it for purposes of their own. The proposal of peace would enable the people of the United States to determine at their coming elections whether they will support those who favor a prolongation of the war or those who wish to bring it to a termination which can but be productive of good to both parties without affecting the honor of either.

I have the honor to be, with high respect, your obedient servant,

R. E. LEE,
General.

HEADQUARTERS ARMY OF NORTHERN VIRGINIA,
Hagerstown, Md., September 12, 1862.

HIS EXCELLENCY PRESIDENT DAVIS,

MR. PRESIDENT: Before crossing the Potomac I considered the advantages of entering Maryland east or west of the Blue. Ridge. In either case it was my intention to march upon this town. By crossing east of the Blue Ridge both Washington and Baltimore would be threatened, which I believed would ensure the withdrawal of the mass of the enemy's troops; north of the Potomac I think this has been accomplished. I had also supposed that as soon as it was known that the army had reached Fredericktown the enemy's forces in the Valley of Virginia, which had retired to Harper's Ferry and Martinsburg, would retreat altogether from the State. In this I was disappointed, and you will perceive from the accompanying order of the 9th instant that Generals Jackson and McLaws have been detached with a view of capturing their forces at each place should they not have retired.

The army has been received in this region with sympathy and kindness.

We have found in this city about fifteen hundred barrels of flour, and I am led to hope that a supply can be gathered from the mills in the country, though I fear we shall have to haul from the Valley of Virginia. The supply of beef has been very small, and we have been able to procure no bacon. A thousand pairs of shoes and some clothing were obtained in Fredericktown, two hundred and fifty pairs in Williamsport, and about four hundred pairs in this city. They will not be sufficient to cover the bare feet of the army.

* * * * * * * * *

R. E. LEE,
General.

HEADQUARTERS ARMY OF NORTHERN VIRGINIA,
Hagerstown, Md., September 13, 1862.

HIS EXCELLENCY PRESIDENT DAVIS, RICHMOND, VA.,

MR. PRESIDENT: I regret that you should have exposed yourself while indisposed to the fatigue of travel, though I should have been highly gratified at an opportunity of conferring with you on many points. You will perceive by the printed address * to the people of Maryland, which has been sent you, that I have not gone contrary to the views expressed by you on the subject. Should there be anything in it to correct, please let me know.

* * * * * * * * *

R. E. LEE,
General.

HEADQUARTERS ARMY OF NORTHERN VIRGINIA,
Camp on the Opequan, near Smoketown, September 23, 1862.

HIS EXCELLENCY PRESIDENT DAVIS, RICHMOND, VA.,

MR. PRESIDENT: My desire for the welfare of the army and the success of the war induces me to trouble you very often. In addition to the matters to which I have recently called your attention, there is another of vital importance to the service. A great number of officers and men borne on the rolls of the army I fear are permanently incapacitated for duty. These should be discharged and their places filled with effective men. Justice would seem to require that some provision should be made for their support, but whether this had better be done now or left to the close of the war you and Congress must determine. Companies whose rolls show a maximum of men cannot be filled by accepting new members when they offer unless the inefficient men be removed, nor can the places of officers unfit for duty be filled until the present incumbents are retired. The subject of recruiting this army is also one of paramount importance. The usual casualties of battle have diminished its

* Included in Chapter XII.

ranks, but its numbers have been greatly decreased by desertion and straggling. This was the main cause of its retiring from Maryland, as it was unable
to cope with advantage with the numerous hosts of the enemy. His ranks are
daily increasing, and it is just reported, on what I consider reliable authority,
that 40,000 joined the army of General McClellan on the day after the battle
of Sharpsburg. We have now abundance of arms ; and if the unarmed regiments in Texas and Arkansas could be brought forward, as well as the conscripts from the different States, they would add greatly to our strength. Our
stragglers are being daily collected, and that is one of the reasons of my being
now stationary. How long they will remain with us or when they will again
disappear it is impossible for me to say.

*   *   *   *   *   *   *   *   *

R. E. LEE,
General Commanding.

HEADQUARTERS ARMY OF NORTHERN VIRGINIA,
Camp on the Opequan, near Smoketown, September 25, 1862.

HIS EXCELLENCY PRESIDENT DAVIS, RICHMOND, VA.,

MR. PRESIDENT : Since my letter of the 23d instant the enemy has been
quiet. He is in occupation of Harper's Ferry, and has troops posted both on
the Maryland and Loudoun Heights. I presume he will reconstruct the railroad bridge over the Potomac, and I see it stated in the Baltimore papers that
a new bridge over the Monocacy has been built. When the railroad is open
to Harper's Ferry he may possibly advance up the Valley, where I shall
endeavor to occupy and detain him.

When I withdrew from Sharpsburg into Virginia it was my intention to
recross the Potomac at Williamsport and move upon Hagerstown, but the
condition of the army prevented ; nor is it yet strong enough to advance
advantageously. Some of the stragglers have been gathered in, but many
have wandered to a distance, feigning sickness, wounds, etc., deceiving the
guards and evading the scouts. Many of them will not stop until they reach
their distant homes.

In a military point of view, the best move, in my opinion, the army could
make would be to advance upon Hagerstown and endeavor to defeat the
enemy at that point. I would not hesitate to make it, even with our diminished
numbers, did the army exhibit its former temper and condition, but, as far as I
am able to judge, the hazard would be great and a reverse disastrous. I am
therefore led to pause.

I have written to General Loring suggesting the advantages, since the enemy
has been driven from the Kanawha Valley, of proceeding down the Monon-
gahela Valley, breaking up the railroad in the vicinity of Clarksburg, Fairmont,

Cheat River, etc., and, should opportunity offer, of continuing his route into Pennsylvania and collecting horses and other necessaries for the army generally. I have told him to keep me advised of his movements should he undertake the expedition, that there may be co-operation, if practicable, between the two armies.

I am, with the highest respect, your obedient servant,

R. E. Lee,
General.

HEADQUARTERS ARMY OF NORTHERN VIRGINIA,
Washington Run, near Winchester, Va., October 2, 1862.

HIS EXCELLENCY PRESIDENT DAVIS,

MR. PRESIDENT: I received last night your letter of the 28th ultimo, and am much obliged to you for the attention given to my requests. I have stated so frequently my opinion of the necessity of improving the discipline of our armies that I need not repeat it. I hope Congress will grant every facility in their power.

In reference to commanders of corps with the rank of lieutenant-general, of which you request my opinion, I can confidently recommend Generals Longstreet and Jackson in this army. My opinion of the merits of General Jackson has been greatly enhanced during this expedition. He is true, honest, and brave, has a single eye to the good of the service, and spares no exertion to accomplish his object. Next to these two officers, I consider General A. P. Hill the best commander with me. He fights his troops well and takes good care of them. At present I do not think that more than two commanders of corps are necessary for this army. I need not remind you of the merits of General E. K. Smith, whom I consider one of our best officers. As regards the appointments for major-generals and brigadier-generals for this army, I have already forwarded to you the names of those whose merits I think have earned promotion. Should you conclude to promote Generals Longstreet and Jackson, major-generals in their places will be required, but I believe you have sufficient names before you to fill the vacancies. Your own knowledge of the claims and qualifications of the officers will, I feel assured, enable you to make the best selection. I do not think it necessary to call your attention to the officers immediately around Richmond, as you are fully aware of their merits.

*   *   *   *   *   *   *   *   *

I am, with the highest respect and esteem, your obedient servant,

R. E. Lee,
General.

HEADQUARTERS ARMY OF NORTHERN VIRGINIA,
October 2, 1862.

GENERAL ORDERS
No. 116.

In reviewing the achievements of the army during the present campaign, the commanding general cannot withhold the expression of his admiration of the indomitable courage it has displayed in battle and its cheerful endurance of privation and hardship on the march. Since your great victories around Richmond you have defeated the enemy at Cedar Mountain, expelled him from the Rappahannock, and after a conflict of three days utterly repulsed him on the plains of Manassas and forced him to take shelter within the fortifications around his capital. Without halting for repose you crossed the Potomac, stormed the heights of Harper's Ferry, made prisoners of more than 11,000 men, and captured upward of seventy-five pieces of artillery, all their small-arms, and other munitions of war. While one corps of the army was thus engaged the other ensured its success by arresting at Boonsboro' the combined armies of the enemy advancing under their favorite general to the relief of their beleaguered comrades. On the field of Sharpsburg, with less than one-third his numbers, you resisted from daylight until dark the whole army of the enemy and repulsed every attack along his entire front of more than four miles in extent. The whole of the following day you stood prepared to resume the conflict on the same ground, and retired next morning without molestation across the Potomac. Two attempts subsequently made by the enemy to follow you across the river have resulted in his complete discomfiture and being driven back with loss. Achievements such as these demanded much valor and patriotism. History records few examples of greater fortitude and endurance than this army has exhibited, and I am commissioned by the President to thank you in the name of the Confederate States for the undying fame you have won for their arms. Much as you have done, much more remains to be accomplished. The enemy again threatens with invasion, and to your tried valor and patriotism the country looks with confidence for deliverance and safety. Your past exploits give assurance that this confidence is not misplaced.

R. E. LEE,
General Commanding.

HEADQUARTERS ARMY OF NORTHERN VIRGINIA,
Camp near Winchester, Va., October 4, 1862.*

HON. GEORGE W. RANDOLPH, SECRETARY OF WAR, RICHMOND, VA.,

SIR: Mrs. Phil Kearny has applied for the sword and horse of Major-general Phil Kearny, which were captured at the time that officer was killed, near Chan-

* Received October 7, 1862.

tilly. The horse and saddle have been turned over to the quartermaster of the army and the sword to the chief of ordnance. I would send them at once as an evidence of the sympathy felt for her bereavement and as a testimony of the appreciation of a gallant soldier, but I have looked upon such articles as public property, and that I had no right to dispose of them except for the benefit of the service. In this case, however, I should like to depart from this rule, provided it is not considered improper by the Department, and I therefore refer the matter for your decision. An early reply is requested.

I am, very respectfully, your obedient servant,

R. E. LEE,
General.

HEADQUARTERS ARMY OF NORTHERN VIRGINIA,
October 6, 1862.

HON. GEORGE W. RANDOLPH, SECRETARY OF WAR, RICHMOND, VA.,

SIR: In view of the probability of the movements of the army, which would render it inconvenient to return the horse, equipments, and sword of the late General Kearny to his widow, in accordance with her request as communicated to you in my letter of the 4th instant, I have caused those articles to be sent within the enemy's lines, to be forwarded to Mrs. Kearny, without waiting for your reply to my letter. Before doing so I caused the horse and equipments to be appraised by a board, and the price fixed for them has been paid to the quartermaster, to await your decision upon the question of returning those articles, as submitted by me in my letter above referred to. The sword, which was a light one with a leather scabbard suitable for a disabled person, I regarded as constituting part of General Kearny's private property, and as such proper to be returned to his family, in accordance with approved usage under such circumstances. Its value will also be paid to the ordnance department should you not approve of its return.

I have the honor to be, very respectfully, your obedient servant,

R. E. LEE,
General.

HEADQUARTERS ARMY OF NORTHERN VIRGINIA,
October 22, 1862.

HIS EXCELLENCY JEFFERSON DAVIS, RICHMOND, VA.,

MR. PRESIDENT: The time is approaching when it becomes necessary to consider what disposition of the troops can best be made for the winter. This must, of course, mainly depend upon the operations of the enemy. But on the supposition that he will do little more this fall than to organize and instruct his new troops, and as the winter advances prepare to advance south of James

River, which now seems to me his most probable plan, some position should be chosen with a view of procuring shelter and provisions for the army and forage for the horses. I have seen no indications to make me believe that General McClellan will advance up the Shenandoah Valley. When this army retires from its present position I think it probable he will occupy Winchester with a sufficient force, and reconstruct the Baltimore and Ohio Railroad between Harper's Ferry and Cumberland. A portion of his force will, no doubt, be retained at Fairfax Court-house and Centreville, and may probably be advanced toward the Rappahannock. At any rate, it will be necessary for us to keep a sufficient force south of the Rappahannock and in front of Richmond, and also one in this valley. We must select points where there is sufficient wood for hutting and fuel for the troops, and within convenient distance from the railroad by which they can be provisioned. A portion of these troops may be placed south of James River, or, if circumstances require it, can operate in Georgia and South Carolina. I should be very glad if Your Excellency would consider this subject and give me the benefit of your views, as well as such directions as you may see fit.

We shall finish by to-morrow, I think, the destruction of as much of the Winchester and Harper's Ferry and Baltimore and Ohio railroads within this valley as we can accomplish without bringing on a battle, which I do not desire to do so near the enemy's base of operations. I wish there was any possibility of my sending back the iron from these roads, but, as there is none within my reach, I have been obliged to injure it as much as possible, to prevent its being relaid. The sills have been taken up and burned, and the bridges and station-houses at Martinsburg, etc. destroyed.

I have to-day ordered General Walker's division to cross the Blue Ridge at Ashby's Gap and take position in the vicinity of Upperville, with a view of checking the incursions of the enemy in that region and watching more closely his movements east of the mountains.

I am, with great respect, Your Excellency's obedient servant,

R. E. LEE,
General.

HEADQUARTERS DEPARTMENT OF NORTHERN VIRGINIA,
November 6, 1862.

LIEUTENANT-GENERAL THOMAS J. JACKSON, COMMANDING CORPS,

GENERAL: Your letter of yesterday from Millwood has been received. The progress of the enemy so far seems to be steadily forward, judging from your reports and those of General Stuart, occupying in his advance the gaps of the Blue Ridge with his right and resting his left on the Orange and Alexandria Railroad. It would seem to be his desire either to detain you in the Valley or to get above you, so as to cut you off from a junction with Longstreet; neither of which must you permit. It will be necessary for you to make every arrangement, so that you may move promptly up the Valley, that the two corps can be kept in communication with each other and unite when necessary. General George H. Steuart will have to evacuate Winchester before you move higher than Front Royal, and I hope you will be able to bring off all the sick that are able to travel. One of the objects of the enemy in proceeding through the counties bordering on the Blue Ridge may be to obtain the forage in that region. You must give the necessary directions to Munford, so that he may regulate his movements by your own. The advantage of the enemy on the eastern slope of the Blue Ridge may be regulated by his force and his facilities for procuring supplies of forage and provision. I do not think he would descend into the Valley except with such force as he would think capable of crushing you, still leaving a sufficient force to oppose Longstreet. I have directed Stuart to watch his movements closely and inform me when he occupies Chester Gap or advances toward Thornton's. In the latter event it will be unwise for the whole of the cavalry to fall back before him to Luray, as that would leave exposed the whole of the country east of the Blue Ridge. I will make inquiries about signal-men and endeavor to establish a line so far as our means will permit. I have heard, however, that one of our signal-officers was captured in Loudoun.

*   *   *   *   *   *   *   *   *

Very respectfully, your obedient servant,

R. E. LEE,
General.

HEADQUARTERS ARMY OF NORTHERN VIRGINIA,
November 9, 1862—1 P. M.

LIEUTENANT-GENERAL THOMAS J. JACKSON, COMMANDING LEFT WING, ETC.,

GENERAL: Your letter of the 7th is at hand. The enemy seems to be massing his troops along the Manassas Railroad in the vicinity of Piedmont, which gives him great facilities for bringing up supplies from Alexandria. It has occurred to me that his object may be to seize upon Strasburg with his main force, to intercept your ascent of the Valley. This would oblige you to cross into the Lost River Valley, or west of it, unless you could force a passage through the Blue Ridge; hence my anxiety for your safety. If you can prevent such a movement of the enemy and operate strongly upon his flank and rear through the gaps of the Blue Ridge, you would certainly, in my opinion, effect the object you propose. A demonstration of crossing into Maryland would serve the same purpose, and might call him back to the Potomac. As my object is to retard and baffle his designs, if it can be accomplished by manœuvring your corps as you propose it will serve my purpose as well as if effected in any other way. With this understanding, you can use your discretion—which I know I can rely upon—in remaining or advancing up the Valley. But I desire you will take precautions to prevent the enemy's occupying the roads west of the Massanutten Mountains, and your demonstration upon his flank might probably be as well made from a position nearer to Strasburg as from that you now occupy. If the enemy should move into the Valley through Thornton's Gap, you must seize the pass through the Massanutten Mountains as soon as you can, while Longstreet will advance through Milman's, which you term Fisher's Gap (on the direct road from Madison Court-house to New Market). But I think his movement upon Front Royal the more probable of the two.

Keep me advised of your movements and intentions, and you must keep always in view the probability of an attack upon Richmond from either north or south, when a concentration of forces will become necessary. The enemy has made no advance south of the Rappahannock line since I last wrote you.

The non-occupation of Martinsburg by the enemy, and his not marching into the Valley from his former base on the Potomac, shows, I think, that his whole force has been drawn from Maryland into Virginia east of the Blue Ridge. His retirement from Snicker's and Ashby's gaps and concentration of his force on the railroad in the vicinity of Manassas Gap must either be for the purpose of supplying it or for making a descent upon Front Royal and Strasburg. I hope, therefore, you will be on your guard.

I am, etc.,

R. E. LEE,
General.

HEADQUARTERS DEPARTMENT OF NORTHERN VIRGINIA,
November 10, 1862—7 P. M.

LIEUTENANT-GENERAL THOMAS J. JACKSON, COMMANDING, ETC.,

GENERAL: Your letter of the 9th instant has been received, and I am glad to learn that your command is in condition to move whenever it becomes necessary. My letter of yesterday will have explained to you my views and informed you that I rely upon your judgment and discretion in determining the time of your departure. As soon as you think that your presence in that portion of the Valley will not retard or prevent the advance of the enemy east of the Blue Ridge, I wish you to advance with all celerity to unite with Longstreet's corps. You must inform yourself of the routes, prepare provision and forage for the occasion, and lose no time in executing your march when it is commenced. As stated in my previous letter, should you find yourself in danger at any time of being cut off from the route west of the Massanutten Mountains, you must move at once.

*   *   *   *   *   *   *   *   *

I have the honor to be, etc.,

R. E. LEE,
General.

HEADQUARTERS DEPARTMENT OF NORTHERN VIRGINIA,
November 12, 1862—8 A. M.

LIEUTENANT-GENERAL THOMAS J. JACKSON, COMMANDING CORPS,

GENERAL: Your letter of the 10th by special courier has been received. In my letter of yesterday in reply to yours of first date I discussed the question of your further delay in the Valley. I cannot add more to what has been said, and it must depend upon the advantages you can effect by operating against the communications of the enemy. He has as yet given no indications of his further movement or direction southward. Whether he will cross the Rappahannock or proceed to Fredericksburg I cannot tell. It is easier for you to determine what damage you can inflict upon him where you are. If you can accomplish nothing but to retain occupation of the Valley, in the apparent and probable need of all our forces southward the force under you is too far from the scene of action. If an advance toward Fredericksburg is discovered, it is plain that you cannot delay longer, and you must be prepared to move at any time. Make your arrangements accordingly, and be prepared to move at any moment. General Stuart has been directed to watch the enemy closely, but you know the difficulty of determining the first movements. You may learn more from the rear than we can in front. It would be grievous for the Valley and its supplies to fall into the hands of the enemy unnecessarily, but we can only act upon probabilities and endeavor to avoid greater evils.

Colonel Davidson, at Staunton, telegraphs that the enemy is within thirty-five miles of that place—one column at McDowell, and one at Rawley Springs, the two columns estimated at from 4000 to 6000 men. He asks for reinforcements; I have none to send him. Have you a disposable force? The Marylanders, if unable to remain at Winchester, might be stationed there.

I am, etc.,

R. E. LEE,

General.

HEADQUARTERS ARMY OF NORTHERN VIRGINIA,
November 14, 1862.

LIEUTENANT-GENERAL THOMAS J. JACKSON, COMMANDING, ETC.,

GENERAL: Your letter of the 10th instant by courier and telegraphic despatch of to-day have been received. The withdrawal of the enemy from the Blue Ridge and concentration at Warrenton and Waterloo show, I think, that he has abandoned his former base and assumed that of the Warrenton and Alexandria Railroad. Your presence, then, in the Valley seems to be too distant from his line of operation to affect his movements should you remain quiescent. If you were able by a movement through Snicker's Gap to threaten his communication north of Manassas Junction, it would have the effect of recalling him.

This, in your condition, would be a hazardous movement, as he could bring a force against you too strong for you to resist, and might intercept your return into the Valley. I do not see, then, what good your continuance in the Valley will effect beyond the support of your troops. It is true it may prevent the occupation of Winchester by a portion of the enemy's forces, but in a military point of view that would accomplish but little beyond the annoyance of the inhabitants, which is much to be lamented. Your detention there until the occurrence of bad weather and deep roads might so break down your command as to render it inefficient for further operations should they become requisite elsewhere. Your remaining in the Valley was based upon the supposition that by operating upon the flank and rear of the enemy you might prevent his progress southward, and so long as you found that this could be effected I considered it advantageous; but when this cannot be accomplished the sooner you make a junction with Longstreet's corps, the better. The question now is whether you can in the present condition of things affect the movements of the enemy. He is in a position to move upon Culpeper, using the Orange and Alexandria Railroad as a line of communication, or to march upon Fredericksburg and establish his base on the Potomac. As you are the best judge of your ability to operate advantageously against him, I leave you to determine the question whether you will continue in your present position or march at once to join Longstreet. I have heard of no movement of the enemy as yet below Kelly's Ford, except a visit of a small party of his cavalry to Fredericksburg on the 8th, when they charged through the town, but were immediately driven back across the river by our cavalry. General Stuart reports this evening that two brigades of the enemy's infantry are at Jeffersonton. Our cavalry still hold the line of Aestham River to Sperryville. The position of Longstreet's corps remains unchanged since you were last informed.

I am, with great respect, your obedient servant,

R. E. LEE,
General.

HEADQUARTERS DEPARTMENT OF NORTHERN VIRGINIA,
Camp near Culpeper Court-house, November 19, 1862—9 A. M.

LIEUTENANT-GENERAL THOMAS J. JACKSON, NEAR WINCHESTER,

GENERAL: Your letter of the 18th has been received. It is certainly important to deceive the enemy as long as possible as to our position and intentions, provided it is rendered certain that a junction can be made before a battle; and this latter point we must always keep in view as necessary to enable us to resist the large force now on the Rappahannock.

As to the place where it may be necessary or best to fight, I cannot now state, as this must be determined by circumstances which may arise. I do not now anticipate making a determined stand north of the North Anna. Longstreet's corps is moving to Fredericksburg, opposite to which place Sumner's corps has arrived.

As before stated, you can remain in the Valley as long as you see that your presence there cripples and embarrasses the general movement of the enemy and yet leaves you free to unite with Longstreet for a battle.

I will advise you from time to time of the movements of the enemy and of mine as far as they can be discovered, and with as little delay as possible; but you must make allowances for the inaccuracy of the first and the delay of the second, and predicate your movements so as to be on the safe side.

I am, most respectfully,

R. E. LEE,
General.

Abstract from Field Return of the Department of Northern Virginia, commanded by GENERAL ROBERT E. LEE, *November 20, 1862; headquarters, Fredericksburg.*

| | Present for duty. | | | | | | | |
| COMMAND. | Infantry. | | Cavalry. | | Artillery. | | Aggregate present. | Aggregate present and absent. |
	Officers.	Men.	Officers.	Men.	Officers.	Men.		
FIRST ARMY CORPS,								
LIEUTENANT-GENERAL LONGSTREET.								
Anderson's division	422	5,717	...	...	...	...	7,646	13,725
McLaws's division	578	7,559	...	...	...	...	9,447	16,278
Pickett's division	551	5,634	...	...	...	...	7,498	15,138
Hood's division	462	5,715	...	...	...	...	7,113	12,734
Ransom's division	270	3,904	...	...	...	...	4,945	8,176
Alexander's battalion of artillery	...	...	...	...	27	517	576	763
Walton's battalion of artillery	...	...	...	...	15	242	274	349
Total	2,283	28,529	...	...	42	759	37,499	67,163
SECOND ARMY CORPS,								
LIEUTENANT-GENERAL JACKSON.								
D. R. Jones's division	407	4,627	...	...	...	...	6,015	12,629
Ewell's division	572	7,018	...	...	...	...	9,122	16,709
D. H. Hill's division	549	7,653	...	...	...	...	9,576	18,526
A. P. Hill's division	723	9,897	...	...	...	...	12,331	21,781
Brown's battalion of artillery	...	...	...	...	23	479	528	697
Post of Winchester	72	767	...	...	...	...	959	1,260
Total	2,323	29,962	...	...	23	479	38,531	71,602
Stuart's cavalry division	...	...	603	8,551	...	...	10,539	15,008
Pendleton's reserve artillery *	...	...	...	...	...	...	...	...
Grand total	4,606	58,491	603	8,551	65	1,238	86,569	153,773

* No return received.

HEADQUARTERS ARMY OF NORTHERN VIRGINIA,
Camp Fredericksburg, November 22, 1862—8 P. M.

GENERAL S. COOPER, ADJUTANT- AND INSPECTOR-GENERAL, RICHMOND, VA.,

GENERAL: I have the honor to report for the information of the President
and Department that General Burnside's army, apparently in full force, is on
the other side of the Rappahannock, opposite this place, stretching from the
banks of the river toward Acquia Creek. I have learned from our scouts sent
toward the Potomac, but who were unable to reach Acquia, that it is reported by
citizens that the enemy were making preparations to reconstruct the wharves at
that place by means of their pontoon-trains. I have not heard of a commencement being made to rebuild the railroad. Their immense wagon-train is
actively engaged, apparently, in provisioning their army, which during the
last three days of rain and cold I know has been a difficult operation, and must
have been attended with suffering among their troops. I have with me two
brigades of Stuart's cavalry, Pendleton's reserve artillery, and four divisions
of Longstreet's corps. The Fifth will be here to-morrow. If the enemy
attempt to cross the river, I shall resist it, though the ground is favorable for
him. Yesterday he summoned the corporate authorities of Fredericksburg to
surrender the city by 5 P. M., and threatened, in the event of its not being
delivered up, to commence to shell the town at 9 A. M. to-day.

Upon the reference of this communication to me, as I was unable to prevent
the city from being cannonaded, I requested General Longstreet to inform the
authorities that they might say that I would not occupy or use the city for military purposes, but that I would resist its occupation by the enemy, and recommended that the women and children be at once removed. Our wagons and
ambulances have been employed all last night and to-day in accomplishing
this object. This morning the authorities were informed that the bombardment would not commence at the hour threatened, but that a definite answer
would be returned in a short time. I have not learned whether it has yet been
received.

*   *   *   *   *   *   *   *   *

I have the honor to be, with great respect, your obedient servant,

R. E. LEE,
General.

HEADQUARTERS ARMY OF NORTHERN VIRGINIA,
Near Fredericksburg, November 25, 1862.

HIS EXCELLENCY PRESIDENT DAVIS, RICHMOND, VA.:

MR. PRESIDENT: I have endeavored in my official communications to the
adjutant- and inspector-general of the army to keep you apprised of the military condition of affairs on this frontier.

For the first two days after my arrival the enemy's forces were being massed on the heights of Stafford, opposite Fredericksburg ; but on the evening of the 22d, which was the second day after my arrival, his camps and trains commenced to move to the rear, and on the morning of the 23d his parks of artillery had all disappeared save four batteries posted on the plateau just opposite the town. Now their force in view is very small. It was generally supposed that this retrograde movement indicated another transfer of operations, but I believe it was made to secure their camps from our fire and for the convenience of obtaining subsistence. I think, from the tone of the Northern papers, it is intended that General Burnside shall advance from Fredericksburg to Richmond, and that he is obliged to wait until he can reconstruct proper landings on the Potomac and rebuild the railroad to the Rappahannock.

All their movements that I have been able to discover look to a concentration at this point, and it appears to me that, should General Burnside change his base of operations, the effect produced in the United States would be almost equivalent to a defeat. I think, therefore, he will persevere in his present course ; and the longer we can delay him and throw him into the winter, the more difficult will be his undertaking. It is for this reason that I have determined to resist him at the outset and to throw every obstacle in the way of his advance. I propose to commence breaking up the railroad as one of the means of retarding him, so as to oblige him to move with a large wagon-train. I fear this measure will produce opposition on the part of the citizens, and may be viewed by this community as an abandonment of their country : I therefore do not wish to undertake it without due consideration, and, should you think it preferable to concentrate the troops nearer to Richmond, I should be glad if you would advise me.

I have waited to the last moment to draw Jackson's corps to me, as I have seen that his presence on their flank has embarrassed their plans and defeated their first purpose of advancing upon Gordonsville and Charlottesville. I think they will now endeavor to get possession of Hanover Junction.

I need not express to you the importance of urging forward all preparations about Richmond, and of uniting all our efforts to resist the great attempt now being made to reach our capital, which, if defeated, may prove the last.

I should like to get some long-range guns from Richmond if any can be obtained on travelling-carriages, and will write to Colonel Gorgas on the subject.

I need not say how glad I should be if your convenience would permit you to visit the army, that I might have the benefit of your views and directions.

I have the honor to be, with great respect, your obedient servant,

R. E. LEE,
General.

HEADQUARTERS DEPARTMENT OF NORTHERN VIRGINIA,
December 2, 1862.
HON. SECRETARY OF WAR, RICHMOND, VA.,

SIR: I have the honor to represent to you that there is still a great want of shoes in the army, between 2000 and 3000 men being at present barefooted. Many have lost their shoes in the long marches over rough roads recently made, and the number forwarded was insufficient to meet the necessities of the troops. I am informed that there is a large number of shoes now in Richmond in the hands of extortioners, who hold them at an extravagant price.

The quartermaster of General Jackson's corps, in which there is the greatest want of shoes, received a proposition from a person in Richmond to furnish 1300 pairs at $15 per pair. Whether these shoes are to be purchased at the prices demanded by the extortioners, or whether any plan can be devised for taking them at a fair price, I submit to your consideration; but I earnestly hope that some effectual means may be adopted to supply the wants of the army as speedily as possible, and avert the sufferings that threaten the troops during the approaching cold and wet weather.

I hope that the quartermaster's department will avail itself of every means to supply the present necessities of the men and to meet the wants that will naturally arise, particularly if active operations continue during the winter. I also respectfully suggest that, in purchasing shoes, care should be taken to prevent imposition, as I am informed by the officers who received those last forwarded that many of them were of a very inferior character and unfit for service.

I am, with high respect, your obedient servant,

R. E. LEE,
General.

[Confidential.]   HEADQUARTERS ARMY OF NORTHERN VIRGINIA,
December 6, 1862.
HIS EXCELLENCY JEFFERSON DAVIS, RICHMOND,

MR. PRESIDENT: The enemy still maintains his position north of the Rappahannock. I can discover no indications of his advancing or of transferring his troops to other positions. Scouts on both of his flanks north of the Rappahannock report no movements, nor have those stationed on the Potomac discovered the collection of transports or the passage of troops down that river.

General Burnside's whole army appears to be encamped between the Rappahannock and Potomac. His apparent inaction suggests the probability that he is waiting for expected operations elsewhere, and I fear troops may be collecting south of James River. Yet I get no reliable information of organized or tried troops being sent to that quarter, nor am I aware of any of their general officers in whom confidence is placed being there in command. There is an evident concentration of troops hitherto disposed in other parts of Virginia, but whether for the purpose of augmenting General Burnside's army or any other I cannot tell.

From the reports forwarded to me by General G. W. Smith, the officers serving there seem to be impressed with its magnitude. If I felt sure of our ability to resist the advance of the enemy south of that river, it would relieve me of great embarrassment, and I should feel better able to oppose the operations which may be contemplated by General Burnside. I presume that the operations in the departments of the West and South will require all the troops in each, but, should there be a lull of the war in these departments, it might be advantageous to leave a sufficient covering force to conceal the movement, and draw an active force, when the exigency arrives, to the vicinity of Richmond. Provisions and forage in the mean time could be collected in Richmond. When the crisis shall have passed those troops could be returned to their departments with reinforcements.

I need not state to you the advantages of a combination of our troops for a battle, if it can be accomplished, and, unless it can be done, we must make up our minds to fight with great odds against us.

I hope Your Excellency will cause me to be advised when, in your judgment, it may become necessary for this army to move nearer Richmond. It was never in better health or in better condition for battle than now. Some shoes, blankets, arms, and accoutrements are still wanting, but we are occasionally receiving small supplies, and I hope all will be provided in time.

There was quite a fall of snow yesterday, which will produce some temporary discomfort.

I have the honor to be, with great respect, your obedient servant,

R. E. LEE,
General.

HEADQUARTERS ARMY OF NORTHERN VIRGINIA.
April 10, 1863.

GENERAL : I have the honor to submit herewith my report of the operations of this army from the time that it moved from Culpeper Court-house, in November, 1862, and including the battle of Fredericksburg.

* * * * * * * * *

I have the honor to be, with great respect, your obedient servant,

R. E. LEE,
General.

GENERAL S. COOPER,
Adjutant- and Inspector-general, Richmond, Va.

REPORT OF GENERAL R. E. LEE OF THE BATTLE OF FREDER-ICKSBURG, DECEMBER 13, 1862.

On November 15 [1862] it was known that the enemy was in motion toward the Orange and Alexandria Railroad, and one regiment of infantry, with a bat: tery of light artillery, was sent to reinforce the garrison at Fredericksburg.

On the 17th it was ascertained that Sumner's corps had marched from Cat-lett's Station in the direction of Falmouth, and information was also received that on the 15th some Federal gunboats and transports had entered Acquia Creek. This looked as if Fredericksburg was again to be occupied, and McLaws's and Ransom's divisions, accompanied by W. H. F. Lee's brigade of cavalry and Lane's battery, were ordered to proceed to that city. To ascer-tain more fully the movements of the enemy, General Stuart was directed to cross the Rappahannock.

On the morning of the 18th he forced a passage at Warrenton Springs in the face of a regiment of cavalry and three pieces of artillery guarding the ford, and reached Warrenton soon after the last of the enemy's column had left. The information he obtained confirmed the previous reports, and it was clear that the whole Federal army, under Major-general Burnside, was moving toward Fredericksburg.

On the morning of the 19th, therefore, the remainder of Longstreet's corps was put in motion for that point.

The advance of General Sumner reached Falmouth on the afternoon of the 17th, and attempted to cross the Rappahannock, but was driven back by Col-onel [William B.] Ball with the Fifteenth Virginia cavalry, four companies of Mississippi infantry, and [Capt. J. W.] Lewis's light battery.

On the 21st it became apparent that General Burnside was concentrating his whole army on the north side of the Rappahannock.

On the same day General Sumner summoned the corporate authorities of Fredericksburg to surrender the place by 5 P. M., and threatened, in case of refusal, to bombard the city at 9 o'clock next morning. The weather had been tempestuous for two days, and a storm was raging at the time of the summons. It was impossible to prevent the execution of the threat to shell the city, as it was completely exposed to the batteries on the Stafford hills, which were beyond our reach. The city authorities were informed that, while our forces would not use the place for military purposes, its occupation by the enemy would be resisted, and directions were given for the removal of the women and children as rapidly as possible. The threatened bombardment did not take place, but in view of the imminence of a collision between the two armies the inhabitants were advised to leave the city, and almost the entire population without a mur-mur abandoned their homes. History presents no instance of a people exhib-iting a purer and more unselfish patriotism or a higher spirit of fortitude and courage than was evinced by the citizens of Fredericksburg. They cheerfully incurred great hardships and privations, and surrendered their homes and property to destruction, rather than yield them into the hands of the enemies of their country.

General Burnside now commenced his preparations to force the passage of the Rappahannock and advance upon Richmond. When his army first began to move toward Fredericksburg, General Jackson, in pursuance of instructions, crossed the Blue Ridge, and placed his corps in the vicinity of Orange Courthouse to enable him more promptly to co-operate with Longstreet.

About November 26 he was directed to advance toward Fredericksburg, and as some Federal gunboats had appeared in the river at Port Royal, and it was possible that an attempt might be made to cross in that vicinity, D. H. Hill's division was stationed near that place, and the rest of Jackson's corps so disposed as to support Hill or Longstreet as occasion might require. The fords of the Rappahannock above Fredericksburg were closely guarded by our cavalry, and the brigade of General W. H. F. Lee was stationed near Port Royal, to watch the river above and below.

On the 28th, General Hampton, guarding the upper Rappahannock, crossed to make a reconnoissance on the enemy's right, and, proceeding as far as Dumfries and Occoquan, encountered and dispersed his cavalry, capturing two squadrons and a number of wagons. About the same time some dismounted men of Beale's regiment, Lee's brigade, crossed in boats below Port Royal to observe the enemy's left, and took a number of prisoners.

On December 5, General D. H. Hill, with some of his field guns, assisted by Major Pelham of Stuart's horse artillery, attacked the gunboats at Port Royal and caused them to retire. With these exceptions no important movement took place, but it became evident that the advance of the enemy would not be long delayed. The interval was employed in strengthening our lines, extending from the river about one and a half miles above Fredericksburg along the range of hills in the rear of the city to the Richmond Railroad. As these hills were commanded by the opposite heights in possession of the enemy, earthworks were constructed upon their crest at the most eligible positions for artillery. These positions were judiciously chosen and fortified, under the direction of Brigadier-general Pendleton, chief of artillery; Colonel Cabell, of McLaws's division; Colonel E. P. Alexander and Captain S. R. Johnston of the Engineers. To prevent gunboats from ascending the river, a battery, protected by intrenchments, was placed on the bank about four miles below the city, in an excellent position, selected by my aide-de-camp Major [T. M. R.] Talcott. The plain of Fredericksburg is so completely commanded by the Stafford Heights that no effectual opposition could be made to the construction of bridges or the passage of the river without exposing our troops to the destructive fire of the numerous batteries of the enemy. At the same time, the narrowness of the Rappahannock, its winding course, and deep bed presented opportunities for laying down bridges at points secure from the fire of our artillery. Our position was therefore selected with a view to resist the enemy's advance after crossing, and the river was guarded only by a force sufficient to impede his movements until the army could be concentrated.

Before dawn on December 11 our signal guns announced that the enemy was in motion. About 2 A. M. he commenced preparations to throw two bridges over the Rappahannock—opposite Fredericksburg and about one and a quarter miles below, near the mouth of Deep Run. Two regiments of Barksdale's brigade, McLaws's division (the Seventeenth and Eighteenth Mississippi), guarded these points, the former, assisted by the Eighth Florida of Anderson's division, being at the upper. The rest of the brigade, with the Third Georgia regiment, also of Anderson's division, was held in reserve in the city. From daybreak until 4 P. M. the troops, sheltered behind the houses on the river-bank, repelled the repeated efforts of the enemy to lay his bridges opposite the town, driving back his working-parties and their supports with great slaughter. At the lower point, where there was no such protection, the enemy was successfully resisted until nearly noon, when, being greatly exposed to the fire of the batteries on the opposite heights and a superior force of infantry on the river-bank, our troops were withdrawn, and about 1 P. M. the bridge was completed.

Soon afterward 150 pieces of artillery opened a furious fire upon the city, causing our troops to retire from the river-bank about 4 P. M. The enemy then crossed in boats and proceeded rapidly to lay down the bridges. His advance into the town was bravely resisted until dark, when our troops were recalled, the necessary time for concentration having been gained.

During the night and the succeeding day the enemy crossed in large numbers at and below the town, secured from material interruption by a dense fog. Our artillery could only be used with effect when the occasional clearing of the mist rendered his columns visible. His batteries on the Stafford Heights fired at intervals upon our position. Longstreet's corps constituted our left, with Anderson's division resting upon the river, and those of McLaws, Pickett, and Hood extending to the right in the order named. Ransom's division supported the batteries on Marye's and Willis's hills, at the foot of which Cobb's brigade of McLaws's division, and the Twenty-fourth North Carolina of Ransom's brigade, were stationed, protected by a stone wall. The immediate care of this point was committed to General Ransom. The Washington Artillery, under Colonel Walton, occupied the redoubts on the crest of Marye's Hill, and those on the heights to the right and left were held by part of the reserve artillery, Colonel E. P. Alexander's battalion, and the division batteries of Anderson, Ransom, and McLaws. A. P. Hill of Jackson's corps was posted between Hood's right and Hamilton's Crossing on the railroad. His front line, consisting of the brigades of Pender, Lane, and Archer, occupied the edge of a wood.

Lieutenant-colonel Walker, with fourteen pieces of artillery, was posted near the right, supported by the Fortieth and Fifty-fifth Virginia regiments of Field's brigade, commanded by Colonel Brockenbrough. Lane's brigade, thrown forward in advance of the general line, held the woods, which here projected into the open ground. Thomas's brigade was stationed behind the interval between Lane and Pender; Gregg's, in rear of that, between Lane and Archer. These two brigades, with the Forty-seventh Virginia regiment and Twenty-second Virginia battalion of Field's brigade, constituted General Hill's reserve. Early's and Taliaferro's divisions composed Jackson's second line; D. H. Hill's division, his reserve. His artillery was distributed along his line in the most eligible positions so as to command the open ground in front. General Stuart, with two brigades of cavalry and his horse artillery, occupied the plain on Jackson's right, extending to Massaponax Creek.

On the morning of the 13th the plain on which the Federal army lay was still enveloped in fog, making it impossible to discern its operations. At an early hour the batteries on the heights of Stafford began to play upon Longstreet's position. Shortly after 9 A. M. the partial raising of the mist disclosed a large force moving in line of battle against Jackson. Dense masses appeared in front of A. P. Hill, stretching far up the river in the direction of Fredericksburg. As they advanced, Major Pelham of Stuart's horse artillery, who was stationed near the Port Royal road with one section, opened a rapid and well-directed enfilade fire, which arrested their progress. Four batteries immediately turned upon him, but he sustained their heavy fire with the unflinching courage that ever distinguished him. Upon his withdrawal the enemy extended his left down the Port Royal road, and his numerous batteries opened with vigor upon Jackson's line. Eliciting no response, his infantry moved forward to seize the position occupied by Lieutenant-colonel Walker. The latter, reserving his fire until their line had approached within less than eight hundred yards, opened upon it with such destructive effect as to cause it to waver, and soon to retreat in confusion.

About 1 P. M. the main attack on our right began by a furious cannonade, under cover of which three compact lines of infantry advanced against Hill's front. They were received, as before, by our batteries, by whose fire they were momentarily checked, but, soon recovering, they pressed forward until, coming within range of our infantry, the contest became fierce and bloody. Archer and Lane repulsed those portions of the line immediately in front of them, but before the interval between these commands could be closed the enemy pressed through in overwhelming numbers and turned the left of Archer and the right of Lane. Attacked in front and flank, two regiments of the former and the brigade of the latter, after a brave and obstinate resistance, gave way. Archer held his line with the First Tennessee, and, with the Fifth Alabama battalion, assisted by the Forty-seventh Virginia regiment and the Twenty-second Virginia battalion, continued the struggle until the arrival of reinforcements. Thomas came gallantly to the relief of Lane, and, joined by the Seventh and part of the Eighteenth North Carolina of that brigade, repulsed the column that had broken Lane's line and drove it back to the railroad.

In the mean time a large force had penetrated the wood as far as Hill's reserve, and encountered Gregg's brigade. The attack was so sudden and unexpected that Orr's rifles, mistaking the enemy for our own troops retiring, were thrown into confusion. While in the act of rallying them that brave soldier and true patriot, Brigadier-general Maxcy Gregg, fell mortally wounded. Colonel Hamilton, upon whom the command devolved, with the four remaining regiments of the brigade and one company of the rifles, met the enemy firmly and checked his further progress. The second line was advancing to the support of the first. Lawton's brigade of Early's division, under Colonel Atkinson, first encountered the enemy, quickly followed on the right and left by the brigades of Trimble (under Colonel Hoke) and Early (under Colonel Walker). Taliaferro's division moved forward at the same time on Early's left, and his right regiment (the Second Virginia, belonging to Paxton's brigade) joined in the attack. The contest in the woods was short and decisive. The enemy was quickly routed and driven out with loss, and, though largely reinforced, he was forced back and pursued to the shelter of the railroad embankment. Here he was gallantly charged by the brigades of Hoke and Atkinson and driven across the plain to his batteries. Atkinson continuing the pursuit too far, his flank became exposed, and at the same time a heavy fire of musketry and artillery was directed against his front. Its ammunition becoming exhausted, and Colonel Atkinson being severely, and Captain E. P. Lawton, [assistant] adjutant-general, mortally, wounded, the brigade was compelled to fall back to the main body, now occupying our original line of battle, with detachments thrown forward to the railroad.

The attack on Hill's left was repulsed by the artillery on that part of the line, against which the enemy directed a hot fire from twenty-four guns. One brigade advanced up Deep Run, sheltered by its banks from our batteries, but was charged and put to flight by the Sixteenth North Carolina of Pender's brigade, assisted by the Fifty-fourth and Fifty-seventh North Carolina of Law's brigade, Hood's division.

The repulse of the enemy on our right was decisive, and the attack was not renewed, but his batteries kept up an active fire at intervals, and sharpshooters skirmished along the front during the rest of the afternoon.

While these events were transpiring on our right the enemy, in formidable numbers, made repeated and desperate assaults upon the left of our line.

About 11 A. M., having massed his troops under cover of the houses of Fredericksburg, he moved forward in strong columns to seize Marye's and Willis's hills. General Ransom advanced Cooke's brigade to the top of the hill, and placed his own, with the exception of the Twenty-fourth Carolina, a short distance in the rear. All the batteries on the Stafford Heights directed their fire upon the positions occupied by our artillery, with a view to silence it and cover the movement of the infantry. Without replying to this furious cannonade our batteries poured a rapid and destructive fire into the dense lines of the enemy as they advanced to the attack, frequently breaking their ranks and forcing them to retreat to the shelter of the houses. Six times did the enemy, notwithstanding the havoc caused by our batteries, press on with great determination to within one hundred yards of the foot of the hill, but here, encountering the deadly fire of our infantry, his columns were broken and fled in confusion to the town.

In the third assault the brave and lamented Brigadier-general Thomas R. R. Cobb fell at the head of his gallant troops, and almost at the same moment Brigadier-general Cooke was borne from the field severely wounded. Fearing that Cobb's brigade might exhaust its ammunition, General Longstreet had directed General Kershaw to take two regiments to its support. Arriving after the fall of General Cobb, he assumed command, his troops taking position on the crest and at the foot of the hill, to which point General Ransom also advanced three other regiments. The Washington Artillery, which had sustained the heavy fire of artillery and infantry with unshaken steadiness and contributed much to the repulse of the enemy, having exhausted its ammunition, was relieved about 4 P. M. by Colonel Alexander's battalion. The latter occupied the position during the rest of the engagement, and by its well-directed fire rendered great assistance in repelling the assaults made in the afternoon, the last of which occurred shortly before dark. This effort met the fate of those that preceded it, and when night closed in the shattered masses of the enemy had disappeared in the town, leaving the field covered with dead and wounded. Anderson's division supported the batteries on Longstreet's left, and, though not engaged, was exposed throughout the day to a hot artillery fire, which it sustained with steady courage.

During the night our lines were strengthened by the construction of earthworks at exposed points, and preparations made to receive the enemy next day.

The 14th, however, passed without a renewal of the attack. The enemy's batteries on both sides of the river played upon our lines at intervals, our own firing but little. The sharpshooters on each side skirmished occasionally along the front.

On the 15th the enemy still retained his position, apparently ready for battle, but the day passed as the preceding.

The attack on the 13th had been so easily repulsed, and by so small a part of our army, that it was not supposed the enemy would limit his efforts to an attempt which, in view of the magnitude of his preparations and the extent of his force, seemed to be comparatively insignificant. Believing, therefore, that he would attack us, it was not deemed expedient to lose the advantages of our position and expose the troops to the fire of his inaccessible batteries beyond the river by advancing against him; but we were necessarily ignorant of the extent to which he had suffered, and only became aware of it when, on the morning of the 16th, it was discovered that he had availed himself of the darkness of night and the prevalence of a violent storm of wind and rain to recross the river. The town was immediately reoccupied and our position on the river-bank resumed.

In the engagement more than 900 prisoners and 9000 stand of arms were taken. A large quantity of ammunition was found at Fredericksburg.

The extent of our casualties will appear from the accompanying report of the medical director. We have again to deplore the loss of valuable lives. In Brigadier-generals Gregg and Cobb the Confederacy has lost two of its noblest citizens and the army two of its bravest and most distinguished officers. The country consents to the sacrifice of such men as these, and the gallant soldiers who fell with them, only to secure the inestimable blessing they died to obtain.

The troops displayed at Fredericksburg in a high degree the spirit and courage that distinguished them throughout the campaign, while the calmness and steadiness with which orders were obeyed and manœuvres executed in the midst of battle evinced the discipline of a veteran army.

The artillery rendered efficient service on every part of the field, and greatly assisted in the defeat of the enemy. The batteries were exposed to an unusually heavy fire of artillery and infantry, which officers and men sustained with a coolness and courage worthy of the highest praise. Those on our right, being without defensive works, suffered more severely. Among those who fell was Lieutenant-colonel [Lewis M.] Coleman, First Regiment Virginia artillery, who was mortally wounded while bravely discharging his duty.

To the vigilance, boldness, and energy of General Stuart and his cavalry is chiefly due the early and valuable information of the movements of the enemy. His reconnoissances frequently extended within the Federal lines, resulting in skirmishes and engagements in which the cavalry was greatly distinguished. In the battle of Fredericksburg the cavalry effectually guarded our right, annoying the enemy and embarrassing his movements by hanging on his flank and attacking when opportunity occurred. The nature of the ground and the relative positions of the armies prevented them from doing more.

To Generals Longstreet and Jackson great praise is due for the disposition and management of their respective corps. Their quick perception enabled them to discover the projected assaults upon their positions, and their ready skill to devise the best means to resist them. Besides their services in the field —which every battle of the campaign from Richmond to Fredericksburg has served to illustrate—I am also indebted to them for valuable counsel, both as regards the general operations of the army and the execution of the particular measures adopted.

To division and brigade commanders I must also express my thanks for the prompt, intelligent, and determined manner in which they executed their several parts.

To the officers of the general staff—Brigadier-general R. H. Chilton, adjutant- and inspector-general, assisted by Major [Henry E.] Peyton; Lieutenant-colonel [James L.] Corley, chief quartermaster; Lieutenant-colonel [Robert G.] Cole, chief commissary; Surgeon Guild, medical director; and Lieutenant-colonel B. G. Baldwin, chief of ordnance—were committed the care of their respective departments and the charge of supplying the demands of each. They were always in the field, anticipating, as far as possible, the wants of the troops.

My personal staff were unremittingly engaged in conveying and bringing information from all parts of the field. Colonel [Armistead L.] Long was particularly useful before and during the battle in posting and securing the artillery, in which he was untiringly aided by Captain S. R. Johnston, of the Provisional Engineers; Majors [T. M. R.] Talcott and [Charles S.] Venable, in examining the ground and the approaches of the enemy; Majors [Walter H.] Taylor and [Charles] Marshall in communicating orders and intelligence.

I have the honor to be, very respectfully, your obedient servant,

R. E. LEE,
General.

Abstract from Return of the Department of Northern Virginia, GENERAL R. E. LEE *commanding, for Dec. 10, 1862, Fredericksburg Campaign, Dec. 15, 1862.*

COMMAND.	Present for duty.		Aggregate present.
	Officers.	Men.	
FIRST ARMY CORPS.			
LIEUT.-GEN. LONGSTREET.			
General staff	13	. .	13
Staff	15	. .	15
Anderson's division	556	7,083	9,373
Hood's division	539	6,795	8,569
McLaws's division	587	7,311	9,285
Pickett's division	707	6,860	9,001
Ransom's division	260	3,595	4,304
Alexander's and Walton's battalions of artillery	37	586	672
Total	2,714	32,230	41,232
SECOND ARMY CORPS.			
LIEUT.-GEN. T. J. JACKSON.			
Staff	13	. .	13
Ewell's division	616	7,100	9,209
A. P. Hill's division	811	10,743	12,978
D. H. Hill's division	617	8,327	10,164
Jackson's division	479	4,526	6,067
Brown's battalion of artillery	24	449	513
Total	2,560	31,145	38,944
Stuart's cavalry division	634	8,512	10,016
Pendleton's reserve artillery	41	677	752
Grand total	5,949	72,564	90,944

List of the Regiments, Brigades, Divisions, and Batteries composing the First Corps, Army of Northern Virginia, LIEUTENANT-GENERAL JAMES LONGSTREET *commanding, December 20, 1862.*

ANDERSON'S DIVISION.

Wilcox's Brigade.

8th Alabama, Col. Y. L. Royston.
9th Alabama, Col. Samuel Henry.
10th Alabama, Col. W. H. Forney.
11th Alabama, Col. J. C. C. Sanders.
14th Alabama, Lieut.-col. L. Pinckard.

Mahone's Brigade.

6th Virginia, Col. G. T. Rogers.
12th Virginia, Col. D. A. Weisiger.
16th Virginia, Lieut.-col. J. H. Ham.
41st Virginia, Col. W. A. Parham.
61st Virginia, Col. V. D. Groner.

Featherston's Brigade.

12th Mississippi, Col. William H. Taylor.
16th Mississippi, Col. Carnot Posey.
19th Mississippi, Maj. John Mullins.
2d Mississippi Battalion, Lieut.-col. T. B. Manlove.

Wright's Brigade.

3d Georgia, Col. Edward J. Walker.
22d Georgia, Col. R. H. Jones.
48th Georgia, Col. William Gibson.
2d Georgia Battalion, Maj. G. W. Ross.

Perry's Brigade.

2d Florida, Lieut.-col. L. G. Pyles.
5th Florida, Col. J. C. Hately.
8th Florida, Lieut.-col. T. B. Lamar.

Artillery.

Donaldsonville Artillery, Capt. V. Maurin.
Grandy's battery, Capt. C. R. Grandy.
Huger's battery, Capt. Frank Huger.
Lewis's battery, Capt. John W. Lewis.

McLAWS'S DIVISION.

Kershaw's Brigade.

2d South Carolina, Col. John D. Kennedy.
3d South Carolina, Col. James D. Nance.
7th South Carolina, Col. D. Wyatt Aiken.
8th South Carolina, Col. John W. Henagan.
15th South Carolina, Col. W. D. De Saussure.
3d South Carolina (James's) Battalion, Lieut.-col. W. G. Rice.

Semmes's Brigade.

10th Georgia, Lieut.-col. J. B. Weems.
50th Georgia, Col. W. R. Manning.
51st Georgia, Col. William M. Slaughter.
53d Georgia, Col. James P. Simms.

Cobb's Brigade.

16th Georgia, Col. Goode Bryan.
18th Georgia, Col. W. T. Wofford.
24th Georgia, Col. Robert McMillan.
Cobb Legion, Lieut.-col. L. J. Glenn.
Phillips's Legion, Col. W. Phillips.

Barksdale's Brigade.

13th Mississippi, Col. J. W. Carter.
17th Mississippi, Col. W. D. Holder.
18th Mississippi, Col. T. M. Griffin.
21st Mississippi, Col. B. G. Humphreys.

Artillery.

Manly's battery, Capt. B. C. Manly.
Read's battery, Capt. J. P. W. Read.
Richmond Howitzers, Capt. E. S. McCarthy.
Troup Artillery, Capt. H. H. Carlton.

PICKETT'S DIVISION.

Garnett's Brigade.

8th Virginia, Col. Eppa Hunton.
18th Virginia, Col. R. E. Withers.
19th Virginia, Lieut.-col. Henry Gantt.
28th Virginia, Col. R. C. Allen.
56th Virginia, Col. W. D. Stuart.

Armistead's Brigade.

9th Virginia, Lieut.-col. J. S. Gilliam.
14th Virginia, Col. J. G. Hodges.
38th Virginia, Col. E. C. Edmonds.
53d Virginia, Col. H. B. Tomlin.
57th Virginia, Col. David Dyer.

Kemper's Brigade.

1st Virginia, Col. L. B. Williams, Jr.
3d Virginia, Col. Joseph Mayo, Jr.
7th Virginia, Col. W. T. Patton.
11th Virginia, Col. David Funsten.
24th Virginia, Col. William R. Terry.

Jenkins's Brigade.

1st South Carolina Volunteers, Col. W. H. Duncan.
2d South Carolina (Rifles), Col. Thomas Thomson.
5th South Carolina, Col. A. Coward.
6th South Carolina, Col. John Bratton.
Hampton Legion, Col. M. W. Gary.
Palmetto Sharpshooters, Col. Joseph Walker.

Corse's Brigade.

15th Virginia, Col. T. P. August.
17th Virginia, Col. Morton Marye.
30th Virginia, Col. A. T. Harrison.
32d Virginia, Col. E. B. Montague.

Artillery.

Dearing's battery, Capt. James Dearing.
Macon's battery, Capt. M. C. Macon.
Stribling's battery, Capt. R. M. Stribling.

HOOD'S DIVISION.

Robertson's Brigade.

3d Arkansas, Col. Van H. Manning.
1st Texas, Col. A. T. Rainey.
4th Texas, Col. J. C. G. Key.
5th Texas, Col. R. M. Powell.

Law's Brigade.

4th Alabama, Col. P. D. Bowles.
44th Alabama, Col. C. A. Derby.
6th North Carolina, Col. Isaac E. Avery.
54th North Carolina, Col. J. C. S. McDowell.
57th North Carolina, Col. A. C. Godwin.

Anderson's Brigade.

1st Georgia (Regulars), Col. W. J. Magill.
7th Georgia, Col. W. W. White.
8th Georgia, Col. L. M. Lamar.
9th Georgia, Col. Benjamin Beck.
11th Georgia, Col. F. H. Little.

Toombs's Brigade.

2d Georgia, Lieut.-col. Skidmore Harris.
15th Georgia, Maj. P. J. Shannon.
17th Georgia, Col. H. L. Benning.
20th Georgia, Col. J. B. Cumming.

Artillery.

German Light Battery, Capt. W. K. Bachman.
Palmetto Light Battery, Capt. H. R. Garden.
Rowan Artillery, Capt. James Reilly.

RANSOM'S DIVISION.

Ransom's Brigade.

24th North Carolina, Col. William J. Clarke.
25th North Carolina, Col. H. M. Rutledge.
35th North Carolina, Col. M. W. Ransom.
49th North Carolina, Col. Lee M. McAfee.

Cooke's Brigade.

15th North Carolina, Col. H. A. Dowd.
27th North Carolina, Col. John A. Gilmer, Jr.
46th North Carolina, Col. E. D. Hall.
48th North Carolina, Col. R. C. Hill.

Artillery.

Branch's battery, Capt. J. R. Branch.
Cooper's battery, Capt. R. L. Cooper.

[RESERVE ARTILLERY.]

Alexander's battalion, Lieut.-col. E. Porter Alexander.
Washington Artillery, Col. J. B. Walton.

HEADQUARTERS FIRST ARMY CORPS,
December 19,* 1862.

In the foregoing list, where a junior officer is apparently in command of a regiment, it is because vacancies exist in those commands which have not yet been filled.

Respectfully,

G. MOXLEY SORREL,
Assistant Adjutant-general.

List of Regimental and Battery Commanders, by Brigades and Divisions, of the Second Army Corps, LIEUT.-GEN. THOMAS J. JACKSON *commanding, December 20, 1862.*

EWELL'S DIVISION.
Maj.-gen. RICHARD S. EWELL.

First Brigade.

Brig.-gen. A. R. Lawton.

13th Georgia, Col. J. M. Smith.
26th Georgia, Col. E. N. Atkinson.
31st Georgia, Col. C. A. Evans.
38th Georgia, [Lieut.-] col. L. J. Parr.†
60th Georgia, Col. W. H. Stiles.
61st Georgia, Col. J. H. Lamar.

Second Brigade.

Brig.-gen. Jubal A. Early.

13th Virginia, Col. J. A. Walker.
25th Virginia, Col. George H. Smith.
31st Virginia, Col. John S. Hoffman.
44th Virginia, Col. William C. Scott.
49th Virginia, Col. William Smith.
52d Virginia, Col. M. G. Harman.
58th Virginia, Col. F. H. Board.

Third Brigade.

Brig.-gen. I. R. Trimble.

15th Alabama, Col. James Cantey.
12th Georgia, Col. Z. T. Conner.
21st Georgia, Col. J. T. Mercer.
21st North Carolina, R. F. Hoke.

Fourth Brigade.

Brig.-gen. Harry T. Hays.

5th Louisiana, Col. Henry Forno.
6th Louisiana, Col. W. Monaghan.
7th Louisiana, Col. D. B. Penn.
8th Louisiana, Col. H. B. Kelly.
9th Louisiana, Col. L. A. Stafford.

Artillery.

Charlottesville (Virginia) Artillery, Capt. James McD. Carrington.
Chesapeake (Maryland) Artillery, Capt. W. D. Brown.
Courtney (Virginia) Artillery, Capt. J. W. Latimer.
Dement's (First Maryland) Battery, Capt. William F. Dement.
Louisiana Guard Artillery, Capt. L. E. D'Aquin.
Staunton (Virginia) Artillery, Capt. W. L. Balthis.

* This roster is indorsed as of December 10, 1862.
† J. D. Mathews was appointed colonel December 13, 1862.

D. H. HILL'S DIVISION.
Maj.-gen. D. H. HILL.

First Brigade.

Brig.-gen. R. E. Rodes.

3d Alabama, Col. Cullen A. Battle.
5th Alabama, Lieut.-col. Edwin L. Hobson.
6th Alabama, Col. John B. Gordon.
12th Alabama, Lieut.-col. Samuel B. Pickens.
26th Alabama, Lieut.-col. Edward A. O'Neal.

Second Brigade.

Brig.-gen. George Doles.

4th Georgia, Col. Philip Cook.
44th Georgia, Col. John B. Estes.
1st North Carolina, Col. John A. McDowell.
3d North Carolina, Col. William L. De Rosset.

Third Brigade.

Brig.-gen. A. H. Colquitt.

13th Alabama, Col. B. D. Fry.
6th Georgia, Col. John T. Lofton.
23d Georgia, Col. E. F. Best.
27th Georgia, Col. C. T. Zachry.
28th Georgia, Maj. Tully Graybill.

Fourth Brigade.

Brig.-gen. A. Iverson.

5th North Carolina, Lieut.-col. P. J. Sinclair.
12th North Carolina, Col. Benjamin O. Wade.
20th North Carolina, Lieut.-col. William H. Toon.
23d North Carolina, Col. Daniel H. Christie.

Fifth Brigade.

Brig.-gen. S. D. Ramseur.

2d North Carolina, Col. W. P. Bynum.
4th North Carolina, Col. Bryan Grimes.
14th North Carolina, Col. R. T. Bennett.
30th North Carolina, Col. F. M. Parker.

Artillery.

Maj. H. P. JONES.

Hardaway's battery, Capt. R. A. Hardaway.
Jeff. Davis (Alabama) Artillery, Capt. J. W. Bondurant.
King William (Virginia) Artillery, Capt. T. H. Carter.
Morris (Virginia) Artillery, Capt. R. C. M. Page.
Orange (Virginia) Artillery, Capt. C. W. Fry.

A. P. HILL'S DIVISION.
Maj.-gen. A. P. HILL.

First Brigade.

Brig.-gen. C. W. Field.

40th Virginia, Col. J. M. Brockenbrough.
47th Virginia, Col. R. M. Mayo.
55th Virginia, Col. F. Mallory.
2d Virginia Battalion, Maj. E. P. Tayloe.

Second Brigade.

Brig.-gen. Maxcy Gregg.

1st South Carolina, Provisional Army, Col. D. H. Hamilton.
12th South Carolina, Lieut.-col. Cadwalader Jones.
13th South Carolina, Lieut.-col. O. E. Edwards.
14th South Carolina, Lieut.-col. Samuel McGowan.
Orr's Rifles, Lieut.-col. J. M. Perrin.

Third Brigade.

Brig.-gen. E. L. Thomas.

14th Georgia, Col. R. W. Folsom.
35th Georgia, Col. B. H. Holt.
45th Georgia, Col. T. J. Simmons.
49th Georgia, Col. A. J. Lane.

Fourth Brigade.

Brig.-gen. J. H. Lane.

7th North Carolina, Col. E. G. Haywood.
18th North Carolina, Lieut.-col. T. J. Purdie.
28th North Carolina, Lieut.-col. S. D. Lowe.
33d North Carolina, Col. C. M. Avery.
37th North Carolina, Col. W. M. Barbour.

Fifth Brigade.

Brig.-gen. J. J. Archer.

5th Alabama Battalion, Maj. A. S. Van de Graaff.
19th Georgia, Col. W. W. Boyd.
1st Tennessee, Provisional Army, Col. P. Turney.
7th Tennessee, Col. John F. Goodner.
14th Tennessee, Col. William McComb.

Sixth Brigade.

Brig.-gen. W. D. Pender.

13th North Carolina, Col. A. M. Scales.
16th North Carolina, Col. J. S. McElroy.
22d North Carolina, Col. James Conner.
34th North Carolina, Col. W. L. J. Lowrance.
38th North Carolina, Col. W. J. Hoke.

Artillery.

Lieut.-col. R. L. WALKER.

Branch Artillery, Capt. A. C. Latham.
Crenshaw Battery, Capt. William G. Crenshaw.
Fredericksburg Artillery, Capt. Carter M. Braxton.
Johnson Battery, Capt. Marmaduke Johnson.
Letcher Battery, Capt. Greenlee Davidson.
Pee Dee Artillery, Capt. D. G. McIntosh.
Purcell Battery, Capt. William J. Pegram.

JACKSON'S DIVISION.

Lieut.-gen. THOMAS J. JACKSON.

First Brigade.

Brig.-gen. E. F. Paxton.

2d Virginia,* Capt. J. Q. A. Nadenbousch.
4th Virginia, Col. Charles A. Ronald.
5th Virginia, Lieut.-col. J. H. S. Funk.
27th Virginia, Col. James K. Edmondson.
33d Virginia, Lieut.-col. E. G. Lee.

Second Brigade.

Brig.-gen. J. R. Jones.

21st Virginia,* Capt. W. R. Berkeley.
42d Virginia,* Capt. B. W. Leigh.†
48th Virginia, Col. T. S. Garnett.
1st Virginia Battalion,* Provisional Army, Confederate States, Capt. D. B. Bridgford.

Third Brigade.

Brig.-gen. William B. Taliaferro.

47th Alabama, Col. J. W. Jackson.
48th Alabama, Col. J. L. Sheffield.
10th Virginia, Col. E. T. H. Warren.
23d Virginia, Col. A. G. Taliaferro.
37th Virginia, Col. T. V. Williams.

Fourth Brigade.

1st Louisiana Volunteers, Col. W. R. Shivers.
2d Louisiana, Col. J. M. Williams.
10th Louisiana, Col. M. de Marigny.
14th Louisiana, Col. Zebulon York.
15th Louisiana, Col. Edmund Pendleton.

* No field officer.　　　　† On rolls and registers as captain First Virginia Battalion.

Artillery.

Carpenter's battery, Capt. Joseph Carpenter.
Danville Artillery, Capt. G. W. Wooding.
Hampden Artillery, Capt. W. H. Caskie.
Lee Artillery, Capt. C. I. Raine.
Lusk Battery, Capt. J. A. M. Lusk.

ARTILLERY CORPS.

Col. J. THOMPSON BROWN.

Brooke's (Virginia) Battery, Capt. J. V. Brooke.
Powhatan (Virginia) Artillery, Capt. W. J. Dance.
Richmond Howitzers, 2d Company, Capt. D. Watson.
Richmond Howitzers, 3d Company, Capt. B. H. Smith, Jr.
Rockbridge (Virginia) Artillery, Capt. W. T. Poague.
Salem (Virginia) Artillery, Capt. A. Hupp.

HEADQUARTERS ARMY OF NORTHERN VIRGINIA,
January 10, 1863.

HON. JAMES A. SEDDON, SECRETARY OF WAR, RICHMOND, VA.,

SIR: I have the honor to represent to you the absolute necessity that exists, in my opinion, to increase our armies if we desire to oppose effectual resistance to the vast numbers that the enemy is now precipitating upon us. It has occurred to me that the people are not fully aware of their danger, nor of the importance of making every exertion to put fresh troops in the field at once, and that if the facts were presented by those whose position best enables them to know the urgency of the case, they and the State authorities would be stimulated to make greater efforts. I trust, therefore, that it may not be deemed improper by the Department to communicate these facts to the governors of the several States, that they may give efficient aid to the enrolling officers within their limits and arouse the people to a sense of the vital importance of the subject.

The success with which our efforts have been crowned, under the blessing of God, should not betray our people into the dangerous delusion that the armies now in the field are sufficient to bring this war to a successful and speedy termination. While the spirit of our soldiers is unabated, their ranks have been greatly thinned by the casualties of battle and the diseases of the camp. Losses in battle are rendered much heavier by reason of our being compelled to encounter the enemy with inferior numbers; so that every man who remains out of service increases the dangers to which the brave men who have so well borne the burden of the war are exposed.

The great increase of the enemy's forces will augment the disparity of numbers to such a degree that victory, if attained, can only be achieved by a terrible expenditure of the most precious blood of the country. This blood will be upon the head of the thousands of able-bodied men who remain at home in safety and ease while their fellow-citizens are bravely confronting the enemy in the field or enduring with noble fortitude the hardships and privations of the march and camp. Justice to these brave men, as well as the most urgent considerations of public safety, imperatively demand that the ranks of our army should be immediately filled.

The country has yet to learn how often advantages, secured at the expense of many valuable lives, have failed to produce their legitimate results by reason of our inability to prosecute them against the reinforcements which the superior numbers of the enemy enable him to interpose between the defeat of an army and its ruin.

More than once have most promising opportunities been lost for want of men to take advantage of them, and victory itself has been made to put on the appearance of defeat because our diminished and exhausted troops have been unable to renew a successful struggle against fresh numbers of the enemy. The lives of our soldiers are too precious to be sacrificed in the attainment of successes that inflict no loss upon the enemy beyond the actual loss in battle. Every victory should bring us nearer to the great end which it is the object of this war to reach.

The people of the Confederate States have it in their power to prevent a recurrence of these misfortunes, and render less remote the termination of this desolating war, at much smaller expense of treasure, suffering, and blood than must attend its prosecution with inadequate numbers. They must put forth their full strength at once. Let them hear the appeal of their defenders for help, and drive into the ranks, from very shame, those who will not heed the dictates of honor and of patriotism. Let the State authorities take the matter in hand and see that no man able to bear arms be allowed to evade his duty.

In view of the vast increase of the forces of the enemy, of the savage and brutal policy he has proclaimed, which leaves us no alternative but success or degradation worse than death, if we would save the honor of our families from pollution, our social system from destruction, let every effort be made, every means be employed, to fill and maintain the ranks of our armies, until God, in his mercy, shall bless us with the establishment of our independence.

I have the honor to be, very respectfully, your obedient servant,

R. E. LEE,
General.

HEADQUARTERS CAMP NEAR FREDERICKSBURG,
January 13, 1863.

HIS EXCELLENCY JEFFERSON DAVIS, PRESIDENT OF THE CONFEDERATE STATES, RICHMOND, VA.,

MR. PRESIDENT: I have had the honor to receive your despatch of yesterday.

For several days past there have been general indications of some move-ment by the army of Burnside, but nothing sufficiently definite to designate it if true. Rumors are abundant, but whether it is intended to retire, advance, or transfer it elsewhere I cannot ascertain. I am pretty sure that the whole army is between the Rappahannock and the Potomac. No considerable portion ought to have been able to leave without my knowing it. Reinforcements of infantry and artillery have reached it from Washington. Wharves are still being constructed at Potomac Creek. The army has recently been more con-centrated, its land-communication with Alexandria more strongly guarded, and its right flank more extended toward the Orange and Alexandria Railroad. Cattle are being driven down on the Maryland side and crossed over on steam-ers to Acquia. No winter quarters are being erected, but the men are covering themselves, constructing chimneys to tents, etc.

There are a great many vessels of all sorts in the Potomac, but not more than enough to supply so large a force. It is said by their army that their transports were sent off with General Banks, and that there are not enough now to move it.

Citizens in Stafford and King George counties are not allowed to leave their dwellings. Persons even going to mill are guarded.

You may have remarked that recent Northern papers are silent as to its movements. It is said this is by order. I have hoped from day to day to have been able to discover what is contemplated, and to be guided in my move-ments accordingly. I think by spring, if not before, they will move upon James River. In the mean time they will endeavor to damage our railroads, etc. in North Carolina and get possession of Wilmington and Charleston.

Should General Burnside retire from his present position, I have intended to throw part of this army into North Carolina, and with another endeavor to clear the valley of the Shenandoah. I did not wish to move until the designs of the enemy were developed. I have hoped that General Smith, with the troops at his disposal, could keep the enemy in North Carolina in check in the mean time. I still hope so. Since you seem to think my presence there would be of service, I will endeavor to go on as soon as I can.

All the troops in that State should be concentrated as near as possible to the threatened points. Charleston will not be attacked until Wilmington is cap-tured. General Beauregard can therefore fight them at both points. As far as I have been able to judge, I have apprehended the movements in North Carolina were intended more as a feint to withdraw troops from this point, when General Burnside could move at once upon Richmond. Telegraph me your wishes.

With great respect, your obedient servant,

R. E. Lee,
General.

EXECUTIVE DEPARTMENT, C. S. A., RICHMOND, VA.,
January 22, 1863.

GENERAL R. E. LEE, COMMANDING, ETC., FREDERICKSBURG, VA.,

GENERAL: I have the honor to acknowledge the receipt of yours of the 19th, covering correspondence with General Halleck, and am pleased at the manner in which you presented the matter which had been submitted to you in connection with the atrocities of Milroy. If General Halleck should fulfil his promise, information recently received here does not permit me to doubt that he will have no opportunity to escape on the ground that Milroy has not executed his barbarous threats.

Yours of the 21st has also been received, and, after reading it, my opinion is that you would not be justified at this time in making further detachments from your command. Should the enemy succeed in crossing the river either above or below the long line occupied by you, at the same time holding a strong reserve opposite to Fredericksburg, it would make your retrograde movement, for the purpose of attacking the force he had thrown over, hazardous, by all the difficulties which would attend the exposure both of your flank and rear. The rain which is now falling must render the roads in that region impracticable for heavy artillery, and it may be that the movements which are observed are only changes of position for the establishment of winter cantonments.

We have nothing from North Carolina to develop the purpose of the enemy there, and it may well be that the late storms have interfered with his programme if it all tended to an attack upon Wilmington.

Intelligence from Tennessee is less cheering than we had anticipated, except that the cavalry is still successful against the enemy's shipping.

As ever, your friend,

JEFFERSON DAVIS.

HEADQUARTERS ARMY OF NORTHERN VIRGINIA,
September 23, 1863.

GENERAL: I have the honor to transmit herewith my report of the operations of this army from the time the enemy crossed the Rappahannock on April 28th last, to his retreat over that river on the night of May 5th, embracing the battles of Chancellorsville, Salem Church, etc. I also forward the reports of the several commanding officers of corps, divisions, brigades, and regiments, and the returns of the medical and ordnance departments, together with a map of the scene of operations. The accompanying reports and other documents are enumerated in a schedule annexed to my report.

Very respectfully, your obedient servant,

R. E. LEE,
General.

GENERAL S. COOPER,
Adjt.- and Insp.-gen., Richmond, Va.

REPORT OF GENERAL R. E. LEE OF BATTLE OF CHANCEL-LORSVILLE, VA., MAY 1 TO 3, 1863.

GENERAL: After the battle of Fredericksburg the army remained encamped on the south side of the Rappahannock until the latter part of April. The Federal army occupied the north side of the river opposite Fredericksburg, extending to the Potomac. Two brigades of [R. H.] Anderson's division—those of Generals [William] Mahone and [Carnot] Posey—were stationed near the United States Mine (or Bark Mill) Ford, and a third, under General [C. M.] Wilcox, guarded Banks's Ford. The cavalry was distributed on both flanks, Fitzhugh Lee's brigade picketing the Rappahannock above the mouth of the Rapidan, and W. H. F. Lee's near Port Royal. Hampton's brigade had been sent into the interior to recruit. General [James] Longstreet, with two divisions of his corps, was detached for service south of the James River in February, and did not rejoin the army until after the battle of Chancellorsville.

With the exception of the engagement between Fitz Lee's brigade and the enemy's cavalry near Kelly's Ford on March 17th, of which a brief report has been already forwarded to the Department, nothing of interest transpired during this period of inactivity.

On April 14th intelligence was received that the enemy's cavalry was concentrating on the upper Rappahannock. Their efforts to establish themselves on the south side of the river were successfully resisted by Fitzhugh Lee's brigade and two regiments of W. H. F. Lee's, the whole under the immediate command of General Stuart.

About the 21st small bodies of infantry appeared at Kelly's Ford and the Rappahannock bridge, and almost at the same time a demonstration was made opposite Port Royal, where a party of infantry crossed the river about the 23d. These movements were evidently intended to conceal the designs of the enemy, but, taken in connection with the reports of scouts, indicated that the Federal army, now commanded by Major-general Hooker, was about to resume active operations.

At 5.30 A. M. on April 28th the enemy crossed the Rappahannock in boats near Fredericksburg, and, driving off the pickets on the river, proceeded to lay down a pontoon bridge a short distance below the mouth of Deep Run. Later in the forenoon another bridge was constructed about a mile below the first. A considerable force crossed on these bridges during the day, and was massed out of view under the high banks of the river. The bridges, as well as the troops, were effectually protected from our artillery by the depth of the riverbed and the narrowness of the stream, while the batteries on the opposite heights completely commanded the wide plain between our lines and the river. As in the first battle of Fredericksburg, it was thought best to select positions with a view to resist the advance of the enemy, rather than incur the heavy loss that would attend any attempt to prevent his crossing. Our dispositions were accordingly made as on the former occasion.

No demonstration was made opposite any other part of our lines at Fredericksburg, and the strength of the force that had crossed and its apparent indisposition to attack indicated that the principal effort of the enemy would be made in some other quarter. This impression was confirmed by intelligence received from General Stuart that a large body of infantry and artillery was passing up the river. During the forenoon of the 29th that officer reported that the enemy had crossed in force near Kelly's Ford on the preceding evening. Later in the day he announced that a heavy column was moving from Kelly's toward Germanna Ford on the Rapidan, and another toward Ely's Ford on that river. The routes they were pursuing after crossing the Rapidan converge near Chancellorsville, whence several roads lead to the rear of our position at Fredericksburg.

On the night of the 29th, General Anderson was directed to proceed toward Chancellorsville and dispose Wright's brigade and the troops from the Bark Mill Ford to cover these roads. Arriving at Chancellorsville about midnight, he found the commands of Generals Mahone and Posey already there, having been withdrawn from the Bark Mill Ford with the exception of a small guard.

Learning that the enemy had crossed the Rapidan and were approaching in strong force, General Anderson retired early on the morning of the 30th to the intersection of the Mine and plank roads near Tabernacle Church, and began to intrench himself. The enemy's cavalry skirmished with his rear-guard as he left Chancellorsville, but, being vigorously repulsed by Mahone's brigade, offered no further opposition to his march. Mahone was placed on the old turnpike, Wright and Posey on the plank road.

In the mean time, General Stuart had been directed to endeavor to impede the progress of the column marching by way of Germanna Ford. Detaching W. H. F. Lee with his two regiments (the Ninth and Thirteenth Virginia) to oppose the main body of the enemy's cavalry, General Stuart crossed the Rapidan at Raccoon Ford with Fitz Lee's brigade on the night of the 29th. Halting to give his men a few hours' repose, he ordered Colonel [Thomas H.] Owen with the Third Virginia cavalry to throw himself in front of the enemy, while the rest of the brigade attacked his right flank at the Wilderness Tavern, between Germanna Ford and Chancellorsville. By this means the march of this column was delayed until 12 M., when, learning that the one from Ely's Ford had already reached Chancellorsville, General Stuart marched by Todd's Tavern toward Spottsylvania Court-house to put himself in communication with the main body of the army, and Colonel Owen fell back upon General **Anderson.**

The enemy in our front near Fredericksburg continued inactive, and it was now apparent that the main attack would be made upon our flank and rear. It was therefore determined to leave sufficient troops to hold our lines, and with the main body of the army to give battle to the approaching column. Early's division of Jackson's corps and Barksdale's brigade of McLaws's division, with part of the reserve artillery under General [W. N.] Pendleton, were entrusted with the defence of our position at Fredericksburg, and at midnight of the 30th, General McLaws marched with the rest of his command toward Chancellorsville. General Jackson followed at dawn next morning with the remaining divisions of his corps. He reached the position occupied by General Anderson at 8 A. M., and immediately began preparations to advance.

At 11 A. M. the troops moved forward upon the plank and old turnpike roads, Anderson, with the brigades of Wright and Posey, leading on the former, Mc-Laws, with his three brigades, preceded by Mahone's, on the latter. Generals Wilcox and Perry of Anderson's division co-operated with McLaws. Jackson's troops followed Anderson on the plank road. Colonel Alexander's battalion of artillery accompanied the advance. The enemy was soon encountered on both roads, and heavy skirmishing with infantry and artillery ensued, our troops pressing steadily forward. A strong attack upon General McLaws was repulsed with spirit by Semmes's brigade, and General Wright, by direction of General Anderson, diverging to the left of the plank road, marched by way of the unfinished railroad from Fredericksburg to Gordonsville and turned the enemy's right. His whole line thereupon retreated rapidly, vigorously pursued by our troops until they arrived within about one mile of Chancellorsville. Here the enemy had assumed a position of great natural strength, surrounded on all sides by a dense forest filled with a tangled undergrowth, in the midst of which breastworks of logs had been constructed, with trees felled in front so as to form an almost impenetrable abatis. His artillery swept the few narrow roads by which his position could be approached from the front, and commanded the adjacent woods. The left of his line extended from Chancellorsville toward the Rappahannock, covering the Bark Mill Ford, where he communicated with the north bank of the river by a pontoon bridge. His right stretched westward along the Germanna Ford road more than two miles. Darkness was approaching before the strength and extent of his line could be ascertained, and as the nature of the country rendered it hazardous to attack by night, our troops were halted and formed in line of battle in front of Chancellorsville at right angles to the plank road, extending on the right to the Mine road and to the left in the direction of the Catharine Furnace. Colonel [William C.] Wickham, with the Fourth Virginia cavalry and Colonel Owen's regiment, was stationed between the Mine road and the Rappahannock. The rest of the cavalry was upon our left flank.

It was evident that a direct attack upon the enemy would be attended with great difficulty and loss, in view of the strength of his position and his superiority of numbers. It was therefore resolved to endeavor to turn his right flank and gain his rear, leaving a force in front to hold him in check and conceal the movement. The execution of this plan was entrusted to Lieutenant-general Jackson with his three divisions. The commands of Generals McLaws and Anderson, with the exception of Wilcox's brigade, which during the night had been ordered back to Banks's Ford, remained in front of the enemy.

Early on the morning of the 2d, General Jackson marched by the Furnace and Brock roads, his movement being effectually covered by Fitz Lee's cavalry, under General Stuart in person. As the rear of the train was passing the Furnace a large force of the enemy advanced from Chancellorsville and attempted its capture. General Jackson had left the Twenty-third Georgia regiment, under Colonel [E. F.] Best, at this point to guard his flank, and upon the approach of the enemy Lieutenant-colonel J. T. Brown, whose artillery was passing at the time, placed a battery in position to aid in checking his advance. A small number of men who were marching to join their commands, including Captain [W. S.] Moore with two companies of the Fourteenth Tennessee regiment of Archer's brigade, reported to Colonel Brown and supported his guns. The enemy was kept back by this small force until the train had passed, but his superior numbers enabled him subsequently to surround and capture the greater part of the Twenty-third Georgia regiment. General Anderson was directed to send a brigade to resist the further progress of this column, and detached General Posey for that purpose. General Posey became warmly engaged with a superior force, but, being reinforced by General [A. R.] Wright, the enemy's advance was arrested.

After a long and fatiguing march General Jackson's leading division, under General Rodes, reached the old turnpike, about three miles in rear of Chancellorsville, at 4 P. M. As the different divisions arrived they were formed at right angles to the road—Rodes in front, Trimble's division, under Brigadier-general [R. E.] Colston, in the second, and A. P. Hill's in the third line.

At 6 P. M. the advance was ordered. The enemy was taken by surprise and fled after a brief resistance. General Rodes's men pushed forward with great vigor and enthusiasm, followed closely by the second and third lines. Position after position was carried, the guns captured, and every effort of the enemy to rally defeated by the impetuous rush of our troops. In the ardor of pursuit through the thick and tangled woods the first and second lines at last became mingled and moved on together as one. The enemy made a stand at a line of breastworks across the road at the house of Melzie Chancellor, but the troops of Rodes and Colston dashed over the intrenchments together, and the flight and pursuit were resumed, and continued until our advance was arrested by the abatis in front of the line of works near the central position at Chancellorsville. It was now dark, and General Jackson ordered the third line, under

General [A. P.] Hill, to advance to the front and relieve the troops of Rodes and Colston, who were completely blended and in such disorder, from their rapid advance through intricate woods and over broken ground, that it was necessary to re-form them. As Hill's men moved forward General Jackson, with his staff and escort, returning from the extreme front, met his skirmishers advancing, and in the obscurity of the night were mistaken for the enemy and fired upon. Captain [J. K.] Boswell, chief engineer of the corps, and several others were killed and a number wounded. General Jackson himself received a severe injury and was borne from the field. The command devolved upon Major-general Hill, whose division, under General Heth, was advanced to the line of intrenchments which had been reached by Rodes and Colston. A furious fire of artillery was opened upon them by the enemy, under cover of which his infantry advanced to the attack. They were handsomely repulsed by the Fifty-fifth Virginia regiment, under Colonel [Francis] Mallory, who was killed while bravely leading his men. General Hill was soon afterward disabled, and Major-general Stuart, who had been directed by General Jackson to seize the road to Ely's Ford, in rear of the enemy, was sent for to take command. At this time the right of Hill's division was attacked by the column of the enemy already mentioned as having penetrated to the Furnace, which had been recalled to Chancellorsville to avoid being cut off by the advance of Jackson. This attack was gallantly met and repulsed by the Eighteenth and Twenty-eighth and a portion of the Thirty-third North Carolina regiments, Lane's brigade.

Upon General Stuart's arrival soon afterward the command was turned over to him by General Hill. He immediately proceeded to reconnoitre the ground and make himself acquainted with the disposition of the troops. The darkness of the night and the difficulty of moving through the woods and undergrowth rendered it advisable to defer further operations until morning, and the troops rested on their arms in line of battle. Colonel [S.] Crutchfield, chief of artillery of the corps, was severely wounded, and Colonel [E. P.] Alexander, senior artillery officer present, was engaged during the entire night in selecting positions for our batteries.

As soon as the sound of cannon gave notice of Jackson's attack on the enemy's right, our troops in front of Chancellorsville were ordered to press him strongly on the left, to prevent reinforcements being sent to the point assailed. They were directed not to attack in force unless a favorable opportunity should present itself, and, while continuing to cover the roads leading from their respective positions toward Chancellorsville, to incline to the left, so as to connect with Jackson's right as he closed in upon the centre. These orders were well executed, our troops advancing up to the enemy's intrenchments, while several batteries played with good effect upon his lines until prevented by the increasing darkness.

Early on the morning of the 3d, General Stuart renewed the attack upon the enemy, who had strengthened his right during the night with additional breast-works, while a large number of guns, protected by intrenchments, were posted so as to sweep the woods through which our troops had to advance. Hill's division was in front, with Colston in the second line and Rodes in the third. The second and third lines soon advanced to the support of the first, and the whole became hotly engaged. The breastworks at which the attack was suspended the preceding evening were carried by assault under a terrible fire of musketry and artillery. In rear of these breastworks was a barricade, from which the enemy was quickly driven. The troops on the left of the plank road, pressing through the woods, attacked and broke the next line, while those on the right bravely assailed the extensive earthworks behind which the enemy's artillery was posted. Three times were these works carried, and as often were the brave assailants compelled to abandon them—twice by the retirement of the troops on their left, who fell back after a gallant struggle with superior numbers, and once by a movement of the enemy on their right caused by the advance of General Anderson. The left, being reinforced, finally succeeded in driving back the enemy, and the artillery under Lieutenant-colonels [T. H.] Carter and [H. P.] Jones, being thrown forward to occupy favorable positions secured by the advance of the infantry, began to play with great precision and effect. Anderson in the mean time pressed gallantly forward directly upon Chancellorsville, his right resting upon the plank road and his left extending around toward the Furnace, while McLaws made a strong demonstration to the right of the road. As the troops advancing upon the enemy's front and right converged upon his central position, Anderson effected a junction with Jackson's corps, and the whole line pressed irresistibly on. The enemy was driven from all his fortified positions with heavy loss in killed, wounded, and prisoners, and retreated toward the Rappahannock. By 10 A. M. we were in full possession of the field.

The troops, having become somewhat scattered by the difficulties of the ground and the ardor of the contest, were immediately re-formed preparatory to renewing the attack. The enemy had withdrawn to a strong position nearer to the Rappahannock, which he had previously fortified. His superiority of numbers, the unfavorable nature of the ground, which was densely wooded, and the condition of our troops after the arduous and sanguinary conflict in which they had been engaged, rendered great caution necessary. Our preparations were just completed when further operations were arrested by intelligence received from Fredericksburg.

General Early had been instructed, in the event of the enemy withdrawing from his front and moving up the river, to join the main body of the army with so much of his command as could be spared from the defence of his lines. This order was repeated on the 2d, but by a misapprehension on the part of the officer conveying it, General Early was directed to move unconditionally. Leaving Hays's brigade and one regiment of Barksdale's at Fredericksburg, and directing a part of General Pendleton's artillery to be sent to the rear in compliance with the order delivered to him, General Early moved with the rest of his command toward Chancellorsville. As soon as his withdrawal was perceived the enemy began to give evidence of an intention to advance, but, the mistake in the transmission of the order being corrected, General Early returned to his original position.

The line to be defended by Barksdale's brigade extended from the Rappahannock above Fredericksburg to the rear of Howisen's house, a distance of more than two miles. The artillery was posted along the heights in rear of the town.

Before dawn on the morning of the 3d, General Barksdale reported to General Early that the enemy had occupied Fredericksburg in large force and laid down a bridge at the town. Hays's brigade was sent to his support and placed on his extreme left, with the exception of one regiment stationed on the right of his line behind Howisen's house. Seven companies of the Twenty-first Mississippi regiment were posted by General Barksdale between the Marye House and the plank road, the Eighteenth and the three other companies of the Twenty-first occupied the telegraph road at the foot of Marye's Hill, the two remaining regiments of the brigade being farther to the right on the hills near Howisen's house. The enemy made a demonstration against the extreme right, which was easily repulsed by General Early. Soon afterward a column moved from Fredericksburg along the river-bank, as if to gain the heights on the extreme left, which commanded those immediately in rear of the town. This attempt was foiled by General Hays and the arrival of General Wilcox from Banks's Ford, who deployed a few skirmishers on the hill near Taylor's house and opened on the enemy with a section of artillery. Very soon the enemy advanced in large force against Marye's and the hills to the right and left of it. Two assaults were gallantly repulsed by Barksdale's men and the artillery. After the second a flag of truce was sent from the town to obtain permission to provide for the wounded.

Three heavy lines advanced immediately upon the return of the flag and renewed the attack. They were bravely repulsed on the right and left, but the small force at the foot of Marye's Hill, overpowered by more than ten times their numbers, was captured after a heroic resistance and the hill carried. Eight pieces of artillery were taken on Marye's and the adjacent heights. The remainder of Barksdale's brigade, together with that of General Hays and the artillery on the right, retired down the telegraph road. The success of the enemy enabled him to threaten our communications by moving down the telegraph road or to come upon our rear at Chancellorsville by the plank road. He at first advanced on the former, but was checked by General Early, who had halted the commands of Barksdale and Hays, with the artillery, about two miles from Marye's Hill and reinforced them with three regiments of Gordon's brigade. The enemy then began to advance up the plank road, his progress being gallantly disputed by the brigade of General Wilcox, who had moved from Banks's Ford as rapidly as possible to the assistance of General Barksdale, but arrived too late to take part in the action. General Wilcox fell back slowly until he reached Salem Church, on the plank road, about five miles from Fredericksburg.

Information of the state of affairs in our rear having reached Chancellorsville, as already stated, General McLaws, with his three brigades and one of General Anderson's, was ordered to reinforce General Wilcox. He arrived at Salem Church early in the afternoon, where he found General Wilcox in line of battle, with a large force of the enemy—consisting, as was reported, of one army corps and part of another, under Major-general Sedgwick—in his front. The brigades of Kershaw and Wofford were placed on the right of Wilcox, those of Semmes and Mahone on his left. The enemy's artillery played vigorously upon our position for some time, when his infantry advanced in three strong lines, the attack being directed mainly against General Wilcox, but partially involving the brigades on his left. The assault was met with the utmost firmness, and after a fierce struggle the first line was repulsed with great slaughter. The second then came forward, but immediately broke under the close and deadly fire which it encountered, and the whole mass fled in confusion to the rear. They were pursued by the brigades of Wilcox and Semmes, which advanced nearly a mile, when they were halted to re-form in the presence of the enemy's reserve, which now appeared in large force. It being quite dark, General Wilcox deemed it imprudent to push the attack with his small numbers, and retired to his original position, the enemy making no attempt to follow.

The next morning General Early advanced along the telegraph road and recaptured Marye's and the adjacent hills without difficulty, thus gaining the rear of the enemy's left. He then proposed to General McLaws that a simultaneous attack should be made by their respective commands, but the latter officer not deeming his force adequate to assail the enemy in front, the proposition was not carried into effect.

In the mean time the enemy had so strengthened his position near Chancellorsville that it was deemed inexpedient to assail it with less than our whole force, which could not be concentrated until we were relieved from the danger that menaced our rear. It was accordingly resolved still further to reinforce the troops in front of General Sedgwick, in order, if possible, to drive him across the Rappahannock.

Accordingly, on the 4th, General Anderson was directed to proceed with his remaining three brigades to join General McLaws, the three divisions of Jackson's corps holding our position at Chancellorsville. Anderson reached Salem Church about noon, and was directed to gain the left flank of the enemy and effect a junction with Early. McLaws's troops were disposed as on the previous day, with orders to hold the enemy in front and to push forward his right brigades as soon as the advance of Anderson and Early should be perceived, so as to connect with them and complete the continuity of our line. Some delay occurred in getting the troops into position, owing to the broken and irregular nature of the ground and the difficulty of ascertaining the disposition of the enemy's forces. The attack did not begin until 6 P. M., when Anderson and Early moved forward and drove General Sedgwick's troops rapidly before them across the plank road in the direction of the Rappahannock. The speedy approach of darkness prevented General McLaws from perceiving the success of the attack until the enemy began to recross the river a short distance below Banks's Ford, where he had laid one of his pontoon bridges. His right brigades, under Kershaw and Wofford, advanced through the woods in the direction of the firing, but the retreat was so rapid that they could only join in the pursuit. A dense fog settled over the field, increasing the obscurity and rendering great caution necessary to avoid collision between our own troops. Their movements were consequently slow. General Wilcox, with Kershaw's brigade and two regiments of his own, accompanied by a battery, proceeded nearly to the river, capturing a number of prisoners and inflicting great damage upon the enemy. General McLaws also directed Colonel [E. P.] Alexander's artillery to fire upon the locality of the enemy's bridge, which was done with good effect.

The next morning it was found that General Sedgwick had made good his escape and removed his bridges. Fredericksburg was also evacuated, and our rear no longer threatened; but as General Sedgwick had it in his power to recross, it was deemed best to leave General Early with his division and Barksdale's brigade to hold our lines as before, McLaws and Anderson being directed to return to Chancellorsville. They reached their destination during the afternoon in the midst of a violent storm, which continued throughout the night and most of the following day.

Preparations were made to assail the enemy's works at daylight on the 6th, but on advancing our skirmishers it was found that under cover of the storm and darkness of the night he had retreated over the river.

A detachment was left to guard the battlefield while the wounded were being removed and the captured property collected. The rest of the army returned to its former position.

The particulars of these operations will be found in the reports of the several commanding officers, which are herewith transmitted. They will show more fully than my limits will suffer me to do the dangers and difficulties which, under God's blessing, were surmounted by the fortitude and valor of our army.

The conduct of the troops cannot be too highly praised. Attacking largely-superior numbers in strongly-intrenched positions, their heroic courage overcame every obstacle of nature and art and achieved a triumph most honorable to our arms.

I commend to the particular notice of the Department the brave officers and men mentioned by their superiors for extraordinary daring and merit, whose names I am unable to enumerate here. Among them will be found some who have passed by a glorious death beyond the reach of praise, but the memory of whose virtues and devoted patriotism will ever be cherished by their grateful countrymen.

The returns of the medical director will show the extent of our loss, which, from the nature of the circumstances attending the engagements, could not be otherwise than severe. Many valuable officers and men were killed or wounded in the faithful discharge of duty. Among the former, Brigadier-general Paxton fell while leading his brigade with conspicuous courage in the assault on the enemy's works at Chancellorsville.

The gallant Brigadier-general Nichols lost a leg.

Brigadier-general McGowan was severely and Brigadier-generals Heth and Pender were slightly wounded in the same engagement. The latter officer led his brigade to the attack under a destructive fire, bearing the colors of a regiment in his own hands up to and over the intrenchments with the most distinguished gallantry.

General Hoke received a painful wound in the action near Fredericksburg.

The movement by which the enemy's position was turned and the fortune of the day decided was conducted by the lamented Lieutenant-general Jackson, who, as has already been stated, was severely wounded near the close of the engagement on Saturday evening. I do not propose here to speak of the character of this illustrious man, since removed from the scene of his eminent usefulness by the hand of an inscrutable but all-wise Providence. I nevertheless desire to pay the tribute of my admiration to the matchless energy and skill that marked this last act of his life, forming as it did a worthy conclusion of that long series of splendid achievements which won for him the lasting love and gratitude of his country.

Major-general A. P. Hill was disabled soon after assuming command, but did not leave the field until the arrival of Major-general Stuart. The latter officer ably discharged the difficult and responsible duties which he was thus unexpectedly called to perform. Assuming the command late in the night, at the close of a fierce engagement, and in the immediate presence of the enemy, necessarily ignorant in a great measure of the disposition of the troops and of the plans of those who had preceded him, General Stuart exhibited great energy, promptness, and intelligence. During the continuance of the engagement the next day he conducted the operations on the left with distinguished capacity and vigor, stimulating and cheering the troops by the example of his own coolness and daring.

While it is impossible to mention all who were conspicuous in the several engagements, it will not be considered an invidious distinction to say that General Jackson after he was wounded, in expressing the satisfaction he derived from the conduct of his whole command, commended to my particular attention the services of Brigadier-general (now Major-general) Rodes and his gallant division.

Major-general Early performed the important and responsible duty entrusted to him in a manner which reflected credit upon himself and his command. Major-general R. H. Anderson was also distinguished for the promptness, courage, and skill with which he and his division executed every order, and Brigadier-general (now Major-general) Wilcox is entitled to especial praise for the judgment and bravery displayed in impeding the advance of General Sedgwick toward Chancellorsville and for the gallant and successful stand at Salem Church.

To the skilful and efficient management of the artillery the successful issue of the contest is in great measure due. The ground was not favorable for its employment, but every suitable position was taken with alacrity, and the operations of the infantry supported and assisted with a spirit and courage not second to their own. It bore a prominent part in the final assault which ended in driving the enemy from the field at Chancellorsville, silencing his batteries, and by a destructive enfilade fire upon his works opened the way for the advance of our troops.

Colonels Crutchfield, Alexander, and [R. L.] Walker, and Lieutenant-colonels [J. T.] Brown, [T. H.] Carter, and [R. S.] Andrews, with the officers and men of their commands, are mentioned as deserving especial commendation. The batteries under General Pendleton also acted with great gallantry.

The cavalry of the army at the time of these operations was much reduced. To its vigilance and energy we were indebted for timely information of the enemy's movements before the battle and for impeding his march to Chancellorsville. It guarded both flanks of the army during the battle at that place, and a portion of it, as has been already stated, rendered valuable service in covering the march of Jackson to the enemy's rear.

The horse artillery accompanied the infantry and participated with credit to itself in the engagement. The nature of the country rendered it impossible for the cavalry to do more.

When the enemy's infantry passed the Rappahannock at Kelly's Ford his cavalry, under General Stoneman, also crossed in large force, and proceeded through Culpeper county toward Gordonsville for the purpose of cutting the railroads to Richmond. General Stuart had nothing to oppose to this movement but two regiments of Brigadier-general W. H. F. Lee's brigade (the

Ninth and Thirteenth Virginia cavalry). General Lee fell back before the overwhelming numbers of the enemy, and after holding the railroad bridge over the Rapidan during May 1st, burned the bridge and retired to Gordonsville at night. The enemy avoided Gordonsville and reached Louisa Court-house on the Central Railroad, which he proceeded to break up. Dividing his force, a part of it also cut the Richmond and Fredericksburg Railroad, and a part proceeded to Columbia, on the James River and Kanawha Canal, with a design of destroying the aqueduct at that place. The small command of General Lee exerted itself vigorously to defeat this purpose. The damage done to the railroads was small and soon repaired, and the canal was saved from injury. The details of his operations will be found in the accompanying memorandum, and are creditable to officers and men.

The loss of the enemy in the battle of Chancellorsville and the other engagements was severe. His dead and a large number of wounded were left on the field. About 5000 prisoners, exclusive of the wounded, were taken, and 13 pieces of artillery, 19,500 stands of arms, 17 colors, and a large quantity of ammunition fell into our hands.

To the members of my staff I am greatly indebted for assistance in observing the movements of the enemy, posting troops, and conveying orders. On so extended and varied a field all were called into requisition, and all evinced the greatest energy and zeal.

R. E. LEE,
General.

HEADQUARTERS, GUINEY'S [STATION], VA.,
May 5, 1863.

AT the close of the battle of Chancellorsville on Sunday the enemy was reported advancing from Fredericksburg in our rear. General McLaws was sent back to arrest his progress, and repulsed him handsomely that afternoon at Tabernacle Church. Learning that this force consisted of two corps under General Sedgwick, I determined to attack it. Leaving a sufficient force to hold General Hooker in check, who had not recrossed the Rappahannock, as was reported, but occupied a strong position in front of the United States Ford, I marched back yesterday with General Anderson, and, uniting with McLaws and Early in the afternoon, succeeded by the blessing of Heaven in driving General Sedgwick over the river. We have reoccupied Fredericksburg, and no enemy remains south of the Rappahannock in its vicinity.

R. E. LEE,
General.

HIS EXCELLENCY PRESIDENT DAVIS.

CHANCELLORSVILLE CAMPAIGN, May 3, 1863.

Abstract from Return of the Army of Northern Virginia, Gen. eral R. E. Lee commanding, for May 20, 1863 ; Station, Fredericksburg, Va.

COMMAND.	Present for duty.		Aggregate present.	Aggregate present and absent.	Aggregate last return.
	Officers.	Men.			
General staff	14	. . .	14	. . .	. . .
Staff	11	. . .	11	. . .	. . .
FIRST ARMY CORPS.					
LIEUT.-GEN. JAMES LONGSTREET.					
Anderson's division	. . .	. . .	8,890	13,726	8,401
McLaws's division	. . .	. . .	8,416	12,889	8,041
Pickett's division	. . .	. . .	7,640	12,113	7,824
Hood's division	. . .	. . .	8,677	12,573	7,265
(Ransom's division detached)	. . .	. . .	. . .	. . .	. . .
Total	. . .	. . .	33,635	51,315	31,544
SECOND ARMY CORPS.					
MAJ.-GEN. A. P. HILL.					
Staff	15	. . .	. . .	. . .	. . .
A. P. Hill's division	. . .	. . .	11,035	18,430	9,940
Rodes's division	. . .	. . .	8,910	15,037	8,191
Early's division	. . .	. . .	7,907	13,081	7,700
Johnson's division	. . .	. . .	6,356	12,008	5,651
Total	. . .	. . .	34,223	58,575	31,492
Stuart's cavalry division *	. . .	. . .	8,193	11,905	7,426
Valley district †	. . .	. . .	. . .	. . .	. . .
Artillery.					
Brig.-gen. Pendleton.					
General reserve	. . .	. . .	786	916	697
First Army corps‡	. . .	. . .	2,307	3,015	2,049
Second Army corps§	. . .	. . .	2,410	3,348	2,264
Total	. . .	. . .	5,503	7,279	5,010
Grand total	. . .	. . .	81,568	129,041	75,472

* One regiment and one company not reported.   † Not reported.
‡ Dearing's battery not reported.   § Two batteries not reported—on picket.

REPORTS OF GENERAL ROBERT E. LEE, C. S. ARMY, COMMANDING ARMY OF NORTHERN VIRGINIA, OF OPERATIONS, JUNE 3D TO AUGUST 4TH, 1863.

CULPEPER COURT-HOUSE,
June 18, 1863.

GENERAL: On the afternoon of the 14th, General Rodes took possession of Martinsburg, capturing several pieces of artillery, more than 200 prisoners, a supply of ammunition, and grain. Our loss, 1 killed and 2 wounded.

R. E. LEE,
General.

GENERAL S. COOPER,
  Adjutant- and Inspector-general.

HEADQUARTERS ARMY OF NORTHERN VIRGINIA,
July 17, 1863.

GENERAL: General Fitz Lee attacked the enemy last evening near Kearneysville and drove him to within a mile of Shepherdstown, when night put an end to the contest. The enemy, under cover of darkness, retired, taking the Charlestown road, leaving many of their wounded in Shepherdstown and the vicinity and their dead on the field. Their loss is reported very heavy. The enemy's force is stated to have been Gregg's division, General [D. McM.] Gregg commanding in person. I regret to state that Colonel James H. Drake of the First Virginia cavalry was mortally wounded in a charge of his regiment.

I have the honor to be, very respectfully, your obedient servant,

R. E. LEE,
General.

GENERAL S. COOPER, Adjt.- and Insp.-general, Richmond, Va.

HEADQUARTERS ARMY OF NORTHERN VIRGINIA,
July 21, 1863.

GENERAL: I have seen in Northern papers what purported to be an official despatch of General [G. G.] Meade, stating that he had captured a brigade of infantry, two pieces of artillery, two caissons, and a large number of small-arms as this army retired to the south bank of the Potomac on the 13th and 14th instants. This despatch has been copied into the Richmond papers, and as its official character may cause it to be believed, I desire to state that it is incorrect. The enemy did not capture any organized body of men on that occasion, but only stragglers and such as were left asleep on the road exhausted by the fatigue and exposure of one of the most inclement nights I have ever known at this season of the year. It rained without cessation, rendering the road by which our troops marched to the bridge at Falling Waters very difficult to pass, and causing so much delay that the last of the troops did not cross the river at the bridge until I P. M. on the 14th. While the column was thus detained on the road a number of men, worn down with fatigue, lay down in barns and by the wayside, and, though officers were sent back to arouse them as the troops moved on, the darkness and rain prevented them from finding all, and many were in this way left behind. Two guns were left in the road. The horses that drew them became exhausted, and the officers went forward to procure others. When they returned the rear of the column had passed the guns so far that it was deemed unsafe to send back for them, and they were thus lost. No arms, cannon, or prisoners were taken by the enemy in battle, but only such as were left behind under the circumstances I have described. The number of stragglers thus lost I am unable to state with accuracy, but it is greatly exaggerated in the despatch referred to.

I am, with great respect, your obedient servant,   R. E. LEE,
                                                              General.

GENERAL S. COOPER,
  Adjt.- and Insp.-gen. C. S. Army, Richmond, Va.

WILLIAMSPORT, June 25, 1863.
HIS EXCELLENCY PRESIDENT DAVIS, RICHMOND,

MR. PRESIDENT: So strong is my conviction of the necessity of activity on our part in military affairs that you will excuse my adverting to the subject again, notwithstanding what I have said in my previous letter of to-day.

It seems to me that we cannot afford to keep our troops awaiting movements of the enemy, but should so employ our own forces as to give occupation to his at points of our selection.

I have observed that extracts from Northern journals, contained in Richmond papers of the 22d instant, state that the yellow fever has appeared at New Berne, and that in consequence the Federal troops are being moved back to Morehead City. If, in fact, the fever is in New Berne, it would tend of itself to prevent active operations from that point. But as I have never heard of the disease being in that city, and as it does not generally break out so early in the season even in localities which are subject to it, I am disposed to doubt the truth of the statement, and regard it as a cover for the withdrawal of the enemy's forces for some other field. The attempt to conceal their movements, as in the case of the withdrawal of the troops from Suffolk, coupled with the fact that nothing has up to this time been undertaken on the North Carolina coast, convinces me that the enemy contemplates nothing important in that region, and that it is unnecessary to keep our troops there to watch him.

If he has been waiting until this time for reinforcements, the probability of their being furnished is greatly diminished by the movements now in progress on our part, and they must at least await the result of our operations. The same course of reasoning is applicable to the question of the probability of the enemy assuming the offensive against Richmond, either on the Peninsula or south of the James. I feel sure, therefore, that the best use that can be made of the troops in Carolina, and those in Virginia now guarding Richmond, would be the prompt assembling of the main body of them, leaving sufficient to prevent raids, together with as many as can be drawn from the army of General Beauregard, at Culpeper Court-house under the command of that officer. I do not think they could more effectually prevent aggressive movements on the part of the enemy in any other way, while their assistance to this army in its operations would be very great.

If the report received from General Buckner of the withdrawal of General Burnside from Kentucky be correct, I think there is nothing to prevent a united movement of the commands of Generals Buckner and Sam Jones into that State. They would render valuable service by collecting and bringing out supplies, if they did no more, and would embarrass the enemy and prevent troops now there from being sent to other points. If they are too weak to attempt this object, they need not be idle ; and I think that if the enemy's forces have in fact been so far weakened as to render present active operations on his part against them improbable, they should go where they can be of immediate service, leaving only a sufficient guard to watch the lines they now hold. They might be sent with benefit to reinforce General Johnston or General Bragg, to constitute a part of the proposed army of General Beauregard at Culpeper Court-house, or they might accomplish good results by going into North-western Virginia. It should never be forgotten that our concentration at any point compels that of the enemy, and, his numbers being limited, tends to relieve all other threatened localities.

I earnestly commend these considerations to the attention of Your Excellency, and trust that you will be at liberty, in your better judgment and with the superior means of information you possess as to our own necessities and the enemy's movements in the distant regions I have mentioned, to give effect to them, either in the way I have suggested or in such other manner as may seem to you more judicious.

I am, with great respect, your obedient servant,

R. E. LEE,
General.

[Enclosure.]

HEADQUARTERS ARMY OF NORTHERN VIRGINIA,
July 4, 1863.

GENERAL ORDERS
No. 74.

I. The army will vacate its position this evening. General A. P. Hill's corps will commence the movement, withdrawing from its position 'after dark, and proceed on the Fairfield road to the pass in the mountains, which it will occupy, selecting the strongest ground for defence toward the east. General Longstreet's corps will follow, and General Ewell's corps bring up the rear. These two latter corps will proceed through and go into camp. General Longstreet's corps will be charged with the escort of the prisoners, and will habitually occupy the centre of the line of march. General Ewell's and General Hill's corps will alternately take the front and rear on the march.

II. The trains which accompany the army will habitually move between the leading and the rear corps, each under the charge of their respective chief quartermasters. Lieutenant-colonel [James L.] Corley, chief quartermaster of the army, will regulate the order in which they shall move. Corps commanders will see that the officers remain with their trains, and that they move steadily and quietly, and that the animals are properly cared for.

III. The artillery of each corps will move under the charge of their respective chiefs of artillery, the whole under the general superintendence of the commander of the artillery of the army.

IV. General Stuart will designate a cavalry command not exceeding two squadrons to precede and follow the army in its line of march, the commander of the advance reporting to the commander of the leading corps, the commander of the rear to the commander of the rear corps. He will direct one or two brigades, as he may think proper, to proceed to Cashtown this afternoon and hold that place until the rear of the army has passed Fairfield, and occupy the gorge in the mountains; after crossing which to proceed in the direction of Greencastle, guarding the right and rear of the army on its march to Hagerstown and Williamsport. General Stuart, with the rest of the cavalry, will this evening take the route to Emmettsburg, and proceed thence toward Cavetown and Boonsboro', guarding the left and rear of the army.

V. The commanding general earnestly exhorts each corps commander to see that every officer exerts the utmost vigilance, steadiness, and boldness during the whole march.   R. E. LEE,
————————   *General.*

HEADQUARTERS ARMY OF NORTHERN VIRGINIA,
August 2, 1863.

GENERAL: On the night of July 31st the enemy laid pontoon bridges at a point below Kelly's Ford and at Rappahannock Station, and crossed the river with two or three divisions of cavalry and a large body of infantry. The cavalry, supported by three brigades of infantry, advanced toward Brandy Station, being retarded in their progress by Hampton's brigade of cavalry, under the command of Colonel [L. S.] Baker of the First North Carolina regiment, which fell back gradually before them to our line of infantry, about two miles this side of Brandy. Our infantry skirmishers were then advanced, and drove the enemy back a mile beyond the station.

Hampton's brigade behaved with its usual gallantry, and was very skilfully handled by Colonel Baker. General Stuart was in the front with the brigade the whole day.

Our loss was small, but among our wounded, I regret to say, are those brave officers—Colonel Baker, commanding the brigade; Colonel [Pierce M. B.] Young of Cobb's Legion, and Colonel [John L.] Black of the First South Carolina cavalry.

I am, etc.,

R. E. Lee,
General.

General S. Cooper,
  Adjutant- and Inspector-general C. S. Army, Richmond, Va.

REPORT OF GENERAL R. E. LEE OF THE GETTYSBURG CAMPAIGN, June to August, 1863.

Heaquarters Army of Northern Virginia,
January —, 1864.

General: I have the honor to submit a detailed report of the operations of this army from the time it left the vicinity of Fredericksburg early in June to its occupation of the line of the Rapidan in August.

Upon the retreat of the Federal army, commanded by Major-general [Joseph] Hooker, from Chancellorsville, it reoccupied the ground north of the Rappahannock opposite Fredericksburg, where it could not be attacked except at a disadvantage. It was determined to draw it from this position, and, if practicable, to transfer the scene of hostilities beyond the Potomac. The execution of this purpose also embraced the expulsion of the force under General [R. H.] Milroy, which had infested the lower Shenandoah Valley during the preceding winter and spring. If unable to attain the valuable results which might be expected to follow a decided advantage gained over the enemy in Maryland or Pennsylvania, it was hoped that we should at least so far disturb his plans for the summer campaign as to prevent its execution during the season of active operations.

The commands of Longstreet and Ewell were put in motion, and encamped around Culpeper Court-house June 7th. As soon as their march was discovered by the enemy he threw a force across the Rappahannock about two miles below Fredericksburg, apparently for the purpose of observation. Hill's corps was left to watch these troops, with instructions to follow the movements of the army as soon as they should retire.

The cavalry, under General [J. E. B.] Stuart, which had been concentrated near Culpeper Court-house, was attacked on June 9th by a large force of Federal cavalry, supported by infantry, which crossed the Rappahannock at Beverly and Kelly's fords. After a severe engagement, which continued from early in the morning until late in the afternoon, the enemy was compelled to recross the river with heavy loss, leaving about 500 prisoners, 3 pieces of artillery, and several colors in our hands.

General Imboden and General Jenkins had been ordered to co-operate in the projected expedition into the Valley—General Imboden, by moving toward Romney with his command to prevent the troops guarding the Baltimore and Ohio Railroad from reinforcing those at Winchester, while General Jenkins advanced directly toward the latter place with his cavalry brigade, supported by a battalion of infantry and a battery of the Maryland line.

General Ewell left Culpeper Court-house on June 10th. He crossed the branches of the Shenandoah near Front Royal, and reached Cedarville on the 12th, where he was joined by General Jenkins. Detaching General Rodes with his division and the greater part of Jenkins's brigade to dislodge a force of the enemy stationed at Berryville, General Ewell with the rest of his command moved upon Winchester, Johnson's division advancing by the Front Royal road—Early's, by the Valley turnpike, which it entered at Newtown, where it was joined by the Maryland troops.

The enemy was driven in on both roads, and our troops halted in line of battle near the town on the evening of the 13th. The same day the force which had occupied Berryville retreated to Winchester on the approach of General Rodes. The following morning General Ewell ordered General Early to carry an intrenched position north-west of Winchester near the Pughtown road, which the latter officer, upon examining the ground, discovered would command the principal fortifications.

To cover the movement of General Early, General Johnson took position between the road to Millwood and that to Berryville, and advanced his skirmishers toward the town. General Early, leaving a portion of his command to engage the enemy's attention, with the remainder gained a favorable position without being perceived, and about 5 P. M. twenty pieces of artillery under Lieutenant-colonel H. P. Jones opened suddenly upon the intrenchments. The enemy's guns were soon silenced. Hays's brigade then advanced to the assault and carried the works by storm, capturing six rifled pieces, two of which were turned upon and dispersed a column which was forming to retake the position.

The enemy immediately abandoned the works on the left of those taken by Hays and retired into his main fortifications, which General Early prepared to assail in the morning. The loss of the advanced works, however, rendered the others untenable, and the enemy retreated in the night, abandoning his sick and wounded, together with his artillery, wagons, and stores. Anticipating such a movement, as soon as he heard of Early's success General Ewell directed General Johnson to occupy with part of his command a point on the Martinsburg road about two and a half miles from Winchester, where he could either intercept the enemy's retreat or aid in an attack should further resistance be offered in the morning. General Johnson marched with Nichols's and part of Steuart's brigades, accompanied by Lieutenant-colonel [R. S.] Andrews with a detachment of his artillery, the Stonewall brigade being ordered to follow.

Finding the road to the place indicated by General Ewell difficult of passage in the darkness, General Johnson pursued that leading by Jordan [Alum ?] Springs to Stephenson's Dépôt, where he took a favorable position on the Martinsburg road about five miles from Winchester. Just as his line was formed the retreating column, consisting of the main body of General Milroy's army, arrived and immediately attacked him. The enemy, though in superior force, consisting of both infantry and cavalry, was gallantly repulsed, and, finding all efforts to cut his way unavailing, he sent strong flanking-parties simultaneously to the right and left, still keeping up a heavy fire in front. The party on the right was driven back and pursued by the Stonewall brigade, which opportunely arrived. That on the left was broken and dispersed by the Second and Tenth Louisiana regiments, aided by the artillery, and in a short time nearly the whole infantry force, amounting to more than 2300 men, with 11 stands of colors, surrendered, the cavalry alone escaping. General Milroy, with a small party of fugitives, fled to Harper's Ferry. The number of prisoners taken in this action exceeded the force engaged under General [Edward] Johnson, who speaks in terms of well-deserved praise of the conduct of the officers and men of his command.

In the mean time, General Rodes marched from Berryville to Martinsburg, reaching the latter place in the afternoon of the 14th. The enemy made a show of resistance, but soon gave way, the cavalry and artillery retreating toward Williamsport, the infantry toward Shepherdstown, under cover of night. The route taken by the latter was not known until it was too late to follow ; but the former were pursued so rapidly, Jenkins's troops leading, that they were forced to abandon five of their six pieces of artillery. About 200 prisoners were taken, but the enemy destroyed most of his stores.

These operations resulted in the expulsion of the enemy from the Valley ; the capture of 4000 prisoners, with a corresponding number of small-arms ; 28 pieces of superior artillery, including those taken by Generals Rodes and Hays ;

about 300 wagons and as many horses, together with a considerable quantity of ordnance, commissary, and quartermaster's stores.

Our entire loss was 47 killed, 219 wounded, and 3 missing.

MARCH INTO PENNSYLVANIA.

On the night of Ewell's appearance at Winchester the enemy in front of A. P. Hill at Fredericksburg recrossed the Rappahannock, and the whole army of General Hooker withdrew from the north side of the river. In order to mislead him as to our intentions, and at the same time protect Hill's corps in its march up the Rappahannock, Longstreet left Culpeper Court-house on the 15th, and, advancing along the eastern side of the Blue Ridge, occupied Ashby's and Snicker's gaps. He had been joined while at Culpeper by General Pickett with three brigades of his division. General Stuart, with three brigades of cavalry, moved on Longstreet's right and took position in front of the gaps. Hampton's and [J. M.] Jones's brigades remained along the Rappahannock and Hazel rivers in front of Culpeper Court-house, with instructions to follow the main body as soon as Hill's corps had passed that point.

On the 17th, Fitz Lee's brigade, under Colonel [Thos. T.] Munford, which was on the road to Snicker's Gap, was attacked near Aldie by the Federal cavalry. The attack was repulsed with loss, and the brigade held its ground until ordered to fall back, its right being threatened by another body coming from Hopewell toward Middleburg. The latter force was driven from Middleburg and pursued toward Hopewell by Robertson's brigade, which arrived about dark. Its retreat was intercepted by W. H. F. Lee's brigade, under Colonel [J. R.] Chambliss, and the greater part of a regiment captured.

During the three succeeding days there was much skirmishing, General Stuart taking a position west of Middleburg, where he awaited the rest of his command.

General [J. M.] Jones arrived on the 19th, and General Hampton in the afternoon of the following day, having repulsed on his march a cavalry force sent to reconnoitre in the direction of Warrenton.

On the 21st the enemy attacked with infantry and cavalry, and obliged General Stuart, after a brave resistance, to fall back to the gaps of the mountains. The enemy retired the next day, having advanced only a short distance beyond Upperville.

In these engagements the cavalry sustained a loss of 510 killed, wounded, and missing. Among them were several valuable officers, whose names are mentioned in General Stuart's report. One piece of artillery was disabled and left on the field. The enemy's loss was heavy. About 400 prisoners were taken and several stands of colors.

The Federal army was apparently guarding the approaches to Washington, and manifested no disposition to assume the offensive.

In the mean time, the progress of Ewell, who was already in Maryland, with Jenkins's cavalry advanced into Pennsylvania as far as Chambersburg, rendered it necessary that the rest of the army should be within supporting distance, and Hill having reached the Valley, Longstreet was withdrawn to the west side of the Shenandoah, and the two corps encamped near Berryville.

General Stuart was directed to hold the mountain-passes with part of his command as long as the enemy remained south of the Potomac, and with the remainder to cross into Maryland and place himself on the right of General Ewell. Upon the suggestion of the former officer that he could damage the enemy and delay his passage of the river by getting in his rear, he was authorized to do so, and it was left to his discretion whether to enter Maryland east or west of the Blue Ridge; but he was instructed to lose no time in placing his command on the right of our column as soon as he should perceive the enemy moving northward.

On the 22d, General Ewell marched into Pennsylvania with Rodes's and Johnson's divisions, preceded by Jenkins's cavalry, taking the road from Hagerstown through Chambersburg to Carlisle, where he arrived on the 27th. Early's division, which had occupied Boonsboro', moved by a parallel road to Greenwood, and, in pursuance of instructions previously given to General Ewell, marched toward York.

On the 24th, Longstreet and Hill were put in motion to follow Ewell, and on the 27th encamped near Chambersburg.

General Imboden, under the orders already referred to, had been operating on Ewell's left while the latter was advancing into Maryland. He drove off the troops guarding the Baltimore and Ohio Railroad, and destroyed all the important bridges on that route from Martinsburg to Cumberland, besides inflicting serious damage upon the Chesapeake and Ohio Canal. He was at Hancock when Longstreet and Hill reached Chambersburg, and was directed to proceed to the latter place by way of McConnellsburg, collecting supplies for the army on his route.

The cavalry force at this time with the army, consisting of Jenkins's brigade and [E. V.] White's battalion, was not greater than was required to accompany the advance of General Ewell and General Early, with whom it performed valuable service, as appears from their reports. It was expected that as soon as the Federal army should cross the Potomac, General Stuart would give notice of its movements, and, nothing having been heard from him since our entrance into Maryland, it was inferred that the enemy had not yet left Virginia. Orders were therefore issued to move upon Harrisburg. The expedition of General Early to York was designed in part to prepare for this undertaking by breaking the railroad between Baltimore and Harrisburg and seizing the bridge over the Susquehanna at Wrightsville. General Early succeeded in the first object, destroying a number of bridges above and below York, but on the approach of the troops sent by him to Wrightsville a body of militia stationed at that place fled across the river and burned the bridge in their retreat. General Early then marched to rejoin his corps.

The advance against Harrisburg was arrested by intelligence received from a scout on the night of the 28th to the effect that the army of General Hooker had crossed the Potomac and was approaching the South Mountains. In the absence of the cavalry it was impossible to ascertain his intentions; but to deter him from advancing farther west and intercepting our communications with Virginia it was determined to concentrate the army east of the mountains.

BATTLE OF GETTYSBURG.

Hill's corps was accordingly ordered to move toward Cashtown on the 29th, and Longstreet to follow the next day, leaving Pickett's division at Chambersburg to guard the rear until relieved by Imboden. General Ewell was recalled from Carlisle, and directed to join the army at Cashtown or Gettysburg as circumstances might require. The advance of the enemy to the latter place was unknown, and the weather being inclement the march was conducted with a view to the comfort of the troops. Heth's division reached Cashtown on the 29th, and the following morning Pettigrew's brigade, sent by General Heth to procure supplies at Gettysburg, found it occupied by the enemy. Being ignorant of the extent of his force, General Pettigrew was unwilling to hazard an attack with his single brigade and returned to Cashtown.

General Hill arrived with Pender's division in the evening, and the following morning (July 1st) advanced with these two divisions, accompanied by Pegram's and McIntosh's battalions of artillery, to ascertain the strength of the enemy, whose force was supposed to consist chiefly of cavalry. The leading division under General Heth found the enemy's videttes about three miles west of Gettysburg, and continued to advance until within a mile of the town, when two brigades were sent forward to reconnoitre. They drove in the advance of the enemy very gallantly, but subsequently encountered largely-superior numbers, and were compelled to retire with loss, Brigadier-general Archer, commanding one of the brigades, being taken prisoner. General Heth then prepared for action, and as soon as Pender arrived to support him was ordered by General Hill to advance. The artillery was placed in position and the engagement opened with vigor. General Heth pressed the enemy steadily back, breaking his first and second lines, and attacking his third with great resolution. About 2.30 P. M. the advance of Ewell's corps, consisting of Rodes's division, with Carter's battalion of artillery, arrived by the Middletown road, and, forming on Heth's left nearly at right angles with his line, became warmly engaged with fresh numbers of the enemy. Heth's troops, having suffered heavily in their protracted contest with a superior force, were relieved by Pender's, and Early, coming up by the Heidlersburg road soon afterward, took position on the left of Rodes, when a general advance was made. The enemy gave way on all sides and was driven through Gettysburg with great loss. Major-general [J. F.] Reynolds, who was in command, was killed. More than 5000 prisoners, exclusive of a large number of wounded, 3 pieces of artillery, and several colors were captured. Among the prisoners were two brigadier-generals, one of whom was badly wounded. Our own loss was heavy, including a number of officers, among whom were Major-general Heth slightly, and Brigadier-general Scales of Pender's division severely, wounded. The enemy retired to a range of hills south of Gettysburg, where he displayed a strong force of infantry and artillery.

It was ascertained from the prisoners that we had been engaged with two corps of the army formerly commanded by General Hooker, and that the remainder of that army, under General [George G.] Meade, was approaching Gettysburg. Without information as to its proximity, the strong position which the enemy had assumed could not be attacked without danger of exposing the four divisions present, already weakened and exhausted by a long and bloody struggle, to overwhelming numbers of fresh troops. General Ewell was therefore instructed to carry the hill occupied by the enemy if he found it practicable, but to avoid a general engagement until the arrival of the other divisions of the army, which were ordered to hasten forward. He decided to await Johnson's division, which had marched from Carlisle by the road west of the mountains to guard the trains of his corps, and consequently did not reach Gettysburg until a late hour.

In the mean time the enemy occupied the point which General Ewell designed to seize, but in what force could not be ascertained, owing to the darkness. An intercepted despatch showed that another corps had halted that afternoon four miles from Gettysburg. Under these circumstances it was decided not to attack until the arrival of Longstreet, two of whose divisions (those of Hood and McLaws) encamped about four miles in rear during the night. Anderson's division of Hill's corps came up after the engagement.

It had not been intended to deliver a general battle so far from our base unless attacked, but, coming unexpectedly upon the whole Federal army, to withdraw through the mountains with our extensive trains would have been difficult and dangerous. At the same time we were unable to await an attack, as the country was unfavorable for collecting supplies in the presence of the enemy, who could restrain our foraging-parties by holding the mountain-passes with local and other troops. A battle had therefore become, in a measure, unavoidable, and the success already gained gave hope of a favorable issue.

The enemy occupied a strong position, with his right upon two commanding elevations adjacent to each other, one south-east and the other, known as Cemetery Hill, immediately south of the town, which lay at its base. His line extended thence upon the high ground along the Emmettsburg road, with a steep ridge in rear, which was also occupied. This ridge was difficult of ascent, particularly the two hills above mentioned as forming its northern extremity, and a third at the other end on which the enemy's left rested. Numerous stone and rail fences along the slope served to afford protection to his troops and impede our advance. In his front the ground was undulating and generally open for about three-quarters of a mile.

General Ewell's corps constituted our left, Johnson's division being opposite the height adjoining Cemetery Hill, Early's in the centre, in front of the north face of the latter, and Rodes upon his right. Hill's corps faced the west side of Cemetery Hill and extended nearly parallel to the Emmettsburg road, making an angle with Ewell's. Pender's division formed his left, Anderson's his right, Heth's, under Brigadier-general Pettigrew, being in reserve. His artillery, under Colonel [R. L.] Walker, was posted in eligible positions along his line. It was determined to make the principal attack upon the enemy's left, and endeavor to gain a position from which it was thought that our artillery could be brought to bear with effect. Longstreet was directed to place the divisions of McLaws and Hood on the right of Hill, partially enveloping the enemy's left, which he was to drive in. General Hill was ordered to threaten the enemy's centre to prevent reinforcements being drawn to either wing, and co-operate with his right division in Longstreet's attack. General Ewell was instructed to make a simultaneous demonstration upon the enemy's right, to be converted into a real attack should opportunity offer.

About 4 P. M. Longstreet's batteries opened, and soon afterward Hood's division, on the extreme right, moved to the attack. McLaws followed somewhat later, four of Anderson's brigades—those of Wilcox, Perry, [A. R.] Wright, and Posey—supporting him on the left in the order named. The enemy was soon driven from his position on the Emmettsburg road to the cover of a ravine and a line of stone fences at the foot of the ridge in his rear. He was dislodged from these after a severe struggle, and retired up the ridge, leaving a number of his batteries in our possession. Wilcox's and Wright's brigades advanced with great gallantry, breaking successive lines of the enemy's infantry and compelling him to abandon much of his artillery. Wilcox reached the foot and Wright gained the crest of the ridge itself, driving the enemy down the opposite side; but, having become separated from McLaws and gone beyond the other two brigades of the division, they were attacked in front and on both flanks and compelled to retire, being unable to bring off any of the captured artillery. McLaws's left also fell back, and, it being now nearly dark, General Longstreet determined to await the arrival of General Pickett. He disposed his command to hold the ground gained on the right, withdrawing his left to the first position from which the enemy had been driven.

Four pieces of artillery, several hundred prisoners, and two regimental flags were taken. As soon as the engagement began on our right General Johnson opened with his artillery, and about two hours later advanced up the hill next to Cemetery Hill with three brigades, the fourth being detained by a demonstration on his left. Soon afterward General Early attacked Cemetery Hill with two brigades, supported by a third, the fourth having been previously detached. The enemy had greatly increased the strength of the positions assailed by Johnson and Early by earthworks.

The troops of the former moved steadily up the steep and rugged ascent under a heavy fire, driving the enemy into his intrenchments, part of which was carried by Steuart's brigade, and a number of prisoners taken. The contest was continued to a late hour, but without further advantage. On Cemetery Hill the attack by Early's leading brigades—those of Hays and Hoke, under Colonel [I. E.] Avery—was made with vigor. Two lines of the enemy's infantry were dislodged from the cover of some stone and board fences on the side of the ascent and driven back into the works on the crest, into which our troops forced their way and seized several pieces of artillery. A heavy force advanced against their right, which was without support, and they were compelled to retire, bringing with them about 100 prisoners and 4 stands of colors. General Ewell had directed General Rodes to attack in concert with Early, covering his right, and had requested Brigadier-general Lane, then commanding Pender's division, to co-operate on the right of Rodes. When the time to attack arrived, General Rodes, not having his troops in position, was unprepared to co-operate with General Early, and before he could get in readiness the latter had been obliged to retire for want of the expected support on his right. General Lane was prepared to give the assistance required of him, and so informed General Rodes, but the latter deemed it useless to advance after the failure of Early's attack.

In this engagement our loss in men and officers was large. Major-generals Hood and Pender, Brigadier-generals [J. M.] Jones, Semmes, G. T. Anderson, and Barksdale, and Colonel Avery, commanding Hoke's brigade, were wounded, the last two mortally. Generals Pender and Semmes died after their removal to Virginia.

The result of this day's operations induced the belief that with proper concert of action, and with the increased support that the positions gained on the right would enable the artillery to render the assaulting columns, we should ultimately succeed, and it was accordingly determined to continue the attack. The general plan was unchanged. Longstreet, reinforced by Pickett's three brigades, which arrived near the battlefield during the afternoon of the 2d, was ordered to attack the next morning, and General Ewell was directed to assail the enemy's right at the same time. The latter during the night reinforced General Johnson with two brigades from Rodes's and one from Early's division.

General Longstreet's dispositions were not completed as early as was expected, but before notice could be sent to General Ewell, General Johnson had already become engaged, and it was too late to recall him. The enemy attempted to recover the works taken the preceding evening, but was repulsed, and General Johnson attacked in turn. After a gallant and prolonged struggle, in which the enemy was forced to abandon part of his intrenchments, General Johnson found himself unable to carry the strongly-fortified crest of the hill. The projected attack on the enemy's left not having been made, he was enabled to hold his right with a force largely superior to that of General Johnson, and finally to threaten his flank and rear, rendering it necessary for him to retire to his original position about 1 P. M.

General Longstreet was delayed by a force occupying the high, rocky hills on the enemy's extreme left, from which his troops could be attacked in reverse as they advanced. His operations had been embarrassed the day previous by the same cause, and he now deemed it necessary to defend his flank and rear with the divisions of Hood and McLaws. He was therefore reinforced by Heth's division and two brigades of Pender's, to the command of which Major-general Trimble was assigned. General Hill was directed to hold his line with the rest of his command, afford General Longstreet further assistance if required, and avail himself of any success that might be gained.

A careful examination was made of the ground secured by Longstreet, and his batteries placed in positions which it was believed would enable them to silence those of the enemy. Hill's artillery and part of Ewell's was ordered to open simultaneously, and the assaulting column to advance under cover of the combined fire of the three. The batteries were directed to be pushed forward as the infantry progressed, protect their flanks, and support their attacks closely.

About 1 P. M., at a given signal, a heavy cannonade was opened and continued for about two hours with marked effect upon the enemy. His batteries replied vigorously at first, but toward the close their fire slackened perceptibly, and General Longstreet ordered forward the column of attack, consisting of Pickett's and Heth's divisions, in two lines, Pickett on the right. Wilcox's brigade marched in rear of Pickett's right to guard that flank, and Heth's was supported by Lane's and Scales's brigades under General Trimble. The troops moved steadily on under a heavy fire of musketry and artillery, the main attack being directed against the enemy's left centre. His batteries reopened as soon as they appeared. Our own, having nearly exhausted their ammunition in the protracted cannonade that preceded the advance of the infantry, were unable to reply or render the necessary support to the attacking party. Owing to this fact, which was unknown to me when the assault took place, the enemy was enabled to throw a strong force of infantry against our left, already wavering under a concentrated fire of artillery from the ridge in front and from Cemetery Hill on the left. It finally gave way, and the right, after penetrating the enemy's lines, entering his advance works and capturing some of his artillery, was attacked simultaneously in front and on both flanks and driven back with heavy loss. The troops were rallied and re-formed, but the enemy did not pursue.

A large number of brave officers and men fell or were captured on this occasion. Of Pickett's three brigade commanders, Generals Armistead and [R. B.] Garnett were killed and General Kemper dangerously wounded. Major-general Trimble and Brigadier-general Pettigrew were also wounded, the former severely.

The movements of the army preceding the battle of Gettysburg had been much embarrassed by the absence of the cavalry. As soon as it was known that the enemy had crossed into Maryland orders were sent to the brigades of [B. H.] Robertson and [Wm. E.] Jones, which had been left to guard the passes of the Blue Ridge, to rejoin the army without delay, and it was expected that General Stuart with the remainder of his command would soon arrive. In the exercise of the discretion given him when Longstreet and Hill marched into Maryland, General Stuart determined to pass around the rear of the Federal army with three brigades and cross the Potomac between it and Washington, believing that he would be able by that route to place himself on our right flank in time to keep us properly advised of the enemy's movements. He marched from Salem on the night of June 24th, intending to pass west of Centreville, but found the enemy's forces so distributed as to render that route impracticable. Adhering to his original plan, he was forced to make a wide détour through Buckland and Brentsville, and crossed the Occoquan at Wolf Run Shoals on the morning of the 27th. Continuing his march through Fairfax Court-house and Dranesville, he arrived at the Potomac below the mouth of Seneca Creek in the evening. He found the river much swollen by the recent rains, but after great exertion gained the Maryland shore before midnight with his whole command. He now ascertained that the Federal army, which he had discovered to be drawing toward the Potomac, had crossed the day before and was moving toward Fredericktown, thus interposing itself between him and our forces.

He accordingly marched northward through Rockville and Westminster to Hanover, Pa., where he arrived on the 30th; but the enemy advanced with equal rapidity on his left, and continued to obstruct communication with our main body.

Supposing from such information as he could obtain that part of the army was at Carlisle, he left Hanover that night and proceeded thither by way of Dover.

He reached Carlisle on July 1st, where he received orders to proceed to Gettysburg. He arrived in the afternoon of the following day and took position on General Ewell's left. His leading brigade, under General Hampton, encountered and repulsed a body of the enemy's cavalry at Hunterstown endeavoring to reach our rear.

General Stuart had several skirmishes during his march, and at Hanover quite a severe engagement took place with a strong force of cavalry, which was finally compelled to withdraw from the town.

The prisoners taken by the cavalry and paroled at various places amounted to about 800, and at Rockville a large train of wagons coming from Washington was intercepted and captured. Many of them were destroyed, but 125, with all the animals of the train, were secured.

The ranks of the cavalry were much reduced by its long and arduous march, repeated conflicts, and insufficient supplies of food and forage, but the day after its arrival at Gettysburg it engaged the enemy's cavalry with unabated spirit and effectually protected our left. In this action Brigadier-general Hampton was seriously wounded while acting with his accustomed gallantry.

Robertson's and Jones's brigades arrived on July 3d, and were stationed upon our right flank. The severe loss sustained by the army and the reduction of its ammunition rendered another attempt to dislodge the enemy inadvisable, and it was therefore determined to withdraw.

The trains, with such of the wounded as could bear removal, were ordered to Williamsport on July 4th, part moving through Cashtown and Greencastle, escorted by General Imboden, and the remainder by the Fairfield road. The army retained its position until dark, when it was put in motion for the Potomac by the last-named route. A heavy rain continued throughout the night, and so much impeded its progress that Ewell's corps, which brought up the rear, did not leave Gettysburg until late in the forenoon of the following day. The enemy offered no serious interruption, and after an arduous march we arrived at Hagerstown in the afternoon of the 6th and morning of July 7th.

The great length of our trains made it difficult to guard them effectually in passing through the mountains, and a number of wagons and ambulances were captured. They succeeded in reaching Williamsport on the 6th, but were unable to cross the Potomac on account of the high stage of water. Here they were attacked by a strong force of cavalry and artillery, which was gallantly repulsed by General Imboden, whose command had been strengthened by several batteries and by two regiments of infantry which had been detached at Winchester to guard prisoners and were returning to the army. While the enemy was being held in check General Stuart arrived with the cavalry, which had performed valuable service in guarding the flanks of the army during the retrograde movement, and after a short engagement drove him from the field. The rains that had prevailed almost without intermission since our entrance into Maryland, and greatly interfered with our movements, had made the Potomac unfordable, and the pontoon bridge left at Falling Waters had been partially destroyed by the enemy. The wounded and prisoners were sent over the river as rapidly as possible in a few ferry-boats, while the trains awaited the subsiding of the waters and the construction of a new pontoon bridge.

On July 8th the enemy's cavalry advanced toward Hagerstown, but was repulsed by General Stuart and pursued as far as Boonsboro. With this exception nothing but occasional skirmishing occurred until the 12th, when the main body of the enemy arrived. The army then took a position previously selected, covering the Potomac from Williamsport to Falling Waters, where it remained for two days, with the enemy immediately in front, manifesting no disposition to attack, but throwing up intrenchments along his whole line.

By the 13th the river at Williamsport, though still deep, was fordable, and a good bridge was completed at Falling Waters, new boats having been constructed and some of the old recovered. As further delay would enable the enemy to obtain reinforcements, and as it was found difficult to procure a sufficient supply of flour for the troops, the working of the mills being interrupted by high water, it was determined to wait an attack no longer. Orders were accordingly given to cross the Potomac that night—Ewell's corps by the ford at Williamsport, and those of Longstreet and Hill on the bridge. The cavalry was directed to relieve the infantry skirmishers and bring up the rear. The movement was much retarded by a severe rain-storm and the darkness of the night. Ewell's corps, having the advantage of a turnpike road, marched with less difficulty, and crossed the river by 8 o'clock the following morning. The condition of the road to the bridge and the time consumed in the passage of the artillery, ammunition-wagons, and ambulances, which could not ford the river, so much delayed the progress of Longstreet and Hill that it was daylight before their troops began to cross. Heth's division was halted about a mile and a half from the bridge to protect the passage of the column.

No interruption was offered by the enemy until about 11 A. M., when his cavalry, supported by artillery, appeared in front of General Heth. A small number in advance of the main body was mistaken for our own cavalry retiring, no notice having been given of the withdrawal of the latter, and was suffered to approach our lines. They were immediately destroyed or captured, with the exception of two or three, but Brigadier-general Pettigrew, an officer of great merit and promise, was mortally wounded in the encounter. He survived his removal to Virginia only a few days.

The bridge being clear, General Heth began to withdraw. The enemy advanced, but his efforts to break our lines were repulsed, and the passage of the river was completed by 1 P. M. Owing to the extent of General Heth's line, some of his men most remote from the bridge were cut off before they could reach it, but the greater part of those taken by the enemy during the movement (supposed to amount in all to about 500) consisted of men from various commands who lingered behind, overcome by previous labors and hardships and the fatigue of a most trying night-march. There was no loss of material except a few broken wagons and two pieces of artillery, which the horses were unable to draw through the deep mud. Other horses were sent back for them, but the rear of the column had passed before their arrival. The army proceeded to the vicinity of Bunker Hill and Darkesville, where it halted to afford the troops repose.

The enemy made no effort to follow except with his cavalry, which crossed the Potomac at Harper's Ferry and advanced to Martinsburg on July 16th. They were attacked by General Fitz Lee with his own and Chambliss's brigades, and driven back with loss.

When the army returned to Virginia it was intended to move into Loudoun, but the Shenandoah was found to be impassable. While waiting for it to subside the enemy crossed the Potomac east of the Blue Ridge and seized the passes we designed to use. As he continued to advance along the eastern slope, apparently with the purpose of cutting us off from the railroad to Richmond, General Longstreet was ordered on July 19th to proceed to Culpeper Court-house by way of Front Royal. He succeeded in passing part of his command over the Shenandoah in time to prevent the occupation of Manassas and Chester gaps by the enemy, whose cavalry had already made its appearance. As soon as a pontoon bridge could be laid down the rest of his corps crossed the river and marched through Chester Gap to Culpeper Court-house, where it arrived on the 24th. He was followed by General A. P. Hill without serious opposition.

General Ewell having been detained in the Valley by an effort to capture a force of the enemy guarding the Baltimore and Ohio Railroad west of Martinsburg, Wright's brigade was left to hold Manassas Gap until his arrival. He reached Front Royal on the 23d with Johnson's and Rodes's divisions, Early's being near Winchester, and found General Wright skirmishing with the enemy's infantry, which had already appeared in Manassas Gap. General Ewell supported Wright with Rodes's division and some artillery, and the enemy was held in check. Finding that the Federal force greatly exceeded his own, General Ewell marched through Thornton's Gap, and ordered Early to move up the Valley by Strasburg and New Market. He encamped near Madison Court-house on July 29th.

The enemy massed his army in the vicinity of Warrenton, and on the night of July 31st his cavalry, with a large supporting force of infantry, crossed the Rappahannock at Rappahannock Station and Kelly's Ford.

The next day they advanced toward Brandy Station, their progress being gallantly resisted by General Stuart with Hampton's brigade, commanded by Colonel [L. S.] Baker, who fell back gradually to our lines about two miles south of Brandy. Our infantry skirmishers advanced and drove the enemy beyond Brandy Station. It was now determined to place the army in a position to enable it more readily to oppose the enemy should he attempt to move southward, that near Culpeper Court-house being one that he could easily avoid. Longstreet and Hill were put in motion August 3d, leaving the cavalry at Culpeper. Ewell had been previously ordered from Madison, and by the 5th the army occupied the line of the Rapidan.

The highest praise is due to both officers and men for their conduct during the campaign. The privations and hardships of the march and camp were cheerfully encountered, and borne with a fortitude unsurpassed by our ancestors in their struggle for independence, while their courage in battle entitles them to rank with the soldiers of any army and of any time. Their forbearance and discipline under strong provocation to retaliate for the cruelty of the enemy to our own citizens is not the least claim to the respect and admiration of their countrymen and of the world.

I forward returns of our loss in killed, wounded, and missing. Many of the latter were killed or wounded in the several assaults at Gettysburg, and necessarily left in the hands of the enemy. I cannot speak of these brave men as their merits and exploits deserve. Some of them are appropriately mentioned in the accompanying reports, and the memory of all will be gratefully and affectionately cherished by the people in whose defence they fell.

The loss of Major-general Pender is severely felt by the army and the country. He served with this army from the beginning of the war, and took a distinguished part in all its engagements. Wounded on several occasions, he never left his command in action until he received the injury that resulted in his death. His promise and usefulness as an officer were only equalled by the purity and excellence of his private life.

Brigadier-generals Armistead, Barksdale, Garnett, and Semmes died as they had lived, discharging the highest duty of patriots with devotion that never faltered and courage that shrank from no danger.

I earnestly commend to the attention of the Government those gallant officers and men whose conduct merited the special commendation of their superiors, but whose names I am unable to mention in this report.

The officers of the general staff of the army were unremittingly engaged in the duties of their respective departments. Much depended on their management and exertion. The labors of the quartermaster's, commissary, and medical departments were more than usually severe. The inspectors-general were also laboriously occupied in their attention to the troops both on the march and in camp, and the officers of engineers showed skill and judgment in expediting the passage of rivers and streams, the swollen condition of which by almost continuous rains called for extraordinary exertion.

The chief of ordnance and his assistants are entitled to praise for the care and watchfulness given to the ordnance trains and ammunition of the army, which in a long march and in many conflicts were always at hand and accessible to the troops.

My thanks are due to my personal staff for the constant aid afforded me at all times on the march and in the field, and their willing discharge of every duty.

There were captured at Gettysburg nearly 7000 prisoners, of whom about 1500 were paroled and the remainder brought to Virginia. Seven pieces of artillery were also secured.

I forward herewith the reports of the corps, division, and other commanders mentioned in the accompanying schedule,* together with maps* of the scene of operations, and one showing the routes pursued by the army.

Respectfully submitted,

R. E. LEE,
General.

GENERAL S. COOPER,
Adjt.- and Insp.-gen. C. S. Army, Richmond, Va.

REPORT OF SURGEON LAFAYETTE GUILD, C. S. ARMY, MEDICAL DIRECTOR, WITH RETURN OF CASUALTIES IN THE ARMY OF NORTHERN VIRGINIA.

MEDICAL DIRECTOR'S OFFICE,
Camp near Culpeper Court-house, July 29, 1863.

SIR: At midnight July 3d, after the fiercest and most sanguinary battle ever fought on this continent, the general commanding gave orders for our army to withdraw from Gettysburg and fall back to Hagerstown. I enclose you a copy of my instructions to the corps [of] medical directors issued on that occasion.† Every available means of transportation was called into requisition for removing the wounded from the field infirmaries, and on the evening of the 4th our ambulance-trains took up their line of march by two routes, guarded as well as could be by our broken-down and inefficient cavalry. One train went by Cashtown, the other by Fairfax. The latter train was attacked by a body of the enemy's cavalry, who destroyed many wagons and paroled the wounded private soldiers, but taking with them all of the officers who fell into their hands. The former train was more fortunate; however, it, too, was attacked by the enemy, and met with some little loss in wagons and prisoners. The poor wounded suffered very much indeed in their rapid removal by day and night over rough roads, through mountain-passes, and across streams toward the Potomac. Those who could be removed from the battlefield and infirmaries were concentrated at Williamsport and transferred to the Virginia bank of the

* On file.   † Not found.

river by rafts and ferry-boats as rapidly as the swollen condition of the stream would permit.

Since my hasty and imperfect letter of the 10th instant from the vicinity of Hagerstown, Md., I have not had time or opportunity to report to you more fully our movements. At Hagerstown, as I informed you in my last letter, we fully expected another battle, and prepared for it. We waited there six long days, nearly every day the two armies engaging in desultory skirmishing. When the enemy made his appearance in force, instead of attacking us, as we expected, he commenced fortifying himself all along our line of battle, his line being little less than a mile from ours.

Our supplies for both men and animals were being rapidly exhausted, and the enemy declining battle by laying aside his muskets and taking to his picks and shovels, orders were given for us to resume our march toward the Potomac on the 13th instant. The army crossed at three points (two fords near Williamsport—very deep and bad fords, the river being swollen, at which quite a number of animals were drowned ; and the pontoon bridge at Falling Waters) without molestation from the enemy, who contented himself with picking up stragglers. Our crossing the river without annoyance evidently shows that the enemy was very badly crippled and could not risk another general engagement. The sufferings of the wounded were distressing. Indeed, the healthiest and most robust suffered extremely in crossing the river.

The head of our column commenced its passage at dark on the 13th instant, and in the afternoon of the 14th the rear-guard reached the south bank.

On July 15th we encamped near Bunker Hill, twelve miles north of Winchester, and remained there until the 21st, refreshing the troops and removing to the rear our sick and wounded from Winchester and Jordan [Alum ?] Springs, at which place I found about 4000 sick and wounded, steps for their removal to Staunton being immediately taken. All who could bear transportation were gotten off by the 22d instant, less than 150 remaining at the two places. Mount Jackson and Harrisonburg have been used simply as wayside hospitals, where the sick and wounded were refreshed with food and wounds re-dressed, medical officers with supplies of all kinds being stationed at the two points.

On the 22d the army resumed its march, the First and Third corps taking different routes to Front Royal and Chester Gap, where they were convalesced and the march continued to this point, where they encamped on the 25th, and are now resting after their arduous night-marches through great inclemency of weather. The Second army corps crossed the Blue Ridge at Thornton's Gap, south of Chester Gap, and will encamp in our vicinity to-day. Considerable sickness has been the consequence of their fatigues and exposure. Diarrhœa, dysentery, continued fever, and rheumatism preponderate. I have prohibited the establishment of a hospital at Culpeper Court-house, but organized a dépôt for the sick and wounded who cannot be treated in camp. Those who should go to general hospital are sent with all despatch to Gordonsville for distribution. The sick and wounded should, in my opinion, by no means be allowed to accumulate at Gordonsville. It is or may be at any time exposed to cavalry raids, and the inhuman enemy invariably, when an opportunity offers, drag our sick and wounded officers (at the sacrifice of their lives) into their own lines.

Mount Jackson and Harrisonburg, in the valley of the Shenandoah, should be abandoned as hospitals, as far as practicable, leaving only those patients whose lives would be endangered by transportation.

I have ordered Surgeon [R. J.] Breckinridge, medical inspector of the army, to proceed to the hospitals near the army where our sick and wounded have been sent since the battle of Gettysburg, and to have all returned to their regiments who are fit for duty. I enclose for your information a copy of my letter of instructions to him and order from the general commanding. The list of casualties has been forwarded to my office, and embrace the whole army with the exception of two brigades, which I have taken steps to have made out.

Our loss at Gettysburg was very heavy indeed, numbering about 14,000 killed and wounded. The consolidated list will be furnished you at an early day.

At the battle of Winchester, fought by General Ewell's corps on June 13th, 14th, and 15th, our loss was comparatively small—42 killed and 210 wounded. I will also forward to you very soon the list of casualties properly prepared.

Complaints are very frequently made by medical officers and officers of the line that many of the sick and wounded who are sent to general hospital are never heard from, the hospital surgeons failing to report deaths, discharges, furloughs, etc. I would again respectfully request that means be adopted for the correction of this neglect of duty on the part of medical officers in general hospital. I am exceedingly anxious to have a personal interview with you relative to some changes in the organization of our corps in the field, particularly in the purveying department. It is impossible for me to visit Richmond at this time, but I hope soon to have an opportunity. My office is exhausted of blank forms. Please have forwarded to me the following, viz.:

* * * * * * * * *

I am, sir, very respectfully, your obedient servant,

L. GUILD,
Medical Director Army of Northern Virginia.

SURGEON-GENERAL S. P. MOORE,
Richmond, Va.

Organization of the Army of Northern Virginia, GENERAL
R. E. LEE *commanding, during the Gettysburg Campaign.*

FIRST CORPS.

LIEUTENANT-GENERAL JAMES LONGSTREET.

McLAWS'S DIVISION:

Major-general Lafayette McLaws.

Kershaw's [1st] Brigade.	*Semmes's [2d] Brigade.*	*Barksdale's [3d] Brigade.*
Brigadier-general J. B. Kershaw.	Brig.-gen. P. J. Semmes (wd.). Colonel Goode Bryan.	Brig.-gen. W. Barksdale (wd.). Colonel B. G. Humphreys.
2d South Carolina.	10th Georgia.	13th Mississippi.
3d South Carolina.	50th Georgia.	17th Mississippi.
7th South Carolina.	51st Georgia.	18th Mississippi.
8th South Carolina.	53d Georgia.	21st Mississippi.
15th South Carolina.		
3d South Carolina Batt.		

Wofford's [4th] Brigade.	*Artillery.*
Brigadier-general W. T. Wofford.	Colonel H. C. Cabell.
16th Georgia.	Carlton's Ga. Bat. (Troup Artillery).
18th Georgia.	Fraser's Ga. Bat. (Pulaski Artillery).
24th Georgia.	McCarthy's Bat.(1st Richmond Howitzers).
Cobb's Georgia Legion.	Manly's North Carolina Battery.
Phillips's Georgia Legion.	

PICKETT'S DIVISION.

Major-general George E. Pickett.

Garnett's [1st] Brigade.	*Armistead's [2d] Brigade.*	*Kemper's [3d] Brigade.*
Brig.-gen. R. B. Garnett (kd.). Major George C. Cabell	Brig.-gen. L. A. Armistead (kd.). Colonel W. R. Aylett.	Brig.-gen. J. L. Kemper (wd.). Colonel Joseph Mayo, Jr.
8th Virginia.	9th Virginia.	1st Virginia.
18th Virginia.	14th Virginia.	3d Virginia.
19th Virginia.	38th Virginia.	7th Virginia.
28th Virginia.	53d Virginia.	11th Virginia.
56th Virginia.	57th Virginia.	24th Virginia.

*Corse's [4th] Brigade.**	*Artillery.*
Brigadier-general M. D. Corse.	Major James Dearing.
15th Virginia.	Blount's Virginia Battery.
17th Virginia.	Caskie's Va. Bat. (Hampden Artillery).
29th Virginia.	Macon's Bat. (Richmond Fayette Art.).
30th Virginia.	Stribling's Va. Bat. (Fauquier Artillery).

HOOD'S DIVISION.

Major-general John B. Hood (wounded).

Law's (1st) Brigade.	*Anderson's (2d) Brigade.*	*Robertson's (3d) Brigade.*
Brig.-gen. E. M. Law. Col. Jas. L. Sheffield.	Brig.-gen. Geo. T. Anderson (wd.). Colonel W. W. White.	Brig.-gen. J. B. Robertson.
4th Alabama.	7th Georgia.	3d Arkansas.
15th Alabama.	8th Georgia.	1st Texas.
44th Alabama.	9th Georgia.	4th Texas.
47th Alabama.	11th Georgia.	5th Texas.
48th Alabama.	59th Georgia.	

* Not engaged at Gettysburg; encamped at Gordonsville July 1st to 8th.

Benning's (4th) Brigade.
Brigadier-general H. L. Benning.
2d Georgia.
15th Georgia.
17th Georgia
20th Georgia.

Artillery.
Major M. W. Henry.
Bachman's S. C. Bat. (German Artillery).
Garden's S. C. Bat. (Palmetto Light Art.).
Latham's N. C. Bat. (Branch Artillery).
Reilly's N. C. Battery (Rowan Artillery).

RESERVE ARTILLERY FIRST CORPS.

Colonel J. B. Walton, Chief of Artillery.

Alexander's Battalion.
Colonel E. P. Alexander.
Jordan's Va. Battery (Bedford Artillery).
Moody's La. Battery (Madison Light Art.).
Parker's Virginia Battery.
Rhett's S. C. Battery (Brooks Artillery).
Taylor's Virginia Battery.
Woolfolk's Va. Battery (Ashland Artillery).

Washington (La.) Artillery.
Major B. F. Eshleman.
Miller's 3d Company.
Norcom's 4th Company.
Richardson's 2d Company.
Squire's 1st Company.

SECOND CORPS.

LIEUTENANT-GENERAL RICHARD S. EWELL.

EARLY'S DIVISION.
Major-general Jubal A. Early.

Hays's [1st] Brigade.

Brig.-gen. Harry T. Hays.

5th Louisiana.
6th Louisiana.
7th Louisiana.
8th Louisiana.
9th Louisiana.

Hoke's [2d] Brigade.
Brig.-gen. R. F. Hoke.
Colonel Isaac E. Avery (wd.).
Colonel A. C. Godwin.

6th North Carolina.
21st North Carolina.
54th North Carolina.
57th North Carolina.
1st North Carolina Battalion.

Smith's [3d] Brigade.
Brig.-gen. William Smith.
Colonel John S. Hoffman.

13th Virginia.
31st Virginia.
49th Virginia.
52d Virginia.
58th Virginia.

Gordon's [4th] Brigade.
Brig.-gen. J. B. Gordon.
13th Georgia.
26th Georgia.
31st Georgia.
38th Georgia.
60th Georgia.
61st Georgia.

Artillery.
Lieutenant-colonel H. P. Jones.
Carrington's Virginia Battery (Charlottesville Artillery).
Garber's Virginia Battery (Staunton Artillery).
Green's Battery (Louisiana Guard Artillery).
Tanner's Virginia Battery (Courtney Artillery).

JOHNSON'S DIVISION.
Major-general Edward Johnson.

Steuart's [1st] Brigade.

Brig.-gen. George H. Steuart.

1st Maryland Battalion.
1st North Carolina.
3d North Carolina.
10th Virginia.
23d Virginia.
37th Virginia.

Nicholl's [2d] Brigade.
Colonel J. M. Williams.
Brig.-gen. A. Iverson. *

1st Louisiana.
2d Louisiana.
10th Louisiana.
14th Louisiana.
15th Louisiana.

Walker's [3d] Brigade.

Brig.-gen. James A. Walker.

2d Virginia.
4th Virginia.
5th Virginia.
27th Virginia.
33d Virginia.

* Assigned July 19th.

Jones's [4th] Brigade.

Brig.-gen. John M. Jones (wd.).
Lieut.-col. R. H. Dungan.
Colonel B. T. Johnson.

21st Virginia.
25th Virginia.
42d Virginia.
44th Virginia.
48th Virginia.
50th Virginia.

Artillery.

Lieutenant-colonel R. S. Andrews.

Brown's Maryland Battery (Chesapeake Artillery).
Carpenter's Virginia Battery (Alleghany Artillery).
Dement's 1st Maryland Battery.
Raine's Virginia Battery (Lee Battery).

RODES'S DIVISION.
Major-general R. E. Rodes.

Daniel's [1st] Brigade.

Brig.-gen. Junius Daniel.

32d North Carolina.
43d North Carolina.
45th North Carolina.
53d North Carolina.
2d North Carolina Battalion.

Iverson's [2d] Brigade.*

Brig.-gen. Alfred Iverson.
Brig.-gen. S. D. Ramseur.

5th North Carolina.
12th North Carolina.
20th North Carolina.
23d North Carolina.

Doles's [3d] Brigade.

Brig.-gen. George Doles.

4th Georgia.
12th Georgia.
21st Georgia.
44th Georgia.

Ramseur's [4th] Brigade.†

Brig.-gen. S. D. Ramseur.

2d North Carolina.
4th North Carolina.
14th North Carolina.
30th North Carolina.

O'Neal's [5th] Brigade.

Brig.-gen. E. A. O'Neal.
Colonel C. A. Battle.

3d Alabama.
5th Alabama.
6th Alabama.
12th Alabama.
16th Alabama.

Artillery.

Lieut.-col. Thomas H. Carter.

Carter's Virginia Battery (King William Artillery).
Fry's Va. Bat. (Orange Art.).
Page's Va. Bat. (Morris Art.).
Reese's Alabama Battery (Jeff. Davis Artillery).

RESERVE ARTILLERY SECOND CORPS.
Colonel J. Thompson Brown, Chief of Artillery.

Brown's Battalion.†

Captain W. J. Dance.

Dance's Va. Battery (Powhatan Artillery).
Hupp's Virginia Battery (Salem Artillery).
Graham's Va. Bat. (Rockbridge Artillery).
Smith's Battery (3d Richmond Howitzers).
Watson's Battery (2d Richmond Howitzers).

Nelson's Battalion.

Lieutenant-colonel William Nelson.

Kirkpatrick's Va. Bat. (Amherst Art.).
Massie's Va. Battery (Fluvanna Art.).
Milledge's Georgia Battery.

THIRD CORPS.
LIEUTENANT-GENERAL AMBROSE P. HILL.

ANDERSON'S DIVISION.
Major-general R. H. Anderson.

Wilcox's [1st] Brigade.

Brig.-gen. C. M. Wilcox.

8th Alabama.
9th Alabama.
10th Alabama.
11th Alabama.
14th Alabama.

Mahone's [2d] Brigade.

Brig.-gen. William Mahone.

6th Virginia.
12th Virginia.
16th Virginia.
41st Virginia.
61st Virginia.

Wright's [3d] Brigade.

Brig.-gen. A. R. Wright.
Captain E. H. Wright.

3d Georgia.
22d Georgia.
48th Georgia.
2d Georgia Battalion.

* Temporarily consolidated July 10, 1863.

† 1st Virginia Artillery.

Perry's [4th] Brigade.

Colonel David Lang.
Brig.-gen. E. A. Perry.

2d Florida.
5th Florida.
8th Florida.

Posey's [5th] Brigade.

Brig.-gen. Carnot Posey.

12th Mississippi.
16th Mississippi.
19th Mississippi.
48th Mississippi.

Artillery (Sumter Batt.).

Major John Lane.

Patterson's Georgia Bat.
Ross's Georgia Battery.
Wingfield's Georgia Bat. (Irwin Artillery).

HETH'S DIVISION.

Major-general Henry Heth.
Brigadier-general J. J. Pettigrew.

*First Brigade.**

Brig.-gen. J. J. Pettigrew (wd.).
Colonel J. K. Marshall.
Col. T. C. Singeltary.

11th North Carolina.
26th North Carolina.
44th North Carolina.†
47th North Carolina.
52d North Carolina.

Second Brigade.

Brig.-gen. Chas. W. Field.
Col. J. M. Brockenbrough.
Brig.-gen. H. H. Walker.‡

40th Virginia.
47th Virginia.
55th Virginia.
22d Virginia Battalion.

*Third Brigade.**

Brig.-gen. James J. Archer.
Colonel B. D. Fry.
Brig.-gen. H. H. Walker.

13th Alabama.
5th Alabama Battalion.
1st Tenn. (Prov. Army).
7th Tennessee.
14th Tennessee.

Fourth Brigade.

Brig.-gen. Jos. R. Davis.

2d Mississippi.
11th Mississippi.
42d Mississippi.
55th North Carolina.

Artillery.

Lieutenant-colonel John J. Garnett.
Major Charles Richardson.

Grandy's Va. Bat. (Norfolk Light Art. Blues).
Lewis's Virginia Battery.
Maurin's La. Battery (Donaldsonville Art.).
Moore's Virginia Battery.

PENDER'S DIVISION.

Major-gen. William D. Pender (wd.).
Brigadier-general James H. Lane.

First Brigade.

Brig.-gen. S. McGowan.
Colonel A. Perrin.

1st South Carolina.
1st South Carolina Rifles.
12th South Carolina.
13th South Carolina.
14th South Carolina.

Second Brigade.§

Brig.-gen. James. H. Lane.

7th North Carolina.
18th North Carolina.
28th North Carolina.
33d North Carolina.
37th North Carolina.

Third Brigade.

Brig.-gen. E. L. Thomas.

14th Georgia.
35th Georgia.
45th Georgia.
49th Georgia.

Fourth Brigade.§

Brig.-gen. A. M. Scales (wd.).
Colonel W. Lee Lowrance.

13th North Carolina.
16th North Carolina.
22d North Carolina.
34th North Carolina.
38th North Carolina.

Artillery.

Major William T. Poague.

Brooke's Virginia Battery.
Graham's North Carolina Battery.
Ward's Miss. Battery (Madison Light Artillery).
Wyatt's Virginia Battery (Albemarle Artillery).

* Temporarily consolidated July 10th, under Pettigrew's command.
† Left at Hanover Junction, and not engaged at Gettysburg.
‡ Assigned July 19th. Appears in return for July 31st as commanding both 2d and 3d brigades.
§ Under Trimble's command July 3d.

RESERVE ARTILLERY THIRD CORPS.

Colonel R. L. Walker, Chief of Artillery.

McIntosh's Battalion.

Major D. G. McIntosh.

Hurt's Ala. Bat. (Hardaway Artillery).
Lusk's Virginia Battery.
Johnson's Virginia Battery.
Rice's Va. Battery (Danville Artillery).

Pegram's Battalion.

Major W. J. Pegram.
Captain E. B. Brunson.

Brander's Va. Battery (Letcher Artillery).
Brunson's S. C. Battery (Pee Dee Art.).
Crenshaw's Virginia Battery.
McGraw's Va. Battery (Purcell Artillery).
Marye's Va. Battery (Fredericksburg Art.).

CAVALRY.

MAJOR-GENERAL J. E. B. STUART.

Hampton's [1st] Brigade.

Brig.-gen. Wade Hampton.
Colonel L. S. Baker.

1st North Carolina.
1st South Carolina.
2d South Carolina.
Cobb's Georgia Legion.
Jeff. Davis Legion.
Phillips's Georgia Legion.

Robertson's [2d] Brigade.

Brig.-gen. B. H. Robertson.*

4th North Carolina.
5th North Carolina.

Fitz Lee's [3d] Brigade.

Colonel Thomas T. Munford.

1st Maryland Battalion (?).
1st Virginia.
2d Virginia.
3d Virginia.
4th Virginia.
5th Virginia.

Jenkins's [4th] Brigade.

Brig.-gen. A. G. Jenkins.

14th Virginia.
16th Virginia.
17th Virginia.
34th Virginia Battalion.
36th Virginia Battalion.

Jones's [5th] Brigade.

Brig.-gen. Wm. E. Jones.

6th Virginia.
7th Virginia.
11th Virginia.
12th Virginia.
35th Virginia Battalion.

W. H. F. Lee's [6th] Brigade.

Colonel J. R. Chambliss.

2d North Carolina.
9th Virginia.
10th Virginia.
13th Virginia.
15th Virginia.

Not Brigaded (?).

Imboden's Command.
43d Virginia (Mosby's) Battalion.

Stuart Horse Artillery. †

Major R. F. Beckham (?).

Breathed's Maryland Battery.
Chew's Virginia Battery.
Griffin's 2d Maryland Battery.
Hart's South Carolina Battery (Washington Artillery).
McGregor's Virginia Battery.
Moorman's Virginia Battery.

* Relieved at his own request August 4, 1863.
† Captain Thomas E. Jackson's battery appears on return for July 31, 1863, as in the cavalry division, but it is not mentioned in reports of the campaign.

Abstract from Return of the Army of Northern Virginia, GEN-ERAL R. E. LEE *commanding, for July 20, 1863—Bunker Hill, Va.*

COMMAND.	Present for duty.		Aggregate present.	Aggregate present and absent.	Aggregate last return.
	Officers.	Men.			
General staff.	16	. . .	16	16	16
FIRST CORPS.					
LIEUT.-GEN. LONGSTREET.					
Staff	11	. . .	11	13	11
McLaws's division*	. . .	. . .	5,647	12,301	5,463
Pickett's division	. . .	. . .	4,696	11,644	. . .
Hood's division	. . .	. . .	5,693	11,428	5,691
Total	. . .	. . .	16,047	35,386	. . .
SECOND CORPS.					
LIEUT.-GEN. EWELL.					
Staff	18	. . .	18	21	. . .
Rodes's division	. . .	. . .	6,223	15,001	5,822
Early's division	. . .	. . .	5,553	13,056	4,791
Johnson's division	. . .	. . .	4,642	12,211	4,194
Total	. . .	. . .	16,436	40,289	14,807
THIRD CORPS.					
LIEUT.-GEN. A. P. HILL.					
Staff	15	. . .	15	16	11
Anderson's division	. . .	. . .	5,820	13,069	5,508
Heth's division†	. . .	. . .	2,388	. . .	2,509
Pender's division	. . .	. . .	3,975	12,855	3,616
Total	. . .	. . .	12,198	25,940	11,644
Artillery.					
Brig.-gen. Pendleton.					
First Army corps	. . .	. . .	1,967	2,900	1,325
Second Army corps	. . .	. . .	1,651	2,660	1,528
Third Army corps ‡	. . .	. . .	1,869	2,724	. . .
Total	. . .	. . .	5,487	8,284	. . .
Stuart's cavalry division ?	. . .	. . .	. . .	. . .	. . .
Grand total	. . .	. . .	50,184	109,915	. . .

* " Present " last return not reported.   † Absent not reported.
‡ " Present " last return not reported.   ? Not reported.

HEADQUARTERS ARMY OF NORTHERN VIRGINIA,
April 27, 1864.

GENERAL: I have the honor to submit a report of the operations of this army on the occasion of the advance of the Federal forces under Major-general Meade, in November, 1863.

After its return from Culpeper, as previously reported, the army occupied the line of the Rapidan without interruption until November 26th. The enemy was encamped in the vicinity of Culpeper Court-house and between that place and the Rappahannock. On the day last mentioned large bodies of troops were observed moving toward the lower fords of the Rapidan, and at a later hour intelligence was received that the enemy had crossed that river in force at Ely's, Culpeper Mine, Germanna, and Jacob's fords. The country in that vicinity was unfavorable for observation, being almost an unbroken forest, and it could not be discovered whether it was the design of the Federal commander to advance toward Richmond or move up the Rapidan upon our right flank.

The army was withdrawn from its lines during the night of the 26th, and put in motion with the intention of falling upon his flank and rear should he attempt the first-mentioned movement, or giving battle should he essay the execution of the second. Lieutenant-general Ewell being absent on account of sickness, his corps was placed under the command of Major-general Early, who was directed to move by the old turnpike and Raccoon Ford roads to Locust Grove. Hill's corps marched down the plank road. Hampton's division of cavalry, accompanied by General Stuart, preceded the advance of the main body. The defence of our line on the Rapidan was entrusted to Fitz Lee's cavalry division.

During the forenoon of the 27th the cavalry in front reported the enemy advancing up the turnpike and plank road, but as it was supposed that it might be only a force thrown out to cover the movement of the main body toward Fredericksburg, the march of the troops was continued. About a mile and a half east of Mine Run, General Hill's leading division, under General Heth, met the cavalry slowly retiring before the enemy. A brigade of infantry was deployed to support the cavalry, and after a brisk skirmish the progress of the enemy was arrested.

In the mean time, Early's division, under General Hays, advanced on the old turnpike to within less than a mile of Locust Grove, and discovered that the enemy's infantry already occupied that place. General Rodes, who had marched by Zoar Church into the Raccoon Ford road, came up soon afterward and took position on the left of Hays. Sharp skirmishing ensued, but as the enemy had an advantageous position and the density of the woods rendered it impossible to ascertain his strength, it was deemed best to defer the attack until the arrival of General Johnson's division. General Johnson marched on the

Raccoon Ford road by Bartlett's mill, and the head of his column had nearly reached General Rodes, when, at a point less than two miles from the mill, his ambulance-train, moving in advance of the rear brigade under General G. H. Steuart, was fired into from the left of the road. General Steuart immediately formed his command and took measures to protect the train. Upon advancing his skirmishers it was discovered that the attacking party consisted of infantry, apparently in considerable force. General Johnson countermarched the other brigades of his division and formed them on the right of General Steuart. After skirmishing for some time, about 4 P. M. he ordered a general advance, and after a sharp engagement the enemy was driven back through the woods and pursued into an open field beyond. The density of the forest rendered it impossible for the troops to preserve their line unbroken in the advance, and prevented the proper concert of action. General Johnson was therefore unable to follow up his success, the numbers of the enemy greatly exceeding his own, and re-formed his troops on the edge of the open ground, which position they continued to hold until dark.

The force of the enemy encountered by General Johnson—consisting, as was afterward ascertained, of one army corps and part of another—crossed the Rapidan at Jacob's Ford, and marched thence by a road which enters the Raccoon Ford road near Payne's farm, where the action took place. The usual precaution had been taken by General Johnson to guard against a flank attack, but owing to the character of the country the presence of the enemy was not discovered until his skirmishers fired upon the ambulance-train. The ground was unfavorable for the use of artillery, but sections of Carpenter's and Dement's batteries participated in the engagement and rendered efficient and valuable service.

Our total loss in killed, wounded, and missing was 545.

Lieutenant-colonel [S. T.] Walton, commanding Twenty-third Virginia regiment, was killed, and Colonel Raleigh T. Colston, commanding Second Virginia regiment, severely wounded, while leading their respective commands with conspicuous gallantry. Colonel Colston has since died. General Johnson mentions with well-merited praise the conduct of those brave and lamented officers.

The promptness with which this unexpected attack was met and repulsed reflects great credit upon General Johnson and the officers and men of his division.

While these events were transpiring information was received from Brigadier-general Rosser, whose brigade of cavalry was guarding the roads leading from Ely's and Germanna fords to Fredericksburg, that the whole Federal army after crossing the Rapidan had moved up the river in the direction of Orange Court-house. General Rosser had attacked a train of wagons near Wilderness Tavern and captured a large number, some of which he brought off, and destroyed the remainder. He also secured 280 mules and 150 prisoners.

Preparations were made to meet the attack which this information led us to expect, but as the enemy did not advance, the army was withdrawn during the night to the west side of Mine Run, where it took up a more favorable position and proceeded to strengthen it with intrenchments.

The next day the enemy appeared on the opposite side of the creek immediately in our front, and skirmishing took place along the whole line, but no attack was made.

On the night of the 28th General Stuart was ordered with Hampton's cavalry to endeavor to gain the rear of the enemy and ascertain his purpose. He penetrated as far as Parker's shop on the plank road, where he attacked and defeated a body of Federal cavalry, but the pursuit was arrested by the intelligence that the movements of the enemy indicated that a general engagement was imminent. He resumed his position on our right flank during the night, having captured more than 100 prisoners and a quantity of military stores.

On the morning of the 29th a heavy fire of artillery was opened upon our lines which was supposed to be preparatory to a general assault, a large force having been previously concentrated opposite our right. Our batteries responded occasionally, but the artillery fire ceased in about an hour, and nothing but the usual skirmishing took place during the remainder of the day.

Believing that the enemy would not abandon an enterprise undertaken with so great a display of force without giving battle, I was unwilling to lose the advantage of our position, and awaited the development of his plans until the night of December 1st, but, finding that he hesitated to bring on an engagement, I determined to move against him on the following morning. The troops were disposed for the purpose before dawn, but as soon as it became light enough to distinguish objects his pickets were found to have disappeared, and on advancing our skirmishers it was discovered that his whole army had retreated under cover of the night. Pursuit was immediately commenced, but on arriving near the river it was found that the Federal army had recrossed at Germanna, Culpeper Mine, and Ely's fords. The withdrawal had no doubt begun the previous afternoon, but was concealed by the dense forest through which the roads of retreat lay. The same cause prevented the efficient use of our cavalry and rendered it necessary for the infantry to pursue with caution. About 500 prisoners fell into our hands.

Our casualties were slight with the exception of those sustained by Johnson's division in the action at Payne's farm. They are stated in the accompanying returns. Among them were several valuable officers whose names are appropriately mentioned in the reports of their superiors.

The army returned to its former position on the Rapidan.

The conduct of both officers and men throughout these operations deserves the highest commendation. The promptness with which they marched to meet the enemy, their uncomplaining fortitude while lying in line of battle for five days exposed without shelter to a drenching storm, followed by intense cold, and their steadiness and cheerful resolution in anticipation of an attack, could not have been excelled.

As has been already stated, the country was very unfavorable for cavalry. Hampton's division rendered good service in guarding our right flank. Fitz Lee's division repulsed several efforts of the Federal cavalry under General Kilpatrick to gain the south side of the Rapidan at Raccoon and Morton's fords in rear of our left.

I cannot conclude without alluding to the wanton destruction of the property of citizens by the enemy. Houses were torn down or rendered uninhabitable, furniture and farming implements broken or destroyed, and many families, most of them in humble circumstances, stripped of all they possessed and left without shelter and without food. I have never witnessed on any previous occasion such entire disregard of the usages of civilized warfare and the dictates of humanity.

I forward herewith the reports of corps, division, and other commanders, and a map of the scene of operations.

Very respectfully, your obedient servant,

R. E. LEE,
General.

GENERAL S. COOPER,
Adjutant- and Inspector-general, Richmond, Va.

CONFIDENTIAL LETTERS OF GENERAL LEE TO THE AUTHORITIES AT RICHMOND DURING THE YEARS 1863, 1864, AND 1865.

THE report just given, covering the campaign of the autumn of 1863, is the last detailed account of his battles ever written by General Lee. From that time forward fighting was too continuous to permit of his writing out the events of the war in detail. Valuable as would have been a report from his hand of the great events of the last year of the war, there is none such in existence, and he has left it to historians to describe the important battles of the Wilderness, Spottsylvania, and Cold Harbor, though in no other engagements of the war did his transcendent military genius more clearly display itself. Fortunately, however, a considerable number of his letters in relation to military events are still in existence. These have been placed at the service of the authors of this work, who take great pleasure in laying them before the reader from the fact that they are full of important information, hitherto unpublished, concerning the military history of the Confederate States.

Many of these letters belong to the period covered by the reports just given, those of the Gettysburg and the subsequent campaign; but, while to some extent they repeat the information contained in those reports, a considerable number of them relate to other subjects, often of great importance. We give the more valuable of these latter, either in full or in the form of extracts which include all that they contain of essential significance, while omitting details of minor importance.

These letters serve to clearly indicate that the attention of General Lee was by no means confined to the management of the Army of Northern Virginia or to the mere planning of campaigns and fighting of battles, but that he had constantly in view the duty of providing for the necessities of his soldiers and perfecting the organization of the army, while acting as military adviser of the President in relation to the affairs of the whole Confederacy, over which he exercised a clear-headed military supervision. There is good reason to believe that many of the successes of the armies of the Confederate States were due to his judicious advice, and that his victories were not confined to Virginia, but that he could properly have claimed a silent share in victorious movements throughout the entire South. General Lee was by no means a mere army-leader. He was a strategist and organizer of the highest grade, and had he never led an army in the field, but confined his powers to cabinet duties at Richmond, he would still have been of incalculable service to the Confederacy, and have wielded all the armies of the nation with the unmatched skill which he displayed in the handling of the corps under his immediate command.

HEADQUARTERS ARMY OF NORTHERN VIRGINIA,
Feb. 5, 1863.

HIS EXCELLENCY JEFFERSON DAVIS, PRESIDENT C. S.,

MR. PRESIDENT: Your Excellency's letter of the 4th inst. has just been received. I yesterday addressed a communication to the Secretary of War giving the reasons which rendered it possible that an attack would be made upon Charleston. In addition, I will say that the fall of Savannah will not carry with it the advantages to the United States Government which would result from the possession of Charleston. It is to be expected, then, that demonstrations will be made against the former city to attract those reinforcements. As soon as the point of attack is ascertained, I would recommend that all the troops which can be spared from the city not in danger should be rapidly thrown to the other, as it is clear that both cities cannot be attacked at the same time. Attempts will be made to deceive by advancing against the point not intended for the real attack such gunboats, vessels, and troops as will not be required against the other, and discrimination will be required to discover the feint. As far as I can learn at this distance, it seems that the iron-clad gunboats of the enemy are south of the Cape Fear River, and that General Foster with his troops has gone south too. I do not think, therefore, that Wilmington is at present in danger of being attacked, though no doubt efforts will be made to detain all of our troops there. They can, however, I think, with safety be detached to Charleston. Should a sufficient force not be left in North Carolina to guard our lines, which cannot under the circumstances be seriously threatened, some regiments of General Wise's brigade might be temporarily ordered to take their place. In case of necessity troops from this army can be sent to Richmond, and if you think the exigency of the south more pressing than here, I will send them at once. In my letter of yesterday to the Secretary of War I stated the reasons why I thought we might expect the advance of General Hooker. The weather to-day is unfavorable for his movements, and it may prove so for some time.

It appears to me that if either Charleston or Savannah is attacked, the rest of the coast may be stripped pretty bare of troops without imprudence. The troops of this army are ready to move at a moment's warning, and all I require is notice when they are wanted. I presume but few of the enemy's troops are left in North Carolina—perhaps not more than enough to guard his positions.

I have the honor to be, with great respect,
Your obdt. servt.,
R. E. LEE,
General.

CAMP NEAR FREDERICKSBURG,
21 March, 1863.

HIS EXCELLENCY JEFFERSON DAVIS, PRESIDENT C. S.,

MR. PRESIDENT: Upon an examination of the Senate bill presented by General Sparrow for the organization of the staff of the army, I think some changes might be made to advantage. These will readily occur to you, and I will therefore allude to them generally.

I think it important, and indeed necessary, to simplify the mechanism of our army as much as possible, yet still to give it sufficient power to move and regulate the whole body. Our armies are necessarily very large in comparison with those we have heretofore had to manage. Some of our divisions exceed the army General Scott entered the city of Mexico with, and our brigades are larger than his divisions. The greatest difficulty I find is in causing orders and regulations to be obeyed. This arises not from a spirit of disobedience, but from ignorance. We therefore have need of a corps of officers to teach others their duty, see to the observance of orders, and to the regularity and precision of all movements. This is accomplished in the French service by their staff corps, educated, instructed, and practised for the purpose. The same circumstances that produced that corps exist in our own army. Can you not shape the staff of our army to produce equally good results? Although the staff of the French army is larger than that proposed by the Senate bill, I am in favor of keeping ours down, as it is so much easier to build up than to reduce if experience renders it necessary. I would therefore assign one general officer to a general commanding in the field, and give to his inspector-general, quartermaster-general, commissary-general, chief of ordnance, and medical director the provisional grade of colonel of cavalry. I would reduce his aides, and give to his chief of staff and inspector-general assistants, as they will never be able to properly attend to their out-door and in-door work, which from the condition of our army, as heretofore stated, is very heavy. I would apply the same principles to the division and brigade staff, placing their chiefs on an equal footing, and giving each a complete organization in itself, so that it can manœuvre independently of the corps or division to which it is habitually attached, and be detached with promptness and facility when required. Each, therefore, in addition to its general staff, should have a surgeon, quartermaster, and commissary and ordnance officers. If you can then fill these positions with proper officers —not the relations and social friends of the commanders, who, however agreeable their company, are not always the most useful—you might hope to have the finest army in the world. I beg you will excuse the liberty of my suggestion,

And believe me, with great respect,

Yr. obt. servt., R. E. LEE,
General.

HEADQUARTERS, May 3, 1863.

JACKSON, GENERAL T. J., Commanding Corps,

GENERAL: I have just received your note informing me that you were wounded. I cannot express my regret at the occurrence. Could I have directed events, I should have chosen for the good of the country to have been disabled in your stead. I congratulate you upon the victory which is due to your skill and energy.

Very respectfully,

Yr. obt. servt.,

R. E. LEE,
General.

HEADQUARTERS ARMY OF NORTHERN VIRGINIA,
June 10, 1863.

HIS EXCELLENCY JEFFERSON DAVIS, RICHMOND,

MR. PRESIDENT: I beg leave to bring to your attention a subject with reference to which I have thought that the course pursued by writers and speakers among us has had a tendency to interfere with our success. I refer to the manner in which the demonstration of a desire for peace at the North has been received in our country.

I think there can be no doubt that journalists and others at the South, to whom the Northern people naturally look for a reflection of our opinions, have met these indications in such wise as to weaken the hands of the advocates of a pacific policy on the part of the Federal Government, and give much encouragement to those who urge a continuance of the war.

Recent political movements in the United States and the comments of influential newspapers upon them have attracted my attention particularly to this subject, which I deem not unworthy of the consideration of Your Excellency, nor inappropriate to be adverted to by me in view of its connection with the situation of military affairs.

Conceding to our enemies the superiority claimed by them in numbers, resources, and all the means and appliances for carrying on the war, we have no right to look for exemption from the military consequences of a vigorous use of these advantages, except by such deliverance as the mercy of Heaven may accord to the courage of our soldiers, the justice of our cause, and the constancy and prayers of our people. While making the most we can of the means of resistance we possess, and gratefully accepting the measure of success with which God has blessed our efforts as an earnest of his approval and favor, it is nevertheless the part of wisdom to carefully measure and husband our strength, and not to expect from it more than in the ordinary course of affairs it is capable of accomplishing. We should not, therefore, conceal from ourselves that our resources in men are constantly diminishing, and the disproportion in this respect between us and our enemies, if they continue united in their efforts to subjugate, is steadily augmenting. The decrease of the aggregate of this army as disclosed by the returns affords an illustration of this fact. Its effective strength varies from time to time, but the falling off in its aggregate shows that its ranks are growing weaker and that its losses are not supplied by recruits.

Under these circumstances we should neglect no honorable means of dividing and weakening our enemies, that they may feel some of the difficulties experienced by ourselves. It seems to me that the most effectual mode of accomplishing this object now within our reach is to give all the encouragement we can, consistently with truth, to the rising peace party of the North.

Nor do I think we should, in this connection, make nice distinction between those who declare for peace unconditionally and those who advocate it as a means of restoring the Union, however much we may prefer the former.

We should bear in mind that the friends of peace at the North must make concessions to the earnest desire that exists in the minds of their countrymen for a restoration of the Union, and that to hold out such a result as an inducement is essential to the success of their party.

Should the belief that peace will bring back the Union become general the war would no longer be supported; and that, after all, is what we are interested in bringing about. When peace is proposed to us it will be time enough to discuss its terms, and it is not the part of prudence to spurn the proposition in advance merely because those who wish to make it believe, or affect to believe, that it will result in bringing us back to the Union. We entertain no such apprehensions, nor doubt that the desire of our people for a distinct and independent national existence will prove as steadfast under the influence of peaceful measures as it has shown itself in the midst of war.

If the views I have indicated meet the approval of Your Excellency, you will best know how to give effect to them. Should you deem them inexpedient or impracticable, I think you will nevertheless agree with me that we should at least carefully abstain from measures or expressions that tend to discourage any party whose purpose is peace.

With this statement of my own opinion on the subject, the length of which you will excuse, I leave to your better judgment to determine the proper course to be pursued.

I am, with great respect,
Your obedient servant,

R. E. LEE,
General.

OPPOSITE WILLIAMSPORT,
June 25, 1863.

HIS EXCELLENCY PRESIDENT DAVIS, RICHMOND,

MR. PRESIDENT: I have received to-day your letter of the 19th instant, and am much gratified by your views in relation to the peace party at the North. It is plain to my understanding that everything that will tend to repress the war feeling in the Federal States will inure to our benefit. I do not know that we can do anything to promote the pacific feeling, but our course ought to be so shaped as not to discourage it.

I am sorry to hear that any controversy has arisen in relation to the exchange of prisoners. That is a matter in which our enemies have an advantage over us. Although we may have more prisoners than they, theirs are maintained at less expense than ours. Moreover, our citizens are much more accessible to them than theirs to us, so that the system of retaliation, if commenced, will not be on an equal basis. Besides, I am not in favor of retaliation except in very extreme cases, and I think it would be better for us to suffer and be right in our own eyes and in the eyes of the world; we will gain more by it in the end. I hope, therefore, some plan may be adopted to prevent a course so repugnant to the feelings of humanity and the sense of right, and that the one you propose may be crowned with success.

You will see that apprehension for the safety of Washington and their own territory has aroused the Federal Government and people to great exertions, and it is incumbent upon us all to call forth all our energies. In addition to the 100,000 troops called for by President Lincoln to defend the frontier of Pennsylvania, you will see that he is concentrating other organized forces in Maryland. It is stated in the papers that they are all being withdrawn from Suffolk, and, according to General Buckner's report, Burnside and his corps are recalled from Kentucky. It is reasonable to suppose that this would be the case if their apprehensions were once aroused.

I think this should liberate the troops in the Carolinas, and enable Generals Buckner and Bragg to accomplish something in Ohio. It is plain that if all the Federal army is concentrated upon this [point], it will result in our accomplishing nothing and being compelled to return to Virginia. If the plan that I suggested the other day, of organizing an army, even in effigy, under General Beauregard at Culpeper Court-house can be carried into effect, much relief will be afforded. If even the brigades in Virginia and North Carolina, which Generals Hill and Elzey think cannot be spared, were ordered there at once, and General Beauregard were sent there, if he had to return to South Carolina, it would do more to protect both States from marauding expeditions of the enemy than anything else.

I have not sufficient troops to maintain my communications, and therefore have to abandon them. I think I can throw General Hooker's army across the Potomac and draw troops from the south, embarrassing their plan of campaign in a measure, if I can do nothing more and have to return.

I still hope that all things will end well for us at Vicksburg. At any rate, every effort should be made to bring about that result.

With great respect, your obedient servant,

R. E. LEE,
General.

HEADQUARTERS ARMY OF NORTHERN VIRGINIA,
Near Hagerstown, Md., July 8, 1863.

HIS EXCELLENCY JEFFERSON DAVIS, PRESIDENT, ETC.,

MR. PRESIDENT: My letter of yesterday will have informed you of the position of this army. Though reduced in numbers by the hardships and battles through which it has passed since leaving the Rappahannock, its condition is good and its confidence unimpaired. Upon crossing the Potomac into Maryland, I had calculated upon the river remaining fordable during the summer, so as to enable me to recross at my pleasure, but a series of storms commencing the day after our entrance into Maryland has placed the river beyond fording stage, and the present storm will keep it so for at least a week. I shall therefore have to accept battle if the enemy offers it, whether I wish to or not; and as the result is in the hands of the sovereign Ruler of the universe, and known to Him only, I deem it prudent to make every arrangement in our power to meet any emergency that may arise. From information gathered from the papers, I believe that the troops from North Carolina and the coast of Virginia under Generals Foster and Dix have been ordered to the Potomac, and that recently additional reinforcements have been sent from the coast of South Carolina to General Banks. If I am correct in my opinion, this will liberate most of the troops in those regions, and, should Your Excellency have not already done so, I earnestly recommend that all that can be spared be concentrated on the upper Rappahannock under General Beauregard, with directions to cross that river and make a demonstration upon Washington. This command will answer the double purpose of affording protection to the capital at Richmond and relieving the pressure upon this army.

I hope Your Excellency will understand that I am not in the least discouraged, or that my faith in the protection of an all-merciful Providence or in the fortitude of this army is at all shaken. But, though conscious that the enemy has been much shattered in the recent battle, I am aware that he can be easily reinforced, while no addition can be made to our numbers. The measure, therefore, that I have recommended is altogether one of a prudential nature.

I am, most respectfully, your obedient servant,

R. E. LEE,
General.

HEADQUARTERS ARMY OF NORTHERN VIRGINIA,
Bunker Hill, Va., July 16, 1863.

HIS EXCELLENCY JEFFERSON DAVIS, PRESIDENT CONFEDERATE STATES,

MR. PRESIDENT : . . . . The army is encamped around this place, where we shall rest to-day. The men are in good health and spirits, but want shoes and clothing badly. I have sent back to endeavor to procure a supply of both, and also horseshoes, for want of which nearly half our cavalry is unserviceable. As soon as these necessary articles are obtained we shall be prepared to resume operations. . . . .

· · · · I share in Your Excellency's regret for the fall of Vicksburg. It will be necessary for us to endeavor to select some point on the Mississippi and fortify it strongly, so that it may be held by a small garrison, which could be supplied with ammunition and provisions to enable it to stand a siege, thus leaving as many troops as possible free to operate against the enemy. I think that in this way a land-attack against such position as we may select can be prevented.

I am, with great respect, Your Excellency's obedient servant,

R. E. LEE,
General.

From a letter to the President, dated September 6, 1863, we select the following extract, with the President's reply :

As regards myself, should you think that the service will be benefited by my repairing to the Army of Tennessee, I will of course submit to your judgment. From your knowledge of all the circumstances of both armies you can come to a more correct conclusion than I can from my point of view. In my conversation with you on this subject when the question was proposed I did not intend to decline the service if desired that I should undertake it, but merely to express the opinion that the duty could be better performed by the officers already in that department.

RICHMOND, September 8 (1863).

GEN. R. E. LEE:

Have considered your letter, believe your presence in the Western army would be worth more than the addition of a corps, but fear the effect of your absence from Virginia. Did not doubt your willingness to do whatever was best for the country, and suggest your aid to determine that question. Have sent you all additional information to aid your further consideration of problems discussed with you here.

JEFFERSON DAVIS.

HEADQUARTERS ARMY OF NORTHERN VIRGINIA,
Sept. 9, 1863.

SEDDON, HON. JAMES A., SECRETARY OF WAR, RICHMOND, VA.,

SIR: The letter of Governor Vance of North Carolina of Aug. 20th, with regard to the causes of dissatisfaction among the North Carolina troops in this army, with your endorsement, has been received. I regret exceedingly the jealousies, heartburnings, and other evil consequences resulting from the crude misstatements of newspaper correspondents, who have necessarily a very limited acquaintance with the facts about which they write, and who magnify the deeds of troops from their own States at the expense of others. But I can see no remedy for this. Men seem to prefer sowing discord to inculcating harmony. In the reports of the officers justice is done to the brave soldiers of North Carolina, whose heroism and devotion have rendered illustrious the name of the State on every battlefield on which the Army of Northern Virginia has been engaged. . . . .

I believe it would be better to have no correspondents of the press with the army. . . . .

I need not say that I will with pleasure aid Governor Vance in removing every reasonable cause of complaint on the part of men who have fought so gallantly and done so much for the cause of our country; and I hope that he will also do all in his power to cultivate a spirit of harmony, and to bring to punishment the disaffected who use these causes of discontent to further their treasonable designs.

I am, with great respect, yr. obt. servt.,

R. E. LEE,
General.

A letter to President Davis, dated Sept. 11, 1863, furnishes the following extract:

The defences around Richmond should now be completed as soon as possible. I did not see any connection or communication between the redoubts for the defence of Drewry's Bluff from a land-attack and the defensive line around Manchester. This is important, and also that there should be obstructions in the river connecting this intermediate line (as it was termed) on both sides of the river. Should the enemy's land forces drive us from Drewry's Bluff, they would remove the obstructions at that point, and, although we might be able to hold the intermediate line, his gunboats could ascend the river and destroy Richmond. I think, too, Colonel Gorgas should commence at once to enlarge his manufacturing arsenals, etc. in the interior, so that if Richmond should fall we would not be destitute. These are only recommended as prudential measures, and such as, should the necessity for them arise, we will then wish had been taken.

Copy of extract of letter from General Longstreet:

HEADQUARTERS, RICHMOND, Sept. 12, 1863.

GENERAL R. E. LEE, *Commanding*,

GENERAL: Henry's artillery has come down here, to my surprise. I have ordered, etc. . . . . Anderson's brigade was so far on its way toward Charleston when your telegram got here that it could not be diverted, and fearing that if I sent Jenkins on to take his place General Beauregard would keep both, I concluded that the wisest and safest plan would be to put Jenkins's brigade in Anderson's place in Hood's division. It has been so arranged. I intended to have suggested before leaving you that our defences around Richmond be so arranged that we might (in the event we should be forced to give up Richmond) hold Drewry's and Chaffin's Bluffs with a garrison of 15,000 or 20,000 men until we could collect army enough here to retake Richmond. I suppose that we might hold our vessels here under the protection of these fortifications until we could recover the city. But if we should give up the river to the enemy, there will be but little prospect of our getting back the capital during the war. As I have never seen the positions of these bluffs, I don't know whether this arrangement is a practicable one. I hope to start West on Monday morning. If I can do anything there, it shall be done promptly. If I cannot, I shall advise you to recall me. If I did not think our move a necessary [one], my regrets at leaving you would be distressing to me, as it seems to be with the officers and men of my command. Believing it to be necessary, I hope to accept it and my other personal inconveniences cheerfully and hopefully. All that we have to be proud of has been accomplished under your eye and under your orders. Our affections for you are stronger, if it is possible for them to be stronger, than our admiration for you.

I remain, general, most respectfully and affectionately, your obedient servant,

J. LONGSTREET,
Lieutenant-general.

In a letter to President Davis, dated September 14, 1863, General Lee refers to affairs in the Western Department in a tone of some dissatisfaction with the depletion of his army:

Everything looks like a concentration of their [the Federal] forces, and it is stated by our scouts that they have learned of the large reduction of this army. I begin to fear that we have lost the use of troops here where they are much needed, and that they have gone where they will do no good. I learn by the papers of to-day that General Rosecrans's army entered Chattanooga on the 9th, and that General Bragg has retired still farther into the interior. It also appears that General Burnside did not move to make a junction with Rose-crans, but marched to Knoxville. General Bragg must therefore either have been misinformed of his movements or he subsequently changed them. Had I been aware that Knoxville was the destination of General Burnside, I should have recommended that General Longstreet should be sent to oppose him, instead of to Atlanta. If General Bragg is unable to bring General Rosecrans to battle, I think it would be better to return General Longstreet to this army, to enable me to oppose the advance of General Meade with a greater prospect of success. And it is a matter worthy of consideration whether General Longstreet's corps will reach General Bragg in time and condition to be of any advantage to him. If the report sent to me by General Cooper since my return from Rich-mond is correct, General Bragg had on the 20th August last 51,101 effective men; General Buckner on the 20th August last, 18,118 effective men; he was to receive from General Johnston 9000 effective men; his total force will there-fore be 76,219—as large a number as, I presume, he can operate with. This is independent of the local troops, which you may recollect he reported as exceed-ing his expectations. Should General Longstreet reach General Bragg in time to aid him in winning a victory and return to this army, it will be well; but should he be detained there without being able to do any good, it will result in evil. I hope you will have the means of judging of this matter and of decid-ing correctly.

To President Davis, September 18, 1863:

I have had the honor to receive your letter of the 16th instant. Should Gen-erals Rosecrans and Burnside unite at Chattanooga, as now seems to be prob-able, and there fortify themselves, they will have, as you say, such vast means at their disposal as to render an attack upon that position by us extremely hazardous. I can see no other way, at this distance, of causing them to aban-don that strong position than that which you suggest of attacking their line of communication. For this purpose their position will be favorable, for although from Stevenson two routes are open to the enemy, one to Memphis and the other to Nashville, from Stevenson to Chattanooga there is but a single route. General Bragg by concentrating his cavalry and sending it to cut the lines of communication beyond Stevenson will cause General Rosecrans to detach largely for its maintenance. Then by moving with his whole force upon a vulnerable point, according to the nature of the ground, he will in all human probability break up his position.

Lee to Davis, September 23, 1863:

I was rejoiced yesterday to learn by a despatch from the War Department of the complete victory gained by General Bragg. I hope he will be able to follow it up, to concentrate his troops, and to operate on the enemy's rear. I infer from the accounts I have seen that Buckner had not joined him. Unless he is occupying a superior force to his own, he ought at once to unite with Bragg, that he may push the advantage gained. If that can be done, Longstreet can successfully move to East Tennessee, open that country, where Sam Jones can unite with him, and thence rejoin me. No time ought now to be lost or wasted. Everything should be done that can be done at once, so that the troops may be speedily returned to this department; as far as I can judge, they will not get here too soon. The enemy is aware of Longstreet's departure. They report in their papers the day he passed through Augusta, and give the position of Ewell's and Hill's corps. General Meade is strengthening himself daily. Our last scouts report the return of the troops sent North to enforce the draft. Nine trains loaded with troops reached Culpeper on Thursday night. Three trains arrived on Monday and three on Tuesday last, in addition to between four and five thousand marching.

HEADQUARTERS, ORANGE,
Sept. 25, 1863.

LIEUTENANT-GENERAL J. LONGSTREET,

GENERAL: If it gives you as much pleasure to receive my warmest congratulations as it does me to convey them, this letter will not have been written in vain. My whole heart and soul have been with you and your brave corps in your late battle. It was natural to hear of Longstreet and Hill charging side by side, and pleasing to find the armies of the East and West vieing with each other in valor and devotion to their country. A complete and glorious victory must ensue under such circumstances. I hope the result will equal the beginning, and that General Bragg will be able to reoccupy Tennessee. I grieve for the gallant dead and mourn for our brave Hood. The names of others have reached me, but I hope the report of their fall may not prove true. Finish the work before you, my dear general, and return to me. I want you badly, and you cannot get back too soon. Your departure was known to the enemy as soon as it occurred. General Meade has been actively engaged collecting his forces, and is now up to the Rapidan. All his troops that were sent North have returned, and reinforcements are daily arriving. His cavalry and engineers are constantly reconnoitering, and a vigorous effort was made Monday and Tuesday to turn our left. We are endeavoring to maintain a bold front, and shall endeavor to delay them all we can till you return.

Present my sincere compliments and admiration to the officers around you, and accept for yourself and command my ardent wishes for the welfare and happiness of all. Very truly yours,

R. E. LEE,
General.

HEADQUARTERS ARMY OF NORTHERN VIRGINIA,
19th Oct., 1863.

LAWTON, BRIG.-GEN. A. R., QUARTERMASTER-GENERAL, RICHMOND, VA.,

GENERAL: I have received your letter of the 12th, and am very glad to find that your exertions to supply the army have been so successful. The want of the supplies of shoes, clothing, overcoats, and blankets is very great. Nothing but my unwillingness to expose the men to the hardships that would have resulted from moving them into Loudoun in their present condition induced me to return to the Rappahannock. But I was averse to marching them over the rough roads of that region, at a season too when frosts are certain and snows probable, unless they were better provided to encounter them without suffering.

I should otherwise have endeavored to detain General Meade near the Potomac, if I could not throw him to the north side.

The supplies that you now have at your disposal for this army will be most welcome, and I trust that your exertions to increase them will meet with full success.

> Very respectfully, your obedient servant,
>
> R. E. LEE,
> *General.*

HEADQUARTERS ARMY OF NORTHERN VIRGINIA,
19 October, 1863.

SEDDON, HON. JAMES A., SEC. OF WAR, RICHMOND, VA.,

SIR: I have had the honor to receive your letter of the 16th inst. I am doubtful as yet whether General Meade will remain on the defensive. . . . .

If General Meade is disposed to remain quiet where he is, it was my intention, provided the army could be supplied with clothing, again to advance and threaten his positions. Nothing prevented my continuing in his front but the destitute condition of the men, thousands of whom are barefooted, a greater number partially shod, and nearly all without overcoats, blankets, or warm clothing. I think the sublimest sight of the war was the cheerfulness and alacrity exhibited by this army in the pursuit of the enemy under all the trials and privations to which it was exposed. . . . .

> Very respectfully, your obedient servant,
>
> R. E. LEE,
> *General.*

HEADQUARTERS ARMY OF NORTHERN VIRGINIA,
October 30, 1863.

HON. JAMES A. SEDDON, SECRETARY OF WAR, RICHMOND,

SIR: Your telegram directing a respite in the cases of Privates Newton and

Scroggins, Forty-first Virginia infantry, is received, and the order has been issued accordingly. At the same time, I beg leave to express my serious apprehension of the consequences of a relapse into that lenient policy which our past experience has shown to be so ruinous to the army, and in the end so much more cruel to the men. Early in the war it was found that stringent measures alone would keep the army together. After a few executions a number of men were pardoned, and the consequence was a recurrence of desertion to a most alarming extent. A return to a sterner discipline was found to be absolutely necessary, and by the executions that have taken place since the proclamation of the President, and by them only, has a stop been put to a spirit that was rapidly growing, that seized eagerly upon the slightest hope of escape from the consequences of crime, and that seriously threatened the existence of the army. A return to the lenient system that formerly prevailed will assuredly be productive of like results in the future, and render still harsher measures necessary hereafter if the army is to continue to exist. I fear that pardons, unless for the best of reasons, will not only make all the blood that has been shed for the maintenance of discipline useless, but will result in the painful necessity of shedding a great deal more. I hope I feel as acutely as any one the pain and sorrow that such events occasion, and I am sure that no one would more willingly dispense with them if they could be avoided; but I am convinced that the only way to prevent them is to visit the offence when committed with the sternest punishment, and leave the offender without hope of escape by making the penalty inevitable. It must be remembered that the punishment of death for desertion is inflicted almost exclusively for the warning of others, and no one without experience can conceive how readily the slightest prospect of escape is embraced.

I have felt it my duty to bring this subject strongly to your attention, as I am satisfied that in it, more than in any other, are involved the strength and efficiency of the army and its ability to cope with the enemy.

And I am further convinced that in a strict adherence to a stern discipline will be found the only means of avoiding the recurrence of these sad occasions.

Very respectfully, your obedient servant,

R. E. Lee,
General.

Headquarters,
6 Nov., 1863.

Letcher, His Excellency John, Governor of Virginia,

Governor : At its late called session the Legislature made an appropriation for the relief of the families of soldiers. I find that there is great suffering among the people in this region for want of the necessaries of life. The farms and gardens have been robbed, stock and hogs killed, and these outrages committed, I am sorry to say, by our own army to some extent, as well as by the Federals. I hear of like destitution in Stafford, where the Federal army alone has been. Would it not be well to forward such supplies of flour and meat as can be obtained to Culpeper Court-house and Fredericksburg, with agents for its distribution to those soldiers' families in distress, so as to relieve their wants during the coming winter ?

Respectfully, your obedient servant,

R. E. LEE,
General.

HEADQUARTERS ARMY OF NORTHERN VIRGINIA,
29th Nov., 1863.

DAVIS, HIS EXCELLENCY JEFFERSON, PRESIDENT CONFED. STATES, RICH-
MOND, VA.,

MR. PRESIDENT: I have the honor to acknowledge the receipt of your letter of the 25th inst., enclosing one from General Bragg. The enemy is in force in my front, and I shall necessarily be brief, but will give you the substance of the views which have suggested themselves to me after much previous reflection on the subjects referred to by General Bragg.

1. I think it a matter of the first importance that our armies now in the field shall be retained in service and recruited by wise and effectual legislation. This cannot be done too soon. The law should not be open to the charge of partiality, and I do not know how this can be accomplished without embracing the whole population capable of bearing arms, with the most limited exemptions, avoiding anything that would look like a distinction of classes. The exemptions of persons of particular and necessary avocations had better be made, as far as possible, by authority of the Department, rather than by special enactment. I think the general exemption of such persons by law is open to much abuse, and many escape service under color of it who are only nominally within the provisions of the law, and who can be taken into service without prejudice to the necessary production of the country. I also am of opinion that the skeleton regiments should be consolidated under the authority of the Department when necessary, and the provision should extend to all arms of the service. If possible, some prospective bounty should be provided for the men who have been, and will be again, retained in service.

As to the imperative necessity for retaining them, and adding sufficiently to their numbers to enable them to cope with the enemy, there can be no doubt, and all the constitutional power of Congress should be fully exerted for this purpose.

2. With reference to mounting the cavalry on Government horses, I should be glad if it could be accomplished, but do not see how the horses could be procured. It is difficult now to meet the wants of our artillery and transportation. But I think the law should invest the Government with complete authority for the time being over every horse mustered into service, and authorize the use of it in such manner as will most promote the public interests, providing at the same time proper compensation for the owners should it be found necessary to deprive them of the use of their horses. A cavalry soldier cannot perform the terms of his enlistment without a horse, and the Government should be able to control the horse on this ground ; and to this extent at least I fully concur in what General Bragg says with reference to depredations, whether committed by cavalry or any other part of the army. Any legislation that can repress this evil would be most beneficial.

3. I am not in favor of increasing the pay of any officer, but think it would be well to allow rations and clothing to company officers and their servants (such as they may lawfully have), and to other officers of like rank and pay with company officers. I see no necessity to extend the law to officers of a higher rank.

4. I think that the evil of officers and men absenting themselves without leave should be provided against, as far as practicable, by legislation. The ordinary mode of punishing by court-martial does not effectually check it, and I do not think General Bragg exaggerates the extent of the practice. In the case of officers I think the law should vacate their commissions by its own operation and subject them to conscription.

5. In this connection I would call your attention to the evils that flow from the absence of officers permanently disabled. Regiments are frequently commanded by captains from this cause, companies by sergeants, and sometimes brigades by majors and lieutenant-colonels. Many officers are borne on the rolls who are unfit for service. It would be harsh to drop them, and yet they prevent the promotion of other officers and interfere with the efficiency of their commands. I would suggest the establishment of an invalid corps to which such officers might be transferred, retaining their rank and pay. This corps might be made useful in many ways and relieve troops fit for field service.

6. I concur in the remarks of General Bragg with reference to the rank of the chief staff officers of our armies and those of the personal staff of commanding generals. The number and rank of the latter should correspond with their duties. These officers have no opportunity of promotion, and their importance is not over-estimated by General Bragg.

7. If any change in our hospital system can diminish the vice of absence without leave, I think it should be made. I do not know the particular features of the system to which General Bragg refers. I think it very important in providing for the personal staff, which should be adequate to the wants of the

officer with whom they serve, that he should be strictly confined to the staff allowed by law.

Respectfully, yr. obt. servt.,

R. E. LEE,
General.

———

HEADQUARTERS ARMY OF NORTHERN VIRGINIA,
December 3, 1863.

HIS EXCELLENCY JEFFERSON DAVIS, PRESIDENT CONFEDERATE STATES,
RICHMOND,

MR. PRESIDENT: I have considered with some anxiety the condition of affairs in Georgia and Tennessee. My knowledge of events has been principally derived from the public papers, and the impressions I have received may be erroneous, but there appears to me to be grounds to apprehend that the enemy may penetrate Georgia and get possession of our dépôts of provisions and important manufactories. I see it stated that General Bragg has been relieved from command, and that General Hardee is only acting until another commander shall be assigned to that army. I know the difficulties that surround this subject, but if General Beauregard is considered suitable for the position, I think he can be replaced at Charleston by General Gilmer. More force, in my opinion, is required in Georgia, and it can only be had, so far as I know, from Mississippi, Mobile, and the department of South Carolina, Georgia, and Florida. The occupation of Cleveland by the enemy cuts off General Longstreet from his base, and unless he succeeds quickly in defeating General Burnside he will have to retire either into Virginia or North Carolina. I see no reason why General Sam Jones should not be ordered to advance to his support, or at least to divert the attention of the column that is said to be moving on Charleston, Tennessee.

I have ventured to trouble Your Excellency with these suggestions, as I know how much your attention is occupied with the general affairs of the country, especially as the session of Congress approaches. I think that every effort should be made to concentrate as large a force as possible under the best commander to ensure the discomfiture of Grant's army. To do this and gain the great advantage that would accrue from it the safety of points practically less important than those endangered by his army must be hazarded. Upon the defence of the country threatened by General Grant depends the safety of the points now held by us on the Atlantic, and they are in as great danger from his successful advance as by the attacks to which they are at present directly subjected.

Very respectfully, your obedient servant,

R. E. LEE,
General.

RICHMOND, Dec. 5, 1863

GENERAL R. E. LEE, ORANGE COURT-HOUSE:

Could you consistently go to Dalton, as heretofore explained?

JEFFERSON DAVIS.

HEADQUARTERS ARMY OF NORTHERN VIRGINIA,
Rapidan, December 7, 1863.

HIS EXCELLENCY JEFFERSON DAVIS, PRESIDENT CONFEDERATE STATES, RICHMOND,

MR. PRESIDENT: I have had the honor to receive your despatch inquiring whether I could go to Dalton. I can, if desired, but of the expediency of the measure you can judge better than I can. Unless it is intended that I should take permanent command, I can see no good that will result, even if in that event any could be accomplished. I also fear that I would not receive cordial co-operation, and I think it necessary if I am withdrawn from here that a commander for this army be sent to it. General Ewell's condition, I fear, is too feeble to undergo the fatigue and labor incident to the position. I hope Your Excellency will not suppose that I am offering any obstacles to any measure you may think necessary. I only seek to give you the opportunity to form your opinion after a full consideration of the subject. I have not that confidence either in my strength or ability that would lead me of my own opinion to undertake the command in question.

I am, with great respect, your obedient servant,

R. E. LEE,
General.

HEADQUARTERS ARMY OF NORTHERN VIRGINIA,
8 Dec., 1863.

WALTON, HON. MOSES, and others,

GENTLEMEN: I have earnestly considered the petitions addressed to the Secretary of War and myself, and, deeply sympathizing in the sufferings of the citizens of Shenandoah, I wish I could see any way of securing them against the ravages of the enemy, the insults to their families, and the loss of their property. We cannot oppose an equal force to the enemy at all points. The safety of some must be hazarded that others considered more vital be defended It would give me great pleasure to increase the force in the Valley, but unless this can be done by the citizens of that region I know not whence at this time it can be attained.

I have forwarded to the Secretary of War your petition, and have written to General Imboden to inquire whether he cannot make such a disposition of his forces as to give greater protection to the lower Valley. I hope this may be done. . . . .

I remain, with great respect, yr. obt. servt.,

R. E. LEE,
General.

HEADQUARTERS ARMY OF NORTHERN VIRGINIA,
December 22, 1863.

MAJOR-GENERAL J. A. EARLY, commanding, etc.,

GENERAL: I telegraphed you to-day with reference to obtaining supplies for the army while the troops are in the Valley, and now write to explain my views more fully. I wish you to avail yourself of the present opportunity to collect and bring away everything that can be made useful to the army from those regions that are open to the enemy, using for this purpose both the cavalry and infantry under your command. I hear that in the lower Valley, and particularly in the country on the south branch of the Potomac, there are a good many cattle, sheep, horses, and hogs. Besides these, there is said to be a quantity of bacon, cloth, and leather, and all these supplies are accessible to and can be used by the enemy. I desire to secure all of them that it is in our power to get, and you will use your command for the purpose of keeping back the enemy while the work is being done. You will buy from all who are willing to sell, and where you cannot buy you must impress and give certificates to the owners. Of course you will not take what is necessary for the subsistence of the people, but leave enough for that, and secure all the rest of the articles named, and any others, such as shoes, horseshoes, and horseshoe nails, that you can get. While so engaged I wish you to subsist the troops on those supplies that are most difficult of transportation, such as bacon, potatoes, and other vegetables, which I hear can be had, sending back those that are easy to transport, such as cattle, particularly sheep and hogs. If you cannot get enough bacon and vegetables, you might use some of the sheep and hogs. You will understand that these instructions have no application to those parts of the country that are accessible to our ordinary agents engaged in procuring supplies. You will make requisition on Major Bell for such transportation as he can furnish, and also try to get additional facilities from the people. The cloth, leather, and other quartermaster stores should be collected as fully as possible, leaving of course enough for the wants of our people. Horses and cattle can be driven back at once. I write to Major Bell by this mail to assist you as far as he is able.

Very respectfully, your obedient servant,

R. E. LEE,
General.

P. S. You will give out that your movement is intended as a military one against the enemy, and of course will do them all the harm you can. You will use all the troops, including those of Imboden and Gilmer, that you may require.   R. E. L.

HIS EXCELLENCY JEFFERSON DAVIS, PRESIDENT CONFEDERATE STATES, RICHMOND,

MR. PRESIDENT: The time is at hand when, if an attempt can be made to capture the enemy's forces at New Berne, it should be done. I can now spare troops for the purpose, which will not be the case as spring approaches. If I have been correctly informed, a brigade from this army with Barton's brigade, Pickett's division, now near Kinston, will be sufficient if the attack can be secretly and suddenly made. New Berne is defended on the land side by a line of intrenchments from the Neuse to the Trent. A redoubt near the Trent protects that flank, while three or four gunboats are relied upon to defend the flank on the Neuse. The garrison has been so long unmolested and experiences such a feeling of security that it is represented as careless. The gunboats are small and indifferent, and do not keep up a head of steam. A bold party could descend the Neuse in boats at night, capture the gunboats, and drive the enemy by their aid from the works on that side of the river, while a force should attack them in front. A large amount of provisions and other supplies are said to be at New Berne, which are much wanted for this army, besides much that is reported in the country that will thus be made accessible to us. The gunboats, aided by the ironclads building on the Neuse and Roanoke, would clear the waters of the enemy and capture their transports, which could be used for transportation. I have not heard what progress is making in the completion of the ironclads or when they will be ready for service. A bold naval officer will be required for the boat-expedition, with suitable men and officers to man the boats and serve the gunboats when captured. Can they be had?

I have sent General Early with two brigades of infantry and two of cavalry under Fitz Lee to Hardy and Hampshire counties, to endeavor to get out some cattle that are reported within the enemy's lines. But the weather has been so unfavorable that I fear he will not meet with much success. The heavy rainstorm will swell all the streams beyond fording, and the cold weather and snow in the mountains will present other obstacles. Many of the infantry are without shoes and the cavalry worn down by their pursuit of Averell. We are now issuing to the troops a fourth of a pound of salt meat, and have only three days' supply at that rate. Two droves of cattle from the West that were reported to be for this army have, I am told, been directed to Richmond. I can learn of no supply of meat on the road to the army, and fear I shall be unable to retain it in the field.

I am, with great respect, your obedient servant,

R. E. LEE,
General.

———

HEADQUARTERS ARMY OF NORTHERN VIRGINIA,
5 Jan., 1864.

NORTHROP, COLONEL L. B., COMMISSARY-GEN., RICHMOND, VA.,

COLONEL: Your letter of the 7th ult. reached here during my absence in Richmond. . . . .

I regret very much to learn that the supply of beef for the army is so nearly exhausted. . . . . No beef has been issued to the cavalry corps by the chief commissary, that I am aware of, for eighteen months. During that time it has supplied itself, and has now, I understand, sufficient to last until the middle of February. . . . .

I cannot adopt your suggestion to employ the organization of your bureau to impress provisions. Neither the law nor regulations of the War Department, in my opinion, give me that power. . . . .

I have the honor to be, with great respect, yr. obt. servt.,

R. E. LEE,
General.

———

[Confidential.]

CAMP ORANGE COURT-HOUSE,
January 16, 1864.

LIEUTENANT-GENERAL J. LONGSTREET,

GENERAL: Your letters of the 10th and 11th instants were handed to me by Captain Gorse last night. I am glad that you are casting about for some way to reach the enemy. If he could be defeated at some point before he is prepared to open the campaign, it would be attended with the greatest advantages. Either of the points mentioned by you would answer. I believe, however, that if Grant could be driven back and Mississippi and Tennessee recovered, it would do more to relieve the country and inspirit our people than the mere capture of Washington. You know how exhausted the country is between here and the Potomac; there is nothing for man or horse. Everything must be carried. How is that to be done with weak transportation on roads in the condition we may expect in March? You know better than I how you will be off in that respect in the West. After you get into Kentucky I suppose provisions can be obtained. But if saddles, etc. could be procured in time, where can the horses be? They cannot be obtained in this section of country, and, as far as my information extends, not in the Confederacy. But let us both quietly and ardently set to work; some good may result, and I will institute inquiries.

There is a part of your letter that gives me uneasiness. That is in relation to your position. Your cavalry, I hope, will keep you informed of any movement against you. After the completion of the Virginia and Tennessee Railroad you will be able to retire with ease, and you had better be prepared in case of necessity. If the enemy follow, with the assistance of General S. Jones you may be able to hit him a hard blow. I would suggest that you have the country examined, routes explored, and strong positions ascertained and improved. There is some report of a projected movement of the enemy next spring by the route from Knoxville, and the abandonment of this to Richmond. It is believed that such a movement will be as successful as that by Grant on Vicksburg. As they have not been able yet to overcome the eighty miles between Washington and Richmond by the shortest road, I hope they will not be able to accomplish the more circuitous route. Not knowing what they intend to do, and what General Johnston can do, has prevented my recommending your return to this army. After hearing that you were in comfortable quarters and had plenty of provisions and forage, I thought it was best you should remain where you are until spring or until it was determined what could be done. I hope you will be able to recruit your corps. In reference to that, how would General Buckner answer for the command of Hood's division, at least until it is seen whether he ever can return to it? . . . .

With kind regards to yourself and all with you,

I am, very truly yours,

R. E. LEE,
General.

HEADQUARTERS ARMY,
18th Jan., 1864.

LAWTON, BRIGADIER-GENERAL A. R., QUARTERMASTER-GENERAL, RICHMOND,

GENERAL: The want of shoes and blankets in this army continues to cause much suffering and to impair its efficiency. In one regiment I am informed that there are only fifty men with serviceable shoes, and a brigade that recently went on picket was compelled to leave several hundred men in camp who were unable to bear the exposure of duty, being destitute of shoes and blankets. . . . .

The supply by running the blockade has become so precarious that I think we should turn our attention chiefly to our own resources, and I should like to be informed how far the latter can be counted upon. . . . .

I trust that no efforts will be spared to develop our own resources of supply, as a further dependence upon those from abroad can result in nothing but increased suffering and want.

I am, with great respect, yr. obt. servt.,

R. E. LEE,
General.

_____

[Confidential.] HEADQUARTERS, January 20, 1864.
MAJOR-GENERAL GEO. E. PICKETT, commanding, etc., Petersburg, Va.,

GENERAL: From all the information I have received, I think the garrison at New Berne can be captured, and I wish it tried, unless upon close examination you find it impracticable. You can use for that purpose Barton's, Kemper's, Corse's, and as much of Ransom's brigades as you can draw to that point. I shall send in addition Hoke's brigade from this army. General Hoke is familiar with the vicinity of New Berne, has recently returned from a visit to that country, and it is mainly upon his information that my opinion has been formed. He will hand you this letter and explain to you the general plan which at this distance appears to me the best. You can modify it according to circumstances developed by investigation and your good judgment. It is proposed that General Barton shall pass south of Trent River and attack the forces said to be stationed behind Brice's Creek, get possession of the railroad to Beaufort, cut off reinforcements from that quarter, and take the town in reverse. General Hoke will move down between the Trent and the Neuse, endeavor to surprise the troops on Bachelor's Creek, silence the guns in the star fort and batteries near the Neuse, and penetrate the town in that direction; Whitford's battalion, or such other force as may be designated, to move down north of the Neuse, occupy if they cannot capture Fort Anderson at Barrington Ferry, and endeavor to take in flank with the batteries the line south of the Neuse, so as to lighten Hoke's work. The night previous to the land-attack Colonel Wood of the navy with 200 men in boats will descend the Neuse and endeavor to surprise and capture the gunboats in that river, and by their aid drive the enemy from their guns. General Whiting will be requested on the day appointed for the attack to threaten Swansborough with the troops he has north of the Cape Fear, so as to fix the attention of the enemy at Morehead City, etc., and to co-operate otherwise in the general plan. Everything will depend upon the secrecy, expedition, and boldness of your movements. General Barton should move first, and be strong enough to resist any combination of the forces from New Berne and Beaufort. The cavalry had better accompany him to cut the telegraph and railroad, gain information, etc. General Hoke with his own brigade should move next, the force north of the Neuse to keep pace with him. Colonel Wood will attend to his part. If successful, everything in New Berne should be sent back to a place of security. In that event, too, it is hoped that by the aid of the gunboats water-transportation can be secured, the enemy driven from Washington, Plymouth, etc., and much subsistence for the army obtained. I wish you therefore to follow up your success. It will also have the happiest effect in North Carolina and inspirit the people. I propose Major Dearing for the command of the artillery of the expedition. With the two battalions of Longstreet's corps near Petersburg there should be twelve 10-pounder Parrotts and two 20-pounder Parrotts; two 20-pounder Parrotts will be sent from Richmond. At Kinston I understand there are four Napoleons and one 3-inch rifle. From Branch's battalion I hope you will get more rifle guns, of which, if possible, you should have about twenty and as many Napoleons as you desire. The guns and ammunition must be sent by railroad and the horses by the common route. See that you have a sufficiency of ammunition and subsistence. I wish you also not to interrupt the general travel of the railroad, but to use the empty trains going south for the transportation of troops, etc. When the day of attack is fixed notify General Whiting. If you have to use the telegraph, merely say, "The day is ——;" name the day of the month—he will comprehend. Commit nothing to the telegraph that will disclose your purpose. You must deceive the enemy as to your purpose, and conceal it from the citizens. As regards the concentration of troops, you may put it on the ground of apprehension of an attack from New Berne. General Hoke will give out that he is going to arrest deserters and recruit his diminished regiments.

Very respectfully, your obedient servant,

R. E. LEE,
General.

[Confidential.]   HEADQUARTERS, 20th January, 1864.
HIS EXCELLENCY JEFFERSON DAVIS, PRESIDENT CONFEDERATE STATES,

MR. PRESIDENT: I have delayed replying to your letter of the 4th until the time arrived for the execution of the attempt on New Berne. I regret very much that the boats on the Neuse and Roanoke are not completed. With their aid, I think, success would be certain. Without them, though the place may be captured, the fruits of the expedition will be lessened and our maintenance of the command of the waters in North Carolina uncertain. I think every effort should be made now to get them into service as soon as possible. You will see by the enclosed letters to Generals Pickett and Whiting the arrangements made for the land-operations. The water-expedition I am willing to trust to Colonel Wood. If he can succeed in capturing the gunboats, I think success will be certain, as it was by aid from the water that I expected Hoke to be mainly assisted.

In view of the opinion expressed in your letter, I would go to North Carolina myself; but I consider my presence here always necessary, especially now when there is such a struggle to keep the army fed and clothed. General Early is still in the Valley. The enemy there has been reinforced by troops from Meade's army and [by] calling down General Averell with his cavalry. I do not know what their intentions are. Report from General Early yesterday stated that Averell with his cavalry had started for Moorefield. I will, however, go to North Carolina if you think it necessary. General Fitz Lee brought out of Hardy 110 prisoners, 250 horses and mules, 27 wagons, and 460 head of cattle. He captured 40 wagons, but 13 turned over on the mountains and had to be abandoned. He had also to leave behind between 100 and 200 head of cattle. The difficulties he encountered were very great, owing to the extreme cold, ice, storms, etc. Nearly all his men were frost-bitten, some badly; many injured by the falling of their horses. He got within six miles of Paddytown, but could not cross the mountains, owing to the icy roads and the smoothness of his horses. He could take with him neither artillery nor wagons.

I am, with great respect, your obedient servant,

R. E. LEE,
General.

[Confidential.]   HEADQUARTERS, ORANGE CO.,
Feb. 3, 1864.

HIS EXCELLENCY JEFFERSON DAVIS, PRESIDENT CONFEDERATE STATES,

MR. PRESIDENT: The approach of spring causes me to consider with anxiety the probable action of the enemy and the possible operations of ours in the ensuing campaign. If we could take the initiative and fall upon them unexpectedly, we might derange their plans and embarrass them the whole summer. There are only two points east of the Mississippi where it now appears this could be done. If Longstreet could be strengthened or given greater mobility than he now possesses, he might penetrate into Kentucky, where he could support himself, cut Grant's communications so as to compel him at least to detach from Johnston's front, and enable him to take the offensive and regain the ground we have lost. I need not dwell upon the advantages of success in that quarter. The whole is apparent to you. Longstreet can be given greater mobility by supplying him with horses and mules to mount his infantry. He can only be strengthened by detaching from Beauregard's, Johnston's, or this army. If I could draw Longstreet secretly and rapidly to me, I might succeed in forcing General Meade back to Washington, and exciting sufficient apprehension at least for their position to weaken any movement against ours. All the cavalry would have to be left in Longstreet's present front, and Jones would have to be strengthened. If the first plan is adopted, supplies will have at once to be accumulated at Bristol or along the Virginia and Tennessee Railroad, ostensibly for Longstreet's present use. If the latter, provision must be made at Gordonsville and Richmond for this army. We are not in a condition, and never have been, in my opinion, to invade the enemy's country with a prospect of permanent benefit. But we can alarm and embarrass him to some extent, and thus prevent his undertaking anything of magnitude against us. I have ventured to suggest these ideas to Your Excellency for consideration, that, viewing the whole subject with your knowledge of the state of things East and West, you may know whether either is feasible or what else can better be done. Time is an important element to our success.

I am, with great respect, your obedient servant,

R. E. LEE,
General.

HEADQUARTERS, February 18, 1864.
HIS EXCELLENCY JEFFERSON DAVIS, PRESIDENT CONFEDERATE STATES, RICHMOND,

MR. PRESIDENT : I have received the despatch forwarded to me to-day from General Longstreet requesting 10,000 men to ensure the capture of Knoxville. I have no information of the practicability of the plan. I think it may be assumed that its defences are stronger now than when it was last attacked, and an attempt to capture it by assault would not only be hazardous, but attended with great loss of life. To reduce it by approaches would require time, and, it seems to me at this distance, render necessary an army sufficient to defeat a relieving force that, now the railroad to Chattanooga has been opened, could be quickly sent from Grant's troops. If a movement could be made to cut off supplies from Knoxville, it would draw out the garrison ; and this appears to me the wiser course. Could supplies be sent if troops were ? For without the former the latter would be unavailing. I wrote to-day to the Secretary of War suggesting that Pickett's division be sent to him in the spring, and that a brigade of Buckner's now at Dalton be returned to its division at once. . . . . .

I am, with great respect, your obedient servant,

R. E. LEE,
General.

HEADQUARTERS ARMY OF NORTHERN VIRGINIA,
March 6, 1864.
HON. JAS. A. SEDDON, SECRETARY OF WAR, RICHMOND,

SIR : I have just received your letter of the 5th instant enclosing a slip from one of the Richmond journals giving an account of the recent attack upon that city, and a copy of some papers found on the dead body of Colonel Dahlgren disclosing the plan and purpose of the enterprise. I concur with you in thinking that a formal publication of these papers should be made under official authority, that our people and the world may know the character of the war our enemies wage against us, and the unchristian and atrocious acts they plot and perpetrate. But I cannot recommend the execution of the prisoners who have fallen into our hands. Assuming that the address and secret orders of Colonel Dahlgren correctly state his designs and intentions, they were not executed, and I believe in a legal point of view acts in addition to intentions are necessary to constitute crime. These papers can only be considered as evidence of his intentions. It does not appear how far his men were cognizant of them, or that his course was sanctioned by his Government. It is only known that his plans were frustrated by a merciful Providence, his forces scattered, and himself killed. I do not think it is right, therefore, to visit upon the captives the guilt of his intentions. I do not pretend to speak the sentiments of the army, which you seem to desire. I presume that the blood boils with indignation in the veins of every officer and man as he reads the account of the barbarous and inhuman plot, and under the impulse of the moment many would counsel extreme measures. But I do not think that reason and reflection would justify such a course. I think it better to do right, even if we suffer in so doing, than to incur the reproach of our consciences and posterity. Nor do I think that under present circumstances policy dictates the execution of these men. It would produce retaliation. How many and better men have we in the enemy's hands than they have in ours! But this consideration should have no weight, provided the course was in itself right. Yet history records instances where such considerations have prevented the execution of marauders and devastators of provinces. It may be pertinent to this subject to refer to the conduct of some of our men in the Valley. I have heard that a party of Gilmer's battalion, after arresting the progress of a train of cars on the Baltimore and Ohio Railroad, took from the passengers their purses and watches. As far as I know, no military object was accomplished after gaining possession of the cars, and the act appears to have been one of plunder. Such conduct is unauthorized and discreditable. Should any of that battalion be captured, the enemy might claim to treat them as highway robbers; what would be our course? I have ordered an investigation of the matter, and hope the report may be untrue.

I am, with great respect, your obedient servant,

R. E. LEE.

[Confidential.] HEADQUARTERS ARMY OF NORTHERN VIRGINIA,
March 8, 1864.

LIEUTENANT-GENERAL JAMES LONGSTREET, commanding, etc., Greenville, Tenn.,

GENERAL: I was in Richmond when your letter arrived, and have been so much occupied by the recent movements of the enemy that it is only to-day that I can reply. I think the enemy's great effort will be in the West, and we must concentrate our strength there to meet them. I see no possibility of mounting your command without stripping all others of animals and rendering them immovable. If horses could be obtained for you, where are the forage and equipments to be procured? The former is not to be had nearer than Georgia. It could not be furnished by the railroad, and I do not think equipments could be impressed through the country. If you and Johnston could unite and move into Middle Tennessee, where I am told provisions and forage can be had, it would cut the armies at Chattanooga and Knoxville in two, and draw them from those points, where either portion could be struck at in succession as opportunity offered. This appears to me at this distance the most feasible plan ; can it be accomplished? By covering your front well with your cavalry, Johnston could move quietly and rapidly through Benton, across the Hiwassee, and then push forward in the direction of Kingston, while you, taking such a route as to be safe from a flank attack, would join him at or after his crossing the Tennessee River. The two commands upon reaching Sparta would be in position to select their future course, would necessitate the evacuation of Chattanooga and Knoxville, and by rapidity and skill unite on either army. I am not sufficiently acquainted with the country to do more than indicate the general plan. The particular routes, passage of rivers, etc. you and Johnston must ascertain and choose. The condition of roads, etc. may oblige you to pass through the western portion of North Carolina, but this you can ascertain, if you do not already know, as well as the distances each column would have to traverse before uniting, their point of junction, time of marching, etc. The agents of the commissary department tell me there is an abundance of provisions and forage in Middle Tennessee, which is corroborated by individuals professing to know that country. But this should be investigated too. It is also believed by those acquainted with the people that upon the entrance of the army into that country its ranks will be recruited by the men from Tennessee and Kentucky who have left it. A victory gained there will open the country to you to the Ohio.

Study the subject, communicate with Johnston, and endeavor to accomplish it or something better. We cannot now pause. I will endeavor to do something here to occupy them if I cannot do more. I hope Alexander has joined you with his new commission. The promotion of the other officers of artillery was ordered as proposed during my last visit to Richmond. Walton retains his former position in the Washington battalion.

Wishing you all success and happiness, I am, very truly,

R. E. LEE,
General.

MILITARY CORRESPONDENCE OF GENERAL LEE DURING THE GRANT CAMPAIGN.

THE letters which follow cover the momentous period from the date of General Grant's taking command of the Army of the Potomac to the surrender of the Army of Northern Virginia in 1865. During this period General Lee returned no formal report of his operations, as in the case of his earlier campaigns. In this final campaign he was in the habit of sending brief despatches to Richmond relating any occurrences of importance. These very imperfectly replace official reports, and have the singular feature of understating, as a rule, the extent of the Confederate successes—a fact which detracts considerably from their historical value. Some few of them are here appended, but the letters which we deem it more important to give are those that relate to the general military interests of the Confederate States. In addition to their suggestions concerning military movements elsewhere than in Virginia, they yield many valuable side-glimpses into the difficulties under which General Lee labored, such as the dearth of provisions, clothing, and arms, the increasing desertions, the lack of recruits, the disaffection in certain sections of the country, and the rapid exhaustion of means of resistance to the North. In none of them does he show a symptom of despair or breathe a thought of giving up the contest. To the last he remained full of resources, energetic, and defiant, and ready to bear upon his shoulders the whole burden of the conduct of the war.

HEADQUARTERS ARMY OF NORTHERN VIRGINIA,
March 30, 1864.

HIS EXCELLENCY J. DAVIS, PRESIDENT CONFEDERATE STATES,

MR. PRESIDENT: Since my former letter on the subject the indications that operations in Virginia will be vigorously prosecuted by the enemy are stronger than they then were. General Grant has returned from the Army in the West. He is at present with the Army of the Potomac, which is being organized and recruited. From the reports of our scouts the impression prevails in that army that he will operate it in the coming campaign. Every train brings it recruits, and it is stated that every available regiment at the North is added to it. It is also reported that General Burnside is organizing a large army at Annapolis, and it seems probable that additional troops are being sent to the Valley. It is stated that preparations are making to rebuild the railroad from Harper's Ferry to Winchester, which would indicate a reoccupation of the latter place. The Baltimore and Ohio Railroad is very closely guarded along its whole extent; no ingress or egress from their lines is permitted to citizens as heretofore; and everything shows secrecy and preparation. Their plans are not sufficiently developed to discover them, but I think we can assume that if General Grant is to direct operations on this frontier, he will concentrate a large force on one or more lines, and prudence dictates that we should make such preparations as are in our power. If an aggressive movement can be made in the West, it will disconcert their plåns and oblige them to conform to ours. But if it cannot, Longstreet should be held in readiness to be thrown rapidly into the Valley if necessary, to counteract any movement in that quarter, in accomplishing which I could unite with him or he unite with me, should circumstances require it, on the Rapidan. The time is also near at hand when I shall require all the troops belonging to this army. I have delayed calling for General Hoke, who besides his own brigade has two regiments of another of this army, under the expectation that the object of his visit to North Carolina may yet be accomplished. I have heard nothing on the subject recently, and if our papers be correct in their information the enemy has thrown reinforcements into that State and the Neuse is barricaded just above New Berne. There is another brigade of this army, General R. Johnston's, at Hanover Junction. I should like as soon as possible to get them back.

I am, with great respect, your most obedient servant,

R. E. Lee,
General.

HEADQUARTERS ORANGE COURT-HOUSE,
April 2, 1864.

HIS EXCELLENCY JEFFERSON DAVIS, PRESIDENT CONFEDERATE STATES,

MR. PRESIDENT: I had a conversation with General Pendleton last evening, who gave me the result of his observations during his late visit to the Army of Tennessee. His report of the condition of that army, the buoyant spirit of the men, and above all the confidence reposed in their leader, gave me unalloyed pleasure. I regret the difficulties in the projected combination and movement of Generals Johnston and Longstreet. Those arising from the scarcity of supplies I can realize. Those arising from the features of the country, the strength or position of the enemy, I cannot properly estimate. They should be examined and judged by the commanders who are to execute the movement. As far as I can judge, the contemplated expedition offers the fairest prospects of valuable results within the limits of the Confederacy, and its success would be attended with the greatest relief. I hope the obstacles to its execution on being closely scanned may not prove insurmountable or may be removed by a modification of the plan. In the mean time, provisions might be accumulated at some suitable point, and if drawn from the country south or west of that point they would always be convenient for the armies north of it. Other preparations might also be made, but if after a full consideration of the subject by General Johnston there should not be, in his opinion, reasonable grounds for expecting success, I would not recommend its execution. He can better compare the difficulties existing to a forward movement with the disadvantages of remaining quiet, and decide between them.

I am, with great respect, your obedient servant,

R. E. LEE,
General.

HEADQUARTERS, April 5, 1864.
HIS EXCELLENCY JEFFERSON DAVIS, PRESIDENT CONFEDERATE STATES,

MR. PRESIDENT: All the information I receive tends to show that the great effort of the enemy in this campaign will be made in Virginia. Nothing as yet has been discovered to develop his plan. Reinforcements are certainly daily arriving to the Army of the Potomac. I cannot ascertain whence they come. Information was received on the 3d from two scouts, derived from citizens along the Orange and Alexandria Railroad, that the troops on the cars said they belonged to Grant's Army of Tennessee. A resident of Culpeper stated that the Eleventh and Twelfth army corps had returned there. I telegraphed to Generals Johnston and Longstreet to know if they were still in the West. I enclose their answers. Both seem to think they are in their front, but preparing to leave. The tone of the Northern papers, as well as the impression prevailing in their armies, go to show that Grant with a large force is to move against Richmond. One of their correspondents at Harrisburg states upon the occasion of the visit of Generals Burnside and Hancock that it was certain that the former would go to North Carolina. They cannot collect the large force they mention for their operations against Richmond without reducing their other armies. This ought to be discovered and taken advantage of by our respective commanders. I infer from the information I receive that Longstreet's corps is in the vicinity of Abingdon and Bristol. It is therefore in position to be thrown West or East.

Unless it is certain that it can be advantageously employed West for a speedy blow, I would recommend that it be returned to this army. The movements and reports of the enemy may be intended to mislead us, and should therefore be carefully observed. But all the information that reaches me goes to strengthen the belief that General Grant is preparing to move against Richmond.

I am, with great respect, your obedient servant,

R. E. LEE,
General.

HEADQUARTERS, April 12, 1864.

MR. PRESIDENT: My anxiety on the subject of provisions for the army is so great that I cannot refrain from expressing it to Your Excellency. I cannot see how we can operate with our present supplies. Any derangement in their arrival or disaster to the railroad would render it impossible for me to keep the army together, and might force a retreat into North Carolina. There is nothing to be had in this section for men or animals. We have rations for the troops to-day and to-morrow. I hope a new supply arrived last night, but I have not yet had a report. Every exertion should be made to supply the dépôts at Richmond and at other points. All pleasure travel should cease and everything be devoted to necessary wants.

I am, with great respect, your obedient servant,

R. E. LEE.
General.

HEADQUARTERS, April 15, 1864.

MR. PRESIDENT: The reports of the scouts are still conflicting as to the character of the reinforcements to the Army of the Potomac and the composition of that of Annapolis under General Burnside. I think it probable that the Eighth corps, which embraces the·troops who have heretofore guarded the line of the Baltimore and Ohio Railroad, the intrenchments around Washington, Alexandria, etc., has been moved up to the Rappahannock, and that an equivalent has been sent to Annapolis from General Meade. Lieutenant-colonel Mosby states that the Eleventh and Twelfth corps, consolidated, have also been sent to General Burnside. But, whatever doubt there may be on these points, I think it certain that the enemy is organizing a large army on the Rappahannock and another at Annapolis, and that the former is intended to move directly on Richmond, while the latter is intended to take it in flank or rear. I think we may also reasonably suppose that the Federal troops that have so long besieged Charleston will, with a portion of their ironclad steamers, be transferred to the James River. I consider that the suspension of the attack on that city was virtually declared when General Gillmore transferred his operations to the St. John's River. It can only be continued during the summer months by the fleet. The expedition of the enemy up Red River has so diminished his forces about New Orleans and Mobile that I think no attack upon the latter city need be apprehended soon, especially as we have reason to hope that he will return from his expedition in a shattered condition. I have thought, therefore, that General Johnston might draw something from Mobile during the summer to strengthen his hands, and that General Beauregard with a portion of his troops might move into North Carolina to oppose General Burnside should he resume his old position in that State, or be ready to advance to the

James River should that route be taken. I do not know what benefit General Buckner can accomplish in his present position. If he is able to advance into Tennessee, reoccupy Knoxville, or unite with General Johnston, great good may be accomplished, but if he can only hold Bristol, I think he had better be called for a season to Richmond. We shall have to glean troops from every quarter to oppose the apparent combination of the enemy. If Richmond could be held secure against the attack from the east, I would propose that I draw Longstreet to me and move right against the enemy on the Rappahannock. Should God give us a crowning victory there, all their plans would be dissipated, and their troops now collecting on the waters of the Chesapeake would be recalled to the defence of Washington. But to make this move I must have provisions and forage. I am not yet able to call to me the cavalry or artillery. If I am obliged to retire from this line, either by a flank movement of the enemy or the want of supplies, great injury will befall us. I have ventured to throw out these suggestions to Your Excellency in order that in surveying the whole field of operations you may consider all the circumstances bearing on the question. Should you determine it is better to divide this army and fall back toward Richmond, I am ready to do so. I, however, see no better plan for the defence of Richmond than that I have proposed.

I am, with great respect, your obedient servant,

R. E. LEE,
General.

HEADQUARTERS, April 16, 1864.
GENERAL BRAXTON BRAGG, commanding Armies C. States,

GENERAL: I have received your letter of the 13th enclosing a copy of a communication from Colonel Gorgas in reference to the large proportion of artillery with this army. I have never found it too large in battle, and it has generally been opposed by about 300 pieces of the enemy of larger calibre, longer range, and with more effective ammunition. If, however, its equipment overtaxes the means of the Ordnance Department, or, as you suggest, its supply of horses cannot be kept up, that decides the question, and no argument on the subject is necessary. Taking the European standard of 3 guns for every 1000 men, based upon the experience of their wars, not ours, the number of guns in this army will fall short, provided the regiments are filled to the minimum allowed by law. I think Colonel Gorgas is correct in not adhering to this standard when the organizations recede from their maximum of strength. Taking his own standard and allowing 5 guns to each brigade, we ought to have 230 guns. Longstreet has 12 brigades, Ewell 13, Hill 14, and the cavalry (including the Carolina brigade being organized) 7 = 46 brigades. Taking Colonel Gorgas's statement as correct, which I have not time to verify, there are in this army 197 guns; with General Longstreet, 27; and in the Washington Artillery (if full), 16 = 240. The excess is not large, but going back to the European standard we have 206 regiments. Taking the minimum and not the maximum of strength (206 × 640 = 131,840), and allowing 3 guns for every 1000 men (131,840 ÷ 3) = 439 guns. Our aggregate present and absent would give us more. I differ from Colonel Gorgas in thinking that 20 guns are too much for the cavalry. In my opinion they are not enough. We should have a battery for each brigade, and a reserve battery for each division; the 7 brigades would require 7 batteries, and the 3 divisions 3 reserve batteries, making 10.

Very respectfully, your obedient servant,

R. E. LEE,
General.

HEADQUARTERS, April 16, 1864.

GENERAL BRAXTON BRAGG, commanding Armies C. States,

GENERAL: I received last evening your letter of the 14th instant by the hands of Major Parker. I trust that the expedition in North Carolina will be attended with success, and that the troops in the department of South ·Carolina, Georgia, and Florida may be made available to oppose the combined operations of the enemy in Virginia. No attack of moment can be made upon Charleston or the southern coast during the summer months, and I think General Johnston can draw with impunity some troops from Mobile to him. Buckner's force, too, might be made available in some way; I fear, as he stands now, it will be lost to us. At present my hands are tied. If I were able to move with the aid of Longstreet and Pickett, the enemy might be driven from the Rappahannock and be obliged to look to the safety of his own capital instead of the assault upon ours. I cannot even draw to me the cavalry or artillery of the army, and the season has arrived when I may be attacked any day. The scarcity of our supplies gives me the greatest uneasiness. All travel should be suspended on the railroad until a sufficiency is secured. I can have a portion of the corn ground into meal for the army if it is sent to me. I do not know whether all can be furnished. The mills are mostly on the Rapidan, and consequently exposed if any movement takes place. It will also increase the hauling, which at this time I should like to avoid if possible. If the meal can be prepared in Richmond, it will be more convenient at this time. If it cannot, we can at least grind part of the corn if sent to us. If we are forced back from our present line, the Central Railroad, Charlottesville, and all the upper country will be exposed, and I fear great injury inflicted on us.

Most respectfully, your obedient servant,

R. E. LEE,
General.

STRENGTH OF THE ARMY PREVIOUS TO WILDERNESS CAMPAIGN.

Abstract from Return of the Army of Northern Virginia, GEN-
ERAL R. E. LEE *commanding, for April 20, 1864; Orange
Court-house, Va.*

COMMAND.	Present for duty. Officers.	Men.	Aggregate present.	Aggregate present and absent.	Aggregate last return.
General staff	12	...	12	12	12
Staff	16	...	16	19	17
SECOND ARMY CORPS. LIEUT.-GEN. EWELL.					
Early's division*	...	...	5,578	9,067	5,529
Johnson's division	...	...	6,383	10,405	6,294
Rodes's division †	...	...	8,733	13,292	8,729
Total	...	...	20,710	32,783	20,569
THIRD ARMY CORPS. LIEUT.-GEN. A. P. HILL.					
Staff	...	...	16	16	15
Anderson's division	...	...	7,910	11,991	7,809
Heth's division	...	...	8,502	14,349	7,951
Wilcox's division	...	...	8,963	12,646	8,946
Total	...	...	25,391	39,002	24,721
Cavalry Corps. Maj.-gen. J. E. B. Stuart.					
Staff	...	...	13	15	13
Hampton's division	...	...	3,815	8,192	3,358
Fitz Lee's division	...	...	5,872	8,715	5,599
Total	...	...	9,700	16,922	8,970
Artillery Brigade. Brig.-gen. W. N. Pendleton.					
First army corps	...	...	465	592	463
Second army corps	...	...	1,977	2,603	1,904
Third army corps	...	...	2,632	3,368	2,568
Cavalry	...	...	473	674	467
Total	...	...	5,547	7,237	5,402
Unattached Commands.					
Valley District ‡	...	...	...	...	...
Maryland Line	...	...	913	1,351	887
Provost Guard	...	...	387	584	387
Battn. Scouts and Couriers	...	...	265	355	274
Total	...	...	1,565	2,290	1,548
Grand total	...	...	62,925	98,246	61,222

* Hoke's brigade detached; not reported.   † Two regiments detached; not reported.   ‡ Not reported.

HEADQUARTERS ARMY OF NORTHERN VIRGINIA,
June 26, 1864.

HIS EXCELLENCY JEFFERSON DAVIS, PRESIDENT CONFEDERATE STATES,

MR. PRESIDENT : I have the honor to acknowledge the receipt of your letter of the 25th instant. General Hunter has escaped Early, and will make good his retreat, as far as I can understand, to Lewisburg. Although his expedition has been partially interrupted, I fear he has not been much punished except by the demoralization of his troops and the loss of some artillery. From his present position he can easily be reorganized and re-equipped, and, unless we have sufficient force to resist him, will repeat his expedition. This would necessitate the return of Early to Staunton. I think it better that he should move down the Valley if he can obtain provisions, which would draw Hunter after him, and may enable him to strike Pope (?) before he can effect a junction with Hunter. If circumstances favor, I should also recommend his crossing the Potomac. I think I can maintain our lines here against General Grant. He does not seem disposed to attack, and has thrown himself strictly on the defensive. I am less uneasy about holding our position than about our ability to procure supplies for the army. I fear the latter difficulty will oblige me to attack General Grant in his intrenchments, which I should not hesitate to do but for the loss it will inevitably entail. A want of success would, in my opinion, be almost fatal, and this causes me to hesitate, in the hope that some relief may be procured without running such great hazard.

I should like much to have the benefit of Your Excellency's good judgment and views upon this subject.

Great benefit might be drawn from the release of our prisoners at Point Lookout if it can be accomplished. The number of men employed for this purpose would necessarily be small, as the whole would have to be transported secretly across the Potomac where it is very broad, the means of doing which must first be procured. I can devote to this purpose the whole of the Marylanders of this army, which would afford a sufficient number of men of excellent material and much experience, but I am at a loss where to find a proper leader. As he would command Maryland troops and operate upon the Maryland soil, it would be well that he should be a Marylander. Of those connected with this army, I consider Colonel Bradley Johnson the most suitable. He is bold and intelligent, ardent and true, and yet I am unable to say whether he possesses all the requisite qualities. Everything in an expedition of this kind would depend upon the leader. I have understood that most of the garrison at Point Lookout is composed of negroes. I should suppose that the commander of such troops would be poor and feeble. A stubborn resistance, therefore, may not reasonably be expected. By taking a company of the Maryland artillery armed as infantry, the dismounted cavalry, and their infantry organization, as many men would be supplied as transportation could be procured for. By throwing them suddenly on the beach with some concert of action among the prisoners, I think the guard might be overpowered, the prisoners liberated and organized, and marched immediately on the route to Washington.

The artillery company could operate the guns captured at the Point. The dismounted cavalry with the released prisoners of that arm could mount themselves on the march, and the infantry would form a respectable force. Such a body of men, under an able leader, though they might not be able without assistance to capture Washington, could march around it and cross the upper Potomac where fordable. I do not think they could cross the river in a body at any point below Washington, unless possibly at Alexandria. Provisions, etc. would have to be collected in the country through which they pass. The operations on the river must be confided to an able naval officer, who I know will be found in Colonel Wood. The subject is one worthy of consideration, and can only be matured by reflection.

The sooner it is put in execution the better if it be deemed practicable.

At this time, as far as I can learn, all the troops in the control of the United States are being sent to Grant, and little or no opposition could be made by those at Washington.

With relation to the project of Marshal Kane, if the matter can be kept secret, which I fear is impossible, should General Early cross the Potomac he might be sent to join him.

Very respectfully, your Excellency's obedient servant,

R. E. LEE,
General.

Abstract from Return of the Army of Northern Virginia, GEN-
ERAL R. E. LEE *commanding, for July 10, 1864; Station
near Petersburg, Va.*

COMMAND.	Present for duty.		Aggregate present.	Aggregate present and absent.	Aggregate last return.
	Officers.	Men.			
DEPARTMENT OF NORTH CARO-LINA, SOUTH CAROLINA, AND VIRGINIA.*					
GEN. P. T. BEAUREGARD commanding.					
General staff	12	...	12	12	12
Johnson's division	...	...	8,403	13,681	8,478
Hoke's division	...	...	6,387	12,668	6,628
Total	...	...	14,790	26,349	15,106
FIRST ARMY CORPS.					
LIEUT.-GEN. R. H. ANDERSON com'd'g.					
Staff	...	...	17	24	17
Pickett's division	...	...	5,862	11,628	5,924
Field's division	...	...	5,952	12,943	5,846
Kershaw's division	...	...	5,791	11,646	5,712
Total	...	...	17,622	36,241	17,499
THIRD ARMY CORPS.					
LIEUT.-GEN. A. P. HILL commanding.					
Staff	...	...	17	17	17
Anderson's division	...	...	7,569	14,380	6,643
Heth's division	...	...	6,288	14,001	6,121
Wilcox's division	...	...	5,581	12,190	5,445
Total	...	...	19,455	40,588	18,226
CAVALRY.					
Hampton's division	...	...	3,570	8,967	
Fitz Lee's division	...	...	1,994	5,889	1,928
W. H. F. Lee's division	...	...	4,929	8,324	3,379
Total	...	...	10,493	23,180	5,307
Of Gen. Beauregard's command	...	...	1,180	1,622	1,247
ARTILLERY.					
BRIG.-GEN. PENDLETON.					
First army corps	...	...	1,919	2,637	1,838
Second army corps †	...	...	818	1,701	817
Third army corps	...	...	2,555	3,475	2,519
Total	...	...	6,472	9,435	6,421
Grand total	...	...	68,844	135,805	62,571

* The Second army corps, Lieutenant-general Early, detached; not reported.
† Part of artillery of Second corps with General Early; not reported.

HEADQUARTERS ARMY OF NORTHERN VIRGINIA,
July 11, 1864.

LIEUTENANT-GENERAL J. A. EARLY, commanding, etc.,

GENERAL: Your letter of the 7th was received this morning. Your movements and arrangements appear to me to have been judicious, and I am glad you did not delay to storm the works at Maryland Heights. It was better to turn them and endeavor to draw from them. I hope you get the Northern papers, as they will keep you advised of their preparations to oppose you. They rely greatly upon General Hunter's force coming in your rear. About the 4th instant, as far as I can judge, he was in the vicinity of Charleston on the Kanawha, with his own, Averell's, and Crooks's commands. To encounter you in your present position he must either ascend the Ohio to Parkersburg and take the railroad to Grafton, thence by the Baltimore and Ohio Railroad, if that is left practicable, or go up to Pittsburg, and thence by the Central Pennsylvania. You will be able to judge of the time that either of these routes will require to bring him in position, and I think that even his whole force, aided by such troops as might join him, would be unable to oppose you successfully.

I ascertained some days ago that on the 6th instant General Grant sent off a portion of his troops, and, as far as I am able to judge, they consisted of Ricketts's division of the Sixth corps, and their destination was Washington City. I think it probable that about a brigade of cavalry without their horses were sent on the night of the 6th to the same point. I learn this morning from our scouts on the James River that about the same number of troops, judging from the transports, descended the river yesterday, and I presume they are bound for Washington City. Whether these belong to the Sixth corps or have been taken from other corps of his army, which I think more probable, I have not yet ascertained. We may, however, assume that a corps or its equivalent has been sent by General Grant to Washington, and I send a special messenger to apprise you of this fact, that you may be on your guard and take this force into consideration with others that may be brought to oppose you. In your further operations you must of course be guided by the circumstances by which you are surrounded and the information you may be able to collect, and must not consider yourself committed to any particular line of conduct, but be governed by your good judgment. Should you find yourself obliged, in consequence of the forces opposed to you, to return to the south side of the Potomac, you can take advantage of the fords east of the Blue Ridge, keeping your cavalry well to your front and causing them to retire by fords between you and Washington. In the event of your recrossing the Potomac, your route through Loudoun will facilitate the procurement of provisions, forage, etc. for your command, and will be otherwise most advantageous, giving you a strong country through which to pass, and enabling you, if pressed, to retire into the Valley and threaten and hang upon the enemy's flank should he push on toward Richmond.

I recommend that you have the fords of the Potomac examined by a competent officer, and held by a small force of cavalry or infantry as you may deem most advisable.

I can tell nothing further of the expedition mentioned to you in my letter of the 3d instant than was stated in that letter, having heard nothing from it since, except that the subject was a matter of general conversation in Richmond, which may tend to frustrate it.

You can retain the special messenger until you may wish to send him back for any purpose. I need not state to you the advantage of striking at the bodies of troops that may be collected to oppose you in detail before they are enabled to unite. None of the forces that I have mentioned, nor any reported in the Northern papers as being likely to oppose you, will be able, in my opinion, to resist you, provided you can strike them before they are strengthened by others. Should you hear of the near approach of General Hunter, and can strike at him before he is reinforced by troops from the East, you can easily remove that obstacle from your path, in my opinion.

Trusting you and our cause to the care of a merciful Providence, I remain,

Very respectfully, your obedient servant,

R. E. LEE,
General.

HEADQUARTERS ARMY OF NORTHERN VIRGINIA,
Petersburg, Va., August 4, 1864.

MR. PRESIDENT: . . . . A scout reported that on Sunday, the 31st ultimo, a body of cavalry estimated at two brigades moved toward the James River in the direction of City Point, and this may be the force of cavalry which has been shipped North. I fear that this force is intended to operate against General Early, and when added to that already opposed to him may be more than he can manage. Their object may be to drive him out of the Valley and complete the devastation they commenced when they were ejected from it. General Grant's plan of operations here appears to be to mine and bombard our lines with a view of driving us from them, and as he is very strongly fortified he can operate with fewer troops and enable him to detach a sufficient force for the purpose indicated. The largest force which I can detach would be Kershaw's and Field's divisions, and that would leave not a man out of the trenches for any emergency which might arise. If it is their intention to endeavor to overwhelm Early, I think it better to detach these troops than to hazard his destruction and that of our railroads, etc. north of Richmond, and therefore submit the question to the better judgment of Your Excellency.....

I am, with great respect, your obedient servant,

R. E. LEE,
General.

HEADQUARTERS ARMY OF NORTHERN VIRGINIA,
August 26, 1864.

GENERAL EARLY,

GENERAL: Your letter of the 23d has been received, and I am much pleased at your having forced the enemy back to Harper's Ferry. This will give protection to the Valley and arrest the travel on the Baltimore and Ohio Railroad. It will, however, have little or no effect upon Grant's operations or prevent reinforcements being sent to him. If Sheridan's force is as large as you suppose, I do not know that you could operate to advantage north of the Potomac. Either Anderson's troops or a portion of yours might, however, be detached to destroy the railroad west of Charlestown, and Fitz Lee might send a portion of his cavalry to cross the Potomac east of the Blue Ridge, as you propose. I cannot detach at present more cavalry from this army; the enemy is too strong in that arm. I am aware that Anderson is the ranking officer, but I apprehend no difficulty on that score. I first intended him to threaten the enemy east of the Blue Ridge, so as to retain near Washington a portion of the enemy's forces. He crossed the mountains at your suggestion, and I think properly. If his troops are not wanted there, he could cross into Loudoun or Fauquier and return to Culpeper. It would add force to the movement of cavalry east of the Blue Ridge. I am in great need of his troops, and if they can be spared from the Valley or cannot operate to advantage there, I will order them back to Richmond. Let me know.

Very respectfully,

R. E. LEE,
General.

HEADQUARTERS ARMY OF NORTHERN VIRGINIA,
September 2, 1864.

HIS EXCELLENCY JEFFERSON DAVIS, PRESIDENT CONFEDERATE STATES,

MR. PRESIDENT: I beg leave to call your attention to the importance of immediate and vigorous measures to increase the strength of our armies, and to some suggestions as to the mode of doing it. The necessity is now great, and will soon be augmented by the results of the coming draft in the United States. As matters now stand, we have no troops disposable to meet movements of the enemy or strike when opportunity presents, without taking them from the trenches and exposing some important point. The enemy's position enables him to move his troops to the right or left without our knowledge until he has reached the point at which he aims, and we are then compelled to hurry our men to meet him, incurring the risk of being too late to check his progress, and the additional risk of the advantage he may derive from their absence. This was fully illustrated in the late demonstration north of the James River, which called troops from our lines here who, if present, might have prevented the occupation of the Weldon Railroad. These rapid and distant movements also fatigue and exhaust our men, greatly impairing their efficiency in battle. It is not necessary, however, to enumerate all the reasons for recruiting our ranks. The necessity is as well known to Your Excellency as to myself, and as much the object of your solicitude. The means of obtaining men for field duty, as far as I can see, are only three: A considerable number could be placed in the ranks by relieving all able-bodied white men employed as teamsters, cooks, mechanics, and laborers, and supplying their places with negroes. I think measures should be taken at once to substitute negroes for whites in every place in the army or connected with it where the former can be used. It seems to me that we must choose between employing negroes ourselves and having them employed against us. A thorough and vigorous inspection of the rolls of exempted and detailed men is in my opinion of immediate importance. I think you will agree with me that no man should be excused from service for any reason not deemed sufficient to entitle one already in service to his discharge. I do not think that the decision of such questions can be made so well by any as by those whose experience with troops has made them acquainted with the urgent claims to relief which are constantly brought to the attention of commanding officers, but which they are forced to deny. For this reason I would recommend that the rolls of exempts and details in each State be inspected by officers of character and influence who have had experience in the field and have had nothing to do with the exemptions and details. If all that I have heard be true, I think it will be found that very different rules of action have been pursued toward men in service and those liable to it in the matter of exemptions and details, and I respectfully recommend that Your Excellency cause reports to be made by the enrolling bureau of the number of men enrolled in each State, the number sent to the field, and the number exempted or detailed. I regard this matter as of the utmost moment. Our ranks are constantly diminishing by battle and disease, and few recruits are received. The consequences are inevitable, and I feel confident that the time has come when no man capable of bearing arms should be excused unless it be for some controlling reason of public necessity. The safety of the country requires this, in my judgment, and hardship to individuals must be disregarded in view of the calamity that would follow to the whole people if our armies meet with disaster. No detail of an arms-bearing man should be continued or granted except for the performance of duty that is indispensable to the army, and that cannot be performed by one not liable to or fit for service. Agricultural details take numbers from the army without any corresponding advantage. I think that the interests of land-owners and cultivators may be relied upon to induce them to provide means for saving their crops if they be sent to the field. If they remain at home, their produce will only benefit the enemy, as our armies will be insufficient to defend them. If the officers and men detailed in the conscript bureau have performed their duties faithfully, they must have already brought out the chief part of those liable to duty, and have nothing to do now except to get such as from time to time reach military age. If this be true, many of these officers and men can be spared to the army. If not, they have been derelict, and should be sent back to the ranks, and their places supplied by others who will be more active. Such a policy will stimulate the energy of this class of men. The last resource is the reserve force. Men of this class can render great service in connection with regular troops by taking their places in trenches, forts, etc., and leaving them free for active operations. I think no time should be lost in bringing out the entire strength of this class, particularly in Virginia and North Carolina. If I had the reserves of Virginia to hold the trenches here, or even to man those below Richmond on the north side of the river, they would render greater service than they can in any other way. They would give me a force to act with on the offensive or defensive, as might be necessary, without weakening any part of our lines. Their mere presence in the works below Richmond would prevent the enemy from making feints in that quarter to draw troops from here, except in such force as to endanger his own lines around Petersburg. But I feel confident that with vigorous effort, and an understanding on the part of the people of the necessity of the case, we could get more of this class than enough for the purpose last indicated. We could make our regular troops here available in the field. The same remarks are applicable to the reserves of North Carolina, who could render similar services at Wilmington, and allow the regular troops to take the field against any force that might land there. I need not remind Your Excellency that the reserves are of great value in connection with our regular troops to prevent disaster, but would be of little avail to retrieve it. For this reason they should be put in service before the numerical superiority of the enemy enables him to inflict a damaging blow upon the regular forces opposed to him. In my opinion the necessity for them will never be more urgent or their services of greater value than now. And I entertain the same views as to the importance of immediately bringing into the regular service every man liable to military duty. It will be too late to do so after our armies meet with disaster, should such, unfortunately, be the case.

I trust Your Excellency will excuse the length and earnestness of this letter in view of the vital importance of its subject, and am confident that you will do all in your power to accomplish the objects I have in view.

With great respect, your obedient servant,

R. E. LEE,
General.

HEADQUARTERS, PETERSBURG,
September 27, 1864.

GENERAL J. A. EARLY, commanding Valley,

GENERAL: Your letter of the 25th instant is received. I very much regret the reverses that have occurred to the army in the Valley, but trust they can be remedied. The arrival of Kershaw will add greatly to your strength, and I have such confidence in the men and officers that I am sure all will unite in the defence of the country. It will require that every one should exert all his energies and strength to meet the emergency. One victory will put all things to rights. You must do all in your power to invigorate your army. Get back all absentees—manœuvre so, if you can, as to keep the enemy in check until you can strike him with all your strength. As far as I can judge at this distance, you have operated more with divisions than with your concentrated strength. Circumstances may have rendered it necessary, but such a course is to be avoided if possible. It will require the greatest watchfulness, the greatest promptness, and the most untiring energy on your part to arrest the progress of the enemy in his present tide of success. All the reserves in the Valley have been ordered to you. Breckenridge will join you or co-operate as circumstances will permit with all his force. Rosser left this morning for Burkeville (intersection of Danville and Southside Railroads), whence he will shape his course as you direct. I have given you all I can. You must use the resources you have so as to gain success. The enemy must be defeated, and I rely upon you to do it. I will endeavor to have shoes, arms, and ammunition supplied you. Set all your officers to work bravely and hopefully, and all will go well. As regards the Western cavalry, I think for the present the best thing you can do is to separate it. Perhaps there is a lack of confidence between officers and men. If you will attach one brigade to Rosser, making him a division, and one to Fitz Lee's division under Wickham, Lomax will be able, I hope, to bring out the rest. ' The men are all good, and only require instruction and discipline. The enemy's force cannot be so greatly superior to yours. His effective infantry I do not think exceeds 12,000 men. We are obliged to fight against great odds. A kind Providence will yet overrule everything for our good. If Colonel Carter's wound incapacitates him for duty, you must select a good chief of artillery for the present.

Wishing you every prosperity and success,

I am very truly yours,

R. E. LEE,
General.

HEADQUARTERS ARMY OF NORTHERN VIRGINIA,
Oct. 21, 1864.

HON. SEC. OF WAR, RICHMOND,

SIR : I consider it very important to supply the garrisons in the forts below Wilmington with thirty days' provisions, in case the enemy should succeed in cutting them off from the city. I directed General Whiting to endeavor to obtain provisions for the purpose in North Carolina, but he has not succeeded in doing so, nor do I know that it is in his power. The amount of subsistence issued to the army in Virginia and North Carolina is not sufficient to enable us to retain what is required for these garrisons for the time indicated. We now get bacon for the troops only once in four days, and the commissary department informed Colonel Cole, chief C. S. of the army, that we must rely on cattle. As the collection of supplies is in the hands of the officers of the C. S. department, Colonel Cole does not know what number of cattle or what amount of provisions he can count upon, so as to make any arrangements to provide for those garrisons from stores that may come into their hands. I think that it would be better that the C. S. department should provide the desired supplies if practicable, and I respectfully ask that you will direct that it be done if it be in the power of that department to accomplish it.

Very respectfully, your obedient servant,

R. E. LEE,
General.

HEAQUARTERS ARMY OF NORTHERN VIRGINIA,
Oct. 24, 1864.

CAPTAIN J. K. MITCHELL, Flag-officer commanding James River Squadron,

CAPTAIN : Your letter of the 23d instant is received, and in compliance with your request I will give you my views as to the service I deem important to be rendered by the navy in the present posture of affairs.

In my opinion, the enemy is already as near Richmond as he can be allowed to come with safety, and it is certain that the defence of the city would be easier did our lines extend lower down the river, and becomes more difficult the farther we are compelled to retire.

If the enemy succeeds in throwing a force to the south bank in rear of General Pickett's lines, it will necessitate not only the withdrawal of General P.'s forces, but also the abandonment of Petersburg and its railroad connections, throwing the whole army back to the defences of Richmond.

I should regard this as a great disaster and as seriously endangering the safety of the city. We should not only lose a large section of country from which our position around Petersburg enables us to draw supplies, but the enemy would be brought nearer to the only remaining line of railway communication between Richmond and the South, upon which the whole army, as well as the population of the city, would have to depend mainly for support. It would make the tenure of the city depend upon our ability to hold this long line of communication against the largely superior forces of the enemy, and, I think, would greatly diminish our prospects of successful defence. It is therefore, in my judgment, a matter of the first moment to prevent such a movement on the part of the enemy ; and I do not know what emergency can arise in the future defence of the city which will more require all the efforts of the army and navy than that which now exists.

I fully appreciate the importance of preserving our fleet, and deprecate any unnecessary exposure of it. But you will perceive the magnitude of the service which it is thought you can render, and determine whether it is sufficient to justify the risk. It is true that the enemy might place torpedoes in your rear while the vessels are on guard down the river at night ; but if you retire it is much easier for him to place them in the river below you, so as to prevent your going down altogether, no matter how great the necessity for your presence below might become. It is therefore very desirable to guard the river as effectually as we can, and I think it can be done so as greatly to diminish the chance of the enemy laying torpedoes if our ironclads can go down as far as Bishop's every night and picket in their rear with small boats and some of the light gunboats.

Our pickets on the north bank extend about half a mile below the lowest battery, and will be able to afford some assistance, as will also those on the south bank. A system of signals should be agreed upon between them and the fleet to give timely notice of any attempt of the enemy to approach the river or launch boats.

We have not sufficient force to picket the banks more effectually. Our batteries on the south side would also tend to deter the enemy from making the attempt you apprehend, and could afford assistance to the fleet.

You of course can best judge of your ability to render the service required.

I can only express my views of its importance, and I trust that if the Department can increase your force of men, or in any other way contribute to render you able to perform this important duty, it will be done. As I said before, I can foresee no state of circumstances in which the fleet can render more important aid in the defence of Richmond that at present by guarding the river below Chaffin's Bluff.

I am, with great respect, your obedient servant,

R. E. LEE,
General.

Organization of the Army of Northern Virginia, commanded by GENERAL R. E. LEE; November 30, 1864.*

FIRST ARMY CORPS.

LIEUTENANT-GENERAL J. LONGSTREET commanding.

PICKETT'S DIVISION.

Major-general George E. Pickett.

Steuart's Brigade.	*Corse's Brigade.*
Brigadier-general George H. Steuart.	Brigadier-general M. D. Corse.
9th Virginia, Colonel J. J. Phillips.	15th Virginia, Lieut.-col. E. M. Morrison.
14th Virginia, Colonel William White.	17th Virginia, Colonel Arthur Herbert.
38th Virginia, Colonel George K. Griggs.	29th Virginia, Colonel James Giles.
53d Virginia, Colonel W. R. Aylett.	30th Virginia, Colonel R. S. Chew.
57th Virginia, Colonel C. R. Fontaine.	32d Virginia, Colonel E. B. Montague.

Hunton's Brigade.	*Terry's Brigade.*
Brigadier-general Eppa Hunton.	Brigadier-general William R. Terry.
8th Virginia, Colonel E. Berkeley.	1st Virginia, Lieut.-col. F. H. Langley.
18th Virginia, Colonel H. A. Carrington.	3d Virginia, Colonel Joseph Mayo, Jr.
19th Virginia, Colonel Henry Gantt.	7th Virginia, Colonel C. C. Flowerree.
28th Virginia, Lt.-col. W. L. Wingfield.	11th Virginia, Captain J. H. Smith.
56th Virginia, Colonel Wm. E. Green.	24th Virginia, Captain W. W. Bentley.

FIELD'S DIVISION.

Major-general C. W. Field.

Anderson's Brigade.	*Law's Brigade.*
Brigadier-general G. T. Anderson.	Colonel W. F. Perry.
7th Georgia, Major John F. Kiser.	4th Alabama, Captain A. D. McInnis.
8th Georgia, Colonel John R. Towers.	15th Alabama, Captain F. K. Schaaf.
9th Georgia, Captain S. A. Jameson.	44th Alabama, Lieut.-col. John A. Jones.
11th Georgia, Colonel F. H. Little.	47th Alabama, Captain H. C. Lindsey.
59th Georgia, Lieut.-col. B. H. Gee.	48th Alabama, Major J. W. Wiggonton.

* Compiled from inspection reports when not otherwise indicated.

Gregg's Brigade.

Colonel F. S. Bass.

3d Arkansas, Lieut.-col. R. S. Taylor.
1st Texas, Captain Wm. A. Bedell.
4th Texas, Lieut.-col. C. M. Winkler.
5th Texas, Captain W. T. Hill.

Benning's Brigade.

Brigadier-general H. L. Benning.

2d Georgia, Captain Thos. Chaffin.
15th Georgia, Captain G. A. Pace.
17th Georgia, Lieut.-col. W. A. Barden.
20th Georgia, Lieut.-col. E. M. Seago.

Bratton's Brigade.

Brigadier-general John Bratton.

1st South Carolina, Colonel J. R. Hagood.
2d South Carolina [Rifles], Colonel R. E. Bowen.
5th South Carolina, Colonel A. Coward.
6th South Carolina, Colonel J. M. Steedman.
Palmetto Sharpshooters, Colonel Joseph Walker.

KERSHAW'S DIVISION.

Major-general J. B. Kershaw.

Wofford's Brigade.

Colonel C. C. Sanders.

16th Georgia, Major J. H. Skelton.*
18th Georgia, Colonel Joseph Armstrong.
24th Georgia, Colonel C. C. Sanders.
3d Georgia Battalion (Sharpshooters), Lt.-col. N. L. Hutchins.
Cobb's Legion, Lieut.-col. L. J. Glenn.*
Phillips's Legion, Lieut.-col. J. Hamilton.*

Humphreys's Brigade.

Major G. B. Gerald.

13th Mississippi, Major G. L. Donald.
17th Mississippi, Captain J. C. Cochran.
18th Mississippi, Lieut. Wm. Baskin.
21st Mississippi, Captain W. H. Dudley.

Bryan's Brigade.

Colonel James P. Simms.

10th Georgia, Colonel W. C. Holt.*
50th Georgia, Colonel P. McGlashan.*
51st Georgia, Lieut.-col. James Dickey.
53d Georgia, Lieut.-col. W. F. Hartsfield.

Conner's Brigade.

Colonel John D. Kennedy.

2d South Carolina, Captain J. D. Graham.
3d South Carolina, Capt. J. K. G. Nance.
7th South Carolina, Captain E. J. Goggans.
8th South Carolina, Captain A. T. Harllee.
15th South Carolina, Major F. S. Lewie.
20th South Carolina, Major J. M. Partlow.
3d S. C. Batt., Captain P. F. Spofford.

SECOND ARMY CORPS.†

THIRD ARMY CORPS.

LIEUTENANT-GENERAL A. P. HILL commanding

MAHONE'S DIVISION.

Major-general William Mahone.

Sanders's Brigade.

Colonel Wm. H. Forney.

8th Alabama, Lieut.-col. John P. Emrich.
9th Alabama, Colonel J. H. King.
10th Alabama, Captain C. W. Brewton.
11th Alabama, Colonel G. E. Tayloe.
14th Alabama, Captain S. G. Perry.

Weisiger's Brigade.

Brigadier-general D. A. Weisiger.

6th Virginia, Colonel George T. Rogers.
12th Virginia, Major J. R. Lewellen.
16th Virginia, Captain S. B. Eley.
41st Virginia, Major W. H. Etheredge.
61st Virginia, Lieut.-col. W. H. Stewart.

* Reported absent on inspection reports, and actual commanders of their regiments not indicated.
† See Army Valley District, following.

Harris's Brigade.

Brigadier-general Nathaniel H. Harris.

12th Mississippi, Lt.-col. T. B. Manlove.
16th Mississippi, Lieut.-col. J. H. Duncan.
19th Mississippi, Colonel R. W. Phipps.
48th Mississippi, Colonel Jas. M. Jayne.

Sorrel's Brigade.

Brigadier-general G. M. Sorrel.

3d Georgia, Captain J. A. Mason.
22d Georgia, Captain George W. Thomas.
48th Georgia, Lieut.-col. M. R. Hall.
64th Georgia, Major W. H. Weems.
2d Georgia Batt., Captain W. F. Walker.
10th Georgia Batt., Captain Wm. A. Greer.

Finegan's Brigade.

Brigadier-general Joseph Finegan.

2d Florida, Captain John B. O'Neill.
5th Florida, Captain J. F. Livingston.
8th Florida, Colonel David Lang.
9th Florida, Colonel J. M. Martin.
10th Florida, Lieut.-col. W. W. Scott.
11th Florida, Colonel T. W. Brevard.

HETH'S DIVISION.

Major-general H. Heth.

Davis's Brigade.

Brigadier-general J. R. Davis.

2d Mississippi, Colonel J. M. Stone.
11th Mississippi, Major R. O. Reynolds.
26th Mississippi, Major T. F. Parker.
42d Mississippi, Lieut.-col. A. M. Nelson.
55th North Carolina, Capt. R. W. Thomas.
1st Confederate Batt., Maj. F. B. McClung.

Cooke's Brigade.

Brigadier-general J. R. Cooke.

15th N. C., Lieut.-col. W. H. Yarborough.
27th North Carolina, Major J. C. Webb.
46th N. C., Lieut.-col. A. C. McAlister.
48th North Carolina, Col. S. H. Walkup.

McRae's Brigade.

Brigadier-general W. McRae.

11th North Carolina, Capt. J. M. Young.
26th North Carolina, Maj. Jas. T. Adams.
44th North Carolina, Maj. C. M. Stedman.
47th North Carolina, Capt. S. W. Mitchell.
52d N. C., Captain W. W. Carmichael.

*Archer's Brigade.**

Colonel R. M. Mayo.

13th Alabama, Colonel James Aiken.
1st Tennessee, Major Felix G. Buchanan.
7th Tennessee, Lieut.-col. S. G. Shepard.
14th Tennessee, Colonel W. McComb.

Walker's Brigade.†

40th Virginia, Captain Hiram E. Coles.
47th Virginia, Captain Charles J. Green.
55th Virginia, Colonel Wm. S. Christian.
2d Maryland Battalion, Captain Joseph L. McAleer.

WILCOX'S DIVISION.

Major-general C. M. Wilcox.

Thomas's Brigade.

Brigadier-general E. L. Thomas.

14th Georgia, Colonel R. P. Lester.
35th Georgia, Lieut.-col. W. H. McCullohs.
45th Georgia, Colonel T. J. Simmons.
49th Georgia, Colonel John T. Jordan.

Lane's Brigade.

Colonel R. V. Cowan.

7th North Carolina, Captain N. A. Pool.
18th North Carolina, Lt.-col. J. W. McGill.
28th North Carolina, Capt. T. V. Apperson.
33d North Carolina, Capt. Riddick Gatling.
37th North Carolina, Major J. L. Bost.

* Appears from return to have commanded also Walker's brigade.
† On return for this date the 22d Virginia Battalion appears as in this brigade.

McGowan's Brigade.

Brigadier-general Samuel McGowan.

1st South Carolina, Col. C. W. McCreary.
12th South Carolina, Captain R. M. Kerr.
13th South Carolina, Col. Isaac F. Hunt.
14th South Carolina, Col. J. N. Brown.
Orr's Rifles, Colonel G. McD. Miller.

Scales's Brigade.

Colonel W. L. J. Lowrance.

13th North Carolina, Maj. E. B. Withers.
16th North Carolina, Col. W. A. Stowe.
22d North Carolina, Col. T. S. Gallaway.
34th North Carolina, Capt. G. M. Norment.
38th North Carolina, Col. John Ashford.

ANDERSON'S CORPS.

LIEUTENANT-GENERAL R. H. ANDERSON.

HOKE'S DIVISION.*

Major-general R. F. Hoke.

Hagood's Brigade.

Brigadier-general J. Hagood.

11th South Carolina, Colonel F. H. Gantt.
21st South Carolina, Col. R. F. Graham.
25th South Carolina, Col. C. A. Simonton.†
27th South Carolina, Col. P. C. Gaillard.†
7th South Carolina Batt., Maj. J. H. Rion.

Colquitt's Brigade.

Brigadier-general A. H. Colquitt.

6th Georgia, Lieut.-col. S. W. Harris.
19th Georgia, Colonel James H. Neal.
23d Georgia, Colonel M. R. Ballenger.
27th Georgia, Captain E. D. Graham.
28th Georgia, Captain J. A. Johnson.

Clingman's Brigade.

Colonel H. McKethan.

8th North Carolina, Lt.-col. R. A. Barrier.
31st North Carolina, Lt.-col. C. W. Knight.
51st N. C., Captain James W. Lippitt.
61st N. C., Lieut.-col. Wm. S. Devane.

Kirkland's Brigade.

Brigadier-general W. W. Kirkland.

17th N. C., Lieut.-col. Thos. H. Sharpe.
42d North Carolina, Col. John E. Brown.
66th N. C., Colonel John H. Nethercutt.

JOHNSON'S DIVISION.

Major-general B. R. Johnson.

Gracie's Brigade.

Brigadier-general A. Gracie, Jr.

41st Alabama, Colonel M. L. Stansel.
43d Alabama, Lieut.-col. J. J. Jolly.
59th Alabama, Lt.-col. G. W. Huguley.
60th Alabama, Lieut.-col. D. S. Troy.
23d Batt. Ala. S. S., Major N. Stallworth.

Ransom's Brigade.

Brigadier-general M. W. Ransom.

24th North Carolina, Major T. D. Love.
25th North Carolina, Col. H. M. Rutledge.
35th North Carolina, Lt.-col. S. B. Taylor.
49th North Carolina, Captain C. H. Dixon.
56th North Carolina, Col. P. F. Faison.

Wise's Brigade.

Colonel J. T. Goode.

26th Virginia, Captain W. R. Perrin.
34th Virginia, Lieut.-col. R. Harrison.
46th Virginia, Captain J. H. White.
59th Virginia, Major R. G. Mosby.

Elliott's Brigade.

Brigadier-general W. H. Wallace.

17th South Carolina, Col. F. W. McMaster.
18th South Carolina, Major R. J. Betsill.
22d S. C., Lieut.-col. W. G. Burt.
23d S. C., Colonel H. L. Benbow.
26th S. C., Colonel A. D. Smith.
Holcombe Legion, Capt. A. B. Woodruff.

* Serving with 1st Army Corps.
† These officers reported as detached in inspection report, etc.

FIRST MILITARY DISTRICT.

BRIGADIER-GENERAL HENRY A. WISE.

Walker's Brigade.

Brigadier-general J. A. Walker.

Batt. Va. Reserves, Col. B. L. Farinholt.
Batt. Va. Reserves, Col. P. M. Henry.
Batt. Va. Reserves, Col. R. A. Booker.
Batt. Va. Reserves, Col. R. E. Withers.
Section of artillery, Major V. Maurin.

Garnett's Brigade.

Lieutenant-colonel J. J. Garnett.

Battalion C. S. Zouaves, Major [F.] De Bordenave.
Batt. Va. Reserves. Major D. J. Godwin.
Co. " H," 8th Georgia Cavalry, Lieutenant A. M. G. Wiggins.
Section of Bradford's Battery, Lieutenant A. J. Cochran.

Post Lynchburg and Detailed Men.

Brigadier-general R. E. Colston.

Petersburg.

Major W. H. Ker.

44th Virginia Batt. (Co. " D"), Captain W. E. Hinton.
2d-class Militia, Captain O. H. Hobson.
Indpt. Signal Corps, Major J. F. Milligan.

Unattached.

Provost-guard Army of Northern Virginia, 1st Va. Batt., Major D. B. Bridgford.
39th Virginia Cavalry Battalion, Major John H. Richardson.

CAVALRY CORPS.

MAJOR-GENERAL WADE HAMPTON commanding.

HAMPTON'S (OLD) DIVISION.

Brigadier-general M. C. Butler.

Butler's Brigade.

Colonel H. K. Aiken.

4th South Carolina, Lt.-col. Wm. Stokes.
5th South Carolina, Captain Z. Davis.
6th South Carolina, Lt.-col. L. P. Miller.

Young's Brigade.

Colonel J. F. Waring.

10th Georgia, Captain L. F. Smith.
Cobb's Georgia Legion, Lt.-col. B. S. King.
Phillips's Ga. Legion, Lt.-col. W. W. Rich.
Jeff. Davis Legion, Major J. F. Lewis.

LEE'S DIVISION.

Major-general W. H. F. Lee.

Chambliss's Brigade.

Colonel R. L. T. Beale.

9th Virginia, Major Samuel A. Swann.
10th Virginia, Lieut.-col. R. A. Caskie.
13th Virginia, Colonel J. C. Phillips.

Barringer's Brigade.

Brigadier-general Rufus Barringer.

1st North Carolina, Colonel W. H. Cheek.
2d North Carolina, Colonel W. P. Roberts.
3d North Carolina, Lt.-col. Roger Moore.
5th North Carolina, Major J. H. McNeill.

Dearing's Brigade.

Brigadier-general J. Dearing.

8th Georgia, Colonel J. R. Griffin.
4th North Carolina, Colonel D. D. Ferebee.
16th North Carolina Battalion, Captain J. R. Lane.

HORSE ARTILLERY.*

Major R. F. Chew.

Graham's Battery, Captain Edward Graham.
Hart's Battery, Lieutenant E. L. Halsey.
McGregor's Battery, Captain Wm. M. McGregor.

ARTILLERY RESERVE, ETC.†

BRIGADIER-GENERAL W. N. PENDLETON commanding.

FIRST CORPS ARTILLERY.

Brigadier-general E. P. Alexander.

Cabell's Battalion.

1st Company Richmond Howitzers, Capt. R. M. Anderson.
Manly's Battery, Captain B. C. Manly.
Pulaski Artillery, First Lieut. M. Callaway.
Troup Artillery, Captain H. H. Carlton.

Huger's Battalion.

Fickling's Battery, Captain W. W. Fickling.
Moody's Battery, Lieut. J. C. Parkinson.
Parker's Battery, Captain W. W. Parker.
Smith's Battery, Captain John D. Smith.
Taylor's Battery, Captain O. B. Taylor.
Woolfolk's Battery, Lieut. J. Woolfolk.

Hardaway's Battalion.

3d Howitzers, Captain B. H. Smith [Jr.].
Dance's Battery, Captain W. J. Dance.
Griffin's Battery, Captain C. B. Griffin.
Rockbridge Artillery, Captain A. Graham.

Haskell's Battalion.

Flanner's Battery, Captain H. G. Flanner.
Garden's Battery, Captain H. R. Garden.
Lamkin's Battery, Captain J. N. Lamkin.
Ramsay's Battery, Captain J. A. Ramsay.

Starke's Battalion.

Giles Artillery, Captain D. A. French.
La. Guard Artillery, Captain C. A. Green.
Matthews Art., Captain A. D. Armistead.

Johnson's Battalion.

Crutter's Battery, Lieut. L. McIntosh.
Fredericksburg Art., Lt. J. [G.] Pollock.

THIRD CORPS ARTILLERY.

Colonel R. L. Walker, Chief of Artillery.

McIntosh's Battalion.

1st Md. Battery, Captain W. F. Dement.
4th Md. Battery, Captain W. S. Chew.
2d Rockbridge Art., Capt. W. K. Donald.
Crenshaw's Battery, Captain T. Ellett.
Rice's Battery, Captain B. Z. Price.

Pegram's Battalion.

Gregg's Battery, Captain Thos. E. Gregg.
Letcher Artillery, Captain T. A. Brander.
Purcell Artillery, Captain Geo. M. Cayce.
Richards's Battery, Captain T. J. Richards.

Poague's Battalion.

Graham's Battery, Captain A. B. Williams.
Utterback's Battery, Capt. A. W. Utterback.
Wyatt's Battery, Capt. Chas. F. Johnston.

Eshleman's Battalion.

1st Co. Washington Art., Capt. E. Owen.
2d Co. Wash. Art., Capt. J. B. Richardson.
3d Co. Washington Art., Capt. A. Hero, Jr.
4th Co. Wash. Art., Capt. Joe Norcom.

Richardson's Battalion.

Donaldsonville Art., Capt. R. P. Landry.
Huger Artillery, Captain J. D. Moore.
Norfolk Light Art., Capt. C. R. Grandy.
Penick's Battery, Captain N. Penick.

Lane's Battalion.

Irwin Artillery, Captain J. T. Wingfield.
Patterson's Battery, Capt. G. M. Patterson.
Ross's Battery, Captain H. M. Ross.

* Johnston's, Thompson's, and Shoemaker's batteries, under Major James Breathed, attached to Rosser's command, Army of the Valley District.
† From returns, and actual commanders not indicated.

Owen's Battalion.

Davidson's Battery, Captain J. H. Chamberlayne.
Dickenson's Battery, Captain [C.] Dickenson.
Otey's Battery, Captain D. N. Walker.

ARTILLERY ANDERSON'S CORPS.

Colonel H. P. Jones.

Moseley's Battalion.

Cumming's Batt., Capt. [J. D.] Cumming.
Miller's Battery, Captain [John] Miller.
Slaten's Battery, Captain [C. W.] Slaten.
Young's Battery, Captain [E. R.] Young.

Coit's Battalion.

Bradford's Batt., Capt. [W. D.] Bradford.
Pegram's Battery, Captain [R. G.] Pegram.
Wright's Battery, Captain [S. T.] Wright.

Blount's Battalion.

Dickerson's Batt., Capt. J. W. Dickerson.
Fauquier Artillery, Capt. W. C. Marshall.
Fayette Artillery, Captain M. C. Macon.
Hampden Artillery, Capt. [J. E.] Sullivan.

Martin's Battalion.

Martin's Battery, Lieut. [S. H.] Pulliam.
Sturdivant's Batt., Lieut. [W. H.] Weisiger.

ARMY VALLEY DISTRICT.*

LIEUTENANT-GENERAL JUBAL A. EARLY commanding.

EARLY'S DIVISION (SECOND CORPS).

Brigadier-general John Pegram.

Pegram's Brigade.

13th Virginia, Lieut.-col. G. A. Goodman.
31st Virginia, Lieut.-col. J. S. Hoffman.
49th Virginia, Lieut.-col. J. C. Gibson.
52d Virginia, Lieut.-col. J. H. Skinner.
58th Virginia, Lieut.-col. J. G. Kasey.

Johnston's Brigade.

Brigadier-general R. D. Johnston.

5th North Carolina, Colonel John W. Lea.
12th North Carolina, Col. H. E. Coleman.
20th North Carolina, Colonel T. F. Toon.
23d North Carolina, Col. C. C. Blacknall.
1st Batt. N. C. S. S., Capt. R. E. Wilson.

Lewis's Brigade.

Brigadier-general W. G. Lewis.

6th North Carolina, Colonel R. F. Webb.
21st North Carolina, Lieut.-col. W. S. Rankin.
54th North Carolina, Col. K. M. Murchison.
57th North Carolina, Lieut.-col. H. C. Jones, Jr.

RODES'S DIVISION† (SECOND CORPS).

Battle's Brigade.

3d Alabama, Colonel C. Forsyth.
5th Alabama, Colonel J. M. Hall.
6th Alabama, Colonel J. N. Lightfoot.
12th Alabama, Colonel S. B. Pickens.
61st Alabama, Colonel W. G. Swanson.

Grimes's Brigade.

32d North Carolina, Col. D. G. Coward.
43d North Carolina, Col. T. S. Kenan.
45th North Carolina, Col. Jno. R. Winston.
53d N. C., Lieut.-col. J. T. Morehead.
2d N. C. Batt., Major J. M. Hancock.

* From returns of the Army of Northern Virginia.
† Only two general officers (brigadier-generals) reported present for duty in the division.

Cox's Brigade.

1st North Carolina, Lt.-col. H. A. Brown.
2d North Carolina, Capt. John P. Cobb.
3d North Carolina, Col. S. D. Thruston.
4th North Carolina, Col. E. A. Osborne.
14th North Carolina, Col. R. T. Bennett.
30th North Carolina, Col. F. M. Parker.

Cook's Brigade.

4th Georgia, Colonel W. H. Willis.
12th Georgia, Lieut.-col. Isaac Hardeman.
21st Georgia, Colonel T. W. Hooper.
44th Georgia, Colonel W. H. Peebles.

GORDON'S DIVISION * (SECOND CORPS).

Major-general John B. Gordon.

Evans's Brigade.

Brigadier-general C. A. Evans.

13th Georgia, Colonel J. H. Baker.
26th Georgia, Colonel E. N. Atkinson.
31st Georgia, Colonel J. H. Lowe.
38th Georgia, Lieut.-col. P. E. Davant.
60th Georgia, Lieut.-col. T. J. Berry.
61st Georgia (no field-officer).
12th Ga. Batt., Lieut.-col. H. D. Capers.

Terry's Brigade.

Brigadier-general William Terry.

2d Virginia, Major C. H. Stewart.
4th Virginia, Major M. D. Bennett.
5th Virginia, Lieut.-col. H. J. Williams.
10th Virginia, Lt.-col. D. H. Lee Martz.
21st Virginia, Colonel W. A. Witcher.
23d Virginia, Colonel A. G. Taliaferro.
25th Virginia, Major Wilson Harper.
27th Virginia, Lieut.-col. C. L. Haynes.
33d Virginia, Colonel A. Spengler.
37th Virginia, Colonel T. V. Williams.
42d Virginia, Colonel R. W. Withers.
44th Virginia, Colonel N. Cobb.
48th Virginia, Colonel R. H. Dungan.

York's Brigade.

Brigadier-general Zebulon York.

1st Louisiana, Lieut.-col. J. Nelligan.
2d Louisiana, Lieut.-col. R. E. Burke.
5th Louisiana, Major A. Hart.
6th Louisiana, Lieut.-col. J. Hanlon.
7th Louisiana, Lieut.-col. D. B. Penn.

8th Louisiana (no field-officer).
9th Louisiana, Colonel Wm. R. Peck.
10th Louisiana, Colonel E. Waggaman.
14th Louisiana, Colonel D. Zable.
15th Louisiana, Colonel E. Pendleton.

WHARTON'S DIVISION † (SECOND CORPS).

Brigadier-general G. C. Wharton.

Patton's Brigade.

22d Virginia, Lieut.-col. G. C. McDonald.
23d Va. Batt., Lieut.-col. C. Derrick.
26th Virginia Batt., Lt.-col. G. M. Edgar.

Smith's Brigade.

36th Virginia, Colonel Thos. Smith.
45th Va. Batt., Lieut.-col. H. M. Beckley.
60th Virginia, Colonel B. H. Jones.

Forsberg's Brigade.

45th Virginia, Major A. M. Davis.
50th Virginia, Colonel A. S. Vanderventer.
51st Virginia, Colonel Aug. Forsberg.
30th Virginia Batt., Lieut.-col. J. Lyle Clarke.

* One major-general and two brigadier-generals reported present for duty.
† Two general officers reported present for duty.

CAVALRY CORPS.*

LOMAX'S DIVISION.

Major-general L. L. Lomax.

Imboden's Brigade.	*McCausland's Brigade.*
Brigadier-general J. D. Imboden.	Brigadier-general J. M. McCausland.
18th Virginia, Colonel G. W. Imboden.	14th Virginia, Colonel J. Cochran.
23d Virginia, Colonel Robert White.	16th Virginia, Colonel M. J. Ferguson.
25th Virginia, Colonel W. M. Hopkins.	17th Virginia, Captain J. S. A. Crawford.
62d Virginia, Colonel G. H. Smith.	21st Virginia, Colonel W. E. Peters.
	22d Virginia, Colonel H. S. Bowen.

Jackson's Brigade.
Colonel William L. Jackson.

19th Virginia, Colonel Wm. L. Jackson.
20th Virginia, Colonel W. W. Arnett.
26th Virginia, Lieut.-col. J. K. Kesler.
37th Virginia Battalion, Lieut.-col. A. C. Dunn.
1st Maryland Batt., Major H. W. Gilmor.

ROSSER'S [FITZ LEE'S] DIVISION.†

Wickham's Brigade.	*Rosser's Brigade.*
1st Virginia, Lieut.-col. W. A. Morgan.	7th Virginia, Colonel R. H. Dulany.
2d Virginia, Colonel T. T. Munford.	11th Virginia, Colonel O. R. Funsten.
3d Virginia, Colonel T. H. Owen.	12th Virginia, Colonel A. W. Harman.
4th Virginia, Lt.-col. W. B. Wooldridge.	35th Va. Batt., Lieut.-col. E. V. White.

Payne's Brigade.

5th Virginia, Colonel R. B. Boston.
6th Virginia, Colonel Julian Harrison.
8th Virginia, Colonel J. M. Corns.
15th Virginia, —— ——.
36th Virginia Battalion, Major J. W. Sweeney.

ARTILLERY.
Colonel Thomas H. Carter, Chief of Artillery.

Nelson's Battalion.	*Braxton's Battalion.*
Kirkpatrick's Battery.	Carpenter's Battery.
Milledge's Battery.	Cooper's Battery.
Snead's Battery.	Hardwicke's Battery.

Cutshaw's Battalion.	*King's Battalion.*
Fry's Battery.	Bryan's Battery.
Garber's Battery.	Chapman's Battery.
Jones's Battery.	Lowry's Battery.

With Lomax.	*With Rosser.*
Griffin's Battery.	Johnston's Battery.
Jackson's Battery.	Shoemaker's Battery.
Lurty's Battery.	Thompson's Battery.
McClanahan's Battery.	

* One major-general and three brigadier-generals reported present for duty.
† No general officers reported present for duty.

HEADQUARTERS ARMY OF NORTHERN VIRGINIA,
27th Oct., 1864.

HON. SEC. OF WAR, RICHMOND,

SIR: I have the honor to acknowledge the receipt of the signal message sent me by your order yesterday. I had supposed that General Grant would make some movement simultaneously with any attack on Wilmington to prevent reinforcements being sent from here, and in that view I consider it important that in such an event General Hardee should reinforce General Bragg with all his available troops, or, on the other hand, should Charleston and not Wilmington be the real point of attack, a demonstration will be made against the others to detain the troops at either from the real point. The officers in command must judge which is the true movement and act accordingly.

I think it would be well that the policy which they are to pursue should be made the subject of an order from the Department directing the one not attacked to reinforce the one who is with all the troops he can spare.

Very resp'lly, yr. obt. servt.,

R. E. LEE,
General.

HEADQUARTERS, TURNBULL'S,
Dec. 5, 1864.

HIS EX. JEFFERSON DAVIS, PRESIDENT C. STATES, RICHMOND,

MR. PRESIDENT: I have received the despatch from General Bragg of the 4th inst, forwarded to me by Mr. B. N. Harrison, stating that there is still time for him to receive any assistance that can be spared. On the 27th ult. General Whiting informed me that General Bragg had carried with him 2700 of the best troops from Wilmington. Since that he has ordered to Charleston a regiment of the North Carolina reserves, and I do not think, so far as I can judge, that more troops can be taken with propriety unless we were certain that all danger of an attack was removed from that point. In addition, I sent General Young with about 400 cavalrymen (without horses), and ordered all those previously sent to Georgia and South Carolina to report to him at Augusta; which Hampton thinks will give him about 800 mounted men, which I thought would strengthen the cavalry very much in that department. General Baker has also gone to General Bragg, so that he will have another good cavalry commander.

I fear I can do nothing more under present circumstances. General Early reports that his scouts stated the Sixth corps had broken camp on the 2d, and taken the cars at Stevenson's Dépôt—said to be going to City Point. From reports received from Longstreet and Ewell last night, I think this corps or a part of it may have reached the north side of James River last night. My last report from scouts on the James was to the 2d. There had been great activity on the river in transportation of supplies, but no troops had passed in any numbers since the 17th ult. Reports of Early and Longstreet have not yet been corroborated, but the whole preparations of the enemy indicate some movement against us. All we want to resist them is men.

With great respect, your obedient servant,

R. E. LEE,
General.

HEADQUARTERS ARMY OF NORTHERN VIRGINIA,
Dec. 11, 1864.

HON. JAMES A. SEDDON, SECRETARY OF WAR, RICHMOND,

SIR: I have been informed by General Stevens that you have consented to the retention of our present negro force until Christmas. This will prove to be some relief, but not sufficient for our wants. My original request was for 5000 laborers: 2200 is the greatest number which ever reported, and those in small bodies at different intervals. The period for which they were first called was thirty days, and subsequently extended to sixty days. A large number of them have deserted, many not serving the first thirty days. Since the expiration of this period the desertions have greatly increased. I cannot state the present strength of the force, but think it cannot exceed 1200. I consequently have not been able to accomplish half I desired. In our present extended line, requiring the troops to be always on duty and prepared for any movements of the enemy, I cannot use them, as formerly, for any work requiring them to leave their trenches. This is the reason why a laboring force is necessary, and unless I can get it for the completion of interior lines of defence, construction of roads, and other work necessary to the existence of an army, I shall be unable to hold my position. Of the negroes called for under the act of Feb. 17, 1864, I have not yet received enough to replace the white teamsters in the army. In fact, we have not received more than sufficient to supply teamsters for the Third corps and a portion of one division. Not one has yet been received for laboring purposes, and to any inquiries on the subject I get no satisfactory reply. I beg, therefore, to call your attention to this matter, which I deem of the greatest importance, and request that prompt measures may be taken to supply this demand.

I am, with great respect, yr. obt. servt.,

R. E. LEE,
General.

NEAR PETERSBURG, Dec. 14, 1864.

MR. PRESIDENT: After sending my despatch to you yesterday, knowing that the snow in the Valley was six inches deep and the weather very cold, and presuming that active operations would necessarily be suspended, I directed Rodes's division to march for Staunton, and requested the quartermaster-general to send cars to convey it to Richmond. It is now on the road, and should reach Staunton to-morrow evening. If the quartermaster's department is active, it should arrive in Richmond Friday morning. A despatch received from General Early last night stated that the scouts just in report that the Nineteenth corps of the enemy had left the Valley, and that the Eighth was under marching orders. The latter might be preparing to move nearer the Baltimore and Ohio Railroad, for I do not think they will strip it of all defence, or both corps may be coming to General Grant. Colonel Withers's scouts report that a New York regiment of infantry and part of the Seventh regiment of cavalry had left the Kanawha for the Valley; but I suppose they might have been intended to replace the garrison at New Creek. I do not know what may be General Grant's next move: his last against the Weldon Railroad and our right flank failed. The expeditions from Plymouth and New Berne against Fort Branch on the Roanoke and Kinston, N. C., have both retreated, before the forces moved against them, back to their former positions. Everything at this time is quiet in the departments of Virginia and North Carolina. If the reports of the prisoners and the statements of Federal officers to the citizens of the country are true, the object of the last expedition was to make a permanent lodgment at Weldon, draw supplies by the Roanoke and Seaboard Railroad, and thence operate against the railroads in North Carolina. General Grant may not now be prepared to break through our centre, as the canal at Dutch Gap is reported nearly completed. As long as he holds so large an army around Richmond, I think it very hazardous to diminish our force. We now can oppose about a division to one of his corps. I fear Savannah is in great danger, and unless our operations there are bold and energetic I am apprehensive of its fall. I hope, though, if all our troops are united Sherman may be repulsed. But there is no time to lose. If the Nineteenth corps does not come to Grant we might spare a division; but if the Nineteenth and Eighth are both drawn to him, we shall require more than we have. I ordered General J. A. Walker with the Virginia reserves from Weldon to Kinston to oppose the movement against that place. He is now on his return to his position on the Danville and Southside roads.

With a firm reliance on our merciful God that He will cause all things to work together for our good,

I remain, with great respect, yr. obt. servt.,

R. E. LEE,
General.

[Telegram from Headquarters A. N. Va.]

HEADQUARTERS ARMY OF NORTHERN VIRGINIA,
Jan. 11, 1865.

HON. J. A. SEDDON:

There is nothing within reach of this army to be impressed. The country is swept clear; our only reliance is upon the railroads. We have but two days' supplies.

R. E. LEE.

———

HEADQUARTERS ARMY OF NORTHERN VIRGINIA,
January 16, 1865.

HON. SEC. OF WAR, RICHMOND,

SIR: I have the honor to acknowledge the receipt of your letter of the 12th inst., with its enclosures. I thank you for your prompt and energetic measures for the relief of the army. As soon as I was informed of the break in our railroad connections I issued the enclosed appeal to the farmers and others in the country accessible by our remaining communications, and sent Major Tannahill to them to obtain all the supplies that could be procured. I am glad to say that, so far as I know, the crisis in relation to this matter is now past.

Very respectfully, your obedient servant,

R. E. LEE,
General.

[Indorsement.]

Noted with pleasure. It was the most effectual mode of obtaining supplies —more effective, I doubt not, than coercive action of the Department.

J. A. S.

JAN. 19, 1865.

———

[Enclosure.]

HEADQUARTERS ARMY OF NORTHERN VIRGINIA,
Jan. 12, 1865.

TO THE FARMERS EAST OF THE BLUE RIDGE AND SOUTH OF JAMES RIVER:

The recent heavy freshet having destroyed a portion of the railroad from Danville to Goldsboro', and thereby cut off temporarily necessary supplies for the Army of Northern Virginia, an appeal is respectfully made to the farmers, millers, and other citizens to furnish with all possible promptness whatever breadstuffs, meats (fresh or salt), and molasses they can spare. Such citizens as Major Robert Tannahill may select are asked to act as agents in purchasing and collecting supplies through the various officers connected with the commissary department on the lines of railroad.

Arrangements have been made to pay promptly for all supplies delivered under this appeal, or to return the same in kind as soon as practicable.

R. E. LEE.

HEADQUARTERS ARMY OF NORTHERN VIRGINIA,
January 19, 1865.

HON. SEC. OF WAR, RICHMOND,

SIR: There is great suffering in the army for want of soap. The neglect of personal cleanliness has occasioned cutaneous diseases to a great extent in many commands. The commissary department has been applied to, but the supply received from it is entirely inadequate. Soap is an article of home manufacture in every family almost. The materials for making it are found in every household, and the art is familiar to all well-trained domestics. I cannot but think that by proper efforts a plan might be devised to meet this want of our soldiers. All that is necessary, I think, is to employ or contract with some intelligent and practical business-men in the different States to ensure a supply. I do not suppose that agents or officers of the C. S. department can succeed as well as private individuals, if it be made to the interest of the latter to procure what we need. I beg that you will endeavor to make some arrangement by which the suffering of the men in this particular can be relieved.

Very respectfully, your obedient servant,

R. E. LEE,
General.

[Circular.]   HEADQUARTERS ARMY OF NORTHERN VIRGINIA,
January 25, 1865.

To arm and equip an additional force of cavalry there is need of carbines, revolvers, pistols, saddles, and other accoutrements of mounted men. Arms and equipments of the kind desired are believed to be held by citizens in sufficient numbers to supply our wants. Many keep them as trophies, and some with the expectation of using them in their own defence. But it should be remembered that arms are now required for use, and that they cannot be made so effectual for the defence of the country in any way as in the hands of organized troops. They are needed to enable our cavalry to cope with the well-armed and equipped cavalry of the enemy, not only in the general service, but in resisting those predatory expeditions which have inflicted so much loss upon the people of the interior. To the patriotic I need make no other appeal than the wants of the service; but I beg to remind those who are reluctant to part with the arms and equipments in their possession that by keeping them they diminish the ability of the army to defend their property, without themselves receiving any benefit from them. I therefore urge all persons not in the service to deliver promptly to some of the officers designated below such arms and equipments (especially those suitable for cavalry) as they may have, and to report to those officers the names of such persons as neglect to surrender those in their possession. Every citizen who prevents a carbine or pistol from remaining unused will render a service to his country. Those who think to retain arms for their own defence should remember that if the army cannot protect them, the arms will be of little use.

While no valid title can be acquired to public arms and equipments except from the Government, it is reported that many persons have ignorantly purchased them from private parties. A fair compensation will therefore be made to all who deliver such arms and equipments to any ordnance officers, officer commanding at a post, officers and agents of the quartermaster and commissary departments at any station, or officers in the enrolling service or connected with the nitre and mining bureau. All these officers are requested, and those connected with this army are directed, to receive and receipt for all arms and equipments, whatever their condition, and forward the same, with a duplicate receipt, to the ordnance department at Richmond, and report their proceedings to these headquarters. The person holding the receipt will be compensated upon presenting it to the ordnance bureau.

While it is hoped that no one will disregard this appeal, all officers connected with the army are required, and all others are requested, to take possession of any public arms and equipments they may find in the hands of persons unwilling to surrender them to the service of the country, and to give receipts therefor. A reasonable allowance for their expenses and trouble will be made to such patriotic citizens as will collect and deliver to any of the officers above designated such arms and equipments as they may find in the hands of persons not in the service, or who will report the same to those officers. A prompt compliance with this call will greatly promote the efficiency and strength of the army, particularly of the cavalry, and render it better able to protect the homes and property of the people from outrage.

R. E. LEE,
General.

HEADQUARTERS, PETERSBURG,
February 4, 1865.

GENERAL S. COOPER, A.- AND I.-GENERAL, RICHMOND, VA.,

GENERAL: I received your telegram of the 1st inst. announcing my confirmation by the Senate as general-in-chief of the armies of the Confederate States. I am indebted alone to the kindness of His Excellency the President for my nomination to this high and arduous office, and wish I had the ability to fill it to advantage. As I have received no instructions as to my duties, I do not know what he desires me to undertake.

I am, respectfully, your obedient servant,

R. E. LEE,
General.

[Telegram.]   HEADQUARTERS ARMY OF NORTHERN VIRGINIA,
                                                 February 6, 1865.

GEN. S. COOPER : The enemy moved in strong force yesterday to Hatcher's
Run.   Part of his infantry, with Gregg's cavalry, crossed and proceeded on the
Vaughan road—the infantry to Cattail Creek, the cavalry to Dinwiddie Court-
house, where its advance encountered a portion of our cavalry and retired.   In
the afternoon parts of Hill's and Gordon's troops demonstrated against the
enemy on the left of Hatcher's Run, near Armstrong's mill.   Finding him
intrenched, they were withdrawn after dark.   During the night the force that
had advanced beyond the creek returned to it, and were reported to be recrossing.   This morning Pegram's division moved down the right bank of the creek
to reconnoitre, when it was vigorously attacked.   The battle was obstinately
contested for several hours, but, General Pegram being killed while bravely
encouraging his men, and Colonel Hoffman wounded, some confusion occurred
and the division was pressed back to its original position.   Evans's division,
ordered by General Gordon to support Pegram, charged the enemy, forced him
back, but was in turn compelled to retire.   Mahone's division arriving, the
enemy was driven rapidly to his defences on Hatcher's Run.

Our loss is reported to be small, that of the enemy not supposed great.

                                                          R. E. LEE,
                                                                General.

                                    ————————

                              HEADQUARTERS ARMY OF NORTHERN VIRGINIA,
                                                 February 8, 1865.

HON. JAS. A. SEDDON, SEC. OF WAR, RICHMOND, VA.,

SIR : All the disposable force of the right wing of the army has been operating against the enemy beyond Hatcher's Run since Sunday.   Yesterday, the
most inclement day of the winter, they had to be retained in line of battle,
having been in the same condition the two previous days and nights.   I regret
to be obliged to state that under these circumstances, heightened by assaults
and fire of the enemy, some of the men had been without meat for three days,
and all were suffering from reduced rations and scant clothing, exposed to battle, cold, hail, and sleet.   I have directed Colonel Cole, chief commissary, who
reports that he has not a pound of meat at his disposal, to visit Richmond and
see if nothing can be done.   If some change is not made and the commissary
department reorganized, I apprehend dire results.   The physical strength of
the men, if their courage survives, must fail under this treatment.   Our cavalry
has to be dispersed for want of forage.   Fitz Lee's and Lomax's divisions are
scattered because supplies cannot be transported where their services are
required.   I had to bring Wm. F. Lee's division forty miles Sunday night to
get him in position.

Taking these facts in connection with the paucity of our numbers, you must not be surprised if calamity befalls us. According to reports of prisoners, we were opposed on Hatcher's Run by the Second and Fifth corps, part of the Ninth, one division of the Sixth, Gregg's division (Third brigade) of cavalry. It was also reported that the Twenty-third corps (Schofield's) reached City Point on the 5th, and that it was present. But this is not confirmed by other reports. At last accounts it was stated to be on the Potomac, delayed by ice. A scout near Alexandria reports it is to march on Gordonsville, General Baker on Kinston. I think it more probable it will join Grant here.

With great respect, your obedient servant,

R. E. LEE,
General.

Respectfully sent to the President for perusal. Please return it.

JOHN C. BRECKENRIDGE,
Secretary of War.

[Indorsement.]

This is too sad to be patiently considered, and cannot have occurred without criminal neglect or gross incapacity. Let supplies be had by purchase or borrowing or other possible mode.

J. D.

HEADQUARTERS CONFEDERATE ARMY,
February 9, 1865.

GENERAL ORDERS, }
No. 1. }

In obedience to General Order No. 3, Adjutant- and Inspector-general's Office, 6th February, 1865, I assume command of the military forces of the Confederate States.

Deeply impressed with the difficulties and responsibilities of the position, and humbly invoking the guidance of Almighty God, I rely for success upon the courage and fortitude of the army, sustained by the patriotism and firmness of the people, confident that their united efforts, under the blessing of Heaven, will secure peace and independence.

The headquarters of the army, to which all special reports and communications will be addressed, will be for the present with the Army of Northern Virginia. The stated and regular returns and reports of each army and department will be forwarded, as heretofore, to the office of the Adjutant- and Inspector-general.

R. E. LEE,
General.

HEADQUARTERS ARMIES OF THE CONFEDERATE STATES,
14 February, 1865.

GENERAL ORDERS, }
   No. 2. }

In entering upon the campaign about to open the general-in-chief feels assured that the soldiers who have so long and so nobly borne the hardships and dangers of the war require no exhortation to respond to the calls of honor and duty.

With the liberty transmitted by their forefathers they have inherited the spirit to defend it.

The choice between war and abject submission is before them.

To such a proposal brave men with arms in their hands can have but one answer. They cannot barter manhood for peace nor the right of self-government for life or property.

But justice to them requires a sterner admonition to those who have abandoned their comrades in the hour of peril.

A last opportunity is afforded them to wipe out the disgrace and escape the punishment of their crimes.

By authority of the President of the Confederate States a pardon is announced to such deserters and men improperly absent as shall return to the commands to which they belong within the shortest possible time, not exceeding twenty days from the publication of this order, at the headquarters of the department in which they may be.

Those who may be prevented by interruption of communication may report within the time specified to the nearest enrolling officer or other officer on duty, to be forwarded as soon as practicable, and upon presenting a certificate from such officer showing compliance with the requirement will receive the pardon hereby offered.

Those who have deserted to the service of the enemy, or who have deserted after having been once pardoned for the same offence, and those who shall desert or absent themselves without authority after the publication of this order, are excluded from its benefits. Nor does the offer of pardon extend to other offences than desertion and absence without permission.

By the same authority it is also declared that no general amnesty will again be granted, and those who refuse to accept the pardon now offered, or who shall hereafter desert or absent themselves without leave, shall suffer such punishment as the courts may impose, and no application for clemency will be entertained.

Taking new resolution from the fate which our enemies intend for us, let every man devote all his energies to the common defence.

Our resources, wisely and vigorously employed, are ample, and with a brave army, sustained by a determined and united people, success with God's assistance cannot be doubtful.

The advantages of the enemy will have but little value if we do not permit them to impair our resolution. Let us then oppose constancy to adversity, fortitude to suffering, and courage to danger, with the firm assurance that He who gave freedom to our fathers will bless the efforts of their children to preserve it.

R. E. LEE,

General.

HEADQUARTERS, PETERSBURG,

Feb. 19, 1865.

HIS EXCELLENCY J. C. BRECKENRIDGE, SECRETARY OF WAR, RICHMOND, VA.,

SIR: The accounts received to-day from South and North Carolina are unfavorable. General Beauregard reports from Winnsborough that four corps of the enemy are advancing on that place, tearing up the Charlotte Railroad, and that they will probably reach Charlotte by the 24th and before he can concentrate his troops there. He states that General Sherman will doubtless move thence on Greensborough, Danville, and Petersburg, or unite with General Schofield at Raleigh or Weldon.

General Bragg reports that General Schofield is now preparing to advance from New Berne to Goldsborough, and that a strong expedition is moving against the Weldon Railroad at Rocky Mount. He says that little or no assistance can be received from the State of North Carolina—that exemptions and reorganizations under late laws have disbanded the State forces, and that they will not be ready for the field for some time.

I do not see how Sherman can make the march anticipated by General Beauregard, but he seems to have everything his own way; which is calculated to cause apprehension. General Beauregard does not say what he proposes or what he can do. I do not know where his troops are or on what lines they are moving. His despatches only give movements of the enemy. He has a difficult task to perform under present circumstances, and one of his best officers, General Hardee, is incapacitated by sickness. I have also heard that his own health is indifferent, though he has never so stated. Should his strength give way, there is no one on duty in the department that could replace him, nor have I any one to send there. General J. E. Johnston is the only officer whom I know who has the confidence of the army and people, and if he was ordered to report to me I would place him there on duty. It is necessary to bring out all our strength, and, I fear, to unite our armies, as separately they do not seem able to make head against the enemy. Everything should be destroyed that cannot be removed out of the reach of Generals Sherman and Schofield. Provisions must be accumulated in Virginia, and every man in all the States must be brought off. I fear it may be necessary to abandon all our cities, and preparation should be made for this contingency.

I have the honor to be, your obedient servant,

R. E. LEE, *General.*

LAST REPORT OF STRENGTH OF THE ARMY EVER MADE BY GENERAL
LEE, PETERSBURG AND APPOMATTOX CAMPAIGN.

Abstract from Return of the Army of Northern Virginia, GEN-
ERAL R. E. LEE *commanding, for Feb. 20, 1865 ; Station,*
Petersburg, Va.

COMMAND.	Aggregate present.	Aggregate present and absent.	Aggregate last return.
LIEUT.-GEN. J. LONGSTREET COMMANDING.			
General staff	12	12	12
Staff	14	18	14
Pickett's division	6,557	9,442	6,520
Field's division	5,732	11,508	5,797
Kershaw's division	4,121	9,179	4,178
Total	16,424	31,147	16,509
MAJ.-GEN. JOHN B. GORDON COMMANDING.			
Staff	...	...	...
Gordon's division	3,334	13,520	3,372
Rodes's division	4,596	12,176	4,445
Early's division	3,196	8,010	2,991
Total	11,126	33,706	10,808
LIEUT.-GEN. A. P. HILL COMMANDING.			
Staff	20	20	18
Mahone's division	5,538	12,854	5,489
Heth's division	5,562	11,852	5,543
Wilcox's division	6,769	11,411	6,822
Total	17,889	36,137	17,872
LIEUT.-GEN. R. H. ANDERSON COMMANDING.			
Johnson's division	7,846	13,642	
LIEUT.-GEN. J. A. EARLY COMMANDING.			
Staff	16	20	18
Wharton's division	1,584	1,735	1,528
General A. L. Long's artillery	457	1,432	743
Lomax's cavalry division	1,790	7,150	1,988
Total	3,847	15,337	4,277
MAJ.-GEN. W. H. F. LEE.			
W. H. F. Lee's division	5,148	9,299	5,107
MAJ.-GEN. FITZHUGH LEE.			
Fitzhugh Lee's division	2,499	9,446	2,519
BRIG.-GEN. J. A. WALKER.			
Defences Richmond and Danville Railroad	1,749	3,269	
Unattached commands	696	1,042	
BRIG.-GEN. W. N. PENDLETON COMMANDING.			
Staff	16	16	
First corps artillery	2,398	3,262	
Third corps artillery	2,227	3,344	
Anderson's artillery	1,462	2,752	
Total	6,113	9,374	
Grand total	73,349	160,411	57,104

Strength of the Army of Northern Virginia, GENERAL ROBT. E. LEE, *C. S. Army, commanding, Feb. 28, 1865, as shown by Inspection Reports.*

TROOPS.	Aggregate present for duty.	Aggregate present.	Aggregate present and absent.	Present effective for the field.
FIRST CORPS.				
Staff	13	13	16	
Pickett's division	6,391	8,073	11,745	6,539
Field's division	4,799	5,650	11,426	4,638
Kershaw's division	1,922	2,447	6,771	1,925
Total First corps	13,125	16,183	29,958	13,102
SECOND CORPS.				
Rodes's division*	2,491	3,135	8,443	2,730
Early's division	2,326	3,001	7,873	2,642
Gordon's division	2,458	3,203	13,228	2,445
Total Second corps	7,275	9,339	29,544	7,817
THIRD CORPS.				
Heth's division	4,429	5,245	11,392	4,401
Wilcox's division	5,222	6,107	11,239	5,242
Mahone's division	4,057	5,413	12,801	4,074
Total Third corps	13,708	16,765	35,432	13,717
Johnson's division	6,813	7,592	12,142	6,762
Fitz Lee's cavalry division	2,021	2,624	9,300	2,015
W. H. F. Lee's cavalry division	2,691	3,257	6,191	1,984
Total cavalry	4,712	5,881	15,491	3,999
Artillery (not reported).				
Grand total	45,633	55,760	122,487	45,397

* Cox's brigade on picket; not included.

[Confidential.]   HEADQUARTERS, PETERSBURG,
                                                      February 21, 1865.

HON. J. C. BRECKENRIDGE, SEC. OF WAR, RICHMOND:

I have had the honor to receive your letter of yesterday's date. I have repeated the orders to the commanding officers to remove and destroy everything in enemy's route. In the event of the necessity of abandoning our position on the James River, I shall endeavor to unite the corps of the army about Burkeville (junction of Southside and Danville Railroad), so as to retain communication with the North and South as long as practicable, and also with the West.

I should think Lynchburg or some point west the most advantageous place to which to remove stores from Richmond. This, however, is a most difficult point at this time to decide, and the place may have to be changed by circumstances.

It was my intention in my former letter to apply for General J. E. Johnston, that I might assign him to duty should circumstances permit. I have had no official report of the condition of General Beauregard's health; it is stated from many sources to be bad : if he should break entirely down, it might be fatal. In that event I should have no one with whom to supply his place. I therefore respectfully request General Johnston may be ordered to report to me, and that I may be informed where he is.

> With great respect, your obt. servt.,

> > > R. E. LEE,
> > > *General.*

                                                   HEADQUARTERS, PETERSBURG,
                                                      Feb. 22, 1865.

HON. J. C. BRECKENRIDGE, SEC. OF WAR, RICHMOND, VA.,

SIR : I have just received your letter of the 21st. I concur fully as to the necessity of defeating Sherman. I hope that General Beauregard will get his troops in hand at least before he can cross the Roanoke. If any additions can be given him, it cannot be south of that stream. The troops in the Valley are scattered for subsistence, nor can they be concentrated for the want of it. The infantry force is very small. At the commencement of winter I think it was reported under 1800. That in Western Virginia you know more about than I do, and there are only two regiments in Western North Carolina. These united would be of some assistance. At the rate that Beauregard supposes Sherman will march, they could not be collected at Greensboro' in time; still, I hope to make some use of them. But you may expect Sheridan to move up the Valley and Stoneman from Knoxville as Sherman draws near Roanoke. What, then, will become of those sections of country? I know of no other troops that could be given to Beauregard. Bragg will be forced back by Schofield, I fear, and until I abandon James River nothing can be sent from this army.

Grant, I think, is now preparing to draw out by his left with the intent of enveloping me. He may wait till his other columns approach nearer, or he may be preparing to anticipate my withdrawal. I cannot tell yet. I am endeavoring to collect supplies convenient to Burkeville. Everything of value should be removed from Richmond. It is of the first importance to save all powder. The cavalry and artillery of the army are still scattered for want of provender, and our supply- and ammunition-trains, which ought to be with the army in case of a sudden movement, are absent collecting provisions and forage, some in Western Virginia and some in North Carolina. You will see to what straits we are reduced. But I trust to work out.

With great respect, your obt. servt.,

R. E. LEE,
General.

[Circular.]
HEADQUARTERS ARMIES OF THE CONFEDERATE STATES,
22d February, 1865.

GENERAL: The spirit which animates our soldiers and the natural courage with which they are so liberally endowed have led to a reliance upon these good qualities to the neglect of those measures which would increase their efficiency and contribute to their safety. Many opportunities have been lost and hundreds of valuable lives uselessly sacrificed for want of a strict observance of discipline.

Its object is to enable an army to bring promptly into action the largest possible number of its men, in good order and under the control of their officers. Its effects are visible in all military history, which records the triumphs of discipline and courage far more frequently than those of numbers and resources.

At no time in the war has the necessity of close attention to this important subject been greater than at present, and at no time has its cultivation promised more valuable results. The proportion of experienced troops is larger in our army than in that of the enemy, while his numbers exceed our own. These are the circumstances most favorable for the display of the advantages of discipline, and in which the power it imparts will be most clearly perceived.

I desire therefore that you will direct every effort to improve the discipline of your troops. This will not only require your own unremitting attention, but also the zealous co-operation of your officers, commissioned and non-commissioned.

The recent law abolishing the system of elections and opening the way to promotion to all who distinguish themselves by the faithful discharge of duty affords a new incentive to officers and men. In addition to the usual and stated instructions, which must be given at all times as fully as circumstances will permit, the importance and utility of thorough discipline should be impressed on officers and men on all occasions by illustrations taken from the experience of the instructor or from other sources of information. They should be made to understand that discipline contributes no less to their safety than to their efficiency. Disastrous surprises and those sudden panics which lead to defeat and the greatest loss of life are of rare occurrence among disciplined troops. It is well known that the greatest number of casualties occur when men become scattered, and especially when they retreat in confusion, as the fire of the enemy is then more deliberate and fatal. The experience of every officer shows that those troops suffer least who attack most vigorously, and that a few men retaining their organization and acting in concert accomplish far more with smaller loss than a larger number scattered and disorganized.

The appearance of a steady, unbroken line is more formidable to the enemy, and renders his aim less accurate and his fire less effective. Orders can be readily transmitted, advantage can be promptly taken of every opportunity, and, all efforts being directed to a common end, the contest will be briefer and success more certain.

Let officers and men be made to feel that they will most effectually secure their safety by remaining steadily at their posts, preserving order, and fighting with coolness and vigor.

Fully impressed with the truth of these views, I call your attention particularly to the accompanying order with reference to the duties of file-closers, which you will immediately carry into execution.

Impress upon your officers that discipline cannot be attained without constant watchfulness on their part. They must attend to the smallest particulars of detail. Men must be habituated to obey or they cannot be controlled in battle, and the neglect of the least important order impairs the proper influence of the officer.

In recommending officers or men for promotion you will always, where other qualifications are equal, give preference to those who show the highest appreciation of the importance of discipline and evince the greatest attention to its requirements.

Very respectfully, your obt. servt.,

R. E. LEE,
General.

———

HEADQUARTERS CONFEDERATE STATES ARMIES,
Feb. 24, 1865.

HIS EXCELLENCY Z. B. VANCE, GOVERNOR OF NORTH CAROLINA, RALEIGH,

GOVERNOR: The state of despondency that now prevails among our people is producing a bad effect upon the troops. Desertions are becoming very frequent, and there is good reason to believe that they are occasioned to a considerable extent by letters written to the soldiers by their friends at home. In the last two weeks several hundred have deserted from Hill's corps, and as the divisions from which the greatest number of desertions have taken place are composed chiefly of troops from North Carolina, they furnish a corresponding proportion of deserters. I think some good can be accomplished by the efforts of influential citizens to change public sentiment and cheer the spirits of the people. It has been discovered that despondent persons represent to their friends in the army that our cause is hopeless, and that they had better provide for themselves. They state that the number of deserters is so large in the several counties that there is no danger to be apprehended from the home-guards. The deserters generally take their arms with them. The greater number are from regiments from the western part of the State. So far as the despondency of the people occasions this sad condition of affairs, I know of no other means of removing it than by the counsel and exhortation of prominent citizens. If they would explain to the people that the cause is not hopeless, that the situation of affairs, though critical, is so to the enemy as well as ourselves, that he has drawn his troops from every other quarter to accomplish his designs against Richmond, and that his defeat now would result in leaving nearly our whole territory open to us; that this great result can be accomplished if all will work diligently, and that his successes are far less valuable in fact than in appearance,—I think our sorely-tried people would be induced to make one more effort to bear their sufferings a little longer, and regain some of the spirit that marked the first two years of the war. If they will, I feel confident that with the blessing of God what seems to be our greatest danger will prove the means of deliverance and safety.

Trusting that you will do all in your power to help us in this great emergency,

I remain, very respectfully, your obt. servt.,

R. E. LEE,
General.

HEADQUARTERS CONFEDERATE STATES ARMIES,
March 9, 1865.
HIS EXCELLENCY Z. B. VANCE, GOVERNOR OF NORTH CAROLINA, RALEIGH,

GOVERNOR : I received your letter of the 2d inst. and return you my sincere thanks for your zealous efforts in behalf of the army and the cause. I have read with pleasure and attention your proclamation and appeal to the people, as also extracts from your addresses. I trust you will infuse into your fellow-citizens the spirit of resolution and patriotism which inspires your own action. I have now no cavalry to spare for the purpose you mention, and regret that I did not receive the suggestion at an earlier period. I think it a very good one, and would have been glad to adopt it. I have sent a force of infantry undei Brigadier-general Johnson [N. D.] to guard the line of the Roanoke and operate as far as practicable in the adjacent counties to arrest deserters. Another detachment of 500 men under Colonel McAllister has been sent to Chatham and Moore counties, in which the bands of deserters were represented to be very numerous. They will, however, operate in other quarters as occasion may require. They are instructed to take no prisoners among those deserters who resist with arms the civil or military authorities. I hope you will raise as large a force of local troops to co-operate with them as you can, and think that the sternest course is the best with the class I have referred to. The immunity which these lawless organizations afford is a great cause of desertion, and they cannot be too sternly dealt with. I hope you will be able to aid General Johnson, who needs all the reinforcements you can give him. If he can check the progress of General Sherman, the effect would be of the greatest value. I hope the late success of General Bragg near Kinston will revive the spirits of the people and render your labors less arduous. The conduct of the widow lady whom you mention deserves the highest commendation. If all our people possessed her spirit, our success I should feel to be assured.

Very respectfully, your obedient servant,

R. E. LEE,
General.

———————

HEADQUARTERS, PETERSBURG, VA.,
March 17, 1865.

HON. JOHN C. BRECKENRIDGE, SEC. OF WAR, RICHMOND, VA.,

SIR: A despatch from Lieutenant-general Taylor at Meridian on the 12th inst. states that he had returned that morning from West Point; that Thomas was reported to be moving with the Fourth army corps and about 12,000 cavalry; that General Maury reports enemy, some 30,000 strong, moving with fleet and by land from Pensacola on Mobile; that about 30,000 bales of cotton in Mobile will be burned as soon as the city is invested; that he has provided for these movements as fully as his resources permitted, but that he had received no aid from Mississippi or Alabama, yet hoped to embarrass the enemy in his efforts to take those States. If the estimate of the enemy's strength is correct, I see little prospect of preserving Mobile, and had previously informed him that he could not rely upon the return of the Army of Tennessee to relieve that city, and suggested the propriety of withdrawing from it, and endeavor to beat the enemy in the field. I hope this course will meet with the approbation of the Department.

General Johnston on the 16th, from Smithfield, reports the Federal army south of the Cape Fear, but near Fayetteville. He had ordered 1000 wagons of the Tennessee army to be used in filling gaps in railroad and 100 wagons to collect supplies in South Carolina for this army. I hope this will furnish some relief.

General Echols at Wytheville, on the 12th, reports that a portion of the troops in East Tennessee had been removed south of Knoxville, destination not known, and that the engineer troops which had commenced to repair the Tennessee Railroad from Knoxville east had been withdrawn and sent to Chattanooga for the purpose, it was thought, of repairing the road toward Atlanta. He also states that an intelligent scout just from Kentucky reports Burbridge's force had been taken to Nashville, and that considerable bodies of troops were passing up the Ohio on their way to Grant. He believed all these reports may be relied on.

The enemy seems still to be collecting a force in the Shenandoah Valley, which indicates another movement as soon as the weather will permit. Rosser's scouts report that there is some cavalry and infantry now at Winchester, and that Hancock has a portion of his new corps at Hall Town. I think these troops are intended to supply the place of those under General Sheridan, which it is plain General Grant has brought to his army. The addition of these three mounted divisions will give such strength to his cavalry, already numerically superior to ours, that it will enable him, I fear, to keep our communications to Richmond broken. Had we been able to use the supplies which Sheridan has destroyed in his late expedition in maintaining our troops in the Valley in a body, if his march could not have been arrested it would at least have been rendered comparatively harmless, and we should have been spared the mortification that has attended it. Now, I do not see how we can sustain even our small force of cavalry around Richmond. I have had this morning to send General William H. F. Lee's division back to Stony Creek, whence I had called it in the last few days, because I cannot provide it with forage. I regret to have to report these difficulties, but think you ought to be apprised of them, in order if there is any remedy it should be applied.

I have the honor to be your obedient servant,

R. E. LEE,
General.

HEADQUARTERS CONFEDERATE STATES ARMIES,
March 27, 1865.

HON. SEC. OF WAR, RICHMOND,

SIR: I have been awaiting the receipt of the order from the Department for raising and organizing the colored troops before taking any action in the matter. I understand that orders have been published in the newspapers, but have not seen them. In the mean time, I have been informed that a number of recruits may be obtained in Petersburg if suitable persons be employed to get them to enlist. . . . .

Very respectfully, your obedient servant,

R. E. LEE,
General.

HEADQUARTERS ARMY OF NORTHERN VIRGINIA,
April 1, 1865.

HON. SEC. OF WAR, RICHMOND,

SIR : After my despatch of last night I received a report from General Pickett, who with three of his own brigades and two of General Johnson's supported the cavalry under General Fitz Lee near Five Forks on the road from Dinwiddie Court-house to the Southside road. After considerable difficulty, and meeting resistance from the enemy at all points, General Pickett forced his way to within less than a mile of Dinwiddie Court-house. By this time it was too dark for further operations, and General Pickett resolved to return to Five Forks to protect his communication with the railroad. He inflicted considerable damage upon the enemy, and took some prisoners. His own loss was severe, including a good many officers. General Terry had his horse killed by a shell, and was disabled himself. General Fitz Lee's and Rosser's divisions were heavily engaged, but their loss was slight. General W. H. F. Lee lost some valuable officers. General Pickett did not retire from the vicinity of Dinwiddie Court-house until early this morning, when, his left flank being threatened by a heavy force, he withdrew to Five Forks, where he took position with General W. H. F. Lee on his right, Fitz Lee and Rosser on his left, with Roberts's brigade on the White Oak road, connecting with General Anderson. The enemy attacked General Roberts with a large force of cavalry, and after being once repulsed drove him back across Hatcher's Run. A large force of infantry, believed to be the Fifteenth corps with other troops, turned General Pickett's left, and drove him back on the White Oak road, separating him from General Fitz Lee, who was compelled to fall back across Hatcher's Run. General Pickett's present position is not known. General Fitz Lee reports that the enemy is massing his infantry heavily behind the cavalry in his front. The infantry that engaged General Anderson yesterday has moved from his front toward our right, and is supposed to participate in the operations above described. Prisoners have been taken to-day from the Twenty-fourth corps, and it is believed that most of the corps is now south of the James. Our loss to-day is not known. A report from Staunton represents that the Eighth corps passed over the Baltimore and Ohio Railroad from the 20th to the 25th ult. General Hancock is at Harper's Ferry with 2000 men. One division of the Tenth corps is at Winchester with about 1000 cavalry. The infantry at Winchester have marching orders, and all these troops are said to be destined for General Grant's army.

The enemy is also reported to have withdrawn all his troops from Wolf Run Shoals and Fairfax Station, and to have concentrated them at Winchester.

Very respectfully, your obedient servant,

R. E. LEE,
General.

PETERSBURG, April 2, 1865.

GEN. J. C. BRECKENRIDGE, SEC. OF WAR:

It is absolutely necessary that we should abandon our position to-night or run the risk of being cut off in the morning. I have given all the orders to officers on both sides of the river, and have taken every precaution that I can to make the movement successful. It will be a difficult operation, but I hope not impracticable. Please give all orders that you find necessary in and about Richmond. The troops will all be directed to Amelia Court-house.

R. E. LEE.

HEADQUARTERS, *via* PETERSBURG,
April 2, 1865.

GENERAL J. C. BRECKENRIDGE:

I see no prospect of doing more than holding our position here till night. I am not certain that I can do that; if I can, I shall withdraw to-night north of the Appomattox, and if possible it will be better to withdraw the whole line to-night from Jones River: the brigades on Hatcher's Run are cut off from us. Enemy have broken through our lines and interposed between us and them, and there is no bridge over which they can cross the Appomattox this side of Goode or Bevel, which are not very far from the Danville Railroad. Our only chance, then, of concentrating our forces is to do so near Danville Railroad, which I shall endeavor to do at once. I advise that all preparations be made for leaving Richmond to-night. I will advise you later according to circumstances.

R. E. LEE.

HEADQUARTERS ARMY OF NORTHERN VIRGINIA,
April 2, 1865.

Generals Longstreet's and Hill's corps will cross the pontoon bridge at Battersea Factory and take the river road, north side of Appomattox, to Bevel's Bridge to-night. General Gordon's corps will cross at Pocahontas and railroad bridge, his troops taking Hickory road, following General Longstreet to Bevel's Bridge, and his wagons taking the Woodpecker road to Old Colville, endeavoring not to interfere with Mahone's troops from Chesterfield Court-house, who will take the same road.   General Mahone's division will take the road to Chesterfield Court-house, thence by Old Colville to Goode's Bridge.   Mahone's wagons will precede him on the same road or take some road to his right.   General Ewell's command will cross the James River at and below Richmond, taking the road to Branch Church, *viâ* Gregory's, to Genito road, *viâ* Genito Bridge, to Amelia Court-house.   The wagons from Richmond will take the Manchester pike and Buckingham road, *viâ* Meadville, to Amelia Court-house.   The movement of all the troops will commence at eight o'clock, the artillery moving out quietly first, infantry following, except the pickets, who will be withdrawn at three o'clock.   The artillery not required with the troops will be moved by the roads prescribed for the wagons or such other as may be most convenient.   Every officer is expected to give his unremitting attention to cause the movement to be made successfully.   By order of General•Lee.

W. H. TAYLOR,
Assistant Adjutant-general.

HEADQUARTERS ARMY OF NORTHERN VIRGINIA,
April 3, 1865, 6.30 P. M.
HEBRON CHURCH, 6 miles from Goode's Ford.

LIEUTENANT-GENERAL EWELL:

When you were directed to cross the Appomattox at Genito Bridge, it was supposed that a pontoon bridge had been laid at that point, as ordered.   But I learn to-day from Mr. Hascall that such is not the case.   Should you not be able to cross at that point or at some bridge higher up, you must take the best road to Rudd's Store on the Goode's Bridge road, and cross the Appomattox on the bridge at that point, and then conform to your original instructions.

This portion of the army is now on its way to Goode's Bridge, the flats at Bevel's Bridge being flooded by high water.   Notify me of your approach to the bridge and passage of the Appomattox by courier to Amelia Court-house or wherever I may be.

I am, very respectfully, your obt. servt,   R. E. LEE,
General.

P. S. 7.30 A. M., APRIL 4TH.   The courier has returned with this note, having been able to learn nothing of you.   I am about to cross the river.   Get to Amelia Court-house as soon as possible, and let me hear from you.

R. E. LEE.

GENERAL LEE'S FAREWELL ADDRESS TO HIS ARMY.

HEADQUARTERS ARMY OF NORTHERN VIRGINIA,
April 10, 1865.

After four years of arduous service, marked by unsurpassed courage and fortitude, the Army of Northern Virginia has been compelled to yield to overwhelming numbers and resources. I need not tell the survivors of so many hard-fought battles, who have remained steadfast to the last, that I have consented to this result from no distrust of them, but, feeling that valor and devotion could accomplish nothing that could compensate for the loss that would have attended the continuation of the contest, I have determined to avoid the useless sacrifice of those whose past services have endeared them to their countrymen.

By the terms of the agreement officers and men can return to their homes, and remain there until exchanged. You will take with you the satisfaction that proceeds from the consciousness of duty faithfully performed ; and I earnestly pray that a merciful God will extend to you his blessing and protection.

With an increasing admiration of your constancy and devotion to your country, and a grateful remembrance of your kind and generous consideration of myself, I bid you an affectionate farewell.

R. E. LEE,
General.

REPORT OF THE SURRENDER AT APPOMATTOX.

NEAR APPOMATTOX COURT-HOUSE, VA.,
April 12, 1865.

HIS EXCELLENCY JEFFERSON DAVIS,

MR. PRESIDENT: It is with pain that I announce to Your Excellency the surrender of the Army of Northern Virginia. The operations which preceded this result will be reported in full. I will therefore only now state that upon arriving at Amelia Court-house on the morning of the 4th with the advance of the army, on the retreat from the lines in front of Richmond and Petersburg, and not finding the supplies ordered to be placed there, nearly twenty-four hours were lost in endeavoring to collect in the country subsistence for men and horses. This delay was fatal, and could not be retrieved. The troops, wearied by continual fighting and marching for several days and nights, obtained neither rest nor refreshment, and on moving on the 5th on the Richmond and Danville Railroad, I found at Jetersville the enemy's cavalry, and learned the approach of his infantry and the general advance of his army toward Burkeville. This deprived us of the use of the railroad, and rendered it impracticable to procure from Danville the supplies ordered to meet us at points of our march. Nothing could be obtained from the adjacent country. Our route to the Roanoke was therefore changed, and the march directed upon Farmville, where supplies were ordered from Lynchburg. The change of route threw the troops over the roads pursued by the artillery and wagon-trains west of the railroad, which impeded our advance and embarrassed our movements. On the morning of the 6th, General Longstreet's corps reached Rice's Station on the Lynchburg Railroad. It was followed by the commands of Generals

R. H. Anderson, Ewell, and Gordon, with orders to close upon it as fast as the progress of the trains would permit or as they could be directed on roads farther west. General Anderson, commanding Pickett's and B. R. Johnson's divisions, became disconnected with Mahone's division, forming the rear of Longstreet. The enemy's cavalry penetrated the line of march through the interval thus left, and attacked the wagon-train moving toward Farmville. This caused serious delay in the march of the centre and rear of the column, and enabled the enemy to mass upon their flank. After successive attacks Anderson's and Ewell's corps were captured or driven from their position. The latter general, with both of his division commanders, Kershaw and Custis Lee, and his brigadiers, were taken prisoners. Gordon, who all the morning, aided by General W. F. Lee's cavalry, had checked the advance of the enemy on the road from Amelia Springs and protected the trains, became exposed to his combined assaults, which he bravely resisted and twice repulsed; but the cavalry having been withdrawn to another part of the line of march, and the enemy, massing heavily on his front and both flanks, renewed the attack about 6 P. M. and drove him from the field in much confusion. The army continued its march during the night, and every effort was made to reorganize the divisions which had been shattered by the day's operations; but, the men being depressed by fatigue and hunger, many threw away their arms, while others followed the wagon-trains and embarrassed their progress. On the morning of the 7th rations were issued to the troops as they passed Farmville, but the safety of the trains requiring their removal upon the approach of the enemy, all could not be supplied. The army, reduced to two corps under Longstreet and Gordon, moved steadily on the road to Appomattox Court-house; thence its march was ordered by Campbell Court-house, through Pittsylvania, toward Danville. The roads were wretched and the progress slow. By great efforts the head of the column reached Appomattox Court-house on the evening of the 8th, and the troops were halted for rest. The march was ordered to be resumed at 1 A. M. on the 9th. Fitz Lee with the cavalry, supported by Gordon, was ordered to drive the enemy from his front, wheel to the left, and cover the passage of the trains, while Longstreet, who from Rice's Station had formed the rear-guard, should close up and hold the position. Two battalions of artillery and the ammunition-wagons were directed to accompany the army, the rest of the artillery and wagons to move toward Lynchburg. In the early part of the night the enemy attacked Walker's artillery-train near Appomattox Station on the Lynchburg Railroad, and were repelled. Shortly afterward their cavalry dashed toward the court-house, till halted by our line. During the night there were indications of a large force massing on our left and front. Fitz Lee was directed to ascertain its strength, and to suspend his advance till daylight if necessary. About 5 A. M. on the 9th, with Gordon on his left, he moved forward and opened the way. A heavy force of the enemy was discovered opposite Gordon's right, which, moving in the direction of Appomattox Court-house, drove back the left of the cavalry and threatened to cut off Gordon from Longstreet, his cavalry at the same time threatening to envelop his left flank. Gordon withdrew across the Appomattox River, and the cavalry advanced on the Lynchburg road and became separated from the army. Learning the condition of affairs on the lines, where I had gone under the expectation of meeting General Grant to learn definitely the terms he proposed in a communication received from him on the 8th, in the event of the surrender of the army, I requested a suspension of hostilities until these terms could be arranged. In the interview which occurred with General Grant in compliance with my request, terms having been agreed on, I surrendered that portion of the Army of Northern Virginia which was on the field, with its arms, artillery, and wagon-trains, the officers and men to be paroled, retaining their side-arms and private effects. I deemed this course the best under all the circumstances by which we were surrounded. On the morning of the 9th, according to the reports of the ordnance officers, there were 7892 organized infantry with arms, with an average of seventy-five rounds of ammunition per man. The artillery, though reduced to 63 pieces with 93 rounds of ammunition, was sufficient. These comprised all the supplies of ordnance that could be relied on in the State of Virginia. I have no accurate report of the cavalry, but believe it did not exceed 2100 effective men. The enemy was more than five times our numbers. If we could have forced our way one day longer, it would have been at a great sacrifice of life, and at its end I did not see how a surrender could have been avoided. We had no subsistence for man or horse, and it could not be gathered in the country. The supplies ordered to Pamplin's Station from Lynchburg could not reach us, and the men, deprived of food and sleep for many days, were worn out and exhausted.

With great respect, your obedient servant,

R. E. LEE,
General.

STRENGTH OF ARMY OF NORTHERN VIRGINIA, AS SHOWN BY PAROLE ROLLS DATED 9TH APRIL, 1865.

COMMAND.	Officers.	Enlisted men.	Aggregate.
GENERAL HEADQUARTERS.			
General Lee, Staff, and Escort	11	87	98
Staff Corps	58	125	183
Total	69	212	281
INFANTRY.			
FIRST CORPS: LIEUT.-GEN. LONGSTREET AND STAFF .	16	. . .	16
Pickett's division: Maj.-gen. Pickett and staff . . .	14	. . .	14
Corse's brigade, Col. A. Herbert	32	262	294
Hunton's brigade, Maj. M. P. Shepard	17	149	166
Steuart's brigade, Brig.-gen. Steuart	46	358	404
Terry's brigade, Maj. W. W. Bentley	11	142	153
Total Pickett's division	120	911	1,031
Field's division, Maj.-gen. Chas. W. Field and staff .	9	. . .	9
Anderson's brigade, Brig.-gen. Anderson	92	895	987
Benning's brigade, Brig.-gen. Benning	76	733	809
Bratton's brigade, Brig.-gen. Bratton	130	1,418	1,548
Perry's (late Laws's) brigade, Brig.-gen. Perry . .	91	892	983
Texas brigade, Col. R. M. Powell	64	553	617
Total Field's division	462	4,491	4,953
Kershaw's division, ——— ——— — and staff . .	4	13	17
DuBose's brigade, Captain J. F. Espy	22	325	347
Humphrey's brigade, Captain G. R. Cherry . . .	20	231	251
Sims's brigade, Captain E. W. Waldron	12	178	190
Total Kershaw's division	58	747	805
Total First corps	656	6,149	6,805
SECOND CORPS: MAJ.-GEN. GORDON, STAFF, ETC.* . .	28	115	143
Grimes's (late Rodes's) division: Maj.-gen. Grimes and staff	13	5	18
Battle's brigade, Col. E. L. Hobson	33	331	364
Cook's brigade, Col. E. A. Nash	28	322	350
Cox's brigade, Brig.-gen. Cox	51	521	572
Grimes's brigade, Col. D. G. Cowand	34	496	530
Archer's battalion, ——— ——— ———	13	52	65
Total Grimes's division	172	1,727	1,899
Early's division: Brig.-gen. Walker and staff . . .	11	1	12
Johnston's [R. D.] brigade, Col. J. W. Lea . . .	30	433	463
Lewis's brigade, Captain John Beard	26	421	447
Walker's (late Pegram's) brig., Maj. H. K. Douglass	42	262	304
Total Early's division	109	1,117	1,226
Second corps, carried forward	309	2,959	3,268

* Provost-guard, couriers, escort, and hospital attendants included.

PAROLE ROLLS—Continued.

COMMAND.	Officers.	Enlisted men.	Aggregate.
Second corps, brought forward	309	2,959	3,268
Gordon's division : Brig.-gen. Evans and staff . . .	10	. . .	10
Evans's brigade, Col. J. H. Lowe	51	790	841
Terry's brigade, Col. T. V. Williams	67	477	544
York's brigade, Col. E. Waggaman	28	345	373
Total Gordon's division	156	1,612	1,768
Total Second corps	465	4,571	5,036
THIRD CORPS :* STAFF AND PROVOST-GUARD	28	119	147
Heth's division : Maj.-gen. H. Heth and staff . . .	15	. . .	15
Cooke's brigade, Brig.-gen. Cooke	70	490	560
Davis's brigade, Brig.-gen. Davis	21	54	75
MacRae's brigade, Brig.-gen. MacRae	42	400	442
McComb's brigade, Brig.-gen. McComb	54	426	480
Total Heth's division	202	1,370	1,572
Mahone's division : Maj.-gen. Mahone and staff . .	13	1	14
Finegan's brigade, Col. D. Lang	64	441	505
Forney's brigade, Brig.-gen. W. H. Forney . . .	72	880	952
Harris's brigade, Brig.-gen. N. H. Harris	33	339	372
Sorrel's brigade, Col. G. E. Tayloe	71	962	1,033
Weisiger's brigade, Brig.-gen. Weisiger	78	583	661
Total Mahone's division	331	3,206	3,537
Wilcox's division : Maj.-gen. Wilcox and staff . . .	12	. . .	12
Lane's brigade, Brig.-gen. Lane	56	514	570
McGowan's brigade, Brig.-gen. McGowan . . .	69	798	867
Scales's brigade, Col. Joseph H. Hyman	92	627	719
Thomas's brigade, Brig.-gen. E. L. Thomas . . .	57	456	513
Total Wilcox's division	286	2,395	2,681
Total Third corps	847	7,090	7,937
ANDERSON'S CORPS : ——— ——— AND STAFF . . .	. . .	24	24
Johnson's division : Maj.-gen. B. R. Johnson and staff	10	. . .	10
Elliott's brigade, Brig.-gen. Wallace	62	568	630
Moody's brigade, Brig.-gen. Moody	63	515	578
Ransom's brigade, Brig.-gen. Ransom	41	394	435
Wise's brigade, Brig.-gen. Wise	72	528	600
Total Anderson's corps	248	2,029	2,277
EWELL'S COMMAND, LT.-COL. THOMAS J. SPENCER . .	19	275	294
Total Infantry	2,235	20,114	22,349

* Attached to First corps after death of A. P. Hill.

PAROLE ROLLS—Continued.

COMMAND.	Officers.	Enlisted men.	Aggregate.
CAVALRY.			
MAJ.-GEN. FITZ LEE AND STAFF	6	1	7
Fitz Lee's division:			
Garry's brigade, Col. A. C. Haskell	61	772	833
Payne's brigade, ——— ———————	6	82	88
Wickham's brigade, ——— ———————	10	177	187
Total Fitz Lee's division	77	1,031	1,108
W. H. F. Lee's division: Maj.-gen. W. H. F. Lee .	7	. 1	8
Barringer's brigade, ———	2	21	23
Beale's brigade, Captain S. H. Burt	22	152	174
Roberts's brigade, Brig.-gen. W. P. Roberts . . .	5	88	93
Total W. H. F. Lee's division	36	262	298
Lomax's division:			
Jackson's brigade	. .	9	9
Total Lomax's division	. .	9	9
Rosser's division: Maj.-gen. Rosser and staff . . .	*8	1	9
Dearing's brigade, Col. A. W. Harman	6	95	101
McCausland's brigade, ——— . . .	1	26	27
Total Rosser's division	15	122	137
Total Cavalry	134	1,425	1,559
ARTILLERY.			
GENERAL HEADQUARTERS: BRIG.-GEN. PENDLETON AND STAFF	12	13	25
First army corps: Brig.-gen. E. P. Alexander and staff	11	36	47
Haskell's battalion, Lt.-col. John C. Haskell. . .	15	139	154
Hughs's battalion, Maj. J. C. Jordan	21	307	328
McIntosh's battalion, Lt.-col. W. M. Owen . . .	14	268	282
Poague's battalion, Lt.-col. Wm. T. Poague . . .	17	279	296
Thirteenth Va. battalion, Capt. D. N. Walker . .	2	10	12
Richardson's battalion, Capt. R. Prosper Landry .	4	77	81
Total First army corps	84	1,116	1,200
Second army corps: Brig.-gen. A. L. Long and staff	8	22	30
Carter's command, Col. T. H. Carter	2	4	6
Braxton's battalion, Lt.-col. Carter M. Braxton . .	7	19	26
Cutshaw's battalion, Capt. C. W. Foy	12	199	211
Hardaway's battalion, Lt.-col. R. A. Hardaway . .	19	382	401
Johnson's battalion, Lt.-col. M. Johnson	8	135	143
Lightfoot's battalion, Asst. Surg. J. B. Coakley . .	1	29	30
Stark's battalion, Lt.-col. A. W. Stark	11	154	165
Total Second army corps	68	944	1,012
Artillery, carried forward	164	2,073	2,237

* Officers whose paroles are signed by Rosser included.

PAROLE ROLLS—Continued.

COMMAND.	Officers.	Enlisted men.	Aggregate.
Artillery, brought forward	164	2,073	2,237
Anderson's corps, Col. H. P. Jones	2	1	3
Blount's battalion, ———— ————————	3	21	24
Cutt's battalion, ———— ————————	.	37	37
Stribling's battalion, ———— ————————	2	8	10
Total Anderson's corps	7	67	74
Miscellaneous:			
Smith's battalion, Capt. W. F. Dement	13	252	265
Total Artillery*	184	2,392	2,576
MISCELLANEOUS TROOPS †	159	1,307	1,466

RECAPITULATION.

	Officers.	Enlisted men.	Aggregate.
General Headquarters	69	212	281
Infantry	2,235	20,114	22,349
Cavalry	134	1,425	1,559
Artillery	184	2,392	2,576
Miscellaneous troops	159	1,307	1,466
Grand total	2,781	25,450	28,231

* Cabell's, King's, Lane's, Nelson's, Pegram's, and Sturdevant's battalions, borne on return for January 31, 1865, are not accounted for by the paroles.
† Composed of detachments of engineers, invalids, naval brigade, provost-guards, etc.

INDEX.

A.

Anderson, G. T., General, 276, 334, 340, 348, 362, 414.

Appomattox Court-house, 415, 417, 419.

Arlington, 31–34, 38, 39, 79, 94, 96.

Army of Northern Virginia, 177, 186, 205, 230, 237, 246, 248; reorganized, 265, 303, 317, 323, 338, 344, 346, 347; losses, 348, 412, 419, 422–425; organization, Sept. 1, 1862, 512–516; return of strength, Sept. 22, 1862, 537; return, Nov. 20, 1862, 549; return, Dec. 10, 1862, 562; organization, Dec. 20, 1862, 563–568; return, May 20, 1863, 584; organization during Gettysburg campaign, 607–611; return, July 20, 1863, 612; return, April 20, 1864, 651; return, July 10, 1864, 654; organization, Nov. 30, 1864, 671; return, Feb. 20, 1865, 682; Feb. 28, 1865, 683; parole rolls, 696–699.

Army of the Potomac, under McDowell, 107; under McClellan, 149, 165, 185, 212; under Burnside, 233, 237; under Hooker, 248, 249; losses, 261; under Meade, 271, 274; under Grant, 322, 323; losses, 341, 344, 345, 347, 348.

Army of Virginia, under Pope, 184.

B.

Beauregard, P. G. T., General, 55, 60, 69, 104; at Manassas, 106–110; at Petersburg, 353, 372, 373, 375, 383, 456.

Blair, F. P., offers R. E. Lee command of United States army, 92, 93, 402.

Boonsboro', 210; battle, 214–216.

Bragg, B., General, 304, 649, 650.

Breckenridge, J. C., General, 348, 353, 355, 357–359, 361, 482, 681, 684, 688–691.

Brown, John, 80, 85, 86.

Bull Run, 106–108, 191, 195, 196, 198, 311.

Burnside, General, 138, 177, 197, 212; at Sharpsburg, 218, 219; in command of Army of Potomac, 233–235; crosses the Rappahannock, 236, 239, 243, 332, 337, 345, 348, 371, 373, 375, 381.

Butler, B. F., General, 62, 104, 138, 146, 325, 346; at Bermuda Hundred, 352; assails Petersburg, 353, 374, 393, 396.

C.

Carter, T. H., Colonel, anecdotes, 385, 386, 420.

Cedar Creek, 364.

Cemetery Ridge, 279, 281, 282, 285–287, 302.

Cerro Gordo, 52, 61, 65.

Chancellorsville, situation, 250; skirmish, 252; battle, 255, 256, 259, 260.

Chapultepec, 60, 61.

Charleston, conflagration of, 134–136; defences, 137, 142, 144.

Chickahominy, 155, 156, 162–164, 169–171, 174, 175, 343, 347, 371, 391, 403.

Christian, B., Hon., 443.

Churubusco, 54, 59, 61.

Coast defences, 136–140.

Cold Harbor, 172; battle, 347–349, 370.

Comanches, 76–78.

Confederacy, formed, 89; commission, 90; army, 104; policy, 203; currency, 246; finances, 266; commission, 402.

THE END.